Making a New World

JOHN TUTINO

Making a New World

FOUNDING CAPITALISM IN THE BAJÍO

AND SPANISH NORTH AMERICA

Duke University Press Durham and London 2011

Duke University Press
gratefully acknowledges the
support of Georgetown University,
which provided funds toward the
production of this book.

Library of Congress Cataloging-in-
Publication Data appear on the
last printed page of this book.

Contents

Chapter 2. Forging Spanish North America: Northward
Expansions, Mining Amalgamations, and Patriarchal
Communities, 1590–1700   121

Chapter 3. New World Revivals: Silver Boom, City Lives,
Awakenings, and Northward Drives, 1680–1760   159

Chapter 4. Reforms, Riots, and Repressions:
The Bajío in the Crisis of the 1760s   228

Maps and Illustrations

Prologue

Making Global History in the Spanish Empire

THE WORLD BECAME WHOLE in the sixteenth century. Population growth, rising trade, and tax collections mandated in silver set off a burgeoning demand for the metal in Ming China just as Spaniards conquered American dominions and found mountains of silver. From the 1550s rising streams of silver from Potosí, high in the Andes, and Zacatecas, far north of Mexico City, flowed west to Europe, to be traded on to China for silks, porcelains, and other goods. Before 1600 a second flow annually sailed west from Acapulco on galleons bound for Manila, again traded for Chinese wares. Silver mined in American colonies of a European empire met a rising Chinese demand, fueling global trade and commercial ways that eventually led to capitalism.[1]

Globalization began in unplanned and little understood encounters among peoples who lived in villages, mining centers, and trading cities ruled by diverse empires, speaking distinct languages and worshipping in varied ways. Around 1500 Ming China included the largest, densest population of any world region; most people there lived by household production in communities linked by growing local markets and regional trade; an empire that took taxes in silver added pressures to put produce into markets, further stimulating trade. At the same time western Europe emerged from the century of depopulation and depression inflicted by the plague of 1348; the sixteenth century saw its populations finally grow again, its cultivation expand, and its trade deepen, while its states continued to fight for survival and dominance, and Iberians led unprecedented overseas expansion. Meanwhile the Americas faced European incursions, bringing devastating diseases and levels of depopulation approaching 90 percent, opening the way for new empires to rule communities once subject to Andean and Mesoamerican states, and to forge new societies in regions where newcomers found economic opportunity among people long free of state rule, now also facing the devastation of smallpox and other Old World infections. Spain's Americas generated silver that fueled global trade; Portuguese Brazil pioneered American sugar and slave plantations that made sugar an Atlantic commodity second only to silver and Africans a growing item of trade.

The expansion of trade linking Europe and Asia, the opening of the Americas to European colonization, and the rise of the African slave trade combined to transform the world. They began a global commercial dynamic that led to capitalism. Britons and their American offspring dominated the world of capitalism after 1800. That has led to enduring presumptions (among Europeans and their offspring) that capitalism was Europe's gift to the world (or plague upon it). Classic authors from Adam Smith to Karl Marx and Max Weber promoted these views, as have recent scholars including Immanuel Wallerstein, Eric Wolf, and Fernand Braudel.[2] Now analysts as different as Dennis Flynn and Arturo Giráldez, Andre Gunder Frank, and Kenneth Pomeranz have emphasized China's commercial dynamism and its central role in stimulating global trade from 1500 to 1800. European primacy was a late development—emerging around 1800.[3] We face a fundamental rethinking of the rise of capitalism.

One conclusion seems set: the accelerating commercialization that began around 1500 was a global process. Ming China was a major participant, as were India, Japan, and the Manila entrepot that tied them to the Americas. European financial centers from Venice to Amsterdam to London were key players, as were the founding Portuguese and Spanish empires, and the Dutch, French, and British regimes that rose to challenge them. No regime, no cartel of merchants designed or ruled the global trade that led the world toward capitalism. There is debate about the relative importance of Europe and Asia and their diverse sub-regions during centuries of foundation; there is debate about why hegemonic power became concentrated in northwest Europe around 1800, and about whether that power was broadly European or mostly British.[4]

In most discussions and debates, the Americas appear as appendages of Europe. Their colonization surely contributed to the rise of Europe; the importance of colonial extractions is debated. How much did silver or the sugar and slave trades fuel (or inhibit) the rise of Europe and differentiate its regions? Yet if silver was essential to early globalization, should we presume that the American societies that produced it in prodigious quantities were peripheral to global dynamism? This analysis rethinks the role of the Americas, especially Spain's Americas, and notably the dynamic region of Spanish North America, in the early globalization of trade, the foundation of capitalist ways, and the conflicts that reshaped global power around 1800.

Potosí led New World production of silver from 1570 to 1640, stimulating trade, grafting a new commercial society onto remnants of the Inca Empire, and forging a hybrid society as important as any European city or Chinese region to global dynamism in the sixteenth and seventeenth centuries.[5] The regions from Querétaro to Guanajuato (the Bajío) and from Zacatecas northward (Spanish North America) in New Spain (now Mexico) formed a secondary core of silver production while Potosí boomed; they led the world in silver mining in the eighteenth century. In a long historic process they created an unprecedented commercial society north of the Mesoamerican empires conquered by Spaniards beginning in 1519. In the fertile Bajío basin and across the arid plateau country stretching far to the north, a new society driven by silver and prospects of commercial gain drew people from Europe, Africa, and Mesoamerica. They built a protean capitalist society pivotal to global trade after 1550 and to the rise of European hegemony after 1770.

The importance of American silver to global trade between 1550 and 1810 is beyond dispute. That the Bajío and Spanish North America produced not only much of that silver but also a protean capitalist society has been suggested by a few.[6] But their views have drowned in a sea of scholarship insisting that capitalism and Spain's Americas were historically antithetical. Perhaps there were flashes of profit-seeking energy among those who financed and operated mines; perhaps the greatest of the mines and refineries were huge enterprises, with great capital investments, and armies of workers set to specialized tasks for monetary remunerations. But the rest of society was devoted to status and honor, not to profit-seeking entrepreneurship. Work was mostly coerced. A powerful state perhaps promoted mining to reap its revenues, but otherwise it strangled innovation and creativity with regulation and a closed Catholic culture.[7] A few life sketches help make it clear that these understandings cannot stand.

Unimagined People Founding Capitalism

Don Fernando de Tapia gained power and acclaim leading settlement at the colonial town of Querétaro, northwest of Mexico City. From the 1520s he encouraged migrants to build homes and claim lands. He promoted irrigation works to water settlers' plots and his estates; he governed under Spanish rule. After 1550 he led troops against Chichimecas, independent natives who fought the northward advance of a burgeoning silver economy. By the 1590s, the wars over, his son don Diego ruled an agricultural and grazing empire, a towering figure at Querétaro as it became a center of cultivation, commerce, and cloth production linking the mines at Zacatecas to Mexico City and the world beyond. Before he died don Diego de Tapia founded the Convent of Santa Clara, endowing it with rich lands and water rights. His daughter and heir doña Luisa ruled the Convent long into the 1600s; a devout abbess, she built Santa Clara into a mortgage bank promoting commercial agricultural development. Honored as founders of Querétaro, the Tapias were not Spanish conquerors. Don Fernando was born Connín, an Otomí trader, tribute collector, and frontiersman who negotiated life under Mexica (Aztec) rule until European newcomers (with Tlaxcalan and other Mesoamerican allies) deposed his native overlords. He took the opportunity to lead Otomí settlement and commercial development at Querétaro—with enduring success.

The richest lands at Querétaro were lush *huertas*, irrigated urban farm gardens built by Otomí settlers in the 1500s and worked by their descendants for centuries. Otomí growers raised fruits and vegetables to sell in local markets, in the raucous mining town of Zacatecas to the north and in Mexico City, the capital of New Spain, to the south. By 1600 Querétaro was a pivot of trade, transportation, and cloth making in a commercial economy promoted by entrepreneurs including the Otomí governor and commercial cultivator don Diego de Tapia, the Portuguese merchant Duarte de Tóvar, and the Spanish textile magnate Juan Rodríguez Galán. Demand for workers grew as decades of plagues left population scarce. Local Otomí along with immigrant Mexica, Otomí, and Tarascans came to work in textile workshops, artisanry, transportation, and other activities that boomed along with silver production. In 1599 Tomás Equina, a Querétaro Otomí, contracted to work for three pesos monthly; so did Baltasar Hernández, a Mexica from Cuautitlán, in 1605. In 1608 Juan Pérez, another Otomí from Querétaro, signed on for four pesos monthly. All took pay in advance and gained food rations to ensure sustenance while they labored. Deep in the American interior, silver stimulated a money economy and a labor market in the Otomí-Spanish-Christian community at Querétaro.

In the 1660s don Diego de la Cruz Saravia operated valuable irrigated properties at Valle de Santiago, west of Querétaro along the great river (also Santiago) that watered the Bajío en route to the Pacific. He lived in a palatial home in the center of Celaya. His wife dressed in Chinese silks embroidered with gold; she wore fine silver and pearl jewelry. Together they owned ten slaves of African ancestry. Don Diego was a leading agricultural entrepreneur; during a lull in the silver economy at nearby Guanajuato he cleared fields and expanded irrigation. He leased rain-fed maize lands to tenants for cash rents; he planted irrigated wheat fields, paying workers salaries and maize rations. Don Diego de la Cruz claimed status as a Spaniard, yet he almost certainly descended from African slaves. So did a number of his employees and others of mixed African and Mesoamerican lineage who settled in the Bajío, built families, and worked as miners, tenants, and laborers. Many who labored the rich but dangerous mines of Guanajuato lived proudly as mulattoes; others of African origins joined Mesoamerican migrants in rural communities and became indios.

After 1780 don José Sánchez Espinosa operated landed properties ranging from the outskirts of Mexico City, through the Bajío around Querétaro and San Miguel, and north across San Luis Potosí and beyond. He raised crops and livestock to sell in northern mining centers, Bajío towns, and Mexico City. In his vast enterprises he too employed tenants for cash rents and workers for salaries, still often paid in advance, still complemented by maize rations. He was a calculating entrepreneur: in pursuit of profit he destroyed his brother-in-law and marginalized his own sons; he manipulated crop prices, raised rents, and drove down wages. In the 1790s at La Griega, just east of Querétaro, his manager don José Regalado Franco faced a working community divided between a Hispanic minority and an Otomí majority. Franco evicted Hispanic tenants to raise rents and expand commercial cropping; meanwhile an Otomí labor captain and an Otomí religious leader kept Otomí workers in the fields as wages fell.

Northwest of Querétaro on the road to San Miguel, Sánchez Espinosa operated Puerto de Nieto, a more ethnically diverse estate community. A few dozen slaves remained there in 1780; when the owner tried to move them northward they refused and forced their own emancipation. Meanwhile most tenants and workers were Spanish and mestizo, mulatto and Otomí, mixing in complex extended families. There too Sánchez Espinosa's manager, don José Toribio Rico, raised rents and pressed evictions, cut wages, and limited rations, using a network of dependent kinsmen whose ethnic diversity mirrored that of the community. Through his managers don José Sánchez Espinosa ruled a vast and profitable agribusiness empire around 1800. An agrarian capitalist, he was also a devout priest, certain that he served God as he took profit in a booming silver economy that stimulated global capitalism.

While the silver economy rose to historic peaks after 1770, Sánchez

Espinosa profited and workers struggled. At the same time the Spanish empire and the Atlantic world faced war and disruption. In the 1790s the French and Haitian revolutions challenged everything. Anxiety promoted debate in New Spain, still booming while a few claimed soaring profits and a growing number labored in insecurity to sustain families. The regime took new revenues; enlightened reformers pressed new ethnic segregations; religious innovators called for rational worship and maligned popular beliefs as superstitions. Into that crucible of prosperity and polarization came the Conde de Colombini, an Italian of enlightened education seeking rest and cure at Querétaro. He had fought across the Mediterranean and the Caribbean in the service of Spain. In 1801 he published a long poem of soaring praise to Our Lady of Pueblito, the Otomí Virgin who brought to the people of Querétaro health in times of disease and rain in years of drought—essential aid in the face of worldly challenges. Colombini saw redemption for a world plagued by war and revolution in a prodigious Otomí Virgin.

In 1808 Napoleon shook the Spanish empire by taking Madrid, ending centuries of legitimate transatlantic sovereignty. Later that year, while drought began to threaten life across the Bajío, doña Josefa de Vergara, a rich widow who never traveled far from Querétaro, began to write a testament. She ordered the City Council to use her landed patrimony to build institutions of social reform. Insisting that she and her husband built their wealth by their own efforts, she would press men to labor, offer credit to craftsmen, subsidize grain in years of dearth, provide nursing in times of epidemic, and protect honorable women from indigence. To doña Josefa worldly action backed by a religion of personal morality and salvation—not devotion to the Virgin—would sustain prosperity and social cohesion at Querétaro and across the Bajío. Before her reform experiment could take hold, in September 1810 the region exploded in an insurgency that brought on a decade of social revolution.

These people and many more participated in a history rarely recognized for its founding innovations and transforming importance. A globally linked, commercially driven, ethnically mixed, patriarchally integrated, and religiously justified—and debated—society began in Querétaro and the Bajío in the sixteenth century. It grew over three centuries, its waves of boom and consolidation linked to cycles of silver production and world trade. The mix of silver mining, irrigated cultivation, and grazing that took form in the Bajío extended north across vast expanses settled by people of European, American, and African ancestry, while independent natives faced, negotiated, and resisted incursions that they often slowed but could not stop. The diverse founders, producers, and worshippers of the Bajío created Spanish North America, a complex commercial society that by 1800 extended deep into Texas, across New Mexico, and up the coast of California to San Francisco.

They formed an early and original salient of capitalism. The history that follows aims to demonstrate how a dynamic commercial society began deep in the interior of New Spain during the sixteenth century. By the late eighteenth century it was one of the few recognizably capitalist domains in the Atlantic world, indeed in the entire world. Production, exchange, and social relations were thoroughly commercial; concentrations of profit-seeking power ruled mining and commerce, cultivation and grazing, orchestrating life in the Bajío and regions reaching far northward.

In contrast to enduring presumptions, the Bajío and Spanish North America were not ruled by a dominant Spanish state; they were not led by men more interested in honor than profit; they did not organize work mostly by coercion. Life was not ruled by rigid castes; communities were not constrained by an imposed Catholicism that inhibited debate. They were instead societies founded and led by powerful, profit-seeking entrepreneurs of diverse ancestry. The regime adapted more often than it imposed. The few who ruled and the many who worked engaged each other in contests shaped more by population dynamics and market power than personal coercions—yet there was no dearth of violence, especially at the frontiers. As diverse peoples migrated and mixed in expanding regional economies, they joined in continuous redefinitions of identities. Catholicism offered a spacious domain of religious belief, difference, and debate, for some sanctifying power and precedence, for most opening ways to adapt, endure, and sometimes challenge a new world in the making.

The Bajío and Spanish North America were not only a center of silver production, important to global dynamism after 1550, and essential after 1700. They were also the site of an early commercial society, where European, African, and Mesoamerican peoples, newcomers all, pressed aside natives (assisted by smallpox and other diseases) while mixing in search of profit and sustenance, and in the process fashioned a New World salient of capitalist social relations. As the lives sketched above suggest, there was much of modern capitalism in the early Bajío and Spanish North America. A close analysis of the region's political economy, social relations, and cultural debates, of its centuries of dynamism and its collapse into revolution in 1810, is a prerequisite to understanding early globalization and the social challenges inherent in nascent capitalism.

Globalizing the Origins of Capitalism

Most of us have been taught to believe, to know, that capitalism—the dynamic commercial ordering of production and society that concentrates power and orders the modern world—was a western invention, that is, a European, mostly British, primarily Protestant invention.[8] Thus the power of Britain and its empire in the nineteenth century and the hegemony of the United States in the twentieth appear almost natural. They generated new ways to accelerate production that made their leaders powerful and their people relatively prosperous. The rest of the world—backward to some, dependent to others, colonized often, desperately poor almost always—needed (and still needs?) to learn from the Anglo-Protestant-capitalist example.

The rethinking of this Eurocentric notion, required by the recognition of Asian dynamism in the rise of globalization after 1500, must be continued and complicated by incorporating the foundational roles of Spain's Americas. Chinese demand for silver was a key stimulus to global trade and commercial ways from 1540 to 1640, and again after 1700.[9] That demand stimulated American production of silver, opened direct trans-Pacific trade from the 1570s, and energized a burgeoning Atlantic economy. The primary way most Europeans gained silver was by trade with Spain's Americas. In the eighteenth century the Bajío fueled the world economy with silver then more important than British textiles to global dynamics. Guanajuato mines and refineries were as large and complex as British textile mills; Querétaro's tobacco factory employed thousands of women as wage workers; Bajío estates were more commercial than most in England. If production and social relations in the Bajío and regions north were orchestrated by profit-seeking entrepreneurs employing workers in deeply commercial ways, is it possible that the Bajío not only was an engine of global dynamism but had produced a society as capitalist as that emerging in Britain during the eighteenth century?

In such an understanding early capitalism becomes a process linking peoples across the globe, with Chinese rulers and merchants, artisans and peasants, and American silver miners, agrarian capitalists, and their working dependents as important as European empire builders, traders, and wage workers. Still, the political and social ramifications of the global acceleration of trade varied in revealing ways. The unprecedented quantities of silver produced by Spain's Americas eventually arrived in China, providing the specie to lubricate trade and fill imperial coffers. The avalanche of silver helped China commercialize, sustain a growing population, and fund the Ming regime. In Spain, the primary European recipient of silver, the precious commodity fueled soaring trade and paid for Hapsburg wars. When flows receded in the 1630s and 1640s the Ming dynasty fell in China while Spain lost Portugal, its Brazilian and African dominions, and Asian trade—and faded from the center of European power relations.[10]

The silver trade was global and shaped by links between Chinese and Spanish empires: both reinforced when silver boomed, both prejudiced when it fell (in the 1640s and again after 1800). Equally important, in American colonies that produced soaring quantities of silver and in European regions that had to trade to gain the silver needed to join global trade (and to compete with Spain), silver helped to bring about transforming social changes. During the global acceleration of 1550 to 1640 Potosí yielded unprecedented amounts of silver high in the Andes, building a commercial economy that latched onto communities grounded in Andean ways of production and exchange. During the same period, important if secondary silver mines at Taxco and Pachuca set off parallel commercial innovations in the heartland of the Aztec empire, while mines at Zacatecas and Guanajuato drove fully commercial development in Spanish North America. Silver landing in Europe passed through Spain to stimulate production and trade in Italian, German, and Low Country city-states.[11]

When Chinese demand for silver revived around 1700, an eighteenth-century acceleration of capitalism combined rising American silver production and dynamic Atlantic trade in sugar, slaves, textiles, and more. Again silver filled the coffers of China and Spain and fueled their trade. Into the eighteenth century Qing China ruled an expanding population (fed in part by local adoptions of American maize and peanuts); it oversaw rising production and trade and a continuing march to the west. Bourbon Spain held its empire while facing challenges from its French ally and British foe. Meanwhile American regions of silver production and European zones of commercial and proto-industrial development accelerated capitalist ways. In the Americas the Bajío and Spanish North America lived a silver boom sustained by commercial cultivation and textile production. In Europe both France and England accelerated cloth production and trade, stimulated by silver, sugar, slaves, and population growth at home. Britain took the lead in industrial innovation late in the century.[12]

Then the 1790s began a time of wars and revolutions in Europe and the Atlantic world: France in revolution set off Napoleonic expansions; Britain, France, and Spain, in varying alliances, fought for Euro-Atlantic power. In the process Haitian slaves freed themselves in a revolution that destroyed the most profitable (and socially degrading) sugar and slave colony in the Caribbean. When Napoleon in 1808 took Madrid (surely in search of silver revenues), he provoked conflicts that led to wars for independence in Spain's American domains, and in 1810 set off a social revolution in the Bajío, the leading silver producer and the most dynamic capitalist region in the Americas.

By 1825 Britain was dominant in Europe in both war and industry. The Americas had broken into nations struggling to find independence. Social revolutions had destroyed the American engines of the Atlantic economy, Haiti and the Bajío. Within Europe and the Atlantic world British hegemony was set in industrialization, war, and other people's revolutions. Decades of conflict enabled Britain, and only Britain, to focus on expansion across South Asia toward China, as the Qing regime faced crises of production and westward expansion along with rising social and political challenges. The British hegemony that marked the nineteenth century had begun.[13] This history of the Bajío and Spanish North America cannot explain all that. But the rise of global trade, the invention of capitalist ways, and the conflicts that drove the great transformation of 1790 to 1830 cannot be understood without examining the origins of capitalism in those key regions of the Americas—and the roots of the social revolution that transformed life there beginning in 1810.

As we turn from Eurocentric presumptions and work to understand the late rise of British and Anglo-American hegemony, there is still much to learn from the best of the scholars who sustain Eurocentric visions. Adam Smith's observation that trade has been an important stimulus to profit and productivity remains essential, a view taken up by Wallerstein, who added the Marxian emphasis that shared trade repeatedly led to contrasting ways of production in different regions, with differing political, social, and cultural outcomes.[14] Marx emphasized that the social relations of production were (and are) vitally important in every society; his historical analyses emphasize that capitalist social relations lead persistently (inevitably?) to concentrating financial-commercial-industrial powers and deepening exploitations of working majorities. (His great error, of course, was the presumption that revolutions would right all that.) Eric Wolf retained Marx's emphasis on social relations of production, and reminded us that even "people without history" (people without strong states, capitalist powers, and historians to serve them) have forced the powerful to adapt to them (at least in limited ways) as capitalism has driven toward hegemony. And Wolf, like Marx, insisted that capitalism only happened when Britons harnessed fossil energy to mechanized industries producing for global trade (protected by an expansive empire). We may debate whether the British industrial, commercial, and imperial breakthrough around 1800 was the beginning of capitalism or the key transition to British hegemony within capitalism, but Marx and Wolf are right that it was a watershed in world history.[15]

Even Max Weber's emphasis on religion and the rise of capitalism remains important, not because Protestant ways underpinned profit-seeking entrepreneurship and lives that honored work, but because Weber reminds us that religion and culture matter in understanding capitalism. Entrepreneurial ways emerged among European and American Catholics and Protestants, as did invocations of the good of hard labor. They flourished in China, India, and Japan among people little influenced by Christianity of any sort. They flourished in the Islamic world. No one religious ethos was aligned with capitalism.[16] Diverse capitalists have understood their worlds in religious ways. Religious visions have repeatedly legitimated power and profit taking; religious responses have regularly guided those who live under capitalism, and sometimes fueled their resistance. Capitalism is an economic system with political linkages, social ramifications, and cultural justifications that are often religious. Weber rightly pointed us to religious understandings. They may not drive capitalism, but they are integral to its daily life.

Fernand Braudel, perhaps the most prolific and innovative modern analyst of the rise of capitalism, remains exceptionally useful, despite his focus on Europe (or because he knew that he focused on Europe). He understood the complexity of European development and the centrality of changing trade to its economic dynamism. He integrated analyses of production and trade, states and empires, social ways and labor relations—and diverse religious visions. In his monumental three-volume work on early modern capitalism, he traced the importance (if not the details) of Europe's engagements with the wider world. He set a foundation grounded in Europe for the analysis of the long and complex global emergence of capitalism.

Braudel emphasized that three levels of economic activity organized early modern life: first and most basic, production for sustenance, "the non-economy, the soil into which capitalism thrusts its roots but which it can never really penetrate"; second and most dynamic, production for exchange, "the favored terrain of the market economy, . . . horizontal communications between different markets; here a degree of automatic co-ordination links supply, demand, and prices"; and third, and increasingly dominant, production ruled by concentrations of financial and commercial power, "the zone of the anti-market, where the great predators roam and the law of the jungle operates. This—today as in the past, before and after the industrial revolution—is the real home of capitalism."[17] Braudel knew that many, perhaps most people around the world produced in important part for family and community sustenance in the early modern world, and that their production helped them to resist the pressures of capitalists and the demands of regimes.[18] He saw the potential for markets to energize shared productivity gains, joining analysts from Adam Smith to Douglass North. And he recognized that the powers driving capitalism concentrated at towering heights, accumulating by taking from the many below.

Braudel's distinction brings clarity to an important historical trajectory: the long-term process—ongoing before the sixteenth century, gaining new dynamism when trade became global—in which capitalists promoted and shaped to their advantage an expanding world of markets, while penetrating and limiting the resistant domains where families and communities produced for sustenance. Ways of production that Braudel separated were increasingly joined in a historic process of integration that over centuries reinforced the powers of capitalist predators, limited the ability of market exchange to generate shared welfare, and eroded the capacity of sustenance producers to keep the autonomies that allowed them to stand resistant (if often poor) in the face of power. The history of the Bajío and Spanish North America illustrates all that, providing a protean example of capitalist social relations. I understand capitalism as a historical trajectory, a process of long-term change, defined by the rising dominance of concentrated economic powers that promote, rule, and reshape market relations, claiming for a powerful few ever more of the gains of exchange, all the while invading, constraining, and eventually eliminating domains of subsistence production, searching for profit while pressing states and cities, communities and families—and churches—to adapt to its ways and interests.

There can be no absolute definition of a historical process as universal, variable, and widely debated as the rise of capitalism. But this adaptation of Braudel's characterization has the advantage of effectively describing far-reaching long-term changes that can be detailed empirically while allowing for important variations that can be investigated empirically. Capitalists may rule financial resources or channels of trade, essential lands or minerals, or key technologies. Markets may be local, regional, or global, controlled by a few predators and limited to favored participants, or open to diverse producers and traders. Makers of sustenance may be cultivators, hunters, or gatherers (including fishers); they may hold ample rich resources or have scarce access to marginal bases of life; they may live mostly outside markets (few are fully autonomous) or regularly engage in work or trade that fuels markets and the profits of others.

Within this understanding of capitalism, questions of population pressures and resource constraints, the rise of fossil fuels and the mechanization of work, remain important.[19] The first two operate as fundamental ecological contexts, the latter two as transformations implemented by capitalists seeking profit and power in an ever more commercial world. This understanding also emphasizes that capitalism does not inherently seek improved productivity or shared material welfare for humanity. It seeks profit and concentrations of power in a widening commercial organization of production and global exchange. Gains in productivity and material welfare have happened, notably where resources were exploited in regions of sparse population (the Bajío and Spanish North America), where technological breakthroughs combined with widening trade and imperial extractions (nineteenth-century Britain, twentieth-century Japan), or where capitalist power combined vast resources, sparse population, technical innovations, widening trade, and imperial assertions (the United States after 1840).

The recent drive of capitalism to bring labor-saving ways to densely populated regions, too often marginalizing growing numbers of desperate people, shows that the goal of profit and power persists, and that the search for productivity focuses on profit, not the welfare of producing peoples. As innovations in public health and medical cures set global populations on course to unprecedented growth (now slowing), their survival and prosperity under a capitalism ruled by labor-saving technologies and dependent on finite fossil fuels remains a question.[20] Braudel's emphasis on the predatory dynamic that drives capitalist concentrations as markets expand requires analyses of the diverse powers that have made and remade the modern world, and the contested and uncertain outcomes as those powers have reconstructed the lives of peoples across the globe.

Thus defined, capitalism drove ever more global trade from 1500 to 1800. New concentrations of wealth and power emerged around the world. Early capitalist societies, where predators ruled expanding markets and commercial ways of work and subsistence production became increasingly marginal, developed in northwest Europe and in the Bajío and Spanish North America. This adaptation of Braudel's conceptualization helps differentiate the dynamic capitalist regions of the Bajío and Spanish North America from Mesoamerican and Andean Spanish America. There too silver drove production and trade, but cultivating communities rooted in pre-Hispanic pasts and reconsolidated under Spanish rule as indigenous republics kept subsistence production resilient (yet never impervious) through the colonial centuries, leaving nascent capitalism to develop as an overlay of real dynamism, dependent upon communities for produce and labor yet limited by the same communities' control of lands and insistence on at least limited subsistence production. This perspective also highlights differences between industrializing capitalist Britain and much of continental Europe, where commercial ways also remained a layer superimposed on entrenched peasant communities, drawing produce and labor from them and thus remaining dependent on them, through the eighteenth century (a fair description of much of China in the same era).[21]

Braudel's vision also solves the dilemma of the slave trade, slavery and capitalism. It is clear that the traffic in Africans and the sugar and slave colonies were ruled by powerful predators profiting from commercial production in expanding markets; they ruled workers priced as commodities, using their produce to profit in an expanding capitalist system.[22] Braudel removed "freedom" and "wages" from the essence of capitalism (as have many capitalists), enabling us to see the slave trade and slave plantations as pivotal to early capitalism, second only to the silver economies as American engines of global dynamism.

Braudel explains the rise of commercial and industrial capitalism in Europe, the focus of his three volumes, by emphasizing the importance of Atlantic trade and the stimulus of silver. Capitalist predators ruled enterprises that promoted markets integrating communities, regions, nations, and empires. They used diverse controls of resources, finance and exchange, machines and labor, in endless combinations. Labor might be free and receive wages, coerced yet commoditized, or attracted, constrained, remunerated, and sustained in other monetized ways. Capitalism accelerated after 1550 as silver-driven trade became global and entrepreneurial predators ruled production, social relations, and cultural understandings in ever wider domains. Recognizing the importance of Chinese demand for silver as demonstrated by Flynn and Giráldez, seeing the multi-centered nature of early globalization as emphasized by Pomeranz, adding an understanding that capitalist social relations came early in the Bajío and Spanish North America, and emphasizing the rising power of capitalists to rule markets and constrain communities of sustenance—this adaptation of Braudel builds on his insights to propose a conceptualization that aims to facilitate analysis of emerging capitalism.

Rethinking the Spanish Empire

Iberian expansion and the Spanish empire were pivotal to early globalization and the origins of capitalism. Iberians led the incorporation of the Americas into global circuits, sending rising flows of silver into dynamic trades. And as with early globalization, no regime and no group of adventuring entrepreneurs imagined or designed the Spanish Empire. As Henry Kamen emphasizes, Iberians did not head out to conquer the Americas, build an empire, and produce silver for global trades. Rather, they joined diverse ventures aiming for immediate gain amid European dynastic conflicts, all linked to emerging trade and the revenues that it might raise. An empire of European power and global reach resulted over the course of the sixteenth century from the military, commercial, diplomatic, and religious engagements of European, Amerindian, and Asian powers, and peoples whom they ruled in complex ways. From unscripted encounters Spain found new power in Europe and the Americas, new profits in silver and trade—powers and profits contested by other Europeans, independent Amerindians, and Asian empires. Spain ruled by negotiating complex global trades and related political, social, and cultural interactions. After Felipe II claimed the crown of Portugal in 1580, his domains included Spain's Americas and their extension to Manila, plus Portugal's Brazil, African enclaves, and Asian trading posts. Around 1600 Madrid claimed an empire of unprecedented global reach.[23] Spain's Hapsburgs joined China's Ming Emperors at the head of the most powerful regimes shaping, and shaped by, decades of founding globalization.

Yet the Spanish Empire remains deeply misunderstood. In an oft-repeated view, conquest led inexorably to coercive exploitations, defined by cultural impositions, leading to constraining closures. Of course there is truth in this vision. Conquests and coercions, exploitations and impositions were everywhere in the foundations of globalization (as in all of history).[24] Spanish monarchs and their imperial delegates aimed to impose their wishes and ways on diverse subjects across the globe. Distance, diversity, and limited coercive powers ensured that they could not. One goal of this history is to detail how regime officials negotiated with entrepreneurs and how both negotiated with diverse working peoples in a key region of the Americas.

Now, Alejandra Irigoin and Regina Grafe have analyzed anew the structure and finances of Spain's empire. They show a regime never absolutist, always in negotiation with commercial elites, creating opportunities and distributing wealth in ways that gave merchants and others a stake in a commercially vibrant empire. With silver production strong, bargaining with "stakeholders" allowed the regime to endure and the Spanish Atlantic economy to flourish, even in the face of the rising military and commercial powers of eighteenth-century France and Britain. For Irigoin and Grafe the Spanish empire was absolutist only in pretense, always in negotiation with key economic players, and never so extractive that it inhibited commercial dynamism.[25]

Their vision points to a new understanding of the regime. Stakeholders included not only merchants who collected revenues but the rich and powerful men who invested in city council seats, and those who bought office as district magistrates. Councilmen were normally merchants and landed entrepreneurs who aimed to oversee the regulation of urban life and elect the judges who led local courts. District magistrates sought office to mix administrative and judicial roles with active trades. The merchants who joined *consulados* (chambers) in Seville, Lima, and Mexico City, and later in Cádiz, Veracruz, Guadalajara, and other cities across the empire to promote trade and settle commercial disputes, were also stakeholders. So were artisans in guilds and native notables who sat as governors, magistrates, and councilmen in Repúblicas de Indios.

All held a stake in the empire; all mixed economic goals with administrative and judicial roles.[26] All bargained to gain and hold benefits, however unequal, under a regime with scant coercive powers. The treasury funded just enough naval force to hold the empire together and protect silver trades. In the Americas military power focused on ports. Elsewhere it depended on militias that reinforced the power of key local interests.[27] Spanish America—especially New Spain, the Bajío, and Spanish North America—generated soaring flows of silver and revenues to the end of the eighteenth century, fueling complex trades with Europe and Asia. Stakeholders in the Spanish American economy shared in those trades and revenues, and in regional and local governance. A few claimed vast wealth; many found ways to prosperity; the majority adapted and negotiated to sustain families and communities.

The regime worked to stabilize all this by mediation. Recourse to coercion was limited, a last and uncertain resort. Stakeholders, whether they were consulado merchants, city councilmen, district magistrates, or village officials, combined entrepreneurial interests and judicial powers. The chance to use judicial power to serve entrepreneurial goals was everywhere. But abuses, especially destabilizing abuses, were limited by the dearth of coercive force and the recognition by powerful entrepreneurs and officials of the need to negotiate with others, whether regional magistrate-traders, urban guildsmen, or indigenous republics, to keep the peace and maintain production. Scholars of New Spain from William Taylor and Woodrow Borah to Felipe Castro Gutiérrez and Brian Owensby have demonstrated that the Spanish colonial regime operated ultimately as a judicial mediator, working to resolve conflicts and limit extreme abuses—stabilizing the inequities inherent in global trade and colonial ways.

An empire generating soaring commercial wealth and regime revenues, encompassing far-flung and diverse communities, with communications slow and military force weak and uncertain, ruled vast domains for three centuries by combining silver production, global trade relations, stakeholder bargaining, and judicial mediation. It was a key participant in the rise of capitalism. Under Spanish political and judicial institutions an early capitalist society that was understood and debated in Catholic religious ways flourished in the Bajío and Spanish North America.

Conflicts Enabling British Hegemony

If capitalism began in global trade, if the Bajío and Spanish North America were the most dynamic and capitalist regions of the Americas as the nineteenth century began, and if the Spanish regime and Catholic culture were compatible with capitalist dynamism, how did Britain and then the United States claim hegemonic roles in global capitalism after 1800? We must seek explanation in changing global trade, imperial conflicts in the Atlantic world and beyond—and in evolving regime powers and political organizations, ways of production and social incorporation, and the cultural visions and debates linked to all that. We must look not only to the histories of regional (and eventually national) societies presumed separate, parallel, and thus comparable but also to the trade, wars, and other interactions that engaged and changed states and societies struggling to find their ways in a globalizing world.[28]

British hegemony came late to capitalism; Braudel reminds us that the global preeminence of London and Britain began only in the 1770s, as industrialization accelerated while new power in India compensated for losses of rule (yet not of trade) in North America.[29] C. H. Bayly details how the combination of capitalist production and national regimes, consolidated in England, the United States, and the Atlantic world around 1800, extended across Europe during the nineteenth century and reached into Asia as the twentieth began.[30] He documents a second stage of globalization.

A fundamental transformation restructured the Atlantic world and global capitalism between 1770 and 1830. It marked a shift from centuries of multi-centered globalization to centuries of North Atlantic hegemony. It ended foundational times in which the Spanish Empire, the Bajío, and Spanish North America were pivotal participants in economic accelerations and social transformations tied to trade with Europe and China, and began a new era of industrial capitalism in which Britain and later the United States claimed the lead in renewed economic dynamism—still tied to China and Asia, the Americas, and Africa.

Parts of that transformation have been widely recognized, deeply analyzed, and regularly debated: industrial innovations in Britain; the British triumph in war against revolutionary and Napoleonic France; the hemispheric conflicts that established national regimes across the Americas and curtailed the Euro-Atlantic empires. Pomeranz has taken up the challenge of analyzing why the second acceleration of global capitalism focused on Britain and not China, emphasizing the advantage of English coal power and Europe's ability to draw on American resources. Less recognized as part of the transformation are the social revolutions that restructured the two leading engines of New World economic dynamism. From 1791 to 1804 the slaves of Saint-Domingue ended slavery, took national sovereignty, and all but ended sugar production and exports.[31] Then from 1810 to 1820 Bajío insurgents assaulted the economy that had slashed their earnings, raised rents, evicted tenants, and challenged patriarchy. They took control of the land, driving a revolution that undermined silver mining and commercial cropping, collapsed state revenues, and slashed entrepreneurial profits in the most capitalist region of the Americas.[32]

Both New World social revolutions exploded amid European political conflicts and Atlantic wars tied to global trade relations and economic transformations. Haitian slaves took arms and freedom in the heat of the French revolution.[33] Those conflicts fueled wars that pitted Britain against France (with Spain a wavering contestant) in a fight for European and Atlantic dominance. The loss of Haiti and its revenues led Napoleon to desperate measures. In 1807 he gained permission from his Spanish ally to march an army to Lisbon, hoping to claim the revenues of Brazil, where sugar and coffee and slavery flourished supplying markets vacated by the collapse of Haiti. The Portuguese monarchy escaped to Río, keeping Brazil's trade and revenues for Britain. Napoleon then took a great gamble, and lost. He attacked his Spanish ally in the spring of 1808, taking Madrid and deposing the monarch, hoping that New Spain's silver revenues would fill his war chest. Instead he set off a crisis of sovereignty in the Spanish empire, breaking the bureaucratic and judicial structures that sustained its trade and revenues. As Irigoin and Grafe show, the break led to conflicts in search of new sovereignties and the revenues to sustain them across the empire. In New Spain disputed rule and uncertain views of the liberal project that led to the Cádiz Constitution of 1812 culminated in Father Hidalgo's insurgency in 1810 and the revolution that followed.[34] Braudel, synthesizing a generation of economic history, concluded that the eighteenth-century rise of the Euro-Atlantic economy peaked and turned to decline in 1812, after two decades of war, soon after the Haitian revolution, and just as Bajío insurgents took down the silver economy that fueled Atlantic and global commerce.[35]

The military, political, and social conflagrations of 1789 to 1824 transformed Atlantic participations in global capitalism. Political sovereignty dispersed across the Americas just as the American engines of capitalism were assaulted by popular revolutions. No wonder the founding fathers of so many American nations felt betrayed by wars for independence that led to political instability and economic collapse. Britain emerged victorious in European warfare and dominant in industrial capitalism. The United States, the first American nation, had struggled for decades to find its way. After 1815 it found political consolidation and an economic dynamism that allowed it to accelerate its European and Asian trades, and in the 1840s to mobilize in war and take vast regions of Spanish North America from Mexico. As a result, Anglo-Americans incorporated and accelerated an expansive continental capitalism integrating mining, irrigated commercial cultivation, and extensive grazing. The wars and social revolutions that reshaped the Atlantic world after 1789 led to British dominance of capitalist production and European imperialism, and to United States hegemony in North America and later in global capitalism, setting Latin America on a course to contested politics and dependent development within capitalism.[36] The social revolution that transformed the Bajío and Spanish North America, undermining capitalist dynamism there just as Mexico claimed independence, was a key part of a global transformation.

A Problem Less Considered: Stabilizing Capitalism

Within this understanding of the rise of global capitalism, the Bajío and Spanish North America were doubly important. Their silver economy drove global trade and stimulated regional capitalist social relations from the sixteenth through the eighteenth centuries. Then after 1770 the Bajío faced reaccelerating capitalist dynamism in a new context of population pressures, generating deepening predations, social dislocations, and cultural polarizations. Mining, textile, and agricultural entrepreneurs took rising profits by assaulting the ways and welfare of the producing majority. Deepening inequities were sustained for decades, until the regime crisis provoked by Napoleon's capture of the Spanish monarchy in 1808 set off revolutionary conflicts in 1810. We must understand both the economic dynamics of capitalism, and the social orchestrations and cultural conversations that organize and stabilize its inherent exploitations. And we must understand how capitalist predations may assault the families and communities that produce everything, undermining the very social arrangements that stabilize enduring inequities—threatening capitalist dynamism, even unleashing conflicts that challenge its primacy in key regions.

Douglass North and his collaborators recognize the dual challenge of understanding capitalism. Their early work focused on the economic institutions that promoted capitalism in Anglo-American contexts, offering them as models to emulate.[37] Now, in *Violence and Social Orders*, they emphasize key differences between early modern and modern capitalism and bring new focus to the institutions that organize and mediate the inequities inherent in unfettered capitalist dynamism (though they do not phrase their insight this way). They make two key points: First, the commercial capitalism that shaped the early modern age developed under regimes that had, whatever their absolutist pretenses, limited powers of coercion—a point that captures the limits of the Spanish empire during its formative role in globalization. By contrast, the new regimes of the age of industrial capitalism, often national, sometimes imperial, built military and police powers not possible in earlier times.[38] Second, in the context of such unprecedented powers of coercion, successful capitalist societies institutionalize not only the property rights that facilitate market exchange but also "open-access institutions"—accessible rights to incorporate to do business, to participate in political life, and to seek judicial redress when all else fails, rights that broaden participation in the gains of capitalism and enable those facing its predations to seek influence in political engagement and redress in court challenges.[39] They recognize, at least implicitly, that the preservation of capitalist dynamism requires political and judicial mediations.

North and his colleagues focus on key institutions that have stabilized modern capitalism: state concentrations of coercive power organized "impersonally" in militaries, police, and prisons, circumscribed by access to incorporation, the political process, and the courts. They recognize that early modern regimes lacked these concentrations of coercion even as they limited rights to incorporation, political participation, and judicial redress. The history of the Bajío and Spanish North America confirms that the powers of coercion were limited within the Spanish Empire. So were rights to incorporation, but they were open to key groups (mine operators, landed entrepreneurs, convent bankers, even indigenous republics) in differing yet important ways. There were also limits on political rights, though they were available to powerful Spaniards in city councils and to native notables in indigenous republics (the latter scarce in Spanish North America). Most important, rights to judicial redress were widely available—and essential to social stabilization.

The history of Bajío and Spanish North America adds new dimensions to our understanding of the orchestration and stabilization of early capitalist ways. Patriarchal hierarchies, ethnic complexities, and religious conversations were pivotal to organizing inequalities and stabilizing predations. Under a regime of limited coercive power, in regions of vital economic importance yet with sparse populations available to labor, bargaining between officials and entrepreneurs organized a commercial economy integrated by patriarchy, fragmented by ethnic complexities, and legitimated in religious debates, all backed by judicial mediations. Those complex orchestrations enabled a dynamic early capitalist society to develop and drive northward for centuries. Only after 1770 did population pressures allow capitalist predators to deny customary remunerations, stimulate social insecurities, threaten working men's patriarchy, and insult popular religious sensibilities, deepening polarizing tensions. The regime responded with a new emphasis on military power, police, and prisons, and soon learned that it needed to sustain judicial and other mediations to maintain capitalist dynamism. The response worked—until the regime broke and revolution exploded to challenge everything.

Capitalism is inherently dynamic, shaping production and social relations to concentrate wealth generated by diverse producers linked in market economies. The paradox of capitalism is that its predations may destabilize its own dynamism. Capitalist persistence requires institutions that organize inequities and mediate conflicts in ways that limit and legitimate predations before they provoke destabilization. North and his colleagues identify key ways of participation and mediation, backed by concentrations of coercion, that have characterized leading nations under industrial capitalism. The history of the Bajío and Spanish North America provides a founding case of how global trade stimulated capitalist social relations, of how these relations were stabilized with limited coercions during centuries of dynamism. The same history reveals how predations were eventually unleashed, briefly kept in check while polarizations deepened, then ultimately led to a shattering revolution.

The patriarchal hierarchies, ethnic complexities, and religious legitimations needed to organize and stabilize protean capitalism in the Bajío and Spanish North America—always backed by judicial mediations—have persisted in diverse ways under modern industrial capitalism. The concentrated coercions and political participations emphasized by North and his colleagues have not replaced but built upon enduring patriarchal hierarchies, ethnic divisions, and religious legitimations—while judicial interventions remain essential, if not always available. As population pressures deepen and capitalist predations proliferate and diversify, the challenges of stabilizing their dynamic exploitations become more complex. By understanding the economic dynamism, social orchestration, and stabilizing mediations of early capitalism in the Bajío and Spanish North America, exploring the deepening polarizations after 1770, and analyzing the breakdown into revolution in 1810, historical inquiry can illuminate processes that gave rise to the formation of global capitalism, the shift to Anglo–North Atlantic hegemony after 1770, and the continuing challenge of stabilizing capitalism's accelerating dynamism and proliferating predations.

There are global implications in the history of the Bajío and Spanish North America. This volume details the emergence of capitalist production, social relations, and cultural conversations to the 1760s, their persistence with deepening polarizations after 1770, and the breakdown into revolution in 1810. A sequel will engage the Bajío revolution and Mexican independence, and the ways they transformed North America and capitalism after 1810. Global connections, Atlantic relations, and North American implications are noted throughout. Still, I focus on globally linked yet regionally based political institutions, economic organizations, social relations, and cultural conversations. The global ramifications sketched here emerged as I saw that a protean capitalist society rose in the interior of North America under Spanish rule—to be transformed after 1810 by a little-recognized social revolution. Few readers will begin this textual odyssey holding these views. I aim to share my understanding through close inquiries into the lives of entrepreneurs and working communities as they negotiated unprecedented historic processes. If my conclusions prove persuasive, others will join me in working out the global implications of this history.

The Bajío, Spanish North America, and Capitalism

This volume, then, explores the Bajío and Spanish North America as a key region driving the creation of capitalism. The chapters mix detailed inquiries into the lives of powerful men (and a few women), the views of contemporaries, and the ways of working communities.[40] This Prologue introduced key characters and raised questions for global history. The Introduction places the Bajío and Spanish North America in the context of global trade, Atlantic empires, and the capitalism they generated. It also previews the approaches that underlie my attempt to write a regional history in global context, integrating production and regime power, patriarchy, ethnicity, and religion.

Part I traces the development of the Bajío and Spanish North America from 1500 to 1770. Chapter 1 focuses on Querétaro from 1500 to 1660, emphasizing its Otomí origins, the impact of silver and Chichimeca wars, and the postwar consolidation of a commercial economy, a patriarchal labor market, and a contested Christian culture. Chapter 2 explores the expansion of silver mining from 1550 to 1700, beginning at Guanajuato and Zacatecas, then far north at Parral. It details developments in the Bajío north and west of Querétaro, focusing on mining at Guanajuato, grazing across the surrounding uplands, and the foundation of patriarchal estate communities on rich irrigated bottomlands. Throughout it engages European, Mesoamerican, and African migrations, amalgamations, and changing identities.

Chapter 3 explores the revival of silver after 1680 at Guanajuato, the rise of industry and trade at San Miguel (then el Grande, now de Allende), and the continuing expansion of Querétaro, still a Spanish-Otomí city of textiles and crafts, cultivation and commerce. By 1760 each city had generated differing ways of entrepreneurship and distinct social relations, ethnic identities, and religious visions. Together they led a dynamic regional economy that generated great wealth, stimulated trade, filled regime coffers, and drove Spanish North America northward—notably through the rugged Sierra Gorda and along Gulf lowlands across the Río Grande and into Texas. Then in the 1760s Atlantic war and a downturn in silver mining brought crisis. Chapter 4 concludes Part I by examining the popular risings that shook the Bajío and nearby areas during pivotal years of conflict. It details how shared postwar challenges set off colonial resistance in the coastal colonies of British North America and the Bajío. It examines the roots, expressions, limits, and repressions of resistance at Guanajuato and other riotous communities. It seeks to explain why the risings in and near the Bajío faced repression in two years, while resistance in British America lived on to fuel the first American war for independence. With the end of resistance in 1767, the Bajío and Spanish North America sat poised to resume capitalist dynamism under Spanish rule.

Part II focuses on the decades from 1770 to 1810, times of renewed economic boom, new population pressure, and unprecedented social and cultural polarization. Parallel chapters explore entrepreneurial power, city lives, rural communities, and religious debates. Chapter 5 engages the life of don José Sánchez Espinosa, a key participant in the small but powerful community of colonial entrepreneurs. He controlled estates from the outskirts of Mexico City, through the eastern

Bajío, and across San Luis Potosí. He ran an integrated commercial enterprise, always in search of profit. His correspondence documents entrepreneurial energy, patriarchal rule, links to other entrepreneurs and regime officials, and his certainty that he served God while accumulating wealth and exerting power. Close examination of the heights of entrepreneurial power shows that leading mine operators, merchants, and landlords colonized the Bourbon regime more than its reformers succeeded in asserting power in New Spain.

Chapter 6 returns to the mining city of Guanajuato, the craft town of San Miguel, and the commercial and industrial city of Querétaro to explore regime reforms and changing ways of urban production, work, and family life during the late colonial boom. It shows the regime offering tax and cost concessions to promote silver production at Guanajuato, helping it reach unprecedented heights. Meanwhile officials favored cloth imports from Spain over textiles made at Querétaro and San Miguel. Mining entrepreneurs profited and merchant clothiers adapted, forging new work relations to sustain production, profit, and social subordination. Patriarchy still controlled much production and most family life; but at Guanajuato's mines and refineries and in Querétaro's huge tobacco factory, new challenges to patriarchy aimed to control workers and limit remuneration.

Chapter 7 turns to rural communities around Querétaro and San Miguel, especially La Griega and Puerto de Nieto. While the Bajío was the most urban region of the Americas in the late eighteenth century, the majority still lived in the countryside, mostly at commercial estates. These rural enterprises and their resident communities generated profits for elite families by feeding grazing communities to the north, mining centers at Guanajuato and Zacatecas, and urban consumers across the Bajío and in Mexico City. From 1770 commercial boom came amid population growth. After a devastating frost and famine in 1785–86, irrigation and cultivation expanded. Slavery, long in decline, ended while new segregation reshaped rural communities. Entrepreneurs pressed wages downward, raised rents, and evicted tenants who could not pay. Overt coercion ended and ethnic segregation deepened while insecurity proliferated in communities facing population pressure. Tensions escalated, yet stability held for decades. In a commercial society fragmented by ethnic diversity, hierarchies of patriarchy linked powerful entrepreneurs and the working poor. Powerful men exploited poor men, while men powerful and poor aimed to rule wives and children. After 1770 insecurity deepened and earnings fell, yet working men acquiesced in their own and their families' exploitation, as long as patriarchal ways survived.

Chapter 8 explores religious life after 1770. The diverse visions of

Catholicism that evolved before 1750 faced a new contender: enlightened rational worship that maligned popular devotions as superstitions. Cultural polarization mixed with proliferating insecurity and deepening exploitation. Yet polarization did not go unmediated: local priests compromised to preserve their roles and revenues; reformers promised education and charity. Some among the powerful and their enlightened allies—the Conde de Colombini gave poetic voice to their views—saw popular devotions as essential to social peace. While social and religious tensions deepened, patriarchy held, and debates about truth and morality persisted, containing conflicts as Bajío capitalism drove past 1800.

The Conclusion links the economic dynamism, patriarchal social relations, ethnic amalgamations, and religious visions of the Bajío to the continuing northward drive of Spanish North America. It offers a case study of California as its last colonial frontier, a Pacific variant of the commercial, ethnic, patriarchal, and Christian assertions, adaptations, and debates that began in the Bajío centuries earlier. It then places New Spain, the Bajío, and Spanish North America in the context of the conflicts that rocked the Americas and the Atlantic world after 1780. An Epilogue points to the coming of the revolution that transformed the Bajío and its role in the world after 1810.

A Note on Terminology

SOME OF THE LANGUAGE USED in this history will surprise even seasoned historians of New Spain. First, I use Mexico only to refer to the capital city and mexicano as an ethnic term for the Nahuatl speakers who lived in the basins around the capital. Mexico did not exist as a nation before 1821; Mexican did not serve as a national identity until after independence, for many not until long after. Referring to New Spain as Mexico and its inhabitants as Mexicans is not only an anachronism but presumes the inevitability of the nation—and one of the key conclusions of my analysis is that the nation was not inevitable.

The term Spaniard refers to those who claimed that status in New Spain, including nearly everyone of Iberian ancestry, and many of mixed origin. Persons arriving from Iberia are called immigrant or peninsular Spaniards (or by the pejorative *gachupínes*)—the standard usage in New Spain. The label Creole was rarely used to identify Spaniards born in New Spain before the wars for independence; I have not seen this usage in private correspondence or judicial records. I refrain from imposing another anachronism that presumes the conflicts of the independence era onto previous centuries. I do preserve the use of *don* or *doña*, titles of honor and minor nobility. They were part of a person's name; their presence says much about a person's status. Equally, I use full titles of nobility; they were the names most used by those who held them—and thus I keep them in Spanish, as I would any name. (There is no evidence, I should add, that a title of nobility—minor or major—deflected anyone from entrepreneurial energy.)

I do not use the English term Indian. *Indio* was a category of subordination and liability for taxation in Spain's empire. People from

Manila were *indios chinos*. Long into the seventeenth century, sources recorded a person's ethnic identity as *mexicano, tarasco,* or *otomí*. Indio was a generic category that combined ethnically and linguistically distinct peoples in the minds and lists of Spaniards. Some people did adopt and adapt identities as indios as the centuries progressed. I use indio, not Indian, as I analyze that process. I aim to avoid imposing on historical developments in New Spain the complex presumptions and debates rooted in present-day ethnic-identity politics.

I use mestizo as it appears in the sources, referring to people of mixed indigenous and Spanish ancestry, generally speaking Spanish and broadly participating in European commercial ways. They proved few in the Bajío and regions north before 1810. Mulattoes were much more numerous and important. Official colonial categories, the famous *casta* paintings, and most modern scholars insist that mulatto refers to peoples of mixed European and African ancestry. In the Bajío and Spanish North America (and I believe across New Spain) most mulattoes mixed African and diverse indigenous ancestries, favored their African heritage by appearance or choice, spoke Spanish, and lived in the Hispanic commercial world—mostly as working subordinates. Ethnic distinctions finer than Spaniard, mestizo, mulatto, and indio (preceded by otomí, tarasco, and mexicano) rarely appear in the sources used here; I avoid them—hoping to avoid unnecessary confusions.

For places and people currently well known—Querétaro, or don José de Gálvez—I aim for standard usage and spelling; for others I use place and personal names as I found them in the sources. They were often variable, so I have opted for the most common usage. I keep all names in Spanish, except for Mexico City; it would confuse too much to call the metropolis (accurately) México.

Introduction

A New World: The Bajío, Spanish

North America, and Global Capitalism

A NEW WORLD BEGAN in the sixteenth century. For three centuries no region was more important to the creation of that world than the Bajío, a fertile basin northwest of Mexico City. A little-settled and often contested frontier between Mesoamerican states to the south and independent peoples to the north, it saw everything change with the arrival of Europeans. Disease, war, and displacement removed most natives. Silver linked the region to rising global trade. Migrants from Mesoamerica and Europe arrived seeking gain; Africans arrived bound to labor. Production, labor, and communities were driven by pursuit of commercial profit. Diverse peoples mixed to forge new and changing identities. Patriarchy orchestrated social hierarchies. Catholicism defined and debated everything. By the eighteenth century the region was dynamically capitalist and socially polarized. Patriarchy persisted, yet faced new pressures and challenges. Catholicism endured while fundamental debates multiplied within its spacious domain. Then in 1810 the Bajío generated a mass insurgency that shook the Spanish empire and became a social revolution that helped create Mexico, transform North America, and redirect global capitalism.

The world made in the Bajío, a basin beginning around Querétaro and extending west across Guanajuato, was new in three fundamental ways. First, immigrant residents, commercial dynamics, social amalgamations, and cultural reconstitutions combined to make life in the

Bajío truly unprecedented locally or elsewhere. Second, while that new society developed in a defined region, it was powerfully and persistently created in response to global linkages: silver trade, the Spanish Empire, and Catholic Christianity. Third, the region, tied to the world by silver, shaped by commercial ways, reshaped by ethnic amalgamations, and integrated by patriarchal hierarchies during three centuries of change, became home to a society that was recognizably capitalist—driven by profit while integrating diverse peoples in commercial social relations that concentrated economic power and deepened exploitation with limited reliance on overt personal coercion.[1]

Globally linked commercial dynamism drove settlement and development in the Bajío. Mesoamericans and Africans built and Europeans usually (but not always) ruled the mines and refineries, cities and textile workshops, irrigated estates and livestock ranches that fueled a burgeoning world economy. Through centuries, silver production peaked, waned, and peaked again. Commercial power ruled throughout. The historic interaction of Europeans, Mesoamericans, Africans, and their mixed descendants produced a society of deep inequality and complex fluidity. Regional culture was ultimately Catholic, while diverse visions of Catholicism contested religious truth and the inequities created at the intersection of power and everyday life.

After 1770 mining, textile production, and commercial cultivation reached historic peaks and held them into the early nineteenth century. By 1800 the Bajío population approached 500,000, its silver mines produced over 5 million pesos annually, its commercial cultivators, cloth makers, and artisans yearly generated taxable goods valued at nearly 6 million pesos. The Bajío was the richest region of the Americas. The mines at Guanajuato and others to the north (also sustained by Bajío grains and cloth) combined to yield most of the 23 million pesos of silver mined annually in New Spain.[2]

Silver fueled global trade; it provoked and financed imperial wars; it helped fund the independence of the United States, which adopted New Spain's peso as its dollar. When France in republican revolution faced England in industrial revolution in wars that began in the 1790s and continued into the nineteenth century, Bajío silver helped finance both belligerents. Napoleon occupied Spain and usurped its monarchy in 1808, in important part aiming to claim New Spain's silver.[3] He set off a transatlantic crisis that led to insurgency in the Bajío in 1810—a rising that became a social revolution, transformed production and social relations across the region, set limits on the Mexican nation, and altered the trajectory of North America and global capitalism.[4]

This book offers a history of the Bajío from the arrival of Europeans after 1500 to the explosion of insurgency in 1810. It analyzes the origins and development of the first fully commercial and eventually capitalist society in the Americas. It explores production, power, social relations, and cultural visions beginning in the sixteenth century; it focuses on the region's eighteenth-century dynamism and deepening polarization. It sees that history as defined by global trade in the context of an Atlantic empire that extended to Asia. It also emphasizes that the Bajío was the foundation of the northward expansion of a deeply commercial and increasingly capitalist Spanish North America. Finally, it aims to understand how capitalist growth and the northward thrust persisted to 1810, while social and cultural polarization deepened and so much of the Atlantic world faced war and revolution.

The analysis details production, work, and everyday life in cities and rural communities from 1500 to 1810. It examines their histories in the context of regime powers that negotiated to facilitate commercial life and maintain social order in an unprecedented new world. It pays particular attention to the organization of production and its links to patriarchal social relations, changing ethnic identities, and debated religious visions—the complex social and cultural web that sustained productive inequities. After 1770 deepening contradictions marked the Bajío. By measures of profit and production, the region drove to new heights during the decades before 1810. Entrepreneurs backed by regime officials seeking revenues ruled a commercial domain integrated by vibrant markets—regional, and Atlantic, and global. Yet the economic dynamism of the late eighteenth century brought pressures to cut wages and other remuneration to mineworkers, cloth makers, and cultivators. Deepening insecurities plagued the majority; patriarchy faced challenges; new segregation divided neighboring communities; polarizing visions of Christian truth debated everything. Working families struggled. Yet stability held to 1810. This history strives to understand all that. A sequel, *Remaking the New World*, will return to the Bajío to explore the insurgency and social revolution that began in 1810, gave birth to the new Mexican nation, and redirected the history of North America, the Atlantic world, and capitalism.

The Bajío and Spanish North America in the Americas

The traditional notion of the Americas as a new world was a European conceit that covered ignorance and aimed to justify conquest and colonization. Diverse peoples inhabited the western hemisphere before Europeans knew them. Complex polities, ways of production, and cultural visions characterized indigenous societies. The Bajío became a new world after 1500 in a very different sense. Society there was built anew, driven by profit-seeking men promoting commercial visions, constituted by peoples from diverse corners of the Atlantic world, and strengthened by economic links that quickly became global. The Bajío began the creation of Spanish North America; together they formed a new and expansive society that played a key role in founding a new world of global interactions shaped by commercial relations—the world of capitalism.

That newness is best illustrated in the contrast with Spanish Mesoamerica, just south. For millennia Mesoamerica had been a domain of settled cultivators, states and empires, trade and integration, and cultural complexity. The celebrated defeat of the Mexica (Aztecs), rulers of the last Mesoamerican empire, by Cortés and his gang of entrepreneurial freebooters led to the conquest and subordination of Mesoamerican states and communities. But the military advantages of horses and iron, the diplomatic advantages of alliance with the Mexica's many enemies, and the ultimate advantage of smallpox and the other diseases that killed so many Mesoamericans and assaulted the survivors' truths combined to allow Europeans to do little more than graft themselves upon the enduring ways of Mesoamerica. Mesoamerican communities, cultigens, languages, and beliefs adapted and persisted for centuries under Spanish rule. Mesoamerica was in its own way an old world—a world that adapted, changed, and endured despite conquest and colonial incorporation.[5] Spanish Mesoamerica was not a new world; it was an attempt, inevitably limited, to harness the peoples and production of Mesoamerica to European ways.[6]

The Bajío and Spanish North America were different. When Europeans arrived in the 1520s the Bajío was a minimally populated frontier, a land contested between the Mexica, the Tarascan state to the west, and the diverse independent peoples, often mobile hunters and gatherers, who held the dry lands to the north. The Mexicas' label for those indomitable stateless peoples announced the depth of the cultural divide: they were Chichimecas, sons of dogs. While conquests and adaptations made Mesoamerican communities the foundation of Spanish Mesoamerica, the native peoples of the Bajío and the arid lands beyond proved a different and more difficult challenge to Europeans' dreams of dominion. Chichimecas were few, independent, and mobile, as resistant to Spanish power as to Mesoamerican polities. They would not become the base of a conquest society. To rule the high plateaus north of Mesoamerica, Europeans needed new means.

They did not find those means alone. Europeans neither initiated nor led the early colonization and settlement of the Bajío. That was left to Otomí peoples. Mesoamericans long subject to the Mexica, groups of Otomí used the cover of Spanish conquest to drive north into coveted lands. They came with Franciscans, but Connín and other Otomí lords ruled, and Otomí people dominated. Later, in the 1540s, Spaniards led by indigenous guides found silver at Zacatecas farther north. From the 1550s Europeans came in droves with livestock, indigenous allies, and African slaves. Responding to Chinese demand, new world silver production drove dynamic global trade, linking the Bajío to worlds far away. The surge of settlement set off conflicts with Chichimecas, who in a violent long run were killed or died of smallpox, a few survivors left in rugged uplands or drowned in a new commercial order.[7]

Spanish Mesoamerica was a conquest society. A European minority ruled an indigenous majority; commercial profit depended on extracting produce and labor from indigenous communities reconstituted as Repúblicas de Indios. Native notables and Spanish clergy remained brokers between two social and cultural sectors melded into one colonial order. In contrast, the Bajío and Spanish North America developed as the first new world in the Americas. It was a colonial creation linked to the far corners of the globe by silver and the markets that it opened. Driven locally by profit-seeking commercial ways, it included people from Mesoamerica, Europe, and Africa. Early on nearly everyone communicated in Spanish, a language of global empire and trade. Diverse people, nearly all new to the region, prayed in churches loyal to Catholic Rome—churches in which many visions of Christianity jostled together in a spacious religious culture. They built a commercial society in the lands of the Chichimecas. The silver of the Bajío and Spanish North America proved an early and enduring stimulus to commercial capitalism. In the new society concentrations of commercial power tied to global trade shaped social relations. Work and life developed in ways that presaged the monetized social relations and exploitations of modern capitalism.

Spanish North America, founded in the Bajío, was neither a variant nor an appendage of Spanish Mesoamerica. The two developed in parallel as distinct colonial orders. The kingdom of New Spain ruled both, and from the combination gained dynamism and resilient strength. The viceroyalty, like the larger Spanish empire, was a loose administrative construct built to collect revenues, promote mining and commerce, and mediate the conflicts that arose when production and trade brought tensions and exploitations to culturally diverse peoples.

The early emergence of two patterns of colonial society in New Spain stimulated the continuing creation of the colonial Americas and the Atlantic world—all tied to global trade. After decades of experiment in the Caribbean, from the 1520s New Spain set the standard for Europeans' American expansion. The conquest and creation of Spanish Mesoamerica led to searches for other indigenous states. The conquest of the Incas created a Spanish-Andean domain; the colonization of the Mayan zones from Yucatán to Guatemala extended Spanish Mesoamerica southward. From the 1550s the silver mines at Potosí in the Andes, at Taxco and Pachuca in Mesoamerica, and at Zacatecas, Guanajuato, and San Luis Potosí in Spanish North America generated unprecedented wealth (tied to trade with China), which other Europeans dreamed of replicating.

When the Portuguese developed Brazil later in the sixteenth century, and the British and French turned to colonial enterprises in the seventeenth, Spanish American precedents were inevitable models. Latecomers aimed to compete with Spanish power by matching its colonial wealth. Their problem was that the Spanish had incorporated all the state-organized peoples of the Americas and claimed all the lands rich in gold and silver (until the Portuguese found gold in southern Brazil in the 1690s). Neither conquest societies like Spanish Mesoamerica and the Andes nor a commercial society like Spanish North America could emerge in the American domains left to the Portuguese, British, and French.

After chaotic early experiments a profitable alternative was found. Sugar and slave colonies had begun on a small scale centuries earlier on the islands of Crete and Cyprus in the eastern Mediterranean to help fund the Crusades. The union of sweetness and bondage migrated westward across the inland sea during late medieval centuries and extended into the Atlantic as part of Portuguese expansion around Africa. On Atlantic islands Africans became the primary victims of slavery. When Iberians crossed the Atlantic, sugar and slave plantations provided an early economic boost in the Spanish Caribbean, until the mainland enterprise of New Spain claimed most attention, energy, and capital. After 1550, while silver drove the economies of Spanish America, the sugar and slave plantation system found a new home in the northeast of Brazil. Genoese capitalists and Portuguese colonists soon demonstrated that the plantations could operate as an engine of colonial wealth second only to silver.[8]

The British and the French, late to the American enterprise, thus knew several models: conquest colonialism based on the incorporation of state-organized indigenous societies; commercial colonialism and the construction of an Atlantic society driven by silver production; and sugar and slave colonialism, equally commercial yet dependent on the slave trade and social relations of bondage. The first British settlers on the Chesapeake imagined a conquest as if Powhatan were Moctezuma; they dreamed that his people would feed Europeans and mine gold for their profit. Those dreams produced years of conflict and death, until the colonists developed tobacco plantations using bound immigrant workers (first indentured Europeans, then African slaves).[9]

Meanwhile, Dutch investors and slave traders helped British planters transform Barbados and then Jamaica into sugar and slave colonies on the model of Brazil, soon followed by the French in Saint-Domingue. Charleston in the Carolinas (after early decades of conflictive trade with indigenous nations) was the first British mainland colony to become a slave plantation society, turning the model to rice and indigo. The praying Puritans of New England appear different, migrating as families, growing their own food, fishing, cutting timber, building ships—all without benefit of a subordinated population. Were they different because they were Puritan? Or were they different because New England had no silver, no climate for plantation crops, no product profitable enough to sustain a slave population? When we see devout Puritan Winthrops in charge in Jamaica, Charleston, and Boston, and find New England staples sustaining slave colonies, it seems that economic prospects shaped colonial differences at least as much as religious visions did.[10]

The Americas developed three fundamental ways of colonial life between 1500 and 1800: the conquest societies of Spanish Mesoamerica and the Andes; the slave plantation colonies of the greater Caribbean, extending from Brazil through the islands to the Chesapeake; and Spanish North America, the dynamic, multicultural, commercial society that began in the Bajío and drove north to include Texas and California in the eighteenth century. There were of course variants within, extensions without, and exceptions everywhere. Coastal Perú and New Spain developed slave plantations as adjuncts to conquest societies; New England was partly a unique colonial domain, and partly an adjunct to slave colonies; New Mexico seemed a distant replica of Spanish Mesoamerica, where Europeans ruled conquered indigenous villagers far to the north of Spanish North America, until the latter's commercial ways arrived in the late eighteenth century.

A fourth pattern of European-indigenous relations proved widespread, enduring, and transforming, but not colonial. Across the vast lands between Spanish New Mexico and British and French coastal settlements, the peoples of the eastern woodlands, the Mississippi basin, and the Great Plains met European traders. Europeans might have imagined this as another route to dominance; yet they traded with independent societies to gain captives, beaver pelts, deerskins, and other goods. Indigenous peoples joined to acquire livestock, guns, cloth, rum, and other goods that they hoped would confirm their independence and bolster them in conflicts with indigenous neighbors. During centuries of trade focused on Spanish New Mexico, the French Mississippi basin, and the British Atlantic seaboard, commerce changed native societies. New diseases devastated populations, disrupted communities, and challenged beliefs. Indigenous peoples were transformed, yet they might hold the upper hand for extended periods. In the long run many were destroyed. But during centuries of interactions the interior of North America was an arena of economic, cultural, and political contact where diverse native and European peoples negotiated exchanges that profited some and altered most lives and cultures—ultimately benefiting Europeans and threatening natives. But Europeans did not rule those vast domains before the nineteenth century. Similar contacts defined life from the sixteenth century to the nineteenth across the interior of South America, where Spaniards and Portuguese competed to engage independent indigenous peoples. Not all colonial contacts led to colonial rule.[11]

Founding Capitalism

The silver of the Spanish Andes, Mesoamerica, and North America, the sugar and other staples of slave colonies, and the furs and skins gained in exchanges with indigenous peoples combined to accelerate trade that expanded to fuel a rising capitalism. Across the diverse domains of Spanish America, silver ruled. Its market expanded suddenly after 1550 as the Ming Empire, including about a quarter of the world's population, demanded taxes in silver. As a result silver was twice as valuable (relative to gold) in China as in Europe during the second half of the sixteenth century. Well into the seventeenth century China drew silver to pay for silks, for porcelains, for anything it could trade to meet an insatiable demand for the metal. It took large amounts from Japan, stimulating production and helping to reshape political power there. It rapidly claimed growing flows from Spain's America, absorbing all the silver that it could produce, first through trade via Europe, the Islamic world, and south Asia, later in direct exchange from Acapulco to Manila.[12]

Spain built the first land empire in the Americas, focusing on incorporating the state-organized peoples from Mesoamerica through the Andes, mobilizing them to produce gold and silver wherever possible. When silver was found north of Mesoamerica at Zacatecas, a new commercial society emerged amid decades of conflict with stateless Chichimecas. Silver drove global trade from 1550 to 1640, stimulating the settlement and development of Spanish America and filling the revenues of a suddenly powerful Spanish empire. It was mined and refined by means ranging from labor drafts rooted in the Inca *mita* at Andean Potosí to free labor rewarded with wages and ore shares at Zacatecas. Silver trade encouraged and funded colonial development; it did not determine its diverse social relations. Where emerging capitalism could build on the ways of existing societies, it did. Where it had to forge new settlements and social relations, it did that too.

Silver, driving the most profitable and the most global of trades, helped to increase the wider trade tapped by those without silver. Slaves made sugar in plantation colonies ruled by different, often warring, European regimes—Spanish Santo Domingo and later Cuba, Portuguese Brazil, British Barbados and Jamaica, and French Saint-Domingue. Spanish, British, and French traders dealt with independent natives to gain furs and skins—commerce that in the seventeenth century was marginal to Spain, important to Britain, and crucial to France. The American societies tied to global silver and Atlantic commodity trade sent diverse products into complex commercial networks. They developed social relations and cultural dynamics at the intersection of global trade, European regime goals and capacities, local resources, and indigenous social, political, and cultural traditions.[13]

European entrepreneurs and regimes promoted and profited from emerging commercial capitalism. In the effort they generated diverse historical experiences at home and overseas. Portugal and its Genoese bankers led early African and Asian trade. Castile oversaw the conquest of Amerindian states and the creation of silver economies. At first the Low Countries were also Hapsburg domains that joined and gained from Castilian expansion. In 1580 Spanish Hapsburgs claimed the crown of Portugal, just as a sugar and slave economy gained momentum in Brazil. The Dutch rebelled in the 1560s to create a trading and manufacturing republic that attacked to usurp Portuguese trade in Asia and plantations and the slave trade that sustained them in Brazil. From the early 1600s the farming and grazing society of England turned to Atlantic expansion, trading with Amerindians, building a New England of farmers and grazers, later creating slave colonies in the islands and on the southern mainland—all advancing trade and manufacturing at home. France soon followed, farming and fishing along the St. Lawrence, trading across the Great Lakes and the Mississippi basin, and bringing sugar and slavery to new heights in Saint-Domingue after 1700, thus also stimulating commerce and manufacturing at home.[14]

A broad pattern emerged. The vast and diverse regions subject to Spain dominated the production of American silver from the sixteenth through the eighteenth centuries. That unparalleled stream of wealth stimulated commercial development across Spain's Americas and world trade, shored up the Spanish regime (which still faced bank-ruptcies when the costs of war and empire exceeded silver flows), and inhibited Iberian industrial development, in large part because silver made it cheaper to buy manufactured goods than to make them. The silver of Spain's Americas instead hastened commercial and industrial development in the Low Countries, France, and England. Textiles and other goods made there passed through Seville and Cadiz, legally and otherwise, traded for American bullion dealt on to China. In the six-teenth century and the early seventeenth it was primarily Potosí in the Andes that spurred European production and Atlantic and Pacific trade, and filled Chinese coffers. After 1700 the Bajío and Spanish North America became the American engines of a silver trade that again enriched the Chinese, now joined by Atlantic sugar and slavery in driving global commerce and European industrialization.[15]

This vision of Atlantic development leads to an understanding of capitalism that begins with the focus of Adam Smith on expanding markets and goes beyond that of Karl Marx on social relations of pro-duction escaping coercion and progressing toward free labor. It ex-tends Fernand Braudel's vision of predatory concentrations of eco-nomic power promoting, penetrating, and reshaping economic and social relations grounded in markets, while pressing to limit produc-tion focused on family and community sustenance. It sees as pivotal the profit-driven commercial linkage of diverse societies with varying polities, ways of production, and cultures. It recognizes that before 1800 regime powers were concentrated in Asia and Europe and re-mained weak across the Americas. Yet economic dynamism was global, focused on European centers of finance and trade, on Chinese markets, trade depots, and treasury offices, and on Potosí, Recife, the Bajío, and Saint-Domingue in the Americas. Intersecting controls of production, trade, and states created concentrations of power that helped shape the diverse societies linked in the larger system.

Notably and emphatically, however, no monarch, no financier, no commercial oligarchy designed the emerging capitalist system; no city, no regime, no empire ruled the growing capitalist network. The coinci-dence of the Spanish conquest of the Americas (ironically the result of a failed expedition to China) and a rising Chinese demand for silver to facilitate internal trade and taxation (at a time when New World production could not be imagined) set the world on a course of un-planned, often conflictive, economic dynamism.[16] No person, society, or culture can claim credit, or take blame, for designing capitalism.

European and Asian states and societies adapted established tradi-tions to the opportunities and costs of the expanding system. For all that seemed new—more powerful monarchies, burgeoning cities, industrialization—Europeans insisted that they lived in an old world. Asians too imagined themselves reinforcing traditional ways. Where states and empires had long ruled in the Americas, across Mesoamerica and the Andes inclusion in Atlantic capitalism built upon, adapted to, transformed—yet in important part preserved—American old worlds. The plantation colonies of Americas seem to have been newer worlds. They combined property in land and people to transform the coasts of Atlantic America and the lives of so many dragged in bondage from Africa to profit European masters, stimulate trade, and fill the coffers of empires. Still, new plantation colonies built on old traditions of Mediterranean slavery. Plantation colonies were old worlds recreated on a new scale in the Americas, where they expanded production and trade, profit and degradation.[17]

The newest world began in the Bajío; during three centuries it expanded northward to create Spanish North America, where the original inhabitants lived free of state powers. After 1521 they were invaded by Otomí migrants and assaulted by Old World diseases. The silver economy took off around 1550, flooding the region with immigrants and livestock. Native Chichimecas died or were displaced by migrants from across the Atlantic basin. Commercial ways, rooted in Europe and Mesoamerica (where they still competed with strong community traditions) and energized by Chinese demand for silver, ruled from the start. In this new world in the making, often-predatory entrepreneurs ruled production of a precious commodity, profiting by meeting a great and growing demand in unseen markets; they developed a regional commercial economy integrating grain, livestock, and cloth production to sustain the silver economy. They forced Africans to migrate, yet slavery failed to endure as a primary means of coercion. And in the Bajío and Spanish North America, no established (and few transplanted) institutions of community rights and self-rule (which held strong across much of Europe, Mesoamerica, the Andes, and Asia) limited entrepreneurial powers and commercial ways.

The subsistence production that Braudel recognized as the entrenched foundation constraining capitalism, the base of resistance to its concentrations of profit and power, proved weak in the Bajío and regions northward, societies forged anew under commercial stimulus. Large landholdings and production for profit quickly became norms. Communities defending historic rights were few. And while slavery and labor drafts were important in the Bajío in the early seventeenth century, they gave way to commercially defined work relations negotiated among entrepreneurs, managers, and diverse working families and communities. Entrepreneurs in mining and estate production gained strength by taking profit in global trade, facilitating concentrations of economic power. But those opportunities came in regions of sparse population where many natives refused to live as dependent producers, most migrants drawn to labor were free Mesoamericans never far from home communities with lands and community rights, and bound Africans lived among a Mesoamerican majority and near a northern frontier of vast openness, uncertain opportunity, and persistent conflict. In a region of unparalleled opportunity for profit and limited potential for coercion, entrepreneurs could not rule without limits. Miners, merchants, and landlords built power in pursuit of profit. They led a commercial society that gave them great strength, but that never allowed them to profit unless they negotiated with diverse working families and communities.

From the sixteenth century the Bajío and Spanish North America developed as commercial societies. Commodity production for profit organized almost everything. Yet regime powers remained weak and personal coercion was limited and declining, while a diverse and mostly transplanted population negotiated to live and produce with few community rights and little claim to land for subsistence cultivation. The result: a protean capitalist society deep in the interior of the Americas.

Elsewhere, persistent struggles between community rights, commercial goals, and regime demands defined early modern ways in societies linked by dynamic trade. It took long and contested struggles over enclosure to eliminate the community rights that restricted commercial life in England. New England began with family cultivation in communities known for their celebrated town meetings. In the remainder of Europe and across the Spanish Andes and Mesoamerica, corporate rights and production for sustenance kept communities strong, or at least resilient, through the eighteenth century. In China empires ruled and traded in a world grounded in landed communities. Commercial ways penetrated everyday life more slowly in all those regions, developing as overlays on deeply peasant societies.[18]

Meanwhile a burgeoning Atlantic economy generated a huge expansion of slavery at the heart of commercial modernity. Opposition to bondage was scarce among European regimes and entrepreneurs before the Haitian revolution of the 1790s showed slavery's ultimate costs. Until then competing Atlantic empires linked and integrated the commercial life of European cities with the dynamic profitability of slave plantations. Along the Atlantic from the Chesapeake to Brazil, slavery sustained production and profit. Arguably it was only in the Bajío and Spanish North America, the Low Countries, and England that commercial social relations ruled life within global capitalism before 1800.

Across the Atlantic world profit-seeking entrepreneurs drove trade that integrated diverse ways of production while competing European states strove to take revenue and consolidate power at home and in colonies. In the Pacific, Chinese demand for silver heightened global trade and Japanese producers took profitable advantage, as dynasties in both countries sought advantage and faced change. All the societies linked by early capitalism changed as trade concentrated profit among some and limited prospects for others. Successful entrepreneurs might reinforce regimes, or dispute their powers. Economic dynamism and political and military power were inevitably linked, but never in simple ways.

The Spanish Empire provides a revealing example. Thanks to colonized territories and the silver trade, the monarchy based in Madrid surged toward Atlantic dominance in the sixteenth century. Its claims to rule extended across much of Europe and the Americas, to Portuguese outposts in Africa and Asia, and to its entrepot in Manila. Key poles of economic power lay in the commercial cities of the Low Countries, at the silver mines of Potosí high in the Andes, and in Manila where American silver met Chinese traders. The Dutch led Europe toward commercial ways in textiles production and other crafts (first within, then outside Spanish power); at Potosí Spaniards used labor drafts of Inca precedent to mine silver in unprecedented quantities; in Manila Chinese traders ruled exchange.[19]

In the eighteenth century Chinese demand for silver soared again, Spanish power waned, and Britain and France contested European and Atlantic dominance. That was the context in which the Bajío and Spanish North America revitalized as American engines of silver, trade, and commercial development. While Spain struggled to remain a contender in imperial wars, France and Britain worked to penetrate the Spanish empire—all aiming to draw historic silver flows away from China and toward Europe.[20] Britain gained the most. The political power and commercial dynamism of London, the money generated by sugar and slavery, the emerging revenues of India, and the trade that penetrated Spanish America all helped to industrialize Lancashire and its "dark satanic mills." Paris gained from the economic dynamism and human degradation of Saint-Domingue and from trade that drew silver from Spanish America. Madrid promoted silver flows from the deep and dangerous mines of Guanajuato and Zacatecas, claiming rising revenues while boosting French and British trade and industry. China continued to drive American silver production and global trade while promoting production, trade, and westward expansion at home, without asserting political power across oceans.

This vision challenges enduring notions of an essentially European capitalism promoting production at home while progressing from coerced to "free" labor (Marx's key contribution to legitimating capitalism). It complicates presumptions that commercial ways and unfettered labor concentrate near centers of regime power.[21] Social relations that were commercial and ever less coercive developed in parallel in the Bajío and England. States promoting trade while ruling entrenched cultivating communities held strong in China, the Andes, Mesoamerica, and continental Europe. Formal coercions taking labor, goods, and taxes from communities retaining rights in the land persisted across eastern Europe and Andean America yet declined in Spanish Mesoamerica. Slavery expanded along Atlantic coasts from Brazil to the Chesapeake, contributing to capital accumulation and capitalism.

The rise of industrial capitalism in eighteenth-century England traditionally defined the emergence of modern capitalism. In the understanding offered here, it marks British dominance of the new era of capitalism that arose in the conflicts of 1750 to 1850. In either perspective it is essential to recognize that industrial textile production linked wage workers in Lancashire mills—poor men, women, and children recently denied land rights by enclosures, thus "freed" to labor—to growing numbers of African slaves on plantations spreading across the southern United States, a nation recently escaped from British rule, newly tied to the transatlantic cotton economy, and driving to take the lands of Creeks and other Amerindians who saw their territories invaded and their trade vanish while slave plantations proliferated.[22] There is no clearer example of capitalism accelerating production and concentrating profit and power by linking diverse ways of production and labor in distant regions ruled by differing, often competing, sometimes warring regimes.

Entrepreneurs seeking to control concentrations of production and trade for profit—Braudel's predators—drove the creation of global capitalism. Regimes sought revenues. Together they worked to integrate markets and control producers' lives, limiting and if possible reducing people's material sustenance, autonomy, security, and mobility, unless they served the interests of profit. In the old, reconstructed, transplanted, and new societies integrated by capitalism, varied resources, technologies, market relations, and cultural traditions generated differing ways of doing work.

No dominant social organization, way of production, regime model, or cultural tendency defines capitalism. Its systematic genius was—and is—the promotion of whatever social relations and cultural constructions best concentrate wealth and power, and their integration into an expanding commercial complex that accelerates those concentrations. Assertions that capitalist accumulations of wealth and power ultimately benefit the many, debatable at best, prosper in the few places where capitalism has allowed shared if unequal prosperity. The masking claim that exploitations imposed by slave plantations, labor drafts, and locked sweatshops are not capitalist is blatantly false, given the importance of these coercions in the dynamics of capitalism. That claim too mostly prospers among the prosperous, legitimating advantages by masking their bases in others' misfortunes.

This analysis suggests a need to distinguish global capitalism, which profits by integrating diverse ways of production and social relations in dispersed societies, and capitalist societies, in which everyday social relations are ruled by concentrations of commercial power and organized mostly by commercial interactions (with coercions set to structure social stability more than to force individual behavior). In such an understanding, the Bajío and Spanish North America helped to found global capitalism in the sixteenth century, became a primary engine of its eighteenth-century dynamism, and generated original capitalist societies. They offer an opportunity to explore a founding case of capitalist dynamism generating deepening exploitations sustained with little overt coercion. Their social and cultural organization deserves careful analysis.

The history that follows details the emergence of capitalism in the Bajío and Spanish North America during three formative centuries. It focuses on explaining how concentrations of economic power developed and persisted with limited and declining use of personal coercion. Capitalist ways with minimal coercion did not produce societies of people simply "free," however, favored by the benefits of market production and content to work to enrich the few. The maintenance of social order, of the stability essential to production, depended on negotiations and adaptations in which concentrations of power shaped and were shaped by patriarchy, ethnic divisions, and religious legitimations.

Historical studies focusing on how coercion structured lives under slavery and other colonial formations offer models of deep research and analytical clarity—and often reveal that even under slavery, social relations allowed negotiations of work and chances at limited mobility, protean family relationships, and ethnic integrations and divisions.[23] Analyses of how enduring inequities were cemented without formal coercion are few. The benefits of "freedom" seem self-evident, the gains of commercial ways universal. The absence of bondage is certainly a gain; but economic concentration, political power, ethnic and racial divisions, and patriarchal impositions remain, leaving life as something other than simply "free." As Braudel reminds us, capitalist concentrations control market exchanges that potentially benefit all, but that historically have served capitalists far more than producers and their families.

How, then, do capitalist societies orchestrate social relations of deep inequity without primary reliance on formal, personal coercion? The Bajío developed from 1500 to 1810 as a commercial society fully integrated into a global capitalist system. The region's complex history allows an exploration of how capitalists built economic concentrations, negotiated with regime powers, structured patriarchal hierarchies, adapted to ethnic amalgamations, and legitimated everything in religious terms. The same history reveals how new commercial dynamism mixed with population pressures after 1770 to generate deepening exploitations and cultural polarizations, tensions negotiated for decades while entrepreneurs in the Bajío and Mexico City profited and capitalism flourished—until the Bajío exploded in conflicts that became a revolution beginning in 1810.

Analytical Foundations: Life and Death, Power and Legitimacy

A history that aims to understand transforming changes in a key region during three centuries, and place them in the context of global and Atlantic developments, must attempt to probe the unfathomable complexity of human affairs. To approach comprehensive analysis, history should integrate production and trade, regime power, social relations, and cultural understandings. The goal is clear, the way uncertain. The remainder of the Introduction outlines the approaches that inform my research and analysis. Readers who prefer to let understanding flow from the narrative may go directly to chapter 1. Those interested in analytical foundations may find the rest of this Introduction useful as a guide.

My work builds on two fundamental and linked premises: First, humans are biological organisms; thus societies at base are material organizations. People inevitably engage in processes of production and consumption to sustain individuals, communities, societies, and polities. Second, societies are equally and inherently cultural constructions; people know their lives and relationships only through shared (and debated) ideas and symbols. History thus must include the ecological processes by which people engage nature to sustain themselves, the social differentiations that organize production and social relations, and the cultural visions through which they understand, legitimate, negotiate, and dispute everything that matters—and analyze all that as it changes over time. The achievement will remain partial. But the goal of an integrated history is too important to relinquish because of the inevitable limits of accessible information and analytical skill.[24]

A historical cultural ecology, Julian Steward emphasized years ago, would detail "subsistence activities and economic arrangements" and "such social, political, and cultural patterns as are empirically determined to be closely connected with these arrangements."[25] More recently Clifford Geertz worried "that cultural analysis, . . . will lose touch with the hard surfaces of life—with the political, social, and stratificatory realities within which men are everywhere contained—and with the biological and physical necessities on which those surfaces rest." His solution: to train "cultural analysis . . . on such realities and such necessities in the first place," and "to look for systematic relationships among diverse phenomena." The goal is "a conception of the relations between the various aspects of human existence . . . in which biological, psychological, sociological, and cultural factors can be treated as variables within a unitary system of analysis."[26]

Analysis must begin with material foundations. People must survive in order to do everything else. Ecological relationships organize the means of life, the combinations of production and exchange that sustain individuals and societies. Historical analysis of the means of life requires knowledge of the environment, the technologies by which people engage and alter that environment, and the social arrangements—including work, surplus extraction, and exchange—that organize their efforts. Powers grounded in controls of resources, key technologies, and ways of exchange are ultimately ecological: they rest upon controls of the means of life; they shape the subsistence production, market exchanges, and predatory concentrations that interact to define capitalism.

In historical societies—from bands of hunters and gatherers to capitalist states—the means of death are structured by equally material coercions. Powers based on violence, on controls of the means of death (like controls of the means of life) may be widely dispersed or highly concentrated; they may sustain a social order or assault it. In early modern times coercive powers defined and enforced bondage and personal freedom. In modern states powers grounded in coercion define and defend rights of political participation, proprietorship, and exchange. Yet violence sometimes threatens all this and more. The dynamics of historical power revolve around a fundamental duality: the inseparable opposition of life and death socially constructed as production and coercion.

In modern societies we conceive of the means of life as economic processes while states orchestrate coercion in political relationships. Together they sustain powers that are analytically distinct and yet inextricable one from the other. Modern states, defined classically by Max Weber as monopolies of coercion, do many things.[27] Douglass North and his colleagues rightly emphasize that early modern regimes rarely approached such monopolies.[28] Still, in the Atlantic empires regimes worked to accumulate coercive power and to monopolize the sanction of its use through militia patents, naval licenses, etc. At a minimum states seek to control and regulate coercion; equally important, they use their power to set norms of proprietorship and mediate disputes. Historical specifics vary. Coercive powers may be monopolized or dispersed; they may rule daily life or lie deep in the background. Only empirical inquiry can discover the nature of historical relationships between powers grounded in the means of life and those grounded in coercion in any community, society, or global system. In New Spain regime powers of coercion were scarce and dispersed; the monopoly to forge a strong state was imagined by Bourbon reformers but never created. Imperial claims to rule, set property rights, and do justice required constant negotiation with stakeholders.[29]

The relationships between ecology and coercion, production and violence—political economy in modern terms—reflect basic material realities: how most people produce to survive while others accumulate; how threats and assertions of violence sustain production and prevailing social relations, or challenge them. Both ecology and coercion are social relationships, ways of organizing interactions among the few who profit and rule and the many who work to survive. Historical relations between powers of production and coercion vary widely: an integrated elite may rule both, or distinct groups may dominate production and regimes, making exploration of the relations between them an essential concern. Equally diverse relationships link entrepreneurs to producers, states to subjects or citizens. History demands empirical investigation of fundamental relationships.

The material links between ecology and coercion, production and violence require a cultural corollary. Again, Weber offers a key insight. He insists that power seeks legitimacy: it strives to be moral. An effective state, in his view, holds a legitimate monopoly of coercion. Thus the material powers of violence essential to states are inextricably tied to rulers' assertions of legitimacy, and to subjects' evaluations of those assertions.[30] The history offered here suggests that not only states but all who exercise power, ecological or coercive, entrepreneurial or political, seek legitimacy. And people subject to power devote parallel energy to evaluating, negotiating, and challenging these assertions. Power and culture are pivotally linked and regularly debated in the domain of legitimacy—that is, of morality.[31]

Historical societies are ecological organizations shaped by coercive interventions: the need to survive shaped by the will to power. They are equally and essentially cultural and moral: people need to know that production and access to essential goods, political power and its constraints, and the social relationships that they circumscribe are just. My argument is not that people live by rules of morality. Rather, it is that people, especially powerful people, create and promote visions that proclaim prevailing ways as just. A critical view may marvel at the human ability to present life-sustaining relationships and destructive exploitations as equally moral. An analytical vision sees history revolving around how materially grounded powers of life and death change in relationship with each other, and with cultural assertions of and debates about the meaning and morality of those powers.[32]

This view too owes much to Geertz, notably his observation that cultural formulations are "fictions," human creations, that seek to be "models of" the world as it is, and "models for" behavior in that world. Such models are inherently ethical. They seek to ground a "powerfully coercive 'ought' . . . in a comprehensively factual 'is.'"[33] They generate ongoing tension between what is and what ought to be. Culture aims to describe, to explain, to legitimate, and to orient action in societies. Because societies are materially grounded, socially differentiated, and culturally constructed, conflict and change often develop when prevailing descriptions, explanations, and justifications fail to capture changing realities of production, coercion, and inequality.[34]

If culture seeks to explain and legitimate the hard material and social realities of life, as Geertz emphasizes, it is improbable that the powerful and the poor—who experience those realities so differently—would construct common understandings. Cultural hegemony imagined as shared knowledge linking and integrating the powerful and the poor is improbable, perhaps impossible.[35] Yet cultural dissonance, the creation and persistence of implacably opposed visions within integrated societies, is also rare. The powerful and the poor are ultimately linked by what divides them—structural relations of inequality grounded in ecological processes that sustain life. Cultures develop as commentaries from divergent perspectives on common yet unequal (often exploitative) roles in shared endeavors. The cultural dynamics of stratified societies are structured by differing visions of common questions, seen from contrasting locations in relationships of material power. The differing visions of the powerful and the poor develop as debates about legitimacy: the morality asserted by those who rule, debated and often reformulated by those who work and serve.

The debates of everyday life repeatedly focus on claims that aim to justify material powers of production and politics. The historical links between power and legitimacy are most often analyzed, following Weber, in the domain of states. Edmund Morgan offers a strong vision of how legitimating fictions changed as the Anglo-American world moved from regimes presuming divine sanction to governments asserting popular sovereignty in the seventeenth and eighteenth centuries. He emphasizes the historical sequence as men in power shifted from asserting legitimacy grounded in the unknowable divine to justifications claiming that those who ruled represented the people subject to their rule—a notion more testable in the world.[36] Still, rule sanctioned by divine right often becomes testable. The Spanish monarchy grounded its power in sanction by God and his Catholic Church. It also insisted that it provided justice and promoted the common good among its subjects, however diverse and distant. The sanction of divinity was hard to test; the promise of justice in the world was testable—and regularly tested in Spain's imperial dominions.[37]

Historically, ecological and economic powers are also legitimated by assertions of ultimate, often divine sanction tied to claims of worldly reciprocity—claims that the few who rule production take profit morally because their powers benefit the majority. And in the domains of production (as with regime powers), assertions of divine sanction and of worldly reciprocity are debatable. Contestable claims of legitimacy and reciprocity also define the domain of patriarchal gender relations: men assert that they rule households because it is God's will, and because they protect and provide for wives and children—claims that wives often contest.[38] Parallel assertions recur in religious conversations in colonial New Spain, as elsewhere. Clergy claimed knowledge of the divine, prescribing sacramental morality to guide Christians to salvation. The church also sanctioned devotions focused on virgins and saints, promising assistance with the trials of everyday life from disease to drought—testable claims.[39] As Geertz and Morgan emphasize, legitimations are fictions that seek to be believable. To assert moral sanction they must be grounded in towering, often inscrutable powers. To be believed they promise gain in the world. All legitimations are debatable; most are debated.[40]

Culture, of course, does more than assert, debate, and negotiate legitimacy. Culture explains and affects action in every aspect of life. It guides birth and death and all the relationships that link them; it defines health and disease and orients approaches to curing; it defines problems and proposes solutions, from when to plant and harvest, to how to gain employment, to how to approach the powers that rule societies and the cosmos. Yet all these aspects of culture are tied to and integrated by debates about legitimacy—often linked to the unknowable divine, normally offering worldly reciprocities—that seek to sanction and sustain powers of production and coercion and the inequities they sustain.

The understanding that material powers are contested through legitimations that are open to debate suggests a revised notion of hegemony. Common visions promoted by the powerful and shared by the poor, locking the latter into subordination marked by "false consciousness," are absent in this history of the Bajío and Spanish North America. By contrast, continuous conversations in which the powerful promote and subordinates debate ultimate sanctions and worldly reciprocities are everywhere. Hegemony is neither an imposed nor a false consciousness. Rather, hegemony rules when assertions of legitimacy—whether by ultimate sanctions, worldly reciprocities, or both—focus and limit the negotiations of power that organize everyday life. The powerful assert that their powers are just; individuals, families, and communities respond by evaluating for themselves the will of the divine and the fulfillment of the promises inherent in claims of reciprocity. Within such hegemony power and its morality are continuously debated and constantly changing. But as long as debates are limited to questions shaped by assertions of legitimacy, power persists.

Of course hegemony may weaken and even collapse, as history's revolutions and other conflicts reveal. Justifications may become so untenable, so demonstrably false, that debates escape their limits. Lived material realities may bluntly contradict legitimating assertions: a regime may collapse into destructive violence that no god could believably sanction; justice may be so poorly served that no claim to provide it remains believable; landlords may profit so blatantly while people starve that no claim to serve the common welfare holds tenable. In the face of such crises, challengers may offer alternative moralities, engaging in new conversations with the populace. Still, culture focuses on legitimating debates linked to materially grounded power relations. The challenge of every crisis is to forge new power relations and a new morality, with the latter believable enough to sustain new hegemonic conversations.

History is thus a domain of power and culture, of continuous contest, periodic conflict, and persistent change. The powerful and their assertions of legitimacy rarely rule unchallenged. Change may flow from contests among the powerful, between the powerful and the populace, of both. Without such contests the powerful would hold more power, and the poor would work more for less—less material welfare, less autonomy, less security, less mobility, and less room to maneuver in cultural contests. Still, most of the time power holds, its controls over the means of life and death legitimated by claims of divinity and reciprocity that are inevitably debated yet rarely falsified.

Globalization and Derived Power

This discussion of power relations focuses on materially grounded, socially constructed, and culturally debated inequalities within societies—the communities, regions, and nations integrated by those relationships. As we recognize the rising importance of global trade and other intersocietal engagements, from war to the spread of world religions, political systems, and ideological visions, we need to think creatively about relations between societies and how those relations affect power and culture within societies. The history of the Bajío and Spanish North America was influenced powerfully by economic links to China, a regime based in Europe, populations that migrated from distant Europe and Africa and nearby Mesoamerica, and a religious culture grounded in Christianity. Almost everything local—everything but natural resources and resistant Chichimecas—was simultaneously global.

The analytical challenge of integrating the global with the local in Spain's Americas too often has been "solved" with presumptions of coercive impositions: Spaniards conquered the American empires and the communities they ruled; they imposed extractive ways; they forced Africans into labor as slaves; they imposed Catholicism. More sophisticated analyses recognized the role of epidemics in weakening indigenous states and communities and facilitating these impositions, but impositions still rule. Yet every scholar knows that conquest, whether in the heartland of the Andean and Mesoamerican empires or beyond their domains, required alliances with native powers and peoples.[41] Where the silver economy developed amid historic Andean and Mesoamerican communities, Europeans had to adapt production to their enduring ways, even after conquest and depopulation.[42] Where the silver economy did not develop, indigenous communities proved more enduring as the base of colonial societies.[43] Slaves were forced to migrate and labor, yet in Spanish American cities and across Spanish North America they steadily found ways to freedom even as they continued to labor.[44] And every close inquiry into the cultural contests of colonial rule shows that Europeans could rarely impose their understandings and indigenous Americans repeatedly adapted their own visions—refusing to be imposed upon.[45]

Coercion, when attempted, proved a crude, often ineffective instrument of power. It provoked changes but rarely controlled their outcomes. A strikingly different presumption about intersocietal relations in a globalizing world, rooted in Adam Smith and still vibrant today, is that long-distance trade stimulates production, productivity, and ultimately human welfare.[46] Every student of Latin America knows that there trade has promoted production, sometimes increased productivity, and rarely promoted the general welfare. Perhaps the great contribution of Immanuel Wallerstein has been to demonstrate that coercion and trade simultaneously and inherently mark most of history.[47] He details how coercions matter, yet rarely achieve their intended goals; how markets stimulate production—and predatory exploitations; how cultural interactions work through complex engagements—with unimagined adaptations the common outcome.

With this understood, the historical challenge is mostly empirical. Concepts learned from Richard Adams guide my inquiries. The first is that power is always a relationship: the powerful always face limits and subordinates always have choices and options (however limited) that allow them to adapt and resist. Simply stated, inequities are real, often enduring, but never absolute. Intersocietal and intrasocietal power relations are inevitably negotiated, however unequally. And their intersections are crucial to history and to historical analysis. To facilitate analysis of those key intersections, Adams provides another key concept: derived power.[48] Simply stated: a regime or group in a given society that derives power from external relationships reinforces itself within that society and restricts others—whether competitors, subordinates, or even superiors.

In the long course of a globalizing history, derived powers most often help to consolidate regimes and economic elites in societies where, if left to local resources, they might face serious competitors or challenges from below. A few examples grounded in early globalization and the Spanish Empire illustrate the tendency: From the sixteenth century through the eighteenth Spain's Hapsburg and Bourbon rulers derived unprecedented revenues from production based in the Americas and trade that spanned the globe. Revenues from outside Spain allowed Spanish monarchs to engage in wars and other activities that would have been far less possible had they relied fully on resources extracted from their subjects in Spain. Colonial resources also helped the Spanish crown to minimize the role of the Cortes, Iberia's historic regional parliaments that negotiated rights for revenues.[49] With externally derived revenues the regime could pay less attention to demands for rights at home, until Napoleon broke the monarchy, the Bajío revolution cut silver flows, and a Cortes returned to bring liberalism to Spain and its fragmenting empire.[50]

As the Dutch Republic and the British and French monarchies saw power concentrate in Spain thanks to rising flows of derived revenues, they knew that they had to seek external resources to compete with Spanish power. They built parallel empires and penetrated Spanish trade (legally or otherwise) to draw revenues (that is, derived power) to their own merchants and regime coffers. In long historic contests each contender faced internal challenges focused on relations between the regime's resources and its subjects' rights, leading to republican rule in the Low Countries, monarchical assertions followed by parliamentary revolution in England, and monarchical absolutism ending in republican revolution in France. This is well-known history, phrased in terms of derived power.[51]

A turn to the Bajío and Spanish North America highlights another face of derived power. There, from the sixteenth through the eighteenth centuries wealth taken from the silver trade funded mining, commercial cultivation, cloth making, and entrepreneurial grazing. The Spanish regime, seeking to maximize the revenues that brought it derived power in Europe, backed American entrepreneurs with naval protection in Atlantic sea lanes, judicial mediations in colonial conflicts, and religious legitimations derived from European Christianity. Normally only men with access to one or more channels of derived power could claim and hold local power in the emerging capitalist society of the Bajío and Spanish North America. There were apparent exceptions: Connín used a frontiersman's knowledge, the ability to mobilize Otomí forces to protect the early silver economy from Chichimeca assaults, and a quick adaptation to commercial ways and Catholic culture to become don Fernando de Tapia, the most powerful man in the sixteenth-century Bajío. A century later don Diego de la Cruz Saravia used local knowledge and entrepreneurial skills to surmount African ancestry and become a leading cultivator sustaining silver mining at Guanajuato. In the process he became a Spaniard, bought African slaves, and dressed his wife in Chinese silks. Neither Connín-Tapia nor de la Cruz Saravia began with access to derived power. They learned to tap it to claim eminence in the globally linked dynamism of the early Bajío.

In the late eighteenth century power derived from soaring silver production, and the trade that it fed kept mining, agricultural, and textile entrepreneurs strong in the Bajío, allowing them to seek greater profits by pressing new poverty and insecurity onto producing families. The Spanish Bourbon regime backed their efforts, limiting administrative demands, offering tax and other concessions, and building new forces of social control, in full recognition that power derived from New Spain's silver revenues and trade kept Spain a participant in European power struggles (even as they limited Spanish economic development).[52] Mutually reinforcing derived powers kept Spain and New Spain locked together, allowing the Bajío economy to soar to new heights while the expansion of Spanish North America reached across California. Only when Napoleon, seeking to claim the derived power of silver for France, broke the Spanish monarchy and undermined the legitimacy of the regime that provided mediations essential to sustaining capitalist dynamism did the collapse of derived political and judicial power (after decades of sustaining deepening exploitation and cultural polarization) set off a revolution that fundamentally altered the roles of Spain and New Spain (as it became Mexico) in a changing capitalist world.

These examples just begin to explore the importance of derived power in the history of societies linked in globalizing processes. They illustrate key ways that intersocietal trade and other ties stimulate production and reinforce the powers that rule the heights of capitalism. We will see that role of derived power again and again in the history of the Bajío and Spanish North America. Yet we will also encounter derived powers aiding subordinate peoples struggling to resist capitalist expansion. Independent Chichimecas, Apaches, and others repeatedly adopted and adapted European weapons, tools, livestock, and aspects of Christian culture to fortify their resistance to entrepreneurial colonizers. The key is to remember that derived powers regularly shape what appear as local social relations of inequality and exploitation.

Integrating Inequality: Axes of Power

When basic questions of power and culture—control of the means of life, control of the means of death, and the debated justifications of both—are set in the context of global interactions and derived powers, and brought to bear on the history of any local, regional, or national society, analytical complexities proliferate. My attempts to understand the Bajío and Spanish North America led me to focus on five axes of power, key relationships that simultaneously linked and divided the powerful and the populace, shaping continuous negotiations of inequalities: (1) Social relations of production tied people into shared productive enterprises and networks of exchange, profiting a few while locking the majority into lives of daily labor. (2) Political relations of administrative bargaining and judicial mediation enabled a few to mix office and entrepreneurship, leaving the majority to seek favor, redress, and most often mediation. (3) A hierarchy of ethnic categories included everyone in a system of sanctioned inequalities, offering benefits to people classed as Spanish, subordination with limited rights to many designated indios, and uncertain dependence to mulattoes and *mestizos*. (4) Patriarchal gender relations linked men in hierarchies of inequality, assigned power to men in households, powerful and poor, and sanctioned women's and children's subordination—integrating inequities within families and across the larger society. And (5) Catholic religious culture included everyone, divided clergy from laity, sanctioned imperial and entrepreneurial powers, and enabled the powerful to proclaim and the poor to debate legitimating visions.

Each axis simultaneously linked and differentiated the powerful and the poor; each organized unequal cooperations that were simultaneously divisive exploitations; each asserted legitimations that evoked debates. While the powerful aimed to rule production and the regime, dominate patriarchal hierarchies, and mold ethnic relations and religious understandings, the populace repeatedly found ways to negotiate production and regime claims, reshape ethnic categories and identities, debate gender relations, and forge alternative religious practices. All five axes of power were essential to life in the Bajío and Spanish North America. Each deserves preliminary exploration.

Social relations of production organize the work that engages environments to gain the necessities of life and produce the material bases of power. Historical inquiry into axes of ecological power must integrate local ways of production and consumption and the networks that tie them to nearby towns, regional cities, and distant societies. Here Braudel's three levels of economic activity—production for sustenance, production for exchange, and production shaped by predatory concentrations of power—intersect with working families' pursuits of autonomy, security, mobility, and material welfare.[53] Subsistence production maximizes autonomy, facilitates trade in local markets, and inhibits capitalist predation. The material welfare of subsistence producers depends most on their resources and the weather; they may live in simple comfort or deep desperation. Production for market exchange should (as emphasized by every economist since Smith) maximize shared welfare and create diverse opportunities that allow mobility, at least (as Braudel reminds us) when producers hold relatively equal resources, and production and exchange are little fettered by monopolists. When capitalists control vast lands, key technologies, and pivotal channels of exchange, producer autonomy diminishes, securities wane, and the gains of specialization and exchange are claimed mostly by powerful predators.

Materially grounded social relations of production are often negotiated in their own terms. Entrepreneurs assert that workers gain ample remuneration; producers regularly dispute their claims. Landlords insist that they provide good lands at fair rents; tenants may see extortion. Economic power holders also offer religious legitimations. Powerful landlords in Mexico City and the Bajío hoarded grain to sell in time of famine, asserting that they did Christian charity by holding food for the worst of times. For their charity they claimed huge profits. The responses of those who spent their last coins on grain, and of those without coin to spend, must be imagined. Braudel emphasizes that capitalists repeatedly justify their accumulations by insisting that everyone gains in market exchange. Their justifications deflect discussions from the capitalists' power to take nearly all those gains, leaving majorities to face vanishing autonomy, declining security, and collapsing welfare, perhaps compensated for by a chance to search for increasingly scarce opportunities. Social relations of production encompass production and work, land and sustenance, profit and exchange, power and survival, and the legitimations proclaimed to make them just—along with the responses of those who struggle to sustain families and communities.

Political relations grounded in coercion organize regime powers and social relations of production. In times of foundation and transformation, conquest and revolution, violence often rules the creation or reconstruction of societies. Subsequently coercion may become institutionalized in regimes and recede into the background. Yet violence remains a foundation of the states that define and defend claims to property and mediate disputes about those claims and much more. Regimes hold or sanction powers of coercion that enable inequality and promise justice. Regimes promise to protect society from external threats; they threaten those who challenge internal order; and they proclaim all that just by divine sanction, popular sovereignty, and worldly reciprocities—often in complex combinations. No historical analysis can ignore social relations of coercion grounded in controls of the means of death and their debated justifications.

In New Spain powers of coercion were notably weak, yet essential to defining property, orchestrating production, bargaining with stakeholders, and mediating disputes over everything. The king and his agents claimed the right to sanction the use of violence, allocate property and possession, and do justice. Yet they never built strong forces of coercion; colonial officials never monopolized violence. Early on coercion was asserted by conqueror-entrepreneurs, Spanish and Mesoamerican. In the Bajío, Otomí and Spaniards fought as allies against Chichimecas while they jockeyed for eminence in a new commercial world. The regime sanctioned outcomes more often than it organized or led northward thrusts that were simultaneously violent and entrepreneurial.

During and after the wars officials worked to confirm claims to silver mines and sanction rights to land and water. Notaries documented every claim to property and all major transactions, from Europeans' first arrival to the end of Spanish rule and long after.[54] From the beginning the regime worked to define and defend rights to property, personal, familial, and corporate. Simultaneously it set up courts to mediate conflicts among the powerful, and between the powerful and poor. By the early seventeenth century regime power organized Spanish cities, indigenous republics (primarily in Mesoamerican regions to the south), and the silver economy. Yet its coercive force remained weak. It focused its limited resources on the naval power to protect the Atlantic passage. Its ability to coerce within colonial society depended on militias led by local entrepreneurs (not certain to defend the regime); in the seventeenth century mulatto militias (not sure to serve the powerful) became important in coastal and mining regions. The result was a regime that sanctioned property, negotiated rule, and mediated conflicts.[55]

The reality, appearance, and legitimacy of state power depended on negotiations among officials and entrepreneurs, magistrates and militias. Repeated conflicts mixed with the shared goal of maintaining the stability essential to the silver economy. The result was a political economy built around two key negotiations: the give and take among entrepreneurs and officials negotiating profit and power for mutual benefit (neither dominating the other); and the mediations between the powerful few and the working majority, often in courts where those seeking profit and power recognized the limits of coercive force and the need to keep subordinates at work. District magistrates were powerful stakeholders and mediators—local judges and merchants at the same time. Most knew or soon learned that to maintain order they had to balance interests among men disputing power and to mediate disputes between powerful men and producing communities.[56]

Bourbon reforms threatened that balance in the 1760s. They increased standing armed forces and built new militias (still dependent on funding and leadership from colonial elites). Early on reforms provoked riots in and near the Bajío; new military forces helped contain them. Afterward officials returned to less disruptive assertions of power, relearning the importance of mediating justice—backed in cities by urban patrols and jails. Sovereignty was still sanctioned by God and delivered as the king's justice. When exploitations deepened and cultural visions polarized after 1780, the regime again expanded militias and city patrols. Yet bargaining with powerful colonials (some of whom still led militias) and judicially mediating conflicts among the populace remained key to stabilizing and legitimating the booming silver economy.[57]

While social relations of production and political relations of coercion are closely linked and structurally basic, materially grounded power relations rarely organize societies unmediated by culturally constructed categories of difference and integration. In the colonial societies formed by early Atlantic capitalism, systems of ranked categories organized the differential inclusion of diverse peoples. In Spain's Americas they emphasized *calidades*—qualities rooted in ancestry. People were to be Spanish, indio, or something between (often mestizo). Colonies dependent on African slaves turned to racial claims, taking visible traits to assert and rank difference. People were white, black, or, again, something in between (mulatto or colored). These rankings aimed to serve the powerful, yet they offered to the colonized and the enslaved room to maneuver—especially when ancestries mixed and visible signs blurred. Whether focused on ancestry, visible race, or combinations of the two, systems of ranked difference aimed to separate people into hierarchies of inequality while incorporating them in colonial production, justifying exploitations with claims of essential difference.

Such claims proved powerful markers in the ethnically stratified colonies of Spanish Mesoamerica and the Andes, where the duality of Spanish and indio separated the powerful few from colonized majorities while tying them together in relations of exploitation. They also flourished in the slave colonies of the greater Caribbean where the powerful were free and mostly white, the majority enslaved and mostly black—and linked in coercive relations of production. Rankings proved complicated and uncertain in the Bajío and Spanish North America. There the regime and the church tried to impose ethnic categories while economic dynamism in regions settled by diverse immigrants brought amalgamations that blurred sharp ethnic lines. Categories proved fluid and changing. Those who ruled and took profit were normally Spanish—in part because those of mixed ancestry who became rich and powerful also became Spanish. Otomí and Tarascan migrants became indios, a generic status that identified colonized peoples of diverse indigenous ancestry and promised limited rights which could be pursued in court. Slaves newly landed from Africa were classed as *negro*—a color code that ignored African diversity. Many of their offspring became mulatto and free. Official classifications presumed that mulattoes mixed Spanish and African ancestry; the evidence from the Bajío and Spanish North America suggests that most had mixed African and Mesoamerican origins. Others of parallel ancestry joined communities of indios. A few mulattoes gained the wealth, land, or office to assert Spanish status. The result was not clear stratification but fragmenting differences constantly renegotiated.[58]

Patriarchy was equally pervasive as an axis of inequality across the Americas and the Atlantic world. Nearly everywhere patriarchal presumptions reserved to men the right to exercise violence. Less universally, but powerfully in European and Hispanic societies, patriarchy promised men the right to rule over women and children in family households.[59] Men produced to provide material sustenance; wives served and provided sex; children served while they awaited the chance to become patriarchs or wives. How and how well men provided and how loyally women and children served—or should serve if men failed to provide—were key questions always debated while patriarchy endured to structure inequities within households, rich and poor.[60]

The history of the Bajío and Spanish North America also reveals that patriarchy operated simultaneously as a social hierarchy linking entrepreneurs, landlords, and powerful officials to the producing poor through managers and local agents. Powerful men enabled dependent men to gain and hold roles in production, community affairs, local governance, religious life. Dominant patriarchs facilitated dependent men's patriarchy, expecting them to acquiesce in their own and their families' subordination—to collaborate in personal and household exploitations. Hierarchical patriarchy was of course debated and contested. It endured as a key relationship, a conversation negotiating and consolidating inequalities through the colonial centuries and long after.[61]

Breakdowns of the social order challenged patriarchy, and breakdowns of patriarchy challenged the social order. Riots engulfed Mexico City in 1692 after weeks of rumors that the viceroy had speculated for profit while drought made grain expensive and scarce. The death of an indigenous woman seeking maize at the public granary sparked violence; angry women demanding justice spread the resistance. When men took the lead, torching the viceregal palace and looting a nearby market, the cry that fueled their angry action called the viceroy a *cornudo*, or cuckold. A commercial and patriarchal social order had failed to feed the populace, failed to serve the common good—the ultimate patriarchal role in a society of commercial inequality. Women suffered, women protested, and men saw the king's colonial agent as a cuckold, a shamed patriarch.[62] Both capitalist and regime powers were patriarchal powers. Failure dishonored patriarchy. After 1770 capitalist predations assaulted working men's patriarchy across the Bajío, leading to social revolution in 1810.

Social relations of production and political relations of coercion are materially based axes of power. Ethnic and racial rankings and patriarchal hierarchies are culturally constructed axes of inequality embedded in production and regime powers. Religion offers, organizes, and debates ultimate explanations, linking cosmic visions to power relations and everyday lives. While every axis of power includes moral justifications and debates, religion defines a privileged domain of moral legitimacy. It explains the unexplainable—the origins of life, its essential meaning, and its ultimate morality—and ties those explanations to life in the world. As the primary language of morality in the Bajío before 1810, religion centered discussions of production and state powers, ethnic roles and rights, and patriarchal relations.

Through the colonial era the church promoted worship emphasizing a sacramental morality that sanctioned patriarchy and popular subordination and promised otherworldly salvation. Simultaneously, popular communities and local clergy focused devotion on virgins and saints who offered assistance with life in the world, notably disease and drought, with fertility in families and fields. The two approaches to religious truth jostled together for centuries, until eighteenth-century proponents of reason insisted that the virgin and the saints could not affect life in the world. To the newly enlightened, popular devotion became superstition. Sacramental worship was the only way to morality and salvation, reasoned action the only way to gain in the world. Religious divisions deepened just as social tensions polarized.

Axes of power linked the powerful and poor in unequal and exploitative reciprocities, vertical relationships that structured and stabilized inequities. They limited the emergence of horizontal solidarities— class, for want of a better term—among the majority in the protean capitalist society of the Bajío and Spanish North America. Among the powerful, family and interest tied merchants to landlords and financiers to officials, surmounting disputes over power, profit, and precedence. Perhaps a dominant class did exert power in Mexico City, the Bajío, and Spanish North America in the eighteenth century. But among the populace differences in local resources, ways of production, ethnic identities, and religious visions made communities, urban and rural, infinitely different. Diverse town neighborhoods and rural communities lived the inequities and exploitations of Bajío capitalism differently, and engaged with differing religious understandings. An integrated class of entrepreneurs and officials ruled through hierarchical relations of production integrated by patriarchy; religion linked the powerful and the poor in debates about right and truth; and judicial mediations dealt with conflicts that were almost always local in communities that might be fragmented, amalgamated, or segregated by ethnicity. A sense of common subordination is hard to find in the Bajío before insurgency began in 1810.[63] Hierarchical power relations and cultural conversations organized history there; they focus my analysis.

The result was a regional history marked by global linkages and local hierarchical negotiations. The powerful worked to profit, control society, and define legitimacy; they never ruled without contest, yet for centuries they ruled. From the plagues of the 1500s to the middle of the eighteenth century entrepreneurs in the Bajío and regions north were always in search of people to work mines and fields, while independent natives resisted just north. Regime power was limited; personal coercion was often ineffective. Social inequities had to be negotiated. Employers made payments in advance and provided maize rations to gain scarce workers. Spaniards conceded status as Spaniards to diverse people who gained wealth. Masters stood by while people bound out of Africa evaded slavery. Powerful patriarchs accepted rich widows as peers; working patriarchs negotiated family life with wives essential to production and reproduction. Clerics claimed privileged access to the divine, and conceded to devotions reshaped by the communities they served.

A dynamic, increasingly capitalist economy tied to a regime of limited coercive power emerged in societies marked by ethnic fluidity and patriarchal hierarchies—all legitimated and debated through a vibrant religious culture. In the Bajío and Spanish North America negotiations of power and legitimacy along axes of integration and difference sustained commercial production and social stability with limited personal coercion during centuries of protean capitalist dynamism, while population remained sparse. After 1770 capitalist production surged again while population pressures mounted. New exploitation mixed with cultural polarization. Tension escalated, yet patriarchal integration, ethnic divisions, and religious legitimations sustained an increasingly fragile social order and the Bajío economy, until regime breakdown in 1808 led to conflicts over nearly everything.

In Search of History: Power Holders, Mediators, and Popular Participations

Understanding the history of the Bajío and Spanish North America requires an understanding of the lives and visions of the powerful, a diverse populace, and those who negotiated between them. The problem, long recognized, is that the powerful and their allies made the historical record. They wrote most texts and took every census; they kept accounts of production and trade, recorded regime rules and court testimonies, generating the archives of power that provide and limit our knowledge. The working poor, state subjects, subordinate ethnic groups, and women and children appear only in records created to serve power. When popular voices broke through, it was often to address power as supplicants or in protest. The first response, of course, is to acknowledge that enduring reality.[64] The next step is to recognize that records of power and texts asserting legitimacy were produced as part of interactions among the powerful and those they aimed to rule. Most documents of power record one side of conversations along axes of inequality; read carefully, they reveal much about silenced people. Powerful men and women claim much attention in the history that follows. Their powers and claims of legitimacy must be analyzed if we are to understand how the majority negotiated lives subject to them.

The records and recollections of district officials, parish clergy, and estate managers provide additional access to negotiations of power and culture. Men all, they mediated between the powerful and the populace. Their superiors expected them to assert power; most learned that to maintain production, keep the peace, and promote stability they had to negotiate with the people they were charged to rule.[65] As key brokers along axes of power, they appear regularly in the history that follows. Their roles and reports reveal much; their mediations were pivotal to sustaining power and production. Texts by clerics and officials proposed and debated ways of ruling and legitimating power; such writings also reflected unrecorded conversations between the powerful and the populace. Also read carefully, texts mediating power and legitimacy reveal elite visions, mediators' roles, and popular retorts.

Still, the historical record remains limited and partial, favoring the powerful. In the rare instances when popular voices and visions are recorded, they come transcribed and often translated by others more favored in the social order. Those glimpses are valuable nonetheless, because they are bits of conversations along axes of power that included the populace, even as the powerful worked to exclude or edit popular voices. The history that follows tries to integrate analyses of production and power, ethnic divisions, gender relations, and religious visions. Limited sources dictate that some sections focus on power and ethnicity, others on production and gender, still others on religious debates. Only after 1770 can the analysis begin to approach an integrated vision of all five axes of power.

Throughout, the lives and voices of prominent men and women appear in detail; a few key brokers and writers emerge clearly. With rare exceptions the populace appears in the texts of the powerful, in the reports of mediators, and in censuses, trial transcripts, labor accounts, tenant lists. Men, women, and children working to survive and understand lives of constant challenge are known mostly in bits. From those bits I attempt to calculate life trajectories and piece together cultural visions that emerge only partially and impersonally. (The work of piecing together fragments is presented in the appendices.)

The lives, goals, and challenges of working people known only in bits and questions are the privileged subjects of this study. They literally produced the history of the Bajío and Spanish North America. For nearly three centuries they worked and negotiated to forge bearable lives and meaningful cultures while the economy they built drove global trade, Atlantic empires, and regional social relations toward capitalism. When after 1770 unfettered power relations unleashed predations that made life ever less bearable for growing numbers, old justifications faced new challenges. Then in 1808 the regime that God had sanctioned for centuries fell to a godless Frenchman. Beginning in 1810 the people of the Bajío fought a social revolution that challenged everything.

PART I

Making a New World

THE BAJÍO AND SPANISH

NORTH AMERICA, 1500–1770

BEFORE 1500 THE BAJÍO was a little-settled basin, a frontier between Mesoamerican states and independent peoples in the interior of North America. By 1750 the same region was a densely settled, increasingly urban, often irrigated, and ultimately commercial zone linked by silver, trade, Christianity, and a Spanish regime to people around the Atlantic and across the globe. Stimulated in large part by Chinese demand for silver, Mesoamericans, Europeans, and Africans built a dynamic commercial society in the Bajío integrating mining, irrigated cultivation, and grazing. Simultaneously frontiers of conflict and commerce pressed northward, as warrior-entrepreneurs sought new mines and new lands. They faced diverse natives, some open to new opportunities, most wary of losing their cherished independence. In an expanding crucible of commercial development and frontier conflict, a new world began.

The four following chapters explore the foundations that shaped the Bajío and their extension into Spanish North America. Before silver, colonial commercial settlement began in and around Querétaro. Otomí lords and migrants led the way, founding a community of irrigated cultivation and emerging trade that was in place in the 1550s when silver dynamism and Chichimeca wars mixed to forge a globally linked economy and a new labor market. The seventeenth century brought northward extensions across the Bajío and far into the continent. Guanajuato became a city of silver and insecurity; rural communities forged ethnic amalgamations while setting patriarchy at the center of social relations. The early eighteenth century brought revivals to silver production and urban communities, religious awakenings, and northward drives. The Bajío and regions north became the richest, most dynamic provinces in New Spain, indeed the Americas; with inevitable times of acceleration and recession, they were engines of a dynamic global economy.

Then the 1750s brought a mining slowdown and Atlantic war, followed in the 1760s by new regime assertions—reforms that provoked popular risings challenging the silver economy and threatened the role of the Bajío in the Spanish empire and world trade. Riotous workers were quickly contained, however. The regime turned to promoting mining and commercial life, and to mediating any conflicts that might threaten them. The decades after 1770 would see capitalism soar in the Bajío, reenergizing northward expansions and deepening social and cultural contradictions.

CHAPTER 1

Founding the Bajío

Otomí Expansion, Chichimeca War, and

Commercial Querétaro, 1500–1660

⊕ THE BAJÍO WITNESSED unprecedented encounters, enduring conflicts, and transforming changes in the sixteenth century. Once a place of towns and cultivators in Mesoamerica's classic past, it was little inhabited and minimally cultivated around 1500. Mesoamerican states fought each other and mobile Chichimecas in a prolonged frontier stalemate. Then, beginning in the 1520s Mesoamericans, Europeans, and Africans arrived from the south, settled the basin, and reconstituted power, production, and culture. The foundation of Querétaro led a historic process. Otomí lords and cultivators built the town, irrigated nearby lands, and began new trades. After silver was found to the north at Zacatecas in the 1540s, Spaniards and their African slaves, Otomí and other Mesoamericans, and vast droves of cattle and sheep invaded the Bajío and the lands stretching north and west. Decades of conflict followed, as Chichimecas resisted and adapted to invasions and opportunities. Spaniards aimed to rule and profit. Yet they relied on Otomí and other native allies to fight Chichimecas, and on Mesoamericans and Africans to build a new economy. European power was uncertain and native subordination was long contested in the early Bajío.

Deep in the American interior Querétaro saw the creation of an Atlantic amalgam of Mesoamericans, Europeans, and Africans. Otomí leaders were surprisingly powerful; Otomí cultivators controlled the best, irrigated lands. Europeans struggled to assert dominance. Africans labored, yet increasingly became free. Immigrant Mexicas, Tarascans, and Otomí came and negotiated new ways of work. Spaniards promoted an Atlantic economy and an Iberian regime, yet they had to negotiate indigenous subordination and African service. Around 1600 a nascent commercial economy, an emerging labor market, and a multicultural society consolidated at Querétaro—the base of an expansive, commercial Spanish North America. Warrior entrepreneurs, Otomí and Spanish, led that foundation. The colonial state was among the many forces shaping early Querétaro and the Bajío, but rarely the most powerful. Officials struggled to favor Spanish allies, fill regime coffers, and mediate among diverse people and interests in times of economic opportunity and persistent conflict. That crucible forged an unprecedented Atlantic economy and New World society.[1]

Before regimes and societies there are geographies. The Valle de los Chichimecas, now the Bajío, lies north of the volcanic axis that links the eastern and western Sierras near Mexico City. Between the Sierras the northern basin and plateau country is potentially fertile, thanks to ancient volcanic soil. Yet the region is dry, and ever drier farther north; every year summer rains give way to winter droughts that periodically last all year. Diverse regional mixes of altitude, soil quality, and moisture set the contexts of historical settlement. The Bajío favored human occupation.[2] While the basins around Mexico City lie 2,200 meters and more above sea level, the Bajío plains sit at 1,600 to 2,000 meters, creating warmer climates. Rainfall is typical of the Mexican highlands, averaging 600 to 700 millimeters a year, mostly in summer. Rivers give the Bajío its great potential. The Lerma originates in the high, cold, and wet Toluca basin west of Mexico City. It flows north through rugged uplands to emerge near Acámbaro and descend into the Bajío. The Río Querétaro begins east of the city for which it is named in mountains beyond the Amascala basin. Perennial springs increase its flow as it falls through the canyon at San Pedro de la Cañada. It passes through Querétaro, flows west to be joined by the stream blessed in the colonial era by Our Lady at Pueblito, gains strength from springs at Apaseo, then joins the Río Laja near Celaya. The Laja begins north of Dolores, flows south by San Miguel, descends through the basin at Chamacuero (now Comonfort), then drops to join the Río Querétaro in the core Bajío basin at Celaya. West of Celaya the combined flows of the Querétaro and Laja enter the Lerma—which becomes the Santiago. Farther west the Turbio River descends from the north around León to add more water, before the great Lerma-Santiago passes into

Lake Chapala. Exiting, it cuts through the western Sierra to the Pacific. Broad fertile basins watered by rivers define the Bajío.

On the Frontier of Mesoamerica

Despite that potential, the Bajío was little settled around 1500. It lay at the northern edge of Mesoamerica, a civilization of intensive cultivation, markets, and organized religion, all sustaining cities and states in conflict. To the north lived peoples whom the Mesoamericans called Chichimecas, mobile hunters and gatherers, warriors resistant to life under state powers. Mesoamericans met Chichimecas in the Bajío, leaving the rich basin a contested frontier, a buffer separating—and linking—peoples in conflict.[3]

The Bajío had once lived the historic trajectory of Mesoamerican agricultural, urban, political, and religious development.[4] Chupícuaro culture flourished between 500 and 200 B.C. along the Lerma River in southern Guanajuato. Its people cultivated, made fine pottery, and built stone temple platforms at ceremonial centers. From A.D. 300, contemporary with the rise of Teotihuacan in the Valley of Mexico, towns and irrigated cultivation extended north through the Bajío to reach Zacatecas and San Luis Potosí. The great northern outpost of classic Mesoamerica was at La Quemada, near Zacatecas. The eastern Bajío, from San Juan del Río through Querétaro to San Miguel and Dolores, was home to many small centers and cultivators who sustained them. Archeology argues links to the imperial metropolis at Teotihuacan. Simultaneously, Teuchitlán north of Lake Chapala ruled as a city of monumental buildings and intensive irrigated agriculture, exerting power across the western Bajío. Through the classic era from A.D. 300 to 900 the Bajío was settled and cultivated, home to diverse peoples within the Mesoamerican political and cultural complex.

The great city of Teotihuacan began to decline after 650. La Quemada fell around 900. Yet while the imperial centers of Teotihuacan and La Quemada struggled, a ceremonial and political center rose between 600 and 900 at Plazuelas, strategically set where mountains looked over the western Bajío basin.[5] Mesoamerican ways persisted in the Bajío, and revived around 1000 with the rise of the Toltec state at Tula, in the Mezquital basin to the southeast. The Toltec presence was strong around Querétaro, its regional center at the village now called Pueblito (a key religious site in colonial times). Smaller Toltec settlements were west of Querétaro at La Magdalena and east at La Griega. Yet the Toltec imprint in the Bajío never matched the earlier

El Cerrito, outside Pueblito, east of Querétaro. Pre-Hispanic temple platform and enduring holy site; an earth-covered ruin in the sixteenth century. (House on summit built in nineteenth century; façade excavated in twenty-first century.)

role of Teotihuacan. There were settlements along the Río Laja near San Miguel and a few outposts in northern Guanajuato. By the 1200s Tula had fallen — and the Toltec centers in the eastern Bajío were in decline.

After the fall of Tula, Otomí communities cultivated across the Mezquital and regions to the west around Xilotepec and north toward the Bajío. Settled and sedentary cultivators, the Otomí had come centuries earlier from regions near the Gulf. They had lived subject to Teotihuacan and then Tula. Often denigrated as primitives, sometimes praised as warriors, they worked the land and fought in their rulers' armies. They proved historic survivors. After the fall of Teotihuacan and Tula local Otomí states negotiated times of conflict and political dispersal. Their polity at Xilotepec only fell to Mexica power in the 1480s. Other Otomí negotiated with the Tarascan regime to the west, seeking advantage in the border zone where the Mexica fought Tarascans for state primacy, while Chichimecas held strong just north in the Bajío.[6]

From the 1200s to the early 1500s the Bajío was a contested frontier. Most of the basin was home to the hunting, gathering, sometimes cultivating, and often warring nomads whom Mesoamericans maligned

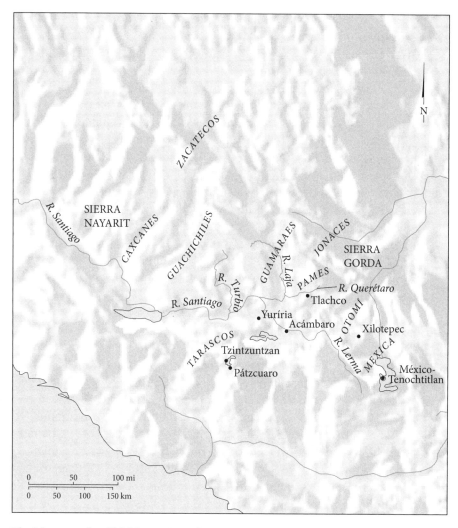

The Mesoamerica-Chichimeca Frontier, ca. 1500

as Chichimecas. They were not one ethnic or linguistic group. The Mexica, Nahuatl speakers who ruled the great city of Tenochtitlan, claimed Chichimeca roots. When they aimed to rule beyond the Valley of Mexico in the 1400s, they drove northward toward the Bajío and their ancestral homelands. They had little success, and denigrated resistant Chichimecas as savage barbarians who would not bow to state powers. A broader meaning of Chichimeca emerges: warriors who ruled, or would not be ruled.

Through the fifteenth century the Mexica marshaled vast armies driven by a religious ideology of sacrificial necessity to assert power and demand tribute from subject lords and cultivating communities—mostly in regions east and south of their island city of Tenochtitlan. Yet Mexica power was always contested, limited, and unstable. The paramount warlords of early-sixteenth-century Mesoamerica never conquered Tlaxcala and Cholula to the east. They were blocked to the west by a Tarascan regime set on the shores of Lake Pátzcuaro at Tzintzuntzan. Within Mexica domains power was negotiated in shifting alliances. As México-Tenochtitlan rose it turned former allies at Texcoco, Tlacopan (Tacuba), and elsewhere into dependents. Conquered peoples resisted, leading to reconquests, new challenges, and uncertain powers. As the sixteenth century began, Mesoamerica was a zone of war, shifting alliances, and contested rule; rising states and established lords asserted religious legitimations while competing to claim work and goods from towns and rural communities.[7] In all that Mesoamerica was not unlike the Europe that would soon send its own warlords with religious legitimations (and commercial goals) into the Mesoamerican crucible.

Through the fifteenth century and into the sixteenth Mexica and Tarascan regimes competed to rule the Bajío; both sent dependent Otomí peoples to settle there. Around 1500 Tarascan frontier power focused at Acámbaro, at the southern edge of the Bajío.[8] The northern thrust of Mexica claims focused on recently conquered Xilotepec. While fighting each other in a frontier stalemate, the Tarascan and Mexica regimes struggled to rule the Otomí peoples who populated the northern margins of Mesoamerica. That left most of the Bajío to Chichimecas. Some were hunting and gathering nomads, minimally clothed, living in caves. Others were mobile cultivators, living in small clusters of huts that Spaniards called *rancherías*. Four groups can be identified in and near the Bajío. Along its western margins Guachichiles roamed the dry hills from the Lerma River, through the Altos de Jalisco, across the Tunal Grande of San Luis Potosí, and north toward Saltillo; Guamares occupied the western and central Bajío, north of the Tarascan outposts, from the Lerma north to San Felipe and east to San Miguel; Jonaces lived deep in the rugged Sierra Gorda of eastern Guanajuato and northern Querétaro. All three groups were nomadic hunter-gatherers and mobile warriors skilled in fighting with bows and arrows.

Pames were different. Linguistic kin of the Otomí, they lived in the southeastern Bajío basins around Querétaro, the eastern uplands near Xichú at the edge of the Sierra Gorda, and south toward Ixmiquilpan in the northern Mezquital. Pames cultivated and traded with the Otomí who lived subject to Nahua rule, and with Tarascans at Acámbaro and Yuriria. If nomadic, hunting and gathering Guachichiles, Guamares, and Jonaces, and settled, cultivating Pames were all Chichimecas, the meaning of Chichimeca becomes clear: they were people living free of state power and ready to fight to remain independent.

As the sixteenth century began, the Bajío was a frontier with a long and complex history. It had lived eras of participation in the state-centered, sedentary, cultivating ways of Mesoamerica; recent times brought rule by independent and mobile hunters and gatherers. Meso-americans and Chichimecas fought and traded. War and trade created knowledge and conflict. People and goods moved back and forth across a frontier that also moved. When Europeans arrived the frontier was contested across the southern Bajío. The Tarascans at Acámbaro aimed to rule and settle Otomí around Yuriria and Apaseo; the Nahua lords of Xilotepec tried to extend Mexica power through outposts of Otomí settlers around Tlachco—later Querétaro. Settlers subject to Mesoamerican states were expected to defend the frontier, cultivate maize and cotton, and weave mats that they paid as tributes. Still, neither the Mexica nor Tarascans ruled the frontier. The southeastern Bajío remained home to independent Pame cultivators; nomadic Guamares and Guachichiles ruled the central and western basin and nearby uplands; Jonaces held strong in the Sierra Gorda.

Otomí Querétaro, 1520–1550

The Spanish-Tlaxcalan conquest of Tenochtitlan, the center of Mexica rule, set off fundamental changes in the Bajío. Mexica power collapsed. Tarascan rulers resisted briefly and then negotiated uncertain alliances with the newcomers. Spaniards scrambled to assert sovereignty, challenging each other while struggling to rule diverse indigenous peoples. In the Bajío competing Spanish forces claimed sovereignty over Nahua lords at Xilotepec and Tarascans at Acámbaro. Meanwhile two salients thrust north beyond the limits of Mexica and Tarascan rule. Spaniards led by Nuño de Guzmán drove northwest into Jalisco with infamous violence, taking slaves wherever they went. Simultaneously, Otomí lords and settlers drove north with Franciscan allies to assert independence and promote settlement around Tlachco-Querétaro. In the Bajío "Spanish" occupation began as Otomí expansion.

When don Fernando Cortés and his freebooters invaded Nahua domains, forged alliances with outlying city-states, and conquered the Mexica at Tenochtitlan from 1519 to 1521, they collapsed the structures of power, alliance, and war that shaped Mesoamerica. They brought smallpox and other Eurasian diseases that devastated a population previously untouched and lacking immunities. Cortés and his native allies destroyed the most assertive state in Mesoamerica in two years. The first smallpox epidemic came in 1520, amid that conflict, killing about a third of the population and leaving survivors scarred to remind all of its deadly assault. Smallpox facilitated conquest and Spanish rule. Together they assaulted truth. Warlords from unknown lands, serving unseen sovereigns and an unimagined God while untouched by devastating plagues, claimed to rule. The powerful fell; their gods failed; people died. Truth became false; the unimagined became real.[9] In the 1520s Mesoamerica, long a domain of instability, became a place of incomprehensible death, conflict, uncertainty, and for a few, opportunity.

Vastly outnumbered in lands and among peoples they barely knew, Spaniards aimed to rule by adapting Mesoamerican ways of lordship. The *encomienda* grants that organized early Spanish sovereignty gave to favored Spaniards the right to take tribute in goods and labor from native lords and their people. Under encomiendas indigenous production, social ways, and tributes would persist, to the extent possible amid depopulation and demands for Christianization. Some encomienda grants recognized native lords in place at conquest; some deposed ruling Nahuas, Tarascans, and others and replaced them with lords recently displaced in indigenous conquests. Otomí lords often found Spanish conquest a way back to power, subject to Spanish overlords.[10]

After the fall of Tenochtitlan, Cortés awarded Xilotepec in encomienda in 1522. With rule and tribute collection uncertain on the northern frontier, the grant changed hands until it settled with Juan Jaramillo in 1523. Jaramillo, however, faced persistent challenges to his right to take tribute from Xilotepec's dependents at Tlachco (Querétaro). Otomí resistance and Spanish challengers limited his powers.[11] It was the Otomí Connín, later baptized don Fernando de Tapia, who led expansion into the Bajío, according to sources that his power shaped. By the 1550s he ruled an Otomí community entrenched at Querétaro.

Connín was born at Nopala, a town subject to Mexica rule at Xilotepec. Some texts call him a minor noble, others an assertive commoner. Some see a *calpixque*, an agent of Mexica power collecting tribute from Otomí settlers at Tlachco. Others see a *pochtecatl*, trading with the Otomí at Tlachco and among dispersed Chichimeca— buying skins and bows-and-arrows in exchange for salt and cotton cloth. There is a plausible integration: many a commoner sought noble status by serving higher lords, before and after the conquest; many an agent of empire traded for himself and his overlords, before and after the conquest. What seems clear is that Connín was an entrepreneurial frontiersman. He lived at a border, integrating peoples on both sides.

He served overlords when useful; he served himself when possible. After the fall of the Mexica, while Spaniards struggled to establish rule at Mexica Xilotepec and Tarascan Acámbaro, around 1530 Connín and others led a growing number of Otomí to settle the river basin lands of the Bajío, notably at Tlachco, the future Querétaro.

While Connín and his kin, allies, and dependents settled Tlachco, Spaniards disputed conquest and rights to rule and take tributes. In the 1520s Nuño de Guzmán aimed to rival Cortés and the first conquerors of the Mexica. Guzmán began his quest along the Pánuco River, north of Veracruz. He focused less on establishing rule and more on assaulting dispersed communities, taking slaves to sell in Caribbean islands facing depopulation. He later drove inland across the Bajío and into the Tarascan heartland. He fought to build a New Galicia on Tarascan domains and among peoples north and west, aiming to rival Cortés's New Spain. Failing to control the Tarascan core, Guzmán turned on Jalisco to the northwest, again taking slaves in native communities while he fought fragmented local rulers.[12]

In 1532 Guzmán included Querétaro (Tarascan for Tlachco) in the encomienda he gave Hernán Pérez de Bocanegra at Acámbaro, reviving Tarascan claims to the Otomí outpost. For decades Jaramillo and his heirs at Xilotepec would dispute encomienda rights to Tlachco-Querétaro with Bocanegra and his heirs at Acámbaro, allowing Connín-Tapia to work between them. He allied with Bocanegra to escape the lords of Xilotepec; Bocanegra brought Connín to baptism as Tapia and recognized him as lord of Querétaro. In response the Jaramillos pursued Xilotepec's rights over Tlachco, aiming to bring Tapia to dependence.

While Guzmán pressed conquest and slaving north into Jalisco and Bocanegra and the Jaramillos disputed encomienda rights over Querétaro, Connín led Otomí communities in settling the eastern Bajío in the 1530s. With Franciscans based at Acámbaro, he brought settlers and convents to Apaseo (an old Tarascan-Otomí outpost), to San Miguel north on the Río Laja, and to Xichú northeast at the base of the rugged Sierra Gorda. Connín worked in alliance with the Spaniards Martín Jofre (whose name would mark an important estate north of Querétaro in the eighteenth century and after), multiple members of the Rico family (whose descendant managed Puerto de Nieto after 1790), and don Juan Alanís de Sánchez (perhaps the first of the great land-engrossing, entrepreneurial priests of the Bajío, imaginably an ancestor of don José Sánchez Espinosa). Also with Franciscan allies, Connín first founded a Querétaro that mixed Otomí and Pames in the canyon later christened San Pedro de la Cañada. The Pames refusal to tolerate the newcomers in their fortress home and the promise of irrigation along the river just west soon moved the center of Otomí power and production to its modern basin site at Querétaro. The eastern Bajío remained a frontier of complex interactions—with Spaniards as new participants, but far from simply dominant.[13]

Meanwhile, early in the 1540s Guzmán's brutality and slaving led to an alliance of resistance among peoples dispersed around Jalisco. Elder sages promised to restore native lords and rich fields, revealing that many rebels lived in stratified, cultivating communities, "en policía," Spaniards then said. Cycles of native resistance and Spanish attack led to a vast mobilization of native peoples led by Caxcanes, cultivators living under multiple lords, and including stateless Guachichiles to the east and Zacatecos to the north. A punitive expedition followed, led by New Spain's first viceroy, don Antonio Mendoza. It included famed conquerors like Pedro de Alvarado (who died in the effort). It also mobilized tens of thousands of Mesoamerican allies led by native lords, mounted on Spanish horses, wielding firearms, and expecting reward for their effort. A great Spanish-Mesoamerican assault at Mixtón crushed Caxcan and Zacateco resistance. The victors, European and Mesoamerican, took captives as slaves (just as the Crown outlawed indigenous slavery). Escaped Caxcanes dispersed along with Zacatecos. In the wake of the punitive campaign don Diego de Ibarra and Juan de Tolosa continued north to discover the rich silver mines of Zacatecas in 1546.[14]

Less violent occupations shaped the eastern Bajío. While Otomí, Pames, and others settled to cultivate along riverbanks, Viceroy Mendoza began to grant lands for grazing on the Amascala plain east of Querétaro and across the basins north and west. The region consolidated its early structure: an Otomí town surrounded by Spaniards' estates. The name Querétaro asserted links to Tarascan Acámbaro and a refusal to be Tlachco, subject to Xilotepec. Parallel extensions of Otomí cultivation and Spanish grazing spread west of Querétaro around Apaseo. Farther west Agustinian friars began to build the great San Nicolás estate near Yuriria, at the northern limit of Tarascan settlement. The 1540s were a decade of relative peace and emerging prosperity in the Bajío—a sharp contrast to the violence raging just west. Yet there were precipitants of conflicts to come. Extensive deer hunting to provide meat and skins for new residents and new trade threatened the sustenance of Chichimecas and opened ecological space for invasive Old World livestock.[15]

As the 1540s closed, it seemed that resistance around Jalisco was over, Otomí settlement in the eastern Bajío was set, and silver would provide riches at Zacatecas. The regime aimed to curtail the power

of Spanish encomenderos and native lords. It worked to limit encomienda tributes and block inheritance rights; when they endured, encomiendas became pensions run by the regime. Officials also aimed to
limit native lords by founding indigenous republics: councils of *principales* (nobles), annually electing governors, *alcaldes* (magistrates),
and *regidores* (councilmen). By 1550 Querétaro was a republic, proud
of markets, streets, and plazas, and a water system driving a grist mill
and irrigating rich *huertas* (urban gardens).[16]

With the republic in place, the regime worked to blunt don Fernando
de Tapia's power. In 1550 Mendoza, near the end of fifteen years as
viceroy, sent an Otomí noble from Tepejí to investigate Querétaro.
Tapia was not named, but a "Governor and Cacique" was accused of
taking excess tribute from Otomí and Chichimecas and making them
work without pay. The same unnamed lord was said to have allowed
Chichimecas to persist in "sacrifices, drunken revels, and idolatries"—
that is, in traditional rituals and festivals. In August, the inquest done,
Tapia was ordered to take only the tributes listed in the assessment of
1546.[17] Meanwhile Mendoza confirmed the right of the Otomí to stay
at Querétaro. He licensed a weekly Saturday market; he ordered Spaniards and Otomí lords to pay the republic to use the grist mill. A year
later, aiming to protect Otomí lands and crops, Mendoza's successor
don Luis de Velasco decreed that Spaniards could take land and graze
livestock around Querétaro only with his license.[18]

Complex interests were at play. The lords of Xilotepec complained
that Otomí families rushed to Querétaro, where they found better
land and lesser tributes. Equal tributes would stop the migration.[19]
Amid that dispute Velasco confirmed possession of the Xilotepec encomienda by the widow doña Beatriz Jaramillo; she received two-thirds,
her daughter one-third. In November 1551 Velasco ousted don Fernando de Tapia as governor of Querétaro, replacing him with a native
of Xilotepec who was ordered to end excess tribute and labor without pay, promote "the common good," and "end drunken revelries,
sacrifices, and other public sins." How Tapia took tributes so limited
that they encouraged migration yet so excessive that they exploited
commoners is not addressed. Clarity came in April 1552. The widow
Jaramillo married don Francisco de Velasco, the Viceroy's brother. The
highest official in New Spain then confirmed his brother's possession
of her share of the Xilotepec encomienda.[20] The viceroy aimed to limit
Tapia power and strengthen his newly married brother's access to Querétaro's tribute.

Yet just as Velasco aimed to end Tapia's Otomí lordship, the silver
bonanza at Zacatecas brought accelerating northward migration and

intensifying conflict with Chichimecas. The viceroy faced a dilemma. He knew well the two ways of northward expansion. His daughter had married don Diego de Ibarra, long involved in slaving and pivotal to mining at Zacatecas; his brother had married the widow Jaramillo, gaining encomienda rights limited by the power of the Tapias, who led the more peaceful expansion of settlement around Querétaro. Velasco promoted mining at Zacatecas; he sanctioned war against Chichimecas—as a defensive measure. He also recognized that he could not fight Chichimecas without the Tapias who led Otomí warriors into battle while Querétaro sustained the fight and mining at Zacatecas.

By 1554 don Fernando was again governor at Querétaro. The Jaramillos and their allies, including the lords of Xilotepec, again tried to assert rights at Querétaro. They backed the claims of Chichimeca lords against Tapia. But as conflict escalated Tapia could not be ousted.[21] He gave lands long claimed by the lords of Xilotepec to the Querétaro republic; he bought for himself properties earlier granted to enterprising Spaniards. Complaints of his excesses still reached Velasco, but in the face of war the viceroy could only try to limit Tapia's power—he could not curtail it. Late in 1555, traveling south of Querétaro, Velasco reminded Tapia to pay the Otomí workers who served on his "croplands and other enterprises," and to compensate the carriers who delivered produce around the region. His rights to labor were held within a four-league (twelve-mile) limit, a zone more than sufficient to his enterprises.[22]

Three years later Tapia faced a challenge that revealed much about the Otomí conqueror and the inability of the regime to curb him during Chichimeca wars. In 1558 the Otomí of San Miguel Huimilpan, south of Querétaro, accused Tapia of taking lands and forcing them to live and work at Querétaro. They recalled living happily dispersed across uplands between Xilotepec and Querétaro. Then in 1535 Tapia and don Nicolás de San Luis, accompanied by Franciscan friars, congregated them in a village and granted them all the land in their valley. Velasco confirmed the grant in 1551. Now Tapia took their land and forced them to Querétaro. Velasco reconfirmed the rights of Huimilpan. At the inspection implementing the villagers' possession, however, Tapia denounced the Otomí of Huimilpan as rebels.[23] In 1564 Chichimecas at Jurica, just outside Querétaro, also accused Tapia of taking land and forcing them to work. Again Velasco ordered Tapia to stop but could not blunt his power.[24] The rights of Chichimecas who refrained from war were respected; yet Tapia was essential to the fight against many more independent Chichimecas. He could be cautioned, not curbed. He lived until at least 1571, for over forty years a key participant in the founding of the Bajío.[25] He ruled Querétaro before silver

The Bajío in the Sixteenth Century

created a global economy and Spaniards came north with new vigor, provoking rising conflicts with native peoples. His power remained essential to Spanish settlement and the silver economy once those conflicts began.

Silver and Chichimeca Wars

Silver brought economic dynamism, accelerating migration, and escalating conflict to the Bajío and the lands north. Europeans came to the Americas with a sharp eye for specie. When the Ming Empire mandated that only silver would serve as money for tax payments in densely populated China, its value soared, as did demand around the globe.[26] Spaniards in the Americas could not know why global demand was insatiable; they quickly sensed its dramatic stimulus. Dreams of gain drew untold numbers of Europeans and Mesoamericans north toward the mines, along with African slaves and their mixed offspring. Conflict escalated along roads heading north and around the mines at Zacatecas, as Guamares, Guachichiles, Zacatecos, and others faced invasions of people and livestock.[27] Soon after the Zacatecas strikes, silver was also found in rugged uplands at Guanajuato, just north of the Bajío basin.[28] Spaniards again rushed to stake claims and met resistant Chichimecas.

The resulting conflicts are captured in a petition by Juan de Jaso el Viejo, who came north from Mexico City to become a leading miner at Guanajuato. He swore in 1557, "five years ago, more or less, I discovered a number of mines in these mountains . . . which I revealed . . . to others who came with me as dependents, . . . I distributed rights to mines to those I believed would work them well, taking some for myself and my children, surveying and registering everything." Jaso then accepted a charge from Viceroy Velasco to "round up the Chichimecas, which has required long and hard effort, and damaged my interests in the mines which were taken by others; I rounded up more than four hundred and took them to Pénjamo, where they now live." Jaso's reward: while he cleared Guanajuato of Chichimecas, "many people who live at the mines, with little fear of God and less conscience, have invaded my claims." He demanded that the usurpers "be punished accoriding to the laws."[29] A powerful Spaniard found mines and staked claims for himself and his sons and daughters. He fought to clear the zone of Chichimecas and saw others take his mines. Jaso demanded that his claims be preserved, insisting that without Chichimeca removal, mining could not flourish. His efforts to contain native resistance should be rewarded, not punished.[30]

The titles granted in 1557 to Guanajuato mines show powerful men claiming mines for themselves, their kin, and their allies. Lesser men prospected without titles. While Spaniards and others (including a Nápoles) disputed claims and fought Chichimecas, the underlying challenge was labor. Chichimecas would not serve, so Jaso removed them. Early mining worked at the surface, facilitating the work of poor prospectors. Soon, however, the need to follow veins into mountains and refine large quantities of low-grade ore by amalgamation with mercury required a growing number of workers.[31] Pero Fernández Valenciano claimed lands for a "crew (*cuadrilla*) of people to refine metals." Juan de Goyre registered sites he had "taken and begun to populate in order to build mills to crush ore, to incorporate mercury, and to separate it, and to build residences, and houses for a crew of negros and for *indios*, along with sheds to guard silver, and another for a foundry."[32]

In the face of Chichimeca resistance, recruiting indios meant drawing migrants from Mesoamerica. By the 1560s Guanajuato had chapels and hospitals for Otomí, Tarascan, and Mexica newcomers. An image of Our Lady of the Rosary, brought by Spaniards, was placed first in the Mexica hospital. When the Tarascan chapel was ready in 1562 she moved there to serve a larger community. She became Our Lady of Guanajuato as the Tarascan chapel became the parish church for the mining community. The risks of mining amid warfare made the migrant virgin a key protector of Europeans and Mesoamericans alike. The viceroy named a district magistrate to inspect claims, collect taxes, and do justice; a parish priest reported to the bishop of Michoacán. Neither Spaniards nor Mesoamericans had a council in sixteenth-century Guanajuato—a contrast with Otomí Querétaro.[33]

With limited success drawing Mesoamericans to the mines, Spaniards bought African slaves. A report from around 1560 noted 1,035 Spaniards and 1,762 enslaved Africans in the bishopric of Michoacán, and lamented 20 runaways in the Sierra de Guanajuato; Viceroy Velasco ordered 150 indigenous fighters to mobilize with bows and arrows "en busca de dichos negros."[34] When his successor don Martín Enríquez signed a charter in 1575 offering land and a Spanish council to promote settlement at León, just west of Guanajuato, the challege was to defend against Chichimecas. In 1580, when Spaniards and free mulattoes asked for new support for settlement at León, they argued a need to fight "the many mulattoes and mestizos who commit sinful public outrages in disservice of God, many of whom go about . . . with firearms, . . . swords, and other weapons and commit endless and grave crimes."[35] Reports around 1580 suggest four to eight hundred slaves working at Guanajuato; a petition in 1584 argued a need for eight hundred slaves. Yet when Spaniards set costly African slaves to mining, many escaped. Pedro de Yrasso, a leading miner, saw liabilities in sending Africans into the mines: "we have seen from experience that a *negro* dies quickly when sent into a mine to extract metal."[36] All workers risked death in the mines; African slaves cost large investments, and Spaniards preferred that Mesoamericans risk life and health underground.

In 1570 Viceroy Enríquez tried another solution. A labor draft, a *repartimiento*, ordered Tarascan communities, ranging from the old capital at Tzintzuntzan on Lake Pátzcuaro to Jiquilpan in the west and Yuriria in the east, to send 4 percent of their men in shifts to work at Guanajuato. The goal was 487 workers every week, paid to work but not to travel. Twice-yearly treks would disrupt family life and local production. Everyone but Guanajuato's miners objected. Tarascans resisted, while their numbers plummeted as disease struck.[37] During decades of war, mining carried on at Guanajuato; it rarely flourished.

Silver offered a chance at wealth to men fortunate enough to gain claims and find workers. Mining offered steadier profits to others who financed mines, and good prospects to those who supplied food, clothing, tools, and livestock. In 1550 Acámbaro, Apaseo, and Querétaro, already settled along the rivers of the southeastern Bajío, sat ready to supply mines, miners, and workers at Zacatecas and Guanajuato. Caravans drove north with maize, flour, cloth, and tools, surrounded by herds of sheep, horses, and cattle. To Guamares, Guachichiles, and Zacatecos the supply trains of the 1550s were both an invasion and an invitation; the tens of thousands of livestock, whether herded together or escaped to roam and multiply across vast plateaus, were both a problem and an opportunity.

Hunting and gathering was always precarious across the dry country between the Sierras. Animals were small and scarce, and scarcer still after the deer hunt of the 1540s. Plants were few and periodically decimated by drought. Human populations remained sparse. The thousands of horses, tens of thousands of cattle, and hundreds of thousands of sheep that invaded from the 1550s grazed on the plant life that sustained Chichimecas and their traditional prey. Chichimeca survival was threatened—and facilitated. To war-hardened hunters and gatherers the response to invasion by Spaniards, Mesoamericans, and vast herds of livestock was obvious: they began to hunt livestock and gather food and cloth from caravans crossing their homelands. For Guamares, Guachichiles, and Zacatecos the invasion brought opportunity. New ways of hunting and gathering fueled decades of war.[38]

To Spaniards and Otomí seeking gain in mining and the supply economy, Chichimeca livestock hunting and cloth gathering were theft and savagery. The 1550s began wars that escalated into the 1580s, only to end as the 1590s began. Over the years Spanish policies and Chichimeca ways changed. Mining expanded in fits and starts while conflict raged. Spanish North America and its silver economy began in decades of war; during later centuries they would expand northward, always at war with independent peoples on the northern frontier.

Silver production and Chichimeca resistance rose as don Luis de Velasco became New Spain's second viceroy. His rule from 1550 to 1565 framed the first stage of a long era of conflict. He aimed to promote silver production, facilitating the activities of his son-in law don Diego de Ibarra, a leading miner and refiner at Zacatecas. Yet Velasco had to work with policies set by Carlos V and the "pro-Indian party" led by Bartolomé de las Casas. In 1549 the emperor had outlawed military advances into native territories; in 1555 he decreed that only peaceful evangelization could bring independent people into Christian society. Velasco found a way. He promoted mining at Zacatecas and exploration all around, seeking new mines and grazing estates to sustain them. If Chichimecas resisted, Spaniards would fight "defensive" wars—thus "just" wars. In 1554 don Francisco de Ibarra, don Diego's son, drove north of Zacatecas, setting off escalating conflicts that he answered with deadly force.[39]

Meanwhile, Velasco had to protect the route that linked Zacatecas to Querétaro, Mexico City, and the world beyond. Into the 1550s he relied heavily on Otomí lords like don Fernando de Tapia and don Nicolás de San Luis. The latter was honored with a grant of nobility and commission as a captain for capturing the Chichimeca war leader Maxorro.[40] Still, the fighting continued. Velasco concluded that he had to accelerate Spanish settlement on the road to the mines. San Miguel lay in a corner of hills where basins extended north and south along the Laja river, and east toward Querétaro. Otomí had settled there in the 1530s, proselytized by Franciscans from the 1540s. Spaniards claimed land there from the early 1550s, provoking complaints from the Otomí. Velasco sanctioned Spanish claims in 1555. Fifty settlers, armed and ready to fight Chichimecas, gained house lots, irrigated gardens, croplands, and grazing sites. Fifty native workers from Acámbaro and Querétaro built a new town center. Two indigenous governors—don Juan de San Miguel for the Otomí, don Domingo for Tarascans and Chichimecas—oversaw native residents. Then in 1559 Velasco gave San Miguel a Spanish council; it would be a Spanish town. So would San Felipe, a day's journey northwest, where the Bajío uplands met the dry country extending north. Led by Velasco's brother don Francisco, in 1562 Spaniards there got a council, town lots, croplands, and grazing sites to guard the road to Zacatecas.[41]

Velasco's approach was clear: promote mining and protect the roads connecting mines to the Bajío and Atlantic trade; drive north in search of new riches; and respond with "defensive" force when Zacatecos and others hunted livestock, gathered cloth, and blocked development. Conflict escalated. After Carlos abdicated in favor of his son Felipe II, king and viceroy became more aggressive. The early 1560s saw silver production peak at Zacatecas while nearby estates faced rising attacks. Don Alonso de Zorita, a judge on the High Court in Mexico City, proposed a solution. With "pro-Indian" views, Zorita called for more Spanish settlement and peaceful evangelization of Chichimecas. He promised to end escalating conflicts and promote mining. But his plan required treasury funds and Velasco rejected it.[42]

He instead turned to Captain Pedro de Ahumada Sámano, who promised a war of pacification without cost to the treasury. Warriors who "defended" mining and commercial settlement would gain Chichimeca captives as reward. Velasco had opened the way in 1560, when he authorized taking Chichimeca captives who could be held for six years, skirting the prohibition of enslavement with a euphemism. Chichimeca "hunting" became a primary Spanish activity.[43] What Zacateco or Guachichil warrior would live more than six years after capture and incorporation into a Spanish society laden with diseases deadly to Amerindians? Who would count the years of bondage among the few who lived longer?

Ahumada also planned to take advantage of differences among native peoples. He knew that the Caxcanes, leaders of the Mixtón war in the 1540s, "were political people like the Mexicas, . . . they plant fields and live in fixed villages." They had adapted to defeat by Mendoza's army. Some labored at Zacatecas; others fought Chichimecas. The latter were different. "The people of the Guachichil nations live naked and wander like arabs and savages without fixed homes." They were not "political," armies could not defeat them; they rarely served as effective allies. Nations among them claimed home domains; to protect them they mixed alliances and conflicts that might work to Spanish advantage. In a complex new world Ahumada offered a war of assault and retreat, killing warriors and taking captives, his activities funded by sales of captives legally not slaves. Mining and war would expand together.[44]

In the late 1560s Felipe II, facing revolt in the Netherlands and other European conflicts, turned against his father's defense of native rights (however limited) to embrace a policy of "economic utility." He sent don Francisco de Toledo to Perú and don Martín Enríquez to New Spain as viceroys charged with promoting mining and raising revenues. In 1569 Enríquez called a council of clergy in Mexico City to demand approval of offensive war against Chichimecas. The churchmen complied, and sanctioned holding captives for fourteen years—a term that few would outlive. The 1570s brought rising conflicts promoted and funded by hunts for Chichimeca captives. They were taken by the thousands, and war escalated.[45]

Conflict limited cultivation and grazing around Zacatecas, leaving the Bajío to sustain the mining economy. When war began in the 1550s the Otomí around Querétaro were ready to supply staples and fight Chichimecas. At Yuriria, Agustinian friars oversaw construction of a dam and canals to irrigate a vast convent estate and water small plots for hundreds of Tarascan families. Again native migrants gained irrigated lands. But at Querétaro, Connín-Tapia led commercial development while Franciscans preached and gave hospital care. At Yuriria the Agustinians were devout preachers and estate builders, claiming commercial cultivation for their convent estate.[46] Both Otomí-Franciscan Querétaro and Tarascan-Agustinian Yuriria channeled indigenous production to sustain mining in years of conflict.

In the 1570s Enríquez concluded that new settlements in the Bajío might serve as bulwarks against Chichimecas and bases for increased cultivation to support mining and grazing farther north. In 1570 he chartered Celaya, where the Laja and Querétaro rivers met. León, on the Turbio River west of Guanajuato, came in 1576. Irapuato, in the central basin south of Guanajuato between Celaya and León, began as war waned in 1589.[47] In the basin towns founded during the wars, Enríquez and his successors sanctioned Spanish power. From Celaya to León and at every new foundation in between, Spaniards ruled local councils, the best irrigated lands, and outlying grazing sites. Indigenous settlers were welcomed and a few (most near Celaya, secondarily around León) gained rights and lands as indigenous republics. But as basin lands were settled during Chichimeca wars, Spaniards ruled and Mesoamericans faced dependence. Querétaro would not be replicated.[48]

New Spanish settlements brought strength against Chichimecas and an expanding agricultural and pastoral economy. Along the Laja, Querétaro, and Lerma rivers, Spaniards gained lands measured in *caballerías*, each equal to about 40 hectares (100 acres). Settlers holding one or more grants fronting rivers joined to build irrigation systems, first at Celaya, later reaching west. They raised wheat and built mills. Beyond the reach of irrigation they grazed livestock. Spanish settlements raised European products—wheat and livestock—to supply local towns and mines at Guanajuato and Zacatecas. Inevitably, expanding cultivation and grazing heightened threats to and opportunities for Chichimecas. The war in the Bajío did not pit Spaniards against "Indians." Rather, cultivators and grazers (Spaniards, Otomí, Tarascans) fought hunters and gatherers (Guamares, Guachichiles, and others). Don Fernando de Tapia (Connín) and his son don Diego joined Spaniards to defend settlement, cultivation, a commercial economy, and Spanish rule. The Otomí lords' ability to mobilize fighters against Chichimecas and to orient production to support mining strengthened Tapia power at Querétaro, even as Spanish settlers took precedence on the bottomlands expanding west.

At the heart of the conflict was the drive to create a silver-led commercial economy. In 1574 don Pedro de Moya y Contreras, archbishop of Mexico City and the leading churchman in New Spain, made that clear. Writing to the king in his Council of the Indies, he began:

the most important revenue and source of wealth your majesty has in this land comes from the rights and taxes on the silver miners extract. We can even say that everything you have here comes from silver alone, because if mining ceased there would be no gain from tributes in maize, cloth, or anything else. They would have no value and fall back to their old prices, which for Spaniards was too little to support your courts and officials, and among natives was nothing because every exchange was mere barter. As a result, by helping miners and supporting silver refining, everything grows in value and quality and the taxes and revenues of your majesty are assured and will continue to grow. Commerce will be greater, its payments and taxes also greater; farmers will be stimulated to expand their fields. The conclusion: the land cannot thrive nor your majesty take revenue without mining.

The archbishop saw two necessities: cheap mercury and "stopping these indios at war." With peace and prosperity, "Spaniards and natives alike would populate many settlements, travel the roads with security, and foodstuffs would be cheap. Everyone would go about rich and content." To promote these commercial goals the bishop (backed by all the religious but the Dominicans, the order of Bartolomé de las Casas) called for offensive war against Chichimecas. They must be attacked; captives would be "slaves for as long as they lived" and thus gain the benefit of "our Holy Mother Church." Some would die, but they were "highway robbers and murderers." It was "less inconvenient that a few indios who justly deserve it die than that Spaniards traveling the roads or living at the estates and farms be killed." In 1574 the churchmen of New Spain justified war without quarter in defense of the silver economy.[49]

Yet offensive war and slaving without euphemism brought the frontier no closer to peace during the next decade. Hernando de Robles reported that he had taken more than a thousand captives and sent them to labor under Franciscan oversight around Querétaro and Acámbaro. Meanwhile, from 1778 to 1782 Chichimecas "killed more than a thousand people, among them peaceful *indios*, Spaniards, *negros*, mulatos, and mestizos, men, women, and children, inflicting on them the most cruel deaths I have ever heard of, read about, or seen." In addition, "they have burned and devastated nineteen settlements of peaceful, Christian *indios*, along with sixteen estates grazing cattle and sheep, leaving nothing behind. They set fire to churches, burning images and altars, . . . The number of livestock they have taken or killed is infinite and of incalculable value, as is the loss to the owners." Robles added that while Chichimeca assaults escalated many began to live on European livestock; growing numbers fought on horseback with European firearms.[50]

After decades of violence Spanish leaders began to see that independent people whose ways of life were under siege, whose mobility facilitated resistance, and who nimbly adapted to new means of sustenance and new ways of warfare would not be subjugated by force. A radical rethinking of policy began. In 1580 Viceroy Enríquez wrote to his successor, the Conde de Coruña, that war was feeding on itself with no end in sight. Coruña arrived with permission to spend treasury funds to promote new settlements that he hoped might limit slaving and break the cycle of violence. Many voices called for change; rising costs brought officials to consider change, culminating in the program offered in 1585 by none other than Archbishop Moya y Contreras, then interim viceroy. He presented the problem of Chichimeca resistance to the Third Council of New Spain's bishops. Prelates and heads of religious orders reversed their vision of a decade earlier, now condemning "the war of blood and fire." They called for a program of pacification led by clergy who would preach and teach settled ways to Chichimecas while Spaniards led commercial development. The bishops published their new vision before approval by the Council of the Indies. It was the first proposal seen by Viceroy Marqués de Villamanrique, who adopted the program in 1787.[51]

For decades Spaniards and Otomí, Guamares, Guachichiles, and Zacatecos all killed with savagery. Mostly they killed men—warriors or potential warriors. All worked to capture women and children, incorporating them in production and reproduction. Martial patriarchy shaped Chichimeca wars; manly warfare and the capture of women and children promoted patriarchy, production, and reproduction among all contenders. The "theft" of people, livestock, foodstuffs, and cloth shaped the ecology of conflict. Guamares, Guachichiles, and Zacatecos hunted Spanish and Otomí men and gathered their women and children, livestock and produce. Spaniards and Otomí hunted Chichimeca men and gathered Chichimeca women and children—and took back livestock and produce when they could.

Finally pacification began in the late 1580s. New policies sanctioned by the bishops and adopted by Viceroy Villamanrique and his successor don Luis de Velasco, the Younger, backed the change. A new generation of commanders led by Miguel Caldera proved pivotal to implementation. Caldera was a mestizo, son of a Spanish settler at Zacatecas and a Chichimeca mother (ally or captive?). He fought Chichimecas for decades and knew that the war was self-sustaining. Chichimecas lived by "stealing" Spanish women and children, food, cloth, and livestock. Spanish and Otomí soldiers prospered by "capturing" Chichimeca women and children and by reclaiming food, cloth, and animals. Archbishop Moya y Contreras, Viceroys Villamanrique and Velasco the Younger, and the mestizo Captain Caldera all finally recognized that the only way to end the war was to end the war.[52]

Underlying pacification was an ecological transformation of Chichimeca life. From the 1550s Chichimecas hunted and gathered wheat, maize, cloth, horses, cattle, and sheep, and faced disease and depopulation.[53] While a generation of warriors—Spanish, Otomí, mestizo, and Chichimeca—lived fighting, Chichimecas died in devastating numbers, and the survivors lived ever more dependent on crops and livestock. New policies built on that dependence. In the late 1580s Caldera and others offered surviving Chichimecas a new deal: they could settle under the supervision of clergy and get land, seed, cloth, and lessons in planting, clothmaking, and Christianity. Dependent for a generation on grain and livestock, natives would become farmers and grazers. Decades of war and disease had proven destructive. Mines in San Luis Potosí opened by Caldera in the 1590s drew new waves of Spaniards north. Mesoamerican migrants from Tlaxcala, who were granted councils, lands, and livestock, came to live across lands from Zacatecas and San Luis Potosí to Saltillo.[54] Whether Chichimecas saw Tlaxcalans as models, competitors, or invaders is unknown. In a radically new world many Chichimecas concluded that settlement under clerical oversight was the best deal available.

Decades of conflict gave way in the 1590s to pacification. Mining consolidated in an inverted triangle, its southern point at Guanajuato, its northern extensions reaching past Zacatecas to the northwest and San Luis Potosí in the northeast. Across Bajío basin lands from San Juan del Río through Querétaro to Celaya and beyond, a culturally complex society of irrigated planting and vast grazing emerged from decades of war. Otomí growers and grazers around Querétaro, Tarascan and Augustinian growers at Yuriria, and Spanish growers and grazers from Celaya to San Miguel to León could focus on crops and livestock to supply the mines that made New Spain pivotal to the Spanish empire and global trade.

Chichimeca War and Nascent Capitalism:
A View from San Miguel

The violence that forged Spanish North America peaked in the early 1580s. Two participants penned revealing analyses of the challenges of war and settlement in 1582. Father Juan Antonio Velázquez, pastor at San Miguel, wrote to Felipe II, aiming to dissuade the king from destructive policies. Francisco Ramos de Córdoba, notary at Xilotepec, produced a long description of Querétaro, responding to the king's request for detailed information. Velázquez offered a clear understanding of the roots, challenges, and consequences of the Chichimeca wars; Ramos reported Querétaro's complex history and emerging promise, even while war raged.

Velázquez identified himself as a "priest with benefice at the town San Miguel de los Chichimecas." The town that gained fame as San Miguel el Grande in the colonial era and San Miguel de Allende after independence was "de los Chichimecas" in 1582.[55] Velázquez did not say how long he had served the frontier outpost; he did emphasize: "I am friend of many indios and their leaders, including Copuces and Guamaraes and their Captain don Juan, Maculias and their Captain don Alonso, and some Guachichiles and the Captains called Naguadame and Atanatoya . . . the last two not baptized and without Christian names."[56] The priest at San Miguel knew Chichimecas who had come to Christianity and others who refrained.

Velázquez lamented "the great and continuous damages these faithless native attackers have inflicted on the lands and subjects of your majesty across this frontier, the costs of the war against them in people and revenue, and that the plague not only has not ended, but has grown and continues to grow every day thanks to the audacity and great success of our enemy and the little resistance and punishment we place upon them. All this promises enduring problems and the future ruin of the kingdom."[57] Having gained the monarch's attention, the cleric aimed to educate him. Chichimeca lands began thirty leagues (ninety miles) northwest of the viceregal capital. San Juan del Río, Xichú, Querétaro, Apaseo, Acámbaro, and Yuririapúndaro were "the last native towns that remain at peace." Just beyond was "a land at war" beginning at Celaya, and including San Miguel, Guanajuato, León, and San Felipe. The early settlements led by Franciscans, Augustians, and their Otomí and Tarascan allies remained at peace. The places settled as Spanish bulwarks after 1550 faced war.[58]

Velázquez knew the region's history. "In the Chichimecas' province there are clear signs that once the land was cultivated, leaving us certain that the region was settled in earlier times by people inclined to build and to live in settled culture. Now, all of that is absent; the present residents build nothing and sow small and scattered plots." Two views explained the change: most believed "that indigenous bowmen conquered the earlier inhabitants who worked the land, forcing them to flee toward Mexico City." Others argued that a "great plague or drought" had emptied the basin, allowing the "bowmen" to move in. The explanations were not mutually exclusive; no modern scholar has done better.

The priest then sketched Chichimeca ways—in the prejudices of his day. Diverse nations spoke many languages; none kept fixed settlements, each claimed a domain and fought to protect it. "They have no kind of church nor other place of worship, no priests, nor do they recognize any law or rule; as a result they have no towns nor any set homes—they live without human regulation." Instead, "like beasts, they wander across the land." To mobilize for war, "an old man or old woman takes a drink made of the herb root we call peyote, which for a long time deprives them of reason. While out of their minds, the devil appears in their imagination . . . and they come out to report what the devil has ordered."[59] Chichimecas were not settled, they did not cultivate, they lacked politics and religion as Spaniards knew them—and they served peyote-induced devils.

Velázquez did find ways to admire among the "savages." They were naked, dirty, and lazy, yet they promoted "chastity." A father could execute any man who took his daughter before a ceremony had provided patriarchal sanction and proof of the bride's virginity. Chichimecas were monogamous, though many allowed divorce and second unions. The priest then repeated that the men were skilled warriors, using long bows-and-arrows with deadly aim in wars among themselves and in raids against Spaniards and other Christians.[60] Europeans and Mesoamericans easily understood the Chichimecas' martial patriarchy.

The priest then turned to changes under way as Chichimecas adapted to European and Mesoamerican invasions. "They live by the hunt, and on wild fruits, roots, and insects. Those who have taken our cows and mares live better because they kill many cows and even mares and mules for food. They steal livestock and carry them north where they guard them in corrals like ours and slaughter them when needed. . . . In order to herd and guard livestock, some indios go about on horseback." Some "think they are cattlemen." Hunting and gathering Chichimecas developed "a taste for beef."[61] Still, the priest told his king that they remained savages: they ate meat raw; some killed and ate captives taken in war—not only men but "young and pretty Spanish women . . . after they made use of them."[62]

Such people had to be pacified. They might be few in number: "rarely are they found in groups of even two hundred people." The problem was that in the Bajío and around the mines Chichimecas remained defiant and ready to draw people farther north into the conflict. "In lands to the north, natives remain more numerous; that is where those near the frontier recruit allies to join in assaults. Many come eagerly attracted by the chance to take clothing and cattle still rare in their northern homelands."[63] Velázquez knew that local raiders took livestock because they ate beef and rode horses, but he asked why they raided for cloth when they continued to live and fight naked. They sent it north, in trade or as tribute, building alliances with people who lived beyond contact with Europeans and the silver economy. Those northern links kept war alive, drawing in unseen people, sometimes as raiders, often as traders. The challenge could only escalate, unless it was solved.

Velázquez then turned to the war and how to end it. Most Chichimecas had first greeted Spaniards in peace, especially if they brought gifts of food and clothing. Then hunters and gatherers developed a taste for beef and a desire for cloth to trade, while Spanish slaving turned skirmishes into a war that fed on itself. Men fought to capture women: "one of the greatest motives driving these barbarians to hate us and make war" was "seeing their women and children despoiled." Seeking vengeance and replacements, "they take to the roads to inflict what damage and death they can, and because they face a shortage of women, they reserve for themselves the native and mulatto women they find in the crews of the cart caravans they rob."[64] The conflict became self-sustaining as raids reached south to Acámbaro, even Xilotepec. Chichimecas took twenty thousand cattle and an equal number of horses every year. They were adept fighting on horseback, shooting arrows with skill and beginning to master firearms. Velázquez feared that they would be joined by runaway Africans, already skilled horsemen; then the threat would be uncontainable. Meanwhile people far to the north were discovering European cloth and livestock. They would find ways to obtain them, provoking further raiding unless conflict gave way to settlement and trade.[65]

In a third chapter Velázquez offered a plan for peace. The king must support a policy of settlement including Chichimecas, Spaniards, and Mesoamericans. Slaving had to stop, ending the cycle of raiding and retribution. Then Chichimecas dependent on cloth and livestock had to be supplied with clothing and food while they learned to plant and make cloth. Velázquez knew of Chichimeca men who farmed and women who wove; he expected most to adapt slowly, as they were accustomed to lives without such regular work. Still, if depredations ended and lands, tools, and instruction were provided, they would adapt.[66]

The priest added an incentive. The settlement of surviving Chichimecas would open vast spaces for grazing and settlement by Spaniards and Mesoamericans. Spaniards should be married men granted land; they must not raid indigenous communities. Still, Velázquez recognized that conflict would persist at the northern frontier. Thus Spaniards must settle, cultivate, keep livestock, and remain armed to defend the frontier. And they should be joined by "friendly indios" who would settle in communities, cultivate, and live an example of Christian ways. The frontier would be pacified by settlement that left everyone dependent on cultivation and grazing, living in monogamous patriarchal families.[67]

In a last chapter Velázquez promised great benefits. Legitimacy came first: "God would see his evangelical promise kept." With peace the priest saw a land "abundant in mines and rich ores." The result: "in a few years there will rise in this region a new kingdom that will not be accounted as small or poor among the great and rich domains of Europe because, as we have shown, the land is temperate, rich in mines, fertile, healthy and with room for everything." He foresaw "growing gains for the royal treasury . . . increases in the royal fifths, and revenues from sales of mercury and of *negros* from Cape Verde."[68] In all this he would be proven right—including in foreseeing a growing trade in African slaves. The sale of Spanish goods would also grow, "because there will be more silver." Atlantic commerce would soar, "because silver by its nature flows and connects the entire world; with silver in abundance everyone is freed and finds gain. Once the land here is open and secure . . . settlement will expand so much that fleets coming from Europe will bring many more ships laden with goods, rapidly raising royal revenues. This conquest will draw northward uncounted carts loaded with cloth, and they will return full of silver."[69] All that also proved true, though after a few decades most cloth came from northwest Europe. Spanish North America stimulated European production and global capitalism. Spanish kings got their revenues; for a long time that proved enough.

Did Velázquez's vision and program influence changing policies? He worried that his first report, shipped on the fleet in 1582, did not arrive, so he sent a copy in 1583. It did reach the Council of the Indies; who read it is not known. The priest at San Miguel understood the promise of silver and the cost of Chichimeca wars; much that he proposed became policy. His projections also proved true: with pacification in the 1590s, silver boomed and commercial settlement drove northward, filling royal coffers, stimulating world trade and European production. Velázquez was a good historian, a competent (but not sympathetic) anthropologist, and a clear predictor of Spanish North America's future.

Querétaro during Chichimeca Wars: One Report, Two Visions

Otomí Querétaro proved essential to fighting Chichimecas and supplying the silver economy. Francisco Ramos de Córdoba's *Relación Geográfica* (1582) offers a detailed view of Querétaro in wartime. Felipe II called for reports from across the empire. His councilors asked a series of questions about indigenous history and the conquest, local society, production, and religion. Ramos de Córdoba traveled from Xilotepec to Querétaro to take up the task in a two-month stay. His report opens with sharply negative images shaped by deep Spanish prejudices, perhaps hardened by Xilotepec's resentment of Querétaro's independence and prosperity. Later sections portray a much admired Otomí Querétaro.[70]

Ramos began with basics: a district magistrate represented the regime at Querétaro, reporting to the viceroy in Mexico City. Indigenous republics ruled local affairs at Querétaro and San Juan de Río to the southeast. Querétaro paid tributes to Xilotepec's encomendero, but recognized no dependence on native lords there. Franciscans of the Michoacán Province led religious life. In a population mostly Otomí, "There are among them some of the Mexica nation, though few; they have been converted into Otomí and speak their language; all have become one." The rugged Sierra Gorda, just northeast, remained home to unconquered Chichimecas. Ramos reported fifty Spanish households, most at Querétaro, a few at San Juan del Río. They struggled to keep grazing estates in the face of Chichimeca attacks.[71]

Ramos told the origins of Querétaro with Connín (don Fernando de Tapia) the hero.[72] Writing during wars in which don Fernando and his son don Diego de Tapia led Otomí troops against Chichimecas and channeled Otomí production to sustain mining, Tapia eminence was truth. Ramos then lamented "the many deaths of Spaniards as well as *indios, negros,* and other sorts of people, along with clergy of the Order of San Francisco that the barbarians have inflicted." Chichimeca assaults stymied settlement as "many have lost properties and goods, and vacated their lands in fear of patent danger."[73] Chichimecas killed Spanish, Otomí, and African men. When Chichimecas captured women, "they took them alive, . . . as they have a shortage." Ramos compared Chichimeca fighters, mounted and mobile, to hardened veterans of Spain's Italian wars.[74]

His first description of the Otomí was bleak: "all are of low intelligence . . . they know no honor . . . they are curious of nothing . . . they are filthy in their clothing and eating, of vile and cowardly ways. They are very barbaric and slow to understanding the good customs they are taught." They lie and steal, even from priests. Then he clarified: "They are great thieves, though they take little from each other; they destroy Spaniards by taking horses and mares, sheep and cows, because they love to eat and meat is their favorite food, and among meats they most like beef."[75] Even while joining Spaniards against Chichimecas, the Otomí were barbarians, stealing Spanish livestock. Ramos struggled with Otomí work habits: "At work they are lazy, though in comparison with the other nations of this land they are energetic workers. . . . They are most dedicated to work in the fields. . . . They prefer to live in distant and forested places where no one can see them, mostly to avoid labor. . . . They value wages little." They often work and leave without waiting to be paid.[76] Querétaro's Otomí worked hard in their own affairs, resisted labor for Spaniards, and in 1582 saw little gain in wages.

Ramos drew a scathing portrait of Otomí culture. "They are hugely superstitious." They believe in "powerful witches" and other "ridiculous things."[77] "Neither fathers and sons nor husbands and wives respect each other."[78] "In lust they are very hot, women and men, and women give themselves too easily. They are especially fond of *negros* and mulattoes, and others like them, and when one of these asks for their body you know they will answer yes; they refuse Spaniards as if they were enemies."[79] Amid prejudice Ramos offered revelation. The Otomí were not properly patriarchal; they clung to native rites and rituals; they were open in sexual relations. He resented Otomí women's openness to men of African ancestry, while they refused Spaniards. The resentment was surely sexual, and more. Most African men came to the Bajío as slaves; sex with Otomí women produced free children.

Ramos concluded his early narrative with this: "Their vices . . . are rooted in becoming drunk every day, especially on festival days. The more important the leader the greater the drinking. Women are more temperate."[80] Again, revelation lurks in prejudice. The Otomí drank too much: primarily men, and notably lords on days of religious devotion. To Ramos and most Spaniards this was debauchery. Among Otomí and other natives, alcohol (or peyote) led to states closer to the divine—states appropriate to men, and especially to men who ruled. There was patriarchy among the Otomí, a patriarchy alien to Ramos.

Then Ramos's tone changed. It was time to note the good customs of the Otomí.[81] On old religious practices, "they worshipped the stone gods of the Mexica," yet local Otomí rites ruled: "They had a god of water and good rains . . . made of sticks and dressed in rich cloths; they offered it everything they harvested and made."[82] People looked to divine powers to sustain life. An Ancient Father and an Ancient Mother, both represented by figures of stick, richly dressed, ruled reproduction.[83] "They honored greatly a stone idol in the figure of a man they called Eday, which is to say lord of the winds; they believed he had created the entire universe."[84] Powers shaping the universe, ruling reproduction, and enabling production defined Otomí religion. A great annual festival tied worship to everyday life: "They had a great festival held in time to celebrate their harvests, called Tascameme . . . which means festival of the white bread (*pan blanco*), a very ancient celebration and one of great solemnity. Then, everyone offered the Ancient Mother shares of the fruits of their harvests."[85] The Mother of reproduction was honored for her role in production. The same festival readied men for martial roles: "On every feast day and at the festival of Tascameme . . . the governor required all men . . . to train in the use of weapons."[86]

In times of crisis the Otomí turned to powers ruling production and reproduction. "Where bad weather threatened, everyone climbed the hills and made offerings to their gods." Penance meant bloodletting "in separate houses only for men; and while they did penance, their wives let blood at home."[87] Ramos ended his description of religion by distancing the Otomí from the Mexica's sacrifical practices: "The people of the Otomí nation did not sacrifice to anyone, except when they went to war under Mexica flags."[88]

In Ramos's new vision the Querétaro Otomí had become good Christians: "They are so attached to our religion that they take great care to participate every Sunday and feast day; . . . they travel two or three leagues to hear mass. . . . At Easter they attend to confesion with great diligence and become upset if anything, even a just cause, blocks access to absolution or communion." If they fail to attain standards set by the clergy, it is not for lack of effort or desire. Nor do they fail to support the church: "They have built a great number of sumptuous churches and provided them with many rich ornaments. They support the clergy, especially the Franciscans, . . . giving them everything needed for life with great energy and love."[89]

Ramos added that the Otomí had built a community of productivity beyond any in New Spain, equal to the best in Spain: "At Querétaro . . . the natives have built a canal to irrigate their huertas, and to power a mill that belongs to the community. Most of the water benefits the natives by irrigating chiles and the other crops that sustain them."[90] Otomí farmers grew maize, "their wheat," frijoles "like chickpeas," and chiles, "their pepper." They got salt from Michoacán. "In everything else they have what they need in abundance, even planting the cotton that clothes them."[91] The Querétaro Otomí also adopted European goods. Surrounded by Spanish livestock, they learned to eat meat: "they have a great taste for beef and eat it daily, having money to buy it." "Chickens from Castile" were everywhere, with six thousand consumed yearly in Querétaro.[92] The Franciscans were intermediaries in dietary and economic exchange. They kept a large huerta raising European fruits and vegetables. "They supply everyone." Meanwhile the Tapias founded a hospital to care for the Otomí in time of disease, endowed it with nine thousand sheep, and charged the Franciscans to oversee the flock and minister to the ill.[93] Otomí huertas raised native staples and avocados, along with Old World grapes, figs, pomegranates, peaches, lemons, limes, oranges, apples, and pears. They sold fruit in Mexico City. Europeans admired the herb—natehee in Otomí, tlatlacistli in Nahuatl, famed for healing wounds—a key resource in time of war.[94]

Ramos closed with a vision of earthly paradise: "Querétaro is one of the most beautiful, sumptuous, and luxuriant towns in all New Spain; there is such great abundance of fruits of Castile, I doubt any place in Spain produces more." He praised "the great quantity of grapes of the kind grown around Seville." The Otomí enjoyed a hybrid paradise of cultivation and commerce: "When the fruits are harvested, the town becomes an earthly paradise, . . . The natives take profit and are rich, because Spanish and *indio* merchants come from Mexico City and many other places to buy grapes, and they pay good prices."[95]

Ramos's report first detailed a vision of Querétaro's Otomí as barbaric, filthy, idolatrous, and lazy. His revised vision portrayed their religious practices as understandable, their reception of Christianity as positive, their response to European crops as creative, their economy as strong. In the early 1580s Querétaro's Otomí were productive, self-sufficient, commercially engaged, and essential to fighting Chichimecas and sustaining the silver economy. Otomí power and production shaped Spanish North America at Querétaro.

Postwar Settlements: Mines, Missions, and Commercial Development

Querétaro emerged from war ready to profit from the silver boom that held strong into the seventeenth century. Production at Zacatecas peaked in the 1570s, stayed solid through the 1590s, and then soared to new heights from 1615 to 1635.[96] Supplemented by Guanajuato from the 1550s and San Luis Potosí in the 1590s, Zacatecas led a globalizing economy that stimulated regional markets. Irrigated fields raised maize and wheat, fruits and vegetables at Querétaro and across the basin stretching west. By 1635, at the peak of the silver boom, over 60 percent of the grain consumed at Zacatecas was wheat, and over

80 percent of that came from the Bajío.[97] While Zacatecas silver drove trade, Querétaro became a pivot of cultivation, cloth making, commerce, transportation. Together they forged the complex, multicultural, deeply commercial society of Spanish North America.

Key developments at the end of the Chichimeca wars shaped Querétaro's primacy in the Bajío. Mining proved limited at nearby Guanajuato. As conflicts waned, a report in 1593 called its mines "collapsed." Many workers had left for more promising digs at San Luis Potosí. A survey in 1597 reported 652 adult men at Guanajuato: 29 Spaniards, 42 African slaves, and 415 indigenous workers. The prosperous mines at Zacatecas had 34 Spaniards, 130 slaves, and 1,014 native laborers.[98] After the war the stimulus of silver came from the north, promoting cultivation, crafts, and trade in the Bajío. Querétaro consolidated as the commercial pivot of Spanish North America. While much of the capital that financed mining at Zacatecas and trade at Querétaro came from Mexico City, commerce, cloth making, and cultivation at Querétaro were in the hands of local people—Otomí, Spanish, and others.[99]

Meanwhile, just northeast of Querétaro the rugged uplands and canyons of the Sierra Gorda remained a refuge for indigenous peoples living free of colonial rule. The Chichimeca wars did not end with a Spanish-Otomí victory. There was no conquest, no moment when the regime and its allies ruled and rebel fighters acquiesced in subordination. The war ended with a stalemate and a new negotiation of power and everyday life. Spaniards and Otomí lords expected Chichimecas to live like most Otomí, subordinate cultivators in a colonial order. After decades of war the silver economy and Otomí Querétaro flourished. Chichimeca numbers had plummeted: men fell in war; women and children taken captive lived in Hispanic society. Most of all, smallpox and other diseases killed indigenous peoples drawn into contact with Atlantic newcomers. By the 1590s the independent peoples fused in Spanish and Mesoamerican minds as Chichimecas were few and dependent on grain, cloth, and livestock. And they knew that the world of Spanish power and silver production would not recede before their resistance.

Some began to try mission life. In 1583 Franciscans set a convent at San Pedro Tolimán, east of Querétaro, at the southern edge of the Sierra Gorda. They offered a way to settled lives for Pames and Jonaces exhausted by decades of war.[100] The Jesuits, a new order committed to proselytizing in expanding Spanish and Portuguese empires, came late to New Spain. While conflict raged they preached nomadically across the Bajío and at Zacatecas. When they could, they took up the challenge of settling and incorporating Chichimecas in the new world of Spanish North America. In 1590 the Jesuit don Gonzalo de Tapia—

a name laden with meaning locally—worked at San Luis de la Paz, a place founded in the 1550s to defend the route to Zacatecas. The goal, a Jesuit chronicler said, was "to win the *indios* and give them a social life, . . . unite them in groups, . . . teach them how reasonable it was to plant crops, provide for sustenance," and "build homes around the church." Chichimecas must become sedentary Christian cultivators.[101]

The regime would pay; missions cost less than war. To support Tapia an expedition came north in 1594 from the Jesuit base at Tepozotlán near Mexico City. It included Otomí from near Tepozotlán, granted lands and tribute exemptions to settle among the Chichimecas, Pames, Otomí, Tarascans, and Nahuas already at San Luis de la Paz. At first the Jesuits worked among thirty Chichimeca families; a year later they reported ninety baptisms and the marriage of nearly seventy couples. Chichimeca youths went to school. The community built a mission compound including a church, convent, workshops, and residences.[102] It seemed a promising start.

With the mission offering a settled peace, Spaniards claimed lands around San Luis de la Paz, built grazing estates, and staffed them with African slaves, free mulattoes, and migrant Mesoamericans. Mining carried on at nearby Pozos and Xichú and flourished just north at San Luis Potosí. Mission settlement brought commercial life to the northeast margin of the Bajío. San Luis de la Paz became a base for long contacts with the independent people who retreated into the Sierra Gorda at the end of the war. Some came down from the mountains, in the Jesuits' view seeking Christianity, joining in the annual Easter Passion, reenacting the sacrifice that defined sacramental Catholicism. At the gathering in 1613 nine hundred indigenous Christians confessed and six hundred took communion. How many were transplanted Mesoamericans, settled Chichimecas, or people from the Sierra is unknown.[103]

The mission aimed to settle mobile and independent people in communities, teach them to cultivate, and convert them to Christianity. They would live in patriarchal couples sanctioned by marriage, produce to sustain themselves, and labor for the community and at nearby estates. A chronicler emphasized that the goal was to end "the abusive drink and armed disputes among them," and to promote "the pleasure of labor in community works and for their own welfare, for monetary gain, and in their own fields."[104]

The alternative was retreat into the Sierra. For the uncounted numbers who chose independence, the mission at San Luis de la Paz, the Franciscan outpost at Xichú de los Indios (near mines of the same name), and the Agustinian and Franciscan missions that later developed on the southern flanks of the Sierra from Cadereita to Jalpán, Tolimán, and beyond became sites of interaction. People of the Sierra engaged the Hispanic, commercial, Christian world, adapted what they wanted when they wanted and stayed independent. Through the seventeenth century the people of the Sierra visited missions, sometimes for months or years. They came seeking Christianity, often accepting baptism while learning to cultivate and acquiring tools and craft skills. Missionaries wrote of great success. Yet sooner or later most who came returned to the Sierra. Frustrated clergy then lamented perverse influences. A pattern emerged: in time of drought and scarcity, or when wars among natives led some to seek security, indigenous families and even whole communities went to the missions. They sought food, tools, livestock, and sanctuary; they tried the knowledge offered by Christianity. But when drought passed or enemies receded they returned to the Sierra—taking with them the European ways and Christian practices they found most useful.[105]

The Sierra Gorda became an enclave of of indigenous independence, linked to but not ruled by colonial society. The missions mediated an enduring relationship—a failure if the goal was native subordination; a success if the need was to contain independent people and allow commercial development in the Bajío. The outcome set a new frontier. San Luis de la Paz and other missions on the edge of the Sierra separated and integrated the commercial Bajío and independent natives in the uplands just northeast. Farther north the early 1600s saw the foundation of missions at Valle del Maíz and Rioverde in eastern San Luis Potosí, separating mines and developing estates from still-independent natives in the Sierras and coastal lowlands.[106] A similar frontier of conflict and contact developed after the Chichimeca wars in the rugged uplands north and northwest of Guadalajara, south and southwest of Zacatecas. There the presidio and Tlaxcalan settlement of Colotlán became a point of containment and contact with still-independent people in the Sierra de Nayarit.[107] With mountain refuges of native independence contained to the east and west, with the coastal lowlands beyond left aside, the highland plateaus from the Bajío north were open to Mesoamerican and Spanish settlement and commercial development.

Around 1600, with mining limited at Guanajuato and the Sierra Gorda set as a refuge for those who could not abide subordination, Querétaro flourished as a center of production and trade and the Otomí faced difficulties and opportunities.[108] In 1590 the native republic began to rebuild crumbling Casas Reales, the seat of local government.[109] Don Diego de Tapia, the founder's son, remained the pivot of local power. Like his father a proud Christian and ally of the Franciscans, he had fought Chichimecas in the name of the Spanish crown. He raised wheat, horses, cattle, and sheep. He dressed as a Spanish

Franciscan church and convent, Querétaro, sixteenth to eighteenth centuries.

gentleman; he was the richest and most powerful man in the eastern Bajío. All the while he was an Otomí lord, recognized as a cacique by the Spanish regime, repeatedly elected governor of the República de Indios—the only council at Querétaro as the seventeenth century began.

Don Luis de Velasco the Younger (like his father four decades earlier) feared Tapia power. In 1591 he ousted Tapia as governor of the Querétaro republic; he accused don Diego of taking excess tribute and using community property for personal gain. Removal would "avoid factionalism, drunkenness, concubinage, and other public sins that offend God Our Lord."[110] Don Diego de Tapia, like his father, was accused of taking too much from Otomí Querétaro and allowing customs contrary to Christianity. He was too powerful, both exploiting and protecting the Otomí community.

Tapia was not the only prosperous and powerful Otomí. He allied in marriage and entrepreneurship with the Martín clan and others who honored God and the friars, sat as judges and councilmen of the indigenous republic, developed irrigated wheat lands and grazing estates, and profited in the commercial economy. Seven Martín men appeared in work contracts between 1589 and 1609. Don Estéban Martín proclaimed himself an *indio principal*, noble and fluent in Spanish. Three others were *vecinos*, citizens, including Diego Martín, who operated grazing estates. Antón Martín gained thirteen hundred pesos for five years' service managing don Diego de Tapia's estates. Francisco Martín, a mestizo, labored.[111]

While a few Otomí ruled and prospered, the majority cultivated and labored in the commercial economy. The system of dams and canals so admired by Ramos in 1582 stretched along the river from La Cañada in the east through Querétaro to Apaseo in the west and remained the foundation of Otomí life. Irrigated huertas fed families and supplied growing markets. Exotic trees lined those rich urban gardens, yielding fruits of European origins, while native maize, frijoles, chiles, and cotton flourished within. Huertas were an Atlantic amalgam, raising American and European crops to sustain Otomí families, the city they founded, and the mining economy that linked them to the world. Others sought opportunity in the countryside. Before the war migrant Otomí had settled the Amascala plain to the east; during the wars most took refuge in Querétaro. In 1591 don Diego de Tapia lamented that new migrants were resettling the fertile plain without order; he proposed to charter a town to organize their arrival.[112]

Spaniards also came to Querétaro in new numbers, seeking profit and preeminence. Access to favor in Mexico City brought grants of cropland and grazing sites. Many aimed to trade in the economy that linked the Bajío and the silver mines to the world. An explosion of sheepgrazing brought another way of gain; as flocks around Querétaro approached a million head, entrepreneurs built *obrajes*, large workshops making woolen cloth.[113] By diverse means a Spanish elite settled in. Denied local rule by Querétaro's status as a República de Indios, they focused on commercial cultivation and grazing, cloth making, trade, and transportation. To prosper they had to work with don Diego de Tapia.

In March 1591 Tapia and don Estéban Martín, then governor, led a delegation to the court of Duarte de Tóvar, lieutenant to Querétaro's district magistrate. The Otomí republic offered to donate to don Pedro de Quesada more than a caballería (forty hectares) of land with water rights along the road to Celaya, as thanks for "many and good works worthy of great reward." The most powerful Otomí lord and landlord at Querétaro led the republic in asking Tóvar, a Spanish merchant-magistrate, to approve a gift of irrigated lands to Quesada, the Spaniard who received Querétaro's encomienda tributes. Tóvar approved the gift, which was confirmed by Viceroy Velasco in 1596.[114] In 1595 Tapia, again governor, appeared before Tóvar, still the magistrate's lieutenant, to state that the community grist mill long leased to Bartolomé Martín was in disrepair. Tapia sought and Tóvar approved a new lease; bidding drove the annual rent from 210 pesos to 550 pesos and delivered the mill to Juan Rodríguez Galán, Spaniard and textile entrepreneur.[115] The Otomí republic gained income, the mill was repaired, and passed from Otomí to Spanish hands.

Similar leases became commonplace, allowing Tapia and the republic to promote and profit from the commercial economy while helping Spanish entrepreneurs get into business. Early in 1598 the community *meson*, a way station for merchants and muleteers heading north, was leased to Nicolás Martín, a prosperous Otomí. Months later the slaughterhouse went to a Spaniard, Martín de Ugarte, in a contract that obliged the community to provide workers to whom Ugarte would pay one to two reales daily.[116] In June the republic owed the treasury for tributes not paid by men who had died or left. The solution: sell a caballería of land with water rights to don Diego de Tapia for three hundred pesos.[117] The treasury (and encomendero Quesada) got paid, the community found debt relief, and Tapia added to his lands. The next month Duarte de Tóvar appeared as administrator of the community hospital, an institution founded and endowed with land and herds by the Tapias. He leased its flock of over eleven thousand sheep to a Spaniard, Pedro Hernández Gato, for ninety-one pesos per thousand head—one thousand pesos yearly.[118] The deals continued. In 1605 don Diego de Tapia, again governor, led the Otomí in donating a town lot to Tóvar as thanks for twelve years as hospital administrator. Three years later Tapia and the republic sold a similar lot to Diego de Villapadierna for 124 pesos.[119] Land and economic opportunity flowed from Otomí to Spaniards. Ties to Tapia brought donations as thanks for "service"; others paid cash to gain lands and opportunities.

The integration of community resources and Spanish entrepreneurship extended to crop production. In October 1598 the Otomí republic (without Tapia) formed a company with Francisco Hernández to cultivate community lands west of town. He would complete needed repairs and plant wheat, maize, chile, and other crops. The community promised eight *gañanes* (resident workers), a *boyero* to care for oxen, "and all the *indios* and other people needed to work the farm . . . paying them as *indios* would pay *gañanes* and other *indios* who worked for them, with Francisco Hernández paying them nothing." Hernández provided oxen, yokes, and plows; the community delivered irrigation water, in turns that it shared with don Diego de Tapia (again governor) and don Pedro de Quesada (still encomendero). Hernández (essentially an entrepreneurial sharecropper) gained a third of all harvests, the Otomí community two-thirds.[120]

The community lands west of Querétaro created income for the republic. In a time of sparse population and commercial expansion, the market economy took hold. Early in 1599 don Diego de Tapia led a delegation to court to swap a piece of community land with Quesada, the encomendero. The trade consolidated land and water rights for Quesada, the community, and Tapia, leaving all with contiguous irrigated holdings.[121] Tapia, Quesada, and Hernández (who managed the community lands) all gained; the Otomí republic would receive its share of the crops. The Otomí majority would labor.

An entrepreneurial elite emerged at Querétaro. The Otomí lord and governor, landlord, and entrepreneur don Diego de Tapia was the key player. He used Otomí rights to lordship, his office as governor of the republic, indigenous traditions of labor service, new ways of wage work, community lands, and private properties to promote his own power and profit in the emerging commercial economy. Don Pedro de Quesada used encomienda tribute rights (grounded in Mesoamerican traditions, then redirected to Spaniards by claims of conquest) to provide capital that would support land acquisition and agricultural entrepreneurship. Duarte de Tóvar combined office, trade, and management of the Otomí-Franciscan hospital to promote his interests. Profit backed by power was the goal of all; the Otomí Tapia and the Europeans Quesada and Tóvar were becoming capitalists. Yet their power had limits. Nowhere in the deals do we see the irrigated huertas that sustained the Otomí majority. Tapia knew the Otomí republic; he understood the need to protect the huertas and sustain the republic with income. As the seventeenth century began, don Diego de Tapia still ruled at Querétaro.

Through his brokerage a community of Spanish entrepreneurs flourished. The merchant, magistrate, and financier Duarte de Tóvar (surely Portuguese) managed the hospital that cared for the Otomí sick and poor. He represented the republic in a suit to guard its water rights. After 1600 he invested in land, becoming a leading sheep grazer as Querétaro became a center of cloth production. Two sons followed his lead. One, Luis de Tóvar, joined the miller and textile maker Juan Rodríguez Galán after 1600 in a company to import goods from Castile and China. Luis later used his earnings to buy land extending around Querétaro, near San Miguel, and north to Nuevo León. His brother, Capitán Antonio de Echaide, traded and served as district magistrate, first at San Miguel, then at Texcoco near Mexico City.[122]

Others took parallel paths. Pedro Carvallo (surely Carvalho, also Portuguese) began as an immigrant cashier for an established merchant; later he opened a store at Querétaro in company with Mexico City merchants, then sold it in 1602 to buy land and become a wheat grower and sheep grazer.[123] Gonzalo de Cárdenas came from Castile in the 1580s; he leased lands from the indigenous hospital to become a leading grazer—backed by Duarte de Tóvar.[124] After 1600 Cárdenas men took the lead in claiming lands and building grazing estates in eastern San Luis Potosí.[125] Don Pedro de Quesada used encomienda tributes first to finance commercial cultivation; then around 1600 he sold his lands near Querétaro to fund mining at Xichú, on the edge of the Sierra Gorda.[126] Hernando de Galván offers a final example. An immigrant from Galicia, he grazed sheep on leased lands in the 1590s. At his death in 1602 he owned vast grazing sites reaching north from San Miguel. His widow, Francisca de Espíndola, ruled family affairs into the 1620s. Her sons then took over; into the 1640s they partnered with Duarte de Tóvar's sons, all linked to officials and financiers in Mexico City.[127] A Spanish commercial community began to prosper in Otomí Querétaro.

A Protean Labor Market, 1590–1610:
Obligation, Ethnicity, and Patriarchy

After the Chichimeca wars the silver economy held strong for decades; opportunities proved plentiful for Otomí and Spanish entrepreneurs at Querétaro. The challenge was labor. Population was sparse in the wake of wars and epidemics. The Otomí majority worked irrigated huertas, protected by the Otomí republic; few aimed to labor for others. In that context a labor market began at Querétaro. Along with the commercial work relations that developed simultaneously in mining and refining at Zacatecas,[128] Querétaro's labor market set a foundation of monetized labor that would persist to shape Spanish North America.

The formal, coercive institutions that organized labor to the south across Spanish Mesoamerica were tried in Querétaro and across the Bajío, but they generated little labor there. By the 1590s encomiendas were pensions, providing no claims to labor. The draft called the repartimiento aimed to send rotating gangs to mines, urban construction projects, and rural harvests, insisting that employers pay for the work. But drafts did not recruit workers sufficient for mining at Guanajuato. Querétaro proved especially resistant. Men like the Tapias preferred to employ (the viceroys Velasco would say exploit) local workers in their own enterprises; they had little incentive to organize work gangs for Spaniards.

Slavery did force Africans to Querétaro. Between 1590 and 1630 fifty-four enslaved men and thirty-one women were sold there. The average age of men was eighteen; their average value 356 pesos. Slave women were older, averaging twenty-one, and more valuable: their average price of 373 pesos reflected the value of potential children (by law also slaves).[129] Slaves were expensive workers. A healthy young adult cost the equivalent of ten years' wages, and the slave still had to be fed and clothed if the owner was to keep the investment and gain the work that cost so much. Yet across the Bajío from Querétaro to Guanajuato slaves proved hard to keep during and after Chichimeca wars. The eighty-five sales over four decades suggest that fewer than a hundred African slaves labored at any time at Querétaro near the beginning of the seventeenth century, a small part of the working population.

In that context most work had to be negotiated and paid. Querétaro courts wrote nearly 300 labor contracts between 1588 and 1609, most after 1598. They reveal over 150 employers, over 300 workers, and over 400 labor relationships (many contracts recorded shifts from one employer to another). The contracts document a protean labor market with a few large employers and many more with one or two workers. Most employers were European, but some were Otomí and others free mulattoes. Most workers were Mesoamerican, but Chichimecas, Africans, and Europeans also labored.[130]

For too long scholars and others have looked at work relations in terms of two dichotomies: coerced and free, unpaid and paid, with slaves defining one pole as coerced and unpaid, wage workers the opposite pole as free and paid. Historical labor relations have been more complex, with incentives lurking amid coercion, pressures shaping freedom, and remuneration ranging from dismal to ample.[131] The early labor market at Querétaro reveals a world of complex negotiations, where choices and pressures mingled and remunerations mixed cash and goods, often paid in advance—all commercially driven.

The contracts reveal a dominant way of work: an employer advanced cash or goods, often cloth or livestock, to a worker who promised to work at a set salary for the time needed to repay the advance. While working, the employee also received food and sometimes housing.[132] Employers and workers often negotiated advances informally. If the worker failed to provide the work or aimed to change employers, then employer and worker went to court to set a contract. Sometimes it was a judicial mandate to complete service. Often it recorded a new employer's agreement to pay an old debt and take on the worker for a new term—until old and new advances were paid in work. In cases of extreme recalcitrance, of workers taking advances and working minimally, an offender might be jailed and sentenced to labor in shackles in one of Querétaro's two large obrajes. Coercion was not the essence of the system, nor the experience of most workers; it was the judicially mandated result for a few who took advances, refused to work, and flouted contract obligations.

These relations created obligated labor, neither coerced nor free in any simple way. Advance payment revealed (and valued) workers' advantage in a commercial economy desperate for labor. Contractual enforcement—imprisonment in extreme cases—showed that employers had leverage in courts committed to the commercial economy. Obligated labor had roots in Mesoamerica and Europe. Under the Mexica regime that ruled most Otomí before 1520, many labored to meet obligations. People facing drought and dearth took food from lords, creating obligations to serve. Debts from failed trade also led to obligation and work; so did criminal convictions. Obligated labor for a lifetime or less, personal dependence that was not heritable, was common in Mesoamerica.[133]

Obligated labor also built on European precedents. Many sailors who worked the merchant vessels and warships that linked Spain and New Spain gained salaries in advance, contracting to serve for food and a bunk while crossing the Atlantic. For many advance payment was a way to get to Veracruz or another American port, there to escape obligations and seek opportunity in the interior—often in the Bajío or the mining regions north. Labor based on advanced payment, followed often by an evasion of work, was well known to men who arrived from Europe.[134] With Mesoamerican and European precedents, the labor market that was built on advanced payment and obligated service at Querétaro around 1600 was an Atlantic hybrid fashioned in a new silver-driven commercial economy.

Two contracts illustrate common elements of obligated labor. In 1605 Baltasar Hernández, a Mexica from Cuautitlán near Mexico City, speaking Spanish, appeared in the Querétaro district magistrate's court. Baltasar admitted receiving from Domingo de Chávez an advance of forty-six pesos "given in *reales* (coin) so that he would serve." But Baltasar worked only a few months. As a result "he was jailed for evasion of service." Now Juan Rodríguez Galán, the obraje operator, paid Chávez the remaining thirty-six pesos and advanced Baltasar six more for clothing, extending the obligation. Baltasar now contracted to work for three pesos monthly, plus food, and Rodríguez agreed not to fire him.[135]

In 1608 Juan Pérez, Otomí and born in Querétaro, contracted to serve Juan de Cuadros. Earlier, Cuadros "had given him many pesos in gold in advance of his service." But Juan "fled" and Cuadros brought him to court with records documenting seventy pesos in advances. Briefly jailed, Juan signed to serve Cuadros for four pesos monthly, plus food. The high salary discounted the obligation; the brief jailing told Juan the obligation was serious. The contract ended stating that if he fled again, Juan would pay the cost of capture and face a longer obligation in confinement.[136] Obligated labor was paid in advance, hard to enforce, and subject to judicial sanction. It ruled while labor scarcity favored workers, commercial opportunity drove economic expansion, and judicial power backed employers' efforts. It was unequal, exploitative, in extreme cases coerced, and continually negotiated.

Landed, commercial, mining, and textile entrepreneurs—many mixing roles—were leading employers, engaging three-quarters of all workers at Querétaro.[137] Merchants had limited labor needs. Estate operators and mining entrepreneurs contracted laborers whom they employed outside of town. Cultivators found workers for nearby wheat farms; grazers took on herdsmen for distant sites. Mine operators recruited labor for digs as near as Escanela, as distant as Xichú and San Luis Potosí. For agricultural and mining entrepreneurs the workers contracted at Querétaro were part of larger groups. In contrast, the cloth makers operating local obrajes concentrated labor at Querétaro. They were the largest employers in town.

Querétaro was a base for muleteers and carters, also important employers. So were craftsmen in the Otomí town. Blacksmiths supported the transport sector and much else. Millers, bakers, butchers, even a pastry chef fed local residents. Shoemakers, tailors, and hat makers clothed them. A barber-surgeon offered cures. A master of writing served the commercial economy. All employed a worker or two around 1600. Regime officials, the indigenous republic, and the church employed a few more. Diverse employers, large and small, set the demand for workers that created a labor market.

Most employers claimed status as vecinos—Spanish citizens of Querétaro. Duarte de Tóvar, his sons, and their commercial allies contracted workers. So did don Diego de Tapia, Otomí lord, often governor of the Indigenous Republic, and landed entrepreneur. He recruited four workers plus a manager, and sold the debts of two others between 1596 and 1608.[138] He was not the only indigenous employer. There were many Martíns. In 1600 Juan Bautista Martín, alcalde of the Otomí republic, paid forty-two pesos to recruit Diego Equena.[139] In 1607 don Nicolás de San Luis, Governor of the Republic, received thirty-seven pesos to cover an advance to Cristobal Yuye—who went to work for Juan Garcia.[140] Not every Otomí employer was noble or an official: Mateo Juárez, a muleteer, advanced to José Exiní forty pesos in 1601;

Francisco Erini took payment to end Gabriel Equenguín's obligation in 1603; later Diego Hernández gained payments to allow Pablo Garcia and Pablo Martín to move on.[141]

Nor were Spaniards and Otomí the only employers. Juan Francisco, a mulatto, advanced thirty-three pesos to gain the labor of Diego Martín, an obligation he later sold to Diego de Santillano.[142] In 1606 Agustín Álvarez, a mulatto muleteer, advanced sixty-four pesos to Baltasar García—part in cash, part in honey that García would sell while traveling with Álvarez's commercial caravan.[143] Women also appeared as employers, though rarely. Ana María, a pastry maker, paid thirty-four pesos in 1606 to gain the service of Juan Francisco, covering old work obligations and a fine for stealing a horse and saddle. He was shackled, at least until a guarantor appeared.[144] María del Rincón, a vecina and presumably Spanish, contracted for the service of three indigenous workers in 1609, one from Mexico City and two described as minors, all paid less than the usual rate of three pesos monthly. None got advances, suggesting a poor employer and desperate dependents.[145] While Spanish entrepreneurs and Otomí lords ruled Queréretaro's early labor market, people of every sort joined in.

Employers struggled to attract workers and hold them. Over a third of all employers in the contracts had paid advances without written documentation.[146] When they failed to gain the promised labor they went to court for enforcement—or to document payment from a new employer ready to take on an obligation and a new promise of labor. Most contracts recorded prior obligations and unmet service; they threatened new debts and coercions if labor was not done. In a few cases, most in the obrajes, the court mandated shackles.

The obrajes played a pivotal role in Querétaro's labor market. They used wool from the vast herds of sheep grazing nearby to produce the coarse woolen cloth used to make sacks to transport nearly everything. They needed full-time workers to clean wool, spin it, and weave it into cloth. The merchant and miller Juan Rodríguez Galán operated an obraje that he sold to Antón de Arango in 1598. They disputed the deal, and Rodríguez owned the workshop again from 1603. The two joined in 62 contracts, advancing over 3,200 pesos to create obligations of nearly 1,200 months' labor—62 contracts to create the equivalent of ten years' work by ten workers, at a cost of 320 pesos each. Juan de Chavarría operated the other large obraje in town. He advanced 2,223 pesos in 56 contracts to gain obligations totaling 780 months' labor—equal to ten years' work by 6.5 workers at 342 pesos each.[147]

Advances to create labor obligations cost slightly less than buying an African slave, presuming that the slave would labor for ten years. Yet Querétaro's *obrajeros* had to contract with nearly 120 men, and a few women, to claim the equivalent of ten years of service by about 18 workers. Obraje workers were mobile; they came and went, making labor contracting a constant concern. Not surprisingly, salaries rose— holding near 2.5 pesos monthly in the late 1590s, approaching 3 pesos monthly by 1609. Advances also had to rise, or they created obligations promising less labor. When a new employer bought an old obligation, a higher salary meant that the worker owed less labor. The Querétaro labor market, like all labor markets, was a domain of inequality—but it was a domain of negotiated inequality.

An inspection in 1604 of the obraje recently reacquired by Rodríguez Galán shows that contracts involved only part of the workforce.[148] Among sixty-one workers, eighteen were subject to enclosure, twelve labored under contract, and twenty-five worked voluntarily. More is known about a group of thirty-two workers. Nineteen were voluntary laborers who gained advances and generally owed less than six months' labor at salaries averaging over three pesos monthly. Thirteen enclosed workers owed similar terms of work, at salaries averaging only 2.8 pesos. The obraje advanced more and paid higher wages to those free to come and go.

Many stayed. While most workers, voluntary and enclosed, owed less than six months' labor, in 1604 many in both groups had worked in obrajes for over five years. Those subject to enclosure averaged just over five years; voluntary workers were there on average nearly a year longer. Workers paid in advance and free to leave provided the steadiest service. In a complex, salaried, obligated, and negotiated labor market, advances to men and a few women were essential to gain workers. Those less diligent providing labor might see obligations set into contracts; the most recalcitrant, and a few convicted of crime, faced enclosure. Advances without contract or coercion proved the best route to long labor service.

In a labor market remuneration calculated in money defines relations between employers and workers. At Querétaro the salaries paid in addition to food rations were key indicators of work negotiations. The contracts record nearly three hundred salaries, most between 1598 and 1609.[149] In 1598 the dominant salary was two pesos a month. A year later those gaining three pesos exceeded those earning only two pesos, and by 1600 three pesos monthly was the dominant salary. During later years growing numbers earned four, five, and more pesos monthly. Salaries rose, increasing remuneration and decreasing the work owed for advances. Querétaro developed a labor market in which workers claimed real gains.

A growing minority earned eight or more pesos monthly. They were managers, foremen, overseers of transport caravans, and skilled craftsmen. Often but not always Hispanic, they worked for advances in the same way as the indigenous majority. In 1601 Juan de la Serna contracted to work for a hundred pesos yearly, over eight pesos monthly, as a blacksmith in Francisco Hernández's shop. Juan called himself a mestizo, criollo de la Habana—of mixed ancestry, born in Cuba. He may have been of indigenous and Spanish ancestry. Or perhaps the label mestizo, criollo de la Habana was an evasion of African ancestry in a new town. Juan took a twelve-peso advance, and Hernández agreed not to fire him without cause, or he would owe the dismissed worker all hundred pesos. To employ a skilled worker, obligation struck employer and worker alike.

Workers at Querétaro were very diverse, a situation masked by the label *indio*. Around 1600 indio was not an ethnic identity; it was a regime category marking as conquered and subject to tribute all natives of the Americas. Among 310 identifiable workers at Querétaro, over 80 percent were indios; the rest were divided among mulattoes, mestizos, and vecinos, plus three *indios chinos* (Asians).[150] Looking within and beyond the category of indio, the regional, ethnic, and linguistic origins of Querétaro's workers were notably varied and changing. About 60 percent were Otomí, yet only 43 percent of the Otomí were from Querétaro. Most native workers were Mesoamerican migrants drawn north to a new commercial world.[151]

The mix of Querétaro natives and indigenous immigrants changed over the years. From 1598 to 1600 locals predominated, joined by a few Chichimecas. A large minority of migrants mixed about even numbers from Otomí zones just south, Tarascan communities to the southwest, and Mexica regions farther south and east. By 1606 migrants outnumbered locals in Querétaro's labor market. Those from distant Otomí communities and Mexicas from around Mexico City and Puebla came in steady numbers; Tarascans became less common. The result was an Otomí-Mexica community of workers, a process noted in Ramos's report of 1582. Querétaro's separation from Michoacán and its links to the Mexica world around the colonial capital shaped indigenous migration. Otomí language and identity held strong into the seventeenth century, reinforced by Tapia power, the indigenous republic, Otomí families cultivating huertas, and the primacy of Otomí men, local and immigrant, in the labor market.

Yet Otomí continuity came with changes. Names and Spanish-language skills suggest revealing adaptations.[152] Indigenous workers used three naming patterns: Christian names with native surnames, Christian names with Spanish surnames, and dual Christian saints' names. Indigenous surnames held strong from 1598 to 1600, then diminished. It appears that indigenous naming persisted through the

Chichimeca wars. Conflict consolidated Tapia power, Otomí huertas, and traditional naming—all linked to the broader cultural persistence lamented in Ramos's *Relación*.

Still, the largest group of indios in the labor contracts, ninety people of diverse ethnic and linguistic origins, displayed Hispanic surnames—García, Hernández, etc. They were a growing presence from 1598 to 1609. Some may have been the offspring of Spanish fathers, raised by indigenous mothers while keeping Spanish patronyms, speaking indigenous languages, and classed as indios by Querétaro judges. Diego García contracted to work, with rights to come and go, in Juan de Chavarría's obraje in 1603. García was indigenous, born in Mexico City of Nahua ancestry and able to speak Spanish. He stated that he had been born in the house of Francisco García Barzallo, whose patronym he shared.[153] Could a Spaniard's son be indio as the seventeenth century began? Apparently. Was young Diego García becoming mestizo? Probably. He emphasized his surname, his birth in a Spaniard's household, and his Spanish-language skills. Still, the contract labeled him indio.

Others used the dual saints' names that the clergy promoted to mark indios. Of diverse regional, ethnic, and linguistic ancestry, perhaps they were the beginning of generations that would adapt—at least in naming—to the norms of the Church. But when Marcos Antonio, born at Puebla (a Spanish city in a Nahua region), contracted in 1606 he offered that he was "indio mestizado ladino en castellano"—indigenous yet mixed and fluent in Spanish. He recorded that he was son of Diego Carrillo, a mestizo, vecino of Puebla.[154] Bearing the dual saints' names that would become a mark of the colonial indigenous majority, Marcos Antonio emphasized that he was a mestizo's son. Could a mestizo become an indio?

When language skills—the persistence of indigenous tongues or the use of Spanish—are seen in the light of naming practices, new distinctions and questions emerge. Almost none with native surnames spoke Spanish. They remained rooted in indigenous cultures even as they joined the labor market. In contrast, many people with Hispanic surnames and dual saints' names spoke Spanish. Over a quarter of indios with Spanish surnames spoke Spanish; a third of those using dual saints' names contracted in Spanish. Important numbers were adapting to the colonial order. Yet we are left with questions. Were men with Hispanic surnames and speaking Spanish becoming mestizos? Were people of Otomí, Mexica, or Tarascan origin who displayed dual saints' names, spoke Spanish, and worked in the new commercial world becoming indios—adapting an identity of colonial dependence?

While salaries rose and ethnic complexities proliferated, patriarchy was embedded in labor relations at Querétaro. Patriarchy had a long history in Europe and Mesoamerica. The reports in 1582 by the priest Velázquez at San Miguel and the notary Ramos at Querétaro noted key similarities and differences. Velázquez admired Chichimeca fathers' attempts to control their daughters; the martial roles of men in Otomí society seemed appropriate to Ramos. But the Otomí failure to restrict sexual relations to monogamous unions sanctioned by marriage was unacceptable, as was Otomí women's sexual independence. With Chichimeca wars over, the regime aimed to end native men's martial roles. Patriarchy would be limited to rule within producing households. Otomí men would labor for advances, salaries, rations, and precedence in families sanctioned by marriage.

The district magistrate's court at Querétaro promoted patriarchy as it regulated labor relations. Only 15 percent of the contracts included sentences for criminal offenses, totaling about 10 percent of work relations.[155] Criminal sentences were marginal sources of labor, more important in the 1590s, fading toward 1610. Most often violent crime led to forced labor. Yet crimes against patriarchy were a close second, with theft and other property crimes far behind. Most crimes against patriarchy were convictions for living *amancebado*—outside church-sanctioned marriage. One man had "stolen" a woman and was living out of wedlock. The "theft" could only have been against her father's patriarchal rights, for the woman had lived freely with her partner for years—until the court righted the situation by sentencing the unwed man to labor. In 1603 Inés Hernández, a Spanish-speaking india, was sentenced to labor for three pesos monthly. She owed nearly seventy pesos, forty-five advanced by a former employer, the rest "a fine imposed by the judge of the pueblo"—the indigenous court—"for repeated concubinage."[156] In 1582 Ramos's report lamented the Otomí failure to adopt proper patriarchy, and especially women's independence in choosing partners. Around 1600 the courts saw a solution in sentences to labor.

Labor and patriarchy also linked when husbands and wives contracted to work jointly. Paid labor was mostly men's work. Still, fifty-one women appeared in the contracts: six working alone and thirty-three as husbands' dependents; twelve did not work but appeared as guarantors. Patriarchy did not mean that women did not labor; it meant that most women worked without pay under their husband's rule. When husbands contracted to provide joint labor, the wife usually got a lesser salary (only one gained equal pay). The contracts reveal a dual approach to locking patriarchy into labor relations: men and women who refused church-sanctioned patriarchy were separated; married men who accumulated advances but did not provide the work might be drawn into contracts that required wives to work beside them for lesser pay. Patriarchy's advantage to the man was reinforced, as was the wife's dependence.

A dozen women appeared as guarantors, six with husbands and six alone.[157] Wives guaranteeing with husbands had likely brought resources to the union; perhaps too their inclusion emphasized that married patriarchs were reliable participants in market relations. The six women who guaranteed alone had huertas, market stalls, or other enterprises to be tapped if the worker did not meet obligations. The Querétaro labor market was not a space of gender exclusion: a few women were employers, a few more guaranteed men's debts; more worked as husbands' dependents. Labor relations promoted household patriarchy.

Most often men labored to gain advances, salaries, and food, strengthening claims to household patriarchy. Obligated, salaried work sustained rule over wives and children in sacramentally sanctioned marriages. Working patriarchs acquiesced in their own dependence and that of the households they ruled. Two contracts illustrate how patriarchy cemented labor relations. In June 1599 Tomás Equina, Otomí and from Querétaro, contracted to work off twelve pesos, a fine imposed by the Otomí court for wounding his wife, María Enegui. He would labor for four months at a salary of three pesos, unless his wife chose to work with him (the option was hers). She would earn two pesos monthly; together they would fullfil the obligagion in only ten weeks. María could stay home and extend her husband's service; she could work with him for lesser pay and end his obligation sooner. Her decision is unknown.[158] The court recognized patriarchy and a victimized wife's limited choices.

A decade later another contract implemented the patriarchal ideal almost perfectly. Gaspar Juárez, an Otomí born in Querétaro, speaking through an interpreter, had been jailed. He owed over forty pesos, first to Álvaro Hernández, then to Luis and Lucas Ruíz de Peralta. All hoped to gain labor that Gaspar had long evaded. In September 1609 he contracted to serve Miguel Gallardo at 3.5 pesos monthly. The first guarantor was Gaspar's wife, Juana Paula. A second guarantee came from Juan Gabriel, an Otomí also born in Querétaro, and his wife Catalina Méndez. The contract stated that Juan Gabriel was a good guarantor because he was married and worked as a shepherd for Tomás González Figueroa, Alférez (Standard Bearer) of the Valladolid (Michoacán) council and a leading landed entrepreneur around Querétaro.[159] Household patriarchy was becoming the definition of secure dependence.

By 1610 Querétaro was a place of Otomí rule and irrigated huertas, a town where diverse entrepreneurs profited from estate cultivation and textile production, along with trade, and transportation, and where a a labor market was rapidly developing. Otomí lords and officials joined in commercial production and trade. Hispanic traders and clothmakers, transport contractors, and craftsmen joined in work relations shaped by labor scarcity, advanced payments, obligations, and last-resort coercions, mostly in obrajes. As criminal sentences and overt coercion became less central to labor relations, patriarchy increasingly defined the ties between employers, workers, and dependent families. Production and work were commercial, obligated, negotiated, and patriarchal.

During the decades that followed, salaries rose and criminal sentences to labor declined. The costs of labor in the obrajes rose, yet more than other enterprises they needed a large and permanent workforce. By the 1640s most obrajes relied on African slaves, who remained at the core of their operations past 1700.[160] Yet Querétaro did not become a slave society. Obrajes were profitable enough to afford slaves and enough like prisons to contain them. Elsewhere in and around Querétaro, labor was commercial, mostly voluntary, sometimes contracted, deeply patriarchal, and often obligated by advance payments.

Consolidating Querétaro, 1600–1640

From 1590 to 1610 commercial ways took root at Querétaro, promoted by Otomí and Spanish entrepreneurs. While silver flowed from Zacatecas and San Luis Potosí to Europe and China, cloth making, irrigated cultivation, and grazing flourished. A labor market developed as entrepreneurs paid for work, usually in advance and nearly always by men, mostly Otomí. As capitalism emerged it changed. Soon after 1600 it became clear that the Tapia's fusion of Otomí lordship and entreneurship would not continue. Don Diego had no male heir. His sisters and his widow had married into the Martín clan; they lamented that Spaniards saw them as "*indias*," not noble Christians. Don Fernando and don Diego built power as Otomí lords, founding settlers, commanders against Chichimecas, and entrepreneurs. With no male successor in a patriarchal society, Don Diego consolidated his croplands, water rights, and grazing properties to found the Convent of Santa Clara de Jesús. His daughter and heir became a nun and entered as doña Luisa de Espíritu Santo.[161]

Santa Clara preserved and transformed the Tapia legacy. During the seventeenth century the convent operated the most valuable estates around Querétaro. For decades doña Luisa lived as Santa Clara's leading resident, often ruling as abbess, sustained by the family estates,

Santa Clara Convent, Querétaro, seventeenth to eighteenth centuries.

daily honoring the God who sanctioned her family's rise to power. Santa Clara preserved the Otomí-Christian alliance that was key to Tapia eminence. But it was an institution of the colonial church; by the 1620s it was the leading mortgage bank in the Bajío, funding Spanish entrepreneurs, including many whom don Diego had helped toward power and profit. The convent continued the key relationship in which Tapias allied with the church to promote commercial ways at Querétaro. But without Tapias leading local government and business — without their brokering among regime officers, Spanish entrepreneurs, the Otomí republic, and the Otomí majority — Spaniards asserted rising power while most Otomí struggled.

Into the seventeenth century Otomí power focused on the republic — the only local government, still in control of important lands and water rights. Its revenues sustained local worship and funded diverse enterprises, often using rents gained by leasing land and other resources to Spanish entrepreneurs. By an assessment made in 1614 the community owed 407 pesos cash and 203 *fanegas* of maize in annual tribute. Of that, 100 pesos and 50 fanegas funded the local Franciscans convent and parish. Another 77 pesos and 50 fanegas went to the Franciscan mission at San Pedro Tolimán, at the edge of the Sierra Gorda. The Archbishop in Mexico City gained 20 fanegas in tithe. That left 230 pesos and 83 fanegas, about half, to the encomendero don Luis de Quesada. He used his earnings to fund diverse enterprises. He paid 100 pesos to Juan Rodríguez Galán, merchant and textile entrepreneur, 135 pesos to Bernardo Murillo, and 146 pesos to Antonio de Echaide—one of Duarte de Tóvar's merchant sons.[162] The tax revenues generated by Querétaro's Otomí republic funded local religion, pacification of the Sierra, and local business—a mix that would persist.[163]

The community also forged joint ventures with Spanish entrepreneurs. Early in 1622 the republic extended Cristóbal Sánchez's lease to operate a community farm. Days later a delegation finalized a deal with Juan de Guevara, a local merchant, to provide "cloth . . . for advances."[164] The farm was leased to one Spaniard while another advanced cloth to the Otomí working the land, creating obligations essential to gaining their labor. Two Spaniards and the republic shared produce and profits; working Otomí got advances in cloth, calculated in cash, accounted against future work. The republic joined in obligated labor relations.

Scarce financial resources increasingly challenged the republic, however. Sometime before 1624 it took control of three caballerías (120 hectares) of irrigated cropland near the Santa Clara holdings. Since Lázaro Martín had vacated the property, "there have been many years in which we could not work it; it has sat fallow as we cannot afford to build a farm or estate, for lack of resources." So in 1624 the republic decided to "sell" the lands as a "perpetual lease." In public auction Diego Montañez, a local Spaniard, bid 1,100 pesos—committing to pay 27 pesos, 4 reales a year (in perpetuity) to "own" the property. Doña Luisa de Tapia, cacica y principal, sister of Santa Clara, guaranteed the lease.[165] The community gained little; at prevailing prices the annual payment equaled less than fifteen fanegas of maize for prime irrigated lands that would harvest hundreds of fanegas yearly. Was the republic that poor? Or was this another deal in which the republic passed resources to favored Spaniards? The role of doña Luisa suggests the latter.

A final episode illustrates the difficulties faced by the Otomí republic in a developing commercial economy. In June 1629 the Otomí governor don Baltasar Martín appeared before the district magistrate don Juan Fernando de Caraveo. Martín lamented that community operation of an "irrigated farm" yielded but 461 pesos yearly. He called for a lease, including land, equipment, and "indios laborios." A first bid of 800 pesos yearly came from Caraveo, the magistrate overseeing the auction. Two other Spaniards, Francisco Díaz and Alonso de Casas, drove the bidding to 1,010 pesos per year. Then the Otomí governor Martín stepped in, offering the same rent, paid in advance, and insisting that he needed the lease to cover 1,350 pesos due for past tributes. Bidding continued, allowing Alonso de Casas to offer 1,011 pesos yearly and in advance. One more peso won him the lease for four years.[166]

The cost of tribute inhibited the republic's ability to finance production on valuable lands. Leases brought profit to favored Spaniards and income to the republic. They became locked in joint ventures; Spanish entrepreneurs profited most, while the Otomí republic retained land rights and gained income to pay tributes that funded local worship and the encomendero's projects. The Otomí majority continued to work huertas and to labor for advances, wages, and rations in town and at nearby estates.

New World Religion: Convent Capitalism, Sacramental Worship, and an Otomí Virgin

Ever since Connín and his Otomí followers settled Querétaro with Franciscan allies, Christianity had asserted its understanding of the cosmos and worldly life in the Bajío. Every aspect of the development of Querétaro as an Otomí-Spanish commercial society linked to Christian understandings and legitimations. Tapias and Franciscans, the Otomí republic and Spanish entrepreneurs—all promoted Christianity and Church institutions. Throughout, the Otomí majority proved independent and selective in engaging Catholicism. Ramos's report made that clear. By 1600 nearly everyone at Querétaro professed Christianity. Still, Spaniards and the clergy worried about the religious commitments of the majority. During the Chichimeca wars reliance on Otomí fighters led Spaniards to limit cultural pressures on essential allies. After pacification, as commercial life deepened, Spaniards and Otomí debated a complex religious culture. Catholic institutions proliferated, as did independent adaptations—including devotion to an Otomí Virgin, Our Lady of Pueblito.

For most of a century Connín (don Fernando de Tapia) and his son don Diego ruled as Otomí lords, fought Chichimecas, led commercial development, and promoted baptismal conversion and sacramental worship. Their efforts culminated in the Convent of Santa Clara. The Martíns and other Otomí nobles also founded religious institutions, endowing them with land and livestock in a rush of early-seventeenth-century convent building. The transfer of estates built by Otomí lords to church institutions reinforced commercial ways and Catholic legitimations.[167] By the 1630s key institutions were in place: Franciscans of the Michoacán province led religious life at Querétaro; facing a fine plaza, their temple was the parish church for Spaniard and Otomí alike, sustained by tributes, donations, a huerta, and flocks of sheep. Blocks west, doña Luisa de Tapia led the sisters of Santa Clara, supported by family estates and mortgage earnings. Just east of the plaza, Jesuits educated sons of local notables.[168]

All preached a post-reformation Catholicism keyed on sacraments and saints, sin and salvation, penance and communion. They insisted that men be devout patriarchs, ruling and sustaining families. Women must be chaste and obedient, marrying to provide their husbands with sex, service, and legitimate heirs—or entering convents to serve God through investment and prayer. Devotion to the Virgin Mother was central. These women, like all good women, must be chaste and obedient; they served and comforted by interceding with God and Christ. Friars and Jesuits, diocesan priests and Santa Clara nuns might debate emphases, but few questioned core prescriptions: patriarchs and wives, priests and nuns would live in hierarchical order—avoiding sin, seeking sacraments, honoring God and the Virgin, sanctioning power, inequality, work, stability. Wealth was legitimate and left to legitimate heirs. Those who worked would live in patriarchal families and honor legitimate power.[169]

Cultural authority was easier to assert than to impose. While church institutions proliferated, promoted by the regime, by clerical authorities, by Otomí elites, and by devout Spaniards, the people forged a complex popular culture. At Querétaro and nearby Celaya slaves of African ancestry and their free mulatto offspring mixed with Mesoamericans and Europeans in everyday life. Between 1611 and 1615 Celaya saw a spate of denunciations to the Inquisition—many self-denunciations—that revealed popular beliefs and practices challenging the prescriptions that legitimated power. A group of Spanish women, most poor, many pregnant out of wedlock and without patriarchs to protect and provide, engaged African slaves, men and women, along with indigenous curers, mostly women, in search of potions, spells, and cures. They aimed to punish or attract powerful men, to divert rivals, to cure ills. They were experimental, trying the offerings of every tradition. They lived a hybrid popular culture in which Spanish women, African men and women, a few mestizos, and Mesoamerican women sought gain in a world of Hispanic, commercial, patriarchal power.[170]

Among the Querétaro Otomí the early seventeenth century brought a new indigenous Catholicism, promoted, sanctioned, but never controlled by the church. Ramos's report outlined indigenous religious visions that included a founding deity of ultimate power, along with divine forces that guided production and reproduction and daily life, and offered ways of penance to atone for transgressions. Indigenous worship also offered assistance with health, fertility and childbirth, drought, and famine. Ramos insisted that Querétaro's Otomí had taken up Christianity with fervor. They knew the power of God; in times of deadly epidemics and constant warfare they turned to penance and communion as the way to salvation. Still Ramos worried about Otomí "idolatries"; he reported no devotion to saints or the Virgin. No Christian intermediary yet dealt with worldly challenges; old ways held strong when the Otomí sought aid in the 1580s.

In the 1630s a Franciscan friar, Sebastián Gallegos, lamenting enduring indigenous rites, aimed to capture Otomí needs for protection and tie them to Christianity. He sculpted a humble Christ placed in a rustic chapel on a huerta near the Santa Clara convent. El Señor de la Huertecilla—Lord of the Little Garden—drew growing devotion among people cultivating urban gardens.[171] A figure of Christian male power, he offered protection and aid to Otomí cultivators. Gallegos then sculpted Our Lady of the Immaculate Conception for the villagers at San Francisco Galileo, called Pueblito, just west of Querétaro. She would join the several Virgins who focused popular devotion in New Spain. Soon after the conquest of Tenochtitlan, amid disease, depopulation, and anxiety, rural Mexicas found the Virgin they came to know as Guadalupe near the temple of Tonantzin, a powerful Mesoamerican mother divinity. Nahuas, Spaniards, Franciscans, and other clergy debated the power and meaning of Guadalupe for a century. Then in the 1640s elites and clergy in New Spain's capital began to celebrate her powers, promoting a devotion to be shared by Spaniards and Mesoamericans.[172] In the 1630s there was no sign of Guadalupe in Otomí Querétaro.

Outside Pueblito rose an earth-covered pyramid, reminding all that this was an important place in a hazy past. During the sixteenth century Franciscans preached in the village by the pyramid. A stream passed by, but this was not a place of lush huertas. In the 1630s friars worried that villagers baptized children, attended Mass, and took sacraments, yet mixed Christianity with "idolatry." An eighteenth-century chronicle stated: "although they offered outward appearances as Catholics, in their huts and forest solitudes they kept truly gentile rites." Pueblito was a "deplorable origin of idolatries, lamentable spring of superstitions, abominable source of idols." People climbed the "hand-made mountain . . . to consult their oracles and offer incense as tribute to the devil."[173] The people of Pueblito were not yet Christian in the eyes of their clergy.

Gallegos offered Our Lady of the Immaculate Conception, royally robed and crowned. She held the infant Christ, also richly robed and crowned, yet overshadowed by his mother. St. Francis of Assisi, the Franciscan founder, appears at her feet, in plain robe, dwarfed by her size, her magnificence, her power. Perhaps the friar aimed to promote the Virgin as the chaste, serving mother of God—to further clerical and patriarchal power, orthodox devotion, and Otomí obedience. But the image emphasized the power of the Virgin, the dependency of Christ, and the service of the Franciscan founder. Whatever the friar's plan, Our Lady of Pueblito became a religious force serving the Otomí at Pueblito and all around. As her chronicler wrote, "the most pious Lady showed herself so generous and so favorable to so many rude and barbarous people . . . she converted the seminary of idolatries and supersticiones into a home of miracles, a heaven of prodigies."[174] She was a vital female force, serving villagers in the face of drought and disease, promoting fertility in families and fields. She defined Pueblito, where residents built a chapel that was "the shared place of propitiation for all the people of the region, where they find consolation for every affliction."[175]

The Franciscan sculptor hoped that Our Lady of Pueblito would claim the Otomí for Christianity. She succeeded. Yet the Otomí made her an agent of a deeply Otomí Christianity. They went to her when ill, and she cured. They sought her help in childbirth, and she delivered healthy children. They asked her aid when rains failed and streams ran dry, and she watered their crops. As Tapia power waned and the republic slid into a secondary role in the commercial economy, the poorest Otomí found a maternal Virgin to aid them with the challenges of life. Querétaro's Otomí forged a Christian devotion to serve their needs. Our Lady at Pueblito helped them to worship independently and to negotiate, at times to contest Spanish Christian power and culture.[176]

During the decades after the Chichimeca wars a commercial economy and a complex Catholic culture took shape at Querétaro. Otomí lords and Hispanic entrepreneurs endowed convents that preached sacramental Catholicism and funded commercial life. Otomí families with huertas looked for protection from a humble Christ. And the poorest Otomí, grappling with the uncertainties of climate, disease, and a new commercial world, found hope and help in the Virgin at Pueblito. Meanwhile, outside the sanction of the church, sorceries and cures offered aid to diverse people facing subordination in a patriarchal society. All these devotions and adaptations engaged each other in a commercial society of ethnic fluidity. In time Our Lady at Pueblito would define Querétaro Catholicism.

In the first half of the seventeenth century Querétaro flourished as the commercial pivot of the Bajío and Spanish North America, a place of trade, cloth making, cultivation, and devotion. The Otomí republic was the only local government; Otomí families cultivated huertas and made cotton cloth; the Otomí Virgin at Pueblito shaped popular religious life. Still, Spanish power was rising: Spaniards ruled commerce and became leading landowners; they operated obrajes with African slaves; they dreamed of political power.

In 1621 the High Court in Mexico City complained that a lawyer working in Querétaro facilitated too many suits by Otomí against Spaniards.[177] In 1631 Querétaro gained formal independence from Xilotepec, confirming Querétaro's importance in the silver economy (and the old head town's decline).[178] In 1640 the republic got viceregal backing to collect tributes from "the many natives . . . who work for Spaniards in town and across the countryside, who owe large sums past due." When the republic sent collectors they were "mistreated in acts and words." The viceroy ordered payment. Still, the growing number of Otomí working in Spaniards' enterprises and at rural estates challenged republican power at Querétaro.[179]

The middle of the seventeenth century brought two new assertions of Spanish power, both contested, both successful in part, and both limited in ways that allowed the Otomí republic to evade full subordination. The first came from Santa Clara. The sisters continued to run the Tapia properties; their lending financed others' commercial cultivation. In 1640 they built a dam in the canyon to the east, increasing the flow of water to their estates and those of other Spaniards. In the 1650s the sisters claimed all the water in the river and the canals. They demanded payment from all users, Otomí families cultivating huertas and Spaniards leasing lands from the republic. The High Court in Mexico City limited the sisters' claim, granting them only the water not used by huertas or the republic; they could charge only Spanish cultivators.[180] The sisters of Santa Clara pursued profit; the Tapia legacy served Spanish commercialism; only the regime protected Otomí rights.

That protection had limits. In 1655 Querétaro's Spanish merchants, landlords, and professionals petitioned for a city charter. The 1640s had brought a decline of the silver trade, the separation of Portugal and its domains, and the revolt of Cataluña. Desperate for funds, the monarchy offered concessions for cash. Spaniards at Querétaro offered three thousand pesos for a city charter with jurisdiction over the urban center and the countryside around. The viceroy raised the price to four thousand pesos, took the funds, and limited Spanish jurisdiction to the city center. The huertas of San Sebastián, north of the river, remained subject to the Otomí republic, which still led Querétaro's Otomí community. From the 1650s on Otomí and Spanish councils shared—and negotiated—rule in the commercial pivot of the Bajío.[181]

Founding Querétaro, the Bajío, and Spanish North America

After more than a century of founding participation in an Atlantic economy, Querétaro was a place where Otomí and Spaniards jostled each other to produce, to profit, and to rule. Otomí huertas supplied local markets, Mexico City, and northern mines. Otomí without huertas, Mesoamerican migrants, and free mulattoes negotiated a labor market; African slaves labored in obrajes. Sacramental Catholicism, hybrid popular cures and sorceries, and Otomí devotion to the Lord of the Huerta and the Virgin at Pueblito shaped a complex religious culture. Spaniards asserted power and Otomí contested everything—in government, production, social relations, and religion. In all that, a new world began.

What began at Querétaro shaped the Bajío and regions north: Entrepreneurs negotiating with a colonial regime built a commercial society driven by silver and focused on irrigated cultivation, extensive grazing, and textile production. People from Europe, Africa, and Mesoamerica built Querétaro. They fought together against Chichimecas, who fell before a flood of migrants, livestock, and diseases. Production and work relations were commercial and patriarchal. Catholicism provided many ways to understand changing lives. All of this would characterize the Bajío and Spanish North America for centuries.

Still, Querétaro was unique. The role of the Otomí in leading settlement, building irrigation and huertas, and fighting Chichimecas led to enduring Otomí importance in local rule and commercial cultivation, roles rarely replicated by Mesoamericans elsewhere in the Bajío or the dry zones to the north. At Querétaro a commercial, patriarchal, Catholic society was shaped by a Spanish-Otomí dichotomy. Across the rest of the Bajío and Spanish North America, Spaniards would rule commercial, patriarchal, and Catholic communities shaped more by ethnic amalgamations than dichotomous polarizations.

CHAPTER 2

Forging Spanish North America

Northward Expansions, Mining Amalgamations,

and Patriarchal Communities, 1590–1700

THE SEVENTEENTH CENTURY brought a second wave of north-ward expansion, driving the conflicts and opportunities that shaped Spanish North America far beyond the Bajío. Silver mining boomed after 1590. Merchants based in Mexico City, mostly immi-grants from Spain (and Portugal, a Hapsburg domain from 1580 to 1640), profited in trade with Seville, Manila, and European and Asian worlds beyond. Viceregal authorities promoted mining and trade, claimed revenues for the crown, and mediated conflicts as they could.[1] Hapsburg Spain took unprecedented revenues, ruled soaring trade, and set its European competitors on a dual quest: to build replicas of Spanish power and gain access to Spanish silver.[2]

New Spain's two societies adapted to the stimulus of silver. In Meso-america epidemics drove native populations toward their nadir after 1590. Among scarce survivors, indigenous republics confirmed rights to community land and local rule; they became refuges of adaptation and survival for indigenous peoples, languages, and cultures as they negotiated subordination and inevitably changed. On lands vacated around congregated villages, Spanish entrepreneurs claimed property and built estates—raising wheat, sugar, and livestock to supply cities and mining centers. Indigenous republics jostled emerging estates across the countryside, disputing land, labor, and trade; the regime

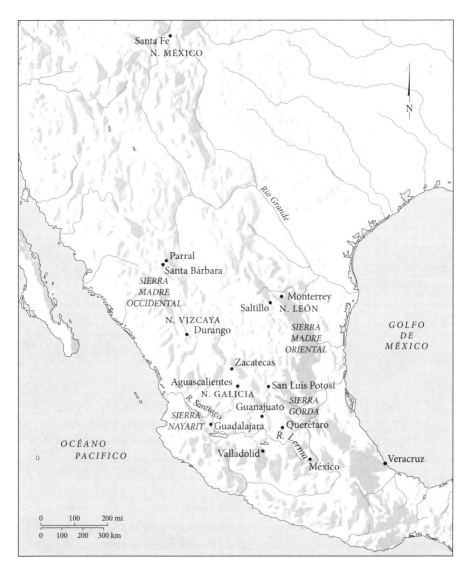

Spanish North America in the Seventeenth Century

promoted commercial development, defended indigenous republics, and founded courts to mediate inevitable disputes.[3] Commercial ways latched onto Mesoamerican communities; Christianity sanctioned and debated everything. After a century of unimagined opportunity for Spaniards and devastating depopulation among Mesoamericans, a re- markable stability set in. Spanish Mesoamerica would prove a society of enduring duality.

The North remained more dynamic, expansive, and conflictive.

Most of New Spain's silver came from Zacatecas and other northern mines; it was then shipped to be minted and taxed in Mexico City before entering global trade. As Chichimeca wars ended, discoveries at San Luis Potosí accelerated northern production and raised hopes for new bonanzas. Mining held strong at Zacatecas through the 1630s, while prospectors pressed north looking for the next great find. In the process they set growing herds of livestock to graze across the dry plateaus still home to independent natives—recreating the invasions and opportunities that had set off Chichimeca wars in the Bajío.

In the 1630s Parral became the next silver boomtown; the expansion of Spanish North America accelerated northward. As Chinese demand for silver waned in the 1640s, new domains of mining, irrigation, and grazing recapitulated the economic developments, social conflicts, and cultural changes begun around Querétaro and Zacatecas after 1550. Across a new North, warrior-entrepreneurs hunted resistant natives while mission clergy called them to settled lives of Christian service. Amid uncertain engagements, periodic wars, and recurrent plagues, native numbers again plunged. Among people without traditions of structured, ruled, and settled life, Spaniards founded few indigenous republics. Migrants from Iberia, Mesoamerica, and Africa came north, mixing in a population divided between a few entrepreneurs and numerous producers, most living in mining camps and estate communities.

Zacatecas and Parral kept the silver economy alive to 1680. In the Bajío, Guanajuato continued as a secondary mining center—a place of dreams, social insecurity, and ethnic mixing. A few claimed riches and developed vast properties across nearby uplands, building a new north in the Bajío. Querétaro remained a center of trade, textiles, and huertas, where Spaniards and Otomí contested power and culture. And across the rich basin lands west of Querétaro and south of Guanajuato irrigation expanded along with new communities of cultivators, most living as estate dependents. Amid profit seeking, ethnic mixing, and changing identities, patriarchy shaped communities in the Bajío and regions north. It structured inequities that channeled profits to a few and kept the majority at work. After 1600 a commercial, patriarchal, and ethnically fluid society expanded beyond Querétaro. Spanish North America sank deep roots in the Bajío and drove northward.

Northward Expansions

Chinese demand created growing markets for the silver mined at Zacatecas after 1550, drawing Europeans, Africans, and Mesoamericans north along with livestock and diseases, setting off Chichimeca wars and encouraging Bajío development, thus beginning ways of production, conflict, and social life that would mark the north for centuries. Powerful men mixed office holding, military command, strategic marriages, and entrepreneurship to profit from mining, build landed patrimonies, and establish dominant families. They drew financing from Mexico City; they bought African slaves; and they recruited Mesoamerican migrants to work in mines, refining, and estate communities by offering ore shares (for dangerous underground labor), salary advances, wages, and food rations to men who would labor in a commercial economy short of workers. They drove Spanish North America northward in search of new mines and new estates, always in the face of resistant independent peoples.[4]

Among the founders of Zacatecas who gained wealth, power, and acclaim, don Cristóbal de Oñate had been lieutenant governor of New Galicia. He combined his office and mining to build thirteen mills for refining silver and buy more than a hundred African slaves. Don Juan de Tolosa, credited as the discoverer of Zacatecas's silver, married doña Isabel Cortés, daughter of Cortés and one of Moctezuma's daughters. Don Diego de Ibarra married a daughter of the first viceroy don Luis de Velasco and gained regime favors, land grants, and access to financing. His son don Francisco led expeditions north into Nueva Vizcaya, which don Diego later governed. Oñate's son, don Juan, later led an expedition that set the Spanish presence in New Mexico in 1598, serving as that province's first governor.[5]

The stimulus of silver was strong enough that Zacatecas boomed and led northward expansion even while Chichimeca wars raged.[6] But Guachichil and Zacateca assaults and livestock gathering limited rural settlement and estate development. During decades of conflict Zacatecas depended on the Bajío for essential staples. When the wars quieted, Zacatecas miners and traders began to claim land; they developed irrigation where streams allowed and set livestock to graze all around, creating integrated enterprises linking estates, mines, and refineries. Pedro Mateos de Ortega left Spain in the late 1570s. By 1590 he traded and held office in Mexico City; later that decade he did business in San Luis Potosí and Zacatecas. From 1593 to 1609 he and his son claimed twenty sites to graze cattle, three sites for sheep, plus seventy-six caballerías for cultivation—a total of 41,000 hectares between the Bajío and Zacatecas. They built vast estates focused at Ciénega de Mata; their heirs expanded the holdings to over 160,000 hectares by the 1670s. They populated them with slaves who herded livestock, staffed an obraje, and worked in a slaughterhouse at Zacatecas. Numerous tenants paid ten to thirty pesos to cultivate the land.

Eventually locked into an entail by the Rincón Gallardo family, these enterprises and others less imposing supplied Zacatecas and sold wool to Querétaro obrajes. They profited men who held office in Spanish councils at Zacatecas and towns like Lagos and Aguascalientes. Many left legacies to found church institutions, including a Jesuit college at Zacatecas sustained by its own rich estates.[7]

Facing sparse and resistant local populations, Zacatecas's miners and estate builders had to draw workers north. They owned about eight hundred African slaves around 1600. During boom decades before 1600 Mateos and Rincón family entrepreneurs regularly bought (and sometimes sold) slaves for four hundred pesos or more. In 1656, a time of slowdown, sixty-eight slaves sold for prices between 250 and 300 pesos; in 1685, with renewed boom, forty-eight changed hands at prices from 300 to 350 pesos. Ciénega de Mata's slave population peaked at 123 in 1683. Through the boom of the early seventeenth century and long after, slaves of African ancestry (many noted as mulatto by mid-century) provided a core of permanent workers at Zacatecas and nearby estates. Still, they were too valuable to send into dangerous mines.[8]

As a result the majority of workers in Zacatecas were drawn from Mesoamerica. Early on the town had barrios of Tlaxcalans, Mexicas, and Texcocans, and two for Tarascans. Most worked in *cuadrillas*, gangs living on properties that entrepreneurs developed as *haciendas de minas*, silver refineries and residential compounds. Workers were always scarce; they gained *pepenas* (shares of the ore they mined) in addition to advances, cash wages, and food staples for their labor in the dangerous shafts that generated profit for a few and drove world trade. A raucous boomtown atmosphere ruled: the powerful enjoyed luxuries from Europe and Asia; a few workers gained a bit of the same. There were periodic combats between cuadrillas, disputes among men who competed for a chance in a place of prospects, dangers, and uncertainties.[9]

In the early 1600s fifteen hundred Spaniards and three thousand others—Africans, Mesoamericans, and their mixed offspring—lived and worked at Zacatecas. About seventeen hundred mineworkers produced silver. They drew wheat and other sustenance from the Bajío and tools, textiles, and luxuries from New Spain, Europe, and Asia. To about 1635 Chinese demand for silver held strong. By 1640 the historically high prices paid by the Ming treasury had fallen, while older mines at Zacatecas faced rising costs. Local production waned and power shifted to Mexico City, where financiers tied to Atlantic trade funded production at lower levels.[10] In mining and mine labor, in estate building and ethnic mixing, in reliance on the Bajío for cloth and grain, Zacatecas set a model that would be replicated across Spanish North America.

Dreams of another Zacatecas sent men north across dry plateau country. By the 1580s they reached the villages of the upper Río Grande valley, a place they named New Mexico. There Europeans led by the younger Oñate found a world where settled villagers (soon named Pueblos) faced hunters and gatherers all around—a world of endemic conflict not unlike the Bajío when Mexica, Otomí, and Tarascans faced Chichimecas in war and trade after 1550. New Mexico would mark the northernmost reach of New Spain for centuries. A few warrior-entrepreneurs accompanied by Franciscans claimed sovereignty. They struggled to rule a world where cultivating communities engaged in war and trade with independent, often nomadic peoples. Europeans brought livestock (horses, sheep, and cattle), new tools and weapons, new possibilities for alliance, new religious understandings, and new diseases. Spanish officials confirmed Pueblo rights to land and self-rule as republics, asking Christianization, tribute, and service in return. Spaniards and Franciscans lived among Pueblos, strengthening villagers in their conflicts and trade with Navajos, Apaches, and others. An outpost where European horses and sheep, tools and weapons, cloth and beliefs could be bought or stolen, New Mexico drew independent natives from near and far, across plains stretching east and mountain basins reaching north, setting off far-reaching changes in worlds Europeans rarely saw.

Franciscans pressed Pueblos to abandon old worships, including life-sustaining interactions with Corn Mothers. In exchange the friars offered sacraments and access to saints and the Virgin Mary; eventually Guadalupe came to offer protection. Spaniards insisted there as elsewhere that Pueblo men relinquish patriarchal powers rooted in war and privileged access to divine powers; they challenged Pueblo women's rights to maintain hearths, cultivate fields, and pursue sexual freedom. Martial patriarchy and sexual independence would give way to dependent, monogamous, patriarchal families: men would lead households as providers who cultivated and earned wages; they would gain dominion over wives in sacramental unions, and over the children they generated.

But in New Mexico those pressures played out in a region lacking silver, where Franciscans and Pueblos together faced independent natives in a continuous mix of war and trade—recurrent conflicts in which men killed men, and captured and "adopted" women and children. New Mexico lived centuries of "Chichimeca wars." Everyone changed: Spaniards struggled to hold the nothern outpost and claim Pueblo peoples for Christianity. Pueblos gained tools, livestock, and allies against independent peoples while they adapted ancient knowledge in a world of new diseases, broken truths, and proclaimed certainties, including the promise of Christian salvation in a time of deadly epidemics. Navajos gained sheep to become herders and weavers; Apaches and others claimed horses and weapons that made them fierce warriors. Seventeenth-century New Mexico saw Spanish persistence and endemic instability that exploded in Pueblo rebellion in 1680.[11]

Spaniards never found rich mines in New Mexico, but their tenuous and contested presence there allowed the Sierras and high plateaus between the Bajío and the Río Grande to become the vast domain of a continuing search for silver.[12] From the 1560s the Ibarras used wealth taken at Zacatecas to lead treks that inevitably included Africans and Mesoamericans. They focused on basins near the Río Florida, eight hundred kilometers north of Zacatecas along the trail to New Mexico. Tantalized by small silver strikes at Indé, drawn by opportunities for irrigated planting nearby, with grazing lands all around—and finding native peoples interested in tools, cloth, and animals, intrigued by God and the saints, but resistant to settled dependence—the newcomers named the province for Santa Bárbara. She was famous for finding silver, protecting the devout from disease and nature's malevolence, and fighting peoples the Europeans called barbarians.[13]

From the 1580s through the 1620s there were no bonanzas beyond Zacatecas; small strikes kept the search alive. Spaniards kept coming, along with African slaves and free mulattoes, migrant Mesoamericans and their mixed offspring. Entrepreneurs were often regime officials like Francisco de Ibarra and Francisco de Urdiñola; they aimed to cultivate where streams allowed irrigation. They set livestock grazing everywhere. Herds multiplied, again threatened hunting and gathering, and offered new ways of native survival. Franciscans and Jesuits built missions, offering Christianity and settled lives to natives facing invasion by Atlantic peoples, Old World livestock, and deadly diseases. Tepehuanes, Conchos, Tarahumaras, and many others had to respond. Some experimented with mission life; others tried mine labor or estate dependence; still others retreated to isolated canyons. All learned of profit-seeking newcomers lusting for silver, dependent on livestock, and demanding labor, while honoring a new god and insisting on new truths. Meanwhile smallpox and other diseases brought waves of death.[14]

Into the 1600s the boom in Zacatecas and the absence of bonanza farther north limited incursions. Prospectors tried promising sites and moved on. Hispanic settlements were islands in spaces still indigenous, yet invaded by livestock and disease. Newcomers and natives negotiated demands and adaptations. Spanish officials awarded native peoples to warlord-entrepreneurs in grants called encomiendas and re-partimientos. Yet it was difficult to take tribute and labor from people who came and went. When conflict erupted, captives were key prizes on all sides. In vast spaces populated by mobile natives, any claim to tribute, trade, or labor required a mix of force, incentive, and negotiation with local headmen.[15]

Simmering conflicts exploded in the Tepehuan rebellion of 1616. Many rebel leaders had engaged the Spanish world; some were mestizos, most knew Hispanic ways. Rebel communities kept European tools and livestock, and the elements of Christianity that they found persuasive. In wars that preserved martial patriarchy, men were killed, women and children captured. The Tepehuan rising led to stalemate in 1619; resistant communities took amnesties and gifts of food, cloth, and livestock. The regime accelerated mission projects, again pressing independent peoples to live as monogamous Christian cultivators, dependent on the clergy and available to labor.[16]

Then the 1630s brought bonanza at Parral, north of the Tepehuan homelands and nearer to Tarahumaras, Conchos, and others who now faced rising pressures. While Zacatecas declined, Parral drew entrepreneurs, financiers, and workers.[17] Chinese demand for silver was waning, but the silver economy of northern New Spain was firmly established. New digs at Parral almost certainly yielded richer ores for less cost than older and deeper mines at Zacatecas. Silver mining and the trade that it fueled carried on. A new road helped oxcarts roll north from Mexico City and Querétaro. Financiers in the viceregal capital funded Parral's merchants and miners, including many arriving from Spain. They negotiated and married with local landlords (often also local officials) who controlled workers, food supplies, and livestock products. A small clique of entrepreneurs ruled mining; most were Spanish, many from Spain, but at least one mulatto and one mestizo were prominent among them. As mining boomed at Parral it stimulated riverside irrigation and cultivation at Santa Bárbara and San Bartolomé along with grazing all around. Migrants came in droves: Spaniards to profit, African slaves, free mulattoes, and Mesoamericans to labor. They mixed to generate more free mulattoes. Local natives drawn from missions also labored, as did Conchos, who quickly divided between those who tried working with Spaniards and others who resisted. Slaves and free mulattoes, migrant Mesoamericans, mission residents, and independent Conchos never ended labor scarcity. Nor did punitive expeditions and barely disguised slaving. A constantly changing mix of coercion and negotiations marked the landscape of northern labor.[18]

Miners, estate builders, officials, and missionaries all pressed northern natives to settle, convert, and work. Attempts to make independent people labor led to bondage for men taken in combat; demands for draft labor from mobile natives granted in "encomiendas" became licenses to hunt independent workers, or to demand them from missions where natives had settled, baptized children, and labored to sustain themselves and the mission community. The enticements that drew some Conchos—still independent, some baptized, others not—to work and trade in the new commercial world in the 1630s gave way in 1644 to decades of conflict and coercion.[19]

Silver production continued. As diseases, coercion, and conflicts left local natives scarce and recalcitrant after 1650, workers were drawn in drafts from Jesuit missions among the Yaqui on the Pacific coast, even from Pueblo communities in New Mexico. Men taken in wars with independent peoples near Parral and around New Mexico were sent to labor. Geographically and culturally diverse peoples—Mesoamericans migrating north hoping for a new chance; Africans dragged north as slaves and their free mulatto offspring; natives linked to missions near and far—all discovered the silver economy through labor. Coercion mixed with opportunity; work in the mines was dangerous, but it also offered ore shares and a chance at prosperity. In refineries rough stone crushers and noxious mercury made work so dangerous that slaves rarely labored there. Other men did—because they were coerced, drawn by advances, or left with no alternative after a long trek. Among northern natives, invasions, coercion, and diseases again shaped hurried adaptations. Some Tarahumara welcomed missionaries who built irrigation works, provided livestock, and offered new truths; other resisted, or stayed for a time and left. Conchos faced pressures and incentives to labor in the mines and nearby; many tried mission life for a time, adopted horses and firearms, and turned to resistant engagements.

Parral boomed in the 1630s and 1640s, slowed, and then held solid to about 1680. During the early boom slavery and labor drafts combined with the incentive of advances, salaries, ore shares, and food rations to bring a population that grew to around ten thousand. When the boom receded, slaves became scarce; epidemics and flight reduced the number of local natives who might be captured or drafted. Attempts to recruit mission workers reached from the local Tarahumara to Yaqui Sonora and New Mexico. Experimental adaptations ruled, while disease devastated natives. Tarahumaras and others went to missions for food in times of drought, for protection against native foes, and for help in resisting the demands of miners and estate operators. They often left when difficulties passed, taking new skills in cultivation and stock grazing, cloth making, and Christian worship to lives of independence.

Through the second half of the seventeenth century slaves and their free mulatto offspring, migrant Mesoamericans, and people escaping missions all mixed at northern estates combining irrigated cropping and stock grazing. They forged ethnically diverse communities that consolidated as mining faded at Parral after 1680. Meanwhile a diverse religious culture emerged. In the 1660s many Tarahumara turned to Guadalupe, offered to them and so many others as a protector of indigenous peoples. In unsanctioned popular cultures Mesoamerican, mulatto, and locally native women and men swapped remedies and potions to fend off disease and assert power against patriarchs.[20] Spanish North America, founded in the Bajío and Zacatecas and then stretched toward New Mexico, redeveloped around Parral during the seventeenth century. Its silver drove New Spain's commercial economy. People came north, a few finding wealth and power, more forced to labor, most seeking a chance at better lives of work and worship. At the same time Atlantic migrations still brought diseases that inflicted death and depopulation rates nearing 90 percent on northern natives.[21] Seventeenth-century Parral and Santa Bárbara would be eerily familiar to any who knew the sixteenth-century history of the Bajío and Zacatecas.

In the 1680s northward expansion faced new challenges. As mining waned at Parral, New Mexican Pueblos allied with independent nomads—often former foes—to expel Hispanic officials, priests, traders, and settlers, killing many while asserting a revived indigenous culture infused with Christian elements. A few years later French interlopers landed on the Texas coast, offering natives trade and new alliances. The news passed quickly among independent peoples, reaching New Mexico and Parral, worrying Spaniards, perhaps inspiring natives. And as mining faded, as Pueblos rebelled, and as rumor of imperial challenges spread, many Tarahumara also turned to war in the 1680s. Like the Tepehuanes before, they were led by men who had tried Christianity and its commercial ways, and now fought for independence. They rejected Hispanic rule while they used chosen pieces of European culture—livestock, weapons, and Christian beliefs—to reject subordination and exploitation. They promoted martial patriarchy, insisting that men fight and not acquiesce like women. Men were not men, rebels insisted, if they lived with one wife in mission communities. Tarahumaras fought in waves: warring when Spaniards were vulnerable, retreating when struck by drought and smallpox, returning to fight when they could. In the 1690s Spaniards reasserted rule among Tarahumaras and New Mexico's Pueblos as the Europeans and their often mixed dependents gained enough indigenous allies to press rebels to new dependence at missions, pueblos, and estate communities. The alternative was flight to isolated retreats, engaging commercial and Christian ways without living subject to them.[22]

Toward the end of the seventeenth century, what began in the Bajío and at Zacatecas had been replicated across regions far to the north. As mining waned at Parral and flight and disease left few independent natives, the Santa Bárbara countryside was a place of landed estates. Communities mixed families of diverse ancestry, many called mulatto. Men gained access to land, salaries, advances of cloth (accounted in money against their salaries), and grain rations. Missions struggled; people of mixed ancestry often became majorities there too. A few independent natives held out in isolated uplands, visiting missions and working seasonally at estates. During a late-century recession in the silver economy, landlords, estate communities, and missions changed to survive. When mining surged again after 1700 at Santa Eulalia, farther north near Chihuahua on the road to New Mexico, Santa Bárbara reenergized to supply a resurgent commercial economy.[23]

The North in the Bajío: Guanajuato and the Uplands

While commercial ways and frontier conflicts drove northward, a new North consolidated in the Bajío. It focused on mining at Guanajuato and grazing across upland basins from San Miguel to San Felipe to León. Through the seventeenth century Guanajuato was a secondary mining center, an unsettled place of limited changes. Yet a few men took wealth and built landed patrimonies. Their mining and grazing enterprises forged a Bajío North beyond the zones of indigenous settlement and irrigated cultivation that shaped the region along the Mesoamerican frontier from Querétaro to Yuriria. Across that new North ethnic diversity, amalgamation, and new identities shaped mining and grazing communities.

From the 1550s a district magistrate promoted mining and collected revenues at Guanajuato; no council organized local rule through the first half of the seventeenth century. A parish priest ministered from the chapel of the Tarascan hospital. The dreams and risks of mining and the comings and goings of workers created a community of insecurity. In 1585 the first Jesuit to preach there reported that "greed rules these mines; the people live freely in licentious sin."[24] The next century brought constant calls for a Jesuit presence to settle the rau-

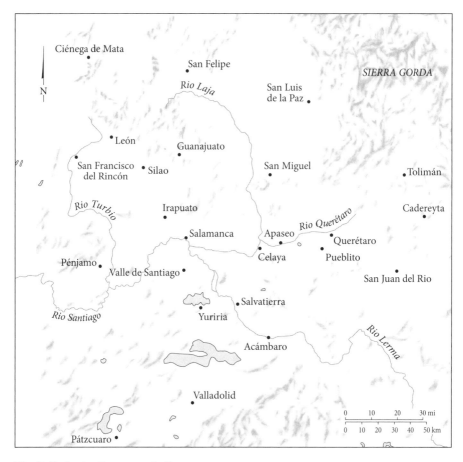

The Bajío in the Seventeenth Century

cous community.[25] But the regime funded missions to pacify indigenous peoples, not mineworkers, and no donor found resources to endow a Jesuit college at Guanajuato.

During the first quarter of the seventeenth century, while mining flourished at Zacatecas (which had a Spanish council and a Jesuit college) and while Querétaro (with an Otomí council and a Jesuit college) boomed as a center of trade, textiles, and cultivation, Guanajuato lived times of uncertainty. Entrepreneurs were often officials tied to merchants, administrators, and judges in Mexico City. If the sixteenth century was a time of warrior-entrepreneurs in New Spain's north, the early seventeenth brought an era of official-entrepreneurs. As Chichimeca wars gave way to regime consolidation, men who linked entrepreneurship, administration, and justice were strategically placed to weather the negotiations essential to power and profit. Their chal-

San Juan de Rayas mine, Guanajuato, seventeenth century; church of Mellado mine in background, eighteenth century.

lenge, as disease drove Mesoamerican populations toward their lowest levels, was to recruit and hold workers sufficient to the hard and often deadly labor of mining and refining silver.

As the new century began, Pedro de Busto and his partner Diego de Burgos led mining at Guanajuato. They traded together, importing iron and wine—one a necessity of mining, the other a salve for hard labor and reward for small bonanzas. They operated two of eight *haciendas de beneficio*, refining mills that were also residential compounds for workers. Another was run by Francisco de Velasco; had another kinsman of the Viceroys Velasco, father and son, found a way into rich business? Busto, Burgos, Velasco, and others paid men in their cuadrillas with ore shares and salaries. Living in refinery compounds, workers were dependent partners in a risky business. Among the early entrepreneurs Busto, a Spanish immigrant, founded a family that navigated the seventeenth century and profited enough after 1700 to claim titled distinction.[26]

After 1610 a new generation of entrepreneurs focused on the extended Altamirano family. From 1611 to 1617 Doctor don Hernán Carrillo Altamirano, a lawyer before the Mexico City High Court, claimed vast lands around León, west of Guanajuato; between 1617 and 1625 don Juan Altamirano gained more. Meanwhile the district magistrate don

Pedro Lorenzo de Castillo acquired additional lands in the western Bajío, later bought by don Rodrigo Mejía Altamirano. In the 1620s Carrillo Altamirano held key roles in Mexico City. He led militia troops that quelled food riots in 1624; he conspired to oust Viceroy Marqués de Gelves. He traveled to Spain and published a tract insisting that the protection of natives required limits on district magistrates and labor drafts—leaving workers to deal directly with employers. In 1631 Carillo Altamirano was back in Guanajuato serving as royal treasurer; his Altamirano and Mejía kin operated mines and refineries in Guana-juato and Marfil along with rural properties at nearby Silao, León just west, and San Miguel to the east. Combining office and entrepreneur-ship, local influence and imperial politics, the Altamiranos accumu-lated power at Guanajuato.[27] When the bishop of Michoacán visited in 1631, they were the most powerful men in a canyon community of many mines, twelve refineries, and eight hundred communicants in-cluding Europeans, mulattoes, and Mesoamericans.[28]

The first decades of the seventeenth century were times of strong de-mand for silver, creating entrepreneurial opportunity limited by labor scarcity. The ability to recruit and keep cuadrillas was as important as regime connections in building power at Guanajuato. Parish regis-ters recorded births, marriages, and deaths by cuadrilla. Before 1625 twenty-two cuadrillas registered at least thirty people each. Four with more than two hundred registrants accounted for 36 percent of the community; eleven with more than a hundred accounted for 64 per-cent. One clan wielded enormous labor power. Don Juan Mejía Alta-mirano led the largest cuadrilla with nearly five hundred workers; together four Altamiranos ruled a quarter of the working community at Guanajuato.[29]

After 1625 the parish identified people less as members of cuadri-llas, more as residents of refinery compounds. Were working commu-nities becoming more tied to places of residence? The second quarter of the century also brought a limited dispersal of power among min-ing entrepreneurs. Four refineries registering over two hundred resi-dents still included almost 35 percent of the total, but the seven with over a hundred people included only 45 percent. Working communities were smaller and entrepreneurial leadership dispersed, but the Mejía-Altamirano clan retained five refineries registering 250 dependents. More powerful after 1625 were don Damián de Villavicencio, whose one property registered 340 people; the Ahedo clan, with three hacien-das and 596 registrants; and resurgent Bustos whose four properties registered 635. Half the people listed in Guanajuato parish records in the second quarter of the century lived at compounds ruled by four entrepreneurial clans.[30]

From 1600 to 1650 the majority of the workers at Guanajuato were Mesoamericans. The disruptions of depopulation and disputes over land and labor in home communities led them to move north to try life at Guanajuato. Before 1625 parish records there recorded a population nearly 40 percent Tarascan, almost 30 percent Otomí, and over 15 percent Mexica. Nearly 85 percent of the community kept Mesoamerican ethnic identities; 12 percent reported African origins, of whom 3.7 percent were enslaved negros and 8.5 percent free mulattoes. Only 1 percent was mestizo and fewer claimed Spanish status.[31] Early in the seventeenth century Guanajuato had a powerful but limited Spanish presence, a small African population, and a large Mesoamerican majority.

During the fifteen years after 1625 the population recorded as Mesoamerican fell: Tarascans to 25 percent, Otomí to 20 percent, Mexicas to less than 15. The Mesoamerican total dropped from 85 to 60 percent. Meanwhile an influx of slaves drove the population of African ancestry toward 20 percent while mestizos approached 8 percent. Spaniards finally exceeded 1 percent. Increasing slave numbers suggest mining prosperity; the reduction of Mesoamerican migrants perhaps reflected a stabilization of home communities as population hit historic lows around 1625. At Guanajuato growing numbers of free mulattoes (10.4 percent), mestizos (7.8 percent), and people without designation (5.7 percent) suggest that slaves found ways to freedom, diverse people mixed, and many grappled with uncertain identities.

The new trends continued through the 1640s and into the 1650s. The proportion of Tarascans fell to 20 percent and of Otomí to 18, while Mexicas held steady just under 15 percent—leaving Mesoamericans a bare majority at mid-century. Fewer slaves arrived while many found freedom: free mulattoes approached 15 percent of Guanajuato's population around mid-century; negros and mulattoes, slave and free, combined to total 18 percent. Mestizos held at 8 percent. And suddenly nearly 14 percent claimed Spanish status.[32] It is possible that prosperity brought a flood of Spanish immigrants. But more likely, prosperous mestizos and mulattoes took Spanish status while Mesoamericans and Africans mixed to become mulattoes.

In 1650 the Spanish elite of Guanajuato finally gained a city charter and a council to represent its interests. Yet as mining weakened after 1640, entrepreneurial families took divergent paths. The Altamiranos had accumulated vast lands across the uplands from San Miguel to León. The properties concentrated in the inheritance of doña Juana Altamirano y Mejía, who married don Carlos de Luna y Arellano, a Spaniard already titled and landed as Mariscal de Castilla, serving as Corregidor (colonial magistrate) in Mexico City. The couple fused title and properties in a patrimony that lived to the end of the colonial era. They left mining to live by the less spectacular but more secure profits of their estates. In the late seventeenth century they grazed great herds of sheep and cattle while a few tenants cultivated.[33] In contrast, the Ahedos worked the Rayas mine through the middle decades of the seventeenth century and then faded from the records. Another don Damián de Villavicencio sat on the Guanajuato council in the 1690s; then his lineage lost eminence. The Busto clan continued in mining. Busto men held office and militia commands in the 1690s, and when mining boomed again after 1700 they profited enough to gain title as Marqués de San Clemente.[34]

After 1650 there was also a radical shift in ethnic labeling at Guanajuato. Suddenly few were entered as Mesoamerican. From 1655 to 1669 parish registers listed less than 5 percent as Tarascan, less than 3 percent as Otomí, less than 4 percent as Mexica. Combined, only 12 percent were entered as Mesoamerican. Meanwhile the proportion of people registered as *indios ladinos*, of indigenous ancestry and speaking Spanish, rose from 6 percent before 1655 to nearly 40 percent after. Then in the 1670s and 1680s Mesoamericans fell to less than 4 percent while ladinos approached 50 percent. The number of slaves continued to fall, while free blacks and mulattoes rose to over 20 percent in the 1650s and 1660s and held over 18 percent into the 1680s. Mestizos rose from 8 percent into the 1660s to 12 percent in the 1670s and 1680s. Spaniards jumped to nearly 20 percent in the 1650s and 1660s—only to fall back to 14 percent in the 1670s and 1680s.

After 1650 Mesoamerican identities all but disappeared at Guanajuato. Many of Mesoamerican ancestry became hispanized indios. People marked by African ancestry held near 20 percent, while slavery all but vanished. A growing number asserted Spanish and mestizo status. Another shift began in the 1680s as mining began to revive. Migration brought Mesoamericans back to 8 percent while mestizos rose from 12 to 14 percent, unidentified people to over 8 percent, and Spaniards from 14 to nearly 20 percent; at the same time people of African ancestry held near 18 percent, and indios fell from 50 to just 30 percent.[35]

The people of Guanajuato lived dependent on mining and the powerful patriarchs who ruled nearly everything. A majority of diverse Mesoamerican ethnic and linguistic origins mixed with a large minority of African origin. Marriage records show that Spaniards were 98 percent endogamous. Did they avoid ethnic mixing—or use wealth to assert Spanish status, whatever their ancestry and whomever they married? Among Mesoamericans during the first half of the century Otomí were 93 percent endogamous, Tarascans 90 percent, the Mexica 81 percent—fewer and farther from home, they mixed more. Negros were only 61 percent endogamous; they knew that an indigenous wife was free, as were her children. Mulattoes were 84 percent endogamous. During the second half of the century a growing number of mestizos appear to have been 91 percent endogamous, while those defined as indios ladinos were 95 percent endogamous.[36] But endogamy is an elusive concept among people defined by mixing and new identities. Over the century the working majority at Guanajuato became hispanized, spoke Spanish, and lived in a commercial world. People claimed and debated diverse identities. Spaniard, indio, mestizo, and mulatto were all colonial creations, not ancestral ethnicities. Accelerating amalgamations and changing identities defined seventeenth-century Guanajuato.

It remained an unsettled mining town in a mountain canyon. A report on religious institutions in 1657 documented that sodalities dedicated to Nuestra Señora del Rosario (or de Guanajuato) and other devotions of aid and comfort earned over 13,000 pesos yearly; four hospitals earned over 4,000 pesos yearly. Meanwhile, sacramental worship earned 11,500 pesos, prayers for souls in purgatory 2,700. At Guanajuato, with profits always uncertain and labor laden with danger, even the rich dedicated their money to devotions promising help with the tribulations of daily life.[37]

Still, social stability proved elusive. In the 1670s the city of dreams and insecurities saw pitched battles between cuadrillas of mineworkers, mobilized by captains who served leading entrepreneurs (similar to combats reported earlier at Zacatecas). Perhaps they were promoted by powerful men looking for an edge over rivals in difficult times; perhaps they were driven by working men seeking gain and a release of frustrations when work was scarce. In 1676 the Jesuit José Vidal offered a three-week mission to settle and convert contentious and often violent crowds. He reported: "These riots are occasions of disgraceful hurt; three or four thousand people fight with brazen barbarity, each trying to kill as many of the other side as they can." He preached penance and forgiveness; the first night of his mission ended with mass flagellations. There was "such a disordered mass of people in the streets it looked like judgement day; nothing was heard but voices asking pardon." During the weeks that followed, Vidal drew indios and mulattoes, pickmen and haulers, to penance and reconciliation. At the end he counted 2,500 taking communion—many fewer than had joined earlier battles. For a moment, though, the mission turned mineworkers from battle to flagellation, penance, and communion.[38] It is doubtful that peace and devotion endured.

In the 1690s Guanajuato remained a place of promise and risk. In

1691 the need to honor the marriage of Carlos II, Spain's last Hapsburg, called for contributions from the local elite. The council, militia officers, and treasury officials, institutionally and individually (including don Damián de Villavicencio and two captains Bustos, don
Francisco and don Nicolás), contributed a total of 820 pesos. A small
clique of patriarchs who continued to mix office, command, and entrepreneurship provided over half the 1,570 pesos collected. They likely
concentrated a similar portion of Guanajuato's wealth. Another eight
men contributed as mine operators: the Franciscan who managed the
Rayas mines after the order took them for debts gave 100 pesos; seven
others paid only 10 pesos each. Mining without backing in office and
command seems less than profitable. Over thirty merchants paid from
2 to 30 pesos, an average of 12 each. None was rich. The exception
seems Francisco Martín, the one merchant classed as indio. He gave
50 pesos—the same as leading Spanish councilmen. The name Martín
hints at roots in Querétaro's Otomí elite; his prosperity suggests that in
a community of many indios ladinos, a merchant indio found advantage. Last on the list came don Antonio de Sardaneta who gave 4 pesos;
his future riches could not be imagined in that small gift.[39]

There was no great wealth in Guanajuato as the seventeenth century
ended. The city in the canyon remained a place of unmet prospects,
hard labor, and ethnic fluidity. But its mines had stimulated settlement across the rural Bajío. From the 1550s through the 1640s, during
the Chichimeca wars and after, towns developed in a ring surrounding the mining city. To the south Querétaro, Celaya, and Yuriria mixed
Hispanic and indigenous settlers who provided sustenance to Zacatecas and strength against Chichimecas. East, north, and west of Guanajuato, San Miguel, San Felipe, and León began as fortresses against
Chichimecas and became sites of mixed settlement and estate development after the war.[40]

Beyond the commotion of Guanajuato, towns like San Miguel and
León remained small, home to local landholders, artisans, and diverse cultivators. Spanish councils ran local affairs. There were no indigenous republics, no community lands at San Miguel or San Felipe,
though a few men spoke as indigenous officials, apparently accepted
by all as useful intermediaries. There were landed republics at León,
but they lived in the shadow of the Hispanic town and surrounded by
estate communities. Across the northern Bajío countryside, sparse and
slowly growing populations lived as estate dependents, mixing people
of every ancestry, most serving as herdsmen and small tenants.

There were thirty-six Spanish households at San Miguel in 1619 and
sixty-two in 1639, suggesting a Hispanic population growing from
about two hundred to over three hundred. Most lived in town, joined

by a few indigenous families and a growing number of mestizos, African slaves, and free mulattoes. North, east, and south of town nearly fifty estates mostly grazed livestock in 1631. A bishops' census reported estate communities of Africans, Mesoamericans, and their mixed offspring but left them uncounted. A report in 1639 indicated two thousand rural residents around San Miguel, about thirty-five per estate, perhaps seven families each. Puerto de Nieto, owned in the 1630s by the heirs of Juan Caballero, raised maize and cattle. In 1649 a parish survey estimated San Miguel's parish at 2,500 communicants; total population exceeded 3,000, mostly Otomí and Mexica, mulattoes, and a few mestizos at sixty-two rural estates.[41]

Across rolling uplands from San Miguel through San Felipe to León and reaching north toward Zacatecas, the second half of the seventeenth century brought both a concentration and a dispersal of landholdings. The Mariscales de Castillo accumulated multiple patrimonies by strategic marriages, assembling vast estates that dominated the countryside north of San Miguel. Similar unions built the Rincón Gallardo's Ciénega de Mata holdings that began around San Felipe, extended through Lagos, and reached toward Aguascalientes. Other families faced dispersed inheritances and economic challenges and saw their holdings divide. As a result the Mariscales and the Rincón Gallardos shared the northern countryside with modest estates held by professionals (often lawyers and bureaucrats) and clergy (often parish priests). In decades of fluctuating silver production, estate operators large and small usually left cultivation to tenants and focused commercial operations on stock grazing, using herdsmen of African ancestry, some still slaves and many others free.

Landlords aiming to organize and sustain their estate residents' dependence built chapels and paid priests to serve growing communities; churches at the Rincón Gallardos' Ciénega de Mata and the Mariscales' La Erre gained designation as extensions of parishes at Lagos and San Miguel. La Erre's registers recorded many marriages between mulattoes and indios ladinos. They also showed large numbers of Otomí marrying Otomí, as migrants continued to arrive from Querétaro farther south. Newcomers reinforced Otomí language, identity, and endogamy, and kept alive knowledge of the rights of people classed as indios. Some used that knowledge to seek independence. In the 1680s a group of Otomí on estate lands near Santa María del Río, between San Miguel and San Luis Potosí, mixed established residents and recent migrants. They went to court seeking land, a church, and a council—rights as an indigenous republic. After a long suit and difficult negotiations they became the community of San Nicolás de Tierranueva in 1712. Around 1690 seven hundred men living on and near the

Mariscales' estates north of San Miguel announced themselves as indio (Otomí, ladino, or both) and also sued for republican rights. Facing a more powerful landlord, they failed.[42]

Across the northern Bajío countryside estate communities ruled. Amalgamations accelerated, while migration kept Otomí identity alive. Some residents sought independence as indigenous republics; a few succeeded. Most adapted to life as estate dependents. Around 1700 most northerners in the Bajío and beyond lived in estate communities where tenants raised grains and herdsmen produced livestock products for mines and nearby towns. When mining surged again after 1700, estates from Guanajuato to Chihuahua reenergized as commercial enterprises.

New Communities on the Bottomlands

Very different rural communities developed during the seventeenth century on the bottomlands south of Guanajuato and west of Querétaro. Along the rivers that defined the basin, rich soils were open to irrigation. The demand generated by the mines at Guanajuato and Zacatecas encouraged settlement there during boom times and long after. Profit-seeking entrepreneurs ruled estate development; settlements again mixed diverse Mesoamericans with minorities of African ancestry. The bottomlands were like Querétaro in their focus on irrigated cultivation and dense rural settlement; they were like the new North in the primacy of Spanish power, the dearth of native republics, and the acceleration of ethnic mixing.

Celaya was the first Spanish irrigation community on the bottomlands. Chartered in 1570 amid Chichimeca wars, the town sat near the junction of the rivers arriving from San Miguel to the north and Querétaro to the east, on their way to join the Lerma flowing west. Settlers gained town lots and plots of land *(caballerías)* of 40 hectares subject to irrigation. Dams, diversions, and canals were built by indigenous workers drafted from Acámbaro to the south, and from small communities set around the new town. Celaya raised growing wheat harvests during the Chichimeca conflicts and long after.[43]

After pacification, with silver strong at Zacatecas, continuing at Guanajuato, and later booming at Parral, demand for Bajío wheat grew. In 1602 Salamanca was chartered as a Spanish town on the north bank of the Lerma, at its northmost thrust into the Bajío before it turns west toward the Pacific. The goal was to develop irrigated wheat farms along the river and on plains south of the new settlement—including the rich Valle de Santiago. The next half-century brought expanding irrigation and new Spanish towns: Salvatierra southeast of Salamanca in 1644; Valle de Santiago on the plain across the Lerma in 1649.

These basin lands, just north of the Agustinians' San Nicolás estate and the Tarascan community at Yuriria, were earlier used as grazing sites. As demand for wheat increased, Spanish cultivators built towns and irrigated fields, drawing workers and tenants from Mesoamerican communities to the south. Demand at Zacatecas drove the expansion of cultivation through the 1630s; the shift of mining to Parral continued it.[44] Later, mining revived at Zacatecas in the 1660s, and there and at Sombrerete in the 1680s. Demand for Bajío wheat persisted with peaks and troughs.[45] Through the century Salamanca, Salvatierra, and Valle de Santiago became cultivating communities ruled by Hispanic entrepreneurs, worked by people of Mesoamerican and African ancestry, and integrated by patriarchy.

An Entrepreneurial Patriarch—and Patriarchal Production

Don Diego de la Cruz Saravia was one of the most successful entrepreneurs at Valle de Santiago. After his death in 1669 an inventory detailed his properties, his wealth, his commercial orientation, and the social relations that generated profit at his diverse holdings. He was almost certainly the son of Diego de la Cruz, who in 1631 lived at Salamanca and operated three farms harvesting sixteen hundred *cargas* of wheat on fields across the Lerma.[46] By the 1660s don Diego de la Cruz Saravia lived with his wife, doña Ynés Luisa de Vergara y Moncayo, and two minor children, don Manuel and doña María de Saravia y Vergara, in a great stone house in the center of Celaya with three patios and nineteen rooms.[47]

Ten slaves of African ancestry served the household: two aging men and another near his working prime; two elderly women plus one forty and ill; and the mulatta Ana, thirty-six, with three sons. Richly housed and served by slaves, the de la Cruz Saravias enjoyed the trappings of wealth. The inventory included a gold necklace inlaid with emeralds, valued at nearly 1,200 pesos; four gowns embroidered with gold and silver, together valued at 480 pesos; two pairs of diamond earrings valued at 86 pesos; and a string of pearls valued at 60 pesos. The luxuries that advertised wealth and power in the Bajío came from Europe, the Americas, and Asia. All the gowns and jewels were accounted the patriarch's property. Surely doña Luisa wore them, often while riding in an elegant carriage valued at 300 pesos. The Celaya home, slaves, and luxuries (plus town lands held for speculation or future development) were valued at nearly 12,000 pesos, almost 20 percent of an estate totaling 58,427 pesos.[48]

The great house, slaves, jewels, silver, gowns, and carriage combined with the titles of don and doña to announce aristocracy. Yet the ornaments of power were but a preface to an inventory documenting that aristocratic sheen came from entrepreneurship in a commercial economy. After the house, the slaves, and the rich personal items came a list of fifty-eight documents titling lands, water rights, obraje sites, and livestock brands. Another six bundles of papers detailed land disputes adjudicated in court. Any notion that the viceregal regime did not document land rights, or that entrepreneurs were inattentive to property titles, vanishes in the encounter with the de la Cruz inventory.[49]

De la Cruz Saravia's properties included irrigated wheat farms, maize fields relying on rainfall, grazing sites, and lands awaiting development. Their values reflected commercial potential. Eleven caballerías of irrigated wheat fields averaged 2,000 pesos each, 22,000 pesos in total—half of productive property, a third of the estate. A caballería of scrub not open to irrigation was worth 75 pesos and used to pasture oxen. Between the extremes, a caballería of land without irrigation and sown in maize was worth 400 to 500 pesos. Investment in irrigation, an allocation of labor that allowed wheat production, maximized land value.[50]

The enterprise was profitable. Don Diego ran the wheat farms with salaried workers. He leased maize lands to indigenous tenants and commercial growers, who often sublet to indigenous tenants. Most pastures and livestock were leased. His earnings from marketed crops and rents, minus costs of management and labor, were 7.5 percent of the value of his productive properties. He charged rents to commercial tenants at the same rate. Annual profits of 7 to 8 percent on productive capital supported an elegant urban lifestyle for the patriarch and his family.[51]

Don Diego organized production in diverse ways. He employed dependent laborers in wheat fields, paying salaries plus maize rations of about 12 fanegas yearly, just enough to feed a family. The inventory lists nine employees as *sirvientes*, each owed by the estate an average of 12 pesos, 5 reales (1 peso equals 8 reales). A larger group of 16, called indios, owed an average of 26 pesos, 7 reales, to the estate. The custom of recruiting workers with salary advances remained. Some worked off their debts and remained at work awaiting new payments; others retained debts and obligations to labor.[52] Another twenty-one men labored at de la Cruz Saravia's maize farms and grazing lands. Seven faced obligations totaling 34 pesos, less than five pesos each;

fourteen others awaited payment of 212 pesos, about 15 pesos each.[53] De la Cruz Saravia had to attract workers to wheat farms with large advances and maize rations. The men who raised maize and cared for livestock were less heavily obligated, their debts few and small. They lived among forty-five tenant families, cultivating crops and keeping gardens while working seasonally in estate fields. Advances and obligations were less needed where access to land complemented labor.

Among forty-five tenants, six were opening new fields and were charged no rents. Most others paid 11 to 30 pesos, indicating holdings sufficient to sustain a family and perhaps market a small surplus. The rentals brought income to de la Cruz Saravia, and kept on his properties a growing population of families cultivating to sustain themselves and available to work seasonally in estate fields. Offering undeveloped lands at no charge brought settlers, expanded the pool of seasonal hands, and opened new fields at no cost to the entrepreneur. Aiming to expand production and recruit workers, don Diego negotiated rent collections. Among thirty-nine tenants owing 740 pesos yearly, nineteen fell short by a total of 70 pesos in 1669. The entrepreneur absorbed the shortfall, held his tenants, kept his labor force, and profited.[54]

He also leased lands to commercial tenants, again negotiating to promote estate development. The largest leasehold, worth nearly 1,750 pesos, brought 250 pesos annual rent: 100 pesos in cash, 150 in contracted improvements. The cash rent was low, less than 6 percent of value. The projected rent was high, over 14 percent, reflecting the value to be added by improvements. The next-largest holding, worth 1,200 pesos, paid only 40 pesos—another low rent promoting development. Most leaseholds were valued from 250 to 700 pesos, with rents calculated at 7.5 percent of value. Indigenous subtenants, *terrazgueros*, worked most commercial leaseholds. There were thirty-six such households at Ajolote, six at Sotelillos, and four at San Agustín del Sauce. Elsewhere the inventory noted uncounted *jacales de indios*.[55] A hierarchy of Hispanic and indigenous employees, large and small tenants, and indigenous subtenants sustained commercial cultivation at de la Cruz Saravia's estates.

What these complex social relations of production shared was patriarchy. Among dependent laborers and tenants the more prosperous were Hispanic, the poorest mostly indigenous. All were men: every manager, every sirviente owed unpaid earnings, every indio indebted and obligated to work, every tenant, large and small. Saravia's exclusive allocation to men of roles in management, cultivation, and labor worked as a patriarchal chain tying producing households to commercial enterprises. If only men had access to the means of production and sustenance, women and children had no option but to live, work, and serve subject to dependent patriarchs. Wives and youths inevitably worked. Women kept gardens and yard animals; they made cloth and clothing; they did the endless work of grinding maize to make tortillas. Children also labored: boys assisting fathers in the fields, girls joining mothers in daily labors. But only family patriarchs (and youths soon to be patriarchs) gained advances, wages, and rations from the estate; only patriarchs could lease lands—commercial ranchos or subsistence plots. Working patriarchs depended on de la Cruz Saravia or his commercial tenants. By acquiescing in dependence, working men solidified patriarchal rule in producing households. Hierarchies of patriarchy embedded in commercial cultivation orchestrated production at don Diego de la Cruz Saravia's Valle de Santiago estates in the 1660s.

Patriarchal Communities on the Bottomlands

Social relations defined by patriarchy shaped life across the bottomlands. Parish censuses from 1683 detail family organization at Salamanca, Salvatierra, and Valle de Santiago, all seventeenth-century foundations that became irrigation settlements divided between town-dwelling Hispanic elites and cultivating communities of indios on estate lands. A few African slaves and free mulattoes were noted, along with fewer mestizos. Attention to ethnic labels was limited. In contrast, clerical enumerators carefully recorded gender and marital status. Male heads of household focused the listings; wives followed, with the possessive notation "su mujer"—his woman. Children old enough to confess, and to work (usually at seven), were identified by sex, as were widows and widowers. As the seventeenth century neared its end, patriarchy was the primary axis of social hierarchy on the bottomlands; ethnic identities seem to have been secondary, uncertain, and changing.[56]

Salamanca was the oldest of the three parishes, founded in 1602. In the following decades its residents gained fifty-seven land grants, thirty-one subject to irrigation. Some built estates across the Lerma on the plain called Valle de Santiago. In 1649 a town of that name was chartered near lands in rapid development. Many left Salamanca for the new town. Working families left behind petitioned to found the indigenous community of Santa María Nativitas; in 1655 they won lands vacated by those who left.[57] Salamanca and Valle de Santiago were closely linked in the 1680s. Kinship integrated leading families; Salamanca entrepreneurs held land at Valle de Santiago; parallel social relations shaped both parishes.

In town at Salamanca men headed 80 percent of thirty-two Hispanic households, averaging over seven residents each. Six residences led by women averaged only four persons. Thus nearly 90 percent of the town's Hispanic population lived under patriarchal rule. The Salamanca census also listed forty-five Hispanic households living at rural farms or ranchos. Over 90 percent were patriarchal, and thanks to a few very large households they averaged more than eight residents. At the new town of Valle de Santiago patriarchs also led 80 percent of Hispanic households. They ruled families distinctly smaller than those at Salamanca, averaging fewer than four residents in the recently settled community. Nevertheless, patriarchy defined life in Spanish households at both Salamanca and Valle de Santiago.[58]

There were four small indigenous republics around Salamanca. Newly settled Santa María Nativitas had fifty households with ninety-five residents old enough to confess; 95 percent of households were patriarchal, usually consisting of a young man and his wife (and perhaps small children). Across the four communities households averaged 2.6 residents: a patriarch, his wife, and less than one child old enough to confess. In total, communities provided lands and self-rule to only 128 small indigenous families near Salamanca.[59]

The majority of indigenous families at Salamanca and all at Valle de Santiago lived on farms and ranches. There were fifty properties around the older settlement at Salamanca, twenty-nine near Valle de Santiago. The share of patriarchal households approached 95 percent and households remained small, averaging only 2.5 residents. Most estate communities were small, with ten or fewer households. But Valle de Santiago had a few properties with larger settlements; a majority of rural families there lived at nine estates with ten to thirty-three households.[60] Patriarchal Hispanic families lived by the labor of patriarchal indigenous families: at Salamanca 349 small indigenous households sustained 81 large Hispanic households; at Valle de Santiago 287 small indigenous households sustained 111 small Hispanic households.

Of course everyday social relations were more complex than census averages. Not every patriarch profiting from rural production in the area around Salamanca and Valle de Santiago lived there. In 1631 Diego de la Cruz lived at Salamanca and operated three farms across the Lerma. When his son don Diego de la Cruz Saravia expanded those holdings to become a leading entrepreneur, he took his family to Celaya. In the 1680s Licenciado don Nicolás de Caballero y Ocío, a leading estate operater at Valle de Santiago, was served by seventeen households and fifty-two people. He was part of a Querétaro clan with great properties at San Miguel and elsewhere. Capitán don Joseph Merino y Arellano was the richest entrepreneur in the bottomlands;

he lived at Valle de Santiago, sustained by estates worked by twenty-eight patriarchal households with seventy-one residents.[61]

A core of leading families linked the Hispanic communities at Salamanca and Valle de Santiago. Joseph Lisarraras was alcalde ordinario (Spanish magistrate) at Salamanca in 1683; a widower, he ruled a household of five dependents (including three doñas named Lisarraras), supported by a rancho with five working households.[62] Nicolás Lisarraras sat on the Valle de Santiago council; Domingo Lisarraras and doña Tomasa Lisarraras, wife of don Juan de Cisneros, lived nearby, sustained by lands near the de la Cruz Saravia holdings.[63] The Pérez de Hoyos and Pérez de Santoyo clan was larger, more complex, and linked to the Lisarraras. Bachiller Domingo Pérez de Hoyos was pastor at Salamanca in 1683. Nearby lived another Domingo Pérez de Hoyos, probably his father, and Juan Pérez Quintana de Hoyos, a brother or cousin. Their three households totaled twenty-one residents. Nearby the widow doña María Pérez de Santoyo led a household of six, including her son Manuel and his wife doña Isabel de Lisarraras. Pablo de Santoyo led a household of five, also nearby.[64] Outside town Lázaro Pérez de Santoyo lived at a rancho, ruling a household of ten plus two working families. He also ran the Rancho de Valtierra, worked by three dependent households. At another Salamanca rancho Alonso Pérez de Santoyo led a household of six, supported by six working families. Nearby the widow Juana de Santoyo headed a household of two daughters and three sons, all Pérez de Santoyo, served by four patriarchal families.[65]

Santoyos also joined the move to Valle de Santiago. There Diego Pérez de Santoyo led a household of four near Juan Andrés Santoyo, recently married and living with his wife. Mariana and Leonor de Santoyo were widows, each with two Santoyo sons. Another Mariana de Santoyo lived at the farm of her husband, Nicolás Fernández Aguado, worked by five dependent households.[66] The Lissarras, Pérez de Hoyos, and Pérez de Santoyos and their kin formed an extended Hispanic clan linking Salamanca and Valle de Santiago; all lived by the work of dependent, patriarchal, mostly indigenous households.

In 1644 the Viceroy Conde de Salvatierra chartered a new town on the north side of the Lerma between Acámbaro and Salamanca, near two small indigenous communities. The charter gave a Spanish Council, house lots, and lands for irrigated cultivation in exchange for 24,000 pesos. The viceroy saw a fine future, thanks to "lands fertilized by a great river that passes through and yielding every crop; the result will be great benefit to the common good, growth of royal revenues, and relief for every need in times of dearth."[67] By 1683 Salvatierra was a place of Spanish estate operators and dependent indigenous families. Hispanic households averaged five residents. Women led a third of those households, significantly more than the 20 percent at Salamanca and Valle de Santiago.[68]

The two indigenous republics at Salvatierra were small, with only 291 communicants. Their households were 95 percent patriarchal and averaged 2.5 residents, parallel to the communities near Salamanca and Valle de Santiago. The rural majority at Salvatierra lived at 32 grain farms with 371 overwhelmingly patriarchal households and 751 residents. Most settlements were small, but over 60 percent of the rural population lived at eight larger properties with more than ten households, including one with eighty-one.

The Salvatierra census emphasizes the link between town eminence and rural property. Don Juan Gerónimo de Sámano led a household of ten, supported by two estates worked by thirty-three patriarchs with young families. Less exalted and more typical were Miguel de Altamirano, don Alonso de Carbajal, and don Diego de Soto. Each ruled a town household of five to seven while operating farms worked by three to five young patriarchs with small families. There were variations: one town patriarch surely struggled to sustain a household of fourteen on the production of four rural laboring patriarchs; a landed family of three lived more comfortably by the work of six households. Francisco Baez employed four patriarchs at a brickworks to support his family of five.[69] At Salvatierra as at Salamanca and Valle de Santiago, small indigenous families worked to sustain larger Spanish households.

At Salvatierra, however, women headed a large minority of Hispanic households. It is uncertain whether life was less patriarchal. Independence was not automatic even when women held property. Doña Thomasa de Sedeño inherited the Labor de Sedeño, but her husband don Joseph Orosco ran the farm. Ownership of the rich Ortíz properties is equally uncertain. Did María Ortíz, who headed a household of five, all women, operate the three farms worked by thirty-three patriarchs and their families? She had no husband and is not listed as a widow. Had she inherited estates, avoided marriage, and become a rural entrepreneur?[70] Or did the estates belong to doña María Ortíz de Covarrubías, married and a dependent in her husband's household?[71]

The Medrano and the Sandi clans reveal clearer and more common situations. They were extended families in which women headed separate households—in the orbit of male kin. In 1683 Bachiller Juan de Medrano was the priest at Salvatierra. Nicolás, Pedro, and Antonia de Medrano each led a nearby household of four to six, all sustained by the Labor de Medrano, worked by ten dependent patriarchs. Pedro and Theresa Sandi each headed households of eight; the family operated two ranchos with eight working families.[72] It is doubtful whether women heading households next to male kin could find real independence.

The women of the Ponce clan confirm that women-headed households often faced dependence, poverty, or both. Doña Gerónima and doña Antonia Ponce each led small households of women only. Neither operated a farm. Ysabel Ponce, no doña but with a dependent Hispanic man in her household, headed a more prosperous household of nine thanks to young Joseph Gutiérrez's economic efforts.[73] It seems that the greater number of women-headed households among Hispanic families at Salvatierra revealed a different way of organizing dependence. Patriarchy still ruled most extended families, even if some women headed separate households. Large Hispanic clans were still sustained by the work of numerous indigenous households. And notably, at Salvatierra as at Salamanca and Valle de Santiago, only men led the households of tenants and workers that produced the crops driving the commercial economy.

By the 1680s patriarchy orchestrated social hierarchies of production in Bajío basin communities. Patriarchy was strong among the prosperous; it was inevitable in the families of tenants and laborers at rural estates. The vagaries of marriage and inheritance allowed a few Spanish women to inherit land; some operated their estates directly. Still, they joined their male kin and neighbors in enforcing patriarchy as a necessary condition of life at rural estates. Only men rented land; only men gained advances, salaries, and rations. Landed men and a few women made patriarchy an inevitable way of life among the working majority.

Patriarchy also orchestrated life around León, northwest of the bottomlands, an area less irrigated and more devoted to grazing. Otomí families settled Rincón around 1600, winning a charter as a republic in 1607.[74] The 1683 census showed two-thirds of the Rincón parish living in communities. With indigenous families working lands gained by inheritance, patriarchy was less absolute: 90 rather than 95 percent. Households were larger, averaging three communicants. At fourteen ranchos, indio households averaged over four residents—again larger than at bottomlands estates. At Rincón in 1683 republican rights had advantages.[75]

In 1685 the León clergy completed a second, more complete census. They excluded the town of León and people classed as Spaniards. Otherwise they covered the jurisdiction, including Rincón and its countryside. This time they listed all residents, not just those who confessed. They distinguished native communities, indigenous families on estates, people of African ancestry, and mestizos. Across the jurisdiction nearly half of all indigenous residents lived in landed republics;

a bare majority lived at commercial properties. Nearly 95 percent of native households at communities and estates were patriarchal. But in communities households approached seven residents each; at estates they averaged only 3.5—parallel to those at basin estates (allowing for the inclusion of young children at León).

The large patriarchal households in León communities included many married sons living under fathers' rule. In 327 patriarchal residences, perhaps compounds rather than households, there were 113 dependent patriarchs. The average population per married patriarch was five—near norms at León estates and across the bottomlands. The large households at León communities document the independence of elder men and the dependence of many married sons. In twenty-three households led by women in León communities, eighteen included dependent patriarchs—young men waiting to claim patriarchy on the death of widowed mothers.[76] Why did so many married young men live in parents' households in communities around León?

They were waiting for land in growing communities with limited resources. The devastating post-contact epidemics were past. Tribute counts show indio populations tripling across the Bajío in the second half of the seventeenth century: from six hundred men in 1644 to two thousand in 1688 at Querétaro; in the Celaya jurisdiction, including the bottomlands, tributaries rose from 2,184 in 1657 to 6,149 in 1698.[77] Growing numbers pressed against limited resources in landed republics. Young men faced a choice. They could wait to inherit in their fathers' (or mothers') households. Or they could move to developing estates, rent land or take employment, and claim household patriarchy free of parental rule. At León, where estate development was limited, many stayed in communities, creating large extended households. Across the bottomlands, where communities were few and estates numerous, commercial growers drew indigenous youths to live and work as dependent patriarchs.

Men—mostly older, landed men—enjoyed preferences in indigenous communities. Men, only men, and usually young men newly married with small families found opportunity at basin estates. The chance to plant drew some to tenancies. Advances (perhaps to pay for a wedding, set up a household, or baptize a child), salaries, and maize rations drew many to labor. They would live as dependent patriarchs, working with wives and children to sustain themselves and generate profits for Hispanic entrepreneurs. Producing patriarchs gained household power while drawing wives and children into dependent labor relations. In estate communities across the Bajío, patriarchy cemented agrarian social relations—holding young, mostly indigenous families in laboring dependence at commercial estates.

Ethnic Adaptations: Spaniards, Indios, and the De la Cruz

With patriarchy the key axis of integration and exploitation in a commercial society, ethnic status remained important, uncertain, negotiated, open to change—and different in different areas of the Bajío. At Querétaro around 1600 diverse Mesoamerican migrants became an integrated underclass that remained Otomí in identity and language. The Otomí republic, Otomí huertas, and Otomí Virgin of Pueblito sustained a dual Spanish-Otomí society where the Bajío had begun on the frontier with Mesoamerica. Across the northern Bajío mining and grazing created communities of ethnic amalgamation. While the few claiming Spanish status ruled (and a slight indigenous majority persisted around León), in mining centers and at grazing estates Spaniards, mestizos, mulattoes, and indigenous peoples mixed in multicultural communities. The bishop of Michoacán visited Rincón in 1631 and lamented, "These *indios* come from all over; most are Otomí yet we attend to them in *mexicano*. In truth they understand little."[78] To the bishop, ethnic mixing and linguistic confusion made every Mesoamerican an indio. He reported similar confusion at Guanajuato, at nearby Santa Ana, and around San Miguel.[79] Some people did retain their native languages and identities. In 1671 an ecclesiastical visitor lamented the lack of clergy who could preach and minister in Otomí at estates north of San Miguel.[80]

The 1685 census of León distinguished 2,326 residents of indigenous republics from 277 mestizos, 724 blacks and mulattoes, and 2,417 indios at estates. Mestizos often worked small ranchos; their households averaged 4.4 residents. Families of African ancestry usually tended stock at grazing estates; they averaged 3.9 per household. The indigenous majority at León estates, mostly tenants and seasonal workers, lived in families averaging only 3.5 residents.[81] At estates around León ethnic distinctions still marked differing lives.

Across the bottomlands amalgamations were advancing in the 1680s. The families that ruled town life and rural estates claimed Spanish status. The rural majority, living in small households and raising the crops to sustain Hispanic families and the commercial economy, fell into a broad category of indios. Yet from the founding in 1649 of Valle de Santiago its baptismal registers documented that indio was a category of amalgamation. Early on the priest recorded indigenous parents and infants by ethno-linguistic group: 65 percent Otomí, 33 percent Tarascan, a few Mexicas, and diverse others. By 1655 ethnic labels were all but gone: nearly every rural resident was recorded as indio. The change happened simultaneously in urban Guanajuato. After a century of mixing in a commercial economy, Mesoamericans without republican rights were becoming indios.

A broader process of ethnic amalgamation was also under way. In baptisms recorded from 1649 to 1660 at Valle de Santiago, among 2,394 parents, godparents, and infants, nearly 80 percent were classed as indigenous (and increasingly as indio). Of the rest 9 percent were entered as Spanish, 8 percent as black or mulatto, 4 percent as mestizo—a total of 21 percent non-indigenous. The 1683 censuses reported a quarter of the population as Hispanic, most in town centers. Nearly everyone else was presumed into an indigenous majority. Few were noted as black or mulatto, fewer as mestizo. To the ecclesiastical census takers of the 1680s there were two categories in the bottomlands: Spanish and indio.

Ethnic reconstructions were everywhere, though the evidence is fragmentary. In the late 1650s a mother listed as india and a father recorded as negro baptized a son as indio; soon after, a negra gave birth to a son by an unknown father, the infant recorded as indio. The parents' goals seem clear; an indio child could not be a slave. Parents of African roots ensured children's freedom with indio status. At Valle de Santiago the priest apparently colluded, entering the parents' preferred category.[82]

Estimating the population of African ancestry in the basin communities is difficult; 9 percent of parents and infants noted in the Valle de Santiago baptismal registers in the 1650s were listed as black or mulatto. They outnumbered Spaniards and were twice as numerous as mestizos. People of African origin were 13 percent of the population in the 1685 León census, a count attentive to ethnic categories. They approached 20 percent in Guanajuato's baptismal registers in the same years. But the 1683 censuses of Salamanca, Valle de Santiago, and Salvatierra—careful to detail patriarchy—were lax about ethnic categories; mulattoes and mestizos were rarely noted.

The parish listings identified only forty-four people as slaves, blacks, or mulattoes and thus of African ancestry. A majority, mostly women, served in Hispanic town households: half slaves, half free. Among the eighteen in rural zones, fourteen were men, of whom eight were slaves and six free.[83] Nearly half of those listed as being of African origin served Gabriel de Valle Alvarado. He led a household of thirteen at Salamanca, including a wife and four kin served by seven women: six of African ancestry, five held as slaves. At his prosperous farm at Valle de Santiago, Valle Alvarado ruled twenty-seven resident workers: thirteen of African ancestry, including six slaves. A free mulatto and two black slaves had married free mulattas, ensuring free children. The estate community also included a mestizo and three indigenous households. Slavery kept people in dependent service—women in the town, men at rural estates. In Valle Alvarado's service people of African ancestry rarely married. When they did, they left free children.[84]

Nearby at Salamanca, Alonso de Zorita Valle, perhaps a relative, also preferred black and mulatto servants. His household of nine included his wife, doña Francisca Esquivel, and his mother, doña María del Valle. A staff of five included two blacks (one male and one female, both named Pérez) along with two mulattoes (a free single woman and a slave man, both named Valle). Valle may have fathered mulatto offspring and given them his name, keeping his son enslaved to ensure his service, freeing his daughter to liberate future generations. Whatever occurred in the household was sustained by the work of two patriarchal indigenous families at the Rancho de la Loma just outside town.[85]

Among those designated with African ancestry in the bottomlands censuses a quarter were named de la Cruz—of the Cross. People of European ancestry showed Spanish patronyms, from the exalted Altamirano to the more common Ortíz. Those of indigenous origin usually had two saints' names—Pedro Juan, Isabel María, etc. (gone were the indigenous patronyms still common at Querétaro around 1600). Yet a fourth of those of African ancestry, men and women, slave and free, had a saint's name followed by de la Cruz. Were slaves and illegitimate mulattoes baptized with reference to Christ's sacrifice as a call to his care? The surname de la Cruz serves as an indicator, imperfect but suggestive, of African ancestry.[86] There were 411 people named de la Cruz in the bottomlands censuses of 1683, 8 percent of a population of 4,939. People of African ancestry probably formed 10 to 20 percent of the basin population in the 1680s.

The roles of the de la Cruz are revealing. A few men and fewer women headed town households. At Salamanca, Miguel de la Cruz led a *casa y familia* that included his wife, Catalina Rodríguez, Joseph de la Cruz and his wife Dominga de la Cruz, Diego Rodríguez and his wife María de la Cruz, and Tomás Juan and his wife Juana de la Cruz. In a large town household the de la Cruz were marrying each other, the Rodríguez, and Tomás Juan—who had no surname and was likely indigenous. Without rural property we may imagine a household of mixed origins, perhaps artisans claiming Hispanic status.[87] Outside Valle de Santiago, Pedro Rico, unmarried, ruled a settlement called Puesto de Rico, or Rico's place. There fourteen patriarchal households included twenty-nine people, among them three married Rico patriarchs and five de la Cruz—a couple, a patriarch, and two wives.[88] It appears that Rico (who may also have been of African origin) let lands to diverse tenants in a community of amalgamation.

In the three Spanish towns six de la Cruz headed households, three men and three women. None were don or doña. In towns where Hispanic women led 10 to 30 percent of households, the de la Cruz women were overrepresented. All the de la Cruz town households remained small, an indication that a few de la Cruz of African ancestry were forming a subordinate segment of Hispanic society. Yet the two patriarchal de la Cruz households were large, one with seven members and the other with nine, the latter linked by marriage to the prosperous Ávilas and through them to the Guineas, whose very name told of African roots.[89] A few de la Cruz found prosperity in Hispanic towns. Still, over 80 percent of the urban de la Cruz were women in service. Their lives mirrored those of the few women listed as being of African ancestry, slave and free.[90]

Over half of the de la Cruz in the censuses lived at rural estates, 8 percent of the population there. They lived in communities that the census makers presumed indigenous: seventy-one de la Cruz men were listed as heads of indio households; eighty-eight de la Cruz women were wives in indio families. At bottomlands estate communities people of African ancestry joined families classed as indio.[91] Smaller numbers of de la Cruz lived in indigenous communities, forming 11 percent of their populations; sixteen community-based patriarchs were named de la Cruz; twenty-three de la Cruz women married indios in the same communities.[92] Even in indigenous republics, where indio status might be closely guarded (it brought rights to land and political participation), the de la Cruz found roles as patriarchs and indigenous patriarchs' wives.

The conclusion is unmistakable: the growing population classed as indio and organized in patriarchal households to sustain commercial production on the bottomlands included not only people of diverse Mesoamerican ancestry but significant numbers (surely 10 percent, perhaps 20) of descendants of African slaves. The indio population of the Bajío was an Atlantic amalgam, organized in patriarchal households living and working primarily at estate communities and in a few indigenous republics. The lives of the de la Cruz in 1683 suggest two ways of amalgamation. A minority found roles in Hispanic society, a few men as patriarchs of limited prosperity, more women as household servants. Most de la Cruz merged into the rural majority to become indio, joining the dependent patriarchal families that labored to sustain the bottomlands economy.

Could a patriarch of African ancestry aspire to more? The life of don Diego de la Cruz Saravia demands a second look. He was son of Diego de la Cruz, a prosperous farmer at Salamanca in 1631. Developing estates with great success, the son became don Diego, married the noble doña Luisa de Vergara y Moncayo, and moved to Celaya, where he built a great house, served by a staff of slaves. It bears asking whether don Diego was of African ancestry, like so many other de la Cruz; whether he moved to Celaya seeking distance from those who knew his origins; whether success allowed him to marry a woman of noble Spanish status. Don Diego's two children were don Manuel and doña María de Saravia y Vergara. They kept their father's Spanish matronym and their mother's noble patronym, rejecting de la Cruz, the mark of African origins. A man of apparent African ancestry could rise to great heights in the seventeenth-century Bajío. When he did, don Diego de la Cruz Saravia's children became Spaniards.

Asserting Difference

Across the bottomlands Spaniards and indios (both including people of African origin) shaped a society of two sectors integrated by patriarchy. Identities remained subject to change, challenge, and uncertainty. A few people, however, expressed notable differences with apparent pride. Near Salamanca the first settlement listed among the "settlements, lands, and farms of natives" was the casa y familia of don Bernabé Butanda. The don was a title only allowed to noble Spaniards and native lords; the name Butanda seems neither Spanish nor Mesoamerican. Yet here was a settlement of "natives" led by a noble. Did don Bernabé descend from a Chichimeca lord who had claimed land and local eminence during or after the sixteenth-century wars? He ruled a household of seven dependents, sustained by properties worked by twenty-seven dependents (including six named de la Cruz): eight patriarchal couples with eleven children. Was Butanda a native lord with commercial properties worked by families mixing indigenous and African ancestry? There was little to distinguish Butanda from a prosperous Spanish patriarch at Salamanca, except his assertion of indigenous nobility, leaving him outside the Spanish town in the 1680s.[93]

The Alcalad family at Valle de Santiago also kept a name that proclaimed difference. Sebastiana de Alcalad, a widow, led a household of five. Three daughters, all named Alcalad, lived with her, along with a son, Matías Cortés. Juana de Alcalad, probably a married daughter, lived nearby with her husband Felipe Jaimes. Felipe's kin Nicolás Jaimes headed another household of two. All lived near the Hispanic elite, yet among the less prosperous.[94] The name Alcalad proclaimed Moorish ancestry, which was not uncommon among migrants from Castile to New Spain. But one might ask why anyone would maintain an assertively Muslim name in a society in which all claimed Christianity and the Inquisition was active. The part of the answer we know is that the family consisted of an assertive woman and her daughters. One suspects a tale of origins, social insertion, and proud difference that would tell much, if only we knew.

Antonio de Guinea also stood out. Head of a family of seven at Salvatierra, he had a name that announced African origins. He led a large and prosperous household including three proud doñas: his wife doña Margarita Ortíz de Covarrubías, doña María Ortíz de Covarrubías, a daughter who took her mother's surname, and doña Luisa de Aguilar (of uncertain relation). Luis Miguel de Guinea followed his father, without nobility and announcing African ancestry. A kinswoman lived in the household of doña María de Contreras, listed as doña Margarita de Guinea—noble and African. There she forged ties to an extended clan of Contreras, Avilas, Camachos, and Guineas that included seven Salvatierra town households—three patriarchal and four led by women. The group was proudly Hispanic and very noble: five household heads were dons or doñas; many more children and dependents carried similar titles.[95] And they included the Guineas. As noted earlier, doña Margarita Ortíz de Covarrubías apparently inherited the prosperous Ortíz estates. She may have married Antonio de Guinea, despite his ancestry, because he was a skilled entrepreneur like don Diego de la Cruz Saravia. Here was another family of African roots claiming a place in the Hispanic elite. Yet while don Diego de la Cruz Saravia fled his (probable) African origins and moved to Celaya, the Guineas wore their name with pride and married into Salvatierra's best families. Ethnic adaptations and amalgamations created complex choices.

Commercial cultivation shaped life across the Bajío basin in the second half of the seventeenth century. Patriarchy organized families powerful and poor, shaping hierarchies of inequality that kept the majority working for the profit of the few. Ethnic identities and differences mattered yet remained negotiated and fluid. Those who gained wealth, most of Spanish ancestry but others with indigenous and African roots, forged an urban Hispanic elite. The working poor, most of Mesoamerican origins and many with African roots, merged in an indio majority. There was benefit to being Spanish, liability to life as an indio or mulatto. Still, economic chances, marriage choices, and ethnic adaptations brought new identities. Property, profit, and patriarchy were less negotiable in organizing power and inequality.

Capitalist Consolidations and End-of-Century Challenges

As the seventeenth century closed, three zones consolidated across the Bajío. At Querétaro and nearby, Otomí language, culture, and huertas held strong while Spaniards asserted power in trade, estate production, and a growing textile industry. Across basin lands to the west, Hispanic minorities ruled irrigated estates worked by indio majorities, both including people of African ancestry. And in northern uplands, including Guanajuato mines and vast grazing estates, diverse peoples mixed in even more complex amalgamations. All were of the Bajío: a society driven by silver, tied to world trade, and marked by ethnic complexity, changing identities, and religious diversity. In everything patriarchy orchestrated inequities that profited a few and set the subordination of producing families.

Consolidation came with changes and challenges. The warrior-entrepreneurs of the sixteenth century gave way to men who were officials and entrepreneurs. Those fortunate enough to claim riches in mining repeatedly invested in landed estates; a few amassed great properties through strategic marriages; others consolidated their power by combining official or priestly roles and estate development. As mining surged and waned, estates held profitable and secure—for the few with vast holdings and for others with good lands, income from office or benefice, and the vision to supply changing markets.

The people who worked in the Bajío economy also changed. Around 1600 most were migrant Mesoamericans who retained languages and identities as Otomí, Tarascans, or Mexica. A minority were African slaves finding ways to become free, often by becoming mulatto. By 1700 the descendants of most Mesoamericans in the Bajío were indios, living as estate dependents and speaking Spanish. Yet the many around Querétaro and others north of San Miguel kept Otomí language and identities. Few slaves arrived from Africa after 1650; yet slaves remained, some locked in Querétaro obrajes, others herding livestock across open lands. Meanwhile many of African ancestry joined amalgamations that led some to labor as free mulattoes in Guanajuato mines, others to join indio families in estate communities. A few became powerful landlords—and Spanish.

Silver stimulated everything; commercial ways ruled. A few men grasped for power: Oñates and Ibarras ruled Zacatecas and led thrusts northward; Altamiranos ruled mining, office, and labor at Guanajuato—their heirs became the vastly landed Mariscales de Castilla. Still, the uncertainties of mining, the continuing conflicts with independent peoples on the northern frontier, and the sparse numbers left by disease in Mesoamerica, across the Bajío, and among native northerners all worked against the power of the powerful. To gain mine-workers, entrepreneurs had to pay ore shares and high wages, often in advance, while providing housing and food rations. To draw settlers to estates don Diego de la Cruz Saravia and the Rincón Gallardos had to rent lands to some and offer advances, salaries, and rations to more. By 1700 commerce shaped the Bajío and Spanish North America. Capitalist goals ruled, but capitalist powers were limited and contested. Cultivators—landlords, tenants, and Otomí working huertas—fed themselves, gaining a cushion against dependence. Workers earned maize rations that provided security of sustenance. There were limits on commercial ways and predatory powers.

There were also challenges.[96] In Spain political men worried as Carlos II struggled to rule without an heir; they expressed mounting frustration as the riches of Spain's empire fueled economic progress mostly among European rivals to the north. After 1648 a series of treaties reflecting Spain's declining power gave Dutch, French, and British traders openings to join Spain's American trade through Seville and Cádiz. As the century ended, continuing flows of silver stimulated industry, trade, and revenues across northwest Europe.[97]

People in New Spain lived their own challenges. The 1680s began waves of native resistance in New Mexico among the Tarahumara, around Parral and elsewhere across the northern frontier. In 1683 pirates sporting Spanish, British, and French names attacked New Spain's key port at Veracruz; they held the city for two weeks, killed and raped wantonly, and only left when the authorities paid a ransom in silver. Then 1688 brought news of French interlopers on the coast of Texas.[98] And 1692 saw riots in New Spain's capital; many of Mexico City's indigenous residents, joined by members of a larger plebian majority, attacked and burned the viceregal palace, then looted adjacent markets and shops—all set off by evidence that powerful speculators were hoarding grain in times of dearth. A week later the most loyal indigenous province of Tlaxcala, famous for joining Cortés to conquer the Mexica, then sending settlers to colonize the north, faced parallel riots as native commoners assaulted the indigenous republic and Spanish officials.[99]

With regime succession uncertain, silver production dropping to historic lows just before 1700, violent intruders on the coasts, and native people asserting independence from northern frontiers to the heart of Mesoamerica, those who expected to rule, profit, or just work for modest prosperity faced frustrating insecurity. Inquisitors took a record number of reports of Hispanic women with mystical visions that challenged orthodoxy.[100] In 1691 Spanish Querétaro experienced a frenzy of sorceries, pregnant virgins, dark demons, and debated remedies.[101]

The conflicts and quandaries of Spain and New Spain coincided with a downturn in the silver economy—the outcome of the waning of Chinese demand for silver after 1640. In the 1680s and 1690s it was easier to see crisis than consolidation on both sides of Spain's Atlantic. Yet during boom times before 1640 and the decades of uncertainty that followed, a protean capitalist society was set in the Bajío and regions north. It was entrepreneurial and commercial, deeply patriarchal, ethnically fluid—and understood, legitimated, and contested by a Catholicism of many visions and voices. At Guanajuato and Zacatecas the 1690s laid foundations for a new century of boom. Silver and the commercial ways that it accelerated would flourish anew in the Bajío and Spanish North America after 1700, as Chinese demand for silver rose again. Spain would promote and benefit from the new boom, maintaining a place in Atlantic power for another century (even as its home economy lagged behind its European neighbors). Stimulated by soaring silver trades, the Bajío and Spanish North America would help lead capitalism toward unprecedented dynamism after 1700.[102]

CHAPTER 3

New World Revivals

Silver Boom, City Lives, Awakenings,

and Northward Drives, 1680–1760

◈ AFTER TWO CENTURIES of commercial formation, social construction, ethnic adaptations, and religious innovations the Bajío and Spanish North America surged as an American engine of the world economy after 1700. Guanajuato became a great mining city; Querétaro and San Miguel boomed as centers of trade and textiles. Commercial agriculture expanded across the basin. Population grew dramatically. Profits soared for a few. Prosperity was real for many. Many more struggled to work and claim enough to sustain families. Times of boom brought promise and change, conflict and uncertainty. Unprecedented opportunities and unimagined changes led to religious awakenings among people grappling with new understandings of life.

By the 1750s the Bajío was the richest region of the Americas. Mines, cities of textiles and trade, and commercial estates drove an economy accelerating toward capitalism. In the countryside growth built on seventeenth-century precedents; new expansions consolidated commercial patriarchy and social stability. In the cities the new century brought disruptive changes. A few men claimed powers that allowed them to operate as predators—sometimes turning on elite rivals, often pressuring those who worked to create the wealth that made them powerful. Working communities faced unprecedented opportunities and difficulties, yet they found ways to negotiate lives of laborious effort. Even as commercial power concentrated, workers remained scarce from the Bajío northward through the 1750s.

Times of boom and change in the Bajío accelerated the northward drive of Spanish North America after 1700. Mining revived first at Zacatecas and at Chihuahua, north of Parral. Migrants followed, as did pressures on independent native peoples to pass through missions, live as Christian dependents, and work in the commercial world. In the first half of the eighteenth century the plateau country from the Bajío to New Mexico was ever more rapidly incorporated into the profit-seeking, patriarchal, culturally complex ways of Spanish North America. Meanwhile a new generation of warrior-entrepreneurs from Querétaro and nearby led assaults on independent peoples in the Sierra Gorda and then drove the search for land, profit, and labor along Gulf lowlands, across the Río Grande, and into Texas.

New Spain's eighteenth-century dynamism came with a new Bourbon dynasty. The regime often gains credit for reviving the silver economy. More important, Chinese demand for silver rose again beginning around 1700. Analysis of mining at Guanajuato and of trade and industry at San Miguel and Querétaro suggests that commercial revival preceded the new regime and its reforms. New Spain's eighteenth-century growth sustained Bourbon rule and early reforms more than the new dynasty stimulated New World revivals. When the Chinese demand for silver waned and the regime instituted reforms more vigorously in the 1760s, it provoked a crisis that threatened the silver economy.

Turn-of-the-Century Challenges

In March 1701 a ship landed at Veracruz with news that the last Spanish Hapsburg, the ailing Carlos II, had died in November. Without a direct heir, he named Felipe de Anjou, a French Bourbon, as successor. The change brought little public debate in New Spain. In April the viceroy, High Court, and Merchant Guild of Mexico City swore loyalty to the new king. But in May the Conde de Moctezuma resigned as viceroy, saying he lacked funds to mobilize New Spain for conflicts to come. In June news came that key members of the Castilian nobility backed Carlos de Austria, a Hapsburg claimant supported by England. The War of Succession was on. England and France raised alliances to fight, mostly on Spanish soil; New Spain's silver was a key prize in a war for Atlantic dominance.[1]

In November the archbishop of Mexico City, as interim viceroy, collected funds for the Bourbon cause. In October 1702 Felipe's first viceroy arrived. The Duque de Albuquerque came on a French warship with orders to send 350,000 pesos to fund Bourbon succession. The convoy that sailed in spring of 1703 carried that much on Crown account, and nearly seven million pesos in trade (most, it was said, heading to "illegal" traders who backed the British-Hapsburg claim). The fleet was attacked off the coast of Spain; the bullion was saved. Felipe took all the silver, aiding his forces and prejudicing merchants on all sides.[2]

Mexico City merchants lost dearly. Through 1703 and 1704 Albuquerque asked them to "donate" to the Bourbon effort. The richest men in New Spain pleaded poverty. Conflict escalated, and became personal when the viceroy backed criminal charges against leading traders. Still, they would not pay. Men who financed mining and through their Consulado (Chamber) farmed the *alcabala* sales tax could not be forced to fund the Bourbon cause. In May 1705 the Council of the Indies instructed Albuquerque to promote "acceptance and love among our subjects." He dropped all charges, offered honors to many, and renewed the alcabala tax farm. Suddenly he collected a million pesos in "loans" that arrived in Brest early in 1707, helping to turn the tide to the Bourbon cause.[3] The merchant financiers of Mexico City ruled New Spain's silver economy. They were essential to any regime in Madrid.[4]

Captain Jean de Monségur, a Basque naval officer, landed in New Spain in 1707, sent by Felipe V to study his new empire. He spent his energy trying to understand the economy that linked New Spain's mines to Europe and Asia. He was awed and troubled by what he saw. Mexico City was the pivot of dynamic global trade. "That famous city is the pivot and warehouse of the richest commerce, . . . the rarest goods of Europe and Asia are found there in abundance; many are consumed locally, the rest are distributed across the vast provinces of the continent it rules."[5] Everyone was a merchant: "one meets entrepreneurs of every status, condition, and sex: bishops, priests, friars, and nuns; people of honor, magistrates, and officials; merchants, craftsmen, and workers; from the Viceroy to the slave everyone is buying and selling, each according to his means, interest, and credit."[6]

Monségur reported the riches of Zacatecas and Parral, noting that few mine operators were rich. They relied on Mexico City merchants for credit and provisions, and the financiers claimed most profits. He estimated annual registered silver at four to five million pesos, 80 percent shipped to Spain in trade or revenues, the rest funding the Spanish Caribbean. Monségur suspected that real output was greater—and would be greater still if officials stopped speculating in the mercury essential to refining. The regime, he insisted, should provide it at a low price and allow merchants to finance mines without interference.

Mine operators would produce more silver, employ more workers, and reduce the wages and ore shares paid to those workers. With better earnings they could drain old mines and produce even more.[7]

Monségur aimed to show how "Spain, in union with France, can profit from the commerce of this rich part of the world."[8] The goal was Spanish-French control of New Spain's silver and trade. The challenge was not British competition but the sway of Chinese and other Asian goods in New Spain's rich markets. Monségur detailed imports of Chinese silks and other fabrics, many embroidered with gold and silver. The Manila trade, sanctioned for more than a century, drew goods from across Asia to Acapulco; Mexico City merchants traded them across New Spain and Perú. To Monségur the silver drained to Asia had to be redirected to stimulate Franco-Spanish Atlantic trade and fill Bourbon coffers.[9]

Monségur punctuated pages of detail with strong conclusions: "The cargo that lands at Acapulco every December or January is merchandise from China and the East Indies, including the coasts of Coromandel and Bengal; they are the same classes of goods sent from Europe to Mexico City, but they cost much less; they rule the market and local consumption, causing irreparable damage to the King and the State."[10] At least three million pesos yearly flowed to Asia, depriving Atlantic routes and regimes of that much trade and revenue. Asian goods held down prices for European imports, further reducing Spanish and French production and revenues. The delivery of Asian goods to Perú, officially illegal, brought pernicious consequences there too.[11] Monségur saw the Manila trade as a Chinese business. The Spanish in Manila depended on Asian traders for goods to ship across the Pacific. "The return trip carries only money."[12] For the Bourbon king that was unacceptable.

The goal was clear: increase silver production and direct the specie to Spain and France. Monségur did not understand the recent rise of the Chinese price for silver that drove demand and stimulated Pacific trades.[13] Nor did he see that silver production was already rising in New Spain. Bonanza at Chihuahua was followed by revival at Zacatecas, Parral, and Guanajuato. New Spain's output, which dipped from 4.5 to 3.6 million pesos yearly in the 1690s, rose to over 5 million pesos after 1700, approaching 6 million by 1710 amid war and regime change.[14] Unprecedented growth had begun.

Can Chinese demand alone explain the sustained increase of production across New Spain—mostly in mines established in the sixteenth century, stagnant after 1640, then explosively productive (despite rising costs) in the eighteenth century? Production grew from almost 6 million pesos yearly in 1710, to an average over 8 million by

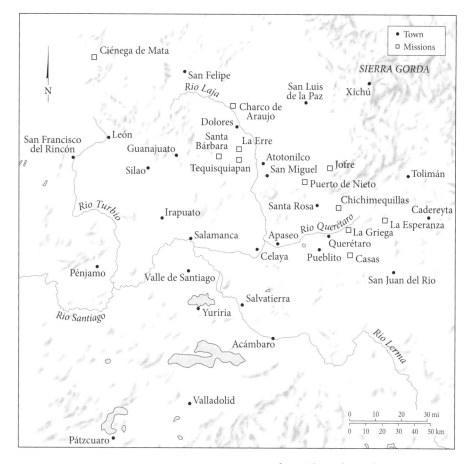

The Bajío in the Eighteenth Century

1725 and a sustained peak of over 12 million pesos from the late 1740s through the 1750s. Most of the growth came at Zacatecas and Guanajuato, the latter becoming for the first time a major engine of the world economy. Its output exceeded a million pesos yearly by 1720, rising to over 3 million in the late 1740s, generating nearly 30 percent of New Spain's silver.[15]

Silver was both a commodity and money, by 1700 essential to regime revenues and global trades everywhere. The revival of old mines once too expensive because of deep shafts and costly drainage responded to a soaring demand for silver and its growing value in a global trade. Chinese demand stimulated production; so did rising revenue needs among Atlantic powers engaged in escalating warfare. The simultaneous rise of populations across Europe and the Americas, in an Atlantic world integrated by local, regional, and oceanic trades, also escalated the demand for money. The population of Europe had plummeted with the great plague of the fourteenth century, expanded in the fifteenth and sixteenth, and stagnated in the seventeenth. The population of the Americas was devastated in the sixteenth century, stabilized in the seventeenth, and began to grow in the eighteenth. Meanwhile exploration, conquest, colonization, and the forced migrations of slavery forged a new commercial world driven by Chinese demand for silver. When after 1700 populations grew simultaneously for the first time on both sides of a commercialized Atlantic, trade flourished, along with demand for silver. The eighteenth century brought a rising demand for silver that was both Asian and European—promoting global trade, competition between European and Asian powers for silver flows, and production in New Spain, the Bajío, and Spanish North America.

The Countryside in the Age of Revivals

All that expansion depended on rural production. As the eighteenth century began, the Bajío had a complex agrarian structure: Otomí families worked rich huertas from La Cañada, through Querétaro to Apaseo, while Spaniards profited from irrigated lands and grazing properties farther out. Around Celaya, Spaniards ruled irrigated cultivation while indigenous villages worked rainfed lands. Farther west, on bottomlands from Salvatierra to Salamanca, Spaniards ran commercial farms worked by patriarchal communities of indios. Just southwest, the Agustinian San Nicolás estate raised great harvests near the Tarascan smallholders of Yuriria, who kept small plots and worked Agustinian fields. Across the north from San Miguel to San Felipe and León, grazing ruled and populations remained sparse. Everywhere Spanish cultivators prospered while majorities—Otomí around Querétaro, Tarascan around Yuriria, indio on the bottomlands, and amalgamating to the north—worked to survive. Across the southern Bajío vast landholdings were rare; the estates of Querétaro's Santa Clara Convent and the Agustinians' San Nicolás were exceptions. The great properties of the Mariscales de Castilla and the Rincón Gallardos dominated drier northern uplands.

The most successful rural enterprises linked estates in the Bajío's diverse zones, and in the north. The holdings of don Juan Caballero y Ocío of Querétaro defined agrarian entrepreneurship as the eighteenth century begain. The origins of his patrimony remain hazy. Puerto de Nieto, east of San Miguel, belonged to the heirs of an earlier Juan Caballero in 1631.[16] Don Juan Caballero y Medina served as a magistrate on Querétaro's first Spanish council in 1655; he later sat as a council-man and chief constable. His son don Juan Caballero y Ocío was born in 1643 and studied with the Jesuits in Querétaro and Mexico City. On his father's death in 1675 he came home to inherit his father's proper-ties and roles as councilman and constable. Five years later he became a priest, keeping his estates and leaving the council. A brother, Licen-ciado don Nicolás de Caballero y Ocío, operated rich lands at Valle de Santiago in 1683, but his holdings paled before those of don Juan.

Caballero wrote a will in 1689.[17] It detailed vast lands devoted to agriculture and grazing and the work relations that sustained them. Nearest Querétaro was La Griega, east of La Cañada on the Amascala plain. It had eleven grazing sites that were now fields for maize and wheat. Stocked with oxen and plows along with horses and carts to haul grain, it had a chapel and granaries to hold accumulating har-vests. Thirty gañanes, Otomí men obligated by advances, labored year round. A cuadrilla of seasonal hands, also Otomí, lived at the estate as well; they gained huts, plots of land, and wages for labor during plant-ing and harvest seasons. Caballero leased out a section called Coyo-tillos for 100 pesos and another called La Venta for 56 pesos, along with two herds of cattle. Like de la Cruz Saravia's Valle de Santiago estates in 1670, Caballero y Ocío's La Griega raised commercial crops with obligated employees and seasonal hands and took rental income for additional earnings.[18]

Puerto de Nieto lay northwest of Queréraro, just over the pass at the eastern limit of San Miguel's jurisdiction. A little-developed grazing property in the 1630s, by the end of the century it was the pivot of Ca-ballero's livestock operations. It included "a great country house with great halls and corridors, along with granaries and many workers' huts; its lands are improved and cultivated, worked by many oxen, native laborers, and everything else necessary." Puerto de Nieto nor-mally held "two thousand fanegas of maize to supply all my hacien-das," grain essential to livestock operations on the arid plateau extend-ing north. Each year Caballero's herdsmen drove the twenty thousand sheep he would sell for slaughter to Puerto de Nieto. There too vast herds concentrated for the annual shearing that supplied wool to obra-jes in Querétaro and San Miguel. Puerto de Nieto's inventory included horses, a hundred mules to haul carts, mule teams to carry maize—and slaves; the estate integrated cultivation and livestock operations, obli-gated workers and slaves of African ancestry. "Domingo the mulatto" leased a farm called Rincón, along with a hundred cows.[19]

To the north Caballero y Ocío owned five grazing estates stretch-ing from San Luis Potosí to Nuevo León and east into Huasteca low-lands. Four great herds of sheep totaled nearly 120,000 head; he leased another 27,000 to the Querétaro Jesuits on newly aquired lands in Nuevo León. His most developed northern estate was Bocas in San Luis Potosí. Grazing over 30,000 sheep, it mixed "slaves . . . with free people, who have accounts in the estate books." There was another "property that raised crops and made charcoal, with a house, workers' huts, oxen, and small dams, all rented for two hundred pesos," along with "several ranchos rented to poor families." While slaves and free workers herded Caballero's sheep, a tenant community emerged at Bocas. Farther north at Santa Ana, Illescas, and an unnamed lamb nursery, Caballero reported mostly sheep and slaves.[20]

Caballero worked vast lands, marketing maize, wheat, sheep, and wool. He employed obligated gañanes and seasonal hands to raise crops at La Griega and Puerto de Nieto; at Bajío estates and at Bocas he leased lands to tenants large and small; and from Puerto de Nieto to Bocas and far to the north, 140 slaves mostly herded sheep. Gañanes gained advances, salaries, and rations, supporting patriarchy in dependent households; squatters gained a hut, access to land, and seasonal wages in a less secure patriarchy; tenants got a chance at uncertain cultivation—and patriarchy.

It is notable that Caballero's 140 slaves remained unemancipated even in a society with openings to freedom all around. Most herded livestock, work that was impossible in shackles. Slaves at Puerto de Nieto lived near Guanajuato and the bottomlands communities, where slaves regularly found ways to freedom in the seventeenth century. Those farther north lived in open country never far from the frontier and its independent natives. Perhaps the priest was a kind master; we know he assured sustenance from Puerto de Nieto's maize harvests. But kindness and sustenance presumably did not suffice to hold slaves. Records from Ciénega de Mata in the early eighteenth century and from Puerto de Nieto in the 1780s reveal that slaves found ways to claim key roles in production while they forged family ties in integrated estate communities.[21] Bondage, like obligated labor, had to be negotiated in the Bajío and Spanish North America.

Caballero y Ocío lived until 1707, operating estates, funding devotions at Querétaro, and promoting northward expansion. His operations paralleled those of the Rincón Gallardo clan. Their sprawling Ciénaga de Mata estates, stretching from the northern Bajío toward Zacatecas, were built in the early seventeenth century. In 1700 they were stragically set to profit when mining soared again at Zacatecas and Guanajuato. Family members fought over control of the great patrimony. The records of their disputes document changing ways of production and labor relations in the early eighteenth century.[22]

Through the seventeenth century Ciénega de Mata mixed cultivation and grazing. The estate left most cropping to tenants; it relied on 123 slaves in 1683 to tend livestock. The most common slave surnames were de la Cruz and de los Reyes, calling on Christ and kings to protect those born without patriarchal protection. The estate sold sheep for mutton from Zacatecas to San Luis Potosí, in the Bajío, and in Mexico City; wool went to Querétaro and San Miguel obrajes. Cattle, horses, and mules found markets across the viceroyalty. All those businesses reenergized with the silver boom and population growth after 1700. Ciénega de Mata profited while slavery declined, giving way to communities of obligated laborers.

In 1704 the number of slaves had fallen to twenty-nine: two-thirds men, two-thirds listed as negro, the rest mulatto. By 1715 economic opportunity led to purchases that increased the slave popoulation at Ciénega de Mata to forty-nine: thirty-two men and seventeen women, three-fourths mulatto, the rest negro. The mean age of men was twenty-six, of women only sixteen. The names de la Cruz and de los Reyes held strong. Among women four were listed as mothers, one as a cook, one as a tortilla maker—classic female roles in patriarchal communities. Among men, there was a range of roles and skills: a mayordomo and his assistant, a muleteer and three coachmen, two blacksmiths and two soapmakers, a tailor, and a cobbler; fourteen tended sheep. Slave men were managers and skilled craftsmen, and were in charge of flocks that produced mutton and wool.[23]

In 1720 slave numbers held at forty-nine, all mulattoes. One had fled; another gained freedom from the owner. In 1727 forty-seven remained. The mean age of thirty men had risen to twenty-nine, all but one noted as mulatto. The seventeen women were all mulattas; their average age was twenty. There were still managers in the group, along with skilled smiths; most tended sheep. Four were disabled. By 1734 the total held at forty-seven but there were two fewer adult men and two fewer adult women, replaced by four infants. Several men had been sent to Querétaro (where obrajes still relied on slaves), several were fugitives, and several were paralyzed or disabled.[24] Slavery persisted at Ciénega de Mata, yet became ever less central to production.

Meanwhile a growing number of free residents labored as sirvientes, receiving advances in cloth and cash accounted against future labor. Most appeared in inventories as owing debts to the estate; a minority were owed by the property. Many were noted as *huidos*, having fled— all owing debts. The 1720 inventory listed 134 obligated residents, with uncounted numbers having fled. In 1727, 171 were in debt and 60 had fled. By 1734 the number of working sirvientes had risen to around 250 and only 40 were noted as having fled. Salaries held near one real per day—4 pesos per month, thus 48 pesos yearly. Total indebtedness rose from 1720 to 1727, then fell in 1734. (The inventories were part of suits over inheritance; they did not come at a common time in cycles of advances and labor—thus changing debt levels likely report only how recently workers had received annual advances.)[25]

A growing number of obligated men worked at the Ciénega de Mata estates. They gained advances accounted in money against work credited in money. The largest advances went to managers, who often owed over 100 pesos. Most workers owed 20 to 40 pesos at any accounting, or less than a year's earnings. Advances did not hold workers at the estates. In 1727, 171 men still working owed 6,184 pesos; 60 who had left owed 1,629 pesos. In 1734, 255 sirvientes owed 4,334 pesos; 40 had left owing 1,080 pesos. Advances to attract workers were a cost of doing business; 20 percent of those advances were lost during times of commercial growth, declining slavery, and scarce labor.

The 250 obligated workers of the 1730s were nearly all men. In 1727 two women, María Magdalena and María Jacinta, owed debts at the Chinampa estate. Their names suggest that they were indias; their rarity indicates that they were widows. At the same property in 1734 shared surnames suggest a community of extended clans. The prominence of the names de la Cruz and de los Reyes among them suggests that many descended from slaves who had long worked the estate. Managers were the best-paid, most heavily indebted employees. Still, the slave Domingo Gómez remained mayordomo at San Juan in 1734. Most obligated workers tended livestock, raised crops, or worked muletrains. Few indebted employees were skilled craftsmen—still a domain of slaves at Ciénega de Mata in the early eighteenth century.

We begin to see why some obligated workers fled and many slaves stayed at Ciénega de Mata. The estate recruited free workers with advances; if they fled they were hard to find, and the estate absorbed their debts as a cost of labor. Slaves did not get advances, but a few rose to be managers, many worked as craftsmen, and most lived with everyday freedom as herdsmen; all watched their kin become free, as slave men reproduced with free women. Advanced payments drew poor but free men to labor as obligated patriarchs; labor scarcity enabled many to move on without working off their obligations. Opportunity, community, family, and a chance at freedom for children kept slaves at work—while slavery declined.

As mining flourished and urban populations grew, those fortunate enough to take profit from risky mining repeatedly invested in lands for commercial cultivation and grazing. Wealth from Guanajuato flowed to estates around nearby León, Valle de Santiago and the bottomlands, and Querétaro.[26] Established owners and new investors opened new fields; where streams allowed they built dams and canals to irrigate growing fields. Maize harvests doubled around León and tripled at Silao during the first half of the eighteenth century; after 1750 wheat production expanded even more rapidly. Land values soared.[27] Grazing gave way to cultivation, pressing livestock northward and often out of the Bajío.

Expanding plantings needed growing estate populations. The social relations of production evident at don Diego de la Cruz Saravia's Valle de Santiago estates in 1671, at Caballero y Ocío's diverse properties in 1689, and at Ciénega de Mata after 1700 were replicated across the Bajío, with local variations. Estates offered plots of nonirrigated land to tenants, inevitably men who planted maize to assert patriarchy and sustain families. Entrepreneurs devoted irrigated land to wheat, recruiting full-time employees with advances, salaries, and maize rations, again enabling workers to assert patriarchy. Seasonal hands for planting and harvesting came from tenants and boys in growing estate communities.

Along the Bajío's southern margins, indigenous communities retained republics and land—sometimes good irrigated land, as at Querétaro and nearby. The eighteenth century brought rapid expansion of irrigation, cultivation, and settlement on estate lands. Around 1750 Otomí families around Querétaro and Tarascans at Yuriria increasingly lived on commercial properties. The bottomlands settled in the seventeenth century saw continued growth, dependence on estate lands, and ever-changing ethnic identities. Dependent patriarchs still led producing families, yet at Salvatierra they increasingly took mulatto identities. At Salamanca and Valle de Santiago the number of mulattoes increased, but indios remained the majority.[28] North of the bottomlands around San Miguel and León the stock grazing that ruled seventeenth-century estate production gave way to growing cultivation: great herds moved north; fields were cleared, and irrigated where possible; tenants planted rain-dependent crops; entrepreneurs recruited obligated workers and seasonal hands from growing estate communities to raise wheat on irrigated fields.[29]

North of San Miguel, estate populations had been growing since the late seventeenth century; to provide religious services the chapel at the Mariscales La Erre estate served as an extension of the San Miguel parish. In 1711 don Álvaro de Ocío y Ocampo, priest and kin to don Juan Caballero y Ocío, bought a small property named La Concepción. He kept two grazing sites and donated a caballería (forty hectares) to found a parish he named for Our Lady of Sorrows: Nuestra Señora de los Dolores. He built a small church and a house and aimed to sell town lots to Spaniards and mestizos. He faced a suit from men who called themselves the governors and caciques of the Otomí communities on nearby estates and demanded lots for themselves. A priest-entrepreneur planned a Spanish town. Otomí leaders intended to live there too, and found support from the bishop at Valladolid and the viceroy. Don Álvaro planned sodalities for penitent Spaniards focused on the Blessed Sacrament and the Virgin's sorrows; Otomí notables founded an indigenous confraternity devoted to the Ascension of Mary and focused on salvation. While the founder struggled to build a parish and develop his estate with loans, Otomí leaders collected funds among the Otomí at nearby estates to support festivals that drew participants from communities all around.[30] Remaining indio proved a way to organize life, at least religious life, in the face of clerical interest and estate power.

The founding pastor at Dolores imagined a parish of Spaniards who ruled laboring indios; from the 1730s to the 1760s the parish registers revealed a community of few Spaniards—fewer than 3 percent, nearly all in town—and a diverse rural population. Nearly three-fourths were recorded as indio, but everywhere they lived with mulattoes and others. Most large estates included Otomí majorities, along with mulatto minorities of 5 to 30 percent; a few communities had mulatto majorities and indio minorities. The amalgamations so prominent earlier in bottomlands communities extended into the uplands around Dolores after 1700. Among the majority of Otomí ancestry (including many who married mulattoes), remaining indio facilitated claims to justice and sustained informal organizations in which Otomí captains organized labor (claiming two reales a day). Otomí governors and caciques lived in Dolores, organizing religious life (and more) through the captains. Priests and other Spaniards resisted indigenous rights. A persistent minority retained mulatto identities.[31] But the value of being indio kept Otomí identity strong around Dolores—in estate communities without councils, without lands, living as tenants and laborers in an expanding commercial world.

Through the first half of the eighteenth century silver mining, population growth, and estate production grew together in delicate balance across the Bajío. Livestock moved north; irrigated cultivation expanded; estate communities grew. But the rural population lagged behind estate labor needs; managers had to draw workers to lives of dependence. In the early 1750s at Juchitlán near Querétaro, Hispanic sirvientes earned four pesos monthly plus maize rations, indigenous gañanes earned three pesos plus rations, and numerous tenants paid eight pesos to plant a fanega of maize, enough to sustain a small family most years. The estate offered access to land, solid wages, and secure rations—all consolidating patriarchy. Tithe receipts from Celaya on the bottomlands and León to the northwest show a slow decline of maize prices from 1700 to the 1760s. Even the peaks brought by periodic years of scarcity held low. The families who raised the harvests at Juchitlán in the 1750s had earnings at least as good as those prevailing at bottomlands estates in the 1670s. Juchitlán's profits in 1752, 5 percent of capital value, were less than those claimed by don Diego de la Cruz Saravia at Valle de Santiago in 1670.[32] As cultivation expanded across the Bajío after 1700, profits perhaps fell and remunerations rose, at least slightly. But profit remained, patriarchy held, and cultivation grew enough to bring a slow but steady decline in staple prices—sustaining the mining boom, perhaps subsidizing it.

Guanajuato: Silver Boom, Unruly Mulattoes, and Penitential Revivals

Long a secondary mining center, Guanajuato became the world's leading producer of silver in the eighteenth century. Entrepreneurs consolidated local power, population grew, and trade soared. The long-sought Jesuit presence finally came. Yet the city in the canyon stayed an unruly boomtown. For every bonanza there were more bankruptcies. Uncertainty and danger defined life. For the few with a chance at riches, for the many in petty trade, and for the many more laboring in deep tunnels subject to flood and collapse or awash in poisonous mercury at refineries, Guanajuato was still a place of hope and risk, chance and insecurity. Its mines yielded steadily rising silver flows from 1700 to 1750, and then faced a downturn in the 1750s as Chinese demand waned (even as New Spain's overall production held strong) before rising again in the 1760s to reach historic peaks in the 1790s.[33]

Guanajuato's eighteenth-century boom had its roots in the 1690s, before the Bourbon accession. Doctor don Juan Diez de Bracamonte deserves much of the credit, as he and his contemporaries could barely sense rising Chinese demand. Born in 1650 into a Guanajuato mining family, he studied locally and in Mexico City to become a priest as well as a lawyer before the High Court there. He was a cleric and a professional, a regime official and an entrepreneur. The Rayas mine had operated since the sixteenth century. In the 1680s it was little profitable, held by the Agustinian convent in Mexico City, having likely been taken for debts. Early in the 1690s the friars asked Diez de Bracamonte to oversee operations, hoping that he might ease relations with creditors. Diez took control in 1694, gaining financing from the Mexico City Cathedral and the Sánchez de Tagle silver bank. He turned the Burras estate into a refinery and between 1694 and 1699 registered 1.2 million pesos of silver. Diez de Bracamonte integrated mining and supply by

San Juan de Rayas mine complex, eighteenth century; Mellado church
in background.

buying rural estates, including Jalpa and Ojo de Agua near León and
grazing lands north in Nuevo León. Well connected, well financed, and
diversified, Diez led a revival that would endure.

Still, he faced constant challenges. The Agustinians' creditors sought
payment, participation, even control. But the greatest challenge came
in draining deep shafts and recruiting, controlling, and paying the
workers essential to drainage, mining, and refining. In the 1690s Guanajuato mineworkers claimed 5 reales daily—nearly 4 pesos per week,
200 pesos yearly if they worked regularly—in addition to ore shares.
To operate Rayas Diez paid 4,000 pesos weekly (suggesting 1,000
workers)—200,000 pesos a year. The five-year production of 1.2 million pesos left but 200,000 pesos after labor costs to pay for credit,
mercury, livestock, timber, and taxes. Production boomed, but profits
were thin and uncertain.

Rivals accused Diez of removing pillars essential to tunnel safety,
taking maximum ores while risking workers' lives. A collapse in 1701
left one dead and many maimed, and unleashed a flood. Diez lost control to a competitor, who could not pay for supplies and labor. Workers
rioted; many left. Diez retook control in 1703 of mines in desperate
shape. He found eight investors who brought their own cuadrillas,
ceding them all income for three months as they drained and restored

the works. Then Diez took on directly the challenges of water and labor. In 1704 drainage required fifteen hand winches and ten drawn by mules to haul water from the depths, all worked by 101 men—a tenth of the labor force. Diez invested twelve thousand pesos to build eight new platforms for mule-operated whims, reducing hand winches to four and thus reducing labor. He further reduced labor by enlarging and extending a tunnel allowing mules to haul ore to the surface. By limiting the number of workers paid wages and ore shares, cutting costs of drainage and ore extraction, Diez revived mining and profits.

Rayas generated silver, profit, and revenues, and sent workers to face danger daily. An inspector reported in 1704: "this mine is the richest jewel of any monarch." Then he added that "only greed for gold and silver could have opened this mine and made work in its depths tolerable; if anywhere in the world there is any place like hell, this is it; dreadful even in a brief visit, where even men accustomed to its depths suffocate and die." The workers who opened tunnels and cut ores, working with gunpowder in the smoke of torches, faced constant heat, hunger, thirst, and danger. Few lived past forty.[34]

Diez worked Rayas until 1715, when appointment as a judge on Mexico City's High Court required him to step aside. He sold estates near León to pay investors and the Crown for mounting debts for mercury. A predator who destroyed competitors' mines and workers' lives, Diez de Bracamonte showed the way to mining revival: investment and innovation, regime backing, inexpensive mercury, and risks shifted to workers even as their pay was cut.[35] He leased Rayas first to a consortium of investors and then to his former managers, don Pedro and don José de Sardaneta. Don José bought control in 1729. He had learned under Diez and married into the Busto family, prominent at Guanajuato for a century. The Bustos operated Cata, Mellado, and other mines near Rayas; from 1724 to 1735 they ruled Guanajuato's first great bonanza. By the 1730s don Francisco Matías Busto was Marqués de San Clemente and a local councilman. In addition to mining he worked estates around León. Sardaneta followed the same path. If he introduced blasting to the mines, as he claimed, he did so as Diez de Bracamonte's manager. Sardaneta built more efficient crushing mills at his refineries. Yet he died in 1741, facing over 500,000 pesos of debts; the Crown placed Rayas in receivership until 1757, when his son don Vicente Manuel de Sardaneta regained control and led a revival that made him Marqués de San Juan de Rayas.[36]

The rise of the Busto and Sardaneta families to great wealth and titled eminence reveals much about Guanajuato after 1700. To some they were heroic entrepreneurs, to others predatory capitalists. They were both, and leading participants in a larger, more complex mining economy. Financing usually came from silver bankers in Mexico City—the Fagoagas, Valdiviesos, and Sánchez de Tagle. At Guanajuato mine operation was linked to refining, and the need to fund and find workers for both. Some entrepreneurs only worked mines; others operated mines and refineries; still others focused on refining only. All joined in commerce or relied on merchants for financing. Refineries were pivotal. They could be mortaged to gain credit; they could house workers; and they were essential to processing by crushing ores, mixing them with mercury (or lead for richer ores), washing the ores, and then separating silver from mercury (or lead) by blasting heat. There were sixty-four refineries at or near Guanajuato during the early eighteenth century; they changed hands so often that during five decades one or more were owned by 208 people—110 were also mine operators, 38 merchants.[37]

A hierarchical entrepreneurial community jostled to profit. The silver bankers in the capital were close to regime officials. The Fagoagas owned the office of the apartado, which oversaw the mandatory separation of gold from silver before coinage and was a secure source of capital. At Guanajuato the Salinas family held the office of assayer, another source of capital to fund trade and refining. Everyone negotiated with the regime to gain mercury in adequate quantity and at an affordable price. The Bustos and the Sardanetas depended on creditors in Mexico City, at least until bonanzas cleared their debts and allowed the accumulations (and revenue payments) that led to titles. They and other leading miners, merchants, and refiners—often the same men— ruled the mining guild and held seats on the city council.[38]

At less exalted levels many more lived in a commercial world of risk and gain. The pickmen and blastmen who earned ore shares worked as lesser partners of mine operators. Merchants and refiners competed to buy their shares, offering silver, cloth, and wine in return. And among the majority who earned only salaries and rations for less skilled labor underground or at refineries, many began the century still living at refinery compounds. There owner-entrepreneurs hoped to gain their loyalty, their labor, and their spending at company stores. From the 1720s, as mining rose and population grew, workers were less scarce and land along the streams in the center of Guanajuato gained value. Owners of refinery compounds began to sell land used for workers' housing. Buyers built new refineries, stores, and shops. Workers and their families dispersed, gaining new independence while facing new costs for housing in an ever more expensive city of boom and struggle.[39]

With all the challenges of financing and labor, silver production at Guanajuato tripled from around one million pesos yearly between 1715 and 1720 to an average of three million pesos by 1750. The population of the city, its mining camps, and outlying zones grew from about 15,000 near 1700 to over 50,000 by mid-century. The urban mining complex reached 32,500 people according to a church census of 1755. In the early 1730s more than 1,000 births annually increased a population also bolstered by migrants. The city then consumed over 50,000 fanegas of maize, 11,000 cargas of wheat flour, 12,000 head of mutton, and 3,400 beef cattle yearly. By the 1760s consumption essentially doubled to 100,000 fanegas of maize, 18,000 loads of flour, 20,000 head of mutton, and 6,000 steers. In 1742 eighty stores offered "cloth, silks, and dry goods from Castilla," forty sold "local goods," and seventy-three more served mine and refinery compounds. A mining deputation represented miners; a commercial deputation organized traders. The district magistrate led a council of two magistrates and sixteen councilmen. Militias included six cavalry companies, plus two of "mulatto militiamen."[40]

Mining required investment, regime backing, mercury, good luck, and a growing population of workers ready to risk life, health, and limb to descend into shafts and work amid blasting and threats of collapse and flood. Pickmen and blasters still got ore shares: they delivered a daily quota to the owner, then gained half of all additional ores as a *partido*. The majority of laborers in mines and at refineries earned only wages, which fell from five to four reales a day during the first half of the eighteenth century. Such remuneration was far beyond the rewards of any other work in the Bajío or probably across the Americas. For these shares and wages miners faced maiming, poisoning, and death. Entrepreneurs faced only the uncertainty of profit or loss, yet they resented having to pay workers' earnings. If wages or ore shares could be reduced, profits rose.[41] Labor relations were a constant source of tension and insecurity. Men worked, drank, gambled, and died young. Patriarchal families were scarce. Many women fended for themselves and their children, facing limited opportunities and enduring insecurities. A census in 1755 reported that the population that endured those challenges was 20 percent Spanish, 10 percent indio, and 70 percent mulatto.[42]

How did the majority at Guanajuato become mulatto? African slaves had labored there from the 1550s, always outnumbered by Mesoamericans. All along, slaves found ways to freedom, sometimes by flight, often by producing children with indigenous women. After 1600 people of African ancestry formed about 15 percent of the population in the basin and at León, while mulattoes peaked at 20 percent in Guanajuato's parish registers. It may be that free mulattoes concentrated at Guanajuato after 1700. But there is no evidence of a loss of mulattoes at nearby León, where a census in 1719 still reported 15 percent of household heads as mulatto, 162 people in a town of trade and crafts.[43]

The explosive increase of mulattoes to form a dominant majority at Guanajuato in the 1750s resulted from continuing amalgamations and adoptions of mulatto identity. When the chapel that once served Otomí migrants was turned over to the Jesuits in the 1730s, the explanation was simple: the Otomí had disappeared by mixing with Africans and other Mesoamericans.[44] But across the bottomlands and the northern Bajío countryside, Otomí mixed with people of African ancestry and became indios. In rural areas indio status brought at least imagined opportunity to seek land and status as republics. In Guanajuato republics offered little to mineworkers. But the regime did promote mulatto militias. Militiamen drilled with arms and gained access to military justice.[45] Perhaps the chance of militia participation was enough to draw men to mulatto identities. Or perhaps being mulatto become a badge of assertion in a raucous community of workers in which African ancestry was denigrated by those who ruled.

A court case begun in 1740 offers rare detail about how slave women continued to free their children. At the isolated Ranchos de San Luisito, near Silao south of Guanajuato, Antonio de la Cruz and his wife claimed status as indios Otomíes while raising an adopted son, the mulatillo Joseph Joaquín. As the boy approached the age to labor, perhaps seven or eight, he faced a judicial inquiry. María Vásquez, a mestiza at the Rancho de los García, claimed to own Joseph Joaquín; he had been born to her slave, the mulatta Teresa de Jesús. The court returned the boy to María, his presumed owner, during the proceedings. Antonio, the adoptive father, worked to keep the boy "out of love for his son." He offered to buy him for two hundred pesos. Backed in court by don Francisco Antonio de Sardaneta y Legaspi, "the rich Guanajuato miner," Antonio won the return of his son.[46] There is much to note: Antonio de la Cruz's name suggests mulatto origins, perhaps even uncertain freedom. Did he assert Otomí status to announce liberty? A powerful Guanajuato miner backed de la Cruz, his rights to an adopted mulatto son, and the boy's freedom. Was it a noble gesture, or an attempt to create an obligation that might recruit another mulatto to work in the mines?

Three years later María Vásquez forced a new inquiry, this time before a judge at León. Antonio and Joseph Joaquín were jailed. The boy admitted that he was son of the mulatta slave Teresa de Jesús; he had been raised by "daddy and nanny"—Antonio and his wife. This time there was no intervention by the powerful. Instead a parade of witnesses testified: Phelipe de Campos, a free mulatto married to a

Spaniard; a mulatto slave, brother to Teresa de Jesús, the biological mother; a Spaniard related to the "indios" of San Luisito; and Josepha Nuñez, a Spaniard who owned a slave woman who had told her of ties of "mutual protection . . . between the indios of the Río Verde and San Luisito ranchos and the runaway slaves." All told the same tale: in the hills at San Luisito southwest of Guanajuato, there were canyons with cabins where slave women fled to deliver babies. Local midwives assisted with births and cared for mothers and infants. Newborns stayed in the ranchos; slave mothers gave up their babies to free them. Antonio de la Cruz admitted that Joseph Joaquín was such a child, given to him and his wife by Teresa de Jesús so that they would raise him "like a son."

By law the case seemed clear. Born to a slave mother, Joseph Joaquín belonged to María Vázquez. But the judge at León was unsure, perhaps reluctant to separate a boy from the only parents he knew, perhaps interested like Sardaneta in promoting mulatto freedom. He recused himself and called a Querétaro judge to settle the case. The new magistrate shifted the focus from birth status to property law, which required title and effective possession. He concluded that "Joseph Joachin was raised and educated as if free—for longer than the law requires." María Vázquez's claim to ownership came too late.[47]

This remarkable case reveals that communities of free people, of diverse and uncertain ancestry and status, regularly helped slave mothers to free their children—and deny slave property to their owners. In 1744 a master chased a slave woman into the same rugged zone, only to find her postpartum, without a baby, denying that a delivery had occurred. The frustrated owner sold the woman in Guanajuato, where she quickly escaped into the urban crowd.[48] This semi-clandestine way to freedom was widely known among slaves. The support for freedom by the miner Sardaneta, by the judges at León and Querétaro, and by the mulatto community at Guanajuato reveals that many were ready to accept the demise of slavery. Youths thus freed found their way to Guanajuato, where risky work might bring prosperity among throngs of mulatto mineworkers.

While free mulatto men and boys did essential, dangerous, and remunerative mine labor, free mulatta women negotiated the uncertainties of the mining community. In her will, executed in 1712, Petrona de Cisneros Matabacas called herself a "free *mulata*, unmarried, and a citizen (*vecina*)" at Guanajuato. She had two "natural children," Joseph Amezquita, married and living at Zacatecas (then in mining boom), and Catalina de Cisneros, fourteen and at home. Petrona owned three large urban lots, each with an ample house. One she left to her son and his daughter; a second went to María de Guadalupe, an orphan girl she had taken in; and the third would become property of "the poorest priest in town." Petrona did not reveal the activities that earned her properties: she may have operated shops, taverns, or boarding houses to profit from the men seeking a chance in the mining community. She owned gold, silver, and pearl jewelry, rich tapestries and fabrics from China, and fine porcelains and other wares from Asia and Europe. And she kept religious objects: a portrait from Burgos, Spain of Christ crucified, and canvases of Our Lady of Guadalupe and Our Lady of Sorrows. Petrona asked for burial in a habit of Saint Francisco. Her estate would pay alms to all who mourned her; the poor priest who gained a house would pray always for her soul.[49] The name of Petrona's father, Matabacas (cow killer), suggests descent from African slaves. In Guanajuato and unmarried, Petrona gained gained ample property and luxuries by means uncertain. She had children, took in orphans (who may have been escaping slave status), and attended to spritual needs in mainstream ways. An independent woman of means, she was proudly a free mulatta.

Petrona was not alone. Nicolasa Muñoz, also a "free *mulatta* citizen," wrote a will at Guanajuato in 1733. She was born out of wedlock at San Miguel to parents now deceased. As a single woman she had two sons, Cayetano and Sebastián Gómez; she later married their father, also Sebastián. Nicolasa insisted that neither she nor her husband brought property to the marriage. At his death she owned a large building with fifteen residences, each with a shop facing the street. The rents sustained her, her sons and grandchildren, and her religious commitments. She left the property to her heirs and mandated continued religious contributions. Nicolasa listed only modest possessions, along with portraits of Guadalupe, Our Lady of Sorrows, and Christ crucified.[50] Again the activities that allowed a life of property and prosperity are not reported. But Nicolasa had come to Guanajuato as a mulatta of uncertain origins and found a way to propertied comfort.

The mulattas' wills reveal a city open to free people of African ancestry, with space for women to gain property and prosperity. Mulattoes went to seek a chance in a place of risks and chances. Petrona found lavish success; Nicolasa gained propertied comfort. Many surely struggled for little gain. Guanajuato was a place of limited patriarchy and ethnic fluidity; people of diverse ancestry and uncertain freedom claimed mulatto status and faced lives of labor and petty trade.

And yet, to the powerful who presumed themselves privileged and Spanish, mulattoes were low and threatening people. That is clear from a dispute involving the Marqués de San Clemente, his twelve-year-old daughter doña María Josepha Marcelina Busto y Moya, her slave servants, and a young immigrant Spaniard who saw his chance in marriage to the noble miner's daughter. In 1747 don José Carlos de Balenchana, a Basque trader, went to the bishop's court in Valladolid with a series of letters in which San Clemente's daughter pledged love and promised to wed. The Marqués stepped in, insisting that there be no marriage. Balenchana asked for church sanction for the union. The case turned on the role of the girl's slave servants. Balenchana insisted that they were go-betweens and that the letters showed the true desires of young doña Marcelina. The Marqués argued that the slave women had drawn his daughter into a web of deceit, taking perverse pleasure in creating a relationship that they knew he would oppose. The role of the slaves and the views of the girl are unknown. San Clemente was adamant. Balenchana's only hope was the church; he won in court but no marriage followed.[51] The mining patriarch ruled. Immigrant dreams, slave interventions, a daughter's goals, and court rulings could not blunt San Clemente's power. Still, the rich patriarch presumed that women whom he owned as slaves were ready and able to control his daughter, create a love relationship against his will, provoke a victory for the suitor in church court, and force him to stop a marriage that he could not abide. Entrepreneurial power ruled. Even so, mining depended on the labor of people asserting African origins, people seen by the powerful as threatening patriarchal good order. Silver created a city of risk and promise, and a perpetual threat of disorder personified to some as mulatto mischief.

Religious exhortations promoted order in defense of power. Missionary colleges founded at Querétaro in the 1680s and Zacatecas in the early 1700s sent friars on penitential circuits; they brought weeks of sermons, processions, and confessions to the streets of Guanajuato.[52] In 1703 don Juan Diez de Bracamonte imagined a Jesuit college; like many before him he was unable to fund his vision.[53] In the 1730s mining soared and a growing number of workers no longer lived on their employers' compounds. One way of controlling workers was waning, as employers found profit by selling, leasing, or developing city lands just as demand for workers rose. It was then that the family of the Marqués de San Clemente, led by doña Josefa Teresa de Busto y Moya, organized funding for a Jesuit college, with the clear goal of improving social control. With her siblings an owner of the Cata and Mellado mines, doña Josefa was the widow of don Manuel de Aranda, a Spanish immigrant financier. He left her a refinery and cereal estate at Silao, the Zamorano hacienda near Querétaro, and grazing properties in the north. With properties worth 300,000 pesos, she pledged a fifth of her ample wealth to bring the Jesuits to Guanajuato.[54]

Seeking official approval in 1731, those who gained most from the mines testified to their goals for the Jesuits, and to their ideas about those who produced the silver that sustained their wealth, power, and presumptions of superiority. Doña Josefa offered a vision of compassion: Jesuits would educate youths, preach to the majority, and hear confessions, bringing "total comfort to the consciences of the citizens."[55] In the following year she emphasized: "mineworkers will receive the comfort their consciences need; they spend so much time and effort in the mines they do not find the spiritual sustenance that comes with missions, sermons, and other virtuous programs."[56]

Priests, entrepreneurs, and officials followed, emphasizing education for the sons of the elite and preaching to constrain the majority. Witness after witness offered increasingly dark visions of people who produced wealth for the Crown, profits for the few, and silver for the world. Bachiller don Francisco Saenz de Goya, pastor of the Guanajuato parish, saw "rude people in need of instruction in the rudiments of the faith." They were "poor mineworkers whose continuous labor allows little time to receive the Holy Sacraments, whether when ill, or to meet their annual obligation to confess and take Holy Communion."[57] Licenciado don José Patricio de Acosta, another priest, said that the Jesuits were needed "so that boys would learn to read, write, and count with perfection." Thus trained, a few would facilitate commercial life. Equally important, Jesuits would preach to "the mineworkers . . . who do not know, as so many do not know, the mysteries that every Christian must know to save themselves." Made into better Christians, "there would not be so many shiftless vagabonds, nor so many crimes and evils in the jurisdiction and nearby — so many now committed repeatedly and atrociously by these ignorant people."[58]

Next appeared the Marqués de San Clemente, joined by don Pedro de Sardaneta y Legaspi, councilman and operator of the Rayas mine. Only San Clemente testified, as if speaking for both and the mining elite in general. He too emphasized the importance of the college for the "large number of honorable families and other superior citizens" who deserve "schooling for their children in the basics of grammar and other liberal arts and sciences." For the rest, "the base people require instruction in the rudiments of the faith and the mysteries necessary to be saved, to live virtuous lives, and to flee from vice." All this would be provided by "the sacred workers . . . of the Society of Jesus." San Clemente offered the Jesuits as holy laborers who would bring religion, virtue, and subordination to rude and faithless workers.[59] Finally, the treasury officer don Anastacio Sebastián Romero Camacho insisted that only Jesuits could stop "the mineworkers' wanton lives of vice and lewdness caused by the total lack of instruction in the rudiments of the Holy Faith."[60] The goal, stated nobly by doña Josefa Teresa and the parish priest and crudely by the men who profited from mining, was clear: the Jesuits would educate the sons of the few—and pacify mineworkers.

In that context the actual funding of the college is revealing. Doña Josefa Teresa, with income from family mines and her husband's estates, gave an endowment of sixty thousand pesos. Her brother the marqués provided ten thousand more, a small sum given his vast wealth. Don Juan de Hiervos, a trader, refiner, and magistrate, added five thousand pesos. No other entrepreneur gave. Instead don José de Sardaneta y Legaspi devised a plan that deflected most of the cost onto workers. A *tanate*, a large basket used to carry ore, was placed at the mouth of every mine. As workers left they would deposit a piece of ore, before the Crown taxed the owners' share, before workers claimed partidos. The baskets collected ore worth 250 pesos weekly, 12,500 pesos yearly, far more than the 2,750 pesos earned annually on the 75,000-peso endowment proudly announced by a few among the elite.[61] Mine operators paid only if their mines prospered; their taxes fell. Workers paid most of the cost of a Jesuit college that aimed to educate elite children and control unruly workers and their families.

Construction took years. In 1738 don Pedro Bautista Lascurain de Retana, a Basque immigrant miner and financier at Guanajuato, adviser and compadre to doña Josefa Teresa, left his estates at Valle de Santiago to the Guanajuato Jesuits on condition that the income (another five to seven thousand pesos yearly) support preaching across the rural Bajío.[62] In 1745 don Juan de Hiervos died. His son-in-law, the rich merchant-landlord don Manuel de la Canal of San Miguel, paid the endowment of five thousand pesos in full, advancing construction and freeing himself of an annual obligation.[63] In 1747 debts forced doña Josefa Teresa to cede the Zamorano estate near Querétaro to don Francisco de Fagoaga and don Manuel de Aldaco, the silver bankers in Mexico City. She moved the charge to other properties and kept paying.

Construction only finished in 1765 at a cost of over 200,000 pesos—most from the ores that workers had placed in baskets as they left shifts of hard labor in the mines.[64] In the interim Jesuits preached on Sundays at the parish church and the Rayas mines, and at Easter in other urban neighborhoods. The year 1760 brought a smallpox epidemic and floods that turned the canyon city into a river of death and destruction; Jesuits nursed the ill, buried the dead, and offered the sacraments. They returned to serve when a plague of matlazahuatl (typhus) ravaged the city in 1762.[65] In 1761 they began roving missions, first in the city and nearby mines, then on circuits across León, north to San Felipe and south to Pénjamo and Cuitzeo in 1762, at Valle de Santiago and Salamanca in 1763, to Apaseo in 1764 and Irapuato in 1765.[66]

After Easter in 1762, as disease threatened life and mining, the Jesuits led a great mission at Guanajuato, beginning at Santa Ana, site of a promising bonanza. In the center they preached and led pentitential parades. Men and women, barefoot and in sackcloth, many bleeding from crowns of thorns, marched toward penance and communion. The Jesuits tried to moderate the most extreme flagellations and took pride in giving communion to over twenty thousand adults and children in the city and its mines.[67] Guanajuato's elite called the Jesuits to educate the children of the few and preach penance and salvation to a rough and resistant majority. Intense missions in times of crisis did reach many. For a moment Jesuit preaching focused those who risked life and limb in mining on penitential introspection—and away from the inequities that structured their lives.

Guanajuato remained a city of riches, risks, and raucous lives, where dreams of wealth relied on hellish labors—and where the powerful and the working poor viewed each other with suspicion. As mining revived in 1764 a new pastor of Guanajuato, don Juan de Dios Fernández de Souza, saw a city little changed by decades of boom, recent recession, or Jesuit preaching: "Guanajuato, confused jumble of craggy peaks . . . all horrible to see, they seem more a home for beasts than for people." The city was an "an abortion of nature . . . refusing to offer sites worthy of human life." In the center all could "admire sumptuous buildings, endless pleasant storefronts, and a confusion of humble structures"; but all around there was only "an assault of straw huts." It was a city resistant to planning, driven by greed, and shaped by risk. "A shelter for people seeking corrupt labor, agitated by a spirit of greed, and driven to hoard riches in an industry of fleeting promises, they perpetually lack even basic comfort." Guanajuato was "refuge of the poor drawn into entrails of silver, the den of vice-ridden men who by their numbers cause confusion and disorder, they recognize no law other than desire, fearlessness, and audacity; a tangle of individuals bound together by infamy, they make a mountain town of brute customs." Yet the pastor also saw Guanajuato as an "opulent vein of endless treasures, rich minerals deposited by God Omnipotent to enrich the public." For a few, at least, the city in the canyon was a "mother of deep talents, gentle ways, and generous souls."[68]

The touring Capuchin friar Franciso de Ajofrín spent July to September of 1764 in Guanajuato. He met with the district magistrate, with don Vicente de Sardaneta y Legaspi, operator of the Rayas mine and leader of the Mining Chamber, and with Father Fernández, whose views Ajofrín came to share.[69] He kept a diary: "Guanajuato, city of confusion . . . it seems more a lair for beasts than a home for men." It was a place of "people on the move and without goals, their numbers grow with the opulence of the mines."[70] Ajofrín visited as Guanajuato came out of recession.[71] He saw a community in production— portrayed in dark hues. "If the mines are in bonanza, entrepreneurs and workers all gamble, spend, and lose whatever they have without end or limit; there is no pickman nor blastman who is not prodigious, spending on luxuries, irrelevancies, and vices every treasure they take from the mines. It is laughable to see these smudged men with faces like devils, black apes ugly to the extreme, dressed up in velvet trousers, a dress coat inlaid with silver and edged with gold over a ruffled Dutch shirt."[72] Laboring in mines that resembled hell, Guanajuato workers were ugly black devils posing as aristocrats.

Ajofrín described a feast sponsored by a "debauched mulato" whose small mine enjoyed a brief bonanza of twelve thousand pesos. "The fame of the strike drew a rabble of wretched nobodies, as always happens with a bonanza. There were almost two thousand, yet no one lacked food or drink, thanks to the great liberality of the mulatto, whose name I don't recall . . . There was such abundance of bread, wine, pulque, meat, fruits, and maize tortillas, so much that ten women got paid."[73] Generosity was bizarre when offered by a mulatto to dark, pretentious workers. With prejudice, Ajofrín confirmed that Guanajuato remained a place of boom and insecurity, of rich elites and mulatto miners, a place where lives of risk limited patriarchy and women worked at what they could. Hugely productive and deeply divided, Guanajuato drove the economy of the Bajío, the Spanish Empire, and the world.

San Miguel: Industry, Awakenings, and Patriarchs at War

A day's travel east of Guanajuato, beyond rugged uplands, sat San Miguel. Founded in the 1550s to guard the road to Zacatecas during the Chichimeca wars, in the seventeenth century it was a small town surrounded by grazing estates. The mining revival of the eighteenth century brought unprecedented opportunities. With good access to markets at Zacatecas and Guanajuato, San Miguel began to earn its name, el Grande. It became a center of industry and trade, home to rich elites who profited and promoted penitential worship. Yet by 1750 deep conflict divided the men who ruled San Miguel. While struggles between the entrepreneurial few and the working majority shaped life at Guanajuato, conflict between elite families divided the powerful at San Miguel.

A small group of entrepreneurs led the rise of San Miguel as an industrial town. Mostly Iberian immigrants and their immediate offspring, they mixed trade, cloth production, and estate operations in integrated enterprises. They married together and with leading clans at Guanajuato and Querétaro. Don Francisco José de Landeta rose first. Locally born of Basque ancestry, he gathered around him don Francisco Antonio de Lanzagorta, a cousin and Basque immigrant, and don Manuel Tomás de la Canal, son of a prosperous merchant in Mexico City. Don Domingo de la Canal had financed mines across Spanish North America since the 1690s. He was among those who gained wealth and honor from the alliance that linked the merchants of Mexico City to the new Bourbon regime. He married a daughter of the prior of the consulado and himself held that leading role from 1716 to 1718. Over the years he added livestock dealing to mining investments.[74] His son don Manuel Tomás moved to San Miguel by 1731 and married the daughter of don Juan de Hiervás, merchant and refiner in Guanajuato. Canal's move to San Miguel reveals the town's dynamism. When don Manuel Tomás's eldest son married a Landeta, the integration of the dominant clan was complete. The Landetas, Lanzagortas, and Canals all held estates nearby and lands extending to the north; they operated textile obrajes, traded in estate produce and cloth, and held seats on the local council. The Canals' capital made them leaders of a provincial enstablishment.

Don Baltásar de Sauto tried to compete. Also a Basque immigrant, he was in San Miguel by 1725. By marrying a Jáuregui he gained an obraje and estates. With a sharp eye to profit, he dealt in cattle and hides, maize and wheat, as well as cloth. He kept a store that sold wares from New Spain, Europe, and China. He invested in mines at Guadalcázar to the north. He served as a magistrate, town councilman, and militia captain. Sauto was everything an entrepreneur could be at San Miguel—except a member of the ruling clan.[75]

For decades entrepreneurial competition brought an industrial and commercial boom. In his *Theatro americano* (1742) don José Antonio Villaseñor y Sánchez exuded praise for San Miguel. He honored its "temperate and healthful climate," "large population," and "abundant and useful commerce." All around were "estates grazing livestock and raising crops" worked by "workers and *gañanes* (dependent *indios*)" and "tenants on the land." A thriving countryside fed vibrant manufacturing. There were "textile *obrajes* and shops making cutlery and everything needed to harness a horse; they make arms like

Canal family mansion, San Miguel el Grande, eighteenth century.

machetes and knives, spurs and and other wares of great interest; the
women dedicate themselves to making pillows, quilts, and other bedding." Textiles, cutlery, leatherwork, and bedding led a thriving manufacturing economy at San Miguel.[76]

Population grew. The jurisdiction included fewer than three thousand people in the 1630s. By the 1740s it exceeded twenty thousand; by
1750 it approached thirty thousand, most in town. Its people were of
mixed origins, living in a commercial world and increasingly mulatto.
A church census of 1754 reported a population two-thirds Hispanic,
mixing Spaniards, mulattoes, and mestizos. A report in 1758 clarified proportions: "this town . . . is a place of very few Spaniards and
huge numbers of mulattoes and other mixes." An indigenous minority,
mostly Otomí, remained, struggling to hold vanishing autonomy by
working small plots near town while spinning yarn for the obrajes. At
San Miguel as at Guanajuato, an urban industrial community led to a
populace increasingly defined as mulatto, while north around the new
parish at Dolores a mixed rural majority negotiated life by remaining
indio.[77]

Rising industrially, San Miguel generated a remarkable religious
awakening. Don Juan Antonio Pérez de Espinosa was born at Querétaro, and educated there and in Mexico City thanks to don Juan

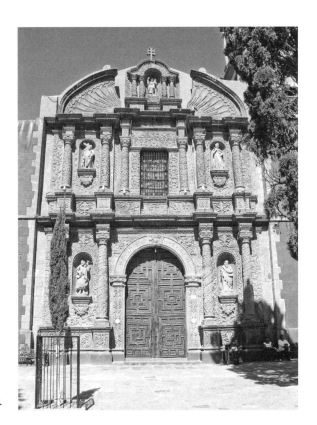

Oratorio de San Felipe Neri, San Miguel el Grande, eighteenth century.

Caballero y Ocío. Ordained by the bishop of Michoacán in 1700, Pérez de Espinosa preached in churches and obrajes at Querétaro until invited to San Miguel for Easter devotions in 1712. His fiery call to prudence, penance, and service struck home. Leading citizens asked him to stay, promising to fund an Oratorio of San Felipe Neri where priests would dedicate lives to prayer and penitence. His sponsors offered the chapel built by a local mulatto brotherhood. (Not consulted, the mulattoes sued and reclaimed the church for one festival a year.) Pérez de Espinosa rebuilt the chapel, added cells for priests, and built gardens where they raised food and offered examples of energetic work. In 1718 the oratorio was complete and Pérez de Espinosa sailed to Europe seeking royal and papal sanction. He succeeded after years of effort, but never returned to New Spain.

Pérez de Espinosa's work was reenergized in 1730 when don Luis Felipe Neri de Alfaro came to San Miguel and the oratorio. Son of a merchant from Mexico City, Alfaro brought drive and money. He gave five thousand pesos to build a chapel for Nuestra Señora de la Salud next to the oratorio. At San Miguel those seeking the Virgin's help in times of crisis approached through the penitential oratorio.

In the 1730s Alfaro founded Escuelas de Cristo, fraternities of leading men dedicated to aiding the poor, comforting the sick, burying the dead, and leading public prayer and penance. Escuelas spread from San Miguel to Guanajuato and León, and north to San Luis Potosí and Zacatecas. Alfaro led the powerful men of San Miguel toward a religion linking introspective penance and charitable service.

In the 1740s Alfaro began to build the Sanctuary of Jesus of Nazareth at Atotonilco in the country north of San Miguel. He bought land at springs along the Río Laja, a spot of beauty that according to Alfaro had become a site of sin and indulgence. He would make the waters spiritually cleansing. He built a fortress-church, a dam to irrigate the land, and a grist mill. Commercial cropping funded penitential worship. Weekly retreats drew men from San Miguel and beyond. Amid life-size replicas of Christ's passion, suffering, and crucifixion, Alfaro relived his savior's suffering; he carried a heavy cross, wore a crown of thorns, and called men on retreat to do the same. Prayer and penitence promoted faith, justice, charity, patience, and hope—virtues inscribed on temple walls inaugurated by Alfaro in 1748. The sanctuary called men to patriarchy: "If we do not teach our sons, we are not fathers—only cruel adversaries." Without service, "only eternal fire awaits."[78]

The awakening at San Miguel promoted a demanding Catholicism of patriarchy, prayer, penance, and service. It was a religion of individual action, of effort linking prayer and service, funded, joined, and promoted by the dominant men of San Miguel. In his will and testament, executed in 1759, the Conde de Casa Loja offered this: "We know that without faith it is impossible to please our Divine Lord, and that no one can attain salvation without fully and inviolably keeping . . . what the Church believes; it is essential that everyone know that faith explicitly and clearly, professing all its mysteries and celebrating them."[79] He proclaimed a religion that was individual, tied to the church, and aimed at personal salvation.

Rich patriarchs and devout priests drove penitential revivalism at San Miguel. A final foundation aimed to incorporate elite women. Don Manuel Tomás de la Canal had tried to build a convent for Capuchin nuns in 1740. When he and his wife died suddenly in 1748 they left nine orphans—the eldest, doña María Josefa Lina, only twelve years old. With her guardian, don Francisco José de Landeta, Conde de la Casa de Loja, she dedicated her inheritance of 58,000 pesos to a convent of Concepcionist sisters. The project was deeply influenced by Alfaro, the young orphan's confessor. Noble guardian, devout orphan, and penitential priest worked together to found a convent named La Purísima, chartered in 1752 and opened in 1756; the first residents included doña María Josefa Lina and three of her sisters. The goal was a

Atotonilco Sanctuary, north of San Miguel el Grande, eighteenth century.

(Below) Christ Crucified, interior of Atotonilco Sanctuary, north of San Miguel, eighteenth century.

refuge where the daughters of men of means would keep *vida común*—communal isolation and ascetic worship. San Miguel's patriarchs spent weeks of penitential devotion at Atotonilco before returning to pursuits of profits and salvation. Their daughters should retreat for life into poverty and devotion, isolated from families and husbands who might divert their wealth. Everything suggests that doña María Josefa Lina joined with unwavering devotion. Few other girls of San Miguel's best families followed her lead.[80]

While mine operators in Guanajuato funded Jesuits to tame an unruly mulatto majority by preaching penitence and adherence to a moral code, at San Miguel the penitential revival called patriarchs and their daughters to prayer, penitence, morality, and service. They focused on their own salvation more than they preached to the majority. Yet if the awakening at San Miguel did not aim at the majority, many surely heard its message. They had to know that powerful patriarchs promoted worship demanding introspective worship, personal responsibility, and charitable service. The awakening paralleled the patriarchs' rise to power; it surely raised questions of responsibility among those who struggled in everyday toil.

Popular devotion at San Miguel remains little known, lost in the shadows of elite-sponsored devotions. The Otomí did support a sodality to promote devotion to Our Lady of the Immaculate Conception, collecting many small contributions, often in goods and labor, to build first a temporary chapel and then a more durable church beginning around 1730. Local Otomí notables led collections and devotions, which included serving meals on Holy Thursday to the local poor (likely Otomí and mulatto)—their own charitable service. In the 1740s the parish priest joined in solidarity, followed by Bachiller don Felipe Neri de Alfaro, founder of the penitential devotions at Atotonilco. Clearly the Otomí at San Miguel sustained worship focused on a serving, caring Virgin.[81] But their devotions never claimed local primacy, as did Our Lady of Pueblito at Querétaro. Worship in estate communities is even less well known. In the 1760s a mulatta named María Guadalupe, famed as a healer, was accused of casting spells on an estate manager. Complaints before church leaders at Valladolid show San Miguel as a center of popular curing that mixed European, Mesoamerican, and African traditions. All was not as priests and patriarchs would wish.[82]

In the 1750s the downturn of mining at Guanajuato cut San Miguel's markets. Many household weavers went out of business. For obraje operators, competition in times of growth gave way to competition for shrinking markets; a war for local dominance ensued. It began with five murders among workers at don Baltásar de Sauto's obraje beginning late in 1756. The accused were jailed but not prosecuted. Sauto wanted his workers back; he wrote to the High Court in Mexico City insisting that the offenders were obligated by debts, some for criminal offenses. They owed him labor and he aimed to collect. Neither justice in general nor justice for the victims—also his workers—was his concern. The inquiry that followed exposed deplorable conditions in Sauto's obraje and began a war among San Miguel's patriarchs.

Five obrajes operated at San Miguel in 1755, with a total of seventy-five looms. Sauto's was the largest with twenty-two, exceeded by the twenty-seven in the two workshops of the Landeta and Canal clan. In the downturn Sauto turned over management to don Domingo de Aldama, an immigrant who cut wages and ended annual allotments of clothing to slaves and apprentices. Owner and manager gave advances, then manipulated wages, rations, and accounts to lengthen terms of work. They forced some to take on the debts of kin who had died or fled. Such practices reduced costs in times of uncertainty. To workers they broke customary agreements of obligated labor. In that context violence escalated.

In August 1758 the viceroy sent a High Court judge, don Diego Antonio Fernández de la Madrid, to investigate. He took Sauto's records and exiled him to Puebla. Inquiry found that Sauto employed four to five hundred people at his obraje and estates. He was a major taxpayer. Some witnesses thought him uniquely exploitative, cutting salaries, extending obligations, whipping men who resisted; others saw standard business practices. The judge called the workers indios, despite local perception that most were mulattoes—thus assuring his jurisdiction. He indicted Sauto, Aldama, and two foremen. While Sauto was jailed in Mexico City, Fernández de la Madrid married a Canal daughter, tying the judge to Sauto's rivals. Conflict dragged on in courts from Mexico City to Seville. The obraje was often closed and operated inefficiently. Finally, Fernández de la Madrid stepped aside. A new inquiry by the corregidor of Querétaro was inconclusive. Sauto was released and regained the obraje in 1760, but his economic ascent and challenge to the dominant clan ended.[83] Sauto may have been uniquely cruel, or perhaps his exploitations were like those in most obrajes in time of downturn—revealed too publicly by a spate of murders. Did the crimes offer the devout patriarchs of the clan of Canals, Lanzagortas, and Landetas a chance to assert charitable justice while assaulting their only competitor?

While patriarchs fought in court, conflict also tore apart the nuns of La Purísima. The founding abbess and doña María Josefa Lina held committed to the vida común, but the majority rebelled against the strict rules. They demanded more independence in life and worship. In 1759 they began a long dispute that stunted recruitment among San

Miguel's leading families and left the convent short of nuns and funds. The penitential ideals of San Miguel's patriarchs, shared by the Canal daughters, did not draw many to La Purísima.[84] San Miguel's elite divided in public, and in the convent devoted to penitential prayer.

The touring Capuchin Ajofrín spent two weeks in San Miguel in September 1764, just after leaving Guanajuato. He lived "with great love and care in the home of . . . Capitán don Báltazar de Sauto, a rich and distinguished gentleman." Ajofrín found the industrial town of San Miguel a respite from Guanajuato's darkness. It enjoyed "a healthy climate, mild airs, and the sweetest waters . . . Its population is large, its commerce rich; . . . most people are Spaniards, mestizos, and mulattoes." He also noted "the good number of Otomí *indios* in the barrios, haciendas, and obrajes."[85] Ajofrín saw fruit all around: "grapefruit, lemons, oranges, *chayotes*, Chinese pomegranates." Most of all, he honored the vibrant commercial and industrial life of San Miguel, as mining grew again to stimulate trade: "There are rich haciendas and livestock farms; in town *barrios* there are great obrajes and shops making exquisite woolens, almost as fine as those of Segovia. There are many tanneries making all kinds of leather wares: cowhides, shoe soles, suedes, chamois, and cordovans. Shops make metal arms and firearms: swords, machetes, shotguns, pistols, and other instruments of war. The women embroider pillows and bed covers, rugs and carpets, with exquisite art. I have seen some as fine as any that can be made in Europe."[86]

While admiring San Miguel, Ajofrín never mentioned its dominant clan and penitential devotions. His list of notables included Sauto, his kin, and allies. He mentioned don Manuel de la Canal only to note a religious endowment. The absence of the Landetas, Canals, and Lanzagortas, of Father Alfaro, and of penitential devotion at Atotonilco seems a purposeful exclusion of men who caused Sauto, Ajofrín's host, such trials. Still, the larger message was that after the war between the patriarchs, San Miguel remained a vibrant place of industry and artisanry, surrounded by flourishing estates. As to popular identities, Ajofrín reported a predominance of mulattoes and a good number of Otomí. He confirmed that what had flourished in the 1740s still flourished in the 1760s, with firearms manufacture new and noteworthy. Industry, trade, obrajes and craft shops, and women quilting and embroidering at home, all ruled by patriarchal entrepreneurs, shaped San Miguel. Certainties of penitential and charitable superiority legitimated lives of power and luxury. The patrarichs' conversations with those who worked to produce their wealth can only be imagined. The views of the mulatto and Otomí majority remain unknown.

Querétaro: Spaniards, Otomí, and the Virgin at Pueblito

Eighteenth-century Querétaro flourished as a place of trade, textiles, haciendas, huertas, Spaniards, and Otomí. The revived stimulus of silver quickened commercial life, expanded industry and cultivation, and helped Spaniards to press their advantage in a city built by Otomí lords and settlers. Entrepreneurs prospered and ruled an assertive Spanish council. The Otomí remained entrenched on their huertas, led by the indigenous republic and served by Our Lady at Pueblito. Two developments in the 1730s illustrate the complexity that shaped and integrated life at Querétaro: Spanish wealth and Otomí labor built a great aqueduct to carry water to the Spanish center, while amid prosperity, disease, and drought, Spanish Querétaro adopted the Virgin of Pueblito. The great project in which Otomí worked to bring water to the Spanish center and the religious inversion in which Spaniards adopted the Otomí Virgin combined to integrate a deeply stratified, culturally divided city. While Guanajuato faced labor conflict and San Miguel lived a war among patriarchs, Querétaro generated wealth and mediated social relations of deepening inequality.

A city of trade, cloth, and cultivation, Querétaro was home to great concentrations of wealth yet little entrenched desperation as the seventeenth century drew to a close. Wealth and dispersed prosperity were legacies of Otomí foundations. The Convent of Santa Clara, founded by the Otomí lord don Diego de Tapia to house his daughter, preserve his fortune, and show his Christian piety, owned the richest irrigated estates in the area. As the economy quickened around 1700 the convent sold its properties to eager entrepreneurs, funding them and many others with mortgage loans. The sisters became the leading bankers in the Bajío.[87] The Otomí majority in the city avoided dependence and desperation thanks to lush, irrigated huertas, and the indigenous republic that defended their lands and water rights.

The other great concentration of property at Querétaro as the century began belonged to don Juan Caballero y Ocío, the priest-landlord with vast holdings built by his seventeenth-century forebears. In 1680 he founded and funded a congregation of priests devoted to Our Lady of Guadalupe at Querétaro. A Mexica-Christian Virgin first worshipped by Nahuas near Mexico City, Guadalupe became a powerful, compassionate mother who brought water amid drought, cure in times of disease, fertility to fields, and children to families. In the 1640s the clergy in Mexico City began to honor Guadalupe, linking colonial elites and indigenous subjects. She served and protected both, integrating and legitimating the colonial order in the Mesoamerican heartland. At Querétaro, Caballero y Ocío offered Guadalupe to Spaniards asserting rule over an Otomí majority devoted to and protected by Our Lady at Pueblito. At Querétaro, Guadalupe's congregation asserted the primacy of Spanish elites.[88] If Caballero hoped she would rival the Franciscan-Otomí worship at Pueblito, he would face disappointment. In 1686 a new sodality reenergized devotion at Pueblito. While the rich priest promoted Guadalupe, endless small contributions from poor devotees kept the Otomí Virgin the focus of everyday worship.[89]

Meanwhile the Franciscan friar Antonio Llinás led a group of clerics from Spain to Querétaro to start a mission college. Born in Mallorca, Llinás had preached in Querétaro and Celaya since the 1660s. He returned to Spain in 1680 (perhaps on the occasion of the founding of Guadalupe's temple), seeking sanction to mount missions to counter what he saw as the failings of Christianity in New Spain: lax devotion, uncertain morality, and the persistence of "infidels," notably in the Sierra Gorda. To Llinás few people in and near the Bajío were fully Christian, whether devoted to Guadalupe or Our Lady at Pueblito.

Llinás arrived in Europe amid the acclaim for the foundation of a missionary college by Portuguese Franciscans; negotiations with his superiors and regime officials won a charter in 1682 to found a replica at Querétaro. Officials selected the site: Llinás preferred San Juan del Río, with easier access to the Sierra Gorda. But Querétaro had the wealth to fund the mission enterprise. While Caballero y Ocío built Guadalupe's temple at Querétaro, honoring the Virgin's appearance in New Spain, the Crown chartered the Franciscan College of Santa Cruz, asserting that there was still much Christianization to be done.[90]

In 1683 a first mission addressed the people of Querétaro in a month of sermons demanding penitential devotion. The friars thought the effort a success; vice persisted, but moved from the public squares. Later that year a second mission brought the same passion to Mexico City—the place most devoted to Guadalupe. The message that Guadalupan Christianity was not sufficiently pure and penitential was clear. A mission in the Sierra Gorda followed, but failed to curtail the independence of its peoples. Perhaps frustrated by limited successes in Querétaro and the Sierra, and by the Pueblo revolt in New Mexico that blocked a turn to the north, the friars of Santa Cruz headed to Puebla and Guatemala.[91]

Into the 1690s the Virgin at Pueblito claimed the devotion of the Otomí majority, while Guadalupe, an immigrant from Mesoamerica funded by the richest man in the Bajío, challenged her primacy. Missionary Franciscans pressed for penitential renewal. Meanwhile the commercial economy of Spanish North America encountered difficulties: mines went into decline, though a few began to revive; the northern outposts faced Pueblo, Tarahumara, and other revolts. In that crucible Querétaro lived a spectacle. Doña Juana de los Reyes, daughter of an honorable Spanish family and a chaste virgin, began to experience troubling symptoms. She seemed possessed; her belly began to expand and expel needles, black wool, and pieces of metal. Franciscans at the Mission College concluded that a sorcerer posing as a curer, Josepha Rámos, La Chuparratones, was responsible for a diabolic possession. Penitential parades ended in exorcisms, and assertions that diabolic spirits named Mozambique and Tongoxoni possessed doña Juana. Evil forces of African and Otomí origin, mobilized by a woman of mixed ancestry, were destroying a virgin of a fine Spanish family. Could missionary Franciscans relieve the siege of evil?[92]

There was debate. Don Juan Caballero y Ocío, Querétaro's rich priestly entrepreneur and Guadalupe's local benefactor, shared the Franciscans' understanding. He invoked Guadalupe, who could not break the devil's hold. The Jesuits, Dominicans, and some parish clergy doubted the role of the devil, blaming La Chuparratones and other sorcerers for doña Juana's troubles. Inquisitors in Mexico City, kept informed by a Querétaro Carmelite, concluded that doña Juana's symptoms were fakery, a heretical blasphemy promoted by local sorcerers and healers. On 27 December 1691 doña Juana gave birth to a son.[93]

The midwife, Mariana de Quadros, declared that "the infant is a son of rational man, not of a beast." She had known for months, she added, that doña Juana was pregnant, as did most women in the neighborhoods. The Franciscans offered a different explanation. During a postpartum exorcism a voice declared: "I Mozambique, Devil from hell, carry the semen of a man and on order of my mistresses I deposited it in the womb of this girl." The African devil served sorcerers led by La Chuparratones. Another virgin birth was announced; more were threatened. Local authorities, linked to the Franciscans by family and interest, arrested La Chuparratones, subjected her to public humiliation and beatings, and gained a confession: she worked with devils, including Cuatzín. For a moment the only debate was whether the devil was African, Otomí, or Mexica.[94]

The Inquisition had begun to deliberate before the delivery. Afterward it concluded that a virgin impregnation could only result from divine intervention, not human sorcerers working through devils (of any ancestry). In January 1692 it prohibited any mention of a virgin birth or a role of the devil from any pulpit. The Inquisitors then proceeded to questions of heresy and blasphemy, seeking "those who buy and sell the herbs pipilzizintlí and peyote." After time passed and calmed local passions, in 1693 both doña Juana and La Chuparratones were brought to Mexico City and jailed by Inquistors, separated from their protectors and collaborators in Querétaro. Doña Juana confessed that she had been impregnated by her brother, who was taken in by the Franciscans as Fray Buenaventura and sent to a convent in Valladolid. She went to La Chuparratones seeking an abortion. The objects expelled from her womb had been inserted to end the pregnancy. When that failed she asked the sorcerer to kill her with potions. This too failed, leading to claims of possession passionately backed by Franciscans and Spanish authorities. Doña Juana was sentenced to a year of seclusion in the Convent of Santa Clara; La Chuparratones took two hundred lashes. The Franciscans were admonished.[95]

The spectacle in the 1690s of pregnant Spanish virgins, popular witches, and dark devils came amid commercial decline and violent assertions of independence by native peoples across the frontier of Spanish North America—a striking parallel to the witch trials soon to engage Salem in distant Massachusetts.[96] At Querétaro, Guadalupe disputed the role of the Virgin at Pueblito while European Franciscans proclaimed the people of Querétaro less than Christian and demanded penitential prostration. Yet it was the newly arrived Franciscans who saw devils everywhere; inquisitors in Mexico City focused on and found human frailty. In the same years a young women of mestizo ancestry emerged from her family's huerta to report mystical conversations with God and translocations to bring truth to natives in Texas and New Mexico. She too endured reports to the Inquisition, yet gained protection from leading friars of the Mission College of Santa Cruz, notably don Antonio Margil de Jesús.[97]

Religious truth was in dispute. While Francisans and Jesuits debated the role of devils, all feared that Otomí, mestizo, and mulatto sorcerers could impregnate a chaste Spanish girl. The Spanish minority had deep worries about the power of the majority in the city, and among independent peoples nearby in the Sierra Gorda and far to the north. Ironically, Franciscans newly arrived from Spain inflamed belief in malevolent devils; New Spain's Inquisition sought moderation, found the underlying truth, and imposed limited punishments that mostly lashed the healer who responded to an honorable virgin's search for an abortion to spare herself, her brother, and her family from the shame of an incestuous pregnancy.

Since the end of the Chichimecas war, Spaniards had worked to claim land, water, and local rule at Otomí Querétaro. The Europeans presumed a moral superiority as honorable patriarchs, devout wives, and chaste daughters. With ethical precedence contradicted by virgin pregnancies in the best Spanish households, clerics blamed dark malevolent witches. The Inquisition found the truth. We may suspect that after taking her lashes, La Chuparratones shared that truth with her neighbors. Spanish elites clung to a fragile moral superiority. After a century of assertion, Spanish power was still contested—in production and rule, honor and truth.

The silver boom and commercial revival of the eighteenth century energized Spanish entrepreneurs and heightened contests between Spaniards, who asserted power and legitimacy, and the Otomí, who sustained production and claimed cultural independence at Querétaro. The textile industry grew: the four obrajes of the 1640s became thirteen by 1718 and twenty-two in 1743. African slaves did most obraje labor in the 1640s; in the early 1700s many remained, but they worked beside convicts sentenced to labor and a growing number of free, obligated workers. Outside obraje walls uncounted numbers spun wool to supply their looms—many were women in rural households. And the obrajes were but part of the cloth industry; Otomí artisans, often families also working huertas, made cloth at home for use and sale.[98]

Obligated workers cultivated expanding commercial fields nearby. Yet many family producers remained: they raised fruits and vegetables on urban huertas; they planted maize as estate tenants; they made cotton goods for markets near and distant. Families with huertas, tenant farms, and artisan shops sent seasonal hands to estate fields and city building sites. Because huertas still sustained the Otomí majority in the city, because Otomí families still ruled cotton weaving, and because obligated labor and tenancies were available at estates, few chose long hours of labor in the obrajes. Slavery and convict labor persisted to force a few to do work that many resisted.

Obraje operators continued to buy slaves in the early eighteenth century. A sample of sixty transactions suggests that purchases peaked in the 1730s (when the Rincón Gallardos sent slaves from Ciénaga de Mata to Querétaro), receded in the 1740s, and then fell precipitously.[99] There is revelation in the details. Most slave men were in their young twenties, laboring in obrajes. Their prices held at 200 pesos each into the 1720s, fell slightly as numbers peaked in the 1730s, and then dropped in the 1740s, when 150 pesos was standard. In the 1730s and 1740s slave youths from twelve to fifteen, who might offer long labor, sold for only 110 to 120 pesos. Slave labor persisted in the obrajes as operators took advantage of falling slave values, while slavery declined across the Bajío because of amalgamations and the presence of diverse ways to freedom.

Slave women were fewer, older, and more valuable in early eighteenth-century Querétaro. When sold they were usually over twenty-five, often over thirty. Their prices averaged over 280 pesos in the 1720s and 1730s, and a few cost 350 pesos. In the 1740s their numbers fell along with their prices, which now averaged 225 pesos (still much more than the price of younger men). Most slave women did household service, the norm in a patriarchal world. They raised their owners' children and served their families in diverse ways—public evidence of rich notability. They raised their own children, still enslaved, some of whom were surely fathered by masters or members of their households. When in 1733 don José de Escandón (among the leading men of Querétaro, as we shall see) served as godfather to a son of don Juan Francisco de la Llata, equally prominent, the newborn received the gift of a slave girl, María de la Trinidad, nine years old, "a little mulatto slave . . . white in color." Two years later de la Llata sold María: "the slave girl has not reconciled herself to please doña Ana Frías, my wife, which has led to many vexations."[100] Oh, to know the full story. Was María white because she was Escandón's child, given away because he would not free her, yet could not keep her in his household? Did María cause "vexations" because she knew she was the daughter of a powerful man and unwilling to live in bound servitude? Or by 1735 was María entering puberty—and facing "vexations" caused by a powerful master in a new household?

As the economy surged, as production expanded and diversified, and as slavery lived its last years of importance, the Otomí republic continued in its mediating role. It still owned the Mesón (travelers' inn), several prime commercial buildings, and the rich lands known as the hacienda de la Comunidad. It leased them out, often by auction, mostly to Spanish entrepreneurs. Thus the republic tapped the commercial economy, earning over a thousand pesos yearly to sustain Otomí community affairs, mostly religious festivals.[101] It also continued to defend Otomí rights, notably the huertas that sustained the urban community. In 1732 it was learned that don Pedro Frejomil y Figueroa, councilman and constable on the Spanish council, had bought a huerta from Bachiller don José Ignacio de la Granada, a priest and Otomí cacique. The property was "across the river," in the jurisdiction of the Otomí republic. Barrio leaders argued that the obraje would do irreparable harm, taking water and polluting huertas. The Otomí governor and council tried an ingenious tactic. They gave power of attorney to don Bernardo de Pereda Torres, Spanish infantry captain, merchant, and obraje operator, to stop construction.[102] Pereda was expected to protect Otomí rights—and limit competition to his own textile enterprise. If only we knew the arguments and the outcome of the suit.

Amid economic expansion Querétaro's leading families and institutions continued to prosper while accommodating successful newcomers. After the death of don Juan Caballero y Ocío in 1707, local leadership passed to his kinsman don Antonio de Ocío y Ocampo. An estate entrepreneur and obraje operator, he sat on the Spanish council, married two daughters to rising entrepreneurs, and sent three others to Santa Clara. There they joined a community living in cloistered comfort, sanctifying local society and promoting estate development as rising endowments funded mortgages for entrepreneurs who purchased estates, expanded cultivation, and built new irrigation works. In 1739 Santa Clara held 274 mortgages totaling 742,000 pesos.[103]

While established elites carried on, newcomers came to compete—and to build ties to already eminent families. Everything came together for don José de Escandón. He left Santander in northern Spain as a youth of thirteen and arrived in Mérida on the Yucatán peninsula in 1715, attached to an elder migrant aiming to trade. Young Escandón joined the military, gained fame in a local skirmish, and moved on. He was in Querétaro by 1721, barely twenty. Three years later he wed doña María Antonia de Ocío y Ocampo, daughter of don Antonio. A dowry of 5,100 pesos facilitated purchase of an obraje worth 38,000 pesos, worked by 16 slaves (worth 3,200 pesos). In 1727 Escandón bought a commercial property on the square facing the Franciscan church and convent. In the early 1730s he bought and sold rural estates and invested in local mines; he was proudly a merchant and obraje operator, sergeant major of the militia, and lieutenant to the corregidor—Querétaro's Spanish district magistrate. Escandón mixed trade, textile production, and estate operation with militia command and important office. He worked closely with don Bernardo de Pereda Torres, a merchant and obraje operator who arrived just before Escandón, also served as the corregidor's lieutenant, and was militia captain (and in 1732 helped the Otomí republic).

When Escandón's wife doña María Antonia Ocío y Ocampo lay gravely ill in 1736, Escandón wrote her will—including a donation of two hundred pesos to Our Lady at Pueblito. Old families and rich newcomers knew the source of cure at Querétaro. This time the appeal failed; in the following year Escandón married doña María Josefa de Llera, daughter of another immigrant merchant, leading estate owner, and Spanish councilman with whom Escandón had business ties. Don José de Escandón became one of the leading men of Querétaro in the 1730s and 1740s.[104] He later led a drive into the Sierra Gorda and beyond, continuing the historic role of the Bajío in the expansion of Spanish North America, gaining honor as the Conde de Sierra Gorda.

Don Pedro Romero de Terreros followed a different route that began in Querétaro and led to wealth and noble title. His uncle don Juan Vázquez de Terreros preceded him from a small town in Extremadura to Querétaro, where he traded with a kinsman who had come even earlier. In the early 1700s Vázquez financed mines with supplies and cloth, gaining silver that he then traded for European and Asian imports, which he then sold in turn from the Bajío to Zacatecas. He bought city houses and rural estates, and sent four daughters with endowments to Santa Clara. Don Pedro was trading with his uncle by 1730 and inherited the business in 1735. In the 1740s his Querétaro trade funded mining at Real del Monte, just north of Mexico City. Financing led to ownership, huge investments in drainage, and unprecedented bonanza in the 1760s. While his kin continued in prominent roles at Querétaro, Romero de Terreros moved to Real de Monte; later his rich and multiply titled progeny settled in Mexico City.[105] Don Pedro became the Conde de Regla, the richest and most landed man in the Americas.

Don Juan Antonio de Urrutía y Arana reversed the journey, taking wealth from Mexico City to sustain prosperity and public service in Querétaro. His father, an immigrant Spaniard, made a fortune in trade in the viceregal capital and gained title as Marqués de la Villa del Villar del Águila. Don Juan Antonio moved to Querétaro, married well, invested in estates, and in the 1720s and 1730s promoted the great aqueduct. Like don Manuel Antonio de la Canal, son of a Mexico City merchant who moved to San Miguel to earn a fortune and assert his eminence, the young Marqués del Villar del Águila took wealth from the capital to claim eminence in the Bajío. So did don Esteban Gómez de Acosta: an immigrant from Galicia, he first traded in Mexico City, gained modest wealth, married into a Querétaro family, and after his wife's death bought the office of Corregidor there for ten thousand pesos. He moved there with his children, holding office as magistrate in the 1740s and 1750s. Economic opportunity and more drew men on the rise to Querétaro.

In 1743 Gómez de Acosta wrote a report revealing deep affection for his adopted city. The population included 1,149 families of Spaniards, 1,203 of mestizos, 692 of blacks and mulattoes, slave and free, and 2,805 of "native Otomí."[106] Of a total of 5,849 families 20 percent were Spanish, 20 percent mestizo, 12 percent mulatto, and 48 percent remained Otomí, not indio. Otomí language and identity held; Hispanic identities divided between Spaniards and mestizos; mulattoes were few. The legacies of Querétaro's Otomí origins remained. Neither the indio status common on the bottomlands nor the mulatto identity that defined and denigrated majorities at Guanajuato and San Miguel ruled at Querétaro. With Otomí holding republican rights and lush huertas, and while slaves of African ancestry still toiled long hours locked in obrajes, Otomí remained a favored identity.

The corregidor Gómez de Acosta's narrative was one of two texts that detailed life at Querétaro around 1740. In 1739 don Francisco

Antonio Navarrete, a Jesuit priest, honored the Marqués del Villar del Águila on completion of the great aqueduct. Four years later Gómez described the city and its environs with unrestrained admiration. Both portrayed Querétaro as nearly utopian, a sharp contrast with contemporary views of Guanajuato. Navarrete began his *Relación peregrina*: "The most noble and loyal city of Santiago de Querétaro, among all the cities of this northern continent is not the most populous, but thanks to mild skies and admirable waters is the most luxuriant; the huertas that surround it in a half moon make it so pleasant and scenic that all the senses take special delight in its elegant beauty."[107] Otomí huertas gave the city its arc of flowering beauty, though Navarrete would not say so. Gómez also gloried in "countless huertas," yet he too failed to state that it was the Otomí who grew "delicious flowers" along with "lush trees that yield ripe fruits they share with their neighbors, all of New Spain, and part of Europe, . . . When the fruit is not fresh, it makes delicate sweets, dried treats, and preserves."[108]

Gómez did note that Spanish agriculture ruled the "beautiful and spacious valley" extending along the river west of the city. "Every bit of land is used for beautiful fields of wheat, barley, and maize, whose abundant harvests bring joy to their owners." He counted eleven *haciendas de trigo*, irrigated with waters that first passed through huertas near the city center. Beyond wheatfields forty-six estates grazed livestock and rented growing numbers of ranchos to small growers.[109] Celebrating the aqueduct that diverted water from Otomí huertas to the Spanish center, Navarrete proposed a new dam in La Cañada to expand estate cultivation.[110] The magistrate and the Jesuit could not avoid Otomí huertas; they preferred and promoted Spanish commercial cultivation.

Both praised Querétaro as a city of industry and trade. Navarrete offered a poetic knot of commerce and cultivation: "Merchants make good money, converting *platillas* [Silesian linens] into *platas* [silver] and smaller coins. Farmers work the land with such enterprise that they and their customers draw sustenance from it."[111] For Gómez de Acosta, the merchant magistrate, "The soul of all republics is the trade and commerce of their citizens." He reported twenty-two obrajes with dozens of workers each, plus numerous family cloth makers and tanneries cutting and finishing fine leather wares. Celebrating the diversity of local industry, he feared overproduction. He called for limits on family production to favor obrajes. In industry as in agriculture large producers dominated, but families found ways to participate, sustain themselves, and limit the power and profits of those who presumed to rule. Gómez de Acosta honored trade as the route of migrant ascent and landed investment: "Many merchants exiled from their homelands come here and find, as if a new mother, the loving shelter of fortunes that continue to grow and yield profit. Others enjoy the most opulent landed estates."[112]

Navarrete and Gómez de Acosta knew that San Pedro de la Cañada, just west, was essential to Querétaro. Navarrete saw utopia. The canyon sent water to the city and its huertas. In addition, "The Cañada is to Querétaro what Aránjuez is to Madrid, Versailles to Paris, Frascati to Rome, . . . because in Cañada Querétaro has every delight; the city is right to see the canyon as the place to play."[113] When Gómez turned to the canyon town, admiration came with a jaundiced eye. Its "native *indios* support themselves with the countless huertas they own and the many and varied fruit trees that create beauty for a league and a half, along with the many other crops their lands yield—all fertilized by river waters on their way to the city. They take fruits and vegetables to sell at the mines of Guanajuato, San Luis Potosí, Zacatecas and other places, acquiring by industrious work great quantities of pesos. It is notable that thanks to their great profits, in two centuries since the conquest, they have refused to sell even one handful of land to a Spaniard, or to allow any to settle among them—with Querétaro so close by." Gómez admired the prosperity of La Cañada's Pames; he resented the exclusion of Spaniards from lands and trades, and the fees they charged the people of Querétaro to bathe in springs that were a favorite retreat. "They are the richest indios in the jurisdiction, very arrogant, audacious, and bold; they refuse to subject themselves to the preaching and teaching of their reverend pastor." The corregidor proposed to appoint "a Lieutenant who will subjugate them, make them meet their Christian duties, obey their superiors and priests, and end their frequent riotous discords, factional spats, and other disturbances." Two centuries after expelling the first Otomí settlers, the Pames of La Cañada still controlled the springs that fed Querétaro's river, huertas, and aqueduct; they profited by trading across the Bajío and in distant mining towns. Navarrete saw utopia, Gómez de Acosta insubordination.[114]

Only Gómez de Acosta addressed life in outlying Otomí towns. He had little to say, and no complaint, when he described San Francisco Galileo, Pueblito, home to the Virgin. Built on a small stream that flowed from uplands to the south, Pueblito lacked huertas. By the 1740s the village had lost much land to nearby haciendas, leaving just enough to plant "the necessities of sustenance." At Huimilpan, in the uplands south, Gómez described "*indios* who maintain themselves comfortably making charcoal, cutting timber, and making good lum-

Querétaro aqueduct, eighteenth century.

ber, all of which they bring to sell in Querétaro." Villagers near Querétaro might be rich and resented at La Cañada, comfortable at Huimilpan, or just surviving at Pueblito. In addition, "most natives, men as well as women, find special support and aid working to spin wool for the obrajes of the city and its district."[115] The textile industry, famous for its city workshops, reached out to incorporate indigenous families in outlying villages. Spinning wool into yarn brought income to prosperous families at La Cañada and to comfortable loggers and sawyers at Huimilpan, while providing needed income to land-starved families at El Pueblito.

Father Navarrete wrote most of all to honor the Marqués del Villar del Águila and the aqueduct that brought water to the center of Querétaro—to the Spanish, the prosperous, the powerful, and those who served them. Before, "though Querétaro had plenty of water . . . it lacked . . . purity." The marqués, "like a skilled physician, recognized all the illnesses the body of the city suffered, and taking its pulse, saw that the gravest disease was not having water to drink while there was so much for irrigation." The torrents cascading from the canyon washed obraje wool and irrigated Otomí huertas, sustaining the economic life of Querétaro. The river was also the city's only sewer. The result was "bad smell, color, and taste"—a constant threat to health. With "these rational motives" the marqués proposed a great aqueduct to capture canyon water before it entered the river, diverting it to the city center with its palatial homes, great convents, and fine squares.[116]

Construction began in 1726. The Spanish council gave 12,000 pesos; other citizens gave 24,000; a benefactor of the Mission College of Santa Cruz gave 3,000; a fine for unstated malfeasance brought 2,500 pesos; and the Marqués de la Villa del Villar del Águila gave 82,987 precisely accounted pesos. Of a total of 124,791 pesos, the Marqués paid nearly two-thirds. Yet the benefactor and his Jesuit admirer knew that there was more to construction than money. The marqués provided constant oversight. "He visited the works at least twice every day, energizing and directing everything, climbing scaffolds, mounting walls, many times with his own hands hauling out debris or delivering stone and brick to the masons. As the public *edificio* [structure] rose, so did public edification, astonished by the marqués's energies."[117] The marqués was a rich donor and active builder.

The work was done in October 1738. Pure water flowed from the canyon, carried thirty-four yards high over forty arches to reach the heights by the Mission College and then flow to homes, convents, and plazas in the center. Great celebrations hailed the generous marqués. City artisans organized a parade highlighted by a boat floating on a crowd of willing hands—making water of Querétaro's workers. Their song of praise ended: "If working well earns the prize of eternal life, then he who has worked so well, may he live, triumph, reign, rule, order, and prevail." Building and working fused as ultimate goods, the way to salvation.[118]

The Otomí republic organized its own parade to remind all that Otomí hands had built the aqueduct. If work was the source of all good, including salvation, none worked more than the Otomí. Their parade began with "kettledrums and trumpets," followed by "a large squad of indigenous infantry, armed with bows and arrows, wearing feathered headdresses, . . . their bodies painted many colors, . . . as they passed reminding all of how they fought in the times of their gentility." The Otomí remembered their warrior origins, "filling hearts with pleasant surprise, calling to mind the deeds of their heroic ancestors." After the young warriors came "indios principales [notables] on horseback, dressed extravagantly in the style of Romans, with rich plumage, harnesses, and saddle blankets." Querétaro's noble Otomí asserted eminence in a classic style that Europeans understood. They also grappled with indigenous identity: in the title of the song they were indios, a label promoted by the regime. In the first phrase they were americanos; later they were Otomí and Chichimecas. In the 1730s the Otomí of Querétaro remembered their warrior origins and insisted that they were Americans—knowing that many wanted to see them as indios.

Their song feigned honor to the marqués for his great work—and boldly contested his claim to have built the aqueduct. Pure water was a gift of God, delivered by Otomí hands:

> As a remedy for all,
> God gave, because He chose to,
> water as the medicine
> of baptismal fonts.
> Water is the shared refuge
> of the soul and of the body,
> washing stains,
> irrigating the land.

And water came by the effort of *indios*:

> Of all the miracles of water,
> we proclaim that
> in imitation of water,
> Indios do prodigious things.
> Indios plant the fields,
> indios harvest wheat,
> indios bake bread
> indios make everything.
> It is certain that if
> these domains lacked indios,
> everything would be scarce
> because indios are the fifth element.

If the point was not clear, they continued:

> From beginning to end,
> indios alone,
> at the cost of hard work,
> gave water to the citizens
> They built the reservoir,
> risking danger
> they built soaring arches and vaults,
> they made buttresses, bricks, and cement.

The conclusion was obvious:

> All the natives
> are so grateful,
> we return to the Spanish
> a river of water, clean and pure.

The cynicism that followed was unmistakable:

> To indios, water gave
> life free of
> cruelties and rude ways,
> of impurities and of sorceries.
> Today, we return the favor,
> because we understand
> that if purity reigns,
> it is because Spaniards live free of vice.

Pure water, like so much else enjoyed by Querétaro's Spaniards, was a "gift" of the Otomí. Spaniards "deserved" the gift because they lived without vice—an absurd assertion that denied Spanish claims to moral superiority.[119] The Otomí honored the aqueduct and reminded all that they had founded Querétaro, had built everything, and would contest any claim of Spanish superiority. Navarrete portrayed the marqués as a rational man doing good works to bring health to Spanish Querétaro. He also recorded the Otomí retort: water was a gift of God delivered by Otomí labor. Rational action for public good drove the noble civic leader; the Otomí knew that God still ruled, and that Otomí labor built what reason imagined.

Navarrete could celebrate rational planning. Both he and the magistrate Gómez de Acosta knew that religion was key to social integration at Querétaro. Both wrote pages to honor convents, churches, and religious benefactors. Gómez remembered don Juan de Caballero y Ocío as founder of the Congregation of Guadalupe. Its endowment of 160,000 pesos, invested in mortgages on commercial estates, rendered 8,000 pesos yearly. Gómez called devotion to Guadalupe universal; then he added that her church included "Our Lord Jesus Christ, on his walk of tormented passion, titled Ecce Homo; He is vulgarly called Lord of the Huerta, having long been kept in a small chapel by simple indios . . . working miracles with the poor, the ill, and the needy." Guadalupe and her priests had captured the Christ who served the Otomí of the huertas: "His cult is greater today."[120] Who drew the Otomí to Guadalupe's temple, the Virgin from afar or the Christ honored by families working huertas?

Gómez praised the Jesuits. Also funded by Caballero y Ocío, they taught sons of the local elite.[121] The convent of Santa Clara de Jesús, the Tapias' legacy, awed Gómez. Original endowments plus dowries of 2,000 to 4,000 pesos paid by every novice funded mortgages that produced "huge revenues" of 40,000 pesos yearly—five times the income of Guadalupe's temple. A capital of 800,000 pesos financed estates while the sisters honored God: "The nuns are of exemplary virtue . . . honoring their sovereign with divine praises in their choir and in the many chapels and saintly exercises they maintain; most praiseworthy, two sisters day and night guard the most holy sacrament."[122]

When Gómez turned to "the prodigious image of Our Lady the Virgin Mary of the Immaculate Conception, known by her home at Pueblito," his tone changed. The Otomí Virgin had but sixteen thousand pesos in endowment, earning eight hundred pesos yearly to keep her sanctuary and fund devotions. Still, year after year endless small contributions sustained Our Lady at Pueblo. "All venerate and adore that most divine image, whose favor and patronage, . . . fire not only the loving hearts of her neighbors, but people in distant regions; her frequent and holy intercessions with God have made her prodigies and miracles commonplace." Gómez left no doubt that Our Lady at Pueblito, in the dusty nearby village, the least endowed of devotions, led spiritual life at Querétaro.[123]

Father Navarrete too gloried in the city's rich convents and hospitals. His tour followed the water from east to west. First came the Mission College of Santa Cruz, then his own Jesuit college. Others noted quickly led to Guadalupe's temple and the Franciscan church and convent that were still the city's main parish in the 1730s. Finally he noted Santa Clara, "enriched and adorned by an inestimable capital of virtue and perfection," confirming the fusion of wealth and virtue the Otomí parodied.[124] Navarrete then turned to "the miraculous images the city venerates for its protection." A stone cross on the main altar of the Franciscan missionary college was "so prodigious." He called "poor indios" the "owners" of the "sovereign image" of the Señor de la Huertacilla held in Guadalupe's temple. He noted Our Lady of Sorrows in the Jesuit church and argued that Guadalupe was "no less divine and admirable," though there is no evidence that either drew popular devotion. Every convent and temple with endowments focused on prayer and sacramental worship, yet included at least one image to serve the populace.[125]

Navarrete concluded his narrative of miraculous images by repeating the truth that everyone at Querétaro knew: in a magnificent temple, two leagues east of the city in the poorest of Otomí villages, ruled "Most Holy Mary with the title of Pueblito . . . She is so admirable and miraculous she is the refuge of all in times of need. Our Lady pays back to the letter the infinite debts that oblige her to serve." She worked as the obligated servant of all the people of Querétaro. In return, "this accumulation of marvels" and "repeated miracles . . . obligates Querétaro's liberal devotion" and gains "famous gratitude."[126]

Navarrete and Gómez saw a religious life in which rich convents promoted sacramental worship while popular devotions dealt with the challenges of everyday life. The *Gaceta de México* reported both. A story in November 1730 began: "On the 19th, the mission fathers of the Convent of Santa Cruz de Querétaro began to proclaim Church doctrine in moral sermons; they have continued for days. We expect abundant and copious spiritual fruits, thanks to the tireless efforts of such zealous apostolic workers." The city mission ended in January 1731 with a "Procession of Blood . . . motivated by general contrition, silent, edifying and mortifying in every step; there were great numbers of penitents, carrying heavy crosses, burdensome chains, sharp rasps, coarse hair-shirts, knotted ropes, . . . clear signs of the ample fruits this rich land can yield when irrigated by doctrine." At the core of the parade were four hundred youths and one hundred university graduates. The *Gaceta* used the language of Querétaro's flourishing irrigated agriculture and productive labor to celebrate a penitential outburst and hopes of abundant spiritual fruits. Yet the festival of penance mostly drew young men of the Spanish center.[127]

In September 1732 the *Gaceta* shared news of Our Lady of Pueblito. In August lightning had struck the Hacienda de Buenavista, five leagues northwest. Thrusting through the portal of the great house, it blew down doors, broke walls and windows, and charged to the estate store where ten workers were taking supplies before returning to their ranchos. Clothes were seared, an infant blown from her mother's arms to a threshing floor well away. Yet none were hurt, "thanks to the intercession of Our Lady of Pueblito, who on that day happened to have stopped at the hacienda."[128] While a few young men joined penitential revivals, the power of Pueblito's Virgin was clear for all to see.

In light of her service, in the 1730s many of Querétaro's prosperous Spaniards, even the sisters of Santa Clara, turned to Our Lady at Pueblito. The adoption bridged the divide between the convent capitalism and sacramental worship promoted by the powerful and the enduring popular commitments to the Virgin and other devotions of propitiation and service. The Franciscan Hermenigildo de Vilaplana, writing in the early 1760s, documented the Spanish turn to Pueblito. He reported that in 1731 a Spaniard riding at night in rugged uplands near Guanajuato had fallen into an abandoned mine. Despairing, he called to the Virgin of Pueblito; at daybreak an indio appeared, raised him from the shaft, and vanished.[129] Our Lady sent an indio to save a Spaniard. In 1733 doña Gertrudis Hurtado de Mendoza faced crisis in childbirth. Her surgeon despaired—and called for our Lady of Pueblito. With her guidance he performed surgery and saved mother and child.[130] The same year Querétaro's Spanish council proclaimed: "every time we face sterility, whether by drought or other plague, each time a disease spreads across the jurisdiction, we will keep the pious custom—the best resort and remedy—of asking protection and assistance from the

Holy Virgin Mary through her miraculous image at Pueblito, which we will carry in solemn procession to the [Querétaro] parish church."[131]

While the Marqués led the council in planning and funding the aqueduct that carried pure water to Spanish Querétaro, droughts and plagues reminded all that challenges beyond human control still threatened everyone. Querétaro's Spaniards demanded that the Virgin at Pueblito come to their churches in times of need. Struggles over her proper home began. The Franciscans, with funds from don Pedro de Urtiaga, a merchant and militia captain she had cured and favored in business, built a new, more lavish church at Pueblito.[132] The friars and Urtiaga promoted devotion among Spanish elites but insisted that the Virgin remain at Pueblito. Other powerful groups pulled her toward the city. In 1736 she lived for months at the convent of Santa Clara, bringing rain in time of drought and curing the abbess. In 1737 a devastating plague of matlazahuatl (typhus) struck. The city's Franciscan pastor became ill, Spanish medicine failed, and the sisters sent him the Virgin's gown—and another miracle cure. That fall lightning struck Santa Clara; thanks to the Virgin, the congregation was spared.[133]

An alliance of friars, rich citizens, and Santa Clara's nuns brought Our Lady at Pueblito to the center of life at Querétaro. Vilaplana chronicled her many interventions: rain in times of drought, cure to the incurably ill, life to mothers and babies in childbirth, extraction from unimaginable accidents. Her power spread to Celaya and Guanajuato, where in 1747 she found rich veins of silver. She served rich and poor, Spanish and Otomí in times of desperation and despair.[134] Spaniards, mestizos, a few mulattoes, and many Otomí worked together amid deepening inequality to make cloth and build an aqueduct, expand irrigation, and cultivate growing harvests. Gómez and Navarrete argued that reason, planning, and good works led to a prosperous and healthy city. But much of life remained beyond understanding and control—for the powerful and the poor. As farming moved beyond river bottoms, it relied on fickle rain. Disease plagued people of all classes and categories, beyond comprehension and without cure.[135] Childbirth remained risky; mother and child could die at any time. The Virgin at Pueblito ruled life out of control.

The Capuchin Ajofrín spent a month in Querétaro in the spring of 1764, first stop on his Bajío tour. "Querétaro is a beautiful, large, opulent, and delightful city."[136] He praised "La Cañada, most fertile and delicious thanks to its huertas and natural delights. In the depths of the canyon runs a copious cristaline river; its waters divide into canals to irrigate and fertilize the lower part of the city [of Querétaro]; the upper part lacks that resource, but enjoys the same or greater benefit thanks to the generous waters carried by the magnificent aqueduct bridge built by the costly labor of the Marqués del Villar del Águila." Ajofrín saw a city of shared waters; he said nothing about divisions between Spaniards and Pames at La Cañada, Spaniards and Otomí in Querétaro. "The city is delightful, fertile, and abundant in every fruit and vegetable. La Cañada is a place of grand recreation, thanks to its forested beauty. The trade and commerce of the city is considerable; in addition to merchants with stores and warehouses, there are many obrajes that make fine woolens, along with flannels, coarse serges, blankets, and rough cotton goods. There are more than a few tanneries that cut all kinds of skins and leathers, making rich suedes, cordovans, chamois, and cowhides. But the greatest commerce is in the abundant wheat, maize, barley, and other crops harvested at the great haciendas all around."[137] Querétaro remained a city of huertas, of trade, textiles, and manufacturing, and of expanding commercial cultivation.

Ajofrín stayed at the Mission College of Santa Cruz. He knew Fray Hermenegildo de Vilaplana, chronicler of the college's mission exploits and of Our Lady at Pueblito miracles. Vilaplana linked sacramental worship and propitiatory devotions at Querétaro. He focused Ajofrín away from social, ethnic, and religious divisions, and toward shared dynamism and devotion. A gracious visitor, Ajofrín honored his hosts' "miraculous cross." It came from the time of the Tapías and linked the mission college to popular devotions: "set on the great altar at the Colegio, it was famous for frequent miracles." Still, on his way out of town, Ajofrín had to stop at Pueblito and acknowledge the Virgin's pivotal role: "They carry her sacred image to Querétaro when they face any calamity, always with happy success."[138] A half-century of silver-driven growth fortified Spanish wealth and power and engergized Otomí production and devotion. And the Virgin at Pueblito integrated the divided city of Querétaro.

Driving North: Texas, the Sierra Gorda, and New Santander

The mix of commercial dynamism and religious energies that shaped the Bajío after 1700 accelerated northward expansion. Mining to feed the world's rising demand for silver stimulated everything; the Bajío focused on cloth making and irrigated cultivation. The search for mines and grazing lands drove north. In the 1740s men from Querétaro and the Bajío marched through the Sierra Gorda, across Gulf lowlands, and into Texas in a thrust at once strategic and military, commercial and religious.

During the seventeenth century the thrust of Spanish North America

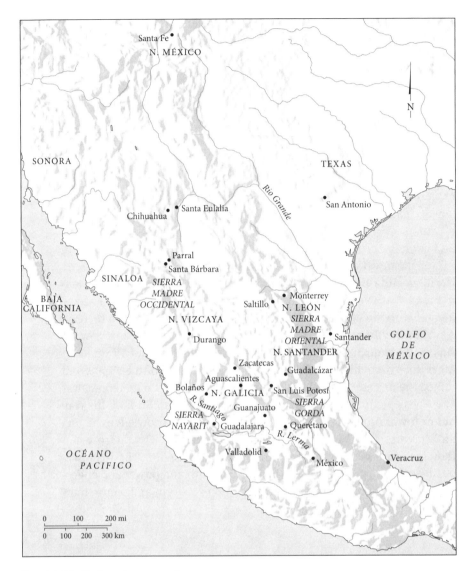

Spanish North America, ca. 1760

focused on the plateau between the Sierras. Silver production flourished at Parral; grazing dominated the countryside except where
streams allowed irrigation. When mining revived from Guanajuato to
far Chihuahua after 1700, settlement, development, and conflict intensified across the uplands. Estates expanded irrigation and cultivation; grazing intensified; migrants came north to mix and negotiate
changing identities. Patriarchy orchestrated almost everything in Hispanic communities, while independent people struggled to stay inde-

pendent. Many tried mission life, mine work, estate dependence, and periodic resistance.[139]

Farther north New Mexico accelerated its engagements with the silver economy. Spaniards and Pueblos joined in allied inequality to produce grains and cloth and to trade with the Apaches, Comanches, Navajos, and other independent peoples who surrounded them. Pueblo cloth and pottery traded south in Chihuahua; independent natives gained horses, tools, and arms in exchange for hides—and captives taken in wars among native peoples. Many captives became serving dependents in Spanish households and Pueblo communities; others were sold to the south to labor in Chihuahua. Relative peace and unequal prosperity held while silver remained strong at Chihuahua to the 1740s; then, as the stimulus of trade faded, Apaches and Comanches increasingly raided to gain the mounts, tools, and weapons that had become essential to their independence. New Mexico faced decades of conflict that reinforced the alliance between the Spanish and the Pueblos. As Apaches raided farther south they become new Chichimecas—their name labeled all who raided commercial settlements.[140]

East and west of the plateau, in rugged Sierras and along Gulf and Pacific lowlands, Hispanic settlement and commercial development was limited in the seventeenth century. To the west the Sierra de Nayarit remained an enclave of native independence between Guadalajara, Zacatecas, and the Pacific. Along the coast stretching northwest, most natives knew Spanish North America through scattered missions; some, notably Yaquis, trekked to labor in mines at Parral. Their lives were not shaped by isolation but by sporadic contacts with commercial ways, often mediated by mission clergy. Northeast of Querétaro the Sierra Gorda remained a parallel enclave of native independence as the eighteenth century began. There and along Gulf lowlands into Texas, indigenous peoples also dealt with Spanish America. Leaders were baptized, used Christian names (at least with Spaniards), and displayed crosses and other Christian signs to show eminence. Independent people traded and raided for livestock, tools, guns, and cloth. They tried new ways of cultivation learned in mission sojourns. They faced each other in struggles for power and resources, drawing Spanish frontiersmen and missionaries into disputes they barely understood.[141]

Like most eighteenth-century revivals, the accelerating northward expansion had its roots in the 1680s. The Franciscan Mission College of Santa Cruz came to Querétaro aiming to Christianize colonial society and convert Sierra Gorda "infidels." The newcomers arrived while Pueblo and Tarahumara resistance frustrated dreams of northern advance. A French threat turned the regime and the college northeastward. René Robert Cavalier, Sieur de la Salle, a land developer and trader based in Canada, hoped to open a Gulf port near the mouth of Mississippi, perhaps to gain access to Spanish silver. In 1685 he left settlers (who may have been the remnants of a weak colony or shipwreck survivors) on Matagorda Bay, far southwest of the Mississippi. Word of his landing passed through native people to Spanish officials. There was little chance that the French might reach Parral; still, a post on the Texas coast would offer natives tools, cloth, and other goods that they might trade for silver gained by trading with—or raiding against—others inland. The regime could not abide the prospect.

Expeditions searched for French settlers, eventually finding a shipwreck and signs of conflict with local natives.[142] The threat, if any, was minimal, but officials decided to send missionaries from Querétaro to Texas. With mining in decline and conflict everywhere across the north, funds were scarce. So they turned to the old "pro-Indian" vision according to which dedicated friars bringing trade, tools, new ways of cultivation, and Christian truth could win natives for Christianity and the Spanish regime, with little force and less cost. From 1690 friars with small military escorts trekked north. Across Texas, natives took livestock, tried mission life, considered Christian truth, and clung to an independence that the Spaniards saw as insubordination. The East Texas missions were abandoned in 1694, a failed experiment. The French founded New Orleans in 1699, opening trade with natives across Texas.[143]

French Louisiana came with the Bourbon ascent to the Spanish throne; for a time Texas seemed less urgent. Northern expansion turned elsewhere. Don Juan Caballero y Ocío, Querétaro's great landed entrepreneur and priestly benefactor, gave 20,000 pesos to found missions in Baja California in 1698; he later sent another 25,000 for a ship to supply the peninsula and trade with the mainland. His aims were deeply religious; he also helped his kinsman don Manuel de Ocío become a leading trader and prospector.[144] Meanwhile, as silver soared with a revival at Zacatecas and strikes at Chihuahua, northward development accelerated on the inland plateau. The mission friars of Querétaro founded a second college (devoted to Guadalupe) at Zacatecas, again aiming to raise alms for the dual mission of preaching penitence to Christians and converting infidels.[145] After leaving East Texas, Querétaro friars joined the reconquest of New Mexico in the 1690s, built missions near the Río Grande north of Saltillo, and sent preachers back into Texas. As before, they found natives both interested and independent; as always, disease assaulted mission populations.

When Louisiana traders reached deep into Texas after 1710 Querétaro missionaries helped respond.[146] From 1715 to 1722 a series of expeditions set Texas as the northeast outpost of Spanish North America. The regime aimed to limit French access to trade; friars from Querétaro and Zacatecas led the way, accompanied by soldier-settlers sent to protect missions and build towns. In 1721 and 1722 leadership and funds came from the Marqués de San Miguel de Aguayo, a frontier entrepreneur. By 1725 missionaries again trekked across forests in East Texas seeking allies and converts. The locals, however, were fine cultivators, nimble negotiators, and skilled at playing Spaniards against Frenchmen. The Nacodoches missions remained fragile outposts in a land of independent natives.[147]

Spanish North America set its northeastern salient at San Antonio de Béjar. There streams allowed irrigated cultivation, and rolling scrublands fed herds of cattle. An indigenous frontier allowed Spaniards to place themselves between coastal hunters and gatherers and the mounted hunters to the west. New Mexican Spaniards were arming Comanches, who pressed rival Apaches south and east. Soldiers and missionaries in and around San Antonio, many from Querétaro, found strategic roles in that world, still shaped by native peoples. San Antonio grew slowly; the capital of Spanish Texas lived in a crucible of native conflicts.[148]

Meanwhile the mountains of Nayarit and the Sierra Gorda remained bastions of native independence close by the Bajío, Zacatecas, and San Luis Potosí. When silver was found in the Tepec highlands of northern Jalisco in 1705, independent natives blocked new bonanzas. Production was frustrated by the people of nearby Nayarit, who confirmed their reputation as "bárbaros." In 1710 Fray Antonio Margil de Jesús, so important at Querétaro and a founder of the Mission College of Guadalupe at Zacatecas, led a mission to pacify Nayarit. He concluded: "the settlement of such miserable people cannot be done through reason, but only with arms."[149] That view set a tone for eighteenth-century expansion. Far from the silver economy, in East Texas and later in California, missions might lead expansion with little military backing and at little cost to the regime. But where the subordination of native peoples was essential to the silver economy, military force shaped incursions.

It took a two-year campaign with Jesuit accompaniment to "pacify" Nayarit from 1720 to 1722. Yet pacification proved to be no more than the containment of independent peoples in rugged uplands. For decades Jesuit missionaries faced persistent frustrations, while the order shaped public texts to announce uncertain successes.[150] Still, silver began to flow from Tepec and Bolaños in the 1730s, followed by bonanza at Bolaños in the late 1740s. In that context don José de Escandón convinced viceregal authorities to sanction military thrusts first into the Sierra Gorda and then along the Gulf to the Río Grande. Friars from Querétaro, Zacatecas, and the new Mission College of San Fernando that opened in Mexico City in 1734 joined. They never ruled.[151]

Attempts to settle and develop the Sierra Gorda began early in the century. A series of military commanders gained land grants to expand commercial grazing while looking for mines. At Maconí in 1715 commanders and native leaders signed a treaty allowing Jonaces to live dispersed and in peace, to labor at new enterprises without pressure to engage in mission life and conversion.[152] In the same years growing Spanish settlements in eastern San Luis Potosí, and the growing herds of livestock grazed there and in lowlands reaching toward the Gulf by landlords often based in the Bajío, provoked both conflict and trade with natives in the sierra and below. The search for mines, lands, and natives to work and convert continued unabated. Without a major silver strike, commercial settlement and native dependence were constantly contested.[153]

Meanwhile Escandón came to Querétaro, married well, and built a fortune in trade and textiles. As sergeant major of Querétaro's militia he contained riots at Celaya and San Miguel, and twice in the Sierra, in 1728 and 1734.[154] He learned to mix coerción and capitalism. In 1740 he won command as colonel of Querétaro's cavalry and infantry. In the following year he was named the viceroy's lieutenant and captain general of the Sierra Gorda, a post that brought military command and jurisdiction over Chichimecas.[155] Escandón began 1743 with an armed tour of the sierra. He led fifty mounted soldiers and two friars from the newest mission college—San Fernando in Mexico City.[156] The mix said everything about Escandón's plan. The military would rule; missionaries would serve.

Escandón produced a report on Sierra settlements and native peoples in the aftermath of his incursion.[157] He had little impact on the regions around San Luis de la Paz, north of Querétaro. Site of the original Jesuit mission that settled Chichimecas and separated the Bajío from the Sierra in the late sixteenth century, it remained a place of Jesuit rule and persistent mining to the east at Xichú, with little military presence. But along the edge of the Sierra, extending east of Querétaro past Tolimán to Cadereyta, Escandón set a powerful military presence amid a growing number of Hispanic settlers and diverse and dispersed natives. Nearly four hundred soldiers made a statement that commercial ways had come to stay—on a line that guarded the road from Querétaro to the Pánuco and the Gulf lowlands.

With armed power set, Escandón aimed to replace Agustinian and Dominican clergy with newcomers, mostly from San Fernando and more closely subject to military rule. The viceroy approved the request in 1744, along with funding for four new missions staffed by San Fernando. Less pleasing to Escandón, mission natives gained rights to councils and lands—some taken from holdings already granted to Hispanic settlers.[158] Escandón opened roads, searched for mines, settled armed colonists, distributed lands, and steered natives toward missions. Some friars were uneasy with the martial emphasis; native peoples resisted, negotiated, and adapted as they could. After the supposed conquest of the Sierra, in 1744 a friar lamented facing "Jonaces, apostate and gentile *indios* who populate the Sierra Gorda," people defined by "aversion to Christian religion and to sociable and rational life," and who spoke "with riotous voices in their Chichimec tongue."[159] As in Nayarit, little was resolved.

Escandón claimed nonetheless to have conquered the Sierra. More accurately, he had led an armed assault against independent peoples; soldiers and settlers helped to develop commercial estates, often set next to missions, thus setting off long conflicts with people newly constrained, but neither subordinated nor pacified. The people of the Sierra would fight for independence into the nineteenth century. In 1750 Fray Junípero Serra came to Xalpan to lead missions struggling to find peace after Escandón's conquest. For Serra and allies like Fray Francisco Palau, dealing between soldiers, settlers, and reluctant natives was training for later roles driving Spanish North America into California.[160]

For Escandón the thrust into the Sierra Gorda was preparation for a larger effort to bring the commercial ways of Spanish North America to the Gulf Coast lowlands from the Pánuco to the Río Grande and beyond. In May 1748 the viceroy Conde de Revillagigedo convened a "Council of War and Treasury." Four days of meetings included five judges of the High Court in Mexico City, five treasury officials, two leaders of a failed attempt to set Spanish power at the mouth of the Nueces—and Escandón, flush with the success of his self-proclaimed conquest of the Sierra Gorda. The key player was the Marqués de Altamira, High Court judge and war inspector, the viceroy's lead counsel on military affairs.[161] Altamira was close to the silver bankers of the Sánchez de Tagle family, and to the Marquéses de San Miguel de Aguayo, founders of Spanish Texas and great northern landowners.

The problem was clear to the assembled officials. The Gulf Coast was "occupied by barbarous nations of enemy *indios*, gentile and apostate Chichimecas." The lowlands remained a refuge of native independence close by the Pánuco River and the Sierra Gorda in the south, the mining regions of San Luis Potosí and the grazing lands of Nuevo León along its mountainous west, and newly opened Texas to the north—"whose governments, provinces, and jurisdictions those barbarians regularly insult with fires, murders, thefts, and all kinds of inhuman atrocities, destroying towns, haciendas, and ranches, blocking roads, communications, and commerce, perverting settled and Christian *indios*—who by their desertion weaken their towns and increase our irreconcilable enemies, the apostates who are always ready for all manner of hostilities"—at great cost to the treasury.

The Council approved 115,700 pesos for a militarized program of settlement to be led by Escandón. As incentives Escandón could distribute "the town lots, lands, and water the law provides, to *indios* and to soldiers and settlers." But the offer to independent natives came with threats. The goal was "their reduction and congregation in towns, and should they refuse—all necessary punishment." Escandón insisted "that they leave the mountains and settle in the towns; there they will be treated like other gentile *indios*, forgetting forever their former crimes. But if that is not done in the time allowed, military campaigns will begin."[162]

In 1748 Escandón led an expedition from Querétaro, through the Sierra, and across coastal hills to the gulf plains. Allies moved in from San Luis Potosí and Nuevo León. They founded Spanish towns, energized commercial life, and pressed natives toward missions and Christian subordination. Escandón traded financing for subordinate command with land engrossers like don Domingo de Unzaga from San Miguel and others from Querétaro and Monterrey. Beyond favored commanders Escandón shared as little as possible. Soldier-settlers got access to town lands, not the ranchos they were promised. There were no Spanish councils; commanders ruled backed by soldiers. Missions rarely got good lands and never gained republican rights. Friars complained that Escandón used them to pacify natives and recruit labor. When they protested he ignored them. Natives who took livestock and fled were branded rebels; many were captured and sent to labor in Querétaro obrajes. Friars negotiated, certain that if they withdrew, natives would face worse; at least they could baptize those who faced death from inevitable plagues. The colonization of the region that Escandón named New Santander for his Spanish homeland replicated the commercial society of Spanish North America: begun in Querétaro, driven by military force in search of profit, settled by Spaniards, mulattoes, and mestizos. Missions allowed invaders to claim a moral high ground and perhaps ease indigenous adaptations; disease hastened native peoples' demise.[163]

Don Agustín López de la Cámara Alta, a military engineer from Spain, toured New Santander in 1757. He detailed the primacy of commercial goals, the dominance of military power, the limits of mission activity, and the complex relations between Hispanic settlers and di-

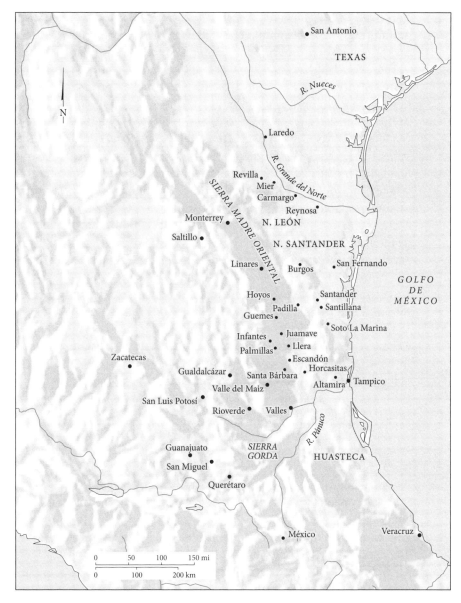

New Santander, ca. 1760

verse natives.[164] The first task of colonization was to contain independent natives. López's report reveals the complexity of the challenge. The lands from the Pánuco to the Río Grande, from the coast to the Sierra, were populated by diverse ethnic and linguistic peoples, "nations" in the language of the day. Mariguanes cultivated around Soto la Marina and Santander in the heart of the zone. Most of their neighbors lived by hunting and gathering aquatic life if near the coast, deer and diverse plants if inland. Native political ways were mostly local and little stratified, shaped by shifting alliances and conflicts.

The people of the gulf were not untouched by Atlantic contacts. North of the Pánuco near Horcasitas lived a small group called the Olives. López reported that they had crossed the gulf from Florida in the 1620s, led by a friar to escape war in their homeland. Once on the western coast they moved often, buffeted by local conflicts. In the 1740s fewer than a hundred survived; they remained Christians and Spanish allies, armed in the Spanish fashion and cultivating when and where they could.[165] At the northern limit of the new colony a group mixing local natives and people of African ancestry—likely shipwreck survivors or escaped Caribbean slaves—held an island at the mouth of the Río Grande. They too were armed like Europeans and blocked access to the great river. In that they served Spanish purposes.[166] Near the center of the new colony more than a dozen grazing properties had developed earlier around Real de Borbón, most owned by Querétaro and San Miguel landlords. Two belonged to the Primos and one to the Querétaro Jesuits; two more had been donated by don Juan de Caballero y Ocío to the Pious Fund that sustained the Jesuits' missions in Baja California. The power of San Miguel landlords was greater: three estates belonged to heirs of don Manuel de la Canal, another to the Conde de Casa Loja—and one to don Baltásar de Sauto, who competed with the Canal clan there too.[167]

Near those properties the Sierras separating Gulf lowlands from inland plateaus were full of natives whom López (like the junta before him) called apostates: people who had tried mission life, accepted baptism, and retreated to independent lives in isolated uplands. They knew European ways—often finding livestock, tools, weapons, and some of Christianity useful. They traded with lowlanders who were still gentiles, sometimes mobilizing them in raids on grazing and trade. To the junta and to López apostates were the most pernicious natives. Their hunting of livestock disrupted life on the grazing estates, becoming ever more important to the highland economy. Conflict between grazers based in the Bajío and apostates from the Sierra offered Escandón the opportunity to invade, extend his power, and build his own estates in the lowlands.

The settlements set by Escandón aimed first to contain the "apostates" in the Sierras and cut their ties to lowlanders. A double line of settlements in the southwest, four in the Sierra Gorda and six in the transition zone where the Sierra met the lowlands, were planned to keep Sierra "apostates" away from coastal "gentiles." To the north Padilla, Real de Borbón, and Burgos were also placed to separate people in the Sierra from lowlanders. Upland apostates had too much independence, too much chance to build alliances among natives, and too much opportunity to disrupt Spanish production and trade. They had to be contained. The first decade of colonization provoked many conflicts led by *serranos*, often with lowland allies. In 1757 life was calming, but challenges remained.

Meanwhile commercial ways spread across the colony. Cultivation, often irrigated, expanded in valleys near the Sierras. Maize went to markets at inland mines in San Luis Potosí and Guadalcázar. Livestock, especially sheep, grazed everywhere, but especially in the central corridor and north along the Río Grande. Salt and salted fish were good trade commodities. Everyone searched for mines in the new colony, but none flourished. At Altamirano, near Tampico and the mouth of the Pánuco, coastal trade grew with Veracruz and Campeche. Three merchants lived there, and so many visited that a *mesón* was built to accommodate them. Escandón focused on Santander and the port that he aimed to open at Soto la Marina. While others faced conflict with serranos and the challenge of colonizing along the Río Grande, he set his military power and commercial interests in the heart of the colony, among cultivating Mariguanes. His estate at Santa Ana already planted thirty fanegas of maize, partly irrigated and yielding harvests reported at two or three hundred grains for every one planted. Close to the coast at Soto la Marina, Escandón's Hacienda de San Juan grazed herds that included over twenty thousand sheep.[168] Spanish North America was extending along Gulf lowlands, and Escandón aimed to take the lead in power and profit.

López de la Cámara Alta reported that most settlers were Spaniards or mulattoes, with mestizos scattered about. Most commanders and paid soldiers were Spaniards; the many who came to plant and graze, expecting grants of property, were mulattoes. In 1757 they still worked lands assigned to settlements, still fought resistant natives. Many were disgruntled. López reflected mulatto settlers' interests in his repeated calls for a distribution of land in property among them.

López wrote in language reminiscent of Monségur's earlier report on Mexico City. Everything was commercial; everyone traded. Among the most common verbs in his text was *comerciar*, as he reported the trade of every settlement.[169] He reflected a language of capitalism when he attributed success to settlers' dedicated work and trade. At San Fernando "there are many rich citizens, and those who do not apply themselves are poor." Along the Río Grande at Mier most were prosperous "because they were very dedicated."[170] Yet López noted unexpected challenges and inverse attractions on the coastal frontier. At Horcasitas settlement was disrupted by the "last year's hurricane." In its wake settlers "do not know how to farm; former shepherds, lazy by nature, . . . live by the wild fruits of the fields."[171] While independent natives resisted settled labor, some Hispanic settlers found attraction in hunting and gathering.

There were larger failures in the colonization project. The goal had been to reach the Nueces and the shores of the Bay of the Holy Spirit, modern Corpus Christi. The soldiers and settlers sent there stopped at the Río Grande, waited months, and turned back for lack of maize. Diverted to Soto la Marina, they strengthened the port community there. The failure to proceed northward served Escandón's power in the heart of the colony. Colonization halted at the Río Grande, mostly on its south bank. Yet herds of over 200,000 head grazed north of the river. López insisted that the lands beyond the river were uninhabitable for lack of water. Yet he reported that vast herds roamed there, tended by natives who guarded stock free of pressure to settle and convert.[172] We glimpse a way of expansion rarely taken, or rarely reported. Spaniards set herds to graze on the lands of hunting and gathering natives who agreed to guard the livestock, surely for shares of the herds. They traded hunting for herding—as long as they were not forced to lead settled lives and adopt Christian beliefs, and not yet plagued by new diseases. The collaboration could not last: more Spaniards, mulattoes, and missionaries, sheep, cattle, and plagues would come. That it was tried says much about frontier goals and native responses when pressures on the latter were limited.

José Hermenegildo Sánchez García arrived in New Santander in 1760, three years after López de Cámara's tour. Sánchez arrived among kin from Linares, inland and upland in Nuevo León. His father and uncles managed estates for landlords based in the Bajío, serving also as militia commanders; Sánchez was a militiaman, likely an estate foreman or tenant, and a schoolteacher, a role of which he was notably proud. He kept a diary focused on the 1760s, which he compiled as a narrative before he died in 1803. He reveals that settlement and commercial development took longer and were more contested than Escandón's triumphalism or López de Cámara's survey suggested.[173]

Before Escandón's incursion the Gulf lowlands were "without Spanish and Christian people, and only populated by barbaric *indios* and a few herdsman who entered seasonally to tend their animals, leading to conflicts with those *indios*." Like Chichimecas two centures earlier, lowland natives hunted Spanish livestock. They gathered periodically in scattered settlements to dance, stimulated by pulque and "peyote, an herb they worship, . . . and in their loss of senses the devil they adore and worship appears . . . coming down from the sky to tell them what to do to destroy the few Christians who have come, to stop them from taking their lands."[174]

Sánchez argued that Escandón's expedition with allies from Querétaro and San Miguel was provoked by "the resistance and uprising of all the missions previously settled on these frontiers of the Sierra Madre." Upland settlers came due to "a time of hunger across this part of America. . . . The dearth of grain began in 1749 [when Escandón invaded], and in 1750 the scarcity was extreme." Apostate natives provoked the invasion, and settlers came only to meet desperate needs. The demise of the natives, long contested, was due in part to battles, and to "the contagion of measles and smallpox, also extreme among them in 1751, 1765, and 1780." Explanation mixed with legitimation.[175]

Once towns were settled Sánchez emphasized that most natives were not pacified but moved to highland refuges and continued to steal horses and sheep, provoking continuing conflicts. One uncle engaged in battles to protect the herds of don Manuel de la Canal; his father did the same in the service of the Querétaro Jesuits. Nearby estates of the Primo brothers of Querétaro faced similar challenges. Sánchez admired the successes of Capitain don Domingo de Unzaga, the land engrosser and militia commander based in San Miguel, owing to his ability to recruit and learn from native guides and spies. The narrative emphasizes conflict between Spanish (and mixed) settlers and native residents; the detail reveals native resistance and collaboration in a world of complex conflicts and commercial settlement. Many indigenous girls were taken into settler households to become Christian and provide service. Sánchez added: "they produced few children." He hints at a mix of imposed collaboration and resistant action that would reveal much about patriarchy in the new colony—if only we knew more.[176]

Unzaga, with allies including Sánchez, his father, and uncles, emphasized pacification and commercial development at Real de Borbón through the 1750s and into the 1760s. Sánchez portrayed a settlement recreating a variant of Spanish North America in the Gulf lowlands: "The land is fertile for every crop, abundant for grazing cattle and sheep, horses and every useful species, . . . Water is scarce but healthful, lying near the surface to facilitate digging wells." An early search for silver, mercury, and iron led "early settlers to open several mine shafts, . . . but not finding profitable ores, now they apply themselves to working the land; planting has brought much profit, and greater permanence to the setlers here." Early on "sheep, horses, and cattle were abundant, but livestock reproduced poorly and most cattle have run off or been lost."[177] A search for silver and a presumption that livestock would flourish on lowland pastures gave way to lives focused on cultivation in support of mines and grazing estates in arid uplands.

Sánchez proclaimed the Sierra around the Real de Borbón pacified by the time of Unzaga's death in 1766. He did the same for the natives at Llera, Escandón, and Horcasitas in 1769, adding that many took passes to return to the Sierra for a month, where they "rob and steal horses; in the end they are tolerated and treated with patience."[178] Driving a commercial new world north into the lands of independent peoples took time and patience in the face of war and disease, but the drive for profitable settlement would not be stopped.

Escandón consolidated power and enterprises around Santander and the port at Soto la Marina. He hoped that the products of the colony would load there for Caribbean and Atlantic markets without passing through Mexico City and Veracruz. Officials knew that such trade would draw silver into Atlantic circuits without the need to pay taxes. Revenue would be lost and internal trade limited; textile shops at Querétaro and across the Bajío, including Escandón's obraje, would face competition from imported cloth. Escandón saw profit in the new port and trade, whatever the threat to his obraje. The regime and the merchants who funded silver mines had much to lose and little to gain. The new port was closed to all but coastal trade. Escandón led the expansion of Spanish North America across Gulf lowlands to the north bank of the Río Grande. The regime made sure that he did not alter the structure of silver mining and commercial expansion, profitably focused on the interior plateau.[179]

While the colonization drew the lowlands from the Sierra Gorda to the Río Grande into the commercial life of Spanish North America, San Antonio developed as its northeast outpost. A town of soldier-settlers and mission neophytes in the 1720s, it grew as Hispanic families trekked there in small numbers. A classic northern mix of Spaniards, mulattoes, and mestizos came seeking land and status as Spaniards. To promote cultivation the Crown settled Canary Islanders with rights to a republic, the first council in Texas. At first resented for their rights to land, irrigation, and a council, islanders soon mixed with soldier-settlers to forge a community. Northerners and islanders married and soon shared council roles. By the 1750s San Antonio mirrored early Querétaro: a town of trade and crafts where families worked irrigated huertas and cattle grazed on outlying scrub. Natives vanished as smallpox killed most who congregated at nearby missions; survivors mixed into the larger community. Local unity strengthened in the face of Apache threats—eighteenth-century Chichimecas who hunted livestock across uplands north and west. They negotiated an offer of mission life organized by Querétaro's College of Santa Cruz, led by Fray Alonso Giraldo de Terreros, funded by his rich cousin, don Pedro Romero de Terreros.[180]

The last words on northeastern expansion go to Fray Simón del Hierro. Born in Zacatecas in 1700 to a father who was a Genoese *azoguero* (silver refiner) and a mother locally born to a father of the same skill, Simón entered the Mission College of Guadalupe in 1719, took first vows in 1720, began to preach in 1723, and became a priest in 1724. In 1727 he joined Fray Antonio Margil de Jesús on a two-year trek of penitential preaching, reaching north to Chihuahua, south through Querétaro to Mexico City, then returning by skirting the unconquered Sierra Gorda through uncolonized Gulf lowlands.[181] Thus began a life of preaching and missions, negotiating between entrepreneurs and people facing pressures to relinquish independence and labor in Christian resignation.

Fray Simón joined an urban mission in Guanajuato in 1745; weeks of preaching in torchlit plazas led to 3,500 confessions. Accompanying Escandón to New Santander in 1748, the mission faced, according to his diaries, the eager approach of some natives and the wary uncertainty of others. Some wanted livestock, land to cultivate, and Christianity if it came with protection from expropriation and forced labors. Fray Simón complained that Escandón did not help the missions; he had no patience with attempts to ease natives into lives of Christian service. Still the priest carried on, sure that his charges were better off with him and Christianity.[182]

In 1762 Fray Simón wrote a long report on the northern missions. He never wavered in his vision: however grasping he found the entrepreneurs and settlers driving northward, natives had to be settled and baptized. He knew that mission congregation led to contagion and death; "in fulfillment of divine decrees we have sent many babies on to Glory by Holy Baptism." He reported native understanding of the link between missions and death: "parents often try to refuse their children's baptism; seeing those blessed with water die repeatedly, they believe that the sacrament killed them." He honored friars "crossing many leagues, usually on foot, so souls can join in eternal surrender."[183]

Fray Simón knew that mission work was embedded in conflicts shaped by politics, production, and cultural contradictions. Reflecting on why missionaries never drew the people of East Texas to settled dependence, he showed keen realism: "They were not Christianized, while others encountered later were, because [in East Texas] we could not take advantage of either of the two means that pressured others to settle. That is, we could not reduce them to settled lives [*policía*] by arms, nor could we give them necessities they lacked while wandering in the wilderness; both approaches were useless in those missions, the first impossible, the second superfluous."

He added: "It is superfluous to try to feed them, because they plant and harvest with such abundance that even our Presidio bought maize and other crops from them; they would only support our missionaries . . . in exchange for tobacco, sweets, and other things they don't produce. . . . when shipments were delayed, they turned to the French for rice, coffee (instead of chocolate), medicine, and other necessities of life." One way to settlement and conversion was by introducing new ways of sustenance; skilled cultivators proved hard to entice. Fray Simón went on: "The other way, changing their traditional politics by force of arms, is also impossible. They outnumber us ten or more to one and wield equal or better arms, firearms and bows; on any threat of violence, especially if they feel vulnerable, they go to French territory and leave us an empty land." Without leverage it was impossible to "exile idolatry" and break "the chains that tie them to the devil." Still, "we await their conversion."[184]

Explaining failure in East Texas, Fray Simón saw how missions worked elsewhere. Where independent people found gain in cultivation and livestock, they might experiment with mission life and Christian truths. Where they faced political and strategic conflicts, access to Spanish allies and arms might be useful; then too natives might seek out missions, soldiers, and Christian truths. Where missions offered sustenance, power, or both they might flourish for a time. But sooner or later missions brought smallpox and other diseases. Strategic advantage for one group led others to seek the same, limiting the gains of mission alliances, often just as diseases became deadly. In time every mission triumph led to depopulation, conflict, and flight, or the integration of survivors at the bottom of Spanish society. Fray Simón was frustrated, yet he and Spanish North America drove on.

A Commercial New World

In the 1750s Guanajuato was a rich and raucous mining center, Querétaro was a dynamic center of trade, textile production, and irrigated farming, and San Miguel's industry sustained vibrant urban life. Towns from Celaya to León were smaller replicas of Querétaro and San Miguel, places of trade and crafts surrounded by commercial estates. In a distance of about 150 kilometers from Querétaro to León, urban populations exceeded 100,000: 32,000 at Guanajuato, 25,000 at Querétaro, 18,000 at San Miguel, 10,000 each at Celaya and León, and

3,000 to 5,000 at several smaller towns. No other region of the Americas had so many places mixing mining, cloth making, crafts, and trade. No other countryside was so commercial, focused on feeding people who sustained globally linked trades.

For two centuries silver drove a commercial economy that shaped the Bajío and Spanish North America. Mines at Guanajuato, Zacatecas, San Luis Potosí, and Chihuahua stimulated local industries and commercial estates and fueled Atlantic trade, promoting commercial life in Europe. The viceregal regime depended on silver revenues, as did the Bourbon monarchy in Spain; both lamented that so much silver passed on to promote production in France and England, and trade and revenues in China. Across the Bajío and Spanish North America mining drove everything; cities and towns were places of trade, crafts, and religious life; commercial estates worked by tenants and laborers ruled the countryside. Indigenous republics were scarce, offering land and self-rule to few. They were important along the borders of Mesoamerica, from Querétaro to Celaya and Yuririapúndaro, but even there estate residents outnumbered villagers by 1750.

Commercial at its colonial birth, the Bajío became increasingly capitalist in the eighteenth century. Profit drove entrepreneurs. Favored mineworkers earned ore shares; others gained cash salaries; all faced pressures to reduce their earnings. What could be more capitalist? Most rural producers were tenants paying cash rents or workers who gained advances against monthly salaries calculated in pesos, plus food rations that were not. Textile producers mixed slaves, obligated employees, family artisans, and women spinning in putting-out deals that reached from city neighborhoods into the countryside. Slaves also labored at isolated estates and as household servants, but they were fewer in number each decade.

Everything was ruled and integrated by entrepreneurs. Had they claimed the power to be predators? Guanajuato mine operators' pressure on workers, the Canal clan's assault on Sauto at San Miguel, and Escandón's entrepreneurial conquest of the Sierra Gorda New Santander were all predatory, if in different ways. Still, mineworkers retained high wages and ore shares; the Sautos survived, though weakened; and the Sierra Gorda remained home to independent peoples, as did most of Texas. Across the Bajío and regions stretching north, men ready to be predators were everywhere. But they continued to face scarce and resilient workers at mines and rural estates, and independent natives as near as Sierra Gorda and across frontiers to the north. Capitalist predation was growing, but it still faced limits that forced continuing negotiations of production, social relations, and religion.

One domain of negotiation focused on ethnic amalgamations and identities. People of varied Mesoamerican ancestry, others descended from African slaves, and a few rooted in Europe mixed in commercial communities. The rich and powerful claimed Spanish status; those who worked adapted diverse identities. A few Spaniards had African blood. Some of Mesoamerican origins retained languages and identities as Otomí, Tarascans, or Mexicas; many more became indios— dependents in a Hispanic world. In town at Querétaro an Otomí majority worked huertas, organized and defended by a resilient republic. Mulatto majorities shaped urban life at Guanajuato and San Miguel. Ethnic categories and identities resisted regime models and changed. They reflected differences of wealth and power, diverse roles in production, and distinct ways of facing subordination—as much as they recorded ancestry.

While ethnic fluidity led to fragmented communities, patriarchy orchestrated most inequalities. It organized family and business among the powerful. It structured life and work in artisan families. In communities of estate dependents, patriarchy defined access to land and labor. Among Querétaro's Otomí patriarchy shaped lives integrating huertas, crafts, and markets. With endless variation, patriarchy shaped enduring inequities, drawing dependent men to negotiate their own and their families' subordination in exchange for household rule.

Yet patriarchy was not always effective. Mineworkers at Guanajuato faced brutal dangers and endemic insecurities in short, rough lives that inhibited patriarchy. Many women found independent if insecure lives in the boomtown. Slaves, convicts, and others locked inside obrajes struggled to assert patriarchy. Where social organization limited patriarchy, tensions were endemic. At Guanajuato workers gained unparalleled earnings to face the daily danger; they were free and rowdy, constant targets of denigration and moral exhortation. Obraje coercions created explosive tensions within. The exceptions highlight the role of patriarchy in integrating production and social stability.

While silver drove commercial dynamism, people negotiated subordination through changing ethnic identities, patriarchy organized deep inequities, and religion was a universal language of debated legitimacy. In the first half of the eighteenth century Bajío Catholicism offered two primary visions: sacramental worship that was ever more penitential, and devotion focused on virgins and saints offering aid to people in need. The powerful funded penitential exhortations demanding personal responsibility from the powerful and the poor. The majority looked to the Virgin of Pueblito and others who promised help in the world.

The church sanctioned both—often in the same churches. Penitential exhortation demanded moral responsibility, while virgins, saints, and popular healers promised aid and comfort. Key variants are notable. At Guanajuato those who profited from mining pressed lives of danger on the laboring majority, aimed to reduce salaries and ore shares, and made workers fund Jesuits who preached peace through penitence. In San Miguel, Canal patriarchs promoted penitential worship that legitimated power and called for charitable service in the world; they announced their morality and their responsabiliity. At Querétaro elites honored sacramental worship and also adopted Our Lady at Pueblito. They joined the Otomí majority in recognizing the risks of everyday life; together they made serving the Virgin a shared devotion that integrated a society of deep ethnic division. In New Santander, Escandón and his allies drove commercial development with military force, ignoring missionaries and assaulting natives with little concern for moral right or popular adaptation. Economic, ethnic, and religious diversity made every Bajío and northern community different. Yet all were part of a dynamic and increasing capitalist economy driving global trade and continental expansion.

CHAPTER 4

Reforms, Riots, and Repressions

The Bajío in the Crisis of the 1760s

❋ THE 1760S SAW UNPRECEDENTED CONFLICTS in the Bajío and nearby provinces. Workers took over mines and plazas at Guanajuato, across San Luis Potosí to the north and at Real del Monte to the southeast. Indigenous women and men rioted at San Luis de la Paz at the edge of the Sierra Gorda. At Valladolid and Pátzcuaro, just south of the Bajío, Tarascans and mulattoes challenged those who presumed to rule. The crisis followed a slump in mining at Guanajuato in the 1750s and the Seven Years' War from 1756 to 1763. After the war the Bourbon regime announced policies designed to increase its revenue and fortify its coercive power, setting off resistance in communities key to the silver economy. It would be easy to presume that the end of Chinese premium prices for silver around 1750 provoked the downturn at Guanajuato.[1] But across New Spain production continued to rise, if slowly, through the 1750s and dipped less than 10 percent in the early 1760s, while flows from Guanajuato rose again, soon leading production across New Spain to unprecedented heights.[2]

If Chinese demand drove the revival of silver after 1700, it appears that during the following decades a quickening Atlantic economy took growing portions of New Spain's rising production—certainly a Bourbon goal. The downturn of the 1750s at Guanajuato appears mostly to have been a crisis of local production, the result of deepening mines and rising costs. The continuing strength of mining across New Spain suggests that declining Chinese demand and prices led to growing

European demand; Europeans needed more silver to buy the same amounts of Chinese goods—and to provide money for their own accelerating commercial economy at home and across Atlantic domains. In that context Britain, France, and Spain disputed European and Atlantic dominance in the Seven Years' War beginning in 1756. In 1763 Britain emerged the apparent victor, gaining Canada; France lost Canada and ceded Louisiana to Spain; Spain felt threatened, lost Cuba briefly, yet emerged with mines intact and vast new North American territories. In the postwar years empires facing debts imposed new taxes on colonial subjects and sought new administrative powers to enforce collection. They set off widespread resistance and popular mobilizations. In British North America the response led to a war for independence in 1776. In New Spain the result was first conciliation, then repression, and finally concessions that allowed a rapid resurgence of the silver economy.

In and around the Bajío mobilizations spread in 1766; popular resistance peaked in the summer of 1767. Then, with widespread uprisings under way, the expulsion of the Jesuits added a new dimension to unprecedented conflicts.[3] Colonial entrepreneurs faced pivotal decisions. A riotous populace called them to join in opposition to a regime taking new revenues, building coercive forces, and removing the Jesuits. They could join a colonial alliance of resistance to the assertive Bourbon state, or they could back the regime against riotous communities—and acquiesce in the expulsion. Everywhere leading entrepreneurs chose the regime and an alliance for repression. They mobilized militias to contain disorder, setting the stage for a tour of punishment led by don José de Gálvez, the visitor general sent to build Bourbon power. Local militias ended riots; Gálvez executed dozens of rebel leaders, imposing lesser penalties on many more. Order returned; mining resumed. Gálvez's reliance on colonial elites to end the riots showed everyone that the regime still had to negotiate to rule.

On a larger stage the conflicts of the 1760s were part of a broad Atlantic crisis. The coastal colonies of British North America mobilized against parallel imperial demands at the same time; conflicts there persisted until they led to the war for independence that created the United States. The cost of the wars of 1756 to 1763 led Spanish and British rulers to seek new revenues and new powers in their colonies. In the Bajío popular mobilization escalated at the heart of the silver economy, only to face an alliance of repression. Colonial rule persisted and the silver economy soared to new heights after 1770. In British North America, in contrast, resistance to imperial demands in the 1760s led to an alliance of colonial elites and communities against British power. They declared independence in 1776, gained it in 1783, and faced decades of struggle to create a nation. Meanwhile, Guanajuato mines and the Bajío economy drove to new heights.

American colonization and the creation of a global economy were pioneered under Iberian sovereignty in the sixteenth century. In the seventeenth century France and England entered the colonial arena and asserted increasing power in Europe, striving to draw silver from Spain's colonies. The eighteenth century brought intensifying Atlantic struggles: France and Britain fought for hegemony, both still aiming to claim the riches flowing from Spain's Americas. The century began with the War of Spanish Succession, which saw England and France fight each other, mostly on Iberian soil, to place a favored claimant on the Spanish throne. The Bourbon accession gave France family ties to a reforming regime in Madrid and favored access to American markets in which sales of French cloth gained silver for France. Continuing rivalry culminated in a new round of European and Atlantic warfare from 1756 to 1763. The Seven Years' War in Europe was the French and Indian War in North America—and a British challenge to Spanish rule in Cuba in 1762. The war and its aftermath set off the imperial demands that led to popular resistance in the Bajío and British North America.

Britain and its colonials expelled France from the North American mainland before Carlos III ascended to the Spanish throne in 1759. He joined the war in 1761 to help his French cousin limit mounting defeats. The British quickly occupied Havana, showing Spain's vulnerability in the Caribbean. But the peace of 1763 revealed the limits of British power. Spain regained Havana and gained New Orleans and control of access to the Mississippi basin. France lost Canada and Louisiana but kept Saint-Domingue and other rich sugar islands. Defeat concentrated French colonialism in rich plantation colonies. Spain shored up its power in North America, ending French sovereignty in New Orleans. In victory Britain gained vast Canadian lands of limited commercial potential. After 1763 England struggled with the costs of enlarged continental colonies; Spain worked to bolster its defenses against British threats. They turned to parallel imperial reforms aimed at fortifying state power and taking new revenues from very different American dominions.[4]

Both provoked resistance among American subjects. Popular resistance to Spanish reforms in and near the Bajío challenged the silver economy, a key engine of Atlantic trade and the essential base of Spain's claims to a continuing place among the European powers. The origins, goals, and defeat of the risings against Bourbon assertions reveal much about the Bajío and its role in New Spain and Spain's empire at the middle of the eighteenth century. The parallel origins and contrasting consequences of the colonial risings against British power in its older mainland colonies during the same years show the 1760s as a turning point in the history of North America and the Atlantic world.[5] For the Bajío and Spanish North America it was a brief conflict that confirmed their long-established centrality in silver production and global trade.

Reform, Resistance, and Conciliation, 1760–1766

Spain's Bourbon rulers aimed to strengthen what every observer saw as weakened powers. Early on they responded to Monségur and others who envisioned New Spain as a fountain of wealth to be tapped more effectively by Spain and its French ally. Silver production must be maximized—and drawn away from China toward Europe. Rising bullion flows must generate growing imperial revenues, pay regime costs in New Spain and across the Caribbean, and deliver a hefty surplus to Madrid. The rest of the silver, over 80 percent, must flow west in trade, exchanged for textiles and other goods, if not Spanish then French— and if French or British, then handled for profit by Spanish middlemen.[6] If more silver flowed toward Europe as the century progressed, the regime proved little able to alter the trajectory of Atlantic development; France and increasingly Britain ruled textile trades. It was easier for Spain to buy cloth produced more cheaply elsewhere; easier to collect taxes than to force an economic transformation as long as the silver flowed.

In New Spain, Bourbon reforms focused on collecting tributes from indios and mulattoes, and enforcing the alcabala sales tax levied on Hispanic commerce. Within the church the regime promoted the power of bishops (whom it appointed) and limited the religious orders, notably Franciscans and Jesuits who seemed too independent to monarchs aiming for absolutism. Meanwhile reformers pressed state power over the entire church, claiming more of the bishops' tithe revenues and insisting that Jesuit estates must pay tithes.[7] Bourbon goals were clear by 1750; implementation remained limited.

Assertions quickened with the ascent of Carlos III in 1759.[8] Atlantic warfare was under way; the new king's French cousin had lost Canada. Carlos arrived with a reputation as the reform ruler of the Kingdom of Naples; he brought along the Marqués de Esquilache, manager of his assertive rule. They hoped to repeat key reforms: centralizing state power, increasing revenues, limiting the church. Their first act, the turn to war in 1761, proved more precipitous than successful; Carlos faced the loss of Havana in 1762. Still, British overextension and exhaustion brought Havana back to Spain in the peace of 1763, along with new control of the Mississippi. The empire and the silver economy held intact.

The years from 1763 to 1765 brought study and debate, culminating in a decree of "free trade" that opened commerce in parts of the empire. It allowed Cuba to trade with diverse Spanish ports, aiming to continue the development of sugar and slave plantations that had energized under brief British rule. The commercial reform was limited, however. There was no change for New Spain. Most silver was mined there; most stayed in channels taxed by the regime and ruled by merchants in Cádiz and Mexico City. It was risky to alter the trade that sustained Spain's imperial coffers and claims to Atlantic power.

A month after announcing open trade for Cuba, Carlos sent don José de Gálvez to New Spain as visitor general, charged with bolstering the power of the regime and its revenues. Established interests in Madrid and among the merchants of Cádiz and Mexico City worried. Gálvez had barely arrived when Carlos faced a challenge at home. The tale is well known: in March 1766 the Madrid rabble rioted against rules that outlawed long cloaks. The goal was to deter disorder, to keep miscreants from hiding weapons and smuggling goods under cloaks as they went about the city. People were livid; a mob ruled for a day, and then Carlos capitulated and fired Esquilache. The inquiry that followed found that Jesuits had orchestrated the riots to show their power against the reforming minister.

Thus told, the tale is improbable, if not unbelievable. Did the people of Madrid take over the city to protest a dress code? Would Carlos dismiss the minister who orchestrated his rule over a dress code and a day of riots? Could Jesuits orchestrate riots and force a quick change of ministers? There was much more to the riots and the fall of Esquilache, much less to the role of the Jesuits. Grain shortages, market manipulations, and tax hikes had fueled rising grievances in Madrid's neighborhoods. The prohibition of cloaks was not the cause of the riots; it was a precipitant. A secret inquiry soon revealed to Carlos that the riots were in part spontaneous outbursts, and in important part provoked, inflamed, and manipulated by key aristocratic and commercial interests threatened by Esquilache's reforms. Powerful men allowed the riots to rage out of control and then urged Esquilache's dismissal. Later, to cover his acquiescence in a coup, Carlos joined in deflecting blame to the Jesuits. The reform impulse was blunted; those who conspired in the background to turn out Esquilache remained powerful. In 1767 the Jesuits would be expelled from Spanish domains, a public assertion of power aimed to cover the weakness revealed when entrenched interests plotted and city people rioted to topple Esquilache.[9]

Between the riots and the expulsion, Bourbon assertions and popular mobilizations shifted to New Spain. Esquilache had sent don José de Gálvez there late in 1765, charged with accelerating reform. Gálvez focused on militia recruitment, tax collection, and a new state monopoly on the cultivation, production, and sale of tobacco products. As Gálvez promoted policies that struck hard upon working people, news came from Spain that a riot had ousted the first minister, the chief reformer—Gálvez's mentor. The powerful interests involved in the riot and coup were hidden; the deflection of blame onto the Jesuits awaited the expulsion decree a year later. The immediate news was clear: popular riots toppled the ministry and blocked reforms.

In that context the summer of 1766 brought assertions of regime power, popular resistance, and negotiated resolutions to the Bajío and nearby provinces. The Bourbon reform impulse had developed over decades. In the 1750s clerical estate operators, including Jesuits, Agustinians, and others, were pressed to pay tithes. Many Franciscans, Jesuits, and others still preaching in parishes were replaced by diocesan clergy appointed by bishops and presumed more loyal (or more fully subject) to the regime. Jesuits resisted tithes and indigenous parishioners protested the shift to diocesan clergy whom they saw as more interested in fees than service. But the regime made gains and protests were contained.[10]

With Spain's entry into war, reform in New Spain focused on militia recruitment. In 1760 and 1761 the viceroy Marqués de Cruillas surveyed New Spain's militias and concluded that many existed mostly on paper, and in honors claimed by local commanders. Units were minimally staffed, little trained, and poorly armed. Cruillas demanded new recruitment and better training; his agents faced opposition from employers wary of losing workers and from artisans and others fearing enlistment and military discipline.[11] The British capture of Havana in 1762 energized Cruillas. Recruitment and mobilization improved from Puebla and Mexico City to the Bajío. In October a company of mulatto lancers from San Miguel marched to defend Orizaba in the highlands above the port of Veracruz. In November they were joined by a cavalry company of their Spanish and mestizo neighbors.[12] While war continued, the threat to New Spain seemed real and resistance to recruitment waned. Men sent to coastal lowlands infested with mosquitos bearing yellow fever learned the truth of the region's deadly reputation.

No invasion came. With peace in 1763 militiamen returned home. Few remembered martial experiences fondly. Separations from families and communities and disruptions of production and labor brought exposure to deadly disease. Men returning to the Bajío faced a regional economy in a slump. They hoped that peace would bring revival, an end to militia recruitment, and reduced demands for revenue. Carlos III and his counselors had other goals; they saw a continuing British threat and thus a need to increase military preparedness in New Spain. They called men to join against British aggression, hoping that strong militias would also increase the regime's power within New Spain. Viceroy Cruillas stressed recruitment, followed by Military Inspector don Juan de Villalba in 1764 and then Visitor General Gálvez in 1765. Employers remained wary and potential recruits resisted, notably in Puebla in 1764 and 1765.[13] The regime aimed to bolster its coercive capacity by strengthening militias; yet it had to negotiate with colonial men, from entrepreneurial elites to urban mulattoes, to assert power. That contradiction endured at the base of the reform effort.

Amid recruitment and resistance, 1764 saw widespread replacement of the district magistrates who served the regime (and traded for themselves) in the provinces. This too was both a revenue measure and an assertion of power: New magistrates bought their offices and worked to recoup costs quickly with aggressive trading. Presumably they would reward the regime with assertive service. Meanwhile, the war crisis past, authorities turned again to removing Franciscans and others from parishes they had long served, replacing them with diocesan priests. Simultaneously officials demanded increased revenues from episcopal coffers. Long a pillar of the regime and a key to mediating conflicts, the church faced new pressures and uncertainties, provoking divisions within.[14]

The arrival of Gálvez late in 1765 added new emphasis on revenues. Maize sold in Hispanic cities and towns began to pay the alcabala, 6 percent of its value at sale. That staple had been exempt as an indigenous crop; now urban consumers would pay a tax on basic sustenance. New monopolies of tobacco and playing cards threatened a multitude of producers and sellers, while adding costs to addictive pleasures common among mineworkers and artisans across the Bajío. And the regime pressed tribute collection from indios defined as *vagos* (not attached to indigenous republics) and from mulattoes. The legal obligation to pay the head tax was not new. But the authorities had rarely effected collection outside the republics, where tribute payment brought access to lands and colonial justice. *Mulatos libres* and indios vagos, without land rights and with limited access to colonial justice, together formed a growing majority in Bajío towns and across the countryside. Reformers aimed to make vagos pay the price of being indio, even as they lacked the rights of living in landed republics. Tributes reminded mulattoes, who did so much labor in the silver economy, and who so often manned militias, that they belonged to no republic, and yet were expected to pay for subordination.[15]

Gálvez's program hit mulattoes hard. Since the late seventeenth century militia service had offered them an approximation of Spanish status, a way up in the colonial order. But when recruitment became intrusive, economically disruptive, and threatened removal to deadly coastal lowlands, resentment escalated. Militia levies, demands for tribute, urban taxes, and new monopolies combined to bring mulattoes to the fore in the risings of 1766 and 1767, revealing the risks of relying on mulatto militiamen to keep the colonial order.

In the summer of 1766 conflict began at Guanajuato. For decades workers there had negotiated dangerous labor and declining pay; many had lost the right to live at refinery compounds, finding new independence while facing rising costs. For months mineworkers—mostly mulattoes—had resisted taxes, monopolies, and militia recruitment. On 17 July they mobilized, a reported forty thousand strong, to take the city and demand "that alcabalas will not be levied . . . on goods like maize, wheat flour, meat, wood, torches, stone, sand, lime, and other goods that have never paid." They refused taxes on the staples of life. If there had to be a tobacco monopoly, it must sell better quality at lower price—and please popular tastes. And they rejected militia recruitment: "news came that soldiers would arrive that day to take a militia census. Not even dead will they enter! This city and its jurisdiction will be free of militia censuses and enlistments." Militia recruitment now challenged the liberty of mineworkers in Guanajuato.[16]

The riot lasted hours and did damage mostly to property. The city council, without effective force and most interested in keeping mining and commerce alive, acceded to the crowd's demands. It then wrote to the viceroy, blaming overzealous tax collectors and tobacco monopolists. In the shadow of the apparent victory of the Madrid populace in ousting Esquilache, the mulatto majority at Guanajuato rebuffed core demands of postwar Bourbon reformers in New Spain. The tide of popular power would embolden others.

August brought a rising of mineworkers at Real del Monte, southeast of the Bajío and north of Mexico City at the eastern edge of the dry Mezquital basin that marked the margins of Mesoamerica. Its mines were surrounded by Otomí communities with republican rights, and lands eroded by the Spanish introduction of sheep.[17] For centuries mining brought opportunities and pressures to the region. Since the 1740s don Pedro Romero de Terreros had invested wealth he gained in trade at Querétaro to dig a deep drainage tunnel, finally hitting bonanza in 1762. He paid ample ore shares and high wages to keep scarce workers in the mines while costly rehabilitation kept production, profits, and remunerations limited during the first years of the boom. Then, in the summer of 1766—perhaps facing increasing costs and thinning ores, certainly aiming to maximize profits—he announced an end to ore shares and began to reduce wages and use gangs of thugs to recruit reluctant workers in mining camps and nearby villages. Romero tried all this after the Esquilache riots and the protests at Guanajuato, both seen as popular victories.[18]

Tense negotiations began in late July. On 14 August Romero conceded ore shares to skilled pickmen, but insisted that day laborers' wages must fall from four to three reales daily. Aiming to divide the workers, Romero provoked a strike that closed the mines in a violent confrontation leading to the death of the district magistrate and a foreman, a close escape by Romero, and a fire that ravaged the works. The next day over three hundred militiamen arrived to stop the violence; a week later don Francisco de Gamboa, a High Court judge, came to investigate and adjudicate. Representing a regime most interested in promoting mining and collecting revenues, he reinstated ore shares and the wage of four reales, citing norms at Guanajuato. Warning against forced recruitment, the judge assuaged the workers' discontent through mediation and again made concessions to keep the work going and silver flowing.[19]

Soon conflict erupted at Valladolid and Pátzcuaro, south of the Bajío. Pátzcuaro had become the center of Tarascan power during the colonial era; Valladolid was built to assert Spanish eminence as seat of the bishop of Michoacán and a district magistrate. Both towns were linked to the Bajío. Tarascan communities sent laborers to mines in Guanajuato and migrant families to estate communities in the Bajío; Valladolid's bishop collected tithes across the Bajío (except Querétaro) and north to San Luis Potosí. Cultivators in Pátzcuaro and Valladolid supplied markets in the Bajío. And the population of the Spanish city, the Tarascan capital, and many outlying republics included a growing number asserting mulatto status.

Early in the 1740s, during war against the British in the Caribbean, mulatto militias were created at Valladolid and Pátzcuaro, forces that were filled in the early 1760s mostly by urban craftsmen.[20] From the 1750s the region struggled with decrees removing clergy of the religious orders from local parishes. Franciscans were the most numerous targets; their Tarascan parishioners resented and sometimes resisted their removal. The Agustinians, with rich estates adjacent to their parish at Yuriria, proved harder to remove. Into those conflicts came a new district magistrate in 1761; he provoked Tarascans (and mulattoes) at Pátzcuaro and favored Spanish (and mulatto) Valladolid. Tensions simmered until the summer of 1766. Then he doubled mulatto tributes and intensified collection. In late August militia recruiters came to en-roll mulattoes and enforce military discipline. Called to assemble in the public square on 1 September, mulattoes rioted and took control of Valladolid. When the district magistrate called on outlying forces to pacify the city, mulatto and indigenous resistance spread to Pátzcuaro. Tensions were diffused only when Bishop don Pedro Sánchez de Tagle negotiated concessions limiting tributes and militia levies.[21]

In the summer of 1766, in the transatlantic shadow of the Esquilache riots, attempts to raise revenues and militias provoked popular ire at Guanajuato, Valladolid, and Pátzcuaro; meanwhile Romero's assault on remunerations set off labor conflict at Real del Monte. Earlier, mu-lattoes saw militia roles as gaining rights—when they led to local drills, honors, and limited actions. Now they resisted recruitment, knowing that they faced mobilizations that could take them away from work and community to serve posts in deadly lowlands. They resented new taxes; at Real del Monte they rioted against pay reductions for dan-gerous labor. They gained indigenous allies, among Otomí villagers who resisted labor drafts around Real del Monte, among Tarascans who resented the loss of Franciscan pastors and other impositions in Pátzcuaro. In every case the popular mobilizations of 1766 led to me-diation and concessions.[22] The new powers sought by Bourbon agents seemed more imagined than effective. Established ways of mediation and negotiation endured, giving heart to working majorities and pause to those who aimed to bolster the regime's power.

Escalating Conflict, Jesuit Expulsion, and Alliance for Repression, 1767

The spring of 1767 brought continuing assertions of popular power at Pátzcuaro and Guanajuato. Conflict spread north of the Bajío across San Luis Potosí. It intensified in late June, when the expulsion of the Jesuits provoked new risings at San Luis de la Paz and complicated on-going conflicts in Guanajuato and San Luis Potosí. In the face of pro-liferating insubordination Visitor General Gálvez rejected the tradi-tion of conciliation and concession. He urged provincial entrepreneurs and officials to join him in an alliance for repression. The conflicts of 1767 reveal much about popular visions; the alliance for repression ex-posed the essence of Bourbon reformers' goals, and the limits of their powers.

The year began with new conflicts at Pátzcuaro. Pedro de Soria Villa-roel was elected governor of the indigenous republic. He was an indio (a status required to hold the position), a blacksmith, married to a Spanish woman, and linked by his name to a prominent Spanish family. Soria aimed to reassert Pátzcuaro's leadership across the Tarascan highlands. He found support among mulattoes in his coalition; he kept close ties with Spanish traders and landlords. He built a cross-class, multiethnic alliance against the power of Valladolid and its district magistrate. Conflict peaked in May and continued with sporadic violence until Soria alienated Pátzcuaro's Spanish elite, the coalition broke, and he fled in July.[23]

At Guanajuato in the spring of 1767, mines and markets carried on. The people showed a bold mood during Holy Week festivities. The district magistrate arrested a few celebrants for what the crowd saw as small offenses. Viewing the official as haughty and demeaning, a rowdy group took the magistrate, threatened to kill him, marched him through the streets in an afternoon of insults, dropped him at his office, and promised to return on Easter Sunday (challenging the magistrate to resurrect his power?). The crowd humiliated a leading Spanish official without repercussion; the magistrate faced the Inquisition.[24]

Soon conflict broke out at San Felipe, north of Guanajuato. Residents in the barrio of Analco had claimed rights as an indigenous republic since 1740, seeking land and self-rule without success. Discontent simmered. In the 1760s a few Spaniards joined mulattoes and indios against gachupínes (the insulting label slung at immigrant Spaniards who often ruled local trade). Conflict peaked on 3 May 1767, when the magistrate's lieutenant (the district magistrate lived at San Miguel) set out to imprison José Patricio Suárez, an indio official at Analco. He fled to a chapel as residents rehearsed for a festival. The official entered and dancers hurled stones, leaving Suárez free in the chapel. The standoff lasted months.[25] The spat at San Felipe would seem a local affair, but for what followed in San Luis Potosí.

Late in May authorities at the mines in San Pedro read decrees from Viceroy Marqués de Croix prohibiting workers from carrying arms and mandating that all without employment take work within a month or face fine, exile, and labor at coastal forts. The message was clear: workers might serve in disciplined militias, but never carry arms independently; they must work—or labor in service of the state. The regulations were not new; why they were proclaimed again in May 1767 is not clear. Officials faced a widening circle of popular independence around Guanajuato. Perhaps they saw San Luis Potosí, an important yet secondary mining area, as the place to reassert power. If so, they miscalculated. The decrees proclaimed at San Pedro provoked riots that sent the local lieutenant into hiding. When the district magistrate announced the same prohibition of arms and mandate to labor in the city of San Luis Potosí, the provincial capital, people in the barrios rioted there too. Into June resistance spread to indigenous towns and upland ranchos that provided supplies and workers to the mines.

On 6 June a throng of mineworkers in San Pedro, nearby rancheros, and people from city barrios and nearby towns occupied San Luis Potosí. They emptied the jail, mostly of men held for criminal offenses. They stoned the Crown offices, the tobacco monopoly, and the homes of officials and merchants. They posted a list of grievances: mineworkers demanded exemption from tributes, the end of alcabalas on grain and other staples, and of the tobacco monopoly (or better quality at lower prices). They claimed the right to carry arms. They insisted that appointment of the magistrate's lieutenant at the mines be subject to their approval. They added that as workers they were the true "owners" of the mines; proprietors only skimmed profits while failing to use designated funds to maintain local worship.

The list of demands then turned to concerns of upland rancheros. Most worked lands without titles; they too insisted that productive use be recognized as a right, for themselves and for indigenous villagers. The rioters at San Luis Potosí linked mineworker, rancher, and village rights. All worked the mines or provided essential supplies. The crowd that took over the provincial capital crossed ethnic lines to assert popular rights against legally demanding yet obviously weak officials. The district magistrate, lacking forces to contain his imagined subjects, capitulated on all grounds. When he asked local merchants and estate operators for armed support, they divided and demurred. When a squad arrived from the south to recruit militias on 16 June, the crowd blocked its work.

The recruiters were an advance guard of a hundred troops trekking north from Querétaro to expel the Jesuits—a state secret to be proclaimed on 25 June. On the 14th the squad stopped at the Jaral hacienda to await arms from Mexico City. While there the commander wrote to don Francisco de Mora, a rich miner, landlord, and captain of the San Luis Potosí militia, asking him to mobilize his troops. The commander also wrote to the lieutenant at Valle de San Francisco, on the way from Jaral and to San Luis Potosí, ordering militias to mobilize there and setting off a riot among residents who presumed that they were being sent against the people of San Luis Potosí.[26]

With troops not fully armed and their numbers limited, the expulsion of the Jesuits was proclaimed on 25 June at San Luis Potosí. The crowd again took over. The secretary of the Spanish Council saw a city "full of *indios* armed with bows and rocks and shouting, 'death to the District Magistrate and all the *gachupines*.'" Officials waited a day and then rounded up the Jesuits. On the 26th a throng of ten thousand blocked the caravan, freed reluctant Jesuits, and returned them to their convent. Again the crowd threatened authorities and emptied the jail. In San Pedro ranchers and mineworkers proclaimed one of their own a new king.[27] Rioters began to challenge the legitimacy of the colonial order.

While insisting on protecting the Jesuits, the crowd at San Luis Potosí turned its anger against immigrant gachupínes, the clique of immigrant merchants and officials most loyal to the Bourbon project. The anti-gachupín turn of the rioters sought an alliance with prosperous provincials. Spaniards with colonial roots faced a challenge and a choice. They could join the populace in resistance, or they could back the regime. Most rallied around don Francisco de Mora as he mobilized regional forces to impose order. The militia commander forged unity among elites and promoted divisions among the populace, recruiting the local Tlaxcalan barrio into his alliance against riotous crowds.

News of regime provocations and popular resistance spread. Conflict began at Guadalcázar, a mining town northeast of San Luis Potosí, on 5 July. As told by the magistrate's lieutenant, at seven o'clock on Sunday evening, "a great number of men and boys entered the public plaza, playing a ball game called *la chueca* [field hockey]." A local curate, "knowing the game was not appropriate to the plaza, and begun only to provoke officials," saw "depraved intentions" and ordered the group to move outside town. Suddenly a game of hockey became a riot; team captains became rebel leaders. The crowd emptied the jail and turned on the store and home of don Juan Antonio Galnares, an immigrant merchant and tobacco monopolist. Rioters broke his door with hatchets and stones, taking cloth and cash as he and his family fled. Resisting a priest's pleas to desist, the men turned on other immigrant merchants and took the funds in the royal offices. Amid the tumult loud voices demanded that the local lieutenant be of colonial birth and that the Conde de Santiago, a leading Mexico City landlord, should become "king of this kingdom."

Near midnight a crowd of five hundred men, women, and boys returned to the plaza. A group of prosperous colonial Spaniards, including the local merchants don Ignacio de Jara and don Santiago de Ortega, met with the leaders. The crowd insisted that its demands be set in text:

> That the position of Lieutenant must go to don Santiago de Ortega.
> That all prisoners freed this night be pardoned, their trials ended.
> That all *gachupínes* living here leave these mines within three days—and forever.
> That there will be no jail, tobacco monopoly, nor alcabalas here.
> That the Conde de Santiago will be crowned king.

The lieutenant resigned in favor of Ortega, who joined Jara and the priest in pacifying the crowd, publicly granting all its demands. Guadalcázar began to calm. On 8 July the deposed lieutenant don José Pérez Platón and his reluctant replacement Ortega signed a report to viceregal authorities defending the resignation of the former and the concessions of the latter.[28] At Guadalcázar rioters again sought alliance with local Spaniards against immigrant merchants and officials. And again rebels demanded a new sovereign, this time naming a distant landed aristocrat who they imagined might share their vision for New Spain.

Soon after the riot at Guadalcázar popular risings took over Venado and La Hedionda. Both were indigenous republics, settled long ago as Tlaxcalan bulwarks against independent peoples; both held vast if arid lands that they defended against developing grazing estates. Conflicts with outsiders fueled divisions within. Amid the rising tide of riots across San Luis Potosí, a dispute over sodality resources at Venado turned into a revolt against the priest and his allies. Treasury offices and merchant shops were sacked. Leaders of the republic were ousted; new officials sent word to nearby La Hedionda seeking allies.[29] While Bourbon assertions faced a challenge in key mining centers, others with diverse grievances in the complex social order of Spanish North America took the opportunity to join the fray.

Across San Luis Potosí rioters took control of the capital, mines, ranchero uplands, and indigenous republics, urban and rural. Anger at new taxes and monopolies, demands for control and fair remuneration at work, claims to lands, and hatred of immigrant merchants fueled resistance. The expulsion of the Jesuits did not cause the risings. It did lead people already rioting to seek alliances with provincial Spaniards—that was the effect (and presumably the goal) of anti-gachupín rhetoric. It was a call for a coalition of colonials against regime reformers and immigrant merchants. But that call came with a radical turn, including proposals for a king of New Spain and demands that workers and producers share ownership of mines and lands. Rather than join the anti-gachupín coalition, provincial Spaniards moved from conciliation and inaction to support for the repression led by don Francisco de Mora.

The risings at San Luis Potosí held strong when news of the expulsion came to the Bajío. There the attempt to remove the Jesuits set off new resistance at San Luis de la Paz and renewed assertions of popular power at Guanajuato. Settled as a mission under Jesuit tutelage at the end of the Chichimeca wars, San Luis de la Paz mixed Mesoamericans and Chichimecas. In 1767 seven Jesuits ministered to over a thousand Spaniards, nearly 1,400 mestizos, about 5,700 residents of Otomí, Tarascan, and Mexica ancestry—and 311 still called Chichimecas. Over the centuries Jesuits built and operated prosperous estates to fund their work; they negotiated between landlords (including themselves) and indigenous families who cultivated community lands and provided seasonal labor at estates. The Jesuits mediated the social order at San Luis de la Paz, a community between the commercial Bajío and the Sierra Gorda, still home to indigenous peoples seeking independence.[30]

Don Felipe Cleere, a treasury official from San Luis Potosí, led the expulsion at San Luis de la Paz. He knew the testy mood of the summer of 1767; he soon learned of the devotion of the people of San Luis de la Paz to their Jesuit pastors. The date of expulsion, 25 June, was a festival and market day that brought throngs to San Luis de la Paz. Cleere waited until visitors headed home and then began.[31] As evening fell, the seven Jesuits surrendered to the orders of their sovereign. Fearing a riot, Cleere planned to take the priests to the San Diego hacienda. Before he could, "*indios* and *chichimecas*" assembled, hurling insults, fireworks [left from the day's festivities], and stones at officials trying to move the Jesuits and at the homes and shops of prosperous Spaniards. Cleere sent the Jesuit rector to calm the crowd, to no avail. Women, men, and children aimed to save their pastors while the Jesuits resisted salvation. A broadside called on the "indigenous republic" to reject "the heresy the king is trying to impose by taking away the fathers of the holy Society." Cleere fled on the 26th, leaving the Jesuits as reluctant yet honored captives of the crowd. Led by an india named Ana Guatemala, the people ruled.

Cleere explained his failure: "the town has only four or five families *de razón* [with reason], among 4,000 *indios* plus the 500 *mecos* [Chichimecas] sheltered in uplands a half-league away. All are devoted to their priests, to whom they owe their upbringing, Christian lessons, and all manner of help." For two hundred years the Jesuits did "the work of zealous pastors, assisting the poor and ill, administering sacraments, constantly preaching in sermons and missions—for which they have earned the fond love of the residents." Cleere also knew the limits of his power. "There is but one company of 100 men, nine leagues away; it is made up of every sort of worker, dispersed in their different labors, making it difficult to call them up quickly, and more difficult to be confident they will move against the Jesuits. My information is that they are equally devoted to the fathers."[32] How could he impose the expulsion on a community devoted to the Jesuits, and without loyal forces?

San Luis de la Paz lived a week of tense stalemate: Cleere was gone but nearby; the Jesuits were hostages and honored pastors of the community. Violence erupted again when news came that a small troop had arrived at the San Diego property on its way to San Luis Potosí. The district magistrate don Juan Antonio Barreda decided to break the standoff at San Luis de la Paz. He called militias from San Miguel and Querétaro; on 10 July they spirited the Jesuits out of the riotous community. In the fight "some natives died."[33] The confrontation at San Luis de la Paz was the only one provoked by the expulsion. Still, the attacks on the homes of prosperous families suggest that other grievances lurked in the community, earlier mediated and moderated by Jesuit conciliation but now thrust into the open by the expulsion.

The conflicts at San Luis de la Paz were under way before any attempt at expulsion began at Guanajuato—engine of the silver economy and home to riotous risings for over a year. Don Fernando de Torijo y Leri, corregidor at Chihuahua, was called south to lead the expulsion at Guanajuato. He set off from Mexico City on 14 June and later reported that heavy downpours and flooded rivers sent him to San Miguel, where a raging river stalled his advance. He did not reach Guanajuato by 25 June, the day set for expulsion. Yet Cleere had no trouble getting to San Luis de la Paz on time. Perhaps Torijo hesitated in the face of rising popular mobilizations. Whatever his reasons, he did not enter the city until 1 July.[34]

By then the people knew why he had come. Torijo asked the district magistrate to mobilize the merchants' militia and others at nearby estates. Secrecy proved impossible. The call to the militias "set off new shouting and riots among the city poor and mineworkers; their violent anger was so extreme that the more active the militiamen became in mounting a defense, the more the masses ran through the streets like unrestrained beasts in a great riot that reached to the peaks above. They shot slings and firearms; our cavalry was so threatened they felt forced to shoot down at the enormous rabble—who from below, using rooftops and terraces, clouded the air with stones." Unable to control the canyon city, Torijo, the district magistrate, and other officials, many wounded, took refuge in the Casas Reales.

From three in the afternoon to midnight a crowd reinforced by throngs streaming in from upland mines besieged the royal offices; militiamen shot back. Torijo reported "several deaths" among rioters and "a few wounds" among officials and militiamen; he emphasized that the forces of order could not stop eight thousand rioters. Guanajuato's geography favored the people who held the heights above a center deep in the canyon. Long-time residents had "never seen such insolence." Torijo offered to die for his sovereign, adding that his sacrifice and that of the militia would not stop the crowd. He awaited the viceroy's orders.[35]

Men, women, and children rose to block the expulsion; they assaulted the stores and homes of the well-to-do. The crowd took casualties but was not deterred. Local clergy tried to pacify the throng by carrying the consecrated host before the angry community, and more stones rained down from the heights surrounding the center. Local Spaniards took arms in urban warfare against the working majority. Violence rose in waves, receded in respites, then spread again; the crowd captured two Jesuits and paraded them on their shoulders to the chapel high above at San Juan de Rayas. The people would have their clergy. The Jesuit rector went to the royal offices to promise "blind compliance with whatever was imposed."[36] Officials believed that three indigenous men led the mob. Two were Chichimecas, or dressed as Chichimecas (enduring symbols of defiance in the Bajío), and armed with bows and arrows. The third was Juan Ciprián, a married man who would become a martyr to the cause.

Late on 2 July, as the populace continued to take casualties and inflict property damage, officials negotiated a truce that was nearly surrender. Torijo would retreat to San Miguel; the Jesuits would stay in Guanajuato. Fleeing officials were stoned as they left. Again the people liberated the Jesuits, whether or not they wanted liberation. The crowd won again, and calm returned to Guanajuato.[37] Officials looked to new tactics. Stealthily they began to arrest the presumed leaders of resistance. Late at night on 10 July an armed squad rounded up the Jesuits and took them out of the city, with no resistance from priests so long desired and only recently established in the mining city. The next day the people rioted again, assaulting the rich and their properties; the populace still controlled the city.

Guanajuato was too important to the silver economy for the regime to leave affairs there. Two years of riot had forced repeated concessions from those who aimed to rule. With the Jesuits gone, officials mobilized militias from León, Silao, Irapuato, Celaya, Salvatierra, and Querétaro. Men who prospered from the commercial economy fueled by Guanajuato's silver took arms to attack riotous mineworkers. The troops drilled for a week. On 25 July, a month after the planned expulsion, they surrounded the city and seventeen hundred militiamen began an occupation that lasted three months. Their first task: remove all silver to safety.[38]

The riots of 1767 in Michoacán, San Luis Potosí, and Guanajuato came after years of resistance to militia recruitment, tax increases, and revenue monopolies. Rioters fought policies that strengthened state power and took new revenue in working communities; anger escalated to challenge colonial rule in strategically important places. Guanajuato and Real del Monte, San Pedro, and Guadalcázar were key mining centers; riots there threatened the silver economy. The risings at Pátzcuaro, San Luis de la Paz, and rural communities across San Luis Potosí turned strategic threats into wider challenges. But resistance was limited. Bajío cities and towns from Querétaro to León remained loyal; their militias mobilized to face crowds at San Luis de la Paz and Guanajuato. Estate communities across the Bajío and San Luis Potosí also refrained from the risings all around them. Knowing who rose and who did not is essential to understanding the roots and the limits of the riots of 1766 and 1767.

Resistance developed in disparate communities: mining centers in the Mezquital, the Bajío, and San Luis Potosí; a center of Tarascan power at Pátzcuaro, a mission community at San Luis Potosí; indigenous and ranchero communities across San Luis Potosí. They seem to have little in common, until viewed in the context of those who did not rebel. There was little resistance across Spanish Mesoamerica, where indigenous republics organized life and negotiated relations with the colonial regime and the commercial economy. There was little mobilization in estate communities in the Bajío and to the north, where hierarchies of patriarchy organized communities of tenant families and obligated laborers in secure dependence (whether identified as indios, mulattoes, or mestizos). Querétaro, the founding settlement and commercial capital of the Bajío and Spanish North America, remained at peace and at work. There, where Spanish Mesoamerica met North America, an Otomí republic organized life for a majority cultivating huertas, while at outlying estates tenancies and labor relations kept growing communities in secure dependence orchestrated by patriarchal families. In sum, indigenous republics mediated social stability in the ethnically bifurcated societies of colonial Mesoamerica, while patriarchal security structured social dependence in ethnically mixed estate communities across the Bajío and North America.

The disparate communities that joined the resistance of 1766 and 1767, in contrast, were marked by social insecurities, ethnic fluidities, and shaky patriarchies, and by absent, limited, or contested republican rights. Guanajuato and other mining centers were famously places of opportunity and danger, ethnic amalgamation, and weak family relations. Tarascan Pátzcuaro had seen Spanish Valladolid challenge its preeminence; its indigenous republics struggled to organize communities including prosperous Spaniards and independent mulattoes. Then, in the decades before the 1760s, the pressure of growing populations on community lands led growing numbers to migrate toward labor at low-country sugar estates. All that challenged the coherence of Tarascan communities and the families within them.[39] San Luis de la Paz, once a mission community, mixed Spaniards, Mesoamericans, and Chichimecas at the edge of the Sierra Gorda, where independent natives still challenged the colonial order. San Luis Potosí mixed rancheros without land rights and indigenous republics of disparate origins, some with vast lands—all challenged by the commercial boom of the eighteenth century. The rebel communities of the 1760s were different in important ways. They shared social insecurities.

Early Bourbon reforms struck those communities of uncertainty hard. Mulattoes who had long seen honor and advantage in militia service learned the disruptive and deadly consequences of coastal assignments, and faced pressure for greater enrollment and new discipline. Increased alcabalas added costs to lives of insecurity. Tobacco and cards were addictive pleasures that compensated lives of dangerous labor; new monopolies raised their costs and threatened the independence of leisure activities. In contrast, the people of indigenous republics across Mesoamerica were ineligible for militia service. They produced much of their own sustenance, rarely paid alcabalas, and were not a focus of tobacco or playing-card monopolies. Tenants in estate communities from the Bajío north also produced their own sustenance; employed workers gained rations as part of compensations for labor. There too Bourbon demands had limited impact. The insecure, mostly mulatto peoples of mining communities were essential to the silver economy and key targets of Bourbon reforms. Mineworkers led the resistance of the 1760s, which extended to nearby communities of ethnic fluidity and social insecurity.

As resistance escalated it responded to perceptions of regime power. In the postwar years opposition to militia recruitment stiffened as the British threat waned and knowledge of deadly lowland assignments spread. Resistance to taxes and monopolies rose with their implementation. The summer of 1766 brought the crisis to a first peak. News of the spring riots that felled Esquilache likely generated a sense that the regime was vulnerable, leading officials to energize reform and emboldening working communities. The first risings at Guanajuato, Real del Monte, and Pátzcuaro proved popular perceptions right. Riots forced mediations that led to concessions; then early popular successes fueled a cycle of regime assertion and popular resistance that extended across San Luis Potosí in 1767. The expulsion of the Jesuits complicated conflicts already under way.

Only at San Luis de la Paz did riots stem directly from the expulsion. Yet rebels everywhere defended the Jesuits—even as they acquiesced in the expulsion. The soldiers of Christ were removed earlier from Portuguese and French domains; the Spanish expulsion could not be a complete surprise. After two centuries spent educating colonial elites and engaging indigenous peoples in missions, the work sustained by estates, the Jesuits acquiesced in 1767. In that they acted like other colonial elites facing state assertion and popular resistance. They mediated when they could; but when the regime forced a choice between power or rebellion, they acquiesced.

Why then did popular rebels claim the Jesuit cause? At San Luis de la Paz, the Jesuits were established pastors. They ruled religious affairs and exerted great influence in politics and economic life. The Jesuits and a Spanish minority prospered; the indigenous majority lived in subordination and poverty. Yet the Jesuits gained legitimacy by mediating between the powerful and the people. They restrained landlords from the most egregious exploitation, guarded limited autonomy for the majority, and mediated when conflicts arose. The expulsion came to San Luis de la Paz as one more attempt to oust respected preachers and impose diocesan priests famous for taking fees and seeking profit. Like many villagers before them, the people of San Luis de la Paz fought the loss of their pastors.

Elsewhere defense of the Jesuits evidenced complex popular goals. Crowds already mobilized to block demands of the Bourbon state saw the expulsion as another assertion of power. Defense of the Jesuits gave rioters a claim to religious legitimacy. Did they understand that the Jesuits were key mediators in the system of conciliation they rose to defend? During decades of itinerant preaching and more regularly after settling into their new college, Guanajuato Jesuits led periodic revivals among a populace facing dangerous labors mixed with raucous diversions. They called for penance, morality, and salvation. They exhorted workers to steady service. Mass participation suggests that the missions served a need—perhaps a respite from work, perhaps a reminder that workers were worthy humans. Jesuits offered a bridge between deadly labor and final salvation. They spoke to real needs.

More broadly, opposition to the expulsion was part of rioters' attempts to forge alliances with more powerful colonials against Bourbon assertions. Defense of Jesuits, anti-gachupín rhetoric, and the call to the Conde de Santiago all asked colonial Spaniards to join in defiance of the reforming regime. The Jesuits and the elites they educated rejected the offer; the former accepted expulsion, the latter—after brief hesitation—joined the repression.

Militias led by provincial elites ended the resistance. Bourbon reformers' attempts to build a state with greater revenue and coercive power provoked riots in key mining centers. Provincial officials first responded with negotiated concessions, revealing the limits of their powers; when conflict escalated in 1767 provincial militias contained the resistance, also demonstrating the limits of regime power. The attempt to strengthen the state revealed to all that the only way to rule

New Spain, to maintain the flow of silver, was by negotiations among officials, entrepreneurs who also led militias, and working communities. When popular power threatened the silver economy, the regime and regional entrepreneurs responded as one. Power had limits in the 1760s; but those limits did not extend to allowing an enduring threat to the prevailing order in the Bajío and Spanish North America.

Inquests, Repressions, and Reformed Reforms, 1767

Visitor General don José de Gálvez let provincial militias contain the riots; powerful colonials had to act publicly to control working colonials fighting the regime's policies. Then the visitor moved to punish the people he blamed for resisting Bourbon goals. In a long report he detailed his inquests, repressions, and policy prescriptions. He revealed much about who threatened the regime, who suffered and died for the effort, how officials viewed rebels, and how the regime aimed to reshape colonial life. First he blamed the Jesuits. They had accepted the expulsion and pacified crowds. But Gálvez knew what his sovereign wanted to read. The problem was the "entrenched power of the Society, resisting tithes; obvious proof of the ambitious greed produced by the self-serving cunning of those priests."[40]

Gálvez also knew that the greatest resistance came at Guanajuato, San Luis Potosí, and Pátzcuaro, where riots long preceded the expulsion. The problem there was "the ancient and constant impunity the peoples of this kingdom have enjoyed; vulgar men of low origin know no brake other than punishment—and this they have not faced for commotions in which great numbers of delinquents disguise themselves in respectability. The people destroy everything; they make whims and audacities into inviolable law, forcing scandalous concessions dictated with deceitful insolence."[41] Gálvez knew that Carlos, trying to reassert power after riots toppled Esquilache, had to blame the Jesuits for the conflicts in New Spain in 1767. He also knew that the deeper challenge was to assert power over people who refused taxes and monopolies, negotiated labor and local rights, and won concessions from officials weak in coercive power. Gálvez aimed to assert state power, end conciliation, and deny workers and communities the ability to demand mediation.[42]

Only after provincial forces quelled local risings and removed the Jesuits did Gálvez begin his tour of inspection and repression, backed by six hundred regular troops—the largest non-militia force ever assembled in New Spain. His route revealed his vision of resistance and the way forward. He began and ended with people he saw as indios; in between he focused on the peoples who labored in the silver economy, often trying to make them into indios.

He began at San Luis de la Paz, the only community that rose in response to the expulsion, and where rebels were most easily marked as indios. He asked the indigenous governor and republic for a list of rebel leaders. Local officials were presumed innocent and invited to blame others. Whether those they named were primarily responsible is uncertain; Gálvez followed their lead. Ana María Guatemala, an indigenous widow, was offered as principal instigator. (Had she come from Guatemala? If so, her move to San Luis de la Paz contains a revealing story.) Among eleven others blamed were four women, two unmarried young men, and don Marcos Pérez de León of the local indigenous elite. Ana María Guatemala, convicted as "principal ringleader of the riots," was hanged along with two married men. Don Marcos's status as a cacique gained him the right to be shot. All were decapitated after execution, their heads displayed for everyone to see, their homes destroyed, their lands sown with salt, and their families expelled from the community. Two single youths took public lashings before facing life exile from home. The rest, including four women, were exiled for a decade. The hangmen were indios from San Luis Potosí, the firing squad from the regiment backing Gálvez. Blame given and sentences done, Gálvez rebuilt local power. Four diocesan priests replaced the Jesuits; denied the thousand-peso stipend paid since the Chichimeca wars, they gained five hundred pesos yearly from confiscated Jesuit estates. The community would pay for services at rates set by the Michoacán diocese. It would also fund the militias Gálvez had ordered to ensure the subordination of "such seditious people."[43]

At San Luis de la Paz, Gálvez worked with the indigenous republic. He allowed its officers to identify culprits and then imposed harsh punishments on a chosen few, including women who challenged patriarchal conventions and led angry crowds. He drew officials of the republic to join in repression, accept diocesan clergy, and fund the Hispanic militia that would contain the community. The republic endured, its autonomy curtailed. Executions, exiles, the toppling of homes, and the salting of land announced that resistance to power and patriarchy brought destruction to family, community, and cultivation.

Having finished at San Luis de la Paz on 18 July, Gálvez might have joined the pacification still incomplete at Guanajuato. He left that task to local officials and provincial militias and marched north to San Luis Potosí, where pacification was nearly done. Don Francisco de Mora and provincial militias had calmed the provincial capital and occupied the mines at San Pedro. Most rebel leaders were in hiding; most workers and rancheros had offered loyalty, though Mora had doubts.

Uneasy calm ruled Guadalcázar. Gálvez arrived in San Luis Potosí on 24 July to spend three months investigating and imposing punishment in the region that had generated the most widespread and enduring risings in 1767. Again he insisted that the officials of indigenous republics deliver lists of rebel leaders. Nearly a thousand were arrested, this time including many indigenous officials.[44]

Before doing more in the provincial capital, Gálvez turned on Analco, the suburb of San Felipe between Guanajuato and San Luis Potosí. Neither reforms nor the expulsion was at issue, but Gálvez aimed to make a quick statement evident in both Guanajuato and San Luis Potosí. He sent sixty troops to arrest the leaders of a "rebellion manipulated by *indios*," including a mestizo, Asencio Martín; an indigenous magistrate, José Patricio Suárez; and a Spanish magistrate, don Miguel de la Puente, an immigrant from Burgos whose crime was "some understandings" with the native magistrate.[45] Convicted as a rebel and blasphemer, the mestizo was executed, his head displayed, his rancho destroyed, his lands salted, and his wife, children, and descendants exiled. The indigenous magistrate and two allies faced life service at coastal forts. Seven others faced six to eight years of the same. The Spanish justice, convicted of complicity, was fined two thousand pesos and sent to serve eight years at Acapulco. Analco would not become a republic; it lost its indigenous magistrate. Gálvez added that if its residents claimed indio status, they must dress and cut their hair "the way *indios* do." They could not ride horses or carry firearms, on pain of a hundred lashes.[46]

Then Gálvez went to Guadalcázar, where a hockey game became "the blackest sedition ever seen in these provinces."[47] Workers challenged taxes and tributes, sacked stores, and denied the sovereignty of Spain's king. Most rebel leaders fled in advance of the troops. "I condemned only four to hang."[48] Mineworkers were mobile and essential to the silver economy. Guadalcázar got off easy, though men facing hanging surely disagreed. Next Gálvez looked to Venado and La Hedionda. Factions there had challenged local clergy on questions of worship and religious resources. For that Gálvez executed twelve leaders and exiled seventy-nine more. In addition, he denied the two indigenous republics rights to their vast lands. Such resources caused "arrogance and discord." The communities kept only remnants; the rest was made available for estate development. The residents retained councils and were reminded to pay tributes. New officials were expected to orchestrate subordination.[49]

Having dealt with outlying communities, Gálvez turned to San Pedro, the heart of resistance in San Luis Potosí. In early August he sentenced eight presumed leaders to death, along with two others from nearby ranchos; forty more faced labor at Veracruz and Havana. Later, in an attempt to discipline nearly four hundred families scattered on ranchos around the mines, Gálvez ordered them congregated at La Soledad. He gave them rights to lands, as long as they paid annual fees to the owners. Not imagined as indios, rancheros neither claimed nor gained republican rights; they did get secure use of land, enabling them to supply mines and provide periodic labor, subject to surveillance in their new community.[50]

Finally, Gálvez returned to the provincial capital of San Luis Potosí. A Spaniard and eight indigenous officials were executed. Another indio leader took two hundred lashes, followed by a life sentence to labor at Acapulco. Eighteen more went to the Pacific port for life, thirty-three for lesser periods. There were executions in the plaza on 6 October; the next day Gálvez hosted a Mass for the souls of the executed: San Luis Potosí's leading citizens came in their finery. The alliance of the regime, provincial elites, and the church could not have been more public.

Then Gálvez began to reform the city. Indigenous barrios lost republican rights, except loyal Tlaxcalilla. He proclaimed the maze of the city streets an obstacle to surveillance, ordering homes destroyed and neighborhoods broken to straighten streets and make plazas square. Meanwhile Gálvez worked to strengthen Spanish rule. He added eight councilmen to the existing two; he divided the city into ten districts (cutting across old indigenous republics) and assigned a Spanish magistrate to each. To back their rule don Francisco de Mora, whose militias contained the risings before Gálvez arrived, became colonel of the Legion of San Carlos. To Gálvez, Mora was "a distinguished and generous subject" who raised more than a thousand troops to defend the regime. Now Mora would provide urban patrols, backed by fifty mounted men ready to ride day or night.[51]

Across San Luis Potosí, Gálvez executed rebel leaders and sent many rioters to labor at ports infamous for deadly diseases. He pursued a new vision of order: Spaniards would rule local councils and commercial life backed by armed force. All who claimed indio status must accept marks of subordination; resistance cost republican rights, land, or both. Among mulattoes so essential to mining, those who led riots faced execution; most escaped punishment if they returned to lives of labor, subject to surveillance.[52]

Gálvez then left for Guanajuato, arriving on 16 October—long after provincial militias had subdued the populace. He saw the city in the canyon as the root of larger disorders: "Everyone knows Guanajuato as the center of treachery, the home of public audacities, the example followed in so many towns and provinces."[53] Militias had imposed peace;

a long roundup jailed nearly six hundred suspects. Gálvez released two hundred, perhaps for lack of evidence, as a gesture of conciliation, or to help with labor shortages. Many of the rest faced severe punishment for what Gálvez called "the repeated scandalous riots and rebellions in which the mob of mineworkers and vile plebeians of the city have committed insults upon its honorable citizens; the rabble's insolence rose to the boldness of refusing to obey the supreme orders of your Majesty."[54]

Gálvez imposed death on nine leaders. Their heads were displayed on pikes at the entrances to the mines, their families exiled from Guanajuato forever; their homes, if they owned any (less certain in the city), were destroyed and the lands salted. Nearly 170 more men were sent to military service and to labor at lowland ports; some also took lashes, while others faced perpetual exile should they survive terms of service.[55] A few men recognized as Spaniards faced convictions for collusion and paid fines. A mine manager paid 300 pesos, six others 150 pesos each, one lesser offender only 50 pesos. The prosperous paid for rebellion in pesos; workers paid with death or the radical disruption of their lives.

Having set "a fear of punishment," Gálvez released the remaining detainees and began to set a new course for rule and labor at Guanajuato. He ended the concessions made earlier in the face of riots. Conciliation was over. "Accustomed to refuse subjection to the sovereign, the mineworkers and common people of Guanajuato" do not "respect the supreme deity in the consecrated host."[56] The problem, Gálvez said, was a lack of "lower officials capable of knowing local problems, solving them, or informing higher authorities." Then he hit the heart of the matter. With weak rule and popular disruptions Guanajuato paid 500,000 to 600,000 pesos in annual taxes on silver. "How much would the city pay with a Magistrate capable of governing with skill and integrity?"[57]

Gálvez's reforms, however, focused more on regime capacity than official integrity. Guanajuato needed strong militias with loyal commanders. The city also required an open road to take silver out—and to march militias in should crowds rise again. The city needed censuses to ensure tribute and tax collections, and it needed armed patrols led by loyal Spanish magistrates. To pay for it all Gálvez fined the city eight thousand pesos (paid by the mining tribunal) and set a tax of one real on every fanega of maize and two reales on every load of wheat sold at the city granary. The people would pay for surveillance aimed to ensure their own subordination.[58]

Gálvez also worried that in Guanajuato, "workers are so mixed in origins and from so many places that it seems impossible to reduce them to good order." The confusion of people, identities, and statuses in a growing and transient population made it hard to collect tributes from indios and mulattoes. Too many people carried mixed identities, creating uncertainties of status that Gálvez believed promoted insubordination. His solution: create armed forces loyal to the regime and capable of enforcing order, and disarm the populace. There would be no "bows, arrows, pikes, nor any other weapons or firearms." He added that "blacksmiths and gunsmiths can no longer make the arms I have prohibited, as they have until now."[59] Denying all working people the right to arms, Gálvez added that indios could not ride horses and must wear "cotton clothing and uncovered braided hair" and never "the Spanish cloak they use to mix with mestizos, mulattoes, and others— on penalty of 100 lashes and a month in jail on the first offense, and perpetual exile from the province for any repeat." Indias must wear "their native skirt *(huipil)*, on penalty of a month in seclusion after being stripped in public if they wear anything else."[60] Gálvez aimed to mark indios and end the mixing of peoples and the negotiation of identities that shaped life at Guanajuato. Rational, enlightened rule apparently required strict ethnic segregation.

Guanajuato silver was too important for Gálvez to stop there. He gave new power to mine operators to make deductions from wages to pay tributes and religious fees. "To assure that mineworkers and refinery laborers in the future will live in peaceful subordination, as they should," he gave managers "the right to correct and punish them domestically [extra-judicially] with fines in less than grave cases." To prevent often skilled and always scarce workers from fleeing discipline or debts, all seeking work would need a "warrant detailing their previous service before they may be admitted to work in another mine or refinery; in everyone's judgment this is the only way to stop the disorders, excesses, and liberties that until now mark the lives of workers in the mining industry."[61] Labor discipline was the key to social peace and silver production; workers would be disarmed, face ethnic segregation, and pay tributes and consumption taxes. Employers could fine workers and limit their movement.

Could decrees alter social relations long shaped by ethnic mixing, labor scarcities, and popular assertions? There were signs that Gálvez's mandates would be challenged. Just before he executed the men selected for exemplary punishment, Gálvez faced the wife of Juan Ciprián, indio and rebel leader. She pleaded for the life of her husband, the father of her children—he was a good patriarch. She offered chickens—sustenance, the currency of everyday life. Gálvez would not stop the execution. He did recognize the public claim of a wife and mother, even as she and her children faced exile from Guanajuato. He refused the chickens and gave the grieving woman a *doblón* worth sixteen pesos—a month's wages in the mines (four months' in the countryside). Later he paid twelve pesos each to five other women widowed by his executions.[62] Gálvez could punish; he could not deny expectations of patriarchy or the claims of widowed mothers. Juan Ciprián's widow drew Gálvez into a public conciliation, the mode of rule he aimed to end.

Juan Ciprián's legacy lived beyond his wife's remonstrance. His severed head was staked on a pike at the Cerro de Buenavista, a gruesome warning to any who might follow him in insubordination. The people drew their own conclusions, taking Juan as a saint, making pilgrimages to his skull, praying, pleading, crying, lighting candles, petitioning favors. The cult grew, despite attempts by civil and church authorities to end it.[63] If Gálvez sought an exemplary execution, the people of Guanajuato found an exemplary life. The martyr to popular power became a way to divine aid. Newly subordinated in life, the workers so essential to the silver economy insistently claimed cultural independence.

As he finished his work in Guanajuato, Gálvez made it clear that his vision of order applied beyond rebel communities. On 10 November he wrote to the district magistrate at San Miguel—a town that had remained at peace, sending militias to discipline rebels at San Luis de la Paz and Guanajuato. Still, Gálvez complained that indios and mulattoes at San Miguel carried arms and evaded tributes. Only mulatto militiamen might be armed; all must pay tributes. Then he added: "The audacity of the *indios* has reached such an extreme that they deny Spaniards exclusive rights of residence and citizenship in the town . . . injuring them in act and word and causing endless unimaginable vexations." People of native ancestry must accept status as indios and return to lives of "subordination and obedience."[64] Ethnic fluidity and uncertainty brought insubordination. It must stop, even at San Miguel, where there was no recent history of challenge to those who ruled.

Finally, Gálvez headed to Pátzcuaro to make a last statement about power and order. The bishop of Michoacán, don Pedro Sánchez de Tagle, had already negotiated peace there. The indigenous governor, Pedro de Soria Villaroel, had joined the pacification, expecting a pardon. Gálvez rebuked the bishop and sent troops to arrest nearly five hundred suspects at Pátzcuaro and nearby. The bishop objected and got a revealing reply. Gálvez rejected the prelate's "charitable mediation" and insisted on "the most important goal" of "exact obedience in the lives of the peoples subject to our august sovereign."[65] Mediation and conciliation must end; power and obedience must shape Spain's richest colony.

Following his troops, Gálvez stopped at Valladolid on 14 November. He sentenced one indigenous rebel to death and one mulatto to exile for life, and then moved on to Pátzcuaro, the center of indigenous and mulatto resistance. He rushed two hundred of the accused to judgment and ordered the execution and decapitation of Governor Soria and a mulatto, Juan Inocencio de Castro, followed by now standard humiliations: heads displayed in public squares, houses destroyed, lands salted, families exiled. Eighteen more, including Soria's Spanish wife, took two hundred lashes and perpetual exile. Others faced lesser whipping, service at ports, and exile. Similar punishments struck officials of the indigenous republics at Uruapan and other towns once allied in resistance. More than 150 faced punishments in and around Pátzcuaro.[66]

Gálvez added now standard regulations: Indios and mulattoes must pay tributes and other taxes; none could carry arms, on threat of death; indios must dress as indios and never ride horses, on pain of lashes. In addition, Gálvez gutted indigenous republics at Pátzcuaro, Uruapan, and nearby. They could no longer elect governors and magistrates; their lands would be overseen by Pátzcuaro's Spanish council; justice would depend on the magistrate's lieutenant or a judge of the Spanish council. And Gálvez denied the communities all right to respond to the regime's decrees with conditions and negotiations. He did not abolish the republics; he prohibited them from serving as republics. Established rights remained a goal, a focus for decades of struggle. To impose his plan Gálvez again created militias led by loyal Spaniards—and again he imposed taxes and fines to make once-resistant people pay the costs of their own containment.[67]

Don José de Gálvez was a state builder. Carlos III sent him to bring more effective rule and revenue collection to New Spain. Before Gálvez could act, the Esquilache riots overthrew the reform ministry in Madrid. The demonstration of the regime's weakness fueled resistance to militia recruitment and revenue demands in New Spain, setting off in the summer of 1766 popular risings that deepened the threat to the regime. Early conciliations led to escalating mobilizations in 1767, when the expulsion of the Jesuits complicated everything. Provincial entrepreneurs might defend the Jesuits and join an alliance of colonial resistance to Bourbon power. Or they might join the Jesuits in accepting the expulsion and join Gálvez in an alliance to contain popular challenges. After short hesitations they chose the alliance for repression. Then Gálvez aimed to set new foundations for Bourbon rule. Power would shift from mediation and conciliation to administration and coercion. Republican rights would be limited; indigenous peoples would live marked as subordinates. Employers gained new power; workers would labor, pay taxes, and fund militias and patrols designed to keep them in their place. But could exemplary punishments, however brutal, followed by new regulations and militias effectively transform Guanajuato, the Bajío, and nearby provinces?

In the short term peace reigned. Repression can work, especially when the powerful unite and resistance is scattered. In the longer run the regime stepped back to mix coercion and conciliation. After 1770 the Bajío, Spanish North America, and New Spain remained loyal colonies; silver production and revenues soared to new heights. Pressures on working families deepened, notably in the Bajío—yet they adapted, labored, and carried on until Napoleon broke the Spanish regime in 1808 and insurgency exploded with new fervor in 1810.

North American Crises, Contrasting Consequences

The North American crises of the 1760s began a watershed. Just as China's premium price and high demand for silver ended, the European powers fought a war for Atlantic dominance. They sought greater shares of the trade and revenues of a quickening Atlantic economy. The conflict brought gains to Britain and losses to France on the North American mainland; Spain's silver economy escaped unscathed and its North American domains expanded. All the European powers faced mounting debts. After the war imperial policies asserted states' power and aimed at raising revenues across the Americas. Resistance to those demands focused in coastal colonies of British North America and mining regions of New Spain. In British America conflicts begun in the 1760s became a war for independence in the 1770s, creating the first American nation in the 1780s, a time of conflict, promise, and uncertainty. In contrast, the risings in the Bajío and nearby were intense yet soon contained, allowing New Spain to resume its role as the American dynamo of the Atlantic economy. The first American nation escaped British rule; the silver economy would persist to shape Spanish power and the Atlantic economy into the nineteenth century.

The reasons are clear. The rioters who challenged the regime and threatened the mining economy in New Spain failed to find allies among prosperous and powerful colonials. Despite attempts to recruit provincial elites—by railing against immigrant gachupínes, defending the Jesuits, proposing the Conde de Santiago as New Spain's king—resistance remained mostly among working people. Those who profited and presumed to rule at first mediated or stood aside. Then they joined an alliance of repression against popular demands. As a result, rebels faced a union of colonial elites and the Spanish regime, while most rural communities remained at work. The riots of 1766 and 1767 were a popular rising blocked by an alliance of the powerful that allowed a calculated repression.

The social relations of resistance proved very different in British America. There colonial merchants and planters led opposition to imperial demands for revenues, to controls on trade, and to rule through military force. Popular communities pressed and tested colonial leaders, but those who expected to rule never lost the initiative within the resistance. They led an alliance that reached into diverse working communities to prosecute the first American war for independence.[68] Why, then, did colonial elites in the Bajío and across New Spain hold loyal to Spain in the 1760s, while so many in British North America joined and led sustained resistance to imperial rule?

The answer, again, is clear: New Spain, especially the Bajío and Spanish North America, produced silver essential to global trade, generating unparalleled revenues for the Spanish monarchy and unmatched wealth for colonial elites. They might quarrel over relative roles, rights, and spoils. But they ultimately understood, and demonstrated in the alliance of repression, that together they profited, while divided they faced uncertainty at best. In contrast, British North America remained a backwater of the Atlantic economy. Silver drove global trade; sugar and slavery formed a second system generating Atlantic riches and revenues. The timber, fish, tobacco, rice, and indigo sold by mainland British colonials were tertiary products. They brought modest wealth to colonial elites. Officials in London saw mainland colonies as financial burdens.[69] Simply stated, New Spain's elites and the Spanish regime had much to preserve in an alliance of colonial rule. In contrast, British North American elites struggled to profit in colonies that British rulers saw as draining state resources: their alliance became fragile in the 1760s and broke in the 1770s.

In this simple explanation complications abound. Two modes of social organization shaped New Spain. Across Mesoamerica, communities assaulted and shrunken by smallpox and other diseases were reconstituted in the sixteenth century as republics with lands and rights to self-rule. A commercial economy grafted onto that base and judicial mediation between Spanish and indigenous republics proved stabilizing for centuries—through the conflicts of the 1760s and the nineteenth-century wars for independence. From the Bajío north the silver economy developed where sparse and independent natives faced diseases and conflicts that forced them off the land. Europeans, Mesoamericans, and Africans were all immigrants there. Over decades Mesoamericans mixed to become indios. Africans found ways out of slavery, often by mixing with neighbors of Mesoamerican ancestry. Some joined as indios in estate communities; others lived as mulattoes in towns and at grazing estates. As frontier conflicts and commercial expansion drove north, most people classed as indios lived as estate dependents; most of African ancestry left slavery behind to live as mulattoes laboring at mines, refineries, and grazing estates.

In the 1760s repúblicas de indios negotiated mounting disputes in colonial courts; peace prevailed across most of Spanish Mesoamerica. In the Bajío and northward, lives of secure dependence shaped by patriarchal families kept the rural majority at work in estate communities. Few indigenous republics and few northern estate communities joined the risings of the 1760s. Resistance focused among mulatto mineworkers who faced danger and insecurity daily, forged patriarchal families with difficulty, and had no chance at republican rights—and among indigenous republics in and around Pátzcuaro facing unique internal tensions and external threats. The risings in New Spain came in strategic places shaped by insecurity; the broader bases of the social order remained solid.

The coastal colonies of mainland British America also lived two ways of social relations—a mostly European North and a slave-based South (with inevitable complications in the middle). Independent natives lived close by everywhere. In that context British colonial politics were more hotly contested, social relations more uncertain—and in slave regions, more blatantly coercive. After joint British and colonial military operations ended French claims to the interior in 1763, colonials expected license to expand into the lands of independent peoples. Ministers in London blocked that expansion, preferring the profits of trade with natives to the costs of the wars that they knew land invasions would provoke. Then Parliament imposed taxes and trade rules that threatened colonial enterprises. Colonials from the powerful to the poor allied to fight taxes and limits on trade and expansion. Where working families were mostly free, alliances were complicated by conflicts over debts, rents, and land rights. Where workers faced slavery, alliances among the free but unequal held strong.

The challenge of sorting out relations among the British regime, colonial elites, and working majorities were complicated by persistent conflicts with independent natives, and by planters' insistence that slavery must endure. During decades of complex conflicts the alliance of colonial elites and imperial rulers essential to imperial rule broke down; in its place an alliance of merchants, planters, and free working families, urban and rural, together resisted imperial claims, indigenous independence, and threats to slavery. The result was an independent United States, enduring slavery, and westward expansion that provoked native resistance and the persistent destruction of independent peoples.[70]

The least complicating factor in the contrasting alliances and out-comes of the North American conflicts of the 1760s was republicanism. For centuries the Spanish regime had shared republican rights with in-digenous peoples across Mesoamerica, a key to negotiating rule and inhibiting resistance in the eighteenth century. The scarcity of republi-can rights in Spanish North America led some to demand them, and to assert indio status in the attempt. Colonial elites held republican rights in the Spanish councils that ruled every major town. Republican ways and goals infused New Spain in the 1760s, organizing power and fuel-ing resistance. No general lack of republican traditions inhibited mobi-lization.

In British America republican rights inhered in provincial assem-blies and town meetings. They were thick on the ground in the North, where communities of European cultivators ruled the countryside. They were scarce across the South, where slave plantations ruled. Since the seventeenth-century English revolution, elections organized representation backed by claims of popular sovereignty. Still, those who sat as town, parish, and provincial leaders and legislators nor-mally came from the prosperous and the propertied.[71] The same sort of men led Spanish councils across New Spain, where they exercised re-publican rights gained by the Crown's recognition (often by purchase) of entrepreneurial success and landed investment. The sharpest differ-ence between the republican traditions of British America and those of New Spain was that the latter granted republican rights to Mesoameri-can communities, legitimated by calls to the common good, facilitated by conciliating courts.[72]

The inclusion of the native majority in landed republics made Span-ish Mesoamerica different from Spanish North America, where inde-pendent natives were subordinated through war and mission trans-formations, and British North America, where natives mostly faced war and marginalization. Southern British colonies kept foundations in slavery while Spanish North Americans adapted to porous bondage and racial amalgamations. Indigenous republics inhibited resistance in New Spain; slavery facilitated cohesion among rebellious colonials in British America. But the contrasting outcomes of the conflicts of the 1760s resulted primarily from the contrasting value of New Spain and British North America to global trade, imperial regimes, and colonial elites. In the face of escalating demands for revenue and more coercive state powers, the men who profited from New Spain's silver economy backed the regime to save the colonial order. In the face of parallel de-mands British America's struggling merchants and planters challenged colonial rule—and England let them go.

New Spain, the Bajío, and Spanish North America were the most valuable colonies in the Americas in the 1760s. Colonial entrepreneurs claimed unparalleled profits; the Spanish monarchy gained revenues that sustained its American rule and the home treasury. Their alliance held, even when the regime's demands escalated and popular rioting threatened silver mining. Resistance was first conciliated, then contained, and finally crushed with focused repressions. Colonial rule was reconsolidated—and the silver economy remained vigorous, poised to soar through decades to come. While the people of the United States struggled to find political stability and prosperity in the new nation, New Spain remained a commercial engine increasingly driving Atlantic trade and European production.

PART II
Forging Atlantic Capitalism

THE BAJÍO, 1770–1810

AFTER 1770 SILVER MINING SOARED to new heights and held them past 1800. An accelerating European economy, just beginning to industrialize, drew silver across the Atlantic; so did Spanish trade and revenue policies. Textile production also rose in the Bajío, despite attempts by the regime to favor Iberian producers. A new tobacco factory became the largest employer at Querétaro; soon a majority of its workers were women. Irrigation and cultivation expanded everywhere. In the realms of production, boom prevailed. After quelling the conflicts of the 1760s the regime backed away from radical changes. It worked to favor mining, increase revenues, and solidify social controls, culminating in the appointment of intendants in 1786. Challenges remained: in 1785 and 1786 drought and frost brought a famine that killed thousands; still, population and production soon revived. The Atlantic wars set off by the French revolution in the 1790s and carried on under Napoleon after 1800 disrupted trade yet stimulated demand for silver and revenues. Silver production, commercial expansion, Spanish rule, and social stability held to 1810.

While British North Americans fought a war for independence and struggled to shape a new United States, while Andean peoples rose in rebellion in the 1780s, and while French citizens and Haitian slaves fought revolutions in the 1790s, the Bajío and Spanish North America mined silver in prodigious quantities and drove the Atlantic economy. From 1770 to 1810 a dynamic capitalism flourished in the Bajío, while leading entrepreneurs increasingly preyed upon the people who worked to sustain everything. Four chapters explore the ways that capitalism soared, assaulted the families and communities that produced everything, and stabilized deepening inequality. Powerful landed entrepreneurs took profits during times of scarcity in urban markets, always certain of their Christian morality. Urban people faced expanding production, declining earnings, and challenges to patriarchy. Rural communities lived the end of slavery, new segregations, evictions, and falling wages. All the while working men clung to a patriarchy that seemed ever more fragile. And everywhere, the powerful, people in between, and the poor debated religious truth and through it social legitimacy. Capitalist expansion came with concentrating wealth, social insecurities, and cultural debates, yet colonial rule, social stability, and northward expansion continued for decades—until everything fell apart after 1808.

CHAPTER 5

Capitalist, Priest, and Patriarch

Don José Sánchez Espinosa and the Great

Family Enterprises of Mexico City, 1780–1810

AFTER 1770 THE BAJÍO and Spanish North America remained a dynamic engine of global capitalism. They were linked to world trades and the Spanish empire by Mexico City, seat of government and financial and commercial capital for all of New Spain. That capital ruled both Spanish Mesoamerica and Spanish North America, tying them to each other and to the world beyond. Financiers there funded mining, claimed profits, shaped trade, and invested in commercial estates. The merchant-financiers of Mexico City and the mine operators at Guanajuato, Real del Monte, Zacatecas, and elsewhere who drove mining and Atlantic and Pacific trades in the eighteenth century were without question profit-seeking investors and entrepreneurs, predatory capitalists by any definition.[1] Still, the risks inherent in local mining and global trades led most successful entrepreneurs to invest in land. Some claimed titles of Spanish nobility. The repeated turn to the land has led to presumptions of a flight from capitalism, of an enduring tradition of honorable lordship that shaped the ways of the powerful in New Spain. In that view colonial entrepreneurship was but a step to noble profligacy, constraining any chance at sustained capitalist ways.[2]

Yet the history of the Bajío and the regions northward is replete with entrepreneurial estate builders from the sixteenth century onward. They were agrarian capitalists taking cash rents and employing dependent workers, permanent and seasonal, in monetized labor relations seeking—and taking—profit in a commercial economy. By the eighteenth century Mexico City was home to a community of great landed capitalists who operated properties for profit in the Mesoamerican basins surrounding the capital as well as across the Bajío and the vast country stretching north. They too were profit-taking predators, speculators in human sustenance, who legitimated their power as a way of Christian charity. After 1770 the heights of economic power in Mexico City, in the Bajío, and across Spanish North America were ever more capitalist in mining, commerce, and the cultivation that sustained everything.

During the first half of the eighteenth century the dynamism of the Bajío drew men of wealth from the capital to Guanajuato, Querétaro, and San Miguel; others took wealth from the Bajío to Mexico City. After 1770, except for the men who directly operated mines at Guanajuato, entrepreneurial power concentrated in the capital. Beginning in 1780 don José Sánchez Espinosa lived in Mexico City and there ruled the vast and profitable landed enterprises built almost a century earlier by don Juan Caballero y Ocío at Querétaro. Sánchez Espinosa's life, family relations, business activities, and roles in Mexico City's entrepreneurial elite show a mix of entrepreneurship, patriarchy, and Christian piety that shaped powers ranging from the capital, through the Bajío, and far to the north.

Power and privilege concentrated in Mexico City. New Spain's capital was the largest city in the Americas in the eighteenth century. There ruled the viceroy and the archbishop. There sat a High Court, the central fiscal offices, and the throngs of lawyers, accountants, and bureaucrats who kept them running. There was the first university in the Americas, the training ground for generations of churchmen and professionals. There an array of artisans and traders made a diverse urban populace.[3] And there lived the richest merchant financiers in the Americas, connected by business and family to the most powerful landed entrepreneurs. The great city was the political, financial, and commercial capital of Spanish Mesoamerica and Spanish North America.

Don José Sánchez Espinosa, like Caballero y Ocío before him, was a priest, patriarch, and entrepreneur. He controlled valuable estates from the outskirts of Mexico City, through La Griega and Puerto de Nieto in the eastern Bajío, to vast expanses in San Luis Potosí. His economic power was immense. His patriarchy constrained his kin, business associates, and hundreds of dependent families, thousands of people all living in communities on his lands and nearby. He understood and justified his power by linking the pursuit of profit and patriarchy to deep religious beliefs. His will to profit and his willingness to exploit others in its pursuit were nothing new among those who ruled. What was different after 1770 was his ability to effect capitalist predations. He imposed more and negotiated less than his predecessors; he proved less interested in funding religious devotions, mission expansions, and charitable works than don Juan Caballero y Ocío had been a century earlier. An inquiry into the life of don José Sánchez Espinosa, his business, his family, his allies, and his powers offers essential insight into the culture of power in Mexico City, the Bajío, and Spanish North America during the decades of boom after 1770.

A Biography of Power

In his pursuit of profit, estate operations, adamant patriarchy, and deep Catholicism, don José Sánchez Espinosa was like most powerful men in Mexico City around 1800. He acquired the properties that sustained his power in less typical ways. Unlike the Condes de Santiago and other old colonial clans, he did not inherit estates built in the early colonial reconstruction, then locked in inalienable entail, tied to a noble title, and passed to generations of patriarchs—and a few widows and unmarried heiresses. Nor was don José the American son of an immigrant Spanish merchant who began in trade, invested in mining, and with luck, perseverance, and capital invested in estates to preserve his family's power. Perhaps he descended from Captain don Lázaro Sánchez de Espinosa, who claimed lands between Xilotepec and the Sierra Gorda in the 1630s, and less directly from Bachiller don Felipe Sánchez de Espinosa, who ran the properties in the 1690s.[4] But don José Sánchez Espinosa (sometimes Sánchez de Espinosa) gained but a limited family inheritance; acquisition of the Caballero y Ocío estates made him a leading agricultural entrepreneur. Sánchez Espinosa lacked the fame and titles that marked the heirs to the first colonial fortunes. He lacked the capital that eased business among newcomers to landed power.[5] Yet few were more powerful after 1780, none more dedicated to the pursuit of profit. Thanks to the survival of vast correspondence and other records, his life and dealings with peers, kin, and dependents are documented with exceptional clarity.[6]

Born in Mexico City in 1757, don José first appeared in the family correspondence in August 1774 as "don Joseph, the boy," then seventeen and traveling with his uncle, don Francisco de Espinosa y Navarijo, at Querétaro.[7] Four years later, don José again joined his uncle in the Bajío, this time to inspect estates. Young don José wrote home, mixing regards to kin with news about estate operations, especially the need for rain to water the crops then dying in the fields.[8] In 1779 he was a bachiller, a youth with education. He kept a house in Mexico City and ran an estate named San Pedro that produced pulque, the indigenous fermented drink, for sale in taverns in Mexico City.[9] Early in 1781 he was Bachiller don Josef Sánchez Espinosa, nephew of Doctor don Francisco Espinosa y Navarijo.[10] In the following year a letter finally mentions that don José is married to doña Mariana and has unnamed "boys."[11] Early letters reveal a youth focused on his uncle and estate production. His wife and children rarely appear.

Don José faced a time of loss and change beginning in the fall of 1781. His uncle don Francisco died that September.[12] Then his wife died in October 1783, identified in death as doña Mariana de la Mora.[13] We can only imagine don José's grief at the loss of the uncle he admired, and of the young mother of his children. But we can document how those deaths brought him power, and the role of patriarch.

From his uncle don José inherited the estates in the Bajío and San Luis Potosí that would ground his power. At death don Francisco de Espinosa y Navarijo was described as "Doctor, Priest, Lawyer before the High Court of New Spain, Lawyer for prisoners held by the Inquisition, and Examiner for the Holy Office of the Faith."[14] He held a doctorate and was an ordained priest. As a lawyer he was licensed to argue before New Spain's High Court and the Inquisition, of which he was an officer. Yet none of these activities found mention in endless letters that focused on estate entrepreneurship.

For decades don Francisco had operated the richest of the properties assembled by don Juan Caballerío y Ocío. La Griega, near Querétaro, focused on cultivation. Puerto de Nieto, near San Miguel, emphasized grazing operations that extended north into San Luis Potosí. Caballero had populated his grazing estates with African slaves to care for growing herds.[15] On his death in 1707 the properties passed to another cleric, don José de Torres y Vergara, archdeacon of the Mexico City Cathedral—moving the center of operations to the capital. His estates remained "the grazing properties named San Agustín de la Griega, in the jurisdiction of Querétaro, and San Nicolás de Puerto de Nieto, in San Miguel el Grande, their northern pasture lands and other properties linked to them."[16] To make the estates inalienable and commit them to pious purposes Torres y Vergara founded an Obra Pía. The properties would operate as a unit: a third of all profits would be shared by his heirs; a third would pay an administrator; and a third would fund pious works, mostly dowries for honorable girls entering convents. Torres y Vergara built an entail, an inalienable patrimony, without state sanction, to guarantee his heirs' landed power and to do good works.

On his death the Obra Pía passed to a nephew, then to the nephew's son, don Francisco de Espinosa y Navarijo. As administrator and one of few heirs, don Francisco operated the estates as if they were his property. His earliest letters, from 1753, document efforts to turn grazing lands at Bocas in San Luis Potosí into estates with communities of tenants, herdsmen, and their families.[17] Don Francisco prosecuted suits over boundaries all the way to the Council of the Indies in Spain—where he won. He claimed that his properties' status as an Obra Pía made them ecclesiastical, thus exempt from the alcabala sales tax. He won that too in the 1760s, just as pressure to increase revenues provoked resistance among so many working families in the Bajío and San Luis Potosí. His agent in Spain congratulated him for channeling income to pious works. Don Francisco knew that most of the money would fund his business affairs.[18] His estates raised grains and livestock. He controlled marketing from Mexico City; he traded with Spain; he kept a store in Querétaro; he lent money at interest. Living in the capital, he could pursue his legal and clerical careers while watching the largest market in the Americas and dealing with other entrepreneurs, including his cousin the Marqués de Rivascacho.[19] Mexico City was the place to live and do business.

Distant estates, however, required periodic inspections. In most years don Francisco undertook a long journey north, usually in August, sometimes as late as October. He spent at least a week at each of his properties in the Bajío and San Luis Potosí, checking production, labor relations, and marketing with resident managers. He brought along the annual shipments of *avíos*, the cloth, shoes, and other goods distributed to employees as part of their recompense, creating obligations to serve in the coming year. Don Francisco obtained many of those supplies in direct trade with Seville and across New Spain. He was proud of the goods he advanced; he liked being present at the distribution. Annual tours combined inspection with demonstrations of his generous power.[20] He also displayed his priestly eminence. Based in the archbishopric of Mexico, his sacramental privileges extended to Querétaro and La Griega. A license to preach and perform sacraments in the bishopric of Michoacán extended his rights to Puerto de Nieto and across San Luis Potosí.[21] He always said Mass and often heard confessions during his tours, aiming to sanctify his power.

During the 1770s don Francisco prepared his nephew don José to succeed him. The youth joined at least three tours of inspection beginning in 1774.[22] Don Francisco also negotiated a fine match for his heir. By 1777 young don José had married doña Mariana de la Mora, daughter of don Francisco de la Mora, key ally of don José de Gálvez in repressing the uprisings in San Luis Potosí in 1767.[23] Mora had taken a fortune in silver during a brief boom at Guadalcázar. Following established business wisdom, he secured his wealth by buying the valuable Peñasco and Angostura estates nearby. Both included irrigated fields and vast pastures. Angostura alone was valued at 400,000 pesos. His wealth, his land, and his service to Gálvez gained Mora the title of Conde de Peñasco. In the 1770s he was the richest and most powerful man in the rapidly developing province of San Luis Potosí.[24] The marriage of doña Mariana and don José linked the region's leading resident landlord and militia commander with the leading operator of San Luis Potosí estates living in Mexico City.

The near-absence of references to doña Mariana in young don José's letters suggests that this was not a love match but a dynastic union, designed to link powerful clans. Doña Mariana's brother would inherit the Peñasco title and estates. Her role was to ease relations between two powerful families, one in Mexico City, the other in the province, operating neighboring properties. During the late 1770s the young couple lived in the home of don Francisco, the aging priest-patriarch who had negotiated the union.[25]

While being groomed to run the Obra Pía and marrying for family interests, don José began to acquire estates. From his mother, don Francisco's sister, he inherited in the late 1770s the haciendas La Teja and Asunción, exceptionally valuable small properties on the western edge of Mexico City. They included numerous well-watered, fertile *chinampas* (not unlike Querétaro's huertas), harvesting grains, fruits, and vegetables at the door of the great urban market.[26] He also began to operate estates northeast of the capital, leasing Hueyapan near Otumba and San Pedro at Apan in 1779. Both were planted with vast fields of maguey; both fermented pulque shipped to urban consumers. In 1794 he would buy both, along with a city tavern to dispense the drink, for 300,000 pesos.[27] Chinampa agriculture and pulque production were rooted in the Mesoamerican past. Don José Sánchez Espinosa joined other entrepreneurs in capitalizing on both in the eighteenth century.

As the 1780s began, don José was a young landed patriarch. He owned small but profitable estates next to New Spain's capital. He leased pulque properties and city taverns. He helped manage the Obra Pía estates in the Bajío and San Luis Potosí, and he had wed the daughter of the most powerful man there. Don José and doña Mariana had two young sons. Then, after a long illness, don Francisco de Espinosa y Navarijo died in September 1781. Don José was his executor and sole heir. The grieving nephew quickly honored his uncle by devoting seven hundred pesos to a perpetual flame at the Oratorio de San Felipe in Mexico City.[28] Just as quickly don José took control of the Obra Pía. He now gained the manager's profits, along with half of the third due the heirs.[29] With full control and half of all profits, don José Sánchez Espinosa became one of New Spain's great landed patriarchs.

It took more than a year to settle the inheritance and complete a limited reorganization. Don José assumed day-to-day management in the summer of 1781, during his uncle's illness. Early in 1782 he reviewed accounts at home. In July he set out on a long inspection that lasted into October, overseeing the settlement of managers' and workers' accounts and trying to resolve boundary disputes.[30] He evaluated all the properties and businesses he had inherited. Earlier he had sold the town properties in Acapulco left by his mother; now he sold his uncle's store in Querétaro. He considered buying two properties that had been Jesuit estates, but the price was too high.[31] His strategy was clear. He sold urban property to focus on estate production for New Spain's most profitable markets: Mexico City and the Bajío.

Too soon, don José faced tragedy again. Early in September 1783 doña Mariana lay gravely ill from an accident; she died a month later. The young patriarch was suddenly a widower with two sons. We know nothing of his emotional response. The correspondence records others' words of condolence. There is no mention of a perpetual flame for his wife.[32]

Don José faced key decisions. Would he marry again? Should he manage his businesses and raise two boys as a young widower? Land and power made him a promising match. A series of letters suggest the complexity of his dilemma. In May 1783 he received a note from doña María Micaela de Arenaza, a young widow in San Miguel. She wrote of business with don José at nearby Puerto de Nieto; she pledged a peso monthly to support devotion to Guadalupe, the young patriarch's favorite cause. She sent greetings from don Domingo de Allende (a trader and father of the future insurgent leader). A second letter written in September reports doña María Micaela's surprise that don José was about to travel and visit her in San Miguel, while his wife lay gravely injured. The widow added quickly that since the visit must be important, she would place herself at his feet and greet him with *abrazos*—embraces. Don José canceled the trip. Doña María Micaela wrote again in October on learning of doña Mariana's death. She shared her sorrow and that of her compadre, don Domingo. She added that since don José was about to visit, she hoped to lift his spirits. Again he canceled. Doña María Micaela wrote a final letter in January 1784. She reported cryptically that her son had left to study in the capital, thanks to funds from don José.[33] Was doña María Micaela a provincial widow with kind concern for don José in trying times? Or was she a woman who was romantically linked to the young patriarch while his wife lived and who imagined more, perhaps marriage, as his wife faced death? Whatever their past ties, her hopes for the future were dashed, as revealed in the sharp tone of her last letter.

The reasons for her disappointment became clear in February 1784. Four months after his wife's death don José Sánchez Espinosa said his first Mass.[34] With sons to assure family succession, he followed don Juan Caballero y Ocío and don Francisco Espinosa y Navarijo into the priesthood. For another generation entrepreneurial power was in the hands of a priest-patriarch. This was not the norm in eighteenth-century New Spain; it was also not unique. The Obra Pía properties were built by Caballero y Ocío and run by Torres y Vergara and Espinosa y Navarijo, all entrepreneurial priest-patriarchs, before passing to Sánchez Espinosa. Don Manuel de la Borda, son and heir of don José de la Borda, a rich miner at Taxco and Zacatecas, took holy orders and ran the family enterprises. The second Conde de Jala, heir to a great pulque fortune, became a priest as a widower in the early 1780s. Capitalism and Catholicism merged in many ways in eighteenth-century New Spain. Entrepreneurial priest-patriarchs took a visible, personal route to that fusion.[35]

Don José Sánchez Espinosa stayed in the capital for three years after his wife's death and his ordination. He may have grieved that long. Perhaps he focused on asserting his role as a priest. Most likely, he hesitated to travel in rural regions during years of killing frosts, enduring drought, deadly famine—and estate profiteering. He relied on a tutor, don Bartolomé, to educate his sons.[36] Only in August 1786, as the first good maize crop in two years ripened in the fields, did don José begin a long-delayed tour of his northern estates. He checked management and accounts; he distributed cloth and other goods among his workers; he settled their accounts. And the patriarch, now a priest, made a point of saying Mass in every estate chapel.[37]

Every arrival created a stir. For two years the people of the Bajío and San Luis Potosí had faced deadly famine. Thousands had died. Don José came just as new crops promised dearth's end. During seasons of scarcity his managers fed estate residents with estate maize, while selling stores from previous years to profit from hunger all around. Now the patriarch arrived bearing goods and priestly powers. His presence emphasized that the hundreds of families living at his estates depended on him for land, wages, food rations, and distributions of cloth. Saying Mass, he asserted that his powers were divinely sanctioned. The profit-seeking landlord, the provider of sustenance, and the servant of God were one. Don José Sánchez Espinosa was certain of that. The people at his estates had to consider the possibility.

The tour that announced his priestly patriarchy also revealed a deep fissure in don José's household. His eldest son, named don Mariano for his mother, refused to send letters to his father during the long trek. He had learned to write, but told his tutor that he did not know what to say. Don Joaquín, the younger son, could not write, yet daily awaited his father's letters and had the tutor write replies.[38] We can only imagine why don José faced strained relations with his first son and primary heir. The tensions would endure.

While becoming a priest, asserting power over estate communities, and struggling with fatherhood, Sánchez Espinosa tried his hand at Atlantic trade. In 1782 he called himself "vecino almacenero"—a wholesaler in trade.[39] At first he finished deals begun by his uncle. Later in the 1780s don José tried new ventures, lamenting that he lacked the cash to join the most profitable deals.[40] As late as 1804 he sent sixteen thousand pesos through an agent traveling to Seville. He aimed to buy paper, wine, glassware, spices, and other goods; the agent protested that with such paltry funds he could not succeed. He closed a harsh exchange by telling don José that he could not work for "an idiot." The accusation of stupidity, coming as wartime disruptions made trade risky, punctuated the end of don José's attempts to deal beyond New Spain.[41] He was never a major merchant. He traded to buy goods for his household, to deliver cloth to estate dependents, and to stock provincial merchants.

Don José Sánchez Espinosa was among the few men—there were even fewer women—who ruled great landed families in Mexico City. He lived in a neighborhood of mansions housing the great clans that dominated the colony.[42] They clustered west and south of the plaza, the seat of government, and the cathedral. They often worked together. In the late 1780s don José did business with the Conde de Jala and the Conde de Regla, leading pulque growers.[43] In 1794 he joined the Marquesa de Jaral, owner of vast estates between the Bajío and San Luis Potosí, in a profitable maize deal.[44] In 1799 he hosted at Puerto de Nieto the Marqués de San Miguel de Aguayo on his way to his Coahuila estates.[45] In 1806 don José did business with the Conde de Santiago, holder of one of New Spain's oldest titles, ruler of the vast Atengo estates in the Valley of Toluca west of the capital.[46] Don José also did favors for clerics and regime officials; touring bishops found hospitality at his estates.[47] He did a small deal with the head of the tobacco monopoly in 1805.[48]

Men and women of less wealth and status came to don José seeking office, funds, or favors. Young men aiming for clerical posts and women hoping for dowries to enter convents wrote repeatedly.[49] Don José helped a tax collector set up in San Luis Potosí in 1805.[50] It was a patriarch's role to deal with constant requests. Some were granted, others not. Most supplicants soon vanished from the correspondence; one relationship endured.

Doña Juana María Cumano traded letters and visits with don José from 1789 until 1812. Her father came from Venice to trade in Mexico City before 1750.[51] Before his death in 1789 don Domingo Cumano ran a store in the capital and another in San Angel, a favorite suburban retreat of Mexico City's elite. He established a three-thousand-peso chaplaincy to support a son who went to the university and became a priest. Doña María married her father's *cajero* (cashier), a young immigrant. But before don Domingo died her husband abandoned her and went north to seek his fortune in Durango, leaving debts and disputes behind.[52] While her father lived doña María ran the store in San Angel, selling pulque supplied by don José and complaining about tax collectors. In 1793 she still struggled with debts left by her husband. Into the early 1800s debts, payments, and mundane affairs of trade filled her letters. She leased lands from don José, which she sublet, and then sought his help collecting rents. In 1805 her letters turned personal. She reported ailments and the relief of recovery. She recalled rushing to see don José before he set off on northern tours. In 1810 doña Juana María invited don José, his sons, and their wives to San Angel for Holy Week. An invitation to Guadalupe's festival came in 1812. All the while the business of the store continued.[53] A relationship begun in business became personal, even affectionate. Don José and doña Juana María shared important religious occasions, and included his family.[54]

The correspondence reveals Sánchez Espinosa's relationships with three women. His wife, doña Mariana, remains a distant image—part of a dynastic marriage. The mother of his sons, the victim of an accident and an early death, is barely known. Doña María Micaela, the widow from San Miguel, appears briefly yet very personally. She knew don José while his wife lived. She shared in grief, offered advice, and perhaps hoped for marriage as the young patriarch faced his wife's death. The widow's hopes vanished when he took holy orders. Doña Juana María Cumano began as a trading dependent; she became Sánchez Espinosa's friend, confidant, and companion on key holidays. Don José married for power and succession. Affection focused on women less equal and more dependent.

Patriarchal power was not free of conflict. A dispute with the Conde de Pérez Gálvez over lands in San Luis Potosí, initiated by don José's uncle, persisted in the courts until won in Seville in 1788. Victory in court did not guarantee rights in the fields. As late as 1800 Pérez Gálvez blocked Sánchez Espinosa's use of the lands in question.[55]

Don José's links to the Condes de Peñasco reveal how elite family relations could become long and painful conflicts, in this case leading to conquest. Doña Mariana's death did not end Sánchez Espinosa's ties to her father, the first Conde de Peñasco. Don José always visited on his treks to San Luis Potosí. He facilitated the Conde's business in the capital. In 1787 they joined to sell three thousand lambs to don Antonio Bassoco, the merchant who supplied Mexico City's slaughterhouses.[56] Cooperation was the purpose of dynastic union, and the priest-patriarch had reason to keep good relations with his father-in-law. Peñasco was the richest, most powerful man in San Luis Potosí. He owned estates that rivaled those of don José there; he remained a mining financier and a power in regime affairs, thanks to ties to don José de Gálvez forged during the repression of 1767.

Cooperation turned into escalating conflict after the Conde's death in 1788. During the next two decades the priest-patriarch, based in Mexico City, took power over his in-laws, a powerful provincial family. The change was perhaps set in motion when Gálvez died in 1787. Don José got the news while in San Luis Potosí. His business manager in the capital reported the death in Spain of "Minister don José de Gálvez, news well received by many."[57] The manager clearly expected don José to join those taking the news as positive: the reforming minister was dead; reasons for good relations with the Peñascos lessened.

Immediately after the Conde's death don José offered to assist the Peñascos. He took over a contract to finance don Bernabé de Zepeda, a miner at Catorce near Matehuala. Peñasco had already invested 350,000 pesos; don José advanced another 30,000 in 1789. To the grieving Peñascos he relieved costly burdens as they settled the founder's estate.[58] In the process he took over one of the late Conde's most profitable businesses. During the early 1790s don José appeared to support his brother-in-law's role as second Conde de Peñasco, offering advice on estate management and marketing as the new noble took on his father's affairs. People in Mexico City seeking introductions to the Conde went through don José.[59] With that cooperation the young Conde took over as the leading resident of San Luis Potosí. His power seemed assured by appointment in 1795 as commanding colonel of the new "Provincial Dragoons of San Luis Potosí." In the second round of Bourbon reforms San Luis Potosí became capital of a new intendancy, a distinction shared with Guanajuato but denied Querétaro. Did the bond between Gálvez and Peñasco bring that honor? When the province gained a new regiment, trained by don Félix Calleja, the second

Conde de Peñasco got command, adding military leadership to economic power.[60] He rewarded Sánchez Espinosa with a contract for uniforms.[61] The Bocas estate, the priest-patriarch's lead property in San Luis Potosí, was home to one of the regiment's battalions. Don José's loyal manager, don Juan Nepomuceno de Oviedo, became captain (and died fighting insurgents in 1812).[62] The second Conde's command channeled profit to don José and allowed him to bring a key northern estate under military discipline.

Apparent cooperation for mutual benefit turned to angry conflict in 1798. The second Conde de Peñasco faced a Junta de Acreedores—a creditors' council. Debts had grown beyond his ability to pay. The Peñasco estates, protected by entail, could not be partitioned, with some ceded or sold to satisfy creditors, preserving the rest free of debt.[63] Mounting obligations ranged from large sums owed major financiers to unpaid salaries and wages due managers and workers. One of the largest debts was due to don Juan José Martínez de Lejarza, owner of an obraje in Querétaro and Sánchez Espinosa's partner in the contract to make uniforms for the San Luis Potosí Dragoons.[64] Had don José stealthily contributed to the Conde's bankruptcy? His takeover of the business of financing Zepeda's mines deprived the Conde of a key source of capital. Did Sánchez Espinosa take his share of payment for the uniform contract, leaving his partner unpaid, and ready to press bankruptcy? Whatever the cause and don José's role, he emerged the beneficiary.

In 1799 the creditors accepted don José's offer to manage the Conde's affairs—in the creditors' interest. Don José seemed a logical choice. A successful entrepreneur with parallel interests in the same region, as a priest his ethics were hard to question. The Peñascos saw differently. They viewed him as a predator who used his influence to profit while burdening the young Conde with debts, and then used ties to creditors, especially Martínez de Lejarza, to take control of Peñasco affairs. Oviedo, don José's manager and the militia captain at Bocas, reported local discontent. Residents of the Peñasco estates were "very insolent and very devoted to their master."[65] The displaced Conde made "troublesome comments, thanks to the pain caused by the loss of his estates."[66] Peñasco and his wife took valuables from the estates and harassed new managers. In 1802 the Conde pleaded for the return of his properties. The creditors refused.[67]

From 1800 the second Conde de Peñasco held a title and command rank in the provincial militia, yet he lived on a stipend from Sánchez Espinosa. In 1805 Peñasco died without heir, a broken man. Don Mariano Sánchez y Mora, don José's first son, the late Conde's nephew, and the founder's grandson, inherited the title and properties.[68] What began as an alliance of powerful families, one in the capital, the other in a key province, culminated in 1805 with the takeover by the Mexico City patriarch of the Peñasco lands, power, and title. Neither the widowed Condesa nor the provincial elite she led responded well. When don Mariano, her nephew and third Conde, asked for command of the provincial militia, he was rebuffed. Instead Calleja, a professional soldier from Spain who had found a home in the province, took over.[69] Don Mariano fared better in the courts and the capital, gaining confirmation of his rights to the Peñasco title and entail. The Mexico City council elected him magistrate.[70]

His aunt the Condesa fought to limit her losses. She asked to keep her jewels and other non-landed properties. She would allow don José to continue to manage her non-entailed estates in exchange for a fixed income—essentially a lease. Don José refused both requests. He won a ruling that the jewels were part of the entail and passed to his son. He convinced a creditors' council that he must continue to manage her properties and pay debts first, with no promise of income to the Condesa.[71] Was she swept aside because she was a woman, a provincial, or an obstacle to the priest-patriarch's ambitions? All surely contributed.

In December 1805, confirmed as Conde de Peñasco, don Mariano set out to claim his inheritance in San Luis Potosí. The trip was a revelation. He passed by San Luis to meet first with Oviedo at Bocas; his father's general manager and militia captain warned the young heir that he would face many opponents. In a letter to Sánchez Espinosa reporting the meeting, Oviedo called don Mariano "el Señor Condesito," my Lord, the little count.[72] If his father's key agent saw him as diminutive, the description common among locals can only be imagined. Their actions spoke clearly. When don Mariano went to town for Christmas, the pastor and town officials greeted him cordially. Local elites snubbed him. He wrote to his father that he believed they were organized by the Condesa and commander Calleja.[73]

After spending the holiday in isolation the young Conde began to take legal and ritual possession of the Peñasco estates. From January through May 1806 he faced at every turn the ire of his widowed aunt and her allies. Legal and other costs took six thousand pesos.[74] Don Mariano became frustrated and angry as weeks of conflict became months. In February he was "every day more anxious to finish in these parts, . . . to leave these people, who every moment make me angrier with their odd and malicious ways."[75] As April began: "I have spent a very sad Holy Week here, despite the many ridiculous things I have seen . . . in processions which might have brought amusement." The long stay in the province was "the most hateful time of my life, thanks to the character of the people I must face."[76] The third Conde de

Peñasco and the provincial society he hoped to lead were fully alienated.

A year later don José Sánchez Espinosa and the Conde de Peñasco, father and son, returned for a joint inspection of their properties in San Luis Potosí.[77] No letter reports the details of the excursion. Did their combined power awe the provincials, containing the overt expressions of disrespect that so angered the young Conde a year earlier? After returning to Mexico City, in April 1808 don José Sánchez Espinosa announced a decision. He had given his younger son don Joaquín management of his pulque estates in 1800; now he would cede to don Mariano management of the Obra Pía, including all the estates from La Griega and Puerto de Nieto in the Bajío to Bocas and its outliers in San Luis Potosí.[78] Don José had ruled the family and its business for nearly three decades. Now he aimed to retire. His younger son would deal in the capital's pulque market. His eldest, now Conde de Peñasco, would take over as patriarch, ruling the combined Obra Pía and Peñasco properties that don José had first fused in a bankruptcy he helped to create.

The retirement proved brief. During the summer of 1808 Mexico City faced the news that Napoleon had invaded Spain, captured the monarchy, and tried to impose his brother as José I. Across Spain and the Americas elites struggled with unprecedented uncertainties. In August Viceroy don José de Iturrigaray called a junta to allow elites in Mexico City a role in reconstituting sovereignty. The young Conde de Peñasco joined the movement. When the meeting was blocked by don Gabriel de Yermo and the capital's merchant militia — who insisted that the viceroyalty must remain dependent on the Junta assembling in Seville — don Mariano fled to the family pulque estates near Apan. He faced exile and exclusion while his young wife struggled with a difficult pregnancy and ill health.[79]

Perhaps don José Sánchez Espinosa opposed his titled son's involvement in the new and risky world of politics. Or perhaps the young Conde's choice of the losing side in 1808 led his father to reclaim power ceded so recently. In the fall of 1809, amid continuing political uncertainties and drought-driven scarcities that promised great profits to strong estate operators, don José wrote to the managers of all the family estates — the inherited properties, the Obra Pía estates, and the Peñasco holdings — ordering that no funds must go to his sons or their wives. The Conde de Peñasco, his brother, and their wives lost control of their own and their father's estates; they would again live as dependents in don José's household, limited to allowances that he gave.[80] The priest-patriarch would rule the family unchallenged through decades of conflict that he could not imagine in 1809. Sánchez Espinosa's landed power enabled him to dominate his kin and do profitable business in the capital and across New Spain. He ruled wives, sons, daughters—even a titled nephew and his widow. From outside don José's power appeared to integrate an extended family and vast enterprises. Those within knew that his power both provoked and contained deep conflicts. Patriarchy organized dominance.

Silver Magnates, Landed Clans, and Regime Officials

Don José Sánchez Espinosa was a key participant in a small community of powerful families based in Mexico City. They ruled the city and the nearby basins of Spanish Mesoamerica, and they exerted great power in the Bajío and regions far to the north. The great families of the colonial metropolis profited from silver and Atlantic trade, operated estates in a commercial economy to sustain patriarchal powers, and shaped the lives of people and communities across vast regions. They were an American entrepreneurial establishment, a ruling class, in an increasingly capitalist world.

Three economic sectors intersected in the great city. Silver production was financed there; silver was minted and taxed there. Long a stimulus of global trade, after 1770 silver flowed in unprecedented quantities from New Spain to benefit the Spanish monarchy, Iberian and American merchants, and traders and producers across Europe and beyond. The silver economy was sustained by a colonial commercial economy grounded in estates focused on supplying Mexico City and other cities engaged in mining, crafts, and trade. And that commercial economy was sustained in turn by thousands of indigenous communities and to the north by innumerable tenants and independent rancheros whose families produced first for sustenance and local markets, yet also provided produce to cities and labor in estate fields.

The three economies that intersected in Mexico City exemplify and revise Braudel's understanding of early capitalism: predatory entrepreneurs ruled global trade, the silver economy, and the commercial activities that sustained them. Meanwhile families in Mesoamerican republics along with the small growers in the north raised sustenance while providing labor and produce to sustain the commercial system stimulated by silver and global trade. They were not separate domains; they linked in a complex system that generated revenues for the regime and focused profit in the hands of powerful men and a few women, most based in Mexico City. They took wealth in the global silver economy, and invested to preserve it in the colonial commercial estate economy—while tapping the surplus production and seasonal labor of families in indigenous republics across Mesoamerica and those living as estate tenants and independent rancheros in regions from the Bajío northward.

The silver economy was driven by the world's thirst for money and focused by the Spanish monarchy's drive for revenues. They combined to create a demand that seemed unlimited (if costs could be contained) even as Chinese prices and demand dropped. The rising demand for silver was first met in the eighteenth century by miners operating in Taxco, Zacatecas, and Guanajuato before 1750, then at Bolaños and Real de Monte around mid-century, and after 1770 again at Guanajuato as well as at Catorce and other centers in the North. Between New Spain's mining centers and the Spanish treasury great merchant-financiers organized and profited from transoceanic trade. Before the 1780s the consulados—merchant guilds—of Seville and Mexico City dominated. Later, with the promotion of what passed as "free trade" within Spanish domains, merchants in other Iberian and American cities claimed increasing shares of trade and wealth (in New Spain notably at the port of Veracruz, where merchants won a new consulado).

Men with the capital to join in transatlantic trade imported metal wares, cloth, wine, and other goods. They earned silver that returned to Spain to buy more imports. The trade was always risky. Knowing markets on two Atlantic shores, with news of demand, purchases, and sales delayed for months, was never easy. Still, those with capital, connections, and luck extracted ample wealth from imperial trade. They often financed silver mines, importing essential supplies and advancing cash for operating expenses, gaining silver to invest in more trade, more financing. The potential profits of mining were enormous. The risks were greater. As shafts drove deep underground, floods or the end of rich veins could bring quick bankruptcy. Those who lost everything in mining far outnumbered those who left with wealth.[81]

Spain's treasury and global trade took mounting wealth in silver from New Spain during the eighteenth century. Production first peaked in the 1740s and held around 12 million pesos yearly through the 1760s; it rose to over 20 million pesos in the early 1780s and held near 23 million pesos yearly through the 1790s and early 1800s. Even the enormous sums taken by the Spanish monarchy as it struggled to survive the warfare of the 1790s and early 1800s did not derail the silver economy.[82]

While the regime and world trade gained rising flows of silver, miners and merchant financiers faced opportunities and risks that made entrepreneurship potentially profitable and exceptionally risky. A few did very well: the Sánchez de Tagle and the Fagoagas in Mexico

City; the Bustos, Sardanetas, and Obregóns of Guanajuato; the first Conde de Peñasco in San Luis Potosí; and notably don Pedro Romero de Terreros, who began trading in Querétaro, financed and then operated mines at Real del Monte, survived the labor wars of 1766, and retired as Conde de Regla, the richest man in New Spain, probably in the Americas. Their fortunes set marks at which many others aimed.[83]

The state controlled the mercury essential to refining silver, using price and access to favor some mines and miners. It used tax exemptions to favor investment when and where it chose. As modern states use control of money and taxes to further their goals, the Spanish regime—dependent on New Spain's silver for much of its revenue and most of its trade—used mercury supplies and tax policies to advance its own interests and those of its allies. The regime's first interest was revenue, and it served that interest well until the collapse of 1808–10.[84]

The silver economy shaped the lives of those who risked its attractions. Most were young immigrant men, often from the mountainous north of Spain. Younger sons in families of limited prospects, they came to New Spain to trade, usually with an uncle of similar origins already in the colony. Thousands came to seek fortune in the eighteenth century. Dozens of the best-connected, most highly skilled, and lucky made money, married a cousin, inherited the business, traded more, and invested in mining—and if they escaped with ample capital, they almost always invested in landed estates.[85] The repeated shift of wealth from trade and mining to estates was not a turn away from entrepreneurship. It was a shift from the risks of the silver economy to the greater security of the colonial commercial economy. In this economy landed patriarchs found profit-seeking entrepreneurship that could maintain a family's wealth, power, status, and honor for decades, even centuries.[86]

The enduring power of the Condes de Santiago Calimaya and a few peers demonstrated the security of landed entrepreneurship. The Santiagos' eminence began with the two Viceroys don Luis de Velasco, father and son. The first ruled in the middle of the sixteenth century, the second at its end. Overseeing the reconstruction of Mesoamerica into New Spain and the foundations of Spanish North America, the Velascos favored kin in mining and trade, granting them lands to build estates later tied into entailed patrimonies linked to noble titles. Judicious marriages, political acumen, and landed entrepreneurship kept the Condes de Santiago at the pinnacle of society in Mexico City for generations.[87]

They remained there in the eighteenth century. In 1732 don Juan Javier Altamirano y Velasco was Conde de Santiago, Marqués de Salinas, and Adelantado de las Islas Filipinas. He held four landed entails built in the late sixteenth century and the early seventeenth. That year he wed doña Ana María Urrutía de Vergara, daughter of a merchant who left her jewels, city mansions, country houses, and mills nearby. Her mother was Marquesa de Salvatierra, whose entailed estates included leading Bajío enterprises.[88] The union fused vast properties. The couple's sole heir, don Juan Lorenzo Gutiérrez Altamirano y Velasco, held all four titles and the vast estates from 1752 to his death in 1793. He was the noble imagined sovereign by rebels in San Luis Potosí in 1767—though there is no hint that he was interested. His Atengo properties, attached to the Santiago title, ruled the southern Valley of Toluca. He worked three flour mills just west of the capital, plus Molino de Flores, a mill and cereal estate near Texcoco to the east. He produced pulque at Tulancalco in the Mezquital. The Salvatierra properties gave him a strong role in the Bajío economy.[89]

The leading landholder among the old families of Mexico City, don Juan Lorenzo had one problem. He left four daughters as heirs. He arranged for the eldest to marry don Cosme de Mier y Trespalacios, a senior justice on the High Court of New Spain. Mier would rule as patriarch and bring links to the regime. But soon after the wedding the heiress died, leaving a second sister, doña María Isabel, to inherit the Santiago title and entails in 1793. She fended off all proposals and ruled the family economy, her youngest sister doña María Josefa managing her affairs. For a time women exercised powers of patriarchy in one of New Spain's most powerful clans.[90]

The third sister married don Ygnacio Leonel Gómez de Cervantes, heir to vast properties in another family that traced its roots to the sixteenth century. He went to court in 1793 and claimed for his wife—and thus for himself—the entailed properties and title of the Marquesado de Salinas. In 1802, when the Condesa de Santiago died, Gómez went to court and claimed the Condado and all its properties for his wife, again for himself. Uniting the properties of the Santiago and Cervantes clans, he fused one of the great landed fortunes accumulated in New Spain. His sons, however, had learned well the lessons of patriarchy. When their mother died in 1809 they went to court, claimed early rights as adults, and ousted their father from control of the titles and estates they stood to inherit. In 1810 they faced insurgent challenges in an unimagined world of conflict.[91]

People who saw titles, city mansions, and leisured wealth might view the Condes de Santiago as beneficiaries of fortunate inheritances. Men who traded in and near the capital knew that the Santiagos' vast inheritances were the landed bases of sharp business practices. They raised wheat, maize, hogs, and pulque. Their mills controlled much of the capital's flour supplies. Letters detail the business of don Juan Lorenzo, Conde de Santiago in the 1780s and early 1790s, and of doña María Josefa, who ran the Condesa's affairs from 1793 until 1802. Both studied production and markets, took every advantage from workers and buyers, and claimed profits that made landed patrimonies into sources of wealth and power.[92] The Condes de Santiago, the Cervantes y Padilla, and a few others survived at the pinnacle of colonial society for generations; they showed the new men who profited in the silver economy the benefits of landed investment and agrarian entrepreneurship.

The Conde de Regla learned those lessons well.[93] Don Pedro Romero de Terreros left Extremadura to join an uncle in trade at Querétaro. His death allowed don Pedro to take over the store, buy an obraje, add a second store at Real del Monte, and begin to finance mines there. He invested over 2,400,000 pesos from 1741 until 1762, when his bonanza came, helping draw the silver economy out of its mid-century slump. From 1741 until his death in 1781 he paid 2,553,129 pesos in taxes and fees to the crown, suggesting silver extraction approaching 20,000,000 pesos. At death he left mining and agricultural properties worth between 4,000,000 and 5,000,000 pesos.[94]

For his contributions to the treasury don Pedro became Conde de Regla. To sustain the family that would carry his name he shifted most of his wealth to landed properties. He began by operating estates to support mining. From the 1750s he financed Jesuit properties near Real del Monte, facilitating the provision of food, livestock, and supplies to his mines. In the 1760s he bought several nearby estates, turning some into silver refineries, cultivating and grazing at others to sustain mining.[95] In the 1770s he became the greatest landowner in New Spain. When the regime expelled the Jesuits in 1767 it expropriated the estates that funded their colleges, seminaries, and missions. Regla had the influence and wealth to obtain the most valuable Jesuit properties. How much he paid is debated. The value of the properties he acquired is not.

When he died in 1781 Regla left three titles and six entails to six children. The eldest son, don Pedro Ramón, became second Conde; the attached entail, worth 1,550,000 pesos, included urban property in the capital, mines and refineries at Real del Monte, and estates valued at 660,000 pesos—primarily the great Santa Lucía property that ruled the northern Valley of Mexico and the nearby Mezquital, between the capital and his mines. The second son, don José María, became Marqués de San Cristóbal. His entail included estates worth nearly 450,000 pesos, some near Real del Monte, others at San Juan del Río in the Bajío, plus distant grazing lands. The first daughter, doña María Micaela, was Marquesa de San Francisco. Her entail approached 600,000 pesos, including 440,000 pesos in lands at Acámbaro in the Bajío. Three younger daughters lacked titles. Each received entails valued at over 600,000 pesos—half in estates, half in urban properties including pulque taverns. Their lands also ranged from the pulque country northeast of Mexico City, through the Mezquital near the family mines, to the Bajío and the north. The family patrimony exceeded 4,400,000 pesos, with landed estates worth 2,534,747 pesos.[96]

The inheritance appeared to fragment the family enterprises. It did not. Doña María Micaela, Marquesa de San Francisco, never married and found independence by spending most of her life in the Bajío, near her estates and away from her brother's power. Her younger sisters found little escape. The second Conde forced doña María Dolores (she fled one wedding, then appeared reluctantly at the next) to marry don Vicente Herrera, a High Court judge. He gained wealth and a powerful family; the second Conde de Regla got access to the heights of regime power. When promotion sent Herrera to the Council of the Indies in Spain, doña María had to go, leaving her estates in her brother's hands. The younger sisters never married; the second Conde managed their properties while they lived, and inherited them when both died before 1800.[97]

Then there was don José María, Marqués de San Cristóbal. He got a title, but the smallest inheritance. A rebellious streak marked his life. Early on he tried a naval career on a warship his father had built for the Spanish Navy. Back in Mexico City he became infamous for sexual escapades. A proposed marriage was blocked by both families and don José fled to Spain. He never wed, but left at least two children in New Spain. Later he gained fame as José Terreros, a physician in Napoleonic Paris who died in 1815 of self-administered drug experiments. All the while his brother the Conde controlled his estates and paid him an allowance.[98]

Only the Bajío estates of his titled sister escaped the second Conde de Regla's control. Like his father he ruled family affairs tightly. A judicious marriage, arranged by his father, added to family power. In 1780 the second Conde wed doña María Josefa Rodríguez de la Cotera, granddaughter and sole heir to the title and landed wealth of the Conde de San Bartolomé de Jala, a pioneer of the commercial pulque business. The marriage set a merger of the two greatest pulque producers and Mexico City tavern operators. The second Conde de Regla ruled landed wealth far beyond what his father left, and his father left the most valuable properties ever assembled in New Spain.[99]

Don Pedro Ramón, titled, vastly landed, and newly married, could have lived high on his near-monopoly of the capital pulque market and on the profits of his many other estates. Election by the Mexico City Council as the city's first magistrate in 1787 confirmed a place in the capital's elite. Yet the second Conde de Regla decided to try to replicate his father's success in mining at Real del Monte. Between 1781 and 1801 he invested 4,668,858 pesos in drainage and other projects. He extracted silver worth only 5,577,451 pesos. He invested more than his father and gained much less silver.[100] The second Conde de Regla challenged established wisdom; he risked an inherited fortune in search of a second bonanza, and predictably faced mounting debts. After 1800 his wife, the Condesa de Jala, took over the properties of the wayward Marqués de San Cristóbal and began to run the pulque business. Power and patriarchy were reinforcing. A failing patriarch could lose power to his wife.[101]

The great landed clans of Mexico City, some with inherited properties, others with estates bought with wealth from the silver economy, and many with both, regularly forged connections with leading men of the regime. The Fagoaga clan was perhaps most successful at taking wealth in the silver economy, investing in estates, and establishing ties with high officials. The family linked financiers, landed entrepreneurs, and high officials in "a colonial establishment."[102] At times great families built links to viceroys. After he returned to Spain the second Conde de Revillagigedo served as the Santiagos' agent from 1789 to 1804.[103] The second Conde de Regla worked closely with don José de Iturrigaray, viceroy from 1803 to 1808.[104] Still, viceroys ruled for brief terms; the patriarchs of Mexico City wanted lasting links to the regime. For greater longevity the viceroys' administrative secretaries were useful: don Yldefonso Antonio Gómez wed a daughter of the first Conde de Jala in the 1750s; don Francisco Fernández de Córdoba wed a daughter of the Marqués de Jaral in the 1780s.[105]

Government in New Spain was ultimately judicial, making ties to High Court judges most valuable. When they sought legal advice entrepreneurial patriarchs often got it from leading jurists. The Condes de Santiago received advice from don Ciriaco González Carbajal, the Conde de Jala from don Baltasar Ladrón de Guevara; the Fagoagas, the Conde de Medina y Torres, and the Condesa de San Mateo Valparaiso all worked with don Francisco Javier de Gamboa.[106] Marriages sealed lasting relationships. The Santiagos kept a High Court judge in the family for most of the century. Don Domingo Balcárcel arrived from Spain in 1721 to join the court; four years later he married a daughter of the Conde de Santiago. By the time of his death in 1783 he had risen to the rank of dean, the top post on the court. Throughout he was a proud member of the Santiago clan. In the 1790s his family in Spain tried to claim one of the Santiagos' titles and an entail, offering a male heir against the inheriting daughters. They failed.[107]

Don Juan Lorenzo, then Conde, did not wait long after Balcárcel's death to forge a new link to the court. Don Cosme de Mier y Trespalacios, also from Spain, came to reinforce metropolitan power—one of Gálvez's reformers. In 1785 he wed doña Juana María de Velasco y Ovando, heir to the Santiago title and entails. Given patriarchal presumptions, don Cosme would rule as Conde de Santiago. His wife's early death in 1785 cost him that fusion of judicial and landed power. It did not cheat the Santiagos. Until his death in 1805 the Condesa and her sisters called him their "brother, don Cosme." He was a trusted legal adviser; he led in public occasions when a patriarch had to appear. He mediated disputes over an inheritance that he had earlier expected to claim. At least once he swayed a decision to favor the Santiagos in a minor affair over debts with a provincial trader. Such direct influence, however, was secondary in the community of interest that linked the most powerful of Mexico City's old landed clans and the High Court.[108]

Newer clans taking riches from the silver economy and investing in landed estates followed the Santiagos in forging links to powerful jurists. Don Francisco Leandro de Viana came to the court from Spain by 1769, one of the first of Gálvez's men sent to reform New Spain. In 1771 he wed doña María Josefa Rodríguez Pablo, a sixteen-year-old claimant to the disputed Condado de Jala—the great pulque fortune. Viana forced arbitration of the inheritance by a panel that included four landed patriarchs (among them the Conde de Santiago and the Marqués de San Miguel de Aguayo), a leading churchman, and Viana's High Court colleague, don Vicente de Herrera. Viana failed to gain the prize for his young wife, but he won a settlement that brought him 150,000 pesos to invest in pulque properties.[109]

Don Vicente de Herrera learned from that settlement. He negotiated to marry doña María Dolores Romero de Terreros, sister of the second Conde de Regla, heir to a valuable entail—a union that she tried to flee but could not prevent.[110] The two appointees to the High Court sent to serve Gálvez and the reform interest who married Mexico City heiresses to acquire valuable lands were the only judges to gain titles of Castille, Viana as Conde de Tepa, Herrera as Conde de Herrera. Both won appointment to the Council of the Indies. And both wrote memorials that cautioned the council not to interfere with the interests of the great families of New Spain—interests that had become their own.[111]

The first Conde de Regla found another way to the heart of the regime. Don Fernando José Mangino was director of the Royal Mint in

Mexico City and manager of the expropriated Jesuit properties in the 1760s and 1770s. Was anyone better placed to help a patriarch taking vast wealth from mining and investing in ex-Jesuit estates? Mangino assisted in key Regla family affairs: the creation of entails, the marriage in 1780 with the Jala clan, and the distribution of titles and entails after the first Conde's death in 1781. Mangino's knowledge of the Regla family business proved indispensable.[112] Yet his close ties to the powerful clan proved no obstacle to administrative advance. In 1787 Mangino won the post of superintendent in Mexico City, chief among the intendants named to fortify regime power. His power rivaled that of the viceroy. When bureaucratic conflict reaffirmed viceregal supremacy, Mangino got a seat on the Council of the Indies.[113]

The entrepreneurial patriarchs of Mexico City forged links to the highest regime officials. After the conflicts of the 1760s, which ended with an alliance of entrepreneurial elites and regime officials that crushed popular resistance, few among the leading entrepreneurs of New Spain mounted loud protests against Bourbon policies. The regime and its reforms were rarely noted in their voluminous correspondence. The entrepreneurs who ruled the intersection of silver production and the commercial economy had little need to protest or complain. Their power led to marriages and other ties that colonized the heights of regime power: the viceroyalty and High Court in Mexico City, the Council of the Indies in Spain. Capitalist patriarchs and the regime's leading men built a community of interest, a symbiosis between the Bourbon state and entrepreneurs in Mexico City, who saw little to fear in the regime they had colonized.

Great Families and Provincial Elites

This portrait of Mexico City's great families focuses on six clans becoming three: Sánchez Espinosa allying with and conquering the Peñascos; the Condes de Santiago allying with the Cervantes y Padilla; the Condes de Regla marrying the Condes de Jala. Together they formed a core part of the Mexico City elite as the eighteenth century ended. Adamantly entrepreneurial and vastly landed, the community of power in the viceregal capital was not fully unified. There were conflicts in and between great families. And the Mexico City elite stratified into two segments. A few great families financed mines, traded across New Spain, and held vast lands extending from near the capital, through the Bajío, and to the north. A larger group lived in the capital as professionals, bureaucrats, and clergy, while operating modest commercial properties nearby.

Family papers, court documents, and estate sales identified 113 families in Mexico City holding 314 estates between 1775 and 1810.[114] Their geographic distribution defined the power of landlords based in Mexico City. They concentrated in five zones: the cereal basins close by the capital, extending southeast to Chalco and west into the Valley of Toluca; the lowland sugar basins near Cuernavaca and Cuautla just south; the pulque zone of the northeast Valley of Mexico, the Mezquital, and Apan; the fertile Bajío to the northwest; and the grazing regions extending north. It is notable that Mexico City families held few estates east around Puebla, west in Michoacán, or south toward Oaxaca. They focused near the capital, in the Bajío, and in the North. Southern Mesoamerica, where indigenous republics held strong, silver was scarce, cities were small, and markets weak, was of little interest.

The greatest concentration of estates lay near the capital. Nearly 45 percent, or 140 of 314 properties, were in the cereal zone; 88, or 28 percent, lay in pulque regions; only 14, less than 5 percent, made sugar. Together 242 of 314 estates, or 77 percent of the total, lay in the near hinterland of the metropolis. There estates tapped the labor of landed republics to raise maize, wheat, sugar, and pulque for the capital's consumers. Landlords in Mexico City held fewer properties in the Bajío and farther north. Owners in the capital held 44 estates in the Bajío and 28 in the country beyond. Northern estates thus accounted for less than a quarter of the holdings of Mexico City elites, but they were very valuable properties held by very powerful families.

The seventeen great families with holdings valued above 500,000 pesos were an elite within the elite, exceptionally rich in estates. Forming 15 percent of the capital's elite families, the 17 most powerful clans held 161 of 314 estates, more than half of the estates linked to the metropolis. The six clans becoming three that are detailed above count as five of the 17 great families (the Peñascos never lived in the capital). They controlled 88 estates—half of the properties of the great families, 30 percent of the holdings of the entire Mexico City elite.[115] The power of the great families was unparalleled, as was the distribution of their holdings. Their landed holdings focused on regions parallel to the mining and estate properties of the Fagoagas—also stretching from the basins around Mexico City, through the Bajío, and across the northern plateau country.[116]

In the cereal zones near the capital great clans held 46 of 140 properties, a third of those of the entire elite (double their "share"). They were absent in sugar production (in part because the Cortés heirs were Neapolitan nobles served by managers in Mexico City).[117] In contrast, great families ruled the pulque economy, holding 54 of 88 properties. Farther north they alone exerted power from Mexico City. They held

38 of 44 estates in the Bajío, 23 of 28 farther north. The great clans joined actively in the cereal economy of Spanish Mesoamerica, tapping labor from indigenous communities to produce grains. They focused locally on pulque estates supplying the capital's taverns. And many joined in the booming economy of the Bajío and Spanish North America, where estates were larger, relied on resident communities, and supplied mining centers, Bajío towns, and the viceregal capital.

Investment decisions, dynastic unions, and the vagaries of inheritance brought varied emphases to the economies of great families. Most dominated estate production in one region yet diversified to participate in other zones. The Condes de Santiago ruled maize and wheat production in the southern Valley of Toluca; they also cultivated grain near Texcoco in the eastern Valley of Mexico, pulque at Tulancalco in the Mezquital, and diverse crops at Salvatierra in the Bajío. Union with the Cervantes brought more concentration in the eastern Valley of Mexico, including cereal estates around Texcoco and pulque properties toward Otumba and Calpulalpan. The long-established Santiago and Cervantes families exerted enormous power in the estate economies that tapped the labor of Mesoamerican communities to supply maize, wheat, and pulque to the capital.[118]

The Condes de Regla and Condes de Jala ruled the pulque economy. The first Conde de Jala pioneered pulque as an estate crop in the first half of the eighteenth century. The Jesuits followed his example.[119] When the first Conde de Regla bought the best of the Jesuit estates, then married his first son to the heir to the Jala fortune, he effected a merger that ruled the capital pulque market. Of the eighty-eight estates in the pulque zone fifty-eight belonged to great families, including fourteen to the Conde de Regla and ten to the Conde de Jala. The Regla properties extended beyond pulque to reach into the Bajío and far north. The expropriation of the Jesuits allowed the richest of silver barons to design a landed patrimony; he concentrated on pulque, complemented by participation in the Bajío and Spanish North America.[120]

The Marquéses de San Miguel de Aguayo and Condes de San Pedro de Alamo, another fused pair of powerful families, dominated landholding and estate operations in the far north around Coahuila while participating in the rural economy around Zacatecas and in the Bajío.[121] Don José Sánchez Espinosa participated in providing cereals and pulque to Mexico City, operated two major Bajío properties, and once in control of the Peñasco estates dominated production in and around San Luis Potosí. A great family strategy becomes clear: dominance in one zone complemented by participation in others brought sustained profit by spreading risks and tapping numerous markets.

Some claimed noble honor, but the great landed patriarchs of Mexico City were entrepreneurs in an age of agrarian capitalism.[122]

The lesser landed families in Mexico City's elite were rich, and certainly elite within New Spain's larger society. To those who struggled daily just to live, they appeared rich and powerful. Yet they lived in the shadow of great families with vast estates, regional dominance, and ties to colonial officials. The 96 lesser landed families held 153 estates—one or two each. Most patrimonies were valued at 200,000 pesos or less, great wealth except when compared to clans with holdings of 500,000 to 5,000,000 pesos. Most secondary elites dealt in cereal and pulque for Mexico City. They competed with great families and with villagers, whom they also employed. They profited, but they lacked the capital to contest the dominance with the great families.

They were provincial patriarchs—important men in Mexico City and its environs, a key province at the center of the dynamic economy of New Spain. They pursued seats on the Mexico City council and rarely married daughters to high officials. They were often lawyers, clerics, and bureaucrats—and also profit-seeking estate operators.[123] Council seats brought power in the city; professional activities gained income to supplement, even to finance, estate operations. Others without such income turned to church lenders to fund estates. Many, notably a group of lawyer-landlords, often served as business managers for great patriarchs while seeking profit on their own as lesser growers in the estate economy.[124] Provincial landlords, often professionals, led the Mexico City council; the great families colonized the highest levels of the regime. Mexico City's provincial elites were like the leading families of Querétaro, San Miguel, and other cities and towns in the Bajío. Rich in many ways and locally influential, they held wealth that paled before that of the great families. Their power was often limited by dependence on the same families.

Entrepreneurship: Don José Sánchez Espinosa in the Commercial Economy

Don José Sánchez Espinosa ruled a great family and joined every segment of the estate economy except sugar. With La Teja and Asunción at the gates of the capital he provisioned the city with grains, fruits, and vegetables. Properties at Otumba and Apan gave him a place in the pulque economy. La Griega and Puerto de Nieto were among the most productive estates in the eastern Bajío. And with the Bocas and Peñasco properties he ruled the livestock economy of San Luis Potosí.

His profit-seeking entrepreneurship illuminates the ways of the great patriarchs of Mexico City at the end of the eighteenth century.

Why leading entrepreneurs avoided sugar deserves notice. The warmer, wetter basins south of the Valley of Mexico began to harvest sugar soon after the conquest; Cortés was among the leading developers. The industry flourished, with ebbs and flows, through the colonial centuries and after. During the late eighteenth century, except for the Cortés heirs, most sugar growers were new merchants, not established patriarchs. The reasons seem clear: sugar required a long growing season, no frost, and ample irrigation, conditions present in the Cuernavaca basin but scarce across the Mexican highlands. Sugar land was thus expensive. Production needed a large number of permanent and skilled workers, many still slaves in the late eighteenth century, along with gangs of seasonal hands for long, difficult harvests. Refining required complex mills. Sugar was the agribusiness with the highest costs of land, equipment, and labor. The market for sugar in Mexico City was ample, but it did not approach the mass demand of pulque; nor did sugar face the periodic scarcity that drove maize to famine prices. Sugar was left to men on the rise, ready to risk a costly business.[125]

Established patriarchs like Sánchez Espinosa preferred to produce cereals, pulque, and livestock. Spaniards began to raise wheat near the capital soon after the conquest. Europeans wanted bread; early cultivators sought profit. For two centuries maize remained mostly an indigenous crop. In the heartland of Mesoamerica around the capital, villagers saw population decline through the sixteenth century. They consolidated landed republics, fed themselves, and supplied maize and pulque to the capital into the eighteenth century. Then population growth began to press against limited village lands. Villagers consumed nearly all their produce—and needed additional earnings to sustain growing families and communities.

Markets opened and labor became available simultaneously. Estate operators in the Valleys of Mexico and Toluca expanded maize cultivation after 1720. During years of ample rains and good crops, commercial growers still faced competition from villagers. But periodically scarce rains reduced crops and drove maize prices to heights painful for consumers and profitable to estate growers. About once a decade drought or frost brought famine, allowing profits of desperation to those with resources to hold grain until years of crisis. Meanwhile labor costs held low as villagers desperate to supplement the produce of shrinking fields worked seasonally in estate fields. When they could they fed themselves and their families with village resources, working for low wages to plant and harvest estate maize and wheat when they could not. After 1700 population growth expanded urban markets, made land scarce in rural communities, and sent labor to commercial growers. Even so, community lands, however limited, subsidized estate profits by sustaining workers and families for part of each year, allowing growers to hire hands as needed for low pay. Periodic scarcity and famine prices did the rest to channel profits to estate growers like Sánchez Espinosa, whose La Teja and Asunción estates sold grains in the capital so close by.[126]

Pulque too was a native product opened to estate production in the eighteenth century; expanding markets and declining village surpluses again brought opportunity to commercial growers. The first Conde de Jala pioneered the conversion of pastures to vast fields of maguey in the northeastern Valley of Mexico, the adjacent Mezquital, and the nearby Apan plains. The Jesuits followed quickly at Santa Lucía. When the Conde de Regla acquired the Jesuit holdings and his son married the Jala heiress, they claimed market dominance—with room for Sánchez Espinosa, the Condes de Santiago, and others to join in.

The labor needs and marketing strategies of pulque were unique. The maguey cactus had to mature for several years before its juice— *tlachique*—was tapped by skilled *tlachiqueros* who oversaw fermentation into pulque. When ready the drink had to reach the city in twenty-four hours or it spoiled. To profit, estates needed vast fields of maguey ready to be tapped, maintaining daily production for tavern goers. Estates periodically employed large numbers to transplant offshoots into great fields, providing a few weeks' income to men and boys from nearby villages. Once transplanted the maturing maguey required no labor for years. When ready, one or two tlachiqueros tapped and fermented the sap; a few muleteers took the pulque to the capital. Costs were low: pulque required only dry land and workers for periodic transplanting. Markets were steady, though profit required city taverns—owned in large numbers by the Condes de Regla and Jala; Sánchez Espinosa had one. With markets growing, the profits of pulque were ample. The problem with pulque was that it profited growers without offering compensating labor to villagers facing land shortages in dry basins where life was always difficult. The pulque zone became a place of conflict after 1810. Still, while the silver economy flourished, the richest landed entrepreneurs took profit there.[127]

The great families sold grain in Mexico City; they ruled the pulque market. In both they operated beside members of the capital's provincial elite. In the larger agro-pastoral economy that linked the capital's markets with the Bajío and grazing lands farther north, great patriarchs were all but alone among participants based in Mexico City, though they faced local competition from elites at Querétaro, San Luis Potosí, and other provincial cities. The turn from grazing to pulque in the northeastern Valley of Mexico and the Mezquital after 1720 sent livestock northward, as did the shift of Bajío estates from grazing to crops at the same time. Grazing and livestock marketing stretched over longer distances, favoring leading landlords. Don José Sánchez Espinosa, a minor seller of grain and pulque in the capital, was a major player in the northern livestock economy. He grazed huge herds of sheep and goats and numerous cattle and horses at the Obra Pía estates and the Peñasco properties in San Luis Potosí. He sold sheep for mutton to feed Mexico City. He sent hides to the city's tanners and tallow to its candle makers. He sold wool to Querétaro obrajes.

The key to the mutton market of Mexico City was the *abasto*: the contract to provide sheep to city slaughterhouses.[128] The city council awarded the contract in return for guaranteed supplies at set prices. While growers profiteered from the maize that fed the city poor, and great landlords ruled pulque with few protections for the drinking public, the meat that fed the more prosperous was regulated. Contract prices did allow consistent profits to producers who delivered large herds. In the early 1780s leading northern grazers like the Marqués de Jaral and the Conde de San Mateo Valparaiso held the abasto. After the devastating frost and famine of 1785 and 1786 killed uncounted livestock and blocked drives to the capital, don Antonio de Bassoco, the richest of Mexico City's merchants, ruled the abasto from the 1790s to 1810. Bassoco married a daughter of the Marqués de Castañiza, tying him to the Fagoagas. He had no estates, but he owned great herds of sheep and paid other grazers for pasture and more sheep. He worked with don Gabriel de Yermo, a rising merchant and landlord strong in the sugar economy, the Marqués de San Miguel de Aguayo, with vast estates in Coahuila, and don José Sánchez Espinosa.[129]

During the 1790s Mexico City annually consumed about 275,000 head. In most years Bassoco supplied 50,000, just under 20 percent. Sánchez Espinosa provided 8,000, over 3 percent. In addition, Bassoco leased pasture at Bocas. The relationship was so regular that it was rarely discussed. Bassoco sent a note confirming that he would take the usual number of sheep at the usual price—2.5 pesos a head. The sheep were delivered to Bassoco's herdsmen in San Luis Potosí. The cash, normally 20,000 pesos, was paid in the capital. The business of supplying the capital's mutton was a joint venture between Bassoco and a group of great grazers, including the priest-patriarch.[130]

Sánchez Espinosa and Bassoco also sold hides and tallow in Mexico City. In 1800 the Peñasco estates shipped 5,667 hides and 1,346 arrobas (25 pounds each) of tallow, the latter to a kinsman, don Antonio de Velasco y Mora.[131] Bassoco annually sold hides worth from 20,000 to 35,000 pesos, mostly to don Martín Angel Michaus, an immigrant merchant who later acquired sugar estates and married into the family of the Condes de Santiago.[132] And while Sánchez Espinosa and Bassoco earned most in large transactions, they also took profit in many small sales. They sold sheep to abasto holders in San Luis Potosí and the Bajío. They supplied mules to muleteers and horses and cattle to small landlords and working rancheros wherever they could.[133]

The same herds that provided lambs for mutton were sheared for wool. At Bocas, Sánchez Espinosa's 100,000 head produced 1,000 to 1,500 arrobas of wool yearly, valued around 3 pesos each. As in most livestock trades, he dealt with preferred buyers over many years. In the early 1780s he continued his uncle's sales to the Querétaro obraje of don Tomás Merino Pablo. When that relationship collapsed in the great famine of 1785 and 1786 don José began to sell his annual clip to don Juan José Martínez de Lejarza, a tie that lasted until 1807. Then another financial crisis led him to shift sales to a third Querétaro obrajero, a link that lasted past 1810.[134]

Wool deals were bartered in cash values. Don José delivered the annual clip from Bocas at an agreed price; in exchange he took cloth of equal value. The textiles stocked estate stores at La Griega and Puerto de Nieto in the Bajío and supplied annual shipments to Bocas. Don José also provided estate residents with cloth and goods from across New Spain and Europe. He obtained textiles, hardware, liquor, and other goods in transatlantic trade; he bought sugar wholesale from estates near Cuautla; he acquired cloth from Puebla and Oaxaca. A shipment to Carbonera near Matehuala in 1795 included goods worth 4,248 pesos: 1,116 pesos of cloth from Zapotec weavers at Villa Alta, Oaxaca; 765 pesos from Puebla workshops; and 765 pesos from Europe, including Silesian linens and cheap calicoes. Buying wholesale, shipping with his own muleteers, selling to estate residents at prevailing prices—higher, of course, in the north—don José found more profit. Landlords who could not supply their northern estates relied on merchants like Bassoco, sharing the profits.[135]

Sánchez Espinosa's Bajío properties, La Griega and Puerto de Nieto, were pivotal to everything. They supplied grain to northern estates, towns in the Bajío, and the city of Guanajuato. In the late eighteenth century they helped feed Mexico City during recurring years of scarcity. La Griega already focused on grains as the eighteenth century began; Puerto de Nieto remained a grazing property. By 1750 don Francisco de Espinosa y Navarijo had sent most of his sheep north to Bocas, settling growing populations at his Bajío estates. He expanded cultivation and irrigation at La Griega east of Querétaro, planting maize on rain-fed lands, irrigating more profitable wheat and chiles. Puerto de Nieto, its rolling lands nestled against uplands east of San Miguel, mostly raised maize. Both harvested maize every January, then held it until prices peaked, often years later. Only in times of scarcity were stocks sold in Querétaro, San Miguel, and other cities and towns in the Bajío, taking maximum profit.

Both estates also sold to more distant consumers. La Griega lay closer to Mexico City and regularly sold chiles there. Here was another native crop, grown mostly by indigenous families into the eighteenth century. But as with maize and pulque, when population growth cut indigenous surpluses, estate growers found new markets. La Griega profited annually selling chiles in the capital. It sent wheat there too, if less regularly. When rains were good and supplies ample, the price did not cover transport. When rains were scarce La Griega was among the first to tap Mexico City demand as prices rose. Puerto de Nieto focused on maize and found consumers in the North, where a drier climate brought frequent scarcity. Periodically Sánchez Espinosa told his managers to sell maize in San Luis Potosí or to estate managers desperate for supplies. He always kept ample stocks for his own northern properties, feeding managers and resident families to sustain livestock production, the source of great earnings. With La Griega and Puerto de Nieto, Sánchez Espinosa profited in a market for grain that reached from the viceregal capital to the far north.[136]

Profit

Operating vast and valuable estates in diverse regions was profitable; four sets of revealing accounts document that. In 1782 the first Conde de Regla's eldest daughter and executor operated all the family estates, pending their distribution among six heirs. She kept records detailing the value and profits of eight sets of estates, mixing pulque operations near the capital and cereal properties in the Bajío. The units reported profits ranging from 2 to 12 percent of inventoried value. The combined rate of 6.5 percent was meaningfully greater than the 5 percent that church lenders gained from mortgages. If the executor's report was accurate, the Regla properties were profitable. And there is reason to suspect that the executor shaped her accounts to limit reported profits. The most valuable landholdings were her estates at San Cristóbal, worth 482,875 pesos. Yet she reported a profit of only 10,775 pesos, just 2 percent. That might reflect a year in which grain was held waiting for higher prices, not the long-term profitability of properties near Acámbaro. Or the low report perhaps resulted from a sharp executor's personal interests. The San Cristóbal estates were to be hers. During the interim administration their profits would be shared with her siblings; income delayed or hidden would be hers alone a year later. If the questionable accounts for San Cristóbal are excluded, the remaining estates gave profits of 8.2 percent in 1782—good profits indeed.[137]

Ample profits were also reported from 1800 to 1806 for the valuable properties of the Marquesado de Vivanco, then operated by a guardian for the minor Marquesa. The estates were bought, like so many others, with wealth from the silver economy. Chapingo, near Texcoco in the eastern Valley of Mexico, produced wheat and maize on irrigated and rain-fed fields. Ojo de Agua was a pulque producer not far to the northeast. Like most cereal estates, Chapingo reported annually varied profits, ranging from 2.8 to 11.6 percent of its inventoried value. The annual mean was 6.4 percent. Ojo de Agua enjoyed the consistent earnings of pulque, its profits ranging from 6.4 to 7.9 percent, and averaging 7.1 percent.[138]

Accounts of many Regla estates during one year and of two Vivanco properties over six years report good profits. Provincials with fewer and less valuable estates generally gained less. The pulque property named Tlateguacan, near Otumba, valued at only 10,000 pesos, earned its owners, professionals in Mexico City, 4 percent on average during six years in the 1790s.[139] The profits of pulque were greater and more regular than those of grains; the profits of great families with many properties in diverse regions were better than those of provincial landlords. The great families did well by landed entrepreneurship; provincials struggled with mortgages and lesser profits.

An account of Sánchez Espinosa's Obra Pía properties for May 1807 to May 1808 also shows ample profits and suggests far greater earnings than he reported.[140] He listed total income of 34,216 pesos: 7,728 from sales of sheep to the San Luis Potosí abasto, 5,392 pesos from rents, 3,780 pesos from wool, and 1,734 from mutton, plus 15,571 pesos from livestock, grains, and other products. He reported expenses of 14,967 pesos: 4,895 pesos in salaries, rations, and goods advanced to managers and permanent workers; and 2,130 pesos to those who sheared sheep, slaughtered livestock, and transported goods. Other "expenses" were not costs of production but allocations of profit: 1,513 pesos in tithes; 1,273 for alcabalas; and 3,939 paid on liens (chaplaincies and charitable bequests). The last "expense" was 1,214 pesos that don José claimed due from past accounts.

Taking the accounts at face value, the profit of 19,248 pesos would have been divided into thirds: 6,416 pesos to don José as administrator; 6,416 pesos shared by don José and a female cousin, the only heirs; and 6,416 pesos for pious works, mostly dowries for girls about to enter convents. But don José decided that 2,000 pesos spent on unspecified litigation should only count against the second and third shares, not his share as manager. Thus in one year he claimed 10,328 pesos: 6,416 pesos as the manager's third; 2,708 for his share as an heir; plus the 1,204 that he said was past due. Such earnings made him one of the richest men in Mexico City. He surely gained much more; how much can only be imagined.

Like the Conde de Regla's daughter and executor, don José managed properties that led to shared proceeds. Both made sure that they shared as little as possible. Annually don José earned 20,000 pesos selling sheep to don Antonio de Bassoco for the Mexico City abasto. No such sum appears in the accounts. Had he "assigned" the sheep to Carbonera, outside the Obra Pía, or to Peñasco, which he managed in his son's name? Did he "define" his sheep as personal property that happened to graze at the Obra Pía and thus exclude sales to the abasto from the income he had to share? On a smaller scale, don José's uncle had exulted in winning exemption from alcabalas on the Obra Pía estates decades earlier. Had the decision been reversed? Or did he claim alcabala payments in the accounts and pocket the 1,273 pesos he reported as an expense? And who could challenge the 1,204 pesos he claimed as his due from the past and the 2,000 pesos he said he spent on litigation?

Accepting that Sánchez Espinosa gained only 10,000 pesos from the Obra Pía properties in 1807–8, his earnings from his personal estates and from control of the Peñasco entail surely brought his income that year to at least 20,000 pesos. Confirmation of his usual participation in the Mexico City abasto would have easily brought the total to nearly 40,000 pesos. To place that wealth in context, if the first Conde de Regla earned only the conservative calculation of 6.4 percent on his estates in the year before he died, he gained over 150,000 pesos. His six heirs would each receive 25,000 pesos yearly after the distribution of the six entails in 1782, except that the second Conde de Regla controlled at least four of the six, taking about 100,000 pesos most years. The income of the two Vivanco estates brought the young Marquesa an average of 20,000 pesos yearly after 1800—as reported by a guardian who surely worked to minimize the noble minor's earnings while he controlled her estates. To place the profits of such great landed clans in context, the highest officials of New Spain generally earned salaries of 5,000 pesos yearly. The managers who ran the estates that generated these profits usually earned from 100 to 200 pesos yearly, and rarely more than 300. The thousands of working families that actually produced the crops and livestock that sustained the great families and the silver economy lived on 40 to 50 pesos yearly. A fair estimate is that the ratio between the profits of the great patriarchs and the incomes of working families around 1800 was 1,000 to 1.

Alexander von Humboldt toured New Spain just after 1800 and saw "the land of inequality. Perhaps nowhere else is there such frightful concentration of fortune, civilization, cultivation, and population. . . . The huge inequality of fortune is seen not only among whites, European and Creole, but is equally manifest among indigenous peoples."[141] The great families of Mexico City, dominant players in New Spain's silver economy and the agrarian capitalism that sustained it, ruled a system that generated great profits and profound inequalities.

Catholic Charity: Legitimating Power, Profit, and Patriarchy

Entrepreneurship and Catholicism were inseparable in the lives of the patriarchs who ruled in Mexico City as the eighteenth century ended.[142] The fusion is obvious in the lives of don Francisco de Espinosa y Navarijo and don José Sánchez Espinosa, priest-patriarchs driven to profit, devout clergymen eager to say Mass and hear confessions in the estate communities that produced their wealth. The Obra Pía estates allocated visible funds to pious works, paying dowries for young nuns and giving alms in the name of Guadalupe. The accounts for 1807–8 detail how Sánchez Espinosa sustained religious lives and activities. Three clerics shared 500 pesos from a chaplaincy; two hospitals shared 226 pesos. Querétaro's Congregation of Guadalupe gained 2,550 for alms for the poor. A relative of the founder got a dowry of 3,000 pesos to enter a convent. Two other aspirants received 400 and 300 pesos. Another 104 pesos supported Capuchin nuns. In a year when Sánchez Espinosa earned profits of at least 10,000 pesos (and likely twice that) from the Obra Pía, he paid over 7,000 pesos to religious and charitable works. He kept another 1,500 pesos dedicated to pious work, gaining working capital by holding them for future use.[143]

Most entrepreneurial patriarchs were not priests; most entails were sanctioned by the monarchy. Still, most landlords funded chaplaincies to support priests who were often kin. Many provided dowries to help poor, respectable girls enter convents. Many also made annual contributions to the poor.[144] Landlords who relied on mortgages from convents to buy estates also, in the process, funded preaching and prayer that legitimated the social order and called the populace to lives of penitential morality.

Beyond the ubiquitous ties among entrepreneurs, clergy, and convents, a fusion of capitalism and Catholicism shaped a language of grain marketing. In most letters Sánchez Espinosa and other entrepreneurs dealt with each other and their managers in a direct language of business. In sales of sheep or wool, even in affairs such as the takeover of the Peñasco properties, the entrepreneurial priest and his correspondents took advantage and profit without obfuscation or justification. But when they dealt in grain, especially when they held maize awaiting the profits of hunger, they used a language of Christian charity. The standard way to profit in grain was detailed by an official in November 1809, as New Spain entered another time of drought and scarcity: "Since most proprietors are powerful, they reserve sales until the months of greatest earnings, from June to October; then they sell slowly and only at their own granaries, awaiting greater advantage with the passing of time."[145] The strategy was clear: hold staples until scarcities and prices peaked—then maximize profits.

When doña María Josefa de Velasco y Ovando ran the Santiago estates for her sister the Condesa, she expressed elite values clearly. In December 1800, amid the maize harvest, she relayed her market strategy to the manager at the Atengo properties that ruled the southern Valley of Toluca: "About the current drop in the price of grain, it is to be expected at this time, as small farmers sell quickly to take care of pressing needs; as we have no such needs, we will not sell now. Better, we must buy as much maize as we can and sell it for profit in the future."[146] Without hesitation doña María Josefa reported how to make money with maize. Don José Sánchez Espinosa and other entrepreneurs gave parallel orders when bountiful harvests drove prices down or when late rains promised scarcity.[147] Every spring and summer, as grain harvested by villagers and rancheros ran out, prices rose and major commercial growers held their stocks.[148] Sooner or later they sent a second standard instruction: maize should be stored awaiting higher prices, but small lots could be sold to "indios" and "the poor" at estate granaries for prevailing—rising—prices. They thus imposed transport costs on desperate buyers. Doña María Josefa de Velasco offered a common justification: she would sell to the poorest of supplicants "so that God may help us."[149]

If rains failed during the next crop cycle, entrepreneurs again halted sales, knowing that a second season of dearth promised famine prices. Meanwhile they joined the viceroy in processions carrying Nuestra Señora de los Remedios (Our Lady of Remedies) or Guadalupe through the streets of the capital. As reported by don José Sánchez Espinosa in April 1801, viceroy and landlords together asked for "divine mercy" and "rain for our fields."[150] While holding grain and waiting for prices to rise, thus driving them higher, elite growers sold small quantities to the poor and called it charity, while joining public processions imploring the Virgin to deliver rains that would bring better crops and lower prices.

Only when convinced that prices had peaked did great landlords order managers to sell large quantities. The goal was maximum profit. But the decision was expressed as charity. Doña María Josefa de Velasco wrote to her agent at Atengo that it was time to sell, because to wait longer would "prejudice the lives of the poor, for whom maize is the sole support of life."[151] While working to create and claim the profits of hunger, don José and the Condesa's sister invoked the Virgin. When supplication failed and prices peaked they sold maize for famine profits—and asserted that they were offering Catholic charity. The letters suggest no hint of hypocrisy. They report a religious culture that made the pursuit of profit based on scarcity and hunger an act of charity—unquestionably legitimate in the Mexico City community of power. The views of the hungry poor are not recorded.

While maize sustained the poor, wheat, often irrigated, fed the comfortable. Years of drought—or blight—still offered opportunities to profit. Don José Sánchez Espinosa sold wheat from La Teja near the capital and La Griega in Querétaro only when prices, normally around four pesos per carga, rose to fifteen or sixteen pesos—near historic peaks. When he was sure they would climb no higher he sent his stocks to the capital.[152] When the *chiaguistle* blight struck in 1799 and 1800, doña María Josefa de Velasco had her manager at Atengo sell only in small quantities, taking advantage of prices around fifteen pesos without bringing them down.[153] Then in August she learned that another grower at Toluca had sold two thousand cargas for only nine pesos each. The market fell to thirteen, costing her large sums. She was irate and called the offending landlord an "immature young gentleman."[154] Perhaps it took a women exercising patriarchal power to express so sharply the linkage of profit and patriarchy that sustained Mexico City's community of power. She found no charity in the young offender's sale, which reduced profits yet made bread more affordable.

Powerful patriarchs (and a few women) led Mexico City's great families after 1770.[155] They tapped the silver economy and colonized the heights of the Bourbon regime. They led a community of landed power that claimed predatory profits in a commercial economy ranging from the capital and the core of Mesoamerica, through the Bajío, and far to the north. They promoted and lived a culture of Catholicism that assured their legitimacy. They were a New World establishment, exemplified by don José Sánchez Espinosa, his allies, and a few peers. Provincial elites in Mexico City, the Bajío, and Spanish North America had no choice but to negotiate from positions of lesser power. Meanwhile producing families across the Bajío—in mining, textile production, and irrigated cultivation—faced deepening dependence, widening insecurities, and declining earnings. For decades working men struggled to hold patriarchy in households struggling to survive and always searching Catholicism for answers.

CHAPTER 6

Production, Patriarchy,

and Polarization in the Cities

Guanajuato, San Miguel, and Querétaro, 1770–1810

MOST OF THE SILVER that drove the economy of New Spain came from Guanajuato, Zacatecas, San Luis Potosí, and regions north. Silver accelerated urbanization, stimulating markets for cloth and commercial crops. Powerful men in Mexico City along with mining, textile, and agricultural entrepreneurs in the Bajío ruled a booming economy after 1770. Still, the late-century boom developed in a changing global context. The premium prices paid by China for silver, stimulating the cycle of 1550 to 1640 and the resurgence of mining after 1700, were gone by 1750. Silver remained vitally important as money and a commodity.[1] Its price declined just as Mexican mines again faced rising costs for tunneling, drainage, and labor. The regime answered with policies that promoted mining by lowering costs for taxes, mercury, and labor; it also worked to draw more silver toward Spain and Europe.

The Bourbons promoted mining, prejudiced colonial textile production, and sought power and revenues while aiming to limit disruptive resistance. Entrepreneurs and officials worked together toward policies of social control that would concentrate the fruits of boom in the hands of the few; the men, women, and rising number of boys who produced silver, cloth, and crops faced declining returns and unprecedented insecurities. Patriarchy remained strong in elite families;

mounting pressures and uncertainties challenged men, women, and children in working households.

Linked histories of boom and dislocation, of entrepreneurs and producers, the few seeking wealth and power and the many working to survive, played out in cities, towns, and rural communities of the Bajío. The region sustained an integrated regional economy; its silver drove burgeoning trades. But it divided internally into zones with different legacies of settlement, ways of production, social organization, and cultural visions. The southern and eastern Bajío focused on the commercial and textile city of Querétaro, still with an Otomí majority in the late eighteenth century. The northern and western Bajío focused on the mining city of Guanajuato; it remained a Hispanic society with a mulatto-indio majority. Prosperity and polarization were everywhere; so were differences that made every community distinct.

Patriarchy remained a dominant ideal, at least among patriarchs. It organized entrepreneurship, in the Bajío as in Mexico City. It orchestrated production in cities and across the countryside. Men were presumed the heads of producing households, working to sustain families; wives and children should serve and assist, in production and in household affairs. The patriarchal ideal did not presume that only men worked. Rather, men would lead working households that incorporated the labors of women and children. Entrepreneurial patriarchs and their managers presumed to deal with producing patriarchs—the heads of working households. Working patriarchs aimed to produce cloth and other goods in the cities and crops in the countryside; wives and children were expected to work, serve, and obey. Thus the key to production and social stability under patriarchy was the link between unequal patriarchs. If entrepreneurial patriarchs allowed working patriarchs the means to provide for and thus rule their families, subordinate men would work loyally for the few who profited. Patriarchy was essential to social stability in the eighteenth-century Bajío.

But what if workingmen could not "provide"—could not gain the work or resources to allow families the necessities of sustenance? If the "failing" was personal, family conflict resulted.[2] Since the beginning, labor at the mines of Guanajuato was so dangerous and insecure that uncertainty about working patriarchs' ability to "provide" was built into the social order grounded in dominant trends in the organization of production. After 1770 deepening structural challenges to working men's patriarchy spread to textile cities and rural communities. The result was an era of polarization and insecurity. Many struggled to sustain patriarchy. Others looked for new ways of work and family life. The Bajío boom after 1770 brought profits to the few and declining earnings to the majority. It also brought new challenges to the patriarchy that orchestrated stability in a deeply unequal regional society. While the boom lasted, elite patriarchs found ways to profit and the majority grappled with unprecedented uncertainties.

Guanajuato: Patriarchs and Producers in the Silver City

Silver mined and refined at Guanajuato soared to new heights after 1770, driving the economy of the Bajío and New Spain, stimulating global and Atlantic trade. A few claimed unimagined riches; the regime gained vast revenues; workers took deadly risks to gain exceptional incomes. Life and work in the silver city were far from typical. They were uniquely risky, uncommonly rewarded, and always contested. After the risings of the 1760s regime officials and silver magnates kept an alliance for power and profit, pressing against workers and their welfare. Polarization had long defined Guanajuato; it deepened after 1770.

The trajectory of Guanajuato silver production is clear. From just over one million pesos yearly around 1720, extraction rose to average three million pesos in the 1740s. It fell to between 2.2 and 2.7 million pesos from 1750 to 1770, and then jumped to average nearly 5 million pesos from 1776 to 1780, a level that fluctuated only slightly until 1810.[3] The soaring production of the 1770s was led by the Sardanetas' Rayas mine. When it flooded in 1780 bonanza was sustained at Valenciana. Both are celebrated cases of eighteenth-century entrepreneurship combining vision, drive, capital, and good luck—and support from the Bourbon state in the form of financial concessions and social controls. There was always an element of gambling in mining. A collapse or flood could turn the most promising investment and the most careful management toward bankruptcy. A fortuitous encounter with a rich vein of ore could turn a wasteful, indebted entrepreneur into a great success. Such uncertainties convinced many investors, notably the men of the Guanajuatos' Septién clan, to finance many mining ventures, hoping that the profits of some and the bonanzas of a few would cover the inevitable collapse of many.[4]

The Bourbon state had a clear interest in mining; silver grounded its power in Europe and the Americas. Its goal was simple: maximize silver production and state revenues. But taxes were a cost of mining. Taxed too much, production might fall and limit revenues. Taxed too little, production might rise but the state's share would decline. The key tax on silver was the *quinto*, the fifth, though the actual rate had been halved to about a tenth. Overall the regime took about 12 to 13 percent of silver production in taxes and fees in the late eighteenth century. But in key cases officials decided that long-term investments in deep shafts and drainage tunnels required tax exemptions. More of the silver extracted could be reinvested in costly works that might eventually bring bonanza and higher revenues. Nearly every great strike at Guanajuato and elsewhere in eighteenth-century New Spain benefited from a tax exemption. The ability to work with the Bourbon state was a key to mining entrepreneurship.

That state monopolized the supply of mercury, essential to refining lower grade ores. New Spain produced no appreciable mercury. To promote and regulate mining, the regime controlled supplies from Spain and central Europe. It could sell mercury dear as a way to claim more of mining wealth; it could sell cheap to stimulate production that could be tapped for revenue in other ways. After the crisis of the 1760s Bourbon reformers took the latter course. They dropped the price of a quintal of mercury from 82 to 76 pesos in 1767, just after quelling Guanajuato's riots. They dropped it again to 41 pesos in 1776.[5] And 1776 began the rise of silver to the peak levels of production sustained to 1810.

The surge of the 1770s was led by revival at Rayas. It had led Guanajuato's silver economy in the 1740s and then declined through the 1750s and 1760s. The first bonanza was facilitated by technological innovation. Don José de Sardaneta expanded the use of blasting powder underground, accelerating excavation while limiting labor demand, and making life more dangerous for the workers who remained. When his son don Vicente Manuel de Sardaneta revived Rayas in the 1770s he took advantage of the regime's new powers to limit workers' earnings.

After Bajío militias crushed and Gálvez punished popular resistance at Guanajuato in 1767, regional elites joined Gálvez to impose new social controls. Together they founded the Príncipe militia regiment, officered by patriarchs at Guanajuato, San Miguel, San Felipe, and León—surrounding mineworkers with loyal forces. Gálvez ordered and Guanajuato's council created a city patrol of forty-six armed men. To fund the new forces Gálvez sanctioned a new tax: one real on every fanega of maize, two reales on every carga of wheat flour sold in the mining city. The levy imposed a charge of 20 to 25 percent on the staples of popular sustenance to create and sustain police charged with controlling the populace.[6]

With new forces of order in place, Sardaneta turned on the workers who produced his wealth. In the early 1770s he ended partidos—the ore shares traditionally claimed by pickmen. Instead of risking life and limb as his working partners, they would labor in the depths for four reales per day, much of which Sardaneta would recapture in his company stores. Four reales a day was a high wage in the Bajío or anywhere in New Spain in the 1770s—more than double the best available in agriculture. But it was much less than mineworkers in Guanajuato customarily received for life-threatening labor underground. The reduction in earnings also struck local trade. Revenue officers complained in 1774 that the cut in earnings at Rayas hurt local storekeepers and limited tax collections on trade. Workers were angry and shopkeepers displeased, but there are no reports of riots like those that blocked the attempt by don Pedro Romero de Terreros to end partidos at Real del Monte in 1766. Instead, backed by the new forces of order, Sardaneta succeeded at Rayas. In 1774 his efforts won him title as Marqués de San Juan de Rayas. His mines' production soared from 1776 to 1780, when unprecedented rains flooded the works, all but closing them for two decades. Our Lady of Guadalupe, even on the silver pedestal built by the Sardanetas, could not save the mines from the forces of nature.[7]

Not every mine operator in Guanajuato shared Sardaneta's goal of seeking profit by ending partidos. Don Manuel José Domínguez de la Fuente, a medical doctor, worked the Guadalupe mine. He struggled with costs and drainage, enjoyed a brief bonanza in 1766 (amid riots that he does not mention), and in 1774 wrote a long memorial offering the regime his views on the challenges of mining. He saw scarce capital as the primary problem, forcing operators to split earnings with financiers. He argued that only mine operators and workers deserved the name of miner. He had no problem paying partidos which made operators and workers partners, however unequal.[8]

To Domínguez de la Fuente, the partido was "exceptionally useful . . . because the owner earns more without paying more; in addition, the worker benefits because by choosing to do a bit more work . . . in a short time he can earn hundreds of pesos. Although that outcome is not common, . . . the possibility brings energy to his work." Domínguez also understood why such an incentive was needed. Labor underground was sometimes deadly and always debilitating. The pickmen, essential to breaking ores, "face grave damage; in a short time they become sick, their lung tissue explodes—we call them cascades." The result: "they never come to enjoy the respect of old age." Still, they labored on: "Poor, they enrich the world. They labor so many can rest. They kill themselves, while everyone else lives." For that, they deserve partidos—which lead them to work longer and harder.[9]

Domínguez did see problems with prevailing labor relations: "Mine stores, called de rayas (of accounts), advance to the workers the necessities of life, debts collected every payday." Obligated labor persisted. "These dispensaries are most useful to the workers. . . . Throughout the week they can take whatever they want and need with confidence and convenience; it is the only inducement that keeps them at a particular mine." But too often advances were not repaid. Workers took more than they earned and left operators to carry debts or lose workers. They left for other mines or other towns, especially when a new bonanza promised work and partidos. "He who becomes gravely ill, which is so frequent, never pays."[10] Advances and unpaid obligations cost mine operators, Domínguez argued. The solution: low-cost working capital, partidos to create incentives (and share profits), and an end to advances—which pay workers for work not done, silver never produced.

Domínguez's views did not prevail. Credit remained scarce, expensive, and controlled by powerful merchants. And while partidos faced continuing attack, advances continued to define labor relations across the Bajío. Partidos favored pickmen, the most skilled and best remunerated mineworkers. Advances benefited the entire workforce. While operators sought to end partidos, and pickmen resisted, the larger reliance on advances and obligations persisted, favoring, as Domínguez de la Fuente insisted, all workers. Two entreprenurial visions competed to reduce labor costs.

The Guanajuato boom continued, led by Valenciana from 1780 to 1810. Don Antonio de Obregón opened the mine in 1760, backed by the storekeeper don Pedro Luciano de Otero. Each held ten shares in an enduring partnership; the other four belonged to don Juan Antonio de Santa Ana, a silent investor. Don Martín de Septién provided credit to Otero, financing operations at Valenciana. The project coincided with Bourbon efforts to promote mining through financial concessions and labor controls. Early on the Valenciana partners continued to pay partidos, attracting workers to an uncertain enterprise. While shafts were driven into unknown ground, partidos gave incentives to workers with little risk to the partners. Obregón and Otero, however, forced the costs of mining onto their workers by requiring that pickmen buy their own candles, picks, and blasting powder—probably at Otero's store. New forces of order facilitated the move against workers' welfare. Obregón, ennobled as Conde de Valenciana, took pride in building a magnificent chapel devoted to San Cayetano, the miners' patron, funded by requiring his workers to give a piece of ore daily (following the precedent set building the Jesuit convent and church). Valenciana yielded 40 percent of Guanajuato's silver in the 1780s, peaking between 1788 and 1791.[11]

While the Rayas and Valenciana enterprises led the Guanajuato boom after 1770, the silver economy was sustained by more numerous but less visible entrepreneurs facing equally contentious workers. There were many middling and small mine operators, inevitably de-

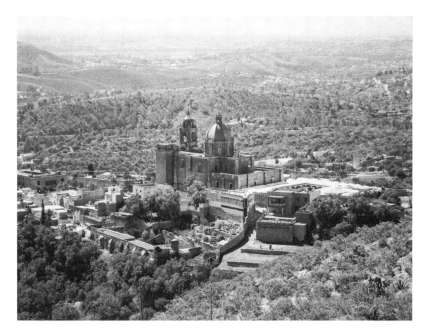

Valenciana mine complex, Guanajuato, eighteenth century.

pendent on merchant financiers. There were independent refiners who aimed to profit by processing ores extracted by mine operators without refineries, by scavengers, and by pickmen still gaining shares. While they competed with each other over profits and earnings, middling mine operators, merchants, and independent refiners joined scavengers and pickmen to oppose the concentration of power among the great entrepreneurs who gained regime concessions, operated mines and refineries, denied ore shares to pickmen, and induced workers to spend wages in company stores.[12] State-backed predatory capitalists were concentrating profits at the expense of a broader community of entrepreneurs and workers who struggled to gain in times of dynamism that mostly benefited the few.

While mining boomed, the regime moved to a second stage of reforms. Gálvez, now Minister of the Indies in Spain, had long aimed to strengthen the regime's power in New Spain. The result in the Bajío, as in Mexico City, was a negotiated, sometimes contentious alliance between officials and colonial elites promoting mining, facilitating entrepreneurship, and prejudicing the work and welfare of the majority. Gálvez's last and most enduring reform was to name intendants, regional magistrates whose arrival created new provincial capitals. They presided over city councils, overseeing administrative, fiscal, military, and judicial affairs. Gálvez named intendants in 1787 at Guanajuato,

Guadalupe mine and refinery, Valenciana complex, Guanajuato, eighteenth century.

Valladolid, and San Luis Potosí, all centers of resistance in 1767. Querétaro, loyal throughout, remained subject to Mexico City.

Gálvez imagined the new officials as agents of the regime in resistant provinces; intendants soon learned that the way to effective rule was cooperation with provincial entrepreneurs. Guanajuato's first intendant, the military engineer don Andrés Amat, took office in 1787 as Valenciana boomed. He knew that his role was to promote mining. With the new tax on consumption taking over 21,000 pesos yearly for social control, he joined Guanajuato's council in efforts to regulate and police the populace. They bought a clock in London and installed it on the parish church to time city life. Led by don Vicente Alamán, operator of the Mellado mine (and father of don Lucas Alamán, the politician and historian of the independence era), they built a poorhouse to contain the indigent and a jail to restrain the criminal.[13]

Gálvez died in 1787, soon after appointing the first intendants. After his passing, cooperation with American elites became policy. Early in 1789 the second Conde de Revillagigedo was appointed viceroy. While he was still in Madrid confidential orders instructed him to create new militias, strengthen Spanish power from Texas to California, review the intendants, and raise revenues while reducing the costs of administration and collection. Revillagigedo wrote a thoughtful response, showing a clear understanding of the prospects of Spanish power in New Spain at a historic juncture—after the independence of the United States and before revolution in France and Haiti began decades of war and social conflict.

In April 1789 the viceroy-elect worried about keeping New Spain a kingdom of Spain. Drawing a key lesson from the independence of British North America, he wrote: "Our arms, even backed by European allies, are not capable of returning New Spain to the king should it throw off its yoke by a general and effective rebellion. And no foreign power is capable of conquering it without the agreement and assistance of the people of the land." Recognizing the power of New Spain's elites, the essential policy was clear: "hold them by illusion and love." New Spain's entrepreneurs had to see their interests as tied to Spanish rule. He emphasized the late Gálvez's error: "the late Minister pressed means completely contrary to these ideas; as a result, he completely exasperated the hearts of the people born in the colony." Gálvez denied office and honor to New Spain's elites, and did so as proud public policy. Revillagigedo insisted that if such exclusions were needed, they should be implemented quietly and without announcement.

Revillagigedo worried about statements attributed to Thomas Jefferson, the United States minister in Paris, which showed a clear understanding of the alienation set off by Gálvez's impositions. In Jefferson's reported view, "the English imagine taking advantage of such disaffection, of the complaints of the Americans, which would bring an imminent danger of losing New Spain." To Revillagigedo and to Jefferson, Gálvez's blunt demands and harsh repressions did not strengthen Spanish rule in New Spain; they threatened it.

Revillagigedo offered solutions. Trade between New Spain and the remaining British colonies should end. Most important, the regime should inspire affection for Spanish rule by promoting "ties of family and interest with Spain" and by creating new militias "in which we surely can employ most of the men of distinction and great wealth in New Spain; as everywhere, it is they who set the tone for the low majority." The goal of strong alliances with American elites made policy of what Gálvez learned reluctantly in harsh conflicts. The essence of colonial rule was an alliance of interest linking the regime and leading colonials.[14] What Gálvez recognized by necessity, and what the great families of Mexico City pursued by interest, Revillagigedo made policy.

In 1790, soon after taking office in Mexico City, Revillagigedo sent a trusted aide to report on Guanajuato. Don Francisco Antonio Mourelle was born in Galicia and served as a naval officer, twice in expeditions to California, once helping to open a new route from San Blas on the Pacific coast of New Spain to Manila (Asian trade still mat-

Workers' entrance, Valenciana mine, Guanajuato, eighteenth century.

tered).[15] Mourelle's report helped shape policies toward Guanajuato and mining for decades. It offers a sharp portrait of power, production, and labor. Arriving in November 1790, Mourelle recoiled at the cramped disorder of the city in the canyon. Lodged in the comfortable home of the councilman don Francisco Marañón, he was invited the next morning by don Antonio de Obregón, Conde de la Valenciana, to explore the depths of the mine that generated so much wealth. The workers' lives shocked Mourelle. He saw "living barbarians who with iron bars, picks, shovels, blasting powder, and other tools penetrate solid rock." He lamented "the sad lives of those living skeletons."[16] Yet he was awed by the six huge whims that raised sacks of ore by day and drew water by night, so that the world's richest mines would not flood.[17]

Moving beyond stark impressions to labor conditions, Mourelle's tone changed little. He saw carriers hauling heavy loads of ore in dark, wet tunnels, up difficult ladders, to platforms where it was loaded and raised by whims. He saw "a degradation of rational men, who carry mineral rock on their shoulders, as if less than beasts." He spoke to "a boy of nine or ten (and not very robust)" who had carried four loads totaling twenty-four arrobas since five in the morning. It was noon, and the boy expected to carry two, perhaps three more loads by the end of his shift at 5:00 p.m. His best effort might earn him three or four reales for a day of backbreaking, potentially deadly labor.[18] That was much more than he might earn from rural day labor, but he faced incalculably greater risks.

The pickmen who blasted and broke rock earned nine reales for a day of hard and risky labor. The pay seemed ample, but Mourelle noted the recent "abolition of *partidos*, followed by a continuous reduction of wages." To preserve its boom and profits in the 1780s the Valenciana had followed the lead set at Rayas and ended ore shares. Mourelle did not know that out of the nine-real wage, pickmen had to buy tools and powder, leaving them with little more than the boys who carried ore. He did learn that the pickmen resented the assault on their independence and earnings. The Valenciana aimed to employ eight hundred workers for every day shift, another eight hundred each night. But only five hundred would currently "go below to waste their lives"; to recruit them "it is often necessary to use the arm of justice to oblige them to enter the mine." The practice, unique to Valenciana, he emphasized, was "a roundup" to force the old, the infirm, and the reluctant underground.[19] While the Valenciana partners cut workers' earnings, the authorities operated as silent partners, dragging workers to the mines.

Mourelle reported that Valenciana annually paid 500,000 pesos in wages, enabling the partners to take 1,000,000 pesos in yearly profits. The workers who blasted, dug, and carried the ore were "the sad victims of greed." Yet his clear vision did not prevent Mourelle from exiting the mine to join a "splendid dinner" with the avaricious partners, and then describing with admiration a new shaft with equally impressive whims—soon to demand the labors of new victims.[20]

Mourelle stayed positive when he noted the "many women who alone are skilled in separating grades of ore, and the others who use hammers to break ore-bearing rocks until they are the size of oranges; they show admirable knowledge distinguishing ore qualities." The mines could not profit without "the laboring women whose efforts make them intelligent in their work."[21] Angered at the degradation and declining earnings of the men and boys who labored underground, Mourelle admired the skilled women who broke and sorted ores in daylight. He knew that declining incomes and deadly conditions threatened working men, inhibited patriarchal households, and contributed to a raucous city. He had no problem with women serving as skilled wageworkers, laboring for cash outside patriarchal households.

Expressing horror at men's degradation underground and admiration for women's contributions, Mourelle knew no alternative but to promote the industry. He saw its global importance with clarity.

"Given the social ways, commerce, and industry to which Europeans have brought us, we cannot take our eyes from these springs [of wealth] that sustain the immense circulation that ultimately flows to bury itself in eastern Asia. There is no option but for the state to provide all possible support to energize them, respect them, and provide them every assistance—despite appeals to the creator [about inhuman conditions]. The decadence [of the mines] would be a mortal wound to all of Europe."[22] Mourelle would not hide the horrors of mine labor; he would not deny falling wages and local coercions. He simply knew that such unconscionable conditions were both consequence and sustenance of the silver trade that fueled Atlantic commerce, European industry, and Chinese wealth. The world of power could not let mining decline at Guanajuato. Despite the horrors of men's and boys' labors underground, despite the threat to patriarchy inherent in women's wage labor, all were essential to feed the avarice of the Valenciana partners and to sustain the regime's revenues, the Atlantic economy, and global trade.

Mourelle saw two problems threatening silver mining: uncertain mercury and scarce timber. Scarce and expensive mercury limited production to the best ores and most efficient enterprises. More and cheaper mercury would allow expansion. He reported an offer to trade California sealskins for Chinese mercury, a trade that the Chinese had refused.[23] Mourelle did not raise the possibility that the Chinese might accept a direct trade of mercury for silver, knowing that such a diversion was unimaginable to a regime insistent on drawing maximum revenues and trade toward Spain and Europe. The problem of mercury would not find a solution soon.

More local, and thus more open to remedy, was the problem of timber. "The scarcity of wood is constantly worsening, and it seems to me that this problem alone will make the ores now being mined too expensive to refine; the forests are now stripped by excessive cutting, . . . and new planting is not imagined by men who think only of their own lives, taking advantage now and leaving their descendants nothing. Thus everything runs toward a rapid destruction." Guanajuato, an engine of eighteenth-century capitalism, faced environmental challenges. Mourelle's solution was to appoint "forest magistrates" to promote reforestation and punish those who cut outside designated areas. Yet he insisted on careful oversight of new officials; otherwise "they will enrich themselves and the mines will quickly decline."[24] Mourelle dealt in contradiction and paradox: imposed misery sustained global wealth; the avarice of entrepreneurs deserved cultivation; the avarice of forest guards (like that of workers) threatened silver production and must be contained.

To conclude, Mourelle returned to his dark vision of Guanajuato: "The population is irregular, growing and declining with the bonanzas of the mines." There could be no stable households, no stable patriarchal families; young people came from elsewhere, labored while they could, and then left "when their health lost, the works will not longer employ them."[25] Ultimately everything was wrong in the great mining city, except silver production: "the dark windows and doors on the fronts of houses; the imperfect and small plazas, the narrow tortuous streets; the small houses of even the rich, low in height because they back up against the hills—ultimately a total chaos in setting buildings, because the land permits no symmetry."[26] Silver mining had to thrive for reasons of state and global wealth; the city and society that it forged at Guanajuato were dark and destructive, disordered, and almost hopeless.

The mine operator Domínguez, writing in 1774, and the imperial inspector Mourelle, visiting in 1790, both emphasized that silver was essential to the Spanish monarchy and the world economy, and that it imposed unconscionable burdens on the workers who produced it. Neither portrayed the working populace of Guanajuato in the tones of ethnic denigration that characterized descriptions by powerful locals and visitors into the 1760s. The worries about who was mulatto or indio, both labels laden with negative characteristics, seem gone. During the late-century boom workers became men, women, and boys; debate focused on remuneration and working conditions.

Despite Gálvez's demand for a sharpening of ethnic identities and segregation, censuses from the early 1790s confirm that Guanajuato continued its course of ethnic fluidity and changing identities. A population that had been mostly mulatto in 1755 generated a majority classed as Spanish in 1790. Even among mineworkers mulattoes had declined to 40 percent, outnumbered by Spaniards and a growing group of mestizos. Indios were fewer than 15 percent (showing the continued demise of the category that Gálvez hoped would mark and contain the rowdy populace); 90 percent were born in the city or its jurisdiction, so the changes did not result from migration. Ethnic status still mattered. But the workers who sustained the global economy were becoming Spanish, escaping the tributes that marked colonial subordination even as they struggled to negotiate deadly labor relations.[27]

The second intendant of Guanajuato was don Juan Antonio de Riaño, like Mourelle a naval officer. He joined an expedition to Pensacola, delivering aid (mostly from New Spain) to those fighting for independence for the United States. In New Orleans he wed one of three Maxent sisters; the others married don Bernardo de Gálvez, nephew of don José de Gálvez and soon viceroy in New Spain, and don Manuel de

Flon, the long-serving intendant at Puebla.[28] After a stint as intendant at Valladolid, Riaño moved to Guanajuato in 1792—a Gálvez family loyalist ready to join Revillagigedo in promoting conciliatory relations with New Spain's pivotal entrepreneurs.

Riaño took office in Guanajuato while the Valenciana partners focused on preserving their bonanza and profits by cutting workers' earning. The intendant followed Mourelle's advice and backed the men who ruled mining. In the 1780s Gálvez sanctioned a mining deputation, granting corporate organization to key entrepreneurs. Soon after taking office Riaño abolished guild rights among Guanajuato's artisans—granting, he insisted, all workers the freedom to work. The regime gave entrepreneurs in Guanajuato the means to organize their interests while denying producers the right to do the same. Workers got the freedom to compete for dangerous work in the face of organized entrepreneurs backed by state power.

Riaño also strengthened the forces of social control. He argued that workers should have the freedom to work, never freedom from work: "The only active commerce that sustains the city is mining, and its employees are by sad necessity rootless people, lacking political education and without Christian learning; this opens them to every vice."[29] The danger and insecurity of mine work created a floating population, rarely able to forge patriarchal family relations. Disorder, irreligion, and vice were inevitable, Riaño asserted. The solution was no longer Jesuit preaching; effective policing was the order of enlightened times. Riaño appointed eleven ward magistrates recruited among city elites, including don Vicente Alamán and don Francisco de Septién, to oversee regular armed patrols. To "conserve good order" the new magistrates were to make census lists; to keep market activity in open plazas and prevent drinking and gaming nearby; to identify vagrants, male and female, and insist that they find work or face jail; and to open schools for all children. The plan began with surveillance and coercion, with but a promise of education.

Resources focused on coercion. Riaño increased armed patrols from forty-six to sixty-three men, announcing their presence with new uniforms. Schools for the poor remained a promise unfulfilled. Riaño saw his efforts to police the working populace a clear success. A city once "restive and insubordinate" was "now docile and obedient." An anonymous complaint to Revillagigedo concluded that Riaño "did not want to hear the petitions brought him by the poor." Not only did Riaño join Guanajuato entrepreneurs to enforce power, he ended the tradition of magistrates hearing popular complaints and mediating solutions to keep the peace. Social order became a matter for police.[30]

Riaño helped the Valenciana partners and others sustain production, profits, and state revenues by controlling workers and limiting their earnings. Valenciana resisted partidos and held pickmen's wages at eight to nine reales daily, still requiring that they buy tools and blasting powder. Workers shared the costs and risks of mining, gaining wages for their efforts. The dearth of workers reported by Mourelle was surmounted slowly. With Rayas flooded, alternative work was limited. Mourelle reported in 1790 that Rayas employed only 189 workers, just enough to hold his claim, while allowing 50 adult scavengers (*buscones*) and 50 boys (*zorros*) to take what they could, dividing the ore with Rayas in a reverse partido.[31] Facing limited alternatives and new controls, workers returned to Valenciana. By 1803 pickmen's wages had risen to ten reales daily—the cost of bringing them back. They remained without partidos and still bought their own candles, picks, and powder.[32]

Having helped Guanajuato entrepreneurs contain workers and reduce their earnings, Riaño turned to the problem of timber. With mountains stripped for five leagues (about fifteen miles) around, Riaño prohibited all forest use other than for mining. Anyone who sent goats to graze in woodlands faced fines that increased with each offense, the proceeds shared with those who reported the offense. Tanners who took bark essential to their craft would be whipped, lashes increasing with each offense. Trees could be cut at the trunk only for mining. Firewood and the green limbs used for charcoal could be taken only from fallen branches and trunks already cut for mining. And no maize could be planted in the forests: new clearings destroyed growing trees; planting in old clearings inhibited new forests.[33]

Riaño's forest policy aimed to preserve timber, promote new growth, and keep wood available and affordable to the mining industry. It prohibited and criminalized activities that sustained working families in and near Guanajuato. Tanners had to seek bark elsewhere; herders had to graze goats farther out; men and women who gathered firewood and made charcoal to sell to miners and urban consumers faced new obstacles; those who would plant a patch of maize in highland clearings found the pursuit of sustenance on public land illegal. Again, policies to promote mining and regime revenues prejudiced the majority.

When Alexander von Humboldt visited Guanajuato in 1803, pickmen's lives remained at risk: "The work that destroys the strongest constitutions most quickly is that of the pickmen who break solid rock with blasting powder; they rarely live past thirty-five years, . . . It is common that they do the job for only five or six years, and then turn to occupations less prejudicial to their health."[34] Yet many took on this damaging labor, thanks to earnings far higher than regional norms, and to Riaño's police and other controls that blocked any negotiation of pay or working conditions. The same year, the intendant reported that Valenciana employed just over 3,000 workers, excluding managers and overseers; 684 pick and blast men gained the top wage of 10 reales daily; 680 haulers earned 6 to 8 reales to carry ore to the whims. Another 266 men gained 5 to 6 reales to care for whims and other machinery and to classify ores as they emerged. And 775 men and boys got only 4 reales daily to perform less demanding tasks. In addition, 720 women labored to separate and classify ores for only 3 reales daily. The skilled women so admired by Mourelle gained wages lower than the least skilled boys. Breaking patriarchal custom brought real savings to Guanajuato entrepreneurs. The result of the alliance of Riaño and the silver magnates was "a decisive fall in both the earnings and the status of the mineworkers of Guanajuato."[35]

The alliance for power and production, organized by Riaño, the city council, and the mining deputation, kept mines profitable and workers underground in the face of danger and declining rewards. Silver production and revenues remained high through the first decade of the nineteenth century. Still, problems emerged. From 1793 wartime disruptions of Atlantic trade kept mercury supplies uncertain; mining production and employment faced uncertainties beyond local control. Overall output held after 1800, but yearly and monthly fluctuations increased, making insecurity a constant companion of magnates' prosperity and workers' survival. As old mines drove deeper underground, the demand for labor increased. Shrinking profit margins focused mine operators ever more on controlling workers' earnings.

During a downturn in 1806 Riaño lamented "the dismay around the mines due to the many workers out of work, the gathering of delinquents finding refuge in rugged uplands, the deserters from the battalion, and the prisoners who have escaped the jail at Irapuato." Years of effort had not created the city of order he imagined. Militiamen did not always serve their betters; jails did not always hold their inmates; forests remained refuges for the indigent. Riaño's proposed solution: thirty-one more patrolmen.[36]

The mines of Guanajuato, Zacatecas, and other silver cities sustained the wealth of New Spain and the power of Spain from the late sixteenth century to the early nineteenth. The workers who mined and refined that silver long enjoyed freedom and high earnings, including ore shares, while laboring in the face of deadly dangers. The alliance of Bourbon reformers and Guanajuato entrepreneurs limited mineworkers' liberties, cut their earnings, and ended partidos, while danger persisted and insecurity proliferated. In towns of boom and bust, wealth and danger, family life had always been less settled and less structured by patriarchal ideals than elsewhere in the Bajío. Around 1800 women were nearly a quarter of the workforce at Guanajuato, laboring outside households for the lowest local wages.

Capitalism flourished in the mining city around 1800. Entrepreneurs backed by the state took windfall profits; the working majority faced the loss of partidos and declining earnings, enduring danger underground and in refineries while employers drew a growing number of women into the labor force—challenging patriarchy and prevailing wage rates. Guanajuato's workers, male and female, paid in risk and insecurity for the boom that sustained the Bajío, New Spain, Spain, and Atlantic trade. A growing number claimed Spanish status and wages held high by regional standards. While the regime and the bonanza held, so did production and polarization at Guanajuato.

The Bajío Economy in the Age of Silver and Free Trade

Guanajuato silver stimulated regional production and trade. Silver production doubled from a mid-century low around 1760 to the late 1770s, dipped in the face of famine in the 1780s, then rose to unprecedented heights in the 1790s, remaining at near historic highs until 1810.[37] Regional commerce grew at a parallel pace, though its increase at Guanajuato lagged because of downward pressure on workers' earnings.[38] Economic expansion did not come automatically. Demographic growth brought expanding markets and populations available to labor, but that growth was sharply curtailed in the famine crisis of 1785 and 1786. When it resumed in the 1790s Atlantic trade faced the disruptive wars of the French revolution, conflicts that persisted with brief interruptions after 1800. From the 1780s the Bajío textile industry faced new pressures. The regime pursued *comercio libre*—free trade within the empire. Reformers favored Iberian cloth production and exports; Bajío manufacturers had to cut costs or lose market share.

Silver boom and population growth drove commercial expansion with little interruption from the late 1760s to the mid-1780s. Then population took a sudden plunge, followed by free trade that challenged cloth makers. When population growth resumed in the 1790s war disrupted Atlantic trade, offering new protections to Bajío textile producers while bringing distortions to the larger Atlantic economy. The sum of all these challenges was that silver held strong and the regional economy soared, but many working families struggled, with notably different trajectories of expansion (or decline) and levels of popular welfare in different zones of the Bajío.

The region's cloth industry had grown to a peak in the middle of the eighteenth century. At San Miguel four large obrajes operated sixty-five looms in 1759. At Querétaro from the 1740s to the 1770s, twenty-five to thirty obrajes worked 250 or more looms. And the obrajes were the core of a larger industry. Large workshops put wool out for spinning to uncounted women and men in rural households while they competed with uncounted numbers of household weavers in cities, villages, and estate communities.

In the 1770s the obrajes faced new pressures. The Bajío countryside completed its historic shift from grazing to cultivation, driving sheep ever farther north. The cost of wool to Querétaro shot up. An arroba that cost seventeen to nineteen reales in September 1778 required twenty to twenty-four reales in May 1779. During the drought, frost, and famine years of 1785 and 1786 sheep could not travel; they died in unprecedented numbers across the north. Wool rose to new peaks; for a time it was not available at any price. During the 1790s and early 1800s an arroba reached twenty-four to twenty-eight reales and peaked at thirty-two to forty-three reales as drought began again in 1809. Wool prices rose 30 percent—excluding drought years when they spiked even higher.[39]

Rising wool prices might have been a cost passed on to consumers, but the 1770s also brought new competition from imported cloth. The Catalan region of Spain was joining the industrial revolution in textiles. From the 1740s cotton production expanded around Barcelona. By the 1780s it concentrated in factories using water power to drive machinery imported from England and France. The regime favored Catalan exports, aiming to draw silver to Spain. In 1780 cloth shipped from Spain to New Spain was exempted from taxes; in 1789 free trade in the empire legalized direct shipments from Barcelona to Veracruz.[40]

The first ship from Barcelona landed at Veracruz in 1785. Arrivals averaged nine a year from 1786 to 1788, rose to sixteen with legalization in 1789, and peaked at twenty-five in 1793. Rising imports challenged cloth makers in the Bajío just as they struggled to recover from the famine of 1785 and 1786. War cut landings to eighteen by 1794, then to fourteen in 1795; imports were depressed from 1794 to 1801, until the Peace of Amiens allowed a flood in 1802, exceeding the previous six years combined. Imports rose in 1803 and 1804, only to fall again in 1805 and 1806. Then 1807 brought another surge, often in neutral ships from the United States. A decline in 1808 proved brief: Napoleon's occupation of Spain brought British ships to New Spain in 1809 and 1810—ships carrying another flood of cloth.[41] The late Bourbon era brought two phases to the Bajío textile industry. From the 1770s to the early 1790s rising wool prices and Catalan imports set high costs and low market prices. Then after 1793 trade blockages and market protections mixed unpredictably with peace, open trade, and floods of imports.

The industry survived rising wool costs and the Catalan threat; it expanded and at times flourished after 1793. And it did both mostly by forcing declining earnings and new insecurities onto the people who made cloth. Faced with rising wool prices and new import competition from the 1770s, the industry had to cut costs. Obrajes had high fixed costs: large buildings, many looms, and permanent workers, some purchased and maintained as slaves, others obligated by advance payments. In 1759 four obrajes worked sixty-five looms at San Miguel; by 1793 only one survived, working seventeen looms. At Querétaro in the 1770s twenty-five to thirty obrajes operated over 250 looms. In the early 1780s twenty workshops still worked 225 looms. Then decline accelerated; in 1791 thirteen obrajes worked but 153 looms.[42] Cutting costs, often by seeking less expensive labor, the obrajes declined—but did not disappear.[43]

Meanwhile the industry turned to household production, a tradition introduced to the Bajío by early Otomí settlers and taken up by mulattoes and mestizos over the centuries. For a long time they were little taxed and rarely counted. In the face of growing cloth imports, household weaving expanded and officials worked to tax it, while Catalan exports were free of taxation. *Trapicheros*, household weavers, remained active in the old woolen centers while obrajes declined. In 1793 at San Miguel one obraje worked only seventeen looms, while 122 looms made woolens in household shops and another fifty-three wove cotton. The same year at Querétaro 181 looms worked in obrajes while 405 household looms wove woolens and another 183 made cotton goods. Household looms were narrow and household production was irregular. Still, after decades of rising wool prices and competition from imports, the household sector probably exceeded obraje output in the old obraje cities.[44]

Elsewhere in the Bajío household weaving expanded, focused on cotton, and far exceeded obraje production.[45] At Acámbaro obraje and household production expanded together. In 1779 eight obrajes worked seventy-one looms; in 1793 ten worked 141 looms—growth in the face of rising wool costs and Catalan imports. Labor costs must have been lower there. In the same years household woolen looms increased from 123 to 137; those making cottons jumped from 142 to 203. At León cloth making concentrated in households. In 1783 cotton looms outnumbered those making woolens, 242 to 108. By 1793 cotton looms had fallen to 187 while woolen looms doubled to 208—perhaps reflecting León's northwest location, nearer to grazing lands. Meanwhile by 1793 new concentrations of family weavers made cotton cloth at Celaya (508 looms), Salamanca (120 looms), San Luis de la Paz (119 looms), and Irapuato and Silao (together 117 looms). Across the Bajío, household cotton production expanded in direct competition with imports.

The sector grew by pressing declining earnings on struggling families. Householders were rarely independent; most labored under merchant-clothiers. Women in rural households spun wool into yarn to supply obraje weavers, sometimes for cash, sometimes for yarn shares. Some household weavers received raw cotton and combined spinning and weaving. Others received yarn made by household spinners and focused on weaving. Often they took fiber or yarn in exchange for delivering a set amount of cloth. The material was sufficient to make that cloth, and more to weave and sell on their own. Merchant-clothiers who controlled supplies of raw cotton along with spinning and weaving got cloth at little cost beyond raw materials. Market uncertainties plagued householders.

Then in 1793 war interrupted transatlantic commerce, cutting cloth imports. While silver production remained vigorous and population was growing again after the dying of 1785 and 1786, Bajío cloth makers regained markets. Querétaro obrajes increased production: sixteen operated 181 looms there in April 1793; by September seventeen worked 227 looms. With brief declines during trade openings in 1796 and 1800, obraje production remained robust at Querétaro into 1802.[46] The household sector also expanded at Querétaro after 1793. About five hundred family looms wove that year. In 1801, at the peak of the boom, Corregidor don Miguel Domínguez reported nearly a thousand looms in *trapiches*. But wartime protection did not last. The Peace of Amiens in 1802 set off a flood of imports that lasted over two years; a report from 1803 suggested that only 650 household looms worked during the peace that brought new imports.[47] In two years production dropped by a third. Then another trade blockage brought new protection to Bajío producers, until another flood of imports surged in 1809.

The silver boom and free trade in textiles affected Bajío cites and towns differently. In the early 1780s Guanajuato maintained the greatest commercial activity, over 1,770,000 pesos yearly, and the highest per capita trade, twenty-seven pesos, over twice the regional average. After 1800 the silver city still led both categories, but total commerce had barely increased and per capita trade had fallen to twenty-four pesos. The downward pressures on worker earnings had consequences. In contrast to Guanajuato, Celaya, San Miguel, and León were towns of crafts and trade, surrounded by agricultural hinterlands. In the 1780s their combined yearly commerce of 2,074,000 pesos exceeded the mining center, but per capita commerce held between six and eight pesos. After 1800 their total commerce averaged 2,340,000 pesos yearly; per capita commerce took divergent trends, with San Miguel falling to near five pesos, Celaya falling slightly to just under eight pesos, and León rising to nearly nine pesos—a gain of 42 percent since the early 1780s. While total and per capita trade fell at San Miguel, they soared at León. Proximity to booming Guanajuato brought commercial advantage.[48]

Querétaro was neither as rich as Guanajuato nor as poor as Celaya, San Miguel, and León. The city of Otomí and Spaniards, cloth makers and huertas, was surrounded by rich, often irrigated estates. In the early 1780s its total commerce was 1,232,000 pesos yearly, its per capita trade over 15 pesos. After 1800 commerce averaged 1,611,000 annually, approaching the level of Guanajuato. And per capita trade was nearly eighteen pesos, twice the level at León. Guanajuato and León combined as an integrated zone, mixing the silver city with the craft town and commercial estates just west. Together their per capita commerce fell slightly from 17.5 in the early 1780s to 17 pesos after 1800. In the first decade of the nineteenth century the city of trade, textiles, and tobacco (as we shall see) at Querétaro and its commercial countryside attained a per capita level of commerce just above that of Guanajuato and León combined. Querétaro lived the most dynamic growth of any zone of the Bajío after 1780; San Miguel faced the sharpest decline.

San Miguel: Monopoly Power and Economic Decline

The textile economy at San Miguel did not do well in the era of silver boom and free trade. León, with similar resources but closer to Guanajuato, took its place in the regional economy. Economic decline, however, did not limit the power of the Canal clan. Canal, Lanzagorta, and Landeta patriarchs tapped Bourbon policies to consolidate local rule. The industrial rise of San Miguel el Grande peaked near the middle of the eighteenth century. A few families then led a city of cloth, cutlery, and leather production; obrajes mixed with household workshops. Entrepreneurial oligarchs developed estates to supply wool and hides; they controlled production in obrajes and by putting-out; they focused on growing markets at Zacatecas and Guanajuato. Flush with wealth, power, and confidence, they sponsored the spiritual awakening that led to the penitential sanctuary at Atotonilco.

Then in the late 1750s San Miguel's patriarchs went to war among themselves. The Canals charged the Sautos with unconscionable exploitations that led to murders in the Sauto obraje. Inquests followed; the Sauto obraje declined; the Canals and their allies stood dominant; and industry at San Miguel declined. The war between the patriarchs shook the local economy in the 1760s, years of recession. When Guanajuato's markets revived in the 1770s they were increasingly supplied by León. The Valenciana partners and their allies invested there. León boomed from the 1770s, enabling the Obregóns and their allies to integrate mining, estate operations, and financial control of growing cloth production.[49] León's rise confirmed San Miguel's demise. In 1777 a visitor saw "obrajes without workers, looms that are not working, while the streets are flooded with vagabonds." He blamed scarce wool and "the insubordination and libertine ways of a town . . . abandoned to vice."[50] The visitor likely learned to blame workers from local entrepreneurs, who were unlikely to attribute economic decline to their own conflicts and competitive failures. In 1783 León had 350 working looms—nearly twice those at San Miguel in the early 1790s.

A municipal budget from the late 1780s shows a town struggling to be modern and manage deep divisions.[51] Most income came from the new taxes on maize and wheat consumption. But 40 percent came from permits for bullfights, public spectacles organized by the city's indigenous community. The plaza became an arena, and indio men fought bulls for audiences of all classes; the Canals could watch from their balconies. Town authority was funded by popular consumption, and by spectacles in which indios risked life in the Spanish sport of manhood. Revenue came from regressive taxes and rituals of inversion that allowed poor men brief and dangerous public moments of patriarchal assertion. When officials in Mexico City argued that bullfights brought only disruption and excess, the San Miguel council insisted that they continue. They brought revenue—and kept the peace.

Town expenditures were also revealing. The largest outlays went to oversee food sales and tax collection. While profiting from the unruly violence of bullfights, the council promoted order with a public clock, a militia, and public works. It contributed little to religious festivals and processions. As we will explore in detail in chapter 8, San Miguel had become a center of enlightened religion; rational action and sacramental devotion shaped the religious culture of elites there in the 1780s. In that spirit the patriarchs of San Miguel aimed to rule a city in decline by providing and taxing essential staples, promoting and taxing festivals of inversion, and keeping time—with militia forces always in reserve.

The militia census of 1792 documented the enduring power of the Canal, Landeta, and Lanzagorta families, and the secondary role of the Sautos. Don Juan María de Lanzagorta owned three haciendas near

San Miguel; his brother don José held another north at Dolores. The Landetas, titled as Condes de la Casa Loja, faced nagging debts yet had two estates at San Miguel and one north at San Felipe. The Canals towered over the local establishment: the patriarch, don José Mariano, held five haciendas around San Miguel and Dolores; kin owned three more.[52] Married among themselves, and with the powerful Septién and Primo y Jordán clan of Querétaro, the three families, with fifteen estates, ruled uncontested at San Miguel.

In contrast, don José Manuel Sauto held three estates and doña María Sauto one more. With four haciendas the Sautos were far from poor.[53] But they could not compete with the Canal establishment—nor could anyone else at San Miguel. Don Domingo Allende was an immigrant entrepreneur, seeking like so many before him to trade, buy estates, and take a place in the elite. In 1792 he owned the Manantiales property. He kept ties to other local gentry, including doña María Micaela de Arenaza, one of the "Arenaza heirs" who owned Puerto de Sosa (near Puerto de Nieto). The trader Allende and the widow Arenaza lived comfortably at San Miguel, in the shadows of the Canal clan.

When Viceroys Revillagigedo and Branciforte turned to strengthen provincial militias, the San Miguel establishment saw opportunity. They proposed a new unit: "the existence of the regiment will finally assure the tranquility of this jurisdiction, so recently disrupted by the lowest class of people who live all around."[54] Apparently the clock, food controls, and rituals of inversion were not checking social ferment.

The regime agreed and the Regimento de la Reina, the Queen's Regiment, was founded in 1794. The viceroy would choose the highest officers, a colonel and lieutenant colonel; the San Miguel council would name captains and lieutenants. Ultimately finances ruled appointments. The San Miguel elite raised over 42,000 pesos; more than 37,000 came from the Canal, Landeta, and Lanzagorta clan. Don Narciso María de la Canal, heir to the patriarch, gave 24,000 pesos; his cousin don Juan María de Lanzagorta gave over 5,600 pesos; their kin combined to give another 7,300 pesos. No other contribution exceeded 1,000 pesos. The heirs of don Domingo de Allende mustered 250 pesos; don José Manuel de Sauto 200 pesos; don Ignacio de Aldama but 100 pesos.[55] The collection to fund San Miguel's militia revealed a sharply stratified elite.

Canal money shaped command. The viceroy named don Narciso María de la Canal regimental colonel and commander of the First Company in San Miguel. Don Juan María de Lanzagorta became lieutenant colonel, leading the Third Company at San Felipe. Five more Canals were captains, placing seven of twelve companies under family command. The Allendes provided four officers: three sons of don Domingo and an Unzaga cousin. One was a company commander, the rest lieutenants under Canal superiors. Two Lámbarris, trading newcomers like the Allendes, also became lieutenants—one under a Canal, the other under an Allende. Don José Manuel de Sauto captained a company at Dolores.[56]

The creation of the militia regiment revealed a provincial elite dominated by the Canal family. The wealth concentrated among the few and the small resources held by men with lesser commands help to explain ongoing conflicts at La Purísima, the convent founded by a Canal daughter, still managed by the Canal patriarch don José Mariano, still struggling with scarce funds and internal spats. Outside the dominant clan few among the local gentry had the wealth to send daughters with dowries to the convent. The money that gained militia commands might have solved the convent's financial needs. Canal patriarchs instead allowed the convent that housed their sisters to remain a place where women lived enclosed and in conflict, struggled with scarce funds, and debated ways of life and devotion. Militia command mattered; their sisters would be honored, contained, and barely sustained.[57]

Penitential devotions had focused religious legitimations at San Miguel during the economic expansion that culminated in the 1750s. After the war between the patriarchs shook local society, followed by the popular risings all around in the 1760s, times of economic decline led to a new focus on rational worship and social coercion. Urban magistrates and regional militias did not create a state monopoly of violence, however. They reinforced coalitions of powerful locals and regime officials, resetting the alliance that crushed the risings of 1767.

The Canals dominated San Miguel. Still, they were provincials, living after 1770 in the shadow of patriarchs in Mexico City. The Mariscales de Castilla still ruled seven huge estates from San Miguel north to Dolores and beyond. The Jaral properties dominated the country from San Felipe north. And don José Sánchez Espinosa's Puerto de Nieto was the largest, most populous estate near San Miguel. When the Canals organized the regiment in 1794 they taxed the local holdings of landlords in Mexico City. They took eighty-two horses from their own properties—24 percent. They claimed ninety-two from Mexico City landlords—27 percent. The largest assessments recognized the landed power of outsiders: twenty-five horses from the Mariscal de Castilla, twenty-four from the Marqués de Jaral, twelve from Sánchez Espinosa's Puerto de Nieto. That left half to be taken from local gentry. The Canals all but monopolized the provision of cash to fund the militia and claim command. They used command and council rule to assess Mexico City patriarchs and lesser San Miguel, Dolores, and San Felipe landlords for three-quarters of the regiment's horses.

They did not rule uncontested. Don José Sánchez Espinosa's correspondence offers rare insight into often testy relations between a powerful patriarch in Mexico City and leading provincials at San Miguel. A long conflict with the Landetas, Condes de la Casa Loja, set the tone. In the 1750s don Franciso de Espinosa y Navarijo claimed vast lands in San Luis Potosí, the Agostadero de Ordóñez. Casa Loja asserted prior title, beginning a suit that lasted half a century. The land became more valuable as mining boomed at Guadalcázar and Catorce, driving commercial development north. The suit was pending when don José became patriarch; he took the case to the Council of the Indies in Spain and won in 1788. Don José prevailed in a transatlantic justice system. The Landetas disputed control on the ground until 1808.[58] Relations between Sánchez Espinosa and the Canals remained sour.

Don José tried to limit the conflict by selling small amounts of maize locally through the Canals in 1786 and 1793. In 1797 he leased a rancho at Puerto de Nieto to don José Landeta, but the deal proved so contentious that Sánchez Espinosa ended it in the following year.[59] The Landetas and Sánchez Espinosa disputed the power to profit from northward expansion. Sánchez Espinosa triumphed, limiting the provincials' access to grazing lands as flocks moved north. Did that also limit the woolen industry at San Miguel, while Sánchez Espinosa sold huge clips of wool in Querétaro, which continued to flourish?

While in conflict with the leading San Miguel patriarchs, Sánchez Espinosa kept ties with less prominent members of the provincial elite, mostly officials and men on the rise. In the 1780s he leased land at Puerto de Nieto to don Domingo Allende and provided pasture and sheep to don Francisco López Cruz, holder of the abasto contract at San Miguel. The latter business became testy when don José's lambs were found among López's flocks. Yet with a dependent, conflict led to negotiation, and López remained at Puerto de Nieto in the 1790s.[60] Don Manuel Lámbarri leased land at Puerto de Nieto in 1792. The next year don Domingo Lámbarri leased pasture at Sánchez Espinosa's estates in San Luis Potosí. In 1799 don Pedro José de Lámbarri rented pasture at Puerto de Nieto, with a mandate to build a fence so that his sheep would not mix with estate flocks.[61] Immigrant traders and subordinate militia officers without extensive lands, the Lámbarris worked to build a livestock trade. They had to pay rent to don José Sánchez Espinosa.

In 1804 don Domingo Lámbarri won the San Miguel abasto, surely with approval of the Canal men who ruled the council. Lámbarri leased land and built a slaughterhouse at Puerto de Nieto, paying 12,655 pesos yearly for land and lambs. Lámbarri and Sánchez Espinosa were unequal partners in a business that the Canal patriarchs would never allow to their foe in Mexico City. Lámbarri dealt between dueling patriarchs; Sánchez Espinosa profited with little risk. The business lasted into 1808, when Sánchez Espinosa decided that he did not earn enough, and that Lámbarri was not deferential enough. Don José ended the lease and left the provincial with a contract that he struggled to fulfill.[62]

In the early 1800s Sánchez Espinosa forged connections to regime officials at San Miguel. Until 1802 Don Francisco Viera was Subdelegado (district magistrate under the Intendent at Guanajuato). In office he leased pastures and a corral at Puerto de Nieto. When he stepped down he asked to keep them another thirteen months to tie up business. Also in 1802 the ex-Subdelegado and tribute collector don Vicente Colmenero bid to rent the Palmagordo rancho at the estate. The royal accountant don Manuel Cabrera leased lands at Puerto de Nieto in the early 1800s.[63] By leasing to local officials Sánchez Espinosa profited while favoring men who sat in justice, collected taxes, and calculated tributes owed by Puerto de Nieto's indios. He worked regularly with the highest officials in the capital. Deals with local officers facilitated business at San Miguel and reminded the Canals that he remained a presence in the province.

The Canal, Lanzagorta, and Landeta patriarchs used landholding, council rule, and militia command to entrench their power after 1780 while the local economy declined, in part because their landed expansion to the north was blocked by Mexico City patriarchs, in part because of competition from León. Neither San Miguel patriarchs nor Sánchez Espinosa suffered. But local weavers saw wool prices soar; artisans watched markets stagnate. The few locals like the Allendes who tried to rise while Canals dueled Mexico City patriarchs faced difficulties. Yet only after the regime crisis of 1808 did a few irate provincials provoke the insurgency that began in 1810. Until the regime broke San Miguel remained a center of concentrated patriarchal powers and exceptional economic decline; food control, festivals of inversion, a clock, and a militia led by dominant patriarchs proved sufficient to keep the peace in the face of deepening popular difficulties.

Querétaro: Power and Prosperity in the Garden City

As the eighteenth century ended, Querétaro was a city of dispersed power and growing prosperity. In contrast with Guanajuato, a place of power, risk, desperation, and death, and with San Miguel, where a closed oligarchy ruled a town in decline, Querétaro struck visitors as a place of riches and remarkable beauty. On his way to Guanajuato in 1790 don Antonio de Mourelle described Querétaro in sharp contrast with his dark portrayal of the mining city: "I found Querétaro at the beginning of a delightful valley, surrounded by orchards that make it even more beautiful; the view is made more exquisite by the soaring arches of the aqueduct linking a nearby canyon to the highest point of the town. . . . I like this place; if one day I retire in New Spain, I will ask that this be the place for my time of rest."[64] A few years later, in 1793, don Carlos de Urrutía saw the city of trade and textiles as "the largest and most opulent in the Intendancy of Mexico . . . It sits at the base of Mount Holy Cross, bordered by an ample river whose waters irrigate the orchards and gardens that are its beauty; its climate is temperate and healthful."[65]

The visitors' strong impressions told much about Querétaro. As the 1790s began, the obrajes faced decline. But obrajes remained, and a growing number of family producers carried on in a restructured cloth industry. Yet neither visitor saw struggling industries; instead both saw a city of huertas and a great aqueduct. The city's Otomí founders built the huertas; the aqueduct announced the eighteenth-century triumph of Spanish power. The visitors saw none of that. They saw a city of lush prosperity and unmatched beauty, a place for rest in retirement. Unknowingly they pointed to a key to Querétaro's prosperity: the Otomí no longer ruled; most faced subordination as the eighteenth century ended. But huertas still shaped city life. Their persistent productivity allowed many of Querétaro's working families to prosper amid the pressures and changes of the 1790s.

Entrepreneurs at Querétaro followed proven paths. Many were immigrants from Spain; most began in trade, often the textile trade. But trade still mixed opportunity and uncertainty, so those who profited continued to invest in land and office. The integration of entrepreneurship, landholding, and office shaped power across New Spain. Still, local variants mattered. Mining ruled entrepreneurship at Guanajuato, slowing the shift to the land and limiting, at least in times of boom, dependence on Mexico City. At San Miguel a small clique ruled, constraining the lives of all not linked to the Canals. Querétaro had a more balanced elite. No great enterprise like the Valenciana dominated local affairs; no clan like the Canals ruled economic and civic life without challenge.[66] The oldest landed fortune at Querétaro, the patrimony built by don Juan Caballería y Ocío, was ruled from Mexico City after 1780 by don José Sánchez Espinosa. The greatest commercial fortune begun in eighteenth-century Querétaro led to the vast mining and landed wealth built by the Conde de Regla, whose heirs also operated from the capital after 1780. And while the family of don José de Escandón retained a role in Querétaro and its countryside, its interests shifted to coastal New Santander. Did less concentrated power facilitate economic dynamism? Did it contribute to the city's shared prosperity? And how did power built at Querétaro but taken to the capital affect life in the province?

Landlords living in Querétaro all but monopolized estate ownership in the city's jurisdiction. Only two of sixty-three haciendas belonged to Mexico City landlords: the Fagoagas' Amascala and don José Sánchez Espinosa's La Griega, near each other east of La Cañada. The remaining sixty-one estates belonged to Querétaro proprietors: forty-two men, three women, and the Carmelites who held the vast Chichimequillas estate north of La Griega. Around San Juan del Río, closer to Mexico City, the Fagoagas, the Conde de Regla, the Condesa de San Mateo Valparaiso, and other capital landlords had properties. Even so, local owners held 80 percent of estates there.[67]

Resident patriarchs ruled the city of huertas and its countryside. The Marqués de la Villa del Villar del Águila, heir to the magnate who funded the great aqueduct, headed the Querétaro elite as the eighteenth century ended. Don Juan Antonio Fernández de Jáuregui and his kin held properties near Querétaro, in the irrigated bottomlands west around Celaya, and the vast and valuable Gugurrón estate (which included an obraje) north between San Miguel and San Luis Potosí. The Marqués held a proprietary seat on the Querétaro council. He raised money to help the city survive the famine of 1785–86. He mediated disputes among landed families and between estates and communities. He collected funds and found supplies for the militia created at Querétaro in the 1790s.[68]

Joining the Marqués at the pinnacle of city power was don Pedro Antonio de Septién, son of a leading financier at Guanajuato. He married a landed heiress in the Primo y Jordán clan, among the oldest at Querétaro, and moved there to control his wife's three estates. He presided over the council as Regidor Decano y Alférez Real, senior councilman and royal standard bearer. Septién and Primo y Jordán kin had additional estates around Querétaro and Celaya, along with extensive holdings north around San Luis de la Paz. Many Primo y Jordán men were priests, which limited neither entrepreneurship nor conflicts with Otomí communities. Don Pedro de Septién was Subdelegado at Celaya from 1796 to 1801; his son don Manuel held the same post at San Luis de la Paz. They sat in justice in towns in the Intendancy of Guanajuato, but in the economic orbit of Querétaro. They integrated office, estate operation, and trade in places where household weavers

expanded production in the face of imports, profiting in the new economy of the Bourbon Bajío.[69]

The Marqués del Villar del Águila was heir to a fortune built in the
early eighteenth century; don Pedro de Septién ruled a clan that fused
new mining money with old landholding. Don José Martínez Moreno
found another route to eminence. When don Pedro Romero de Terreros
left Querétaro to pursue mining at Real del Monte and become Conde
de Regla, he left a proprietary seat on the Querétaro council to a local
branch of his family. Martínez Moreno held that seat from the 1770s to
his death in the 1790s. He and his kin owned two obrajes and four haciendas in and around Querétaro. By 1801 the council seat and family
leadership had passed to a nephew, don Fernando Romero Martínez,
protagonist in a rural labor dispute that revealed mounting social tensions.[70] His cousin in Mexico City, the second Conde de Regla, operated three estates owned by his siblings near San Juan del Río while
his sister, Marquesa de San Francisco, owned the San Cristóbal estates
at Acámbaro. The Romero and Regla family held strong in the southeastern Bajío around 1800.

The Querétaro elite also included many less exalted yet powerful
patriarchs. Don José Ygnacio Villaseñor y Cervantes owned four haciendas: one near Querétaro, the others to the west at Apaseo and
Salvatierra. He was a lawyer, legal adviser to city officials, and magistrate appointed by the council in 1801.[71] Doctor Don Juan Ygnacio de
Briones had one estate at Querétaro and another north at San Luis de
la Paz. He was magistrate in Querétaro in 1801.[72] Don José Antonio
Oyarzábal took another route. He had four haciendas north of Querétaro and the wealth to lend four thousand pesos to famine relief in
1785. He never appears in the lists of Querétaro office holders, suggesting that he never found a secure place in the local elite.[73] More common than a man with many estates but without office were men with
one hacienda, one obraje, and active political lives. Don Melchor de
Noriega, don Francisco Carballido, and don Domingo Fernández were
newcomers who traded and operated obrajes while working to gain
land and political power.[74]

The most successful aspirant to elite power at Querétaro after 1780
was don Juan Antonio de Castillo y Llata. He owned and operated
the Carretas estate and obraje northeast of the city, served as procurador general for the City Council in 1799, commanded the Regiment
of the Sierra Gorda, and announced power and charity by endowing
the city's new free primary school. Castillo y Llata had married the
daughter of don José de Escandón, the Querétaro commander, merchant, and obraje operator who gained fame, title, and landed fortune

by "conquering" the Sierra Gorda and colonizing the coastal lowlands of New Santander.[75] Like don Pedro de Septién, Castillo y Llata showed that the best route to power and prestige at Querétaro wedded entrepreneurship to established power and prestige.

Patriarchy defined all routes to power. Women faced exclusion from the profits of trade and the powers of office. The vagaries of death and inheritance created a few landed women. At Querétaro in 1791 they were very few: three of forty-seven proprietors, holding three of sixty-three estates. One, doña Gertrudis Lleras, loaned four thousand pesos in the relief effort of 1785.[76] Husbands and powerful brothers limited the roles of inheriting women. Powerful women were rare. Few challenged patriarchy as the means of organizing inequality. Yet elite patriarchy was changing at Querétaro late in the eighteenth century. Few patriarchs, old or new, sent daughters to Santa Clara. Novices still came, but growing numbers arrived from outside Querétaro and with limited endowments.[77] But whether the daughters of Querétaro's most powerful patriarchs were finding new independence remains uncertain.

As at San Miguel, the Querétaro militia reflected the structure of the provincial elite. While patriarchs of the Canal clan contributed vast sums and ruled at San Miguel, at Querétaro funding and command were dispersed. Eleven men paid from one to three thousand pesos to buy uniforms in 1795, the largest sum given by the Marqués del Villar del Águila. He was not among the six who would command as captains, all from different families, including the Septiéns and Romeros. When an assembly of landlords met in 1788 to gather horses for the cavalry, fifty-four attended, ten others contributed. The Fagoagas' Atongo estates, the Conde de Regla's Juchitlán, and Sánchez Espinosa's La Griega gave six each; most of the 182 mounts came from local men who gave one to four.[78] Militia command reinforced entrepreneurial patriarchy—and that patriarchy was more widely dispersed at Querétaro. Equally notable, in the 1780s and 1790s coercive power still depended on regime ties with powerful colonials.

Querétaro's merchant and landed patriarchs remained provincials. None competed with the great financiers of Mexico City; none operated estates on the scale of Sánchez Espinosa and others in the capital. Sánchez Espinosa ruled properties built by don Juan de Caballero y Ocío, Querétaro's great entrepreneurial benefactor, a century earlier— and unlike him, don José kept apart from leading Querétaro patriarchs. His letters show no contact with the Septién and Primo y Jordán clan (linked by marriage to the Canals of San Miguel). He paid interest of 150 pesos yearly on 3,000 pesos invested by don José Martínez

Moreno in the Obra Pía estates—an investment, not a relationship. A deal worth a few hundred pesos with a member of the Jáuregui clan led to acrimony.[79]

Sánchez Espinosa's one major business with a leading Querétaro entrepreneur was providing sheep to don Juan Antonio de Castillo y Llata, who held the city slaughterhouse contract from 1804 to 1810. Castillo won the contract but lacked the herds and northern grazing lands to meet the obligation. Don José's control of the Bocas and Peñasco properties in San Luis Potosí allowed him to sell tens of thousands of sheep each year to abasto contractors in San Miguel, Querétaro, and Mexico City. He earned from four to twenty thousand pesos yearly after 1804 selling to Castillo y Llata at Querétaro.[80]

Sánchez Espinosa's flocks and grazing estates also gave him a role in Querétaro's cloth industry. From his acquisition of the Bocas estates in the early 1780s to the outbreak of insurgency in 1810 he sold wool to obrajes. In the early 1780s he dealt with don Tomás Merino Pablo. From the late 1780s into the early 1800s he worked with don Juan José Martínez de Lejarza. Then don Vicente de la Concha took his wool until 1810. Every year Sánchez Espinosa shipped wool south from Bocas. Obraje operators took the clip in trade for a set quantity of cloth, sent to supply Sánchez Espinosa's estate stores. The grazer would sell wool at prevailing (rising) prices; he gained at wholesale cloth that he sold for retail. The grazing landlord had the advantage. He controlled essential wool and ruled northern estate markets. The obraje operators took risks; difficulties in the cloth market brought them losses.

The famine of 1785 and 1786 stopped shipments of wool and cloth between the Bajío and the dry zones to the north, bringing an end to don Tomás Merino's business with Sánchez Espinosa.[81] Sánchez Espinosa's wool business, however, revived. Soon he was in business with Martínez de Lejarza, from Valladolid and owner of a Querétaro obraje. The relationship flourished during the years of expansion after 1793. Don José annually sold from 1,100 to 1,500 arrobas of wool (at 25 pounds per arroba, from 14 to 19 tons) in exchange for cloth valued from 3,300 to 4,500 pesos. Between 1796 and 1802 the Marqués de Jaral, another Mexico City grazer with vast lands north of the Bajío, annually shipped 2,000 to 6,500 arrobas (25 to 80 tons) of wool to the Querétaro obraje of don José del Raso, who returned cloth to supply Jaral estate stores.[82] Grazing entrepreneurs ruled large-scale putting-out deals with Querétaro obraje operators.

The unequal relationship between grazers and obraje operators became clear when Sánchez Espinosa won the contract to supply uniforms to the San Luis Potosí militia in the 1790s. He made Martínez de Lajarza his partner, supplying him with wool and receiving finished cloth from him. Don José took payment for his wool; Martínez got nothing for the cloth. Sánchez Espinosa charged the debt to the Peñasco estates, which he controlled but his son did not yet own. Sánchez Espinosa profited; the obraje manufacturer faced loss; debt burdened the Peñasco enterprises. Like the young Conde de Peñasco, Martínez faced a creditors' council controlled by Sánchez Espinosa. When 1802 brought a flood of imports, Martínez's obraje failed.[83]

Sánchez Espinosa then took his business to don Vicente de la Concha, an aspiring merchant-obrajero. Concha joined the Querétaro militia; in 1807 he won election as business manager of the council. He gained a contract for militia uniforms—and complained when a mobilization disrupted business. He did standard wool-for-cloth barter with Sánchez Espinosa. And from 1808 Concha leased the Coyotillos rancho at La Griega for six hundred pesos yearly. He combined cloth making with landed entrepreneurship, office with militia service. All the while he was a dependent feeding the profits of Sánchez Espinosa.[84]

The Querétaro textile industry profited the great grazers of Mexico City. A few local merchant-clothiers found gain in obraje operations and in financing household cloth makers. But cloth making, still important to production and employment as the eighteenth century ended, was no longer a secure source of profit for Querétaro elites. Before 1750 men on the rise, including don Pedro Romero de Terreros and don José de Escandón, began with obrajes. By 1800 obrajes were still run by men on the make, but turnover was rapid; most operators lasted less than two years.[85] The industry survived, bolstering the wealth of great landed patriarchs in the viceregal capital. The obrajes might remind Querétaro elites of past glories; as the eighteenth century ended they turned elsewhere for profits.

They looked to the countryside. In 1803 don José María Zeláa y Hidalgo, son of an obraje operator and a priest of the Congregation of Guadalupe, wrote in praise of Querétaro. Like many visitors Zeláa began with the huertas. Their water came from "its celebrated Canyon; its leafy orchards and delicious beauty are admired by all who walk its paths." He added: "out of the hills of the Canyon comes a river, fertilizing a great number of huertas." And "it flows through a great canal, serving more than two thousand homes and irrigating equal numbers of orchards and gardens that produce an abundance of all kinds of flowers and fruits, from Europe as well as America." Less glorious but economically as important, as the river flowed west from the city it watered a rich valley where haciendas raised maize, barley, and wheat, and four mills ground flour.[86]

Querétaro appeared an agrarian paradise. While the cloth industry struggled and producers faced deepening difficulties—and great northern grazers profited—thousands of huertas from La Cañada, through Querétaro, to Apaseo, the legacy of Otomí foundations, set an agrarian base in a commercial and industrial city. And Querétaro's patriarchs, however much they joined in trade and manufacturing, focused on agricultural entrepreneurship as the nineteenth century began. While mining showed continued strength and population expanded after 1790, the near-monopoly by Querétaro patriarchs of the nearby countryside brought opportunities for profit. Many expanded irrigation, building dams and canals to open fields to secure cultivation. Those able to take cash from trade invested their own funds. Most turned to convent bankers, often Santa Clara or the Congregation of Guadalupe, taking mortages at 5 percent to expand production. Estates might be mortgaged minimally, or for over 80 percent of value; most were less than 50 percent burdened. Convent bankers funded the expansion of irrigation and cultivation and shared in the profits. The alliance of convents and landed entrepreneurs at the heart of convent capitalism held strong.[87] It was mostly landed elites who rode in the seventy-six elegant coaches that Father Zeláa counted among Querétaro's glories.[88]

Querétaro: Production and Patriarchy in the Working City

Squeezed between Bourbon policies that assaulted the textile industry and the power of entrepreneurs in Mexico City, Querétaro elites pressed against the working majority. To the extent that they could, they demanded more work and greater production from the men and women who made cloth and other goods in the urban economy. In the process entrepreneurs sometimes reinforced patriarchy to exploit working families and sometimes prejudiced patriarchy to drive wages down. During the same years the Spanish city council and viceregal authorities tried to limit the indigenous republic that defended Otomí huertas and rights. From the 1790s new insecurities threatened sustenance and patriarchy among the working people of Querétaro. Still, the city and many of its people prospered, thanks to the diversification of manufacturing to include a large tobacco factory, and to the huertas that still provided a base on the land for many urban families.

The Otomí republic seemed under constant siege after 1770, as long-developing challenges accelerated. It was the only local government from Querétaro's foundation to the 1650s. It held good lands and capital resources into the eighteenth century; it collected local tributes to fund religious festivals—and suits that defended Otomí rights. It gained a public place and strong voice in the festivities that celebrated the great aqueduct in 1738—and challenged Spanish perceptions in public. Early in the 1760s the Spanish council challenged the Otomí republic's right to arrest and jail unruly indios, mestizos, and mulattoes in the Spanish center; the Viceroy Marqués de Croix backed the native magistrates' powers, as long as Spanish magistrates were not present.[89] In 1764 Spanish men aiming to follow San Miguel patriarchs and found an Escuela de Cristo, a penitential religious brotherhood, claimed a chapel devoted to San José in the great Franciscan church on the plaza.[90] The Otomí republic complained to the archbishop, to no avail. Once pastors to the Otomí, the Franciscans now served the powerful.

In 1774 the viceroy again ordered Querétaro's Spanish council to respect the jurisdiction of the Otomí republic. A decade later the corregidor don Juan de Villalva y Velázquez published a new ordinance restricting its rights: it could mount no patrols in the Spanish center, it could appoint no schoolmaster without church approval, it could spend no funds without his approval, and it could deliver no one to an obraje, whether for brief detention or long labor. And most limiting, the republic could collect no revenues beyond the tributes set by the regime. Otomí officials were back in Mexico City in 1799 demanding that their rights be respected, with no sign of endorsement.[91]

All along viceregal authorities worked to control the republic's financial resources. In May 1768, soon after the pacification of the risings at Guanajuato and San Luis de la Paz, Viceroy Croix demanded an account of the holdings of the Otomí republic's treasury. Early in 1782 it still had 16,000 pesos invested in amounts ranging from 11,500 pesos, to 3,000 pesos, plus smaller sums in the estates operated by members of the local elite.[92] In the years that followed, the republic faced, along with others across New Spain, demands that it deposit its funds in the new Banco Nacional de San Carlos, created to fund the debt left by Spain's support for United States independence. Indigenous communities would send deposits to the bank in Spain in exchange for promised annual interest—paid in New Spain—of 6 percent. In theory the return on Querétaro's 16,000 pesos would be 960 pesos yearly, better than the 800 pesos in annual interest that it would gain investing in local mortgages at 5 percent. In November 1784 the Otomí republic granted power of attorney to don Gaspar Melchor de Jovellanos to receive its funds and represent it before the new National Bank.[93] Jovellanos, famed as an intellectual, official, and reformer, is often seen as having inspired the liberal vision that would challenge indigenous towns' rights to hold property in the nineteenth century. In 1784 Querétaro's Otomí trusted him with their funds. The evidence suggests that Jovellanos proved trustworthy; the bank did not.

The Querétaro republic invested 5,971 pesos through Jovellanos in the bank in 1785, earning 364 pesos, or 6 percent. The republic at San Juan del Río deposited 1,602 pesos, gaining 93 pesos interest. By early 1787 Querétaro Otomí had placed 7,500 pesos, the San Juan del Río republic 2,000 pesos, in the bank. For comparison, the two native republics of Mexico City deposited 25,000 pesos, the one at San Luis Potosí 3,750 pesos. Interest payments dropped to 5.5 percent after fees, leaving the Querétaro Otomí with 412 pesos in interest. In 1789 and 1790, 392 pesos had become a set annual yield expected from its investment in San Carlos—5.2 percent on its 7,500 pesos, barely better than local mortgage yields.[94] And when war began in 1793 the bank failed as an effective source of revenue for the Otomí republic. The 291 pesos due for 1793 and again in 1794—much-reduced payments— were not delivered until 1798 and 1799. The bank promised to pay in 1800 and 1801 the 295 pesos due as interest for 1795 and the 351 pesos for 1796. It never did. It promised 270 pesos for 1798 and 223 pesos for 1800, both paid in 1804. Finally, it owed 253 pesos for 1802, paid that sum in 1805, and then paid nothing more, according to accounts completed in 1808.[95] After 1793 bank payments dropped well below Bajío mortgage rates, and they came years late or not at all. It effectively expropriated a large part of the Otomí republic's historic capital.

An account of the Otomí republic's finances for 1808, the last year before drought and regime crisis began to change everything, documents a stunning demise. San Carlos held 6,000 pesos on deposit (1,500 pesos were gone); no interest was paid. The 7,000 pesos invested with the Obregón brothers of San Miguel, both priests, since 1780 now brought no interest—or payment of principal. A suit was under way. Another 1,700 pesos placed at 5 percent on the home of a prominent widow in Querétaro, doña Josefa Ortuña, was caught in a creditors' action, leaving the republic awaiting payment. Only the enduring sisters of Santa Clara still paid the 27 pesos due annually on a small investment. That left the republic dependent on the 224 pesos collected as annual tributes from local indigenous men. The resulting 250 pesos paid for a small contribution to Holy Week festivities, with a surplus of just over 200 pesos going to the provincial treasury to pay for teachers whom the republic could neither choose nor control.[96]

By the first decade of the nineteenth century the Otomí republic had lost key financial resources and revenues, inhibiting its ability to fund and orchestrate local religious life. When a plague hit in 1803 it fell to Corregidor don Miguel Domínguez to organize a religious procession.

He collected half the funds he needed from church institutions and focused on Guadalupe—a questionable choice at Querétaro, so devoted to Our Lady at Pueblito.[97] In the following year the need for funds to reconstruct the church at San Sebastián, the Otomí parish north of the river, led Domínguez to try to collect from prosperous Spaniards who had moved into the neighborhood. Fourteen men came; ten contributed amounts ranging from 1 to 50 pesos.[98] The Otomí republic could no longer support community religious life and local Spaniards proved unwilling, beyond token contributions.

But the republic did not turn against the regime or the prevailing order. In 1803 it proudly spent three hundred pesos to greet the Viceroy. In September 1809 it found five hundred pesos to celebrate the accession of Fernando VII (noting that it had spent the same to honor his father, Carlos IV, in 1789), just as news arrived that the young king had ceded before Napoleon and left his throne for comfortable captivity in Bayonne.[99] In 1810 the Otomí republic stood firm against the Hidalgo revolt that exploded so violently nearby, and it sustained the regime against the insurgency through the next decade.

The payments for celebrations show that the republic could find resources, even as the regime took its traditional funds. The continued honoring of viceroys and kings combined with enduring opposition to insurgency suggests that Otomí notables still found roles working between the Otomí, local Spanish officials and entrepreneurs, and the regime. There are hints about why and how. In 1803 the king in Spain approved the division of the single parish of the Spanish center into four. Diverse peoples had spread to live across a rapidly growing community and they were not well served by the lone Santiago parish.[100] The tribute census of 1807 tells more; the indigenous population of the four parishes of the Spanish city numbered 1,326 male heads of households, almost double the 742 still living in the traditional Otomí parish of San Sebastián across the river. The reasons are clear: most obrajes, tanneries, and household workshops were in the Spanish city. A growing Otomí population moved there to gain work, living among others classed as mestizos and a few mulattoes.[101] As the Otomí dispersed across the city, ever more under entrepreneurial rule, the Spanish council and the viceregal regime pushed to limit the roles and resources of the native republic. We must suspect that the republic collected funds among ever more dispersed Otomí and used them to organize worship and to defend Otomí interests when it could. By such efforts, however informal, the Otomí republic clung to a mediating role in the colonial order.

While indigenous leaders struggled to adapt to changing times, the textile economy faced mounting difficulties. Under the combined pressures of rising wool prices and free trade that brought a flood of imports, the large obrajes faced high fixed costs. Many closed in the 1770s and 1780s; those that survived had to cut costs. One way was to sell slaves. In 1785 a group of investors planned to build an obraje in Durango, far to the north. There, far from the port of Veracruz, imported cloth cost more; there too, vast flocks of sheep grazed nearby to supply wool. But skilled weavers were scarce. The Durango investors turned to Querétaro obraje operators; several sold skilled slaves for the low price of a hundred pesos each, well below the two to three hundred pesos common during the first half of the century. Contracts required that slaves sold to Durango gain the prevailing wage—as if they were free—and be allowed to use their wages to buy freedom.[102] Querétaro obrajeros cut permanent labor; slaves sent to Durango gained a route to freedom, and a facsimile of free labor along the way. Meanwhile apprentice contracts drew a growing number of young workers into the surviving obrajes in the late 1780s. They signed on to train for three years in exchange for sustenance only. One young slave was sent by his owner to apprentice in an obraje—with the right to learn weaving and then use his wages to buy freedom.[103] The demise of slavery at Querétaro was accelerated by the pressures on the obrajes. In the late 1780s and early 1790s a small flurry of local sales mostly dealt in female household servants and their young children, whose prices held at one hundred pesos each.[104]

A census in 1792 reported fifty-five slaves still laboring in ten of Querétaro's sixteen working obrajes. Only seven, all in one shop, were skilled weavers; the rest were general laborers. Slaves then formed but a small part of an obraje workforce that was changing rapidly. In 1778, 1,768 men and boys lived and worked in obrajes just beginning to face high wool costs and import competition. Nearly 85 percent were indio, 8 percent mulatto, 5 percent mestizo, and 2 percent Spanish. By 1792 Spaniards working in obrajes had jumped from 43 to 239, including 10 immigrants from Spain; the largest number, 82, were weavers. Mestizos increased from 88 to 242, with 125 working as skilled weavers, 65 as spinners, and the rest in diverse roles. And mulattoes increased from 136 to 223 (including the 55 slaves), of which 97 were weaving, 24 spinning, and most of the rest doing general labor. There were 81 caciques, noble indios. Native commoners were not listed in a census taken for militia recruitment.[105] Slaves had been reduced to a small part of the obraje workforce, far outnumbered by Spaniards, mestizos, and free mulattoes who came to labor in times of declining production. Were they attracted in the mid-1780s by guaranteed food rations in time of famine? The number of indios laboring in the obrajes had declined. Although they were not counted in the census of 1792, if they remained at 85 percent of the obraje labor force, employment would have soared to nearly 3,800—while the number of working looms declined by half. Had some Otomí claimed mestizo or even Spanish status, as so many Guanajuato mineworkers became Spaniards in the same era? Perhaps. But to some degree, under pressures of rising imports, soaring wool costs, and famine, Hispanic men forced the Otomí out of Querétaro's obrajes, sending them to survive among the growing number of household producers.

Household production soared through the 1780s. In 1793 the 181 looms working in Querétaro obrajes were far outnumbered by the 405 weaving woolens in household shops and the 183 making cotton goods. An official detailed how they worked. Most common were family units—men weaving while women and children spun and did diverse tasks. Couples without children, or with infants too young to help, took in kin or orphans to keep going. A few mixed unrelated adults and children. Compensation came from a merchant clothier or cloth sales. Some took on outwork from obrajes, perhaps shops they had earlier left. All struggled between low payments for putting-out work and falling market prices for cloth.[106]

The result was "self-exploitation." Householders worked longer hours to make more cloth for falling incomes. Self-exploitation was also patriarchal exploitation: men contracted with merchant-clothiers, who were also men, to make cloth for falling compensation (blamed on market pressures). The weaving patriarch—poor, but skilled and empowered within his household by a tie to a merchant clothier—prevailed on his wife, children, and other dependents to work more to meet the contract. The merchant profited; the household patriarch wove and remained the patriarch; his dependents labored long and hard to survive. Household production expanded after 1770 by maintaining patriarchy, incorporating a growing number of dependents, and driving them to work more for declining earnings. In household cloth making patriarchy was the key to social relations of deepening inequity.

The census of 1791 reported seventy-five Spaniards, seventy-eight mestizos, eighteen caciques, and only twelve mulattoes as household cloth makers. If they worked one to two looms each, that left half of household production to Otomí—who were being squeezed there too. Similar trends shaped Querétaro's larger community of household craftsmen (and the craftswomen dependent in their households). Among 583 clothing and leather producers, 244 were Spaniards—of which half were skilled tailors, a quarter hatmakers. Another 229 were mestizos, of which a third were shoemakers, a third tailors. Among forty-six caciques almost half were tailors; among sixty-five mulattoes over half were shoemakers. Were indios squeezed out again? To some degree they were, though we must allow for those of Otomí and African ancestry who claimed Spanish and mestizo status, perhaps to avoid tributes—as had happened in Guanajuato.

Then in 1793 Atlantic war suddenly blocked oceanic trade, setting off renewed expansion in obrajes and among household cloth makers. Population growth kept labor available and malleable; pressures on workers continued. The few remaining slaves in the city began to find freedom; around 1800 there was a flurry of charitable liberations.[107] In the same years obrajes turned away from even three-year apprentice contracts, offering only daily wages to youths who would learn the crafts of cloth making.[108] The goal was flexibility; a textile boom built on wartime protections while the regime promoted free trade could crash at any time. Nor did expansion relieve pressures on those who spun through putting-out contracts. In 1796 a group of Otomí villagers who spun for the obraje of don Tomás López de Ecala sued, complaining that he delivered the same amount of raw wool but unfairly raised the quantity of yarn they had to return—leaving little to sell to support their families. Knowing that officials cared little for their welfare, they argued that new demands prejudiced their ability to pay tribute: magistrates cared about tax collection.[109]

Amid uncertain changes, textile production expanded rapidly after 1793. In 1803 Father Zeláa reported: "the leading trade in the commerce of this city is the production of fine woolens, woven in eighteen *obrajes*. There are also 29 workshops of Spaniards and one hundred ninety eight of *indios* and diverse others that make serges, flannels, sackcloth, rough cottons, and other cotton and woolen wares." He added that there was more to Querétaro industry than cloth: "Eight match makers, five ribbon shops, thirty fine hat makers, and ten tanneries that cut a great number of cordovans and cowhides." Manufacturing fed trade: "In addition, there are thirty eight stores well supplied with cloth from Castille, and many groceries stocked with every commodity and food." Manufacturing and commerce made Querétaro a mandatory stop for traders traveling to *tierradentro*—Spanish North America. Then, as an afterthought, Zeláa noted the royal factory "of cigars and cigarettes" with over 2,500 workers "of both sexes." The city had grown to over 50,000 people by 1800, the equal of Guanajuato and exceeded only by Mexico City.[110]

Zeláa emphasized three forms of urban manufacturing: large workshops weaving woolens and a few tanning leather; household producers making cotton cloth, woolens, and other goods; and the tobacco factory. Each had characteristic labor relations: in obrajes men worked in large shops sustained by women (and some men) spinning at home; in households patriarchal families produced under merchant financiers; in the tobacco factory men and women worked for wages. All faced pressures during the expansion that began in the 1790s.

The proliferation of household production both sustained and threatened patriarchy, Merchant clothiers dealt with male heads of household, weaving patriarchs who took raw wool or spun yarn and agreed to make a set amount of cloth. The patriarch usually wove while his wife and daughters spun; sons learned to weave and helped in every way useful to fill the order. Corregidor Domínguez estimated in 1801 that a thousand household looms needed a weaver plus two to three more workers. The household textile sector thus employed three to four thousand men, women, and children.[111] All worked but the smallest children. To sustain growing families in the face of competitive pressures, weaver-patriarchs urged wives, children, and others to work longer and faster to gain minimal sustenance. Patriarchy was reinforced within families; we can only imagine the conversations within households.

Obrajes maintained different labor relations. The Corregidor reported in 1801, at the peak of expansion, that 19 obrajes worked 280 looms. Domínguez believed that obrajes made cloth worth 500,000 pesos each year: nearly 1,800 pesos per loom, over 80 pesos per worker.[112] They employed 6,000 people, over 20 per loom. About half, all men, worked inside the obrajes as weavers, spinners, and carders. The rest, mostly women, spun at home. The demise of slavery left most men inside the obrajes legally free. In the early 1790s youths were recruited through three-year apprentice contracts that provided guaranteed food and clothing. A second surge of hiring from 1799 to 1801 brought work for daily wages, very low wages. During decades first marked by the pressures of "free trade," then by the opportunities of wartime expansion, Querétaro's obrajes turned increasingly to daily wage labor.[113]

The expansion of weaving required a parallel increase of spinning. Cleaned wool was distributed among women (and fewer men) in urban and rural households. Women spinning for obrajes in putting-out deals usually lived in patriarchal households, urban and rural. Their earnings contributed to their families' sustenance and perhaps brought limited independence from fathers and husbands. Still, the pressures of the times meant that the women labored more to contribute less.

Around 1800 labor relations were very different in the royal tobacco factory, the largest employer in Querétaro. In rapid expansion it radically increased the employment of women wageworkers. While the obrajes employed only men and boys, and the household textile industry sustained and exploited patriarchal working families, the rise of women's wage work in the tobacco factory challenged patriarchy. The tobacco monopoly was central to Bourbon reforms. Its impositions helped set off riots at Guanajuato in 1766. The first factory opened in Mexico City in 1769; production began at Querétaro in 1779. Historically cigar and cigarette making and sales were done in small shops, most by women. The new factories concentrated production and at first employed mostly men. A few women were licensed to operate tobacco shops, selling monopoly products. The goal was revenue. In that the monopoly was a great success: yearly income rose from about 650,000 pesos in the late 1760s, to over 3,000,000 pesos in the 1780s, to approach 4,000,000 pesos around 1800.[114] By then tobacco earnings were second only to silver among sources of revenue for the regime.

The tobacco factories, like silver mining and refining and the largest obrajes, brought specialization and division of labor. A large number of cigarette rollers worked for piece rates, driven down as the monopoly prospered. In 1774 the factory in Mexico City employed over five thousand men and about a thousand women.[115] Wary that so many workers gathered in one factory would press demands and provoke conflicts, the administration chartered the Concordia, a mutual aid society. Workers contributed one real each week to the fund, on which they could draw to help with the costs of marriage, illness, injury, or death.[116] Mutual aid did not cushion falling wages. Having created the largest concentration of workers in the Americas, monopoly managers "cut production costs . . . quite successfully by slashing piece rates between 1779 and 1795."[117] Protest came swiftly. The factory in Mexico City faced workers' resistance in 1780, 1789, and 1791. The managers' first response was to mediate; production had to continue. Then they looked for new ways to cut costs and inhibit resistance. They pursued a dual policy, dispersing production away from Mexico City and shifting to women workers.

Dispersal took time. In 1795 seven thousand of the monopoly's twelve thousand workers remained in Mexico City, with over fifteen hundred in Guadalajara and nearly fourteen hundred in Querétaro. By 1798 the factory in the capital had shrunk to 5,500 workers; Guadalajara had 1,350 and Querétaro nearly 1,500. By 1809 the dispersal was complete. Mexico City retained fewer than 5,500 workers; Querétaro had expanded to over 3,700.[118] After 1800 the Querétaro tobacco factory had the second-largest concentration of workers in the Americas. Most were women. In 1791 men fell to 55 percent of the workers at the factory in Mexico City. Protest continued. An inquest in 1797 led Viceroy Branciforte to recommend "that in the future, no more men will be recruited into the factories, keeping only those indispensable for work women cannot do; we will prefer women, training them in the tasks most appropriate to their sex." The viceroy saw that the shift to women workers called for new services, notably childcare and schools "where we will gather and teach Christian Doctrine to workers' children, to the benefit of religion and the state."[119] As production and work shifted from Mexico City to Querétaro in the late 1790s, it brought a turn toward women workers there too. In 1803 Humboldt reported that women accounted for nineteen hundred of three thousand workers in the Querétaro factory. In the following year they were 1,780 among 2,589; in 1809 they were 2,574 of 3,706—70 percent of an expanding tobacco workforce.[120]

Women working for wages in the tobacco factory, with the factory providing childcare, either were not part of patriarchal households or worked outside them. Either way they challenged patriarchy. The censuses of the early 1790s reveal a large number of women as heads of household in Querétaro. Apprentice contracts show that sons of single mothers were significant among those who entered the obrajes.[121] By the late eighteenth century patriarchal families were a shrinking part of urban society at Querétaro. The tobacco factory tapped a growing population of women seeking work. They accepted lower piece rates with less protest; they proved less riotous than men. In view of women's traditions of riot and resistance in rural New Spain, their acquiescence in the factory needs explanation.[122] The factory offered women a chance to sustain themselves and their children in secure employment with family services. In a city and society defined by patriarchy, while patriarchal families faced deepening pressures, many women found factory labor a bearable option. The tobacco factory employed over 2,500 by 1809.

It is possible to estimate the different working segments of the city's population around 1800. Household weavers with a thousand looms busied four thousand workers—mostly family members. Estimating another thousand dependents too young to work suggests that five thousand of Querétaro's fifty thousand inhabitants lived on the miserable earnings of household cloth production. The obrajes employed about six thousand: three thousand men in the shops, three thousand mostly women spinning in urban and rural households. Estimating that men and boys in obrajes had two dependents each, and that each woman spinning at home sustained one child with her labors, suggests that the obraje sector supported fifteen thousand (most in the city, many in the country). And presuming that eight hundred men in the tobacco factory supported families of four, while eighteen hundred women had one dependent each, suggests that seven thousand people depended on the monopoly. If so, twenty thousand people, 40 percent of Querétaro's population, relied on textiles—production in which patriarchy persisted and imposed deepening pressures and insecurity on families. Another seven thousand, 15 percent of the city, relied on the tobacco factory, mostly on the labors of women. In textiles and tobacco women and men were working producers as the nineteenth century began. In textiles women still labored in patriarchal households; in the tobacco factory they earned wages.

With pressures on patriarchy and family welfare everywhere, the men who ruled Querétaro joined the turn to new social controls. In the 1770s they rebuilt the city jail. In 1803 Father Zeláa described the jail as "very secure," then added, "it does not have enough space." In 1796, amid the wartime boom, the corregidor had divided the city into nine barrios, each with a magistrate; three reported to him, and three each to the Spanish council's two magistrates. In 1803 the city finished a new armory "for the splendor and safety" of the militia.[123] Zelaá did not mention armed patrols among Querétaro's glories. Was the city of gardens, textiles, and tobacco less riotous than Guanajuato? Probably. Did Querétaro lack funds for a police force? Perhaps. Yet the combination of a secure jail, ward magistrates, and militias with a new armory helped to secure urban peace in times of change.

Before 1793 competition from rising imports reduced obraje employment and drove a growing number of household producers to make more cloth for less income; the problem at Querétaro was unemployment and widening poverty. After 1793 war brought growth to obrajes and to household weavers while the tobacco factory expanded. Unemployment was not a problem; employers aimed to increase production and limit remuneration. Don Miguel Domínguez, named corregidor in 1801 after years in the Mexico City bureaucracy, wrote revealing reports on Querétaro labor relations at the peak of the wartime boom.

Obraje employers raised classic complaints: "Another thing I hear from them is that they lack people to work because the poor are so lazy that if they are not forced to labor, they will not do so voluntarily." Having all but eliminated slaves during decades of decline, cloth makers faced new demand for workers after 1793. They saw laziness only cured by coercion. Domínguez saw labor shortages: "the continuous complaints, not only in obrajes but at haciendas and elsewhere, that workers are scarce . . . result in my view from the recent rapid increase in cultivation at the haciendas, and growing production in the obrajes in times of war. The end of trade with Europe has left our manufactures to supply New Spain; as a result production has doubled, even tripled."[124] What employers saw as laziness calling for coercion Domínguez knew as the labor challenges of economic boom.

Domínguez did not mention the explosion of employment at the tobacco factory. Perhaps he was avoiding a project dear to his Bourbon superiors, or believed that the factory's preference for women workers limited its impact on the larger labor market. If so, he was wrong. Women joined in textile production in the household sector; through putting-out they made up nearly half the workers in the obraje sector. To the extent that women took work in the tobacco factory, they gained income outside the cloth sector, perhaps explaining the growing numbers of male spinners. The simultaneous growth of obraje labor, household weaving, and tobaco production made workers less available and less malleable.

To Domínguez the obrajes were objects of special scorn. During his first nine months in office inspections brought him into "some workshops seen in horror, where just the name instills fear; they have become prisons, and they don't produce at the level they should, nor yield the profits they should to their owners nor the state."[125] The obrajes still found ways to coerce workers and were inefficient producers of cloth, profits, and revenues.

Domínguez emphasized that the obrajes paid workers in cash, not cloth; there was debate about whether to pay cash only, or add food rations. Domínguez preferred cash; workers should eat at home with their families. Cash wages consolidated patriarchal households; they also forced workers to pay the high price of food in years of scarcity. While Domínguez aimed to help workers and patriarchal families, he kept a sharp eye on employers' costs. The problem was mostly those "who work locked in obrajes." Men locked into long shifts led to "constant conflict between workers and obraje owners."[126] Not only did locked-in workers generate conflicts that spilled into Domínguez's courts, they could not be good patriarchs—and they cost employers too much. That perception brought Domínguez to a detailed analysis of urban labor relations and the unique role of the obrajes.

The basic problem was obligated labor, and it extended beyond the obrajes. "In all the workshops of this city, in the bakeries, tanneries, craft shops of all sorts, and especially in the large obrajes and the smaller ones called *trapiches*, the pernicious custom of giving laborers, craftsmen, and workers sums of money in advance [endures], with the agreement that they will work off the amount by their personal labor in their craft." As a result of "this corruption . . . the most miserable people of the town have the ability and liberty to gain sums of 30, 40, 60 or more pesos." Some advances went for "real necessities, like . . . marriages, burials, and baptisms." Others went to "optional things . . . for example, to fund participation in a Holy Week parade, to take a role in a neighborhood festival dance, to serve as sponsor at a wedding—in other words any frivolity." Beyond sacramental essentials and social frivolities Domínguez believed that many advances went to "vices and passions." Often equal to many months' wages, advances caused "unimaginable evils."[127]

The Corregidor understood why advances were paid: "Because every employer worries about a shortage of workers," they aimed to "oblige workers and make their labor secure."[128] He also knew that workers rarely repaid advances. The prevailing wage of 1.5 reales daily for unskilled work brought nine reales for a six-day week. A worker might give two or three reales to cover advances; he needed the rest for sustenance. At that rate it would take a year to repay a twenty-peso advance. Often, before advances were covered the worker sought more: "A problem in childbirth or a wife's illness becomes a pretext to take more money." To fund the patriarch in family life, in community festivals, and even in vice, advances were endless, and rarely repaid. The result, Domínguez emphasized, was perpetual debt.[129] What he left unstated—but obvious—was that workers cost employers their wages plus advances that remained unpaid. Advances funded workers' patriarchy and raised the costs of labor. In times of labor scarcity, obligated employment favored workers.

Domínguez found advances most pernicious in the obrajes. Advances were common everywhere, but only the obrajes, fearing the loss of workers and advances, locked in indebted workers. Life inside was violent and destructive. When men were not working, drink and gaming ruled. Fights and wounds were everyday occurrences. "A worker is wounded and his care is entrusted to a local surgeon, often lasting weeks; once the wound is healed, the aggressor by local custom pays four reales daily, two to the surgeon, two to the victim to support them through the time of convalescence. The delinquent, to cover all these costs and to get out of jail, seeks a new advance from an obraje on promise of future work."[130] Life locked into the obrajes was violent, causing wounds which led to new debts and longer periods locked in. The system perpetuated itself.

Most upsetting, locked-in workers could not be good patriarchs. Although "married workers are allowed to sleep with their wives," the Corregidor complained that the concession to married life left children home alone. More generally, obrajes left families without patriarchal oversight. From that, Domínguez insisted, flowed endless calamities. With men locked in, "their wives remain not only unfettered and free, but certain that their husband cannot observe their activities, because they cannot leave the obraje; at the same time, she struggles to support the family on the small amount her husband sends after paying advances, and what she can earn."[131] "In those circumstances, necessity, liberty, solicitation, and opportunity conspire to cause infidelity in marriages. . . . In no other part of the kingdom, including the capital, are there as many adulteries as in this unhappy place." And liberty and infidelity led inevitably to conflict: "the husband, on suspicion or hearing news of his wife's bad conduct, seeks an occasion to take vengeance, leading to discords, suits, wounds, and complaints—in a word every disruption and bad consequence that can be caused by principles grounded in disorder and abomination."[132]

Promoting violence among men, giving liberty to wives, making men violent toward their wives—locked-in labor assaulted the essence of patriarchy. It destroyed patriarchal power over children: "With the man locked in, the family is without a head. As a result, the children lack respect for the father; they know no subordination, nor gain what little education he might give. They live, grow up, and die as brutes." Domínguez saw a final calamity. When a mother went to an obraje to share her husband's bed, "the daughter runs out and does a hundred things it is not necessary to state."[133] To Domínguez patriarchy was essential; only working patriarchs could keep wives at home, educate children, and ensure daughters' chastity. Advances might fund key times in patriarchal lives: marriages, baptisms, and funerals, along with roles in community religious life. But if advances led to debts and workers locked in workshops, patriarchal power was destroyed.

The Corregidor saw coercion as equally destructive. Workers feigned illness and provoked fights with managers, hoping that a magistrate would grant an exit. Workers came to see bosses as "tyrants, rotten with greed, . . . who jail them, whip them, and beat them, in a word, who subject them to the most vile and undignified treatment imaginable." Inside, obrajes split into warring camps; "the boss and his foremen count on a group of workers who are devoted to them; the opposition complains constantly and lives in disgust."[134] Violent and divided workshops were unproductive. Some men escaped, at times through an unguarded door, at times pleading family crisis—a need to attend to a wife or find a wayward child. To leave, they found an ally to guarantee their debt. Many then fled, leaving guarantor and obraje to dispute the obligation. Men in flight went to outlying textile towns: San Juan del Río, Salvatierra, Acámbaro, even Zinapécuaro. If they were found and returned, the costs increased their debt, prolonging the difficulties inherent in locking them into the obrajes.[135]

The solution, Domínguez insisted, was simple: end advances and lock-ins; employers and workers would gain. Advances addressed workers' needs; they rose in the face of labor scarcities that increased workers' bargaining power. "The *indios* and plebians who make up the obraje work forces never save money" to pay tribute or the cost of marriages, baptisms, and funerals. Facing labor shortages, obraje operators like other employers gave advances. But only obrajes locked workers in to force their labor.[136] In Querétaro's tobacco factory "no money is advanced to nearly three thousand persons from the same populace." They paid tributes, married, baptized children, treated illness, and buried their dead without advances. In Mexico City the tobacco factory, the Casa del Apartado (where silver was separated from gold), and innumerable small shops all worked without advances.[137] Domínguez offered no explanation. He might have noted the large number of women in the tobacco factories. They did not pay tributes; they were not patriarchal heads of households. He might have noted too that the factories provided childcare and mutual aid funds, collected from workers to help pay costs that the obrajes addressed with advances.

Ultimately Domínguez recognized that advances were a long tradition at Querétaro, pressed by workers in the face of labor shortages. If advances were essential or at least inevitable, "there should be no lock-in on their account." To prove that advances did not require lock-ins, Domínguez looked to the countryside. Although "agricultural and grazing estates everywhere pay advances to resident workers and day laborers, they have never imagined locking them in. And it is clear that no people are more free than those who live in the country and are always roaming."[138] Domínguez again offered no explanation. He simply insisted that advance payments had to end. Current debts based on past advances had to be paid, in cash or labor: "Otherwise the obraje owners would lose much money." And advances had to end everywhere; otherwise workers would take advances in other towns with labor shortages, pay obligations in Querétaro, and leave. The result would be "a mortal blow caused by a shortage of workers."[139]

Domínguez knew that if advances stopped, workers would need a way to meet the expenses of patriarchal family life. He proposed that obrajes create mutual aid societies (like those in the tobacco factory). He noted that when an obraje worker, his wife, or a child died, workers took a collection to help with funeral costs. Weavers helped weavers; spinners helped spinners; carders helped carders. The Corregidor argued that the custom should extend to marriages and births—the creative moments of patriarchal families. With a shift from informal collections to organized aid, managers would take one real weekly to fund "genuine needs, which will be quickly and surely assisted."[140] In Domínguez's proposal payments would come from workers' wages, not from advances made in addition to wages and rarely repaid. He imagined utopian outcomes: "Then, bosses and workers would live in that sweet liberty that leads to just equilibrium between the authority of the former and the moderate subjugation of the latter." Cruel employers would lack workers; lazy workers would lack work. "Gambling and drunkenness will end"; workers would go home after every shift to rule as patriarchs in well-ordered households.[141]

Domínguez knew that employers would gain more than workers would from his plan. "The owners . . . would be the first to harvest the fruits of this policy, no longer losing the amounts they now lose when so many die or flee still charged with debts. Workers would have to contain their expenses to the level of their wages; they would lose the ability they now have to take exorbitant quantities that they usually waste on useless or pernicious expenditures." The goal was clear: reduce employers' costs and make workers live within their wages. Yet many argued that without advances, labor shortage would follow. Domínguez's answer was that more would be produced by "ten men working by choice and for reward than by twenty forced by rigorous cruelty."[142] Once advances ended, how would employers promote energetic productivity?

Domínguez had plans. With the end of advances the obrajes should turn to piece rates, again following the tobacco factory. If that failed he endorsed a request from obraje owners to allow up to twelve lashes "to contain any lack of subordination."[143] So much for free labor. Domínguez wrote at a time of peak labor demand in 1801. "This is a temporary challenge that will end when the war ends; then, instead of labor shortages, there will be surplus among those who now live in the city."[144] When war ended and production fell employers would be owed large sums by workers whom they no longer needed.

An account in 1804 of workers' debts at the obraje and tannery at the Batán estate, near Pueblito just outside Querétaro, is revealing. Either Domínguez exaggerated the level of individual debts, or they declined after 1801. The obraje's 171 weavers, carders, and spinners owed on average less than 12 pesos each—almost exactly the level owed by the estate's 43 agricultural employees. Four tannery workers owed nearly 20 pesos each; 183 men recruited seasonally from Pueblito and nearby villages owed an average of 5 pesos. Advances remained central to labor recruitment, industrial and agricultural, permanent and seasonal. They gave workers supplements to assist with patriarchal duties. They were an incentive to begin to work, if not to stay at work. Yet they cost the Batán estate and obraje 3,298 pesos more than prevailing wages would have paid.[145] As Domínguez emphasized, advances were a cost that burdened employers and reduced profits.

In 1805 Viceroy don José de Iturrigaray decreed a limit of five pesos on advances and prohibited coercion on the pretext of debts. Did he respond to Domínguez's analysis? After Domínguez wrote, the textile industry faced years of instability. Cloth imports rose to fifteen million pesos yearly in 1802 and 1803, cutting into production and employment at Querétaro. Then imports fell to eight million pesos in 1804 and below three million pesos in 1805 and 1806.[146] The viceroy decreed limits on advances and the end of lock-ins as war again protected markets, increasing production and employment. The goal was to allow employers to hire without costly advances. When imports returned the employers could fire employees without losing debts still owed. These were key concerns when imports rose to nine million pesos in 1807, fell below four million pesos in 1808, then drove to historic peaks of fourteen million pesos yearly as British imports flooded the market in 1809 and 1810.[147] If the viceroy's prohibitions were effective, production could rise with little increase in labor costs and fall with layoffs affordable to employers and costly to workers.

A tribute census completed in 1807 listed sixteen obrajes at Querétaro, the same number as in 1793. There and in a larger number of household workshops, unmarried youths accounted for over 40 percent of working men.[148] That was one way to limit labor costs. Another was to drive down the advances that recruited workers. A lease signed early in 1808 detailed operations at the Tenería obraje, located among the huertas of San Sebastián. There were 121 men in the shop: 28 weavers, 59 carders, and 34 spinners. Another 85 (who may have been men, women, or youths) spun yarn in three cuadrillas at Huimilpan and San Bartolo, in the highlands southwest of the city. A total of 206 workers owed 1,538 pesos—just over 7 pesos each, small advances by historical standards.[149] Perhaps the obligated labor that so long had favored workers, and so often provoked conflicts over debts, was declining as Querétaro industry turned to young wage workers after 1800. The Tenería lease showed a rising merchant ready to take up obraje operation in years of uncertainty. He reimbursed the owner the cost of the advances and committed to pay six hundred pesos in yearly rent. He expected to profit, but the opportunity did not last. The French occupation of Spain later in May 1808 led to a new a flood of British imports in 1809 and 1810. Bajío cloth makers faced renewed pressures and uncertainties.

Alcabala collections show that the market economy remained strong at Querétaro past 1800. The growth of cloth production under wartime protection increased employment with advances and coercions in the obrajes, and with pressures upon working families in the trapiches. The expansion of the tobacco factory offered wage work to hundreds of men and thousands of women, with the security of mutual aid. And thousands of Querétaro families continued to cultivate huertas, the rich urban gardens that defined city life.

Irrigated and intensely cultivated with flowers, fruits, and vegetables sold in city plazas, surrounding towns, and markets from Guanajuato and Zacatecas to Mexico City, the hundreds of huertas at La Cañada, Querétaro, and west at Apaseo provided an agrarian base to urban life. Built by Otomí founders in the sixteenth century, early huertas combined maize cultivation with fruits and vegetables. Over the centuries, as grazing shifted northward and irrigation turned outlying estates to wheat and maize, huertas specialized in vegetables and fruits. The Otomí staunchly defended their huertas and the water that irrigated them. There were conflicts, significant losses, and incursions by Spaniards, mestizos, and mulattoes. An inquiry in the 1750s revealed many such newcomers among the Otomí in the San Sebastián parish; obrajes, tanneries, and other workshops were also interspersed among the huertas there. Spaniards were accused of taking water; tanneries were accused of fouling everyone's water. Yet investigation revealed that even if the huertas were no longer fully Otomí nor purely agricultural, they remained a vibrant part of city life. In the early 1790s the persistence of the Otomí council and huertas sustained a city of two trajectories: In San Sebastián, Otomí separation and endogamy ruled. In the city center people of every origin mixed in a fluid community of workers and artisans. Mesoamerica still jostled North America in urban Querétaro. In 1798 the Otomí of San Sebastián went to court once again to defend huertas and water, and the republican rights that sustained their independence.[150]

Father Zeláa refused to recogize the Otomí among Querétaro's glories. He had to mention the parish of San Sebastián Martyr, heart of the Otomí community. Calling its church "poorly adorned," he conceded that the parish was "respectable enough . . . being one of the most lush and delightful neighborhoods in the city, full of orchards and surrounded by great huertas."[151] Guadalupe's devoted priest admired the legacy of his city's Otomí foundations; he would not recognize the founders' descendants.

With perhaps two thousand Otomí families living on and working huertas, nearly ten thousand of the city's fifty thousand people retained bases in cultivation. They were small commercial growers marketing produce; some had textile and other shops; many women took in spinning. Men worked for wages in obrajes, women in the tobacco factory. The potential mix within families was endless. Some ways of work reinforced patriarchy; others challenged it. Whenever huerta cultivation was part of the mix it limited dependence on industry— whether household weaving, the obrajes, or the tobacco factory. Perhaps that was why employers, large and small, had to offer advances to recruit workers; why obrajes used locks to hold workers and reclaim advances; and why Querétaro's workers negotiated the hard years before 1793 and the expanding yet volatile economy afterward better than their neighbors in San Miguel.

Urban Capitalism

The predatory profit seeking of don José Sánchez Espinosa and other entrepreneurs in Mexico City, Guanajuato, San Miguel, and Querétaro, their alliance for power with the Bourbon regime, their drives to lower earnings among the working majority, and their turn to city patrols and other social controls—in a dynamic, globally linked commercial society shaped by monetized ways of production and labor—combine to illustrate the culmination of capitalism in the Bajío after 1770. Inevitably there were conflicts, contradictions, and complexities. There were conflicts within great families, between them, and between great entrepreneurs and provincial competitors. There were contradictions in the alliance for profit and power: the regime promoted silver mining and prejudiced textile production; it put in place policies designed to assert state dominance and then negotiated as great families forged connections with high officials; intendants sent to rule pursued common goals with provincial elites; new coercive powers meant to strengthen the state relied on entrepreneurs for funds and command.

Complexity also abounded in the mounting pressures that struck the working majority: at Guanajuato mineworkers became Spanish, lost partidos, lived in constant danger, and saw women work in large numbers sorting ore, all while gaining exceptional if declining earnings. In Querétaro obrajes declined and revived, household artisans found new opportunities and pressures that reduced earnings, and the tobacco factory recruited women workers in unprecedented numbers, paying low wages compensated for by childcare and mutual aid. And in Querétaro every pressure was cushioned by huertas that provided an agrarian base to the city of textiles and trade. In both Guanajuato and Querétaro reformers called for an end to obligated labor; the advances that drew men to labor created debts that often went unpaid, increasing employers' costs and workers' earnings. The end of advances would increase profit and curtail endless negotiations over debts, work, and obligations. But obligated labor ended only in the tobacco factory, where most workers were women, childcare was offered, and mutual aid cushioned the insecurities of work and family life.

The tie between patriarchy and obligated labor is clear. When entrepreneurs offered employment to men they provided advances at key times in the lives of working patriarchs: on taking employment, at marriage, at baptisms, and at funerals, and to pay for cures and religious devotions and festivals. Working men consolidated patriarchal roles; they gained earnings above prevailing rates. Ending obligated labor would be difficult. Enforcing work and collecting debts required more effective policing than new patrols provided. Recruiting workers without advances required higher wages. And the attempt would challenge the patriarchal bargains that had structured labor in the Bajío since the sixteenth century. Partidos might end in the most profitable mines; women might work in growing numbers sorting ores and making cigarettes. Obligated labor—the heart of the patriarchal bargain linking entrepreneurs and working men—would endure.

Thus patriarchy remained the dominant way of orchestrating social power in great families and their enterprises, among their provincial dependents and competitors, and in most working households. It remained the pivotal hierarchical link between the powerful and the poor, organizing endless negotiations, conflicts, and conciliations. Yet after 1770 patriarchy faced deepening contradictions: mineworkers remained uncertain patriarchs; household producers faced deepening insecurity; the growth of wage work among women challenged patriarchy directly. Meanwhile the acceleration of capitalism brought parallel opportunites to estate operators and similar pressures to working families across the Bajío countryside.

CHAPTER 7

The Challenge of Capitalism
in Rural Communities

Production, Ethnicity, and Patriarchy

from La Griega to Puerto de Nieto, 1780–1810

IN THE BAJÍO AS ACROSS NEW SPAIN, power concentrated in cities while the population was mostly rural. The separation of city and country was never clear or simple, however. The huertas so important at Querétaro gave the city a rural cast. And cities depended on estates and rural producers in many ways: profit for agricultural entrepreneurs; food for city markets; supplies for mines and craft shops. Rural women took in spinning for urban workshops. City men worked estate harvests. Town magistrates sat in justice at villages and estates. Churches, convents, and clergy concentrated in cities, yet bishops lived on tithes levied on estate harvests, and convents were mortgage banks that funded and profited from estate production. Festivals drew country people to cities; Our Lady at Pueblito made the village west of Querétaro a focus of devotion for people urban and rural, powerful and poor.

Ultimately the integration of the cities and the countryside reflected a deep historical paradox. State power, church institutions, and landed entrepreneurs concentrated in cities that depended on rural production. Cities cannot feed themselves. By the eighteenth century huertas were truck farms providing fruits and vegetables to favored consumers. The staples of sustenance came from the country. In contrast, rural families produced much of their own food and clothing. Rural communities retained at least limited autonomies; powers based in cities worked to constrain those autonomies. Rural families produced sustenance; urban-based estate operators profited by channeling sustenance to city markets. The rural people who sustained everything lived and labored in subordination.

Their subordination was never simple or absolute. Most Bajío estate operators lived in local cities; the most powerful ruled from Mexico City. Most Bajío rural families lived in estate communities; after 1750 republics with community lands held only minorities of the population, even around Querétaro and along the borders with Mesoamerica. For centuries population growth had lagged behind estate development, leading estate operators to offer tenancies, advances, and secure employment structured by patriarchy to attract and hold communities essential to estate production. Thanks to the combination of patriarchy and security, the Bajío countryside remained at peace in the 1760s, while riots shook key cities.

Difficult change came to rural communities across the Bajío after 1770. The silver economy soared, cities expanded, and population growth made rural producers less scarce. Estate operators, like their kin in mining and trade, aimed to boost their profits by reducing workers' earnings and threatening their security. Patriarchy held at the center of the social relations of production while working patriarchs faced new challenges to their ability to sustain families. Contradictions deepened; profits soared while families struggled. But stability held until the regime broke in 1808, followed by two years of dearth that led to insurgency in 1810. Capitalist societies strive to stabilize economic concentrations and deepening exploitations with limited coercion. After 1770 the Bajío, urban and rural, was ever more capitalist.

The transformation of Bajío rural production after 1770 is well known; the changing social relations that brought new tensions to estate communities are less known. Across the eastern Bajío, from La Griega and the Amascala basin to Puerto de Nieto and the uplands around San Miguel, the accelerating pursuit of profit struck estate communities. Hierarchies of patriarchy intersected with changing ethnic relations to organize power, negotiate labor, and sustain production, until an unprecedented mix of social polarization, famine, and regime breakdown brought unimagined crises from 1808 to 1810.

Agrarian Capitalism

Through the second half of the eighteenth century estate communities and cultivation expanded across the Bajío. The Otomí and other indigenous people who had long lived in landed villages along the basin's southern margins remained, increasingly outnumbered by neighbors living and working at estates. Elsewhere in the region landed republics were few; estates mixing Spaniards, mestizos, mulattoes, and indios organized rural life. Population continued to expand despite periodic epidemics and famines. Rural production boomed, sustaining Bajío cities and mines along with towns and estates to the north across Spanish North America. Bajío cultivators also fed Mexico City when scarcity drove up the price of staples there. Market-focused, profit-seeking production soared in a dynamic agrarian capitalism.[1]

In the sixteenth century cultivation had focused on irrigated river plains. Back from the banks, estates mostly grazed sheep and cattle. During the seventeenth century irrigated estates expanded across the bottomlands. By the eighteenth century, as mining, population, and the demand for food surged, cultivation moved far beyond the plains along major rivers. Irrigation expanded along smaller streams, and estates opened fields dependent on irregular rains. Newcomers, often poor tenants, planted rain-fed maize while they and their sons provided seasonal hands to plant and harvest irrigated estate crops, often wheat. The result was the expulsion of sheep to drier pastures in the north, an expansion of maize production on former pastures in the Bajío, and growing populations in estate communities.

By the 1760s the irrigated plains that made the Bajío into New Spain's granary mostly raised wheat, fruits, and vegetables to supply growing urban minorities made prosperous by the mining boom. Maize, the staple of the poor, was left to fields without irrigation, often uplands converted from pasture that yielded good harvests early on and then declined. More and more the food of the poor depended on marginal lands and uncertain rains. When hail, frost, and drought struck together in 1785 and 1786, a devastating famine drove maize prices five times higher than when rains had been good. People took to the roads in a desperate search for food. During two painful years the silver economy slowed, while 15 percent of the people in the Bajío died in an unprecedented famine.

Amid deadly dearth, repeated invocations of Christ and the Virgin came with proud declarations of charitable intent by those who profiteered from hoarded grain. Ecclesiastical capitalists funded new plantings of maize on irrigated lands; they paid for deliveries of grain from coastal lowlands, where drought was less intense but production limited. After the crisis passed, Bajío landlords saw new ways to gain. The profits of scarcity and ecclesiastical mortgages funded new irrigation. Some entrepreneurs planted maize on irrigated fields while many settled more tenants on uplands, expanding maize on marginal lands, collecting rents from families who faced declining yields, and driving tenants and their sons to labor cheaply in estate fields. After 1786 the price of maize never fell to pre-famine levels; in years of plenty a fanega of maize cost 10 to 12 reales, 50 percent more than before 1785.

While landlords increased irrigation and cultivation, they pressured working families and communities. Around Querétaro huertas sustained the urban Otomí, while rural estates mixed Hispanic tenants and employees with Otomí employees and seasonal hands, some recruited in the city. Across the bottomlands small irrigated estates continued to depend on resident communities that mixed migrants from Mesoamerica with people of African ancestry, some classed as indio and others as mulatto. To the north around San Miguel, estates long committed to grazing and limited cultivation still included a few slaves in communities of tenants and grazers. The diverse communities of the eastern Bajío all faced pressures after 1770, yet they faced them in different ways. Still, there was a dominant trend: patriarchal working families lost earnings and rations while paying rising rents on increasingly marginal lands. For centuries patriarchal dependence brought compensating security; now patriarchy structured deepening poverty and unprecedented insecurity.

The Collapse of Slavery at Puerto de Nieto

Slavery was long a part of the history of the Bajío. Beginning in the sixteenth century slaves arrived to labor at Guanajuato, weave in Querétaro obrajes, and care for growing herds at grazing estates. Many found ways out of bondage, becoming mulatto mineworkers or joining bottomlands communities, often as cultivating indios. A few became prosperous landlords and thus Spaniards. Historically in the Bajío, slavery proved more a way to force migration than an enduring labor system. Still, bondage survived into the eighteenth century in Querétaro obrajes and at outlying grazing properties. It collapsed at both in the 1780s amid population growth and commercial acceleration.

A unique view of emancipation comes from Puerto de Nieto, the estate east of San Miguel that don Juan Caballero y Ocío had worked with slaves around 1700 and don José Sánchez Espinosa operated after 1780. The resident community then included dozens of families and hundreds of people. Most were Spaniards and mestizos, often tenants; uncounted indios also lived there, often as subtenants.[2] In the 1770s a number of mulatto slaves remained, most tending livestock. As markets grew, however, the estate shifted from grazing to cultivation, sending livestock north. Early in 1779 don Francisco de Espinosa y Navarijo, the priest of the Mexico City Cathedral Chapter who then ran the Obra Pía estates, ordered a group of slaves and their dependents, twenty-one in all, to move north to Bocas in San Luis Potosí. No longer needed at Puerto de Nieto, they might serve usefully in the north.

The makeup of the group set to move reveals much about the surviving slave population at Puerto de Nieto. Juan de Nono was to go, along with his free wife. Ygnacio Trinidad, his wife Cesárea, and two infants, all slaves, would go. María Sebastiana and six slave children would go. So would three single slave men: Pedro Ponciano, Pedro Ramón, and Bruno, joined "voluntarily," Espinosa y Navarijo insisted, by "old" Manuela Jacinta, María Ventura, and her daughter Ventura, and by María Simona de las Xabones with her baby María Ygnacia.[3]

The group that was to move north included slave men and slave and free women and children. One slave man had a free wife, her ethnicity unstated. Presumptions of patriarchy meant that she would go. There was one slave couple with small children, plus a slave mother with six children (and no identified spouse or father). In addition, three slave men, unmarried, would go with three free women and their free children. Free and not married, the women were to go "voluntarily." The makeup of the group ordered north shows that most men still enslaved at Puerto de Nieto had formed couples with free women, with or without marriage. Their children were free. At Puerto de Nieto in the 1770s slaves still built family relationships to free their children; every generation brought slavery closer to an end. Among those still enslaved, working men were few, dependent women and children many. In the group that was to move, five slave men might work regularly; two slave women had a total of eight children. Two-thirds of the remaining slaves were women and children.

The group provided little labor yet was costly to maintain. It made sense to the entrepreneur to ship his remaining slaves north, where labor scarcity persisted, grazing ruled, and slaves remained valued workers. The slaves soon revealed their own views. In June, Pedro Ponciano, now described as "el viejo" (the old man), ran away. It is not known whether his free companion, "old" Manuela Jacinta, joined him, as the manager reported only the flight of property. Pedro Ponciano's decision is revealing. An elder among slaves at Puerto de Nieto, he could have run earlier. Yet he had remained in the estate community, surely to keep ties to Manuela, a free woman. When ordered north he fled. In the community slavery allowed him a free companion and was apparently bearable. Facing removal to the north and the unhappiness of a companion pressed to go "voluntarily," Pedro Ponciano chose flight.

What "el Viejo" began others continued. In May 1782 two slave women, described only as the wives of Eusebio and José Antonio, fled Puerto de Nieto for Mexico City. They appeared before the Corregidor, chief magistrate of the viceregal capital, denying their slave status. Don José Sánchez Espinosa, now running the Obra Pía estates, convinced the magistrate that the women were slaves. Yet after his legal victory the young landlord did not return the women to Puerto de Nieto. He offered them for sale in Mexico City, but no one bid on married women who had fled and refused to accept slave status.[4] Their fate is unknown.

In September of the same year two young slave men followed the women to the capital. Juan and Bruno also presented themselves in court, arguing that the order to move north to Bocas, separating them from their families, was mistreatment and should bring freedom. They argued in court what "el Viejo" Pedro Ponciano asserted in action: slavery was bearable in the community at Puerto de Nieto; but forced migration was not, and for the youths it was grounds for emancipation. The court rejected their claim and ordered them auctioned to the highest bidder in the capital.[5] Sale would not, of course, return Juan and Bruno to family and community. And with their history of flight, sale proved difficult. They remained in Mexico City, awaiting a buyer. Early in November their mother, María Juliana de Aguilar, wrote to Sánchez Espinosa, apparently in her own hand. She acknowledged her status as a slave. (Her name suggests that she had married a free man named Aguilar; no slave at Puerto de Nieto used a patronym.) She scolded her owner for mistreating her sons.[6] Again the outcome is not known. The two slave wives along with Bruno and Juan were among the throngs seeking asylum or anonymity in Mexico City in the 1780s. When the *Gaceta de Mexico* began in 1785 it was full of notices from those trying to locate and reclaim slaves who had fled to the capital.[7]

By the spring of 1783 Sánchez Espinosa knew he could no longer keep slaves at Puerto de Nieto. Some refused to move north; others fled south to Mexico City, where courts showed no ability to sustain bondage. So the young operator of the Obra Pía estates began to sell his human property at whatever price he could get. Ana María, married to the free indio Salvador Álvarez, bought her freedom for thirty pesos—probably earned by her husband. María Anastasia was a sixteen-year-old slave, daughter of the free mulatto Julián Antonio Córdoba and his slave wife María del Cármen. Her parents paid fifty pesos for her freedom.

The wife of don José Antonio Plaza, the estate manager, paid forty pesos to buy María de los Santos. The slave woman probably served in the manager's household, a role that the purchase maintained. Another slave brought thirty pesos, allowing Plaza to report to Sánchez Espinosa that he had sold four slaves for 150 pesos—less than the value of a single slave earlier in the century. Plaza concluded that only one slave remained: Pedro Norberto—old, ill, and unable to be sold. That assessment is revealing. María del Cármen, wife of the free Julián Antonio Córdoba, mother of the freed María Anastasia, remained a slave. Apparently a slave woman married to a free man and with a free daughter was effectively free.[8]

As the 1780s began, the slaves at Puerto de Nieto kept traditions that had helped free many of their neighbors: slave men and free women produced free offspring; free men and slave women produced slave children whom their fathers could free by purchase. The process left slaves who provided little labor and had many dependents. The owners' first response was to send them north, where they were still valuable as workers. Many refused to move; they considered participation in family and community life at Puerto de Nieto a right. At least five fled, including four who went to court demanding redress. The court's solution was to require the owner to sell irate slaves, and buyers proved hard to find. At that point Sánchez Espinosa sold his remaining slaves for little gain, shedding recalcitrant human property. Social mixing, and the freeing of children every generation, had weakened slavery at Puerto de Nieto. Slave resistance ended it in 1783, when slaves refused to move and Sánchez Espinosa saw that coercion was no longer worth the cost. The demise of slavery came with an acceleration of agrarian capitalism across the Bajío. Freed slaves benefited. Yet the end of bondage was not a sign of gain for all in growing rural communities, as we shall see.

The conflicts that marked the last days of slavery at Puerto de Nieto add complexity to our understanding of patriarchy. No slave had a patronym, at least not in the letters between owner and manager. Those who owned and ruled slaves apparently worked to limit slaves' participation in the patriarchy that organized families, communities, and hierarchies of power. Could men owned by other men be fully men? Could they join the hierarchies that linked unequal patriarchs? Could they claim rule as men, as patriarchs, in working families? Among slaves at Puerto de Nieto, many had companions and children—few were married. Slave men, as property, asserted patriarchy only in limited ways. In contrast, owner and manager recognized ties between enslaved mothers and children. Slave status passed from mother to child, shaping the owner's view. Slavery limited patriarchy and emphasized the roles of slave mothers. That was clear when María Juliana de Aguilar bluntly challenged her owner's treatment of her slave sons. The boys' father, probably a free mulatto dependent on Sánchez Espinosa for land and work, stood back while María Juliana gave no quarter.

Slavery limited men's access to the claims of patriarchy. Yet when the owner tried to force many of Puerto de Nieto's remaining slaves north to Bocas, he and his manager turned to patriarchal assumptions. Suddenly it was useful to give slave men, even those not married to their free companions, patriarchal claims. Only thus might free women and children be induced to join slave men on the trek north. Propertied and powerful men negotiated patriarchy to serve their interests. They denied it to slave men living and working at Puerto de Nieto. But when they decided to force slaves to move and hoped to make free wives, companions, and children go along, the landlords discovered slave men's patriarchal rights. Slaves could be patriarchs if that helped to enforce landlords' power in working families. The turn to patriarchy aimed to cement social inequality as slavery collapsed.

Patriarchy, Amalgamations, and Segregations in Estate Communities

Population growth and the availability of free workers facilitated the end of slavery. Historically obrajes contained slaves by locking them in. The collapse of slavery in obrajes came while operators cut costs in the face of expanding imports. When wartime protection brought boom again in the 1790s, operators advanced wages to free workers, creating pretexts to lock them in, as the Corregidor Domínguez lamented. At estates such control was impossible, as Domínguez also emphasized. Slaves at Puerto de Nieto lived among free people and worked as herdsmen and muleteers, precluding containment. While slavery persisted, ethnic amalgamations, clandestine births, and adoptions had freed children in every generation. Yet family ties also held slaves at estates, and family commitments led those who were asked to move to conclude that the attempt constituted mistreatment, justifying flight and court challenges. Meanwhile Sánchez Espinosa and his manager began to assert patriarchy in slaves' lives.

Diverse ethnic amalgamations shaped society in the Bajío from the beginning, especially north and west of Querétaro (where strong

Otomí foundations inhibited mixing). After the risings of 1767 Don José de Gálvez saw it as essential to enlightened reform to end rampant mixing and enforce ethnic distinctions. Yet not only did amalgamations persist at Guanajuato, but many mulattoes claimed Spanish status there. Mixing also continued in urban Querétaro, though strong Otomí identities remained. And across the countryside around Querétaro and San Miguel, diverse ways of amalgamation and segregation led to unprecedented complexity after 1770. Amalgamations persisted at Puerto de Nieto, integrating mulattoes and indios into the community. At the same time, in the Santa Rosa basin, just east on the way to Querétaro, new segregations separated Spaniards and mestizos from mulattoes and indios in different estate communities. And farther east, at La Griega and most estates on the Amascala plain, segregation separated Spaniards and Otomí within estate communities. As the eighteenth century ended, patriarchy intersected in complex ways with changing ethnic relations in diverse estate communities. The militia censuses of the early 1790s document the Hispanic population of the region.[9]

Less than a decade after the collapse of slavery, in 1792 Puerto de Nieto was a large, ethnically complex community. The census listed 150 households (including only those where at least one spouse was Spanish or mestizo) and 617 people. About half the households were led by men classed as Spaniards, fewer than 40 percent by mestizos, leaving 12 percent headed by mulattoes married to Spaniards or mestizos (mulattoes married to mulattas or indias were excluded, a large uncounted presence). Amalgamation persisted: Spaniards tended to marry Spaniards, but a third of Spanish men and over a third of Spanish women married others (mostly mestizos but also mulattoes and indios). Only half of mestizos wed mestizos; when they married others they preferred Spaniards, yet chose mulattoes and indios more often than Spaniards did. Most revealingly, nine mulatto men had wed Spaniards and seven had married mestizas. The mulattoes of Puerto de Nieto continued to marry into the Spanish-mestizo community. Eight indias also had wed Spaniards and mestizos, revealing an uncounted indigenous sector marrying with the favored majority. After slavery collapsed, Puerto de Nieto remained an amalgamating community.[10]

A traveler heading east from Puerto de Nieto over the pass and into the Santa Rosa basin met a segregating world. The first community in the lowlands below was Buenavista, the estate where Our Lady of Pueblito had protected residents from a lightning strike decades earlier. With 33 households and 152 residents listed in the census (the Querétaro counts listed households headed by Spaniards, mestizos, mulattoes, and indios married to women of those categories), it was a

Spanish-mestizo community. Spaniards and mestizos headed nearly 90 percent of households; Spaniards married Spaniards, mestizos married mestizas. The amalgamation that shaped Puerto de Nieto was all but absent.[11] In 1807 there were forty-seven indigenous employees and eighty-three tenants at Buenavista.[12] How many had come since 1792 is unknown; notably few in the Hispanic community had taken an indigenous spouse. Buenavista was a diverse but segregated community.

So was Jofre, just northeast. It was larger than Puerto de Nieto in 1791, with 186 households and 836 Hispanic residents. In 1807 it included 70 indigenous employees and 128 native tenants. In 1791 Spaniards led most Hispanic households, with mestizos the second-largest group, leaving 22 mulatto households a small minority; 85 percent of Spaniards married Spaniards; 85 percent of mestizos married mestizos. The exceptions saw Spaniards and mestizos marry each other: the few mulattoes never married their Spanish or mestizo neighbors. Jofre was large and ethnically diverse like Puerto de Nieto, yet segregated like Buenavista.[13]

The ethnic amalgamation that facilitated the end of slavery at Puerto de Nieto and promoted integration there in the 1790s was rare at estate communities in Querétaro's jurisdiction. Puerto de Nieto continued the historic fluidity that characterized San Miguel and the northern Bajío. Querétaro, from the start a zone of Spanish-Otomí dichotomy, retained and reasserted the ethnic segregation more common in Spanish Mesoamerica.

In that city and the adjacent countryside, an Otomí majority still lived in indigenous republics: San Sebastián ruled the huertas along the banks of the river north of the city center; San Pedro de la Cañada organized life in the canyon just east; Pueblito orchestrated religious devotion and indigenous life just southwest. San Sebastián and La Cañada were famous for lush huertas; El Pueblito, famous for its Virgin, was infamous for a lack of community lands. There in the 1760s, during a mid-century economic downturn, 57 men contracted to lease a nearby estate for 280 pesos, 5 pesos each, for two years.[14] It did not prove a solution. Close by Querétaro, estates included few resident Spaniards, mestizos, or mulattoes. Most work was done by villagers trekking to labor seasonally, seeking wages to complement their limited cultivation and cloth production. Such ways of production and work mirrored the Mesoamerican basins to the south, where estates without resident communities relied on labor recruited in nearby villages.

Rural Spanish North America began in the basins surrounding Querétaro to the east, north, and west. There large estate communities included Spaniards, mestizos, mulattoes, and Otomí. A census in 1778 showed that beyond the city and the huertas of San Sebastián, most Otomí lived at estates, with Spanish, mestizo, and mulatto neighbors.[15] That diversity did not bring mixing, however. The countryside remained segregated, yet in locally distinct ways. On the Amascala plain east of the city La Griega and other estates included Spanish minorities segregated from indigenous majorities. In the Santa Rosa basin to the northwest, Spaniards and mestizos segregated from mulattoes and indios to inhabit separate estate communities.

A tour of rural Querétaro is revealing. Heading east from the city, the road followed the river up the canyon to San Pedro de la Cañada. Pames settled the area before the conquest and early Otomí settlers tried to build Querétaro there, only to be expelled to the plains below. In the 1750s Corregidor Acosta complained that La Cañada's Pames controlled rich huertas and lush hot-spring baths, blocked Spanish settlement, and charged too much for bathing and recreation. The people of La Cañada preferred segregation.

A small Hispanic community did live at La Cañada. The census of 1778 reported fewer than three hundred Hispanic residents, less than 10 percent of the community. The militia count of 1791 included 127 non-Pames; the tribute list from 1807 reported 498 Pame households. The Pame majority held strong.[16] In 1791, among married heads of Hispanic households, twenty-seven of thirty-one were Spaniards. Two-thirds married Spanish women, but eight had wed mestizas and gained access to huertas. Spanish men at La Cañada included two priests and a schoolmaster, three traders (in one extended family), eleven craftsmen (blacksmiths, hat makers, and candle makers, plus a tailor, a shoemaker, and a sculptor), and five men who managed and worked a gristmill. Eighteen Hispanic cultivators (more than half the heads of household) worked huertas. Twenty of the thirty-three Hispanic heads of households were born at La Cañada, including some men over sixty and others who were only twenty. Eight men (priests, traders, craftsmen, and the schoolmaster) came from Querétaro. The mill managers and workers (who lived in a compound) came from afar. Nearly all the Hispanic cultivators were born at La Cañada, often of mestiza mothers (who likely had inherited huertas from Pame forebears). The small Hispanic community at La Cañada showed a pattern of interest, integration, and segregation. Spaniards married mestizas if the match brought land, or perhaps Pame women who married Spaniards become mestizas. Spaniards not seeking or working huertas kept apart from the indigenous majority.[17]

Climbing out of the canyon east of La Cañada, a traveler soon came to La Griega, the Amascala basin estate operated after 1780 by don José Sánchez Espinosa. In 1791 it had 72 Hispanic families with 322 members. In 1807 there were 191 Otomí households with perhaps 750 members. Among sixty-two Hispanic heads of household in 1791, fifty-four claimed Spanish status, five were mestizos, and three were mulattoes. The Spaniards were adamantly endogamous (94 percent). The few exceptions saw Spaniards wed mestizos, as at La Cañada. No Spaniard or mestizo, male or female, at La Griega in 1791 had married a mulatto or indio. Spanish endogamy was strong; a sharp divide separated Spaniards and the few mestizos from fewer mulattoes and uncounted Otomí.[18] The census of 1778 showed 60 percent of the rural population east of Querétaro as indigenous, a proportion confirmed by labor accounts from 1811.[19] The Spanish community was a minority at an estate with about eight hundred residents in 1791, perhaps a thousand by 1807. La Griega was a large, internally segregated estate community.

North of La Griega, Chichimequillas occupied the end of the Amascala basin, up against the mountains that began the Sierra Gorda. Owned and operated by Querétaro's Carmelites, in 1791 Chichimequillas included 76 Hispanic households with 381 residents. In 1807 it listed 167 Otomí households. Presuming that Hispanic families again made up 40 percent of the total, the estate community included about 950 people in 1791 and over 1,100 by 1807; Chichimequillas was the largest estate community around Querétaro. In 1791 Spaniards headed most Hispanic households, though as thirty-nine of a total of sixty-eight they were less dominant than at La Griega. With seventeen households led by mestizos and ten by mulattoes, Chichimequillas was more diverse. Spaniards and mestizos were 75 percent endogamous; mulatto men did marry Spanish and mestizo women. At the northernmost estate in the Amascala basin, the Hispanic population mixed but again remained separate from the indigenous majority. One mulatto had married an india; otherwise no Hispanic man took an Otomí wife.[20] In the Amascala basin Hispanic and indigenous people lived segregated within estate communities.

Along the road from Querétaro north toward San Luis Potosí, a series of basins included numerous estates and the hamlet of Santa Rosa. Living between the Amascala basin, marked by a sharp dichotomy between Hispanics and Otomí, and Puerto de Nieto, where amalgamation reigned, the Hispanic families of the Santa Rosa basin were creating a newly segregated society as the 1790s began. Six estates dominated the country around Santa Rosa. Don Pedro de Septién, perhaps the richest merchant, landlord, and councilman at Querétaro, owned Juriquilla, La Solana, and San Isidro. Don Francisco Velasco, also a Querétaro landlord, owned Santa Catarina, Monte del Negro, and Buenavista. Each estate complex witnessed new segregation in the 1780s and early 1790s.

Among Septíen's estates Juriquilla lay in the basin center, nearest Querétaro. The census of 1791 reported 33 Hispanic households and 142 residents; the tribute count of 1807 reported sixty-six Otomí households—perhaps 250 residents. In 1791 a few Spaniards managed; most Hispanic men were mulatto cultivators (working beside the uncounted Otomí). Just north and east Septíen's La Solana had 23 Hispanic households and 111 residents—all Spaniards and mestizos—in 1791 (there were 68 Otomí householders in 1807). To the west San Isidro listed four Hispanic households in 1791, surely those of managers dealing with indigenous producers (counted as 43 householders in 1807). Several Spanish and mestizo families had migrated recently from Juriquilla to La Solana, leaving Juriquilla a community where Spaniards ruled mulattoes and Otomí, and La Solana a place where Spaniards and mestizos ruled Otomí without mulatto neighbors.[21]

Parallel migrations and segregation shaped don Francisco Velasco's estates just north. At Santa Catarina, in the basin center, and Monte del Negro in the uplands northeast, among only twenty-one Hispanic households, thirteen were headed by mulattoes in 1791. In 1807 the two estates included sixty-six Otomí employee households and forty Otomí tenants. As at Septíen's Juriquilla, a few Spaniards also managed mulattoes and an Otomí majority. Meanwhile, at Velasco's Buenavista, near the pass to Puerto de Nieto, Spaniards and mestizos lived with an Otomí majority and almost no mulatto neighbors.[22] At the Septíen and Velasco estates recent local migrations led to Spaniards and mestizos being segregated from mulattoes. Spaniards married Spaniards; mestizos married mestizas and sometimes Spaniards. Mulattoes married mulattas or sometimes indias. Spaniards and mestizos lived and married together. Earlier many had lived among mulattoes; but as slavery collapsed, Spaniards and mestizos moved in order to segregate the Hispanic communities at Santa Rosa basin estates. The shift left basin lands to mulattoes; Spaniards and mestizos moved to the margins. A parallel segregation occurred at Jofre farther north, where few mulattoes remained in 1791, and growing numbers of Otomí, including many younger men, remained a minority in 1807.[23] An Otomí underclass, uncounted in the militia list in 1791 but detailed in the tribute census in 1807, labored everywhere around Santa Rosa.

Amid segregating estate communities Santa Rosa grew as an informal town. In 1791 it included nineteen Hispanic households with seventy-two residents. Its church was served by priests at San Sebastián, the Otomí parish of huertas on the north side of Querétaro. Santa Rosa mixed Spaniards, mestizos, mulattoes, and caciques. Most heads of household had come from Querétaro, but men were from as far south as Mexico City and as far north as San Luis Potosí. Women headed over 20 percent of households, a larger proportion than at any estate community. Endogamy was minimal, while segregation prevailed at nearby estates. Most men at Santa Rosa were listed as cultivators, yet the hamlet had no land. Its *labradores* worked estate fields as tenants, employees, or seasonal hands. Santa Rosa was a diverse community, inhabited by people who chose not to live at estates even though they worked estate lands. Their mixing contrasted sharply with the segregation under way at the estates where they worked. Santa Rosa's Hispanic community showed that people less subject to estate power were less committed to patriarchy and ethnic segregation.[24]

The contrasting forms of segregation in the Amascala and Santa Rosa basins bring into focus the amalgamation at Puerto de Nieto. Just west over the pass beyond Santa Rosa, it was a large community under managerial power. Yet the census of 1792 details an integrated community with no signs of recent or emerging segregation. Puerto de Nieto differed sharply from the estate communities in the jurisdiction of Querétaro. Its 150 households and 617 residents made up 75 percent of the Hispanic population living across the basin east of San Miguel, almost 40 percent of all Spaniards and mestizos listed in rural San Miguel.[25] Other properties there included mostly mulatto and Otomí residents. Parish registers at Dolores, north of San Miguel, suggest a population that was a third mulatto and half Otomí. Members of these groups often intermarried, shaping a culture of amalgamation that did not prevent declarations of indio status in suits seeking rights as indigenous republics.[26] Puerto de Nieto had a large Spanish and mestizo population, typical of the Querétaro jurisdiction to the east, and numerous mulatto and indigenous residents, typical of the San Miguel jurisdiction extending west and north. In 1792 they mixed, like the mulatto-indio communities of Spanish North America, rejecting the segregation consolidating around Querétaro.[27]

Ownership cannot explain the difference. Don José Sánchez Espinosa controlled La Griega, the most divided community east of Querétaro, and Puerto de Nieto, the most integrated community in the eastern Bajío. His managers could not force slaves at Puerto de Nieto to move to San Luis Potosí; yet other managers engineered migrations to segregate adjacent estates in the Santa Rosa basin. We can only ask why and how. Segregation of those who claimed indio status and its limited rights was a key part of don José de Gálvez's plan to impose social control after the conflicts of the 1760s at Guanajuato, San Felipe, and elsewhere. In the 1770s the regime worked to limit unions between mulattoes and others, a policy that lamented continuing amalgamations and aimed to implement the segregation that the Spanish enlightenment saw as rational.[28] The Querétaro landlords who ruled the Santa Rosa basin estates shared the urge to separate mulattoes from others in Hispanic estate communities, and found ways to implement segregation as slavery waned. No parallel segregation happened at Puerto de Nieto; no segregating migrations reshaped San Miguel's countryside. Entrepreneurs and their managers had to adapt to local practices, leading to diverse forms of segregation around Querétaro while allowing complex amalgamations to persist around San Miguel and beyond.

Managerial Patriarchy

Meanwhile patriarchy held strong, orchestrating production and the social order during decades of growth amid ethnic mixing and segregation. Patriarchy did more than organize reproduction, production, and consumption in families rich, middling, and poor. It was pivotal to the social relations of production and to societal structures of power and inequality. Patriarchy was more than men asserting power over women, children, and other dependents; it was a structure of hierarchy among men, organizing their inequality and facilitating their ability to exercise power in families at every level of society. Patriarchy cemented inequities across classes and within households. Still, it was not free of challenge and negotiation across the Bajío countryside.

Patriarchy remained the key to stabilizing inequality in estate communities during decades of accelerating capitalism. Yet the same acceleration threatened working men's ability to provide families with material welfare, undermining their claims to household rule. Work relations that strengthened patriarchy led men to acquiesce in their own and their families' subordination; when falling wages, rising rents, and evictions threatened working men's patriarchy, their acquiescence was less sure. Patriarchy continued to orchestrate inequality from La Griega to Puerto de Nieto after 1770. Direct challenges to estate power were rare. Yet in a few revealing contests, subordinate women set themselves against powerful men. Across the eastern Bajío, patriarchy was fundamental, paradoxical, and contested.

The militia censuses of the early 1790s reveal how patriarchy often structured estate management. At La Griega and Chichimequillas in the Amascala basin, resident managers led large, extended, patriarchal clans linking them to over 30 percent of Hispanic estate residents. A similar clan ruled La Solana, the largest, most heavily Hispanic of don Pedro Septién's estates in the Santa Rosa Basin. Parallel power was developing at Puerto de Nieto.[29] Entrepreneurs might recruit managers from large clans already at estate communities; new managers might bring kin with them and forge marriage alliances to create extended family ties. They could favor kin—almost inevitably male kin—with land and work, and presume to gain allegiance. At Chichimequillas, Roque Lozada went further; he facilitated a household textile industry among his kinsmen.[30] Managers used kinship to create networks of patriarchal households that extended their power deep into estate communities.

There were limits to managerial clans. At La Griega and Chichimequillas they organized large Hispanic minorities but did not extend into the Otomí majorities. At Juriquilla, Santa Catarina, and Monte del Negro, segregated communities in the Santa Rosa basin, Spanish managers did not create kinship links with mulatto and Otomí majorities.[31] Where internal division shaped estate communities, managerial patriarchy was limited. Where segregation left mulatto-indio communities, managerial patriarchy was all but absent. Again the uniqueness of Puerto de Nieto is clear. When don José Toribio Rico became manager in 1792 he led a clan related by marriage to Spaniards, mestizos, mulattoes, and indios.

At the same time, extended families of patriarchal kin did not favor managerial rule alone. In every large Hispanic estate community with a dominant managerial clan, there were other clans, less extensive but important, connecting households not tied to management. As managerial clans extended estate power, non-managerial clans contested that power. Patriarchal networks allowed men without kin among managers to work together to combine tenancies, permanent employment, and seasonal wage work, helping them increase production, income, and security. Extended clans backed negotiations with managers; if the latter were too severe they might alienate a large part of the community. At Puerto de Nieto a large network of related households excluded from management mixed tenant cultivation, employment, and textile production.[32] While managerial clans extended estate power, serving the owner and favoring managers' kin, other clans strove to cushion social relations of dependence. Patriarchal hierarchies intersected with local segregation and integration to create distinct histories of power, conflict, and change, while commercial cultivation shaped everything. Uniquely documented histories of power, production, patriarchy, and resistance at La Griega and Puerto de Nieto reveal two paths toward agrarian capitalism—and the regional crisis of 1808–10.

Patriarchy in a Divided Community:
Production and Labor at La Griega

Managers played dual roles in estate communities. Formally they represented the landlord-entrepreneur, organizing production to generate profits. They also led complex communities, negotiating to keep the peace essential to production. Patriarchy was pivotal to both. La Griega's managers served don José Sánchez Espinosa, implementing his power, overseeing production, and pressing residents to labor. The same managers were members of the estate community, linked by patriarchal kinship to resident Hispanic families, overseeing work and life among the Otomí majority. They were brokers negotiating between the owner and a segregated community.

Don Simón Rangel ran La Griega in the 1770s for don Francisco de Espinosa y Navarijo and continued after 1780 under Sánchez Espinosa. Rangel's letters reported planting and harvests, marketing, labor relations, and dealing with tenants. He always addressed his superiors as "my boss." When sickness or death hit the owner's family Rangel sent sorrow and prayers. He always professed to comply with the owners' mandates; he was a most obedient servant. For that he gained a large salary, ample maize rations, and rental of a large rancho. In 1783 Rangel rented another rancho to his son.[33] Early in 1788 he retired to the rancho he leased from La Griega, a change forced by "illnesses."[34] Managerial power had served Rangel and his kin well. In 1791 five Rangel households remained, the largest clan not tied to the new manager, don José Regalado Franco.

Franco led a clan of six households, linked by marriage to four other clans of three to five households each. Soon after taking over the new manager headed a network of at least twenty-one households and ninety-six people, 30 percent of the Hispanic (mostly Spanish) residents at La Griega. Franco did not create that network after becoming manager. Don José Sánchez Espinosa chose him knowing that he was a key patriarch in a clan already strong in the estate community. Franco managed La Griega from the early 1790s past the outbreak of insurgency in 1810; his kin ruled into the 1820s. His letters were like Rangel's, offering deference, obedience, and concern for the welfare of Sánchez Espinosa and his family, plus regular reports on crops, sales, and labor.[35] In 1801 Franco added power and prestige by enrolling as an officer in Querétaro's militia. Yet he worried that mobilization might take him away from the estate.[36] In 1811, the first year covered by available accounts, he earned three hundred pesos yearly, plus fifty-two fanegas of maize—five times the remuneration of the most favored workers.[37]

Don José Regalado Franco managed La Griega, leading a large Hispanic clan in an estate community with a larger Otomí majority. To oversee the divided community Franco mixed management and religion. When rains were late or scarce, threatening crops in estate fields, at tenant ranchos, and in Otomí plots, Franco called on the Virgin. In 1801, after weeks of delay, when rain finally came late in July, "God's will was done."[38] When rains came late again in June 1804 Franco detailed his efforts to address the impending crisis: he had a mass said to María Santísima de la Misión, along with a novena to San Vicente Ferrer. He asked the Madres Capuchinas of Querétaro to pray daily to "Most Holy Mary and her Son." He joined efforts by all of Querétaro's convents invoking "God's intervention."[39] Writing to the priest-patriarch in Mexico City, Franco carefully emphasized that by invoking the Virgin he sought intercession by God, the only source of effective redress.

Franco was the perfect intermediary: he served the landlord—and his own extended family; he pursued profit—and he invoked the Virgin to plead for rains essential to estate crops, the welfare of his clan, and the survival of the Otomí. In a community split between a Spanish minority and an indigenous majority, Franco relied on hierarchal patriarchy to favor his Hispanic kin and their neighbors. Religious invocations were essential to the entire community. Of course patriarchy, segregation, and religious invocations were all backed by Franco's power over production and labor. At La Griega a hierarchy of patriarchy structured power from the landlord through the manager to workers and tenants in the Hispanic minority. Managerial patriarchy, Otomí segregation, and religious integration maintained social peace and profitable production. How they stabilized a community moving toward agrarian capitalism is a history worth telling in detail.

Long planting wheat and chiles on irrigated fields, La Griega had left maize and frijol to rain-fed lands, often worked by tenants who with their sons labored seasonally for wages planting and harvesting estate crops. In the segregated community most Spaniards were tenants or permanent employees. How many Otomí were tenants or employees, permanent or seasonal, is not recorded before 1811.[40] The use of irrigated land for wheat (the staple of prosperous Hispanic consumers) and the relegation of maize (the food of the majority) to land dependent on uncertain rains was common in the Bajío in the 1780s. Entrepreneurs left the staple of the majority susceptible to the frost and drought that had destroyed maize across the Bajío in 1785 and 1786, setting off the great famine.[41]

The winter and spring of 1792 brought a new crisis of production to La Griega. In January the chiaguistle blight destroyed the winter wheat crop. The maize harvest brought disappointing yields. When completed in March it totaled only 3,744 fanegas—low because of poor rains the past summer. Yet Franco found hope. The harvest at La Griega was better than at surrounding estates and villages. La Griega's maize went to storage to await the inevitable price rise. Meanwhile Franco proposed a shift in estate production. With maize at high prices and wheat no longer viable because of chiaguistle, he would plant maize on irrigated fields and build new granaries. Larger and more secure maize harvests on irrigated lands plus expanded storage capacity promised new profits, especially in times of scarcity.[42]

The shift in production brought changing social relations. Franco began to evict long-time tenants. He demanded higher rents, and when tenants could not pay he found others who could, or took the land for estate cultivation. We know details only when protest reached Sánchez Espinosa in Mexico City. Don Melchor agreed to leave La Griega but asked payment for improvements made to his rancho: a stone wall and a wooden fence. He also asked to store his maize at the rancho until prices rose to allow a profit. Franco agreed.[43] Another tenant, identified only as Aguilar, proved less amenable. He turned to don José Antonio Oyarzábal, a leading Querétaro landlord, hoping that intervention by a powerful patron might block eviction. It did not.[44]

The greatest resistance came from doña Gertrudis Villaseñor. She wrote to Sánchez Espinosa early in 1792, the only La Griega tenant to do so. Her letter showed a strong hand and weak spelling. She was literate, though not well educated, and very assertive. She complained that Franco demanded a sharp increase for La Venta, a rancho she had leased for years. She could not pay. Franco offered her other land, but it was not a rancho, lacking a house, water, and a fence. She insisted that only a rancho could compensate the loss of La Venta; she had children and "many animals," she needed a rancho.[45] Framing Franco's demand as unjust while emphasizing that she was a woman with a family in a patriarchal society, doña Gertrudis gained sympathy and compromise. Don José ordered Franco to give her the first open rancho. But she would lose La Venta to cultivation on estate account.[46]

Eviction and a promise did not satisfy doña Gertrudis; she took La Griega to court. In May a Querétaro judge confirmed the estate's right to evict her and gave her a week to vacate. He did order the estate to pay the cost of planting the crop in the field and for any improvements. It was a partial settlement; negotiations continued. Franco offered 147 pesos for 12 fanegas of planted maize, little more than the cost of seed, and nothing for labor. Doña Gertrudis owed unspecified back rents and Franco hoped to balance the cost of seed against them and pay nothing. The court ordered that he pay doña Gertrudis in cash. He would

Rancho de la Venta, La Griega, east of Querétaro, eighteenth century.

wait for back rents. Doña Gertrudis Villaseñor left La Venta in June 1792.[47] In a community structured by patriarchy the most vocal and persistent protest of eviction came from a woman, a Spanish woman honored as doña. Displaced patriarchs left with limited resistance; doña Gertrudis would not go quietly. Patriarchy was not uncontested.

In the years that followed, Franco continued to run La Griega, expanding commercial fields while population grew and urban markets boomed amid wartime protections. In July 1801 he reported plantings in estate fields: thirty fanegas of maize and ten of frijol at San Agustín; thirty-six fanegas of maize and twenty of frijol at La Venta (where planting had tripled since it was taken from doña Gertrudis in 1792). Spring rains were late but finally came; the crop would survive.[48] Yet the rain remained sporadic, and when the harvest was complete in March 1802 it proved disappointing: only 620 fanegas at San Agustín (yielding only 20 to 1), 980 at La Venta (yielding only 27 to 1).[49] In September, with a new crop in the field, Franco reported that rains were ample northwest around San Miguel but poor at La Griega. He blamed a lack of contrition.[50] Who was insufficiently penitent—landlord, manager, tenants, or workers—he did not say. Even penitential worship was linked to rains, harvests, and sustenance.

Poor harvests, always lamented, brought high prices and good profits to those who could hold crops from years of plenty until times of dearth. In July 1805 Franco reported another expansion of production: forty-eight fanegas of maize, eighteen of frijol, and twelve of barley at San Agustín; forty-eight fanegas of maize, twenty of frijol, and fifteen of barley at La Venta. Since 1801 plantings of maize and frijol had increased more than 40 percent; barley was new.[51] Rains were ample in the summer of 1805, the crops a great success. In March 1806 La Griega harvested 10,800 fanegas of maize—a yield of 116 to 1.[52] That brought low prices, but Franco offered no lament. He had ample granaries to hold the harvest until scarcity would bring good profits.

With the expansion of commercial cropping, evictions continued, reducing the number of tenants. The majority of estate workers became laborers, divided between relatively secure salaried employees (sirvientes) and growing numbers of seasonal hands (*alquilados*). Accounts from 1811 detail the change.[53] (By then insurgency had begun around San Miguel, but La Griega remained in production.) Only fifteen tenants remained: one large grower, don Vicente de la Concha, Sánchez Espinosa's partner in textile production; four prosperous rancheros paying from 70 to 125 pesos; four modest rancheros (including a widow) paying 25 to 60 pesos; and six small holders (including one Otomí) paying 10 to 20 pesos. There were 139 sirvientes (58 Hispanic, 81 Otomí), permanent employees paid monthly salaries and weekly maize rations. They were dependent but relatively secure thanks to rations paid in kind, no matter the price. Another sixty-one youths (twenty-two Hispanic, thirty-nine Otomí) worked seasonally as alquilados, most earning wages to supplement their fathers' salaries and rations.

The combination of tenants and sirvientes reveals a total of 153 households at La Griega in 1811: 71 Hispanic and 82 indigenous. The Hispanic community included almost exactly the same number of households as in 1791. But two decades earlier most were tenants. By 1811 over 80 percent were employees. Sons with few opportunities to join in family production labored seasonally for wages in estate fields. That change in production brought a rapid turnover in the Hispanic part of the community. Of forty-one Spanish surnames in the census of 1791, only twelve remained in 1811.

The Otomí community also faced change.[54] The tribute count of 1807 reported 214 Otomí men at La Griega, of whom 191 were married and 23 single. Among them 101 were estate employees; 19 lived without regular employment, available for seasonal labor; and 94 worked for tenants planting at ranchos. The remaining tenants, all but one a Spaniard, had increased commercial cropping, employing a growing number of Otomí. Overall the Otomí increased to nearly 70 percent of residents. Yet young unmarried men were few at La Griega, accounting for only 11 percent of the total (compared to 16 percent at Amascala basin estates and 24 percent across Querétaro's jurisdiction). After 1800 young Otomí men found few opportunities at La Griega and nearby estates. It seems likely that some had gone to urban workshops, where youths were over 40 percent of laborers in 1807, and that others had gone to lands newly opened to cultivation on the margins of the Bajío. Production was growing at La Griega: the Spanish population faced rapid turnover; the Otomí majority grew, yet began to expel its youth for lack of opportunity.

The Francos remained. The managerial clan was not exempt from the shift from tenant production to paid labor. But Francos kept several ranchos and more than their share of secure roles as sirvientes. Other Spaniards had departed, replaced by newcomers seeking work. By 1811 the Otomí were all but excluded from tenancies. Employed sirvientes headed most Otomí households; boys labored seasonally as alquilados, for more weeks and less pay than their Hispanic neighbors. And as more Otomí boys neared manhood they found tenancy impossible and employment scarce. Many had to move.

Yet after the protests against evictions in 1792 the manager reported no resistance to the shift from tenancies to labor. Managerial patriarchy organized the Hispanic minority, negotiating difficult changes; what became of tenants who left is not known. The Hispanic men who replaced them found lives of dependence with limited security. Wages were steady at best, while prices for maize and other staples rose. But rations limited those costs among sirvientes and their families, while they sent sons to the fields to keep households afloat.

The shift from tenancy to labor solidified patriarchy. Widowed women sometimes led tenant households. The accounts of 1811–12 show that all sirvientes and alquilados, Spanish and Otomí, were men. The shift from tenant production, in which women were rare, to paid labor, in which women were absent, confirmed patriarchy in working families. Women remained essential to production in rural households. They kept gardens and yard animals, spun yarn, and made cloth — sometimes for use, often for sale — and every day they turned crops and livestock into family food. When families had access to lands, women worked beside husbands and sons in the fields, especially at harvest time. With the shift from tenancies to paid labor, only men worked the fields and gained remuneration; women kept households and thus subsidized estate profits. While men lost tenant production to face new dependence with steady or falling salaries and limited security, La Griega offered them one gain: only men were paid on estate account; only men would head laboring households.

The way La Griega paid sirvientes also entrenched patriarchal power. Salaries were calculated in pesos: sometimes four, often three, and increasingly two pesos monthly. Part came in cash, part in goods on credit at the estate store. A large part was the annual avío, the distribution of cloth to workers. Cash, goods, and cloth taken over the course of the year were accounted yearly against salaries. If a worker claimed more than his salary allowed, he remained obligated. If he took less, he took cash or held a claim on the estate.

Every year Franco wrote to Sánchez Espinosa detailing the cloth desired by estate residents. Together they assembled a shipment of colonial and imported textiles, some for everyday use, some quite fine. In most years the shipment arrived with the priest-patriarch, to be distributed in his presence in front of workers, their wives, and their families.[55] Every inspection visit included Mass, confessions, the settlement of accounts, and the distribution of cloth. Mass and confessions were intended to sanctify Sánchez Espinosa's power and property. The owner's insistence on hearing workers' confessions shows that he sought access to their beliefs and control of their moral lives. (We may suspect that most shared as little as possible with the intrusive landlord.) The priest-patriarch's presence as accounts were settled announced his rule of production and remuneration. Sánchez Espinosa's oversight of cloth distribution did more.

Historically in Mesoamerica and New Spain men raised crops while women made cloth. Food was the first necessity of sustenance, cloth the second. Even as men claimed patriarchal powers, women's roles making cloth and clothing, preparing food, and rearing children kept them essential to family production. The annual distribution to sirvientes at La Griega gave men privileged access to the cloth that their wives made into clothing. Women gained cloth by dependence on an employed man. Overseeing the annual distribution, the priest-patriarch set his insistence on patriarchy in working households. That reinforcement was part of an implicit bargain. Working men accepted lost tenancies and falling earnings in exchange for strengthened claims to patriarchy. Managers guaranteed that only men would work; only men would gain wages, cloth, and rations. That held Hispanic and Otomí men in laboring subordination at La Griega during the decades before 1810.

Yet that enforcement of patriarchy reached Spanish and Otomí households in different ways. Managerial patriarchy, organized through the extended Franco clan, reached to include much of the Spanish community. But managerial kinship kept apart from the Otomí majority. Instead the Francos engaged the Otomí through informal community leaders. There were no republican rights, no community lands. But key indigenous men served as brokers, negotiating participation in production, labor, and religious life. The list of workers from 1811 included four Otomí notables: José Bartolo, the captain; José Manuel, in the store; Juan Agustín, *el fiscal* (local religious elder); and José Antonio, carpenter.

As captain, José Bartolo organized Otomí men's labor, allowing the manager Franco to deal indirectly with indigenous workers. The captain delivered Otomí men and boys to the fields in numbers sufficient to maintain estate production—and Franco's confidence. José Bartolo also had to deliver wages and working conditions acceptable to Otomí men and boys. He probably used the role of labor captain to consolidate his own network of patriarchal kin (though the lack of surnames blocks certainty). José Manuel had a parallel role in the estate store. When an Otomí sirviente went for cloth, shoes, candles, or food, he dealt with an Otomí clerk. Probably José Manuel was needed because most indigenous men spoke Otomí. And perhaps segregation was so deep that the store needed a Spanish storekeeper for Hispanic employees and an Otomí clerk for indigenous workers. What is clear is that the labor captain and the store clerk were key intermediaries between managers and the Otomí majority at La Griega.

Juan Agustín, fiscal, was the religious leader of the Otomí community. He received a maize ration from the estate but no wages. He was likely an elder, not expected to labor, given maize to sustain his role in religious life. He organized weekly worship and periodic festivals. He too was a broker, working between the religious assertions of the manager and the cultural independence of the Otomí community. He too was essential to the stability of everyday life and production at La Griega. The captain, the clerk, and the fiscal were key links in the hierarchy that negotiated power in the segregated estate community.

The carpenter José Antonio had a different role. He was less a broker, and his skill, along with his exceptional salary and large ration (both greater than those of most Hispanic sirvientes) demonstrated to all that while segregation and discrimination marked La Griega, the liabilities faced by the Otomí were not absolute. If José Antonio could gain skill and great rewards, could not other indios do the same? A key characteristic of segregation in the eastern Bajío as the nineteenth century began was that it was not absolute. At La Griega there was one Otomí tenant, one skilled carpenter. Hispanic men were favored, while indigenous men faced obvious discriminations. But a few Otomí men earned as much as their Hispanic neighbors; many indigenous boys found work and pay beside Hispanic boys. As a result, Otomí workers' lesser wages and rations were less obvious, and perhaps less resented.

As production and labor relations became more capitalist around

1800, the Hispanic minority and the Otomí majority at La Griega faced structural patriarchy reinforced by estate power. An extended patriarchal managerial clan organized dependence among favored Spanish employees and tenants. A labor captain, store clerk, and religious leader organized life in the Otomí community, perhaps through indigenous clans that we cannot see. Patriarchy and ethnic segregation orchestrated power at La Griega. That power sustained commercial production and dependent labor to 1810—and after. Yet it was negotiated and at times contested by indigenous men in the segregated community.

Conflict in Divided Communities: Casas and La Griega

Two conflicts pressed by Otomí at estate communities reveal struggles over labor and cultural life. At Casas (or Lo de Casas), south of Querétaro, Otomí youths challenged labor norms in 1801. At La Griega in 1806 Otomí workers threatened to strike at harvest time if a religious festival was blocked. However segregated, subject to managerial power, and caught in patriarchal bargains, Otomí people found ways to push their goals. Casas was one of four Querétaro estates owned in 1791 by don José Martínez Moreno, *regidor alguacil mayor*, councilman, chief constable, and head of the Querétaro branch of the family led by don Pedro Romero de Terreros, first Conde de Regla.[56] By 1801 the estate and council seat had passed to don Fernando Romero Martínez, a captain in the Querétaro militia. The tribute count of 1807 listed 104 Otomí working at Casas, suggesting a population half that at La Griega—still a larger community than at most haciendas south of Querétaro.[57]

The conflict began when the brothers Julián Santos, Andrés Martín, and José María stood before a Querétaro judge as "tribute paying *indios* and estate workers." The manager at Casas alleged that they owed forty pesos; they argued that they owed no such debt. Their father had died owing that amount. Together they had worked for a year attempting to clear the obligation. They took no wages while suffering verbal and physical abuse. Yet the debt remained. Frustrated, they asked the court for relief. Regime rules limited a worker's debts to five pesos; since the debt was a single obligation against their late father, they asserted that five pesos was all they could owe.[58]

Don Fernando Romero Martínez mounted a vigorous and costly defense in a suit over forty pesos—to the youths a large sum, to the landlord a pittance. He took the case to the High Court in Mexico City, hiring an attorney who surely charged more than forty pesos. Much more than forty pesos was at stake. Three indios appeared to challenge not the concept of obligated labor but the principle that the debts inevitably created by it and regularly left unpaid could pass to heirs. The arguments that followed detailed how advances structured labor and how patriarchy stabilized inequality in a segregated estate community.

The landlord's first defense was that the debt was not inherited from the workers' father. When the last owner, don José Martínez Moreno, died he forgave all workers' debts.[59] That act of charity was of course made with the knowledge that most advances to workers were never collected, as Corregidor Domínguez stated in his report in the same year. The late landlord's forgiveness relieved his estate of uncollectible obligations. And since the debt was not inherited, the estate manager don Pedro Ximénez argued that the three indios were employed like all others. In exchange for labor they received "serge, blue and white sheeting, cottons, shawls, and money in coin, weekly maize rations, and supplements every Thursday—or whenever they needed them." As at La Griega, workers at Casas received the necessities of life—cash, cloth, and food—in exchange for labor. Six witnesses backed the manager: José Camacho, clerk at the estate store; Mariano Loyo, a foreman; Juan Nieto, a Spaniard and assistant manager; Diego Martín, an indio muleteer; and José Ylario and Francisco Valerio, *indios gañanes* (indio estate residents).[60] Three Otomí men testified for the owner, confirming that the men worked and the estate provided (in advance) the essentials of life: the basic bargain of obligated labor and hierarchical patriarchy.

Recent court rulings, however, required precise clarification of the workers' status. A decision in 1791 confirmed that *indios operarios* (indigenous workers) at the Barranca estate of don Tomás López de Ecala were responsible for debts created by advances of cash and cloth.[61] The law limited debts to five pesos only for indios classed as gañanes; it did not apply to *indios de pueblo*, village residents who seasonally went in gangs to plant and harvest estate crops. The owner and manager insisted that the indios were de pueblo, though they were permanently employed at the estate. Residence, they asserted, trumped employment status; thus the debt limit did not apply.[62] Yet two of the three indios who testified for the owner called themselves gañanes, a label that the court recorded without hesitation. Were the witnesses wrong? Was the landlord trying to craft a new designation to avoid limits on debt enforcement?

It appeared that the law and prevailing social designations favored the three indios. So Romero Martínez hired an attorney to write a long, polemical brief detailing his view of Otomí workers at Querétaro estates. It began by stating that "the goal was to defraud the boss of the work and money he had given them, providing for their urgent needs for food and clothing." The three indios had claimed life's necessities and then tried to defraud the estate of the work they owed. According to the brief, the young men could not have done this alone: "these pretensions come out of vicious seductions by influential agitators who perversely led the boys to believe that the debts are unjust." The plaintiffs were not men; they were boys seduced and perverted by unspecified agitators. (Production peaked at Querétaro in 1801 because of wartime protection. Were employers enticing workers away?) Should the indios win, "rule over *indios* and the business of agriculture would face extreme prejudice."[63] The suit over forty pesos was no petty matter.

The brief then turned to social designations and legal distinctions. The debt limit applied to gañanes; workers at Casas were indios laboríos. Gañanes were *ranchados*—born at estates where they lived and worked their entire lives. Laboríos, in contrast, were free to live and work where they pleased. They must pay all debts, in work or cash; the alternative was "to deceive and defraud" their employers. If debts were not enforced no one would plant and harvest crops.[64] The case turned on whether the youths at Casas were gañanes or laboríos. Tribute lists did not help. All indios in the Querétaro jurisdiction remained de pueblo, linked to the urban republic at San Sebastián or outlying communities like Pueblito and La Cañada. Yet most Otomí lived at estates. Did indios no longer living in pueblos retain pueblo status because Otomí elders sought to retain power over families who moved to estates? Had estates accepted that status because it left the republics responsible for collecting tribute? To escape the dilemma the landlord offered the category of laboríos—indios linked to pueblos, but living and working at estates. Not gañanes who could owe only five pesos, laboríos owed whatever they took in advance.

Unsure that the distinction would sway the judges, the brief assaulted the character of indigenous workers: "With such fictions, *indios* present their petitions, always feigning humility and candor." But indios were known liars, and the three youths owed the forty pesos, "knowing that neither these *indios* nor any other worker in the kingdom can live without advance payment." The forty-peso debt was due, in cash or labor, to repay cash and goods freely taken. "This point is done."[65]

To reinforce the point the brief repeated and embellished the manager's description of labor relations: "As is done at all the estates in the district, workers were advanced serge, blue and white sheeting, cottons, shoes, shawls, and money, along with weekly maize rations, the Thursday supplements, and other extraordinary advances—all of which outfit them and provide for their daily needs." The system of advances in cash, cloth, and rations defined labor relations. "Where is this not done, due to necessity? What household is sustained by what family members or dependents earn only by their labors?" The brief gave a clear statement of patriarchal employment: the estate gave men—in advance—the goods necessary to sustain themselves and their families. The exchange of men's service for family sustenance was the pivot of social dependence and labor relations. "It cannot be otherwise with laboring *indios*." Good order and commercial life required that debts be enforced.[66]

Then the brief argued again that the workers in question were neither gañanes, despite the testimony of the landlord's own witnesses, nor de pueblo, despite tribute lists. The lawyer aimed to turn indio de pueblo from a legal category to a labor relation, applying it to "those who live on the wage of two *reales*, or one-and-a-half, from that meeting all their family needs."[67] The village men who came to plant and harvest estate crops suddenly appear as proletarians, living and sustaining households on wages alone. (The brief did not remind the judges of what they knew: most villagers had at least limited lands; wage work at estates supplemented cultivation.) Indios living and working at Querétaro estates were different: managers paid advances to ensure families' sustenance. The system worked only if debts were recognized, even if never repaid (the truth behind testamentary debt relief).

Romero Martínez and his attorney contended that advances and obligations benefited workers. If debts were not recognized, employers would not offer advances. "An *indio* who does not receive them will be incapable of finding twenty pesos a year to clothe himself and his family, a real injury."[68] Cloth ruled at the center of rural labor relations. Maize rations came in kind, outside the structure of advances and obligations. Cash advances were small. It was cloth that created obligations to labor, and set men's power over women and children. The brief stated that cloth advances were essential to workers and their families, confirming patriarchy in dependent households. If that did not sway the judges, the landlord returned to basics: he asked only for the enforcement of legal obligations. The rules of commerce applied to traders, farmers, and indios; debts must be paid or the economy would collapse; if the economy collapsed, how would Spain face the British?[69] The enforcement of obligated patriarchal labor became a key to the survival of Spain's empire.

The brief ended with a rare direct statement of the bargain of patriarchal obligated labor. "If they are not aided with advances to obtain their necessities, as free men they leave the work that employs them; when they take advances, they go to the opposite extreme of enjoying the goods they take while seduced by agitators to deny their debts, taking sustenance and prostituting their most important civil, political, and moral obligations for sustenance, their most important obligation."[70] Men who take advances, work loyally, and rule families are men—good subordinate patriarchs. Men who break the bargain are seduced prostitutes: not patriarchs, not men, but women, the least admired of women.

Indios who challenged obligations had to be stopped. "What will be the lesson learned by the *sirvientes* [Hispanic employees] at Romero Martínez's estate, seeing these three get away without shame, knowing the pride with which they take a judgment that gives them liberty to leave, laughing at the judge and their boss."[71] If indios escaped obligations so would sirvientes; the example could not stand. No longer likened to seduced prostitutes, the three indios suddenly appear as men—proud and free. Were they shameless women because they acted as independent men—not as acquiescent, dependent patriarchs, laboring quietly while ruling their wives and children in subordinate households?

In 1802 the judges agreed that such behavior could not continue. They concluded that the three indios were gañanes, which was obvious in the testimony. The court had no interest in the fine distinctions of terminology that the landlord and his lawyer offered to obscure the law. Instead the judges saw gañanes who had taken advances in exchange for promised work and sued to escape the obligations. The court ordered the men to continue to work, or to find another employer who would pay the debt in exchange for a new obligation to labor. The judges recognized that advance payment was fundamental to labor relations in rural Querétaro—labor relations grounded in patriarchy. The social relations that sustained the Bajío economy had to survive, despite the law limiting debts to five pesos.

Obligated labor structured by patriarchy was one key to social control in Querétaro estate communities; ethnic segregation was the other. A dispute at La Griega reveals how labor relations intersected with cultural oppositions. We know the dispute only through the letters of the manager don José Regalado Franco. Facing a conflict between the goals of don José Sánchez Espinosa in Mexico City and the religious culture of the Otomí community, Franco detailed his struggle to mediate.

The maize harvest that began in December 1805 promised bounty. Workers had already cut and loaded 450 carts. At the usual rate of 24 fanegas per cart, the harvest would approach 11,000 fanegas, one of the best in the estate's history. Additional stalks remained in the field, and the ears had to be husked and the kernels shelled to prepare the crop for storage until the inevitable year of drought brought the profit of high prices. At that crucial moment epidemic struck La Griega. The ill could not work, and others would not do so while they attended families and neighbors. Franco wrote, "I am still unable to conclude the harvest due to the scarcity of workers, who even with money cannot be hired."[72]

The Otomí community, surely led by the captain and the fiscal, asked Franco for permission to organize a religious celebration to limit the ravages of the disease. Franco cautiously approached Sánchez Espinosa, the landlord, priest, and promoter of a rational Catholicism focused on the sacraments (and Guadalupe). He had instructed Franco to end indigenous festivals. Franco knew that whatever the theological question (his letters suggest that he preferred penitential devotion), allowing Otomí families their celebration was essential to peace and production. He wrote at length:

"The *Indiada* [indios, feminized] has asked me to beg your permission to hold their combat [a ritual]. I will be responsible for supervising, taking care to avoid the drunkenness often seen in the festival of San Agustín, patron of the estate. I have done everything in my power to avoid disruptions and riots among them; since I have been in charge there have been no such problems. I ask that you kindly grant permission, and grace us with your presence by coming to lead the benediction in the chapel." Franco favored allowing the festival and asked Sánchez Espinosa to participate. Don José could assert his priestly presence. And "after benediction, there would be great benefit in your hearing confessions."[73] If Sánchez Espinosa heard confessions, he could make the festival more penitential.

If don José did not come, the chaplain José Antonio García could "lead in the chapel," offering benediction and hearing confessions. A priest was part, but only part, of the celebration planned by the Otomí at La Griega. Franco, facing a labor shortage, knew that he had to allow the festival. He wrote for permission and hoped that Sánchez Espinosa would participate. Franco needed Sánchez Espinosa's acquiescence; profit depended on it. Franco's letter is revealing in many ways. The Otomí residents of La Griega had claimed the feast of San Agustín as their own. The saint chosen (perhaps by don Juan Caballero y Ocío) to sanctify proprietorship had become protector of the resident Otomí. They organized festivals that included combats, perhaps variants of the famous rituals of Christians and Moors. They were noted for bouts of drinking that Spaniards saw as unruly, disruptive, and potentially violent, but that Mesoamericans knew brought exalted states close to the divine.[74] In the face of epidemic, the festival was essential to the community and to labor relations.

Franco knew that Sánchez Espinosa saw these celebrations as occasions of drunkenness, disorder, and violence. A cultural gulf divided Sánchez Espinosa from the people who grew his crops at La Griega. Franco, a good broker, wrote carefully. He could not alienate the owner, yet he had to allow the celebration. Permission was essential to show the Otomí at La Griega that the owner and manager cared for their health and welfare. Acceptance of cultural autonomy was necessary to labor relations, thus to estate profits. After pleading for participation, or at least sanction, Franco made it clear that he was already organizing the festival. He had ordered a barrel of *aguardiente* (cane brandy) from La Teja, Sánchez Espinosa's estate near Mexico City. Sánchez Espinosa was not so set against drinking that he refused to profit from it. He did not go to La Griega for benediction and confessions; the festival went on; the harvest was completed, filling Sánchez Espinosa's granaries. How religious disappointment mixed with capitalist pleasure is not recorded.

At the beginning of his letter Franco referred to those demanding the celebration as *la indiada*. He could have said the *indios*. But he wrote to Sánchez Espinosa with a feminine collective reference. Perhaps it was just an accident of language. But given the feminization of references to insubordinate indios in the dispute at Casas in 1801, we may wonder if the feminine reference to the indigenous community was meaningful. In segregated communities around Querétaro, Otomí men were essential workers. They were supported as subordinate patriarchs; if they worked in quiet acquiescence they could rule dependent households. That structure maintained peace, estate production, and owners' profits. When Otomí workers became assertive at Casas and when a conflict about devotion threatened to become a strike at La Griega, owners, lawyers, and managers responded. At Casas resistance began in court, and the landlord responded in court. At La Griega conflict stayed in the community; the manager mediated between the owner and the Otomí majority; negotiation resolved the conflict. In both disputes landlords, lawyers, and managers questioned the manhood of indigenous workers who challenged established power. Patriarchy was a key to stabilizing social inequities deepening in a society driving toward capitalism. Segregation laced with cultural division meant that Spanish patriarchs recognized the manhood of Otomí men only when they acquiesced in laboring subordination. We can only imagine what indigenous men, women, and children thought and said about all this as estate communities across rural Querétaro drove toward capitalism, raising rents, evicting tenants, and lowering remuneration as prices rose.

Profit, Patriarchy—and the Girls' Revolt—at Puerto de Nieto

As the 1780s began, Puerto de Nieto was an estate of Spanish and mestizo tenants, indigenous subtenants, and mulatto slaves tending livestock. In the early 1780s slavery collapsed because it no longer served the owners' search for profit, and because surviving slaves refused to move. Soon after slavery ended, the great frost, drought, and famine of 1785 and 1786 brought struggles to residents and profits to don José Sánchez Espinosa. In that time of uncertainty and opportunity he pressed a transformation parallel to the reorganization at La Griega, shifting from tenancies to commercial cropping. But Puerto de Nieto was less segregated; it was a place of amalgamation. There patriarchy was the central way of social control, organizing managerial power and community adaptations. The only overt resistance reported in the correspondence was a revolt by *las muchachas*—the girls. Where patriarchy was the primary axis of power, resistance was for girls.

When Sánchez Espinosa took over Puerto de Nieto in 1780, don José Antonio Plaza managed the estate. He collected rents and oversaw slaves assigned to stock herding. Early in 1782 the young landlord had enough faith in Plaza to send him to check accounts at La Griega. Soon, however, the owner began to doubt Plaza's ability. Sánchez Espinosa was ready to let slavery end at Puerto de Nieto; he expected to keep his slave property, sending it north to Bocas or profiting from the sale of those who did not move. Instead Plaza's letters, laced with declarations of deference, detailed the collapse of slavery at Puerto de Nieto.[75]

Plaza also narrated his failure to collect rents and defend estate borders. In May 1782, having failed to resolve a dispute with neighboring San Sebastián, Plaza wrote: "in these parts, in these affairs, the name manager carries no weight."[76] Two years later Plaza reported festering boundary disputes, poor harvests, and an inability to collect rents. He enlisted his compadre, don Domingo Allende, the San Miguel merchant, to help, but to no avail.[77] Having documented his own failures, Plaza could not have been surprised when Sánchez Espinosa fired him late in 1784. Plaza kept the large rancho that he leased for 380 pesos yearly.[78] After the end of slavery, management at Puerto de Nieto was rent collection and boundary defense. Plaza's failures cost him his position, but not his tenancy.

Five years later Plaza wrote to Sánchez Espinosa, begging to return. Plaza had applied to manage the Querétaro estates of don Pedro Antonio de Septién, as well as properties held by don Antonio Parada near Temascaltepec to the south. Plaza won neither post. Had word of his failures spread? Plaza abased himself in apologies and begged for a new chance: "you do not need me, yet I always need your protection to maintain my family." Plaza saw himself as "one more prodigal son." He pleaded to return "to my Puerto de Nieto, to your protection, to my father and home."[79] Beyond desperation, Plaza's letter offers a clear statement of how hierarchical patriarchy led men to acquiesce in subordination: he had to serve Sánchez Espinosa at Puerto de Nieto; it was the only way to support his family—the only way he could be a man, a patriarch.

Early in 1785 don Juan José Degollado took over Puerto de Nieto. He ran the estate during the drought, frost, and famine of 1785–86. In the face of such challenges Sánchez Espinosa removed the new manager early in 1787. Where Plaza left quietly and waited five years to plead for a new chance, remonstrance came soon after Degollado's firing—not from the fallen manager but from his angry wife, doña María Guadalupe Zúñiga. She defended her decision to write, saying that her husband was away. She appealed to Sánchez Espinosa's charity, to the saints, and to the memory of don Francisco Espinosa y Navarijo, the first priest-patriarch her husband had served. She complained that her son had quit his studies to assist his father at Puerto de Nieto; now he was left with neither an education nor a post at the estate. Finally a realist, she asked that removal, if unavoidable, be delayed until August to allow the family to arrange its affairs.[80]

Like don José Antonio Plaza, doña María Guadalupe understood patriarchy. Her husband served Sánchez Espinosa in exchange for pay and patriarchy in his own household, for access to positions for his son and others—for provincial eminence for himself and his family. Unlike Plaza, when doña María Guadalupe saw the pact broken she wrote vehemently in defense of her family. She had some success. Her son Joaquín Degollado, an unmarried cultivator in his twenties, without local kin, remained at Puerto de Nieto in 1792.[81] Excluded from management, young Degollado lived as an isolated dependent, unable to exercise even household patriarchy.

The end of slavery, the crisis of 1785–86, and the rapid firing of two managers led to a reorganization of production and a new way of management. In the spring of 1786, while the elder Degollado managed and maize was scarce and costly, the estate planted its first commercial maize crop. In November an early harvest of two hundred fanegas relieved pressing shortages. In January 1787, Degollado gone, the full harvest yielded 2,317 fanegas.[82] That was modest by the standards at La Griega. At Puerto de Nieto it signaled a shift from tenant cropping to commercial cultivation. To oversee the transformation Sánchez Espinosa appointed don Vicente Puente manager in March 1787.

Granary, Labor de Santa María, Puerto de Nieto, east of San Miguel, eighteenth century.

A tenant and former assistant to Plaza, Puente held the title of manager until his death in 1808.[83] His role changed and his power faded over the years, however. In 1790 Sánchez Espinosa named don José Toribio Rico steward at the Labor de Santa María, downstream from the dam, where commercial cropping was expanding. At first Puente and Rico ran separate parts of the property, each reporting to the landlord. While Puente was manager and Rico steward, they worked as equals. When Puente fell ill in 1793 Rico briefly oversaw the entire estate.[84] But Puente and Rico engaged the community at Puerto de Nieto very differently. Born in San Miguel, Puente had leased land before becoming manager. In 1792 he led a clan of two households—his and his son's. The son and a daughter married into the Licea clan—with seven households, one of the largest extended families at the estate. Notably, all the Puentes and Liceas were classed as Spaniards. Plaza, like his predecessors, was Spanish and an outsider. Unlike them he married his children into a large resident clan. Yet his ties to Puerto de Nieto were limited by alliance with a fully Spanish family in a community defined by amalgamation.[85]

Don José Toribio Rico was the ultimate insider. Born at Puerto de Nieto, he belonged to its largest clan. In 1792 eight Rico households had forty-eight members, linked by marriage to another nine-

Irrigated fields, Labor de Santa María, Puerto de Nieto, east of San Miguel.

teen households with ninety-three residents. At a minimum, kinship tied Rico to 15 percent of the population included in the count. And while most Ricos and their kin were Spaniards who married Spaniards, enough of them married mestizos and mulattoes (and some of them were linked to indios) to integrate the managerial clan into the full community.[86] With the shift from tenancies to estate cultivation, management shifted from outsiders to insiders.

Plaza, Degollado, and Puente were tenants who also collected rents. Such managers succeeded when most residents were tenants, subtenants, or slaves caring for livestock. The end of slavery, the shift from grazing, the decline of tenancy, and the growth of commercial cropping called for managers who could deal with cultivators becoming sirvientes, employees paid monthly salaries and maize rations. Part came in cash, part in purchases at the estate store, much in cloth.[87] Dependent workers, paid in wages and goods, gained the means to assert patriarchy and sustain households. Obligated labor structured by patriarchy offered workers dependent security, at Puerto de Nieto as at La Griega. Managers needed large patriarchal clans to extend power deep into the community. At La Griega don José Regalado Franco led a clan embedded in the Spanish minority of a segregated community. At

Puerto de Nieto, Rico led a large clan that extended deep into a more integrated community.

Patriarchal power opened the way to patriarchal negotiation, however. While Puente and Rico used their clans to extend their rule, others built parallel networks to face that rule. In 1792 the linked Alamilla, Arías, López, Monzón, Rodríguez, and Zeballos clans included 23 households and 105 people (Spaniards, mestizos, mulattoes, and indios). They challenged the Rico clan in size and links across the amalgamating community. Renting lands and providing workers to cultivate expanding estate fields, this network of clans not tied to management also developed household industries, making and finishing cloth. Thus might dependent patriarchs work to limit the power of the estate and its managers, creating alternative sources of income—and cloth. Still, the census lists only men as cloth makers. Wives and children joined the work, but the household weavers of Puerto de Nieto claimed power over textiles. Dependent patriarchs built extended-family clans to contest managerial power, also aiming to consolidate household patriarchy.[88]

The men of Puerto de Nieto negotiated at the vortex of a paradox. Some forged links to the managerial Puentes or Ricos, using patriarchal clans to gain benefits by acquiescing in managerial rule. Others formed clans against the managers, seeking allies in negotiation and limited independence in cloth making. None challenged the patriarchy that organized their dependence and gave them rule over women and children in dependent households.

As the 1790s drew toward an end the economic expansion fueled by population growth and wartime protection accelerated. Don José Toribio Rico led Puerto de Nieto into another expansion of commercial cultivation. From May into July 1799 maize grew in the fields and regional stocks seemed ample. The price held at ten reales per fanega, the customary bottom of the market in the Bajío after the crisis of 1785–86 (up from the low of eight reales that had once been common).[89] In November the crop awaiting harvest exceeded three thousand fanegas—a 30 percent increase since 1787. The price held at ten reales at Puerto de Nieto, but had gone to twelve at Querétaro. A sharper increase was expected because rain-fed crops were lost northeast at San Luis de la Paz and Xichú. Rico reported that the workers not harvesting at Puerto de Nieto were clearing pastures to plant more maize the next spring.[90]

The gains of expansion came in the harvest completed early in 1802. Described as modest, it totaled 3,840 fanegas, another 30 percent increase in two years. Again the post-harvest price held at ten reales. Rico sold small quantities to buyers who came to his granaries; otherwise he held the crop, awaiting a rise to twelve reales—the level needed to profit. Then in December 1802 it became clear that the next harvest would be cut by drought; Rico halted sales; the price would soon rise beyond twelve reales.[91] The alternation of good crops and low prices with poor crops and high prices drove commercial cultivation. The year 1802 brought another expansion of estate planting at Puerto de Nieto. In March, Sánchez Espinosa ordered Rico to prepare a list of all tenants and the rents they paid, their livestock, and other property. Until then commercial cropping had expanded by turning pasture to arable land or reclaiming ranchos when they were vacated. Now Sánchez Espinosa raised rents and took ranchos from those who could not pay, as he had done earlier at La Griega.[92]

At La Griega the strongest protest came from doña Gertrudis Villaseñor. At Puerto de Nieto don José Toribio Rico faced revolt by "the girls." A group of young women occupied Rico's residence and refused to leave, insisting that they and their families would not give up their lands.[93] We know the protest only from Rico's report to Sánchez Espinosa; he did not offer details about how a group of girls challenged his power. They knew that Rico's survey was a prelude to evictions. Ranchos allowed families control of production; women joined in family economies, keeping gardens, raising animals, making cloth and clothing, and working fields. A shift from tenant production to employment, even with adequate earnings, would strengthen patriarchy. Only men were sirvientes paid cash, foods, and cloth for labor service; only boys were alquilados paid to plant and harvest crops. Families without ranchos were more dependent, and in them women depended more on husbands. The girls understood and invaded the manager's home to protest the change. Their fathers and brothers either did not participate or came as followers. Men appeared ready to trade the loss of tenant production for dependent security and consolidated patriarchy. They negotiated deepening inequality if it confirmed their patriarchy. The girls protested.

Rico never wrote of the outcome. It is not clear whether he slowed evictions to end the protest, or appealed to men to evict "the girls." He did continue to expand commercial crops. In the spring of 1803 he planted forty-two fanegas; a good crop would yield over four thousand fanegas.[94] At twelve reales, that would bring in six thousand pesos— an ample sum.

The shift to commercial cropping solidified Rico's role as manager. Don Vicente Puente retained the title, but his power waned. In April 1799, as planting began, he gave up the rancho he had leased for years. His accounts were in order, his rents paid.[95] Puente contributed to the expansion of commercial planting, reducing his economic activities while keeping limited oversight. By 1804, however, something was amiss. In February Sánchez Espinosa stripped him of control over finances. All rent collections and major sales went to Rico, supposedly Puente's subordinate. In March don José Regalado Franco wrote from La Griega, accusing Puente of forging Franco's signature to get funds.[96] Sánchez Espinosa requested a private report from Father Juan José Vega, chaplain at Puerto de Nieto. It was the only letter from the cleric in voluminous correspondence; the occasion was ominous.

Vega reported that Puente was living without benefit of marriage with a companion, María Luciana Sanjuanera. The elder manager, his daughter María, her husband Antonio Lepe, and their son Vicente all worked ranchos without paying rent. The release of his original rancho years earlier, it seems, did not curtail Puente's economic activities—it ended his rent payments. Vega added that use of estate resources was common among managers, but Puente had gone far beyond accepted norms.[97] Yet Sánchez Espinosa did not dismiss Puente. Instead he kept the title of manager, while power went to don José Toribio Rico. When Puente died in 1808, his only role was to oversee limited stock grazing and collect rents. He lost 35 animals and collected 2,500 pesos in rents in 1807. Puente managed the shrinking remnants of the old Puerto de Nieto. Rico ruled the expansion of commercial agriculture.

From 1804 Rico seemed an ideal manager. He held the good crop of 1802–3 and the small harvest of 1803–4 until frost struck the maize in the fields in September 1804. With that crop all but lost at Puerto de Nieto and nearby estates, Rico knew what to do. He ended sales to hasten the rise in price.[98] When the spring of 1805 brought "a rigorous drought," he still held large stocks. He sold small amounts to "the poor" who came to the granary, claiming to offer charity while in fact saving transportation costs. Rico lamented that he could not get higher prices "because so many seek profit by bringing maize to the Bajío, selling it everywhere, even in the ranchos, for twelve or fourteen reales per fanega."[99]

The death of don Vicente Puente in 1808 brought Rico the title of manager at Puerto de Nieto, a role he had held for years. His elevation came just as Sánchez Espinosa delegated oversight of the Obra Pía estates to his son, the Conde de Peñasco. Rico wrote to his new young superior, emphasizing his commitment to serve "my kind father and lord."[100] Rico knew that according to the niceties of hierarchical patriarchy he was required to pledge to serve the young Conde. He also knew that power remained with Sánchez Espinosa. As manager, Rico was the key broker in a patriarchal structure. He pressed commercial cultivation forward, holding working men, many of whom were his kin, in subordination by confirming their roles as patriarchs in dependent households. Patriarchy was the key to power in the amalgamating community. Only girls protested—to little effect.

Beyond Puerto de Nieto: Seeking Republics at Santa Bárbara and Tequisquiapan

Beyond Puerto de Nieto, across the countryside from San Miguel to Dolores, few estate residents claimed Spanish status. Most families were of Otomí or African ancestry, often mixing both. Otomí families had migrated over the centuries in search of land and work. Most Africans came as slaves and mixed with indigenous neighbors to generate free offspring. Men classed as indios and mulattoes paid tribute, the mark of subordination in New Spain. Around San Miguel and Dolores nearly all lived as estate dependents.[101]

Higher and drier than the Bajío basins to the south, the lands from San Miguel to Dolores and beyond were among the last to shift from grazing to cultivation. Less fertile and less open to irrigation, estates there turned to farming by settling new tenants on their lands (reversing the process at La Griega and Puerto de Nieto, where tenants were evicted to gain fields for commercial cropping). North of San Miguel families rented land that had to be cleared for planting. Men and boys in tenant families worked for wages in estate fields. Landlords who risked investment in rain-fed maize planned to pay low wages, and pay them only seasonally.

From 1797 to 1799 Charco de Araujo, north of San Miguel on the way to Dolores, opened land for planting maize, taking on tenants while also trying commercial cropping. Dry pasture turned to cultivation proved marginal cropland. Yields were low at the beginning and then fell. They declined on estate fields; they declined more on tenant holdings. Over four years estate planting fell from thirteen to eleven fanegas; tenant planting rose from eight to twenty-one fanegas. Estate yields fell from 70 to 1 to 45 to 1; tenant yields dropped from 74 to 1 to 33 to 1. Charco de Araujo learned the risks of cultivating on dry marginal lands and shifted those risks onto tenant households. Still, demand for maize remained strong, and the estate continued to expand cultivation by settling tenants on ever more marginal lands.

During the transition 60 percent of the families at Charco de Araujo gained income as sirvientes; 40 percent were tenants, many also working for wages. As usual with obligated labor, Charco de Araujo paid monthly salaries, providing cash, food, and cloth before an annual accounting. Yet sirvientes at Charco de Araujo rarely gained year-round employment and faced salaries low by Bajío standards—three pesos monthly or less. Few got advances: most went to managers and skilled employees. So a growing number of families took on tenancies, paying rent to clear land, plant maize and frijol, and gain declining yields. Men at Charco de Araujo struggled to sustain families, their patriarchy far from certain, even at home. In a zone of marginal planting the turn to cultivation after 1785–86 spread insecurity among men grasping for ways to be patriarchs in struggling families.[102]

Some men taking work for declining wages and renting marginal lands answered with demands for community rights. The rolling lands north of San Miguel were dominated by the estates of the Mariscales de Castilla and other large grazers. Resident communities mixed Otomí and mulatto tenants and herders. Since the late seventeenth century estate residents had periodically gone to court to demand republics and lands. Few succeeded. Early in the eighteenth century Dolores was founded as a parish town to give Spaniards, mestizos, and a few mulattoes and Otomí caciques a place to live and worship that would also serve nearby estate communities. Early on an Otomí sodality founded by caciques living in Dolores reached out to estate residents; later the caciques joined Hispanic religious activities at Dolores. After 1790 estate communities faced new pressures in work and production; they searched for new ways to integrate family, community, and religious life.[103] In the early 1800s men from Santa Bárbara and Tequisquiapan went to court claiming status as indios and demanding rights as republics with land, a church, and self-rule.

Santa Bárbara was north of San Miguel in the jurisdiction of Dolores.[104] Don José Gutiérrez, the owner in 1802, was heir to a long line of provincial landlords. The suit began when several men went to court seeking permission to build a chapel. The lead petitioners, José Justo Ríos and Cristóbal Pantaleón López, presented themselves as representing *indios arranchados* at the estate; they were tenant rancheros, indio in status; they spoke Spanish and had Spanish patronyms. (Most rural indios lacked patronyms and used translators in court. Some Otomí near Dolores still required clergy who spoke Otomí; these were not the indios seeking the republic.) Their goal was a chapel; the owner answered that the estate had a chapel to serve residents' needs.[105] In early testimony the plaintiffs insisted that they were indios. They called their community the barrio of Santa Bárbara. They needed a chapel because they lived far from the *casco*, the estate center with a church. They promised to pay for the chapel and sustain worship with contributions collected among "tenant indios." In 1803 the plaintiffs called themselves a "República," their leader a "regidor mayor" (lead councilman). Seeking to build a chapel and take control of worship, the indios of Santa Bárbara claimed to be an indigenous republic with recognized leadership.

To dispute those claims the owner offered testimony from three estate residents, all Spaniards. One was born at Santa Bárbara; the others had come from Celaya and Marfil, near Guanajuato. All stated that there were thirty "casas de indios," totaling about seventy households, at Santa Bárbaro. The casas were extended kin groups, suggesting that indios formed clan networks parallel to those among Spaniards, mestizos, and mulattoes at Puerto de Nieto. The owner's witnesses also stated that the indios did not need a chapel; the owner took care of their spiritual needs. The owner minimized the indigenous population at his property. He offered a list of forty-three married heads of household: thirty-three tenants, nine *arrimados* (subtenants or other dependents), and one *aventurero*, a squatter. He contradicted his own witnesses (who reported seventy indio households), arguing that the community of forty-three households was too small to earn a chapel or status as a republic. The case stalled, the court apparently convinced that the indios at Santa Bárbara were too few to be an independent community.

The suit revived in 1807. Don Bernardino Gutiérrez had inherited the estate from his father. The indio community had grown, likely by tenants settling on former pastures. The plaintiffs declared that they now totaled 800 indigenous residents; the owner recognized 268. Gutiérrez argued that the larger number included families at nearby La Erre and San Marcos, where the number of indio residents exceeded 1,500. La Erre and San Marcos belonged to the Mariscal de Castilla. Gutiérrez aimed to deflect indio demands onto a powerful neighbor; any republic should include lands taken from the Mariscal. Gutiérrez then maligned the plaintiffs. They were *agavillados* (banded, like bandits) with a group at a settlement called La Huerta. The claim to a chapel and republic had no goal other than "to dismember the hacienda from the owners." Pluralizing ownership, Gutiérrez asserted his patriarchal role as head of a landed clan. Should the suit succeed, the plaintiffs would escape patriarchal oversight: "They will be free to pursue their disorders." If they chose their own leaders "who will be fully inclined to drunkenness (as natives usually are), they will live with no one to contain their excesses." The new owner did not challenge the indio status of his dependents; he used it to portray them as seeking the freedom to pursue disorder and drunkenness.

Then Gutiérrez got to the point: if tenants gained pueblo status, the law required that they receive the land and water essential to resident families. He argued that such lands did not exist at his estate; they were available just south at San Marcos. Gutiérrez believed that his dependents had no right to status as a republic—but even if they did, the land should come from the Mariscal de Castilla. While landlords across the eastern Bajío worked to expand profitable production and contain the working majority, conflicts between provincial elites and landlords in Mexico City simmered.

The court ordered a list of indio residents of Santa Bárbara (including neither lands nor dependents of the Mariscal). It showed 67 households with 255 people at the casco; 17 households and 70 people at the Rancho de San Juan; 37 households and 179 people at Señor San Nicolás de los Cilleros; 17 households and 62 people at Rancho de Palacios; and 26 households with 95 people at Rancho de Cerritos. The court recognized five indio settlements with 161 households and 664 people at Santa Bárbara in 1807. The community had grown since 1801, reenergizing the demand for community rights.

The plaintiffs affirmed their status as indios; the owner accepted it; the court recognized it. Each had reasons: for the men living as tenant rancheros, indio status backed the claim to be recognized as a republic with a chapel, a council, and community lands. For the young owner, recognizing the plaintiffs' indio status allowed him to caricature them as drunk and disorderly. For the court, indio status guaranteed that men would pay tributes, a key state interest. Yet these were indios with Spanish patronyms who spoke Spanish; they had long lived among mulattoes in estate communities. They designed a pointed challenge to estate power. They were indios, but not the ethnically segregated, linguistically separate indios of nearby Querétaro or rural Spanish Mesoamerica. They were of Spanish North America, declaring indio status to claim community rights in a regional economy moving toward agrarian capitalism. The record of their suit ends in 1807 with no resolution. Perhaps the court found the community too small to be a republic, or the drought that began in 1808 turned the plaintiffs to more immediate struggles of survival. Surely the Spanish-speaking indio tenants who went to court to claim community rights continued to grapple with marginal cultivation and social insecurity across the dry country north of San Miguel.

A group of men at Tequisquiapan, east of Santa Bárbara, began a nearly identical suit in 1804. In 1792 the estate was a rancho owned by don Feliz de Berber y Vargas, a priest. By 1804 it had been inherited by don Manuel de Berber y Vargas of San Miguel, now called a hacienda thanks to growing cultivation and settlement.[106] In September thirteen men went to court in the name of a community of indios.[107] They argued: "we have long lived at this estate; our parents, grandparents, and ancestors were born here; we were all raised here. We have always lived here, and we have stayed despite the quarrels and conflicts we have faced with don Ylario Zamarripa and Juan de Díos Frías, the principal tenants, over many wrongs."[108] Families long at Tequisquiapan faced difficulties with two major tenants, presumably recruited to raise rents or evict small tenants for commercial cropping. Yet the tenants never reappear in a suit against the owner and demanding a landed republic.

The plaintiffs represented 103 married indio heads of household, patriarchs who with a few widowers, widows, and single men led a community approaching 400. As indios they claimed a right to cultivate land without paying rent, the right of indios in republics. They argued that Tequisquiapan had the land and water to sustain a republic. The owner had a simple answer: creating a pueblo on his lands would cause him "prejudice and wrong."[109]

In a first hearing the indio plaintiffs produced five witnesses. Juan Hermenegildo Valle was an indio widower, eighty-three years old, a muleteer living in San Miguel. He was born at the Rancho de Peñuelas, his ancestral home near Tequisquiapan. Julián Ceferino Vázquez was a Spaniard, married, a fifty-five-year-old cultivator at the Rancho de las Adjuntas. Did he have kin at Tequisquiapan, or was he an ally ready to cross ethnic categories? Asencio de la Cruz called himself an indio ladino, a Spanish speaker. His family came from Tequisquiapan; at sixty-eight, he lived in San Miguel and worked in a textile shop (the name and profession suggest mulatto antecedents). José Feliciano Juárez also called himself an indio ladino, then stated again that he spoke Spanish. Married and living in San Miguel, he was a labrador, probably renting land near town. José Antonio de la Trinidad, fifty-three, indio ladino, labrador, married, and living at San Miguel, completed the group.[110] All testified that the indios of Tequisquiapan were numerous enough to form a landed republic. The witnesses were men, most ready to be indios, yet proud speakers of Spanish, living and working in San Miguel while keeping ties to the community at Tequisquiapan. A Spaniard and four Hispanized indios linked town and country, and stood in court against a local landlord.

Rebuttal began with don José María Cecilio de Berber y Vargas, eldest son and heir of the owner. He claimed immutable rights to property: everything built at the estate must belong to the owner; all who lived there must serve and respect him. "Tenant *rancheros* must be prompt paying rent, . . . They must always live subject to the will of the estate owner, never gaining for themselves the right to rule in the chapel."[111] The suit at Santa Bárbara began over a chapel, yet the owner contended that it was about land. The challenge at Tequisquiapan began as a claim of land, and the owner's son contended that it was also about rule and religion. Land, power, and religion were inseparable—and contested among those who presumed to rule and those who claimed community north of San Miguel after 1800.

The owner followed his son, offering a defense based on legal precedent. He noted that in a recent parallel suit brought by residents at Cruz de Palma, the court had confirmed the property of the Mariscal de Castilla. Don Manuel de Berber y Vargas, a less exalted provincial landlord, expected the same.[112] He found backing by a leading member of the provincial elite. In 1805 don Juan María de Lanzagorta y Landeta testified that with his sisters doña Ygnacia and doña Mariana and his brother don José María—all of San Miguel, all children of don Francisco Antonio de Lanzagorta y Landeta, knight of the Order of Calatrava (and a key member of the Canal clique that ruled San Miguel)—he owned the Petaca estate near Tequisquiapan. He insisted that any grant of land and community status to indios at Tequisquiapan would do irreparable damage to all property owners and all indios in the region. Provincial patriarchs feared escalating conflicts, loss of land, and declining control in estate communities. What indios had to fear is not clear. Life as tenants had become unacceptable. Demands for rising rents on marginal lands left them struggling to sustain households. They sought land, self-rule, and independent worship. What would indios lose? Did Lanzagorta imagine a right to live as subordinate patriarchs?

The indios also found significant, if limited, support. In July 1805 Bachiller don José Manuel de Soria sent a statement backing their demand for land and community. A priest who assisted don Miguel Hidalgo y Costilla at Dolores, Soria stated that Father Hidalgo knew of the conflict and supported the indios. Yet Soria noted carefully that while he and Father Hidalgo backed the men of Tequisquiapan against the owner and tenants, they did not assert the right of all estate indios to independence. Father Hidalgo knew the plight of his rural parishioners. He left his assistant to write on their behalf, offering limited support for rights to land and community.[113] As the suit continued into 1806 the owner raised a new issue. He had long allowed estate residents, including the plaintiffs, the use of the *montes*, or estate woodlands, to gather firewood, make charcoal, and graze animals; now they abused the privilege, destroying the woods.[114] The landlord saw an assault on his property. For struggling tenants, working the woods was part of a desperate search for survival.

In 1807 the case reached the High Court in Mexico City. An experienced Procurador de Indios represented the plaintiffs. He stated that they comprised 143 households and over 400 persons. He asked for community lands, and added that pueblo status would help them to pursue suits against the landlord and others more effectively. And he reported two favorable precedents: two groups of indios (he did not say where) had won land and republican rights from ex-Jesuit estates run by Temporalidades, a regime agency. To deflect the impact of lost lands from the angry owner, the procurador asked the court to grant the plaintiffs' petition, but to take land from several estates. The court ordered a survey of only Tequisquiapan, seeking lands for a community. It charged the surveyor to draw clear boundaries and avoid prejudice to the landlord. The order appears a victory for the indios, yet the order to protect the landlord invited continuing conflict. There is no record of a survey, no evidence of a republic. The dispute at Tequisquiapan continued into the crisis that began in 1808.

The economic transformation and social pressure at Charco de Araujo, along with the suits for land and community at Santa Bárbara, Tequisquiapan, and Cruz de Palma reveal another way toward agrarian capitalism in the country north of San Miguel. There the shift from grazing to cultivation came late, and on marginal lands with limited and declining yields. Landlords still profited by expanding cultivation, offering access to marginal tenancies to families desperate for sustenance. Estates took rents, forcing the insecurity of declining yields onto tenant families. Some of the families went to court asserting rights as indios to create landed republics. Their neighbors surely watched. Landlords resisted, and revealed fractures in provincial society. The challenge to the Mariscal de Castilla at Cruz de Palma failed in the High Court; the great landlord based in Mexico City found protection in court. Provincial proprietors facing similar suits got support from the Canal clique of San Miguel. Father Hidalgo and his assistant cautiously backed the indios of Tequisquiapan against a weak landlord, noting that their support did not extend to a general right to create communities on estate lands.

Before 1810 conflicts stayed in court. Most rural families north of San Miguel descended from Otomí migrants who had mixed with African slaves and their descendants. Indio status allowed them to claim republican rights. They sought redress in the courts, and while the courts temporized they advanced into estate woodlands. While the possibility of judicial mediation and the chance to create community persisted, the hispanized indios north of San Miguel resisted in court. They were frustrated, perhaps angry. They were not rebellious—yet.

Across the eastern Bajío countryside, from the Amascala basin and La Griega east of Querétaro, through the Santa Rosa basin, past Puerto Nieto east of San Miguel, to the uplands stretching to Dolores, diverse estate communities faced accelerating capitalism as the nineteenth century began. Differing resources, legacies of settlement, and access to markets created varied communities. Ethnic complexity was everywhere; different ways of amalgamation and segregation shaped neighboring communities. Patriarchy was also everywhere, reinforced by managers to implement landlords' power. The intersection of locally unique ethnic relations with patriarchal hierarchies made every community different.

Negotiation was also everywhere. Across the Amascala basin east of Querétaro challenges to power focused on indigenous claims. At Casas, Otomí youths protested debts created by obligated labor. At La Griega, the Otomí community threatened a strike to gain a religious festival in time of disease. For their efforts both groups were feminized by men who presumed to rule. Among Spanish tenants at La Griega, staunch protest of eviction in 1792 came from doña Gertrudis Villaseñor. At ethnically amalgamating Puerto de Nieto, protest also came from women: a slave mother protested her slave sons' removal; a manager's wife resisted his firing; the girls occupied the manager's residence to fight a shift from tenant farming to commercial cropping. North of San Miguel, on marginal lands let to struggling tenants facing declining yields, men asserting indio status went to court seeking rights as landed republics. Some forced negotiations. None blocked the changes they protested. Most men acquiesced, adapting to declining earnings and new insecurity as long as they remained patriarchs, however dependent. Men were expected to be men—patriarchs negotiating their own and their families' subordination and exploitation in order to remain patriarchs. The few men who protested were indios, easily feminized in the eyes of managers and landlords. Resistance was an affair of women, girls, and indios.

La Griega and Puerto de Nieto in the Crisis of 1808–1810

Deepening contradictions between profit-seeking production and popular struggles for sustenance and security; between entrepreneurs asserting patriarchy to claim profit and power and producers clinging to patriarchy as their last advantage; and between managers promoting patriarchy to rule communities and dependents seeking community to resist power—all came to a head in the crisis of 1808 to 1810. In May 1808, amid wars for European and Atlantic dominance, the Spanish monarchy fell to Napoleon's armies, breaking legitimate sovereignty across Spain and its American dominions. That summer the worst drought since 1785–86 spread across the highlands from Mexico City to the Bajío. An unprecedented combination of regime crisis and environmental catastrophe in a context of deepening social polarization led to the Hidalgo revolt of September 1810. The insurgency began in the Bajío, became a regional revolution, and led to Mexican independence in 1821.

For don José Sánchez Espinosa, another drought was another opportunity to profit. He charged his managers at La Griega and Puerto de Nieto to hold grain and await the chance for maximum gain. For two years they reported and managed an escalating mix of profit and social dislocations, never imagining that they were worsening contradictions soon to erupt in a revolutionary conflagration.

The spring of 1808 began with promise. Don José Regalado Franco still ruled at La Griega. Don José Toribio Rico finally held the title of manager at Puerto de Nieto. Both spent the early months of the year investing in improvements. At La Griega, where the expansion of commercial cropping began earlier, it was a time of reconstruction. Franco restored the main house, cleaned water tanks, and rebuilt irrigation canals. He had workers to do all that and prepare the fields for planting in April and May.[115] At Puerto de Nieto, Rico continued to expand arable land. In April 1808 he planted "a new field . . . of good size" in the "woodlands." Yet the new field worried him. He knew that fields like it quickly lost fertility. He planned to plant only half the area in maize each year, leaving the rest as pasture to be fertilized by manure. Despite the limited potential of the new fields, expanded cropping promised profit.[116] While proudly reporting renovations, Franco noted the onset of a "terrible drought." Rico, while describing the expansion of fields, reported "rigorous drought." Franco added that the only solution was to seek "remedies" from "the Queen of Heaven."[117] While joining neighbors and dependents seeking aid from the Virgin, the managers focused on production and sales as scarcity loomed. They prayed to the Virgin, and took profit from a population desperate for grain.

Late in April maize still sold at Puerto de Nieto for ten reales. The price approached twelve reales in the cities, but the difference did not cover shipping. By September persistent drought threatened the maize in the fields; the price at the estate reached twelve reales. Rico proposed stopping all sales, holding stocks for the peak to come. Sánchez Espinosa told him to continue small sales at the granaries, taking income while holding most maize for higher prices. Franco was blunt in his report from La Griega. The crop was lost, but the news was not bad. He had over ten thousand fanegas from past harvests, and prices were rising.[118]

October brought Sánchez Espinosa more good news. At Puerto de Nieto rents and limited maize sales brought 4,500 pesos, solid if not spectacular earnings.[119] At La Griega, where drought was more severe, the price of maize shot to twenty-two reales. Franco wrote, "Our neighbors have sealed their granaries and are watching the weather." Prices had more than doubled; rich growers aimed to drive them higher. As fall months passed, Franco's irrigated maize prospered while rain-fed fields died. Prices soared.[120] Water control, ample storage, and the wealth to hold maize until prices peaked were the keys to profitable cultivation. Prayers to the Virgin might serve small growers and desperate consumers. For the agrarian capitalist and his managers, a sharp eye on prices and markets promised profit amid drought.

In March 1809 the granaries at Puerto de Nieto held 15,740 fanegas of maize, accumulated over years. The price after the local harvest held at twelve reales. Rico sold small lots, taking small profits while waiting for higher prices. Then in the summer of 1809, the drought finally struck San Miguel. In November, Rico reported that there would be no maize harvest in the region, except for small amounts on his irrigated fields. The price peaked at 4 pesos (32 reales) per fanega. With people starving all around, Rico opened the granaries. He wrote to Sánchez Espinosa that every day forty to eighty hungry buyers came to spend half a real, perhaps a real, on maize.[121] The specter of famine made good business. If Rico sold 15,000 fanegas of maize for 4 pesos each, he claimed 60,000 pesos—a huge profit if we remember that he called 4,500 pesos a good year. We must imagine the thoughts of people standing in line to buy the little maize they could afford at extortionate prices. Surely they were thankful that there was maize to buy. Yet they must have resented walking long distances, perhaps all the way from San Miguel twenty kilometers west, to pay famine prices for maize and then carry it home. The predatory power of agrarian capitalism was plain to see.

Thanks to irrigation, there were limited harvests in January 1810 at both La Griega (3,400 fanegas) and Puerto de Nieto (1,960 fanegas), for a total of nearly 5,400 fanegas. With scarcity and high prices all around, city councils at San Miguel and Querétaro demanded accounts of estate stocks and pressed for sales to hungry, often angry urban consumers. (Local landlords dominated the councils: the Canal family at San Miguel, don Pedro de Septién and others at Querétaro. Were they suddenly concerned for the common welfare? Or was investigation of the maize market a ritual to mollify a desperate populace, undertaken only after prices peaked?) Rico responded to the inquiry from San Miguel by stating that the combination of his small harvest with stocks on hand gave him 2,760 fanegas for the coming year. He insisted on keeping 1,500 fanegas for estate needs—to pay rations to sirvientes who raised the crops that generated profits. With another 115 fanegas going to the tithe, Rico reported 1,145 fanegas available for sale. He did not say when. Soon after the harvest at La Griega, Franco shipped 3,000 fanegas north to feed residents at Bocas and Sánchez

Espinosa's other estates in San Luis Potosí. He continued to pay rations to the men who worked at La Griega. And he sold small quantities to those who trekked out in search of food, taking profit while holding prices high.[122]

The business of maize in time of scarcity was so good that in the spring of 1810 Franco expanded planting to fifty-four fanegas at San Agustín and fifty-eight at La Venta, historic highs perhaps achieved by taking over fields that tenants could not afford to plant. When rains were late and seed did not germinate he replanted four fanegas at San Agustín and five at La Venta. Two years of drought made oxen scarce; yet plenty of men and boys were ready to work for wages and rations, and Franco kept planting. In July the Querétaro council ordered all maize sent to the city. Franco consulted Sánchez Espinosa, and refused. The two believed that prices would continue to rise; they would not feed the city until hunger assured peak profits.[123]

The drought crisis of 1808 to 1810 deepened long-developing contradictions of agrarian capitalism. For entrepreneurs with irrigated lands, sharp managers, and the funds to hold maize, profits were exceptional. For sirvientes, men paid in cash, cloth, and rations to plant and harvest estate crops, years of drought made the benefits of dependent patriarchy unmistakable. They could feed their families and assert household rule, while people all around faced desperate searches for sustenance. For tenants on rain-fed lands, the liability of lives of dependent insecurity became blatant. They lost crops, owed rents, and joined the growing majority who lived by paying cash for food. For all who had to buy maize, the drought made the costs of agrarian capitalism painfully clear.

Amid the drought, Bajío elites faced a crisis of sovereignty. During the spring and summer of 1810 provincial leaders—including Corregidor don Miguel Domínguez and the merchant-landlord don Pedro Antonio de Septién at Querétaro; lesser elites like don Ignacio de Allende (but not leaders of the Canal clan) at San Miguel; and Father Hidalgo at Dolores—met to discuss how to assert a right to join in reconstituting the sovereignty broken by Napoleon's takeover, as men were doing across Spain. When officials jailed the participants at Querétaro, Allende and Hidalgo provoked the insurrection on 16 September 1810, a rising forever linked to Father Hidalgo.[124]

Why so many men across the Bajío joined the insurgency while others did not is a complex question. All had been regaled with preaching against the "godless" French since the 1790s, preaching that became even more incendiary after Napoleon ousted the Spanish king.[125] All had lived through months of desperate dearth, though they struggled in different ways.

Hidalgo's call to insurrection was heard first at Dolores, parish center of the dry country north of San Miguel. Insurgency began there among deeply insecure tenant cultivators. The rising found early adherents at Puerto de Nieto, where insurgency persisted until 1820. Yet the call to insurrection found little response among the dependent cultivators of La Griega and other communities east of Querétaro in the Amascala basin. Decisions about rebellion reflected complex intersections of production, labor relations, patriarchy, and ethnic diversity. Tenant communities north of San Miguel mixed mulattoes and Hispanized indios, all struggling to assert patriarchy in a society that classed them as lesser men. There dependent insecurity combined with threats to patriarchy—and the failure of efforts to create landed republics—to propel many to insurgency. The sirvientes of La Griega and the Amascala plain divided sharply between Spaniards and Otomí. Most of the married men there, Spanish and Otomí, gained patriarchal security. Otomí youths faced declining opportunities; many moved to the city or to outlying regions in search of opportunities that often came with insecurities.[126] Notably, ethnic segregations made common action difficult around Querétaro. Dependent security reinforced patriarchy; youths seeking opportunities moved; and ethnic separations split communities, undermining common resistance.

At Puerto de Nieto tenants mixed with sirvientes in a community of unique ethnic integration. As tenants men faced insecurity and challenges to patriarchy; as sirvientes they gained security and support for patriarchy. Patriarchy organized in extended family clans helped to strengthen managerial power; it also helped independent clans to contest that power. The only resistance before 1810 came from the girls. The provision of rations during drought years reminded sirviente-patriarchs and their dependents of the gains of service. Men struggling as tenants endured the insecurity and challenges to patriarchy brought by lost crops, rents past due, and the rising cost of buying maize when crops failed. For all that complexity the amalgamating community became a hotbed of insurgency. Integration facilitated common action. In many households, and in every clan, men retaining security and patriarchy were kin to men who faced deepening insecurity and threats to patriarchy. Ties to kin at nearby ranchos made all aware of the price that agrarian capitalism imposed on the wider society—a price evident in long lines of people waiting to pay extortionate prices for maize.

Across the Bajío pressures generated by accelerating agrarian capitalism and then heightened by drought beginning in 1808 struck working families. They generated deep grievances that differed in communities shaped by varying ways of production and distinct ethnic relations, leading some toward insurgency while others stood back. Everything was understood, debated, and negotiated through religious understandings. For some the Hidalgo revolt was a religious crusade.[127] Those who stayed home were no less religious. An exploration of the contradictions of capitalism in the Bajío after 1770 must conclude with the religious beliefs and debates that shaped the understandings and actions of those who lived the crucible that led to the Hidalgo revolt of 1810 and the revolution that followed.

CHAPTER 8

Enlightened Reformers
and Popular Religion

Polarizations and Mediations, 1770–1810

AFTER 1770 PEOPLE ACROSS THE BAJÍO lived new polarizations in an accelerating capitalist economy, challenges they faced
in communities shaped by patriarchy and fragmented by ethnic complexity. They interpreted times of change and uncertainty through
deep religious understandings. Everyone was Christian. Everyone recognized the Church. Yet the Christianity that had developed during
three centuries came out of unequal encounters among Europeans,
Mesoamericans, Africans, and their mixed offspring. By the late eighteenth century they lived a religious culture of many visions and
voices. Most clergy promoted sacramental worship and moral sanctions. Rich testators funded convent capitalism, enabling priests and
nuns to be mortgage bankers. Patriarchs at San Miguel, earlier devoted
to a sharply penitential Catholicism, now turned to an enlightened,
rational vision promoted by reforming churchmen and regime officials. Popular communities, famously the Otomí at Pueblito, kept cults
of propitiation that promised aid and comfort in the struggles of daily
life. All lived within the flexible boundaries of the church.

Religion orchestrated common commitments and contested understandings. It linked people of all ranks and categories, powerful and
poor, offering shared ways to negotiate changing times. Catholic

Christianity was hegemonic across the Bajío as the nineteenth century began, yet divisions deepened and debates escalated.

The Bajío's religious ways emerged from a long history. Sacramental Catholicism and convent capitalism came early, as did the propitiatory devotions that addressed everyday challenges from cultivation to curing. Penitential worship strengthened at San Miguel in the first half of the eighteenth century, just as Querétaro elites adopted devotion to Our Lady at Pueblito, long essential among the Otomí there. After 1770 religion still permeated every aspect of life in the Bajío and New Spain. Powerful entrepreneurs engineered profit amid drought, and believed that they were offering Christian charity. Landlords and managers called on the Virgin to end drought, while they worked to profit from it. The Otomí at La Griega refused to work in the face of plague, unless allowed a festival of appeal and integration.

The diversity of religious voices and visions became more complex in the late eighteenth century. In the age of Atlantic enlightenment, reason asserted a new role in religious understandings. In New Spain reason rarely challenged religion; rather, it reshaped religious visions.[1] It accelerated the emphasis on human action already evident in the penitential and charitable devotion promoted at Atotonilco near San Miguel. Reason supported the morality promoted by sacramental worship; it honored the investments of convent Catholicism. And reason— Catholic, Christian reason—challenged the propitiations, cures, and sorceries at the heart of popular worship. To those who claimed the light of reason, propitiation became superstition, even idolatry. While commercial dynamism brought deepening social polarization, religious culture faced new divisions. Many among the powerful and their enlightened allies denied the validity and value of popular devotions. Difference deepened into polarization; cultural conflicts escalated, pitting an enlightened, reforming few against a deeply religious majority.

Yet elites and reformers also debated how to mediate cultural and social polarization. Some argued for the necessity of popular devotion to propitiatory virgins, notably Our Lady at Pueblito. Others proposed to educate the populace away from "supersticions," while offering worldly charity to cushion social dislocations. Into the first decade of the nineteenth century social and cultural polarization widened; debates about religion and mediation continued. Production, polarization, and social peace persisted, until unimagined crisis struck in 1808.

Religious Reform and Popular Independence

The debates about religion in eighteenth-century New Spain seem clear, especially in Spanish Mesoamerica—the colonial society grounded in the indigenous communities that reached to the southern margins of the Bajío.[2] There a reforming regime and established church faced a Mesoamerican population, mostly still speaking native languages and still living in landed republics. Parish priests remained key brokers. They negotiated with newly assertive regime magistrates and new teachers. Priests, magistrates, and teachers might dispute local eminence; together they promoted more rational, sacramental worship. They saw established community devotions, especially the festivals that combined local solidarity, propitiation, and alcohol-fueled approaches to divinity, as disruptive superstitions.[3] They faced resistance in demands for community control of worship, festivals, teachers, and even priests. Those contests limited reforms; local ways of worship usually persisted.

In the 1750s the regime appointed reforming bishops charged with completing the long process of replacing Franciscans and other clergy of the regular orders with secular priests in indigenous parishes. Resistance came quickly. Parishioners worried about losing old pastors and facing newcomers. Franciscans lived by alms, Jesuits by rich estates; the parish clergy demanded fees for sacramental service. Franciscans and Jesuits promoted devotion to the Virgin (Franciscans led at Pueblito) and saints. New pastors pressed sacramental morality.

In the 1760s the regime began inquiries into indigenous community finances. By the 1780s it concluded that many of them generated surpluses, that expenses should be limited, and that all "surplus" should go to state coffers—to help fund Spain's support of the United States war for independence. The regime saw payments for religious festivals as excessive.[4] Villagers shifted land and other resources from communal control to sodalities, maintaining the festivals that integrated community life. The villagers' success reveals their commitment to their festivals, their ability to negotiate in the face of power, and the acquiescence of many local clerics. Meanwhile the regime promoted schools. The goal was to teach Spanish and the ability to read and write. Communal resources, excess when they funded religious festivals, would pay teachers' salaries. This was not a turn against religion. New schools taught Christian doctrine, Spanish, and literacy, and promoted sacramental morality. Priests were no longer the only outsiders negotiating religious life in indigenous communities. Many villages welcomed the schools and teachers, and demanded control. Teachers,

Spanish, and literacy were fine—if they honored indigenous councils and adapted to local customs.

Amid discussions and negotiations, protests to bishops, and jostling in local communities, little changed. Schools proliferated, mostly in the head towns that were parish centers. Students were often sons of indigenous notables, reinforcing their roles as brokers in the bifurcated world of Spanish Mesoamerica. By 1810 nearly 10 percent of indigenous men were literate in Spanish, a real change. Still, the majority remained illiterate and spoke only native languages. Community payments for religious festivals fell, but sodalities paid and festivals flourished. Reforming priests and teachers adapted to indigenous ways. It was the only way they could collect fees and keep order.

Over the colonial centuries there was a clear trajectory to religious life in Spanish Mesoamerica. No sudden conversion followed the conquest. Neither did indigenous beliefs and devotions simply persist (even masked with Christian façades). Rather, three centuries of Spanish assertion and indigenous adaptation and negotiation led to an eighteenth century in which all asserted Christian identities and negotiated the meanings of Christianity. In the sixteenth century Spaniards proclaimed Santiago and the Virgin as allies in conquest, divine powers that drove and legitimated the colonial enterprise. By the eighteenth century indigenous people and communities had claimed both, especially Our Lady. To the church she was a saintly intercessor; to many indigenous people she was a powerful force in the world. Ultimately Santiago and the Virgin became mediators, brokers sanctioned by the church, patrons to whom indigenous peoples and communities turned in times of difficulty.[5]

Saintly brokers paralleled and legitimated the worldly mediation of indigenous notables, district officials, local priests, and teachers, enabling subordinate communities to negotiate with the regime, and with the divine power that sanctioned its rule. Religious legitimations proclaimed contestable reciprocities: Europeans came to the Americas claiming right based on bringing Christianity to heathens. Indigenous peoples, promised new truths, learned to evaluate rulers' religious commitments and the quality of their truths. Their evaluations went beyond the proclamations and actions of the powerful in the world. People brought to Christianity in the colonial world learned the importance of seeking their own relationships with the Christian divine. As communities made propitiatory and mediating devotions the focus of their Christianity, they claimed direct access to Christian power and independence in worldly cultural negotiations. They did not just evaluate their rulers' and priests' fullfilment of Christian legitimations; villagers made direct contact with powerful virgins, saints, and Christs, seeking their own knowledge of power and legitimacy. Indigenous notables, rural clergy, and local magistrates mediated cultural worlds that intersected, overlapped, and differed in meaningful ways—all Christian.

They negotiated within the institutions and legitimations of the colonial regime, including the Church. Local worship controlled by villagers helped to legitimate and stabilize colonial society in Spanish Mesoamerica. Communities worshipped, however differently, the same Christian God as their rulers; they dealt with the same clergy. As long as villagers negotiated with clergy and sought assistance and mediation through Christian saints and virgins, they remained in the colonial order. They shaped local Christian cultural worlds within that order. As long as they could sustain those worlds they rarely challenged Spanish power.[6]

Most of the rural clergy knew the importance of negotiating with local communities and their religions. Priests might find parishioners' Catholicism insufficiently focused on sacraments and morality, too much concerned with propitiation, intercession, and festivals that used intoxication to move worshippers to states they believed closer to the divine. In propitiations priests saw superstition; in alcohol- and peyote-induced approaches to God they saw debauchery. Yet across Mesoamerica, priests adapted as much as parishioners did. Local peace, parish fees, and the colonial order demanded that. Reforming clergy preached and cajoled; they rarely assaulted the indigenous Christianity that sustained their parishes.

Religious Contests and Mediations: The Bajío's Mesoamerican Fringe

The reforming regime and its clergy also engaged the Bajío and Spanish North America. There too officials sought revenues, and priests preferred a rational, sacramental, moralizing religion. But north of Mesoamerica reformers faced different peoples organized in different communities. Indigenous communities were few and rarely lived as landed, self-governing republics with a resident priest. Most negotiated life and worship in multiethnic cities or in estate communities where the presence of a resident priest was rare. In 1803 there were 3,840 indigenous communities with corporate rights in Spanish Mesoamerica, only 241 across Spanish North America.[7] From the Bajío north most clergy lived and worked in cities and towns; across the countryside priests were few (except at the mission frontier).

If priests were scarce across the North, religion was everywhere.

The challenge is to understand the reforms, adaptations, and nego-tiations of religious life across the Bajío—knowing the limited role of the clergy (and with little evidence about worship in estate commu-nities). The Bajío was of course a zone of transition between Spanish Mesoamerica and the more commercial, fluid society of Spanish North America. Across the southern and eastern flanks of the Bajío—from Tarascan Yuririapúndaro in the west, through multiethnic Celaya, to the Otomí zones of Querétaro, and north to San Luis de la Paz and Xichú—community-based peoples remained important minorities around 1800. They generated religious contests and their clergy kept records, providing an entry into cultural life in the Bajío.

The Intendancy of Guanajuato included about 225,000 residents classed as indios around 1800, two-thirds *laboríos y vagos* (workers and rootless), only one-third *de pueblo* (in communities). Many ac-counted as villagers for tribute collection lived at estates; perhaps only a fourth of Guanajuato's indios lived in republics. Some had small re-sources: Yuririapúndaro collected less than 450 pesos yearly and spent under 300 pesos for all activites, including religious festivals. Apaseo, with rich huertas, annually took in 13,600 pesos and spent 9,400. Apa-seo was exceptional; most Guanajuato villages were poor targets for a regime seeking revenues.[8]

The meaning of being indio varied across the Bajío. A report in 1759 on the central and western zones from Salamanca to Pénjamo noted that most indios spoke Spanish: "All are very Hispanized, understand-ing well the Castillian tongue; I have never heard them speak their native Tarascan." Those in communities enjoyed access to at least lim-ited lands; they were led by local officials who could defend the pueblo in court. To people living in republics, indio status brought limited but important rights—rights that others would seek with limited suc-cess. There were good reasons to be indio.[9] A report from San Felipe (where indios sought republican rights in the 1760s, and paid dearly for the failed effort) detailed a curing ceremony: a communion using peyote, song, and dance, while the man seeking health held a bow and arrow. The rite fused Catholic communion, peyote, and the legendary strength of Chichimeca warriors. The patient died, revived, and gained strength, but was not fully cured.[10] Bajío indios were ready to take what was useful from the Hispanic world, assert indio status when advantageous, and turn to unsanctioned rites and symbols when they promised gain.

Reformers sought change in fluid contexts. Around León they chal-lenged indigenous notables' powers, claimed funds from local trea-suries, and by 1800 placed teachers in all five pueblos.[11] Celaya's large jurisdiction included 100,000 of Guanajuato's 225,000 indios, 29 of its 39 republics. Only 9 had schools after 1800—a sign of poverty, resistance, or both. Schools opened mostly in city barrios; teachers were appointed by negotiation between Spanish and native officials. One, the indio Agustín de la Rosa, gained "fame as an advocate, getting involved in *indios* affairs, writing petitions, going in their name to Mexico City as their defender . . . prosecuting suits to gain his living."[12] Reformers sent teachers; successful teachers served their charges.

In 1790 the priest at Apaseo, the rich Otomí town between Celaya and Querétaro, wrote that the school and teacher in town were fine, but most parishioners lived at distant estates.[13] When estate owners proposed schools, resident communities demanded control. By 1796 the owner of Palmar north of Celaya had built a school and paid the teacher. Indios refused to send their children. They resisted, they said, not because of "laziness and disgust" but because the school served the manager's power. The indios at Palmar named a fiscal to teach their children, avoiding the "estate owner's school."[14]

The city of Querétaro, originally Otomí, still included a majority classed as indio in 1800. It retained a strong indigenous council, ready to negotiate cultural reforms even as it saw its funds drained by the Bank of San Carlos. When Archbishop Lorenzana ordered secularization at San Sebastián in 1768, the Franciscans protested but eventually complied. There is no report of Otomí protest. In 1784 the republics of Querétaro and San Juan del Río paid 7,600 pesos to help Spain support United States independence.[15] Contributions to religious festivals declined. By 1808 Querétaro's 21 pueblos funded only 9 festivals—for a total of only 290 pesos. Meanwhile they built schools and paid teachers. There were no community schools before 1774, five by 1799, and nineteen by 1808. Then Querétaro pueblos reported 3,472 pesos in revenues; 1,185 pesos funded schools and teachers; 1,669 pesos went to the regime.[16] Otomí commoners now paid head taxes to educate local notables' sons, and to fund regime wars.

Who taught mattered. At San Sebastián, Querétaro's urban Otomí parish, rich in huertas, Ignacio Antonio de Tapia and his son Antonio taught through the 1780s and 1790s.[17] The name suggests descent from the Otomí founders; their long tenure indicates that they found a legitimate role. Yet teachers were not always welcome. Archbishop Lizana told the priest at Huimilpan, south of Querétaro, to promote "the public school as much as he could, without losing spirit when few attend, nor pressing parents too hard to send their children." Given the difficulty of gaining school attendance, the pastor should focus on Sunday preaching.[18] Recruiting teachers to outlying posts required extra pay: in urban Querétaro and San Juan del Río they earned 96 pesos a year; at San Pedro de la Cañada, the Pame town east of Querétaro famous for resisting outsiders, 100 pesos; at Amealco, in uplands to the south, 120 pesos.[19]

While schools opened in and around Querétaro cultural conflicts endured, even escalated. Doctor don Augustín Río de Loza served as pastor at San Sebastián during decades of contested reforms. He wrote about his work in 1788. Recalling life before the local school opened in 1774, he insisted that indios could have sent their sons to the school for Spanish boys in Querétaro: "As idiots, they have no commitment to the spiritual or cultural welfare of their children"; they were further inhibited, he insisted, by "the animal drives of their passions . . . drunkenness, insanity, laziness, and other vices." His Otomí parishioners lived "like brutes," ignorant of "Christian doctrine."

The reforming cleric knew the solution. He founded schools in San Sebastián, San Pedro de la Cañada, and San Francisco Galileo (Pueblito). Community funds paid the teachers; parish funds helped with other costs. Local priests supervised, keeping out castas (the Hispanized poor). In 1788 Río de Loza reported success, within limited expectations: "It is a marvel that one meets but a few not ready to receive the sacraments." Sixty boys at San Sebastián knew Spanish (unlikely an innovation in the bicultural city); fewer knew how to "read, write, and assist at mass." The Otomí council worried about costs and sought oversight. It insisted that teachers "teach doctrine to the full numbers . . . corresponding to the hundred peso salary." If numbers fell, so should pay.[20] The priest created schools and maligned their success; the indigenous council saw excess spending and demanded control.

Divisive and degrading views of indigenous parishioners were not limited to Río de Loza. In 1803 a report from Querétaro to the archbishop called the city center a place of fervent devotion, while the countryside lived a "deplorable state of ignorance."[21] Two years later a new pastor at San Sebastián was chastised for living in Mexico City. He collected eighty pesos monthly from Otomí parishioners, yet left preaching and the sacraments to his vicars. He insisted that they performed admirably; the archbishop appointed an interim to serve the parish and collect the salary.[22] Meanwhile Otomí leaders demanded removal of a "defender of natives" named by Corregidor don Miguel Domínguez. They insisted that the defender was "not knowledgeable in forensic matters." More critically, he was not approved by "the community of caciques."[23] Reforming clergy insulted or ignored the Otomí. The Otomí republic tried to control schools and teachers, attorneys, and corporate funds, with declining success.

At the same time the regime kept asserting its power. In 1803 Carlos IV signed an order dividing the Santiago parish that served

Querétaro's center into four, adding Santa Ana, Espíritú Santo, and Divina Pastora to better a serve a growing city.[24] The tribute count of 1807 showed that the four parishes in the center, with obrajes and diverse workshops, had double the Otomí population of San Sebastián, the old Otomí parish among the huertas north of the river.[25] In the following year disease struck the city and death plagued its streets and plazas. Corregidor Domínguez tried to collect funds for a novena in Guadalupe's temple and came up short.[26] The reforming regime could limit the role of the Otomí republic in religious life; replacing its public presence proved more difficult. Still, the republic continued to work in the space left by the regime, mediating through resistant regotiations.

No community was more resistant than San Pedro de la Cañada, infamous for its exclusion of outsiders. While most parish priests named their indigenous assistants—a fiscal who organized worship, a sacristan who kept the church building, and new teachers—the Pames of La Cañada battled with local pastors and distant archbishops from 1763 to 1809, defending their right to name parish leaders.[27] Pastors saw disrespect. In 1795 an outraged priest relayed a tale shared by his predecessor: an indio seeking to join a festival dance entered the church and took a staff from the statue of the Archangel Miguel. The priest saw Pame disrespect for sacred images and for the clergy.[28]

Religious contests were especially intense (and well documented) at San Luis de la Paz and Xichú, north of Querétaro, where the Bajío met the Sierra Gorda. Both were settled in the sixteenth century with indigenous majorities. Both were long overseen by the regular orders: Xichú by Franciscans, San Luis de la Paz by Jesuits. Both mixed migrants from Mesoamerica and conquered Chichimecas. Both faced the removal of established clergy and their replacement by seculars: Xichú losing their Franciscans in 1751, San Luis de la Paz facing the expulsion of the Jesuits in 1767. San Luis de la Paz and Xichú were border communities: San Luis sat where the Bajío basin met the highlands of the Sierra Gorda; Xichú was the deepest thrust of colonial settlement into the Sierra. And the Sierra remained a refuge of Chichimecas, even after don José Escandón's "pacification."

The people of San Luis and Xichú lived at the intersection of the commercial Bajío and the uncolonized Sierra.[29] In 1767 San Luis de la Paz reported 5,725 indios, mixing Otomí, Mexicas, and Tarascos in unknown portions, plus 311 Chichimecas. There were 1,030 residents counted as Spaniards, another 1,369 as mestizos. Among 8,435 residents 30 percent were Hispanic, 70 percent indigenous.[30] Xichú, deep in the Sierra, remained more indigenous. A census in 1776 reported 7,433 as Otomí and 541 "indios Mecos Pames," along with 902 Spaniards, 354 mestizos, 649 mulattoes (plus 20 slaves), and 242 soldiers. The Hispanic population totaled 2,167—just over 20 percent of a total of 9,664.[31]

Xichú had a history of independence that its clergy saw as resistance. In 1734 a pastor reported that "the *indio* Francisco Andrés" led a group including many women in idolatrous ceremonies that used Rosa María—peyote. In 1738 Francisco Andrés carried on, provoking "rebellions and riots," leading the community against nearby estates, ruling elections to the native council. In 1747 he was accused of "witchcraft and disturbances" involving "local women" and sentenced to three years' confinement in the pastor's residence. He fled in 1751 during protests against replacing the Franciscans with secular clergy. Pastors changed; Xichú remained insolent, resisting guidance and even boycotting Mass.[32]

Indigenous religious and political resistance, that is, independence, flared again in 1768 in the aftermath of the conflict that saw San Luis de la Paz protest the expulsion of its Jesuit pastors and face Gálvez's repression. The pastor at Xichú, Bachiller don Joseph Diana, reported two problems: his parishioners blocked the replacement of deteriorating images and they refused to pay the fees in the archbishop's new price list. Felipe González, an indio who led the local republic, had a long history of resistance to the friars. Now he opposed the parish priest and the few local Spaniards, mostly merchants and estate operators. González was an educated, Hispanized indio: he used a Spanish surname; he had served as a teacher at Amealco, south of Querétaro. He wrote protests against priests. His influence reached to estate communities at Tierra Blanca, Santa Catarina, and Cieneguilla.[33]

The pastor complained that Xichú indios had called a Spaniard a "black mulatto dog."[34] The insult struck Spaniards' prejudices. They honored purity of blood and maligned ethnic mixing; they celebrated whiteness and saw blackness as degradation. Chichimecas were "sons of dogs," thus uncivilized. As "black mulatto dogs," Spaniards were dark, mixed, and uncivilized. The insult aimed to wound a man presumed white, pure, and civilized. There was more. The pastor reported that the most threatening "riot of *indios* and *indias*" came when he replaced an image of Our Lady of Sorrows with a new one. To the priest, to whom the statue was an image, the more splendid statue was a gift to parishioners.[35] Riotous resistance showed that it was an object of devotion, property of the indigenous community. Replacing it with a new image, however splendid, challenged cultural control.

The pastor focused his ire on González, political leader of the resistance. Yet behind González the "spiritual leader" was Francisco Andrés, "the Old Christ." Since the 1730s he had led Xichú's indigenous peoples in cultural independence. He was "*indio*," a status confirmed by the absence of a surname. We do not know if he spoke Spanish; he was probably Otomí. Francisco Andrés "says Mass, he makes himself a prophet and saint, he bathes often and *indias* drink the water as a relic, he gives communion using tortillas." Here was an adoption and adaptation of Christian worship, orchestrated by a native Christ during three decades. When local troublemakers were apprehended, the Old Christ Francisco Andrés escaped.[36]

González, the literate, Hispanized indio, ruled Xichú's indigenous council, operating as a broker between native and Hispanic worlds, the community and surrounding estates. He led resistance to the new image of the Virgin, yet he was easily captured. Francisco Andrés lived apart from and in opposition to Hispanic power, and he escaped. Perhaps don Joseph, the local priest, downplayed the role of the Old Christ because he could not grasp him, or because he knew that the Old Christ was so important that it was better to accommodate his flight than provoke a confrontation. For three decades conflict at Xichú abated. The archbishop worked to ensure that local clergy spoke Otomí.[37] Enlightenment demanded Hispanization; negotiation across the cultural divide required adaptation to indigenous independence.

Religious conflict resurfaced in the 1790s at Xichú and San Luis de la Paz. In 1791 the Spanish minority and indigenous majority at Xichú disputed who would carry Nuestra Señora de la Soledad in the Easter procession. In 1794 the local priest gave a new image of Our Lady, which local Spaniards presumed to carry. Indios threatened to riot; the Spaniards proceeded, backed by soldiers. Xichú's indios fled to the highlands. The regime lost tributes; the priest lost fees. Soon reports reached the archbishop that the pastor lived in debauchery, dressed like a criminal, operated an illegal still, carried firearms, and traveled to Mexico City with three women, joining fandangos along the way.[38] Whatever the truth, a deep chasm divided the priest and the Spanish minority from the majority at Xichú.

Then in 1796 a report of indigenous religious independence came from San Luis de la Paz, where the Sierra met the Bajío. The pastor at San Miguel got an anonymous letter detailing that "around 30 indios gathered late at night, a few ringleaders and many more . . . for a diabolical meeting." The leader was "the *indio* Andrés Martínez," mayordomo of the *cofradía* of Señor San Luis, patron saint of San Luis de la Paz. He was backed by his father, Gregorio Martínez, mayordomo of the sodality devoted to Nuestra Señora de la Soledad. Andrés and Gregorio Martínez were prominent in sanctioned religious life, perhaps explaining the anonymous report.[39]

The ceremonies evoked the rites that had persisted at Xichú since at least the 1730s. "They lock themselves in homes and chapels to drink *peyote* and *rosa maría*, herbs that deprive them of their senses and make them crazy; they light candles, dance with puppets, and lash themselves to sacred crosses." Then Andrés Martínez "begins to preach to the others; he washes himself, his feet, hands, and face, then all the rest drink the water . . . They adore him as if he were God, they ask him to perform miracles, raising him in a litter, carrying him to a temple they call Calvary, to the cemetery, and finally to the chapel of Our Lady of Solitude. There is also an *india* . . . they worship her; they raise her on chapel altars, they adore her, they ask her for miracles."[40] Indigenous men claimed roles as clergy; an indigenous girl took the place of the Virgin. The goal was "miracles" and "what they ask"—assistance with the burdens of life.

To demonstrate that the rites could not be Christian, the report added: "they also bury holy crosses with heads of dogs and bones of the dead; they light candles to raise the sick back from the dead; they use the boiled milk of a snake and a herb called *congora* or *covalonga* to kill people they hate."[41] If the appropriation of Christian rites was not sufficient to condemn the accused, the anonymous writer tied the Martínez men and their followers to an underground world of cures and sorceries, even killings. The inquiry that followed found many appropriations of Christianity but few potions and sorceries.

The bishop at Valladolid, Fray Antonio de San Miguel, ordered the pastor at San Luis de la Paz to investigate. Late at night on 29 December 1796 Bachiller don José María de Vicuña burst into the house of the indio Dionisio, alias León the Laboreño (miracle worker). They found fifteen men and uncounted women locked in a room with an altar and many candles. Four silver plates held six pesos of offerings. There were jars of herbs. Two acolytes played guitars. All were arrested.[42] The investigation reported that José Dionisio, an indio from San Miguel and owner of the house at San Luis, had organized the ceremony to collect funds for a Mass to Ecce Homo at San Miguel. The peyote served medicinal needs, he insisted. José Ignacio Ramírez, an indio of nineteen, was more candid. He confirmed that the funds were to pay for a Mass to Our Lord. The peyote was there so that "those who took it would cry, and petition with greater fervor." The music was "to move with more fervor, to plead with more intensity." Ramírez knew of other gatherings that included peyote, processions to El Calvario, and collections of alms, several at the house of Lázaro the Miracle Worker.[43]

Many confirmed the role of peyote in their rites: it was drunk "to plead to God with greater fervor," "to understand God," "to love God," even "to ask pardon of God." Using peyote to draw closer to God lay at the heart of indigenous rites, proudly confirmed even by those facing sanctions. A few were more circumspect, calling peyote "refreshment for the body" or "medicine."[44] Of potions, sorceries, and deaths no confirmation appeared. A different perspective came from Teresa de Jesús Ramírez, an avowed foe of the devotions and wife of one of the accused. She was not identified as india yet she claimed to know the rites, if only by hearsay. She reported that "they take herbs, they sing, they dance, they cry, they do what they please." She noted that the accused earlier faced conflict with a local justice. Then the Miracle Worker and Gregorio and Andrés Martínez fled along with Eugenio Tequesquite, the local jailer, to the Jofre hacienda, where they joined another "lame miracle worker named Antonio." They continued their rites at the estate.[45]

Another anonymous report confirmed the links to estate communities and added new detail: "They also join with *indios* from the Bajío we call *de laborío*, outsiders to our town until these troublemakers sought them out. They came to live here, bringing their resources; they received or bought lands to build houses; they joined in late-night meetings or retreats, especially when these troublesome leaders celebrated election as Governor or Magistrates of the Republic."[46] Jofre was a segregating estate community at the northern end of the Santa Rosa basin. Was that why indios there moved to San Luis de la Paz? In the indigenous republic they gained land and joined local politics—rights that indios around Dolores pursued in court. The ties between Bajío estate residents and the indios at San Luis de la Paz confirm that the striving for religious autonomy linked republics and estate communities.

Additional reports noted the involvement of at least one "*indio* from Querétaro" and a link to Atotonilco. Teresa de Jesús Ramírez defended her husband: "we all join the crew of *mecos* [Chichimecas] that travels to sweep the temple of God every Wednesday and Saturday . . . as we also journey to deliver offerings of stone to build the new façade at the Sanctuary of Our Father Jesus of Nazareth at Atotonilco."[47] Participants in the nocturnal devotions also served the penitential church. The inquiry into the indigenous rites at San Luis de la Paz confirmed the importance of native notables, the centrality of peyote, the participation of women, and the extension of the rites across a wide area of the nearby Bajío. The ties to the estate community at Jofre were clear. So was the role of one indio from San Miguel and another from Querétaro.

The accused blamed their priest for their turn to independent devotions. The remedy: a "zealous and vigorous pastor, very skilled in the [Otomí] language, so he can persuade his rustic flock." The current priest failed to teach "the sacred dogmas of our holy faith," allowing "libertine ways" like "the miserable conditions one sees in France." They proposed a new pastor, Bachiller don Joaquín Zárate, "a man defined by great virtue, skilled in the Otomí language." Blame the priest, threaten parallels to France in irreligious revolution, and demand a pastor skilled in Otomí. It was a defense calculated to persuade church leaders who presumed the power of the clergy and the weakness of native peoples—leaders who when faced with conflict often chose accommodation over doctrinal purity.[48]

In 1800 the investigation ended with a ceremony of reconciliation and promises to end old ways. Most escaped further consequences. Yet two women faced prosecution and public penance, despite the male leadership confirmed by the inquest. Soon after, two indio men from San Luis de la Paz went to court in Mexico City, charged the priest with destroying their chapel, and won compensation.[49] Neither inquest nor reconciliation ended indigenous independence. Across the Bajío's Mesoamerican fringe, reformers challenged persistent indigenous rites that reached into estate communities. Cultural polarization deepened; conflict heightened when priests fought popular independence. But sooner or later the clergy reacted by mediating and accommodating native independence.

Rational Impulses and Popular Devotions

While indigenous communities along the Mesoamerican fringe grasped for a religious independence formally rejected yet repeatedly accommodated by the church and its clergy, a drive toward rational religion took root in San Miguel. The San Felipe Oratorio had promoted penitential devotion since the 1730s. The sanctuary at Atotonilco offered retreats focused on penance and charitable service. The oratorio ran the Colegio de San Francisco de Sales, where twenty to thirty youths (some paying a hundred pesos yearly, others funded by grants) studied for the title of Bachiller and a chance at ordination, to be gained by examination at the university in Mexico City.[50] In the 1770s the colegio was led by Bachiller don Juan Benito Díaz de Gamarra y Dávalos. After years of travel and study in Europe he returned to San Miguel with enlightened mathematical and philosophical visions; he taught a Catholic utilitarianism demanding learning and action in the world.[51] Don Luis Felipe Neri de Alfaro, the force behind penitential worship at Atotonilco, welcomed Gamarra and named him his confessor. Gamarra gave the eulogy at Alfaro's funeral in 1776. The link between the penitential and charitable devotion of the 1740s and the rational, utilitarian worship of the 1770s could not be clearer. Both pressed men toward personal relations with God, and toward action in the world. The tie to Alfaro and the compatability of their views allowed Gamarra to design a new curriculum, linking sacramental Catholicism to scientific reason and worldly action.

Penance, charity, and rational inquiry engaged men in the world. The fundamental conflict was not between penitential and rational Catholicism but between both and the propitiatory devotions that implored representatives (or representations) of the divine to intervene in the world. That conflict emerges clearly in Díaz de Gamarra's reflection on the life of doña María Josefa de la Canal, daughter of the oratory's primary benefactor, founder of the troubled convent of La Purísima. Don Manuel de la Canal and his devout daughter had built the chapel of Our Lady of Loreto, adjacent to the oratorio. Reflecting on that link, Díaz de Gamarra insisted that devotion to Our Lady was not—could not be—propitiatory. Doña María Josefa led an exemplary life, without "extasies, visions, and miracles."[52] To Díaz de Gamarra devotion to the Virgin was fine; expectations that she might bring rain, cures, or other aid were absurd.

Díaz de Gamarra's rational Catholicism gained support from the Canal patriarchs who ruled San Miguel in the late eighteenth century. But the youths sent to take examinations in Mexico City found difficulties. Degrees were few and parishes fewer for prospective priests educated at San Miguel. Perhaps traditional churchmen rejected innovation. Perhaps, too, the canons of the church in the viceregal capital, surrounded by indigenous republics, worried that the rational Catholicism taught at San Miguel would deepen conflicts with people committed to religious independence and propitiatory devotions.

Did the penitential, charitable, rational religious tradition at San Miguel reach beyond its promoters and adherents among landed patriarchs and clerical innovators? Participation in the penitential retreats at Atotonilco suggests that not only the powerful but many among the middling and perhaps the working poor took time from everyday concerns to engage the personal devotions promoted there.[53] The location of Atotonilco among estate communities north of San Miguel, and the role of indigenous peoples from as far away as San Luis de la Paz in building and maintaining the sanctuary, indicate that people across the region knew of the devotion offered there. The call for personal, penitential, sacramental, charitable, and now rational religion—religion that made people responsible for lives in the world—was surely heard by the working poor in San Miguel and its rural environs.

Did the culturally diverse people in estate communities, living in patriarchal clans without the rights of republics, find a religion of personal responsibility attractive? Did they hear the calls for responsibility and action by San Miguel's preachers and patriarchs, and hold them responsible for deepening polarization and deteriorating lives? We know that many among the powerful preached reforming religion. We know that indigenous communities from Celaya, through Querétaro, and north to San Luis de la Paz and Xichú continued to defend and practice independent propitiatory devotions. We know that those devotions reached into estate communities between San Miguel and the Sierra, notably at Jofre. And we know that around Dolores, just north of San Miguel, local caciques had worked to integrate indigenous religious life across the countryside during the early eighteenth century, but that from the 1780s they joined Spanish devotions in town—while outlying communities went to court seeking landed and religious independence.

The people of estate communities, like those in indigenous republics, kept their own religious counsels. We await the sources to tell us whether their beliefs and participations remained focused on the propitiations and shared festivals evident in indigenous republics, tended toward the personal and sacramental approaches promoted at San Miguel, or developed their own independent adaptations of both.

We do know that church leaders and powerful patriarchs promoted reform while parish priests struggled to minimize conflict. A parallel turn to rationalism moderated by negotiation with popular beliefs characterized Inquisitors' continuing engagements with popular cures and sorceries. The Inquisition still took reports of women and men offering potions and cures. They told of indias, mestizas, and mulattas asserting unsanctioned powers in a world of patriarchy. Female sorcerers challenged and sometimes threatened men. Yet men, powerful and poor, regularly sought help from women healers. The unsanctioned world of cures and sorceries carried on in and around Querétaro after 1770 operated through networks of women of all categories: indias, mulattas, mestizas, and españolas, engaging each other and diverse men. Interactions among people whom the official order aimed to separate confirm popular independence, and suggest that the popular devotions documented among indios found resonance among neighbors defined as mulattoes, mestizos, and even Spaniards.

While popular practices persisted, Inquisitors' practices changed. For centuries they had seen dangerous and potentially effective beliefs and practices that had to be repressed. Enlightened Inquisitors saw superstitions to be documented and discouraged, but rarely punished. They saw an underworld of women, mostly poor ethnic subordinates, offering cures and control. They saw patriarchs consulting that world when all else failed. Rational Inquisitors no longer found popular beliefs even worthy of repression. Yet the retreat from repression helped popular cures and sorceries to endure.[54] The cultural chasm widened.

Why did so many among the powerful, the privileged, and their clerical allies find a religion of enlightened reason persuasive, while most of a diverse populace clung to propitiatory devotions and popular cures? Enlightened ideas arriving from Europe provide only part of an explanation. Reformers across New Spain worked hard to preach a rational religion of sacraments and morality. They taught Spanish and the literacy needed to spread rational ways of life and worship. Indigenous villagers and people in diverse communities heard calls for rational sacramental devotion. Yet most rejected them while working for local control and promoting propitiatory worship and popular cures.

No certain explanation is possible. But Clifford Geertz's observation that religion operates as a model of the interaction of the divine and the experienced world, and as a model for action in the same domains, allows for suggestive understandings. Enlightened reason, as the new curriculum at San Miguel emphasized, did not assault religion. Rather, it took emerging scientific approaches of observation, experimentation, and action and aimed to apply them to affairs of the world. Key questions of first origins, ultimate meanings, and moral principles remained unobservable and thus unknowable to science. They persisted as domains of faith and the divine. Enlightened religion aimed to use reason to guide action in domains subject to human control—and to expand those domains where possible.

In that perspective the widening religious gulf in the Bajío becomes understandable. For powerful entrepreneurs who amassed capital and ruled enterprises that dug deep into mountains to extract ores that made them some of the richest people in the world, the world seemed in control, subject to manipulation by rational men. To men and boys who went into bottomless dungeons, risking life and limb while their earnings fell, life was out of control. To agricultural entrepreneurs with the capital to expand irrigation (controlling water), to clear fields and expand production (controlling labor), and to hold crops until prices peaked in times of famine (controlling markets), life seemed in control. To men who tilled fields for declining wages and rations, control was less certain. And among tenant families expelled from the best fields, pressed to clear uplands only to face declining yields on marginal soils—and endure hunger during recurrent years of drought—control was gone.

In the late-eighteenth-century Bajío it was reasonable for mining magnates, agricultural entrepreneurs, merchant clothiers, urban officials, tithe-collecting churchmen, and mortgage-banking churchwomen to feel more in control of life in the world. They worked to increase that control with militias and urban patrols, and clocks to regulate city life. Men of wealth were less ready to commit capital to fund their daughters' lives of cloistered prayer. A growing number found appeals to the Virgin and saints in the face of disease and drought less worthy of attention and endowment. Many among the powerful and their favored allies expanded the domain of reason and focused religion on sacraments, morality, penance, charity, and ultimately personal salvation. But among the working men, women, and children of the Bajío, Spanish, mestizo, mulatto, and indio, there were few signs of increasing control. To the contrary, they faced lost autonomy, declining earnings, deepening insecurity, periodic scarcity, unfathomable illnesses, and new forces of social control with little hope beyond appeal to the virgins or recourse to shadowy healers. In that world of dependence and desperation it was reasonable to emphasize supplications and propitiations to address the uncontrollable uncertainties of everyday life.

Unmistakable evidence that the late eighteenth century brought new control to the powerful and their favored allies, while concentrating insecurity, disease, and death among the working majority, came during the smallpox epidemic that swept New Spain from 1797 to 1799. Smallpox had a long and storied place in the history of the Americas. In the sixteenth century it was essential to conquest and the implantation of colonial societies. Indigenous people died in horrific numbers, while Spaniards lived—and credited their God and His saintly allies. Spaniards established rule while Amerindians died and pondered the power of the newcomers' religion.

After a century of plague-driven depopulation, barely 10 percent of Amerindians survived. Finally smallpox became endemic for them too. It struck periodically, infecting mostly children and killing too many— but far fewer than in the post-conquest century. And finally it killed people of European, Amerindian, and African ancestry in roughly equal portions. While the worst of diseases struck all with equal uncertainty and devastation, people of all ranks turned to propitiatory devotions. At Querétaro wealthy Spaniards and poor Otomí turned together to Our Lady at Pueblito, fueling the rise of that devotion to preeminence in both communities in the first half of the eighteenth century.

In the 1790s, while social polarizations deepened, equality in the face of disease began to end. At Querétaro's central Santiago parish from 1789 to 1795, years of economic transformation without major epidemics, the infant death rate held below 20 percent among Spaniards, approached 30 percent for mestizos and mulattoes, and neared

40 percent for indios. At Otomí San Sebastián rates were higher, approaching 50 percent among the indigenous majority. When smallpox struck in 1797 it killed with similar distinctions: Otomí more than Spaniards, mestizos, and mulattoes—Otomí children most of all.[55] No wonder Querétaro's Otomí were so devoted to Our Lady at Pueblito.

Inoculation came to the Intendancy of Guanajuato during the same smallpox crisis. The enlightened intendant don Juan Antonio de Riaño documented the program as a triumph of reason. Inoculation induced a mild case of smallpox, more survivable than the natural plague. It left its beneficiaries immune to future epidemics. As a result inoculation was far less a risk than leaving children subject to nature's plague. Given the importance of the city of Guanajuato to the imperial economy, inoculation concentrated there. The new scientific medicine focused on the city center, where entrepreneurs, professionals, and clergy lived. In the outlying districts that were home to the men, women, and boys who worked the mines and refineries, inoculation was limited. The results were clear for all to see. Among the powerful and prosperous of the city core, over 11,000 were inoculated, and only 85 died—less than 1 percent. In the same zone nearly 3,000 "natural" cases of smallpox led to 840 deaths—28 percent. In the outlying mining camps only 4,812 were inoculated and 55 died—just over 1 percent. And there 7,722 natural cases struck a working population that suffered 1,329 deaths—17 percent. Overall the city reported 15,827 inoculations with a death rate of 1 percent, and 10,680 natural cases with a death rate of 20 percent.

In the rest of the intendancy inoculation was widespread but less common. Near Guanajuato almost 2,000 were inoculated at Silao and about the same number at Irapuato. Celaya inoculated 1,931, Valle de Santiago 1,457, León 1,257. A few hundred were inoculated in León's outlying settlements, a few dozen in the villages around Celaya. None were reported at San Miguel, Dolores, San Felipe, and San Luis de la Paz—the poorest parts of the intendancy. Outside the mining city only 10 percent of smallpox cases were the result of inoculation, with the usual survival rate of 99 percent; 92,168 mostly young indios and mulattoes, 90 percent of cases, faced natural smallpox and a 20 percent death rate.[56]

Inoculation rewarded the powerful and the prosperous in Guanajuato and in outlying towns. Smallpox struck the working poor of mining camps, towns, and rural communities without benefit of inoculation—without benefit of science. Those favored with inoculation were twenty times more likely to survive than those denied. There can be little doubt that many among the favored saw lives served by science and subject to human control. They responded easily to a religion of sacraments and reason. Meanwhile the working majority faced lives out of control. They just as reasonably clung to devotion to virgins and saints, the only powers that offered aid and compassion to lives of insecurity punctuated by desperation. Access to scientific cures paralleled and reinforced deepening polarities of power and popular welfare. In a commercial society ruled by predatory power relations, the powerful found reason persuasive. The populace found a religion of propitiation essential.

Yet they were never alone in that vision. The polarization of religious views never simply divided the powerful and the poor. Religious life remained within one institutional church. Amid the turn toward rational worship, there were always those among the powerful and the clergy who joined and funded propiatory devotions. In 1803 don José Antonio Zeláa, priest in Querétaro's Congregation of Guadalupe, detailed persistent propitiatory worship, its sanction by the church, its funding by rich and powerful patrons, and its competition with penitential worship in times of crisis.[57] There was no more trying time in the Bajío than the famine of 1785 and 1786. While agricultural entrepreneurs profited (and convinced themselves that they were doing God's charitable work), everyone else faced desperate uncertainty. Thousands died. Small growers had no grain to eat or sell; wage workers had no money to buy grain at prices inflated five times over; merchants could not sell to customers who spent all they had on food; merchant clothiers struggled to maintain production and sales while artisan families and their customers struggled to eat.

In that context of calamity out of control, even the powerful turned to divine patrons. Zeláa reports two revealing cases, one penitential and the other propiatiatory. Penitential worship at Querétaro had never reached the famed levels at San Miguel and Atotonilco. In 1763 a small group of donors built a chapel for an oratorio in the city of trade, textiles, and huertas. It was only during the crisis of 1786 that don Melchor de Noriega, "rich citizen of Querétaro" found the "Christian generosity" to build a new and larger church for Querétaro's oratorio. Amid famine Noriega saw a need to promote penitential worship. Perhaps he expected that deeper penitence might end times of affliction. (We saw a parallel vision held by the manager at La Griega.) Noriega found funds to begin a major building project. He may have profited from scarcity and turned part of his gain to penitential compensation. Before he died in 1795 Noriega spent twenty thousand pesos on the new church. Then doña María Cornelia Codallos took over; the church was almost complete in 1803. Long promoted at San Miguel and Atotonilco, penitential worship came late to Querétaro. It found a patron in a time of famine.[58]

During the same crisis another of Querétaro's powerful men turned his wealth to revive an older propitiatory cult. Zeláa wrote of "the beautiful image of Mary Most Holy" known as the Divina Pastora. "She is worshiped in a very old and badly kept chapel; no one knows when it was built." During the famine crisis of 1785–86 don Francisco Antonio Alday, "republican citizen of this city, in thanks for many and special favors he received . . . through her image," vowed to build "a beautiful vaulted chapel" and a new home for the chaplain who attended the Divine Shepherdess. The result: "In a few years she has become much celebrated for the singular benefits she has brought those devoted to her."[59] Famine could lead rich Querétaro patriarchs to penitential worship or to a virgin shepherdess. When Alday favored a virgin he helped devotion that also served and comforted the desperately poor. Her church became home to one of Querétaro's three new parishes in 1803.

As the nineteenth century began, however, devotion to Our Lady at Pueblito still ruled at Querétaro. Father Zeláa, professionally committed Guadalupe, wrote in 1803 that "the most portentious image of Most Holy Mary, with the title of Pueblito, is venerated in her sanctuary on the outskirts of this city. There she acculumates her glories; there she is the common asylum of every Queretano."[60] In the following year a plague struck and the reforming Corregidor Domínguez "heard the public clamor about the ravages caused by the present disease." The friars at the Mission College of Santa Cruz reported a growing number of confessions. Across Querétaro and San Sebastián "in two weeks of this month there have been more than four hundred burials, mostly infants, but many adults." Even the enlightened Corregidor knew that "the remedy in this grave time of need" was "the protection of the Most Holy Virgin Mary, through her image at Pueblito."[61]

In the early seventeenth century the Virgin at Pueblito converted the poorest of Otomí in the village outside Querétaro. As the nineteenth century began she was the first resort of the city in time of need. Rational religion had spread; penitential devotion grew; but propitiatory devotion to Our Lady at Pueblito held the center of religious life at Querétaro.

Rational reform engaged leading clerics and flourished at San Miguel. Propitiatory devotion remained strong across the Bajío. It focused the religious life of the populace; it claimed funds and devotion from some of the region's most prosperous men and women. Two religious visions competed for preeminence among the powerful; both aimed to engage the populace, and both sought hegemony. They worked very differently. Enlightened reformers honored the rational superiority of the few, the educated, and the powerful; they denigrated popular devotions and aimed to transform the populace through education. Popular communities resisted "rational" impositions and worked for cultural independence. Meanwhile propitiatory devotions held the center of popular worship, honored by many among the clergy and gaining attention among the powerful in times of crisis.

Commercial prosperity and scientific control of smallpox fueled the rational turn among elites. Deepening poverty, insecurity, and recurrent plagues and famines kept propitiatory worship strong among the populace. When the powerful at Querétaro and elsewhere honored propitiatory devotions they led a third tendency, mediating between the visions of the powerful and the devotions of the poor—keeping cultural polarization from becoming a conflictive chasm.

Querétaro Triumphant: An Enlightened Officer's Song to Our Lady at Pueblito

Early in 1801, just as Corregidor Domínguez detailed the social tensions rising amid wartime economic boom at Querétaro, there appeared in Mexico City a long poem entitled *Querétaro triunfante*, published with ecclesiastical and viceregal sanction. The author was don Francisco María Colombini y Camayori, Conde de Colombini, a captain in Spain's military. Of Italian origin, Colombini proudly listed ties to enlightened academies in Florence, Valterra, Modena, and Corregio, and membership in the Real Sociedad Económica de Amigos de la Patria in Guatemala. He insisted that his readers know he was a man of enlightenment, a man of reason, a man of the modern age.[62]

His epic sang praises to Our Lady at Pueblito. A long prose footnote deep in the text told why: stationed in Havana in 1793, Colombini began to suffer "a fierce asthma of the third level, in Greek called Orthopnaea, the strongest and hardest to cure." He saw leading physicians in Havana, Veracruz, Puebla, and Mexico City. He went to Querétaro in November 1797, hoping that the dry climate might help. Nearly a year later, in September 1798, he knew no relief; the asthma seemed worse. Then "a most devout lady" sent Colombini a replica of Nuestra Señora de Pueblito, challenging the officer to seek "her most powerful assistance, as no human effort had helped." Remembering youthful devotion to Our Lady of the Immaculate Conception, he called on the Virgin of Pueblito, "pledging to be her majesty's perpetual slave, promoting her worship and devotion everywhere." Not cured, Colom-

Church of Our Lady of Pueblito, east of Querétaro, eighteenth century.

bini went to her sanctuary, arriving "so weak, it was difficult to step down from the coach." Then, "having with total confidence and live faith adored the Divine Lady in her healthful aura, I became at that moment so well that I returned to the city without anxiety or fatigue, to the amazement of the friends who accompanied me." By November Colombini was well; he left Querétaro to rejoin his troops.

The asthma returned in Mexico City, worsened as Colombini marched toward the coast, and became grave as he neared Veracruz. He returned to Querétaro and the Sanctuary at Pueblito in March 1800, and regained his health in nine days of devotions. He then wrote his song, published early the next year.[63] Colombini provides rare testimony of how a man of enlightenment came to Pueblito. Taught as a boy to worship Our Lady, he was led to reason by education and Atlantic experience, and reason led him to every scientific cure. Science failed and he suffered until a woman sent a replica of Our Lady of Pueblito. Not cured, he went to the Virgin's sanctuary and promised to serve as her slave if she cured him. She did, and he left to join his troops. When the malady returned he retreated to Pueblito. The Virgin cured him again—and he kept his promise of service by writing an ode to her powers.

Image of Our Lady of Pueblito, modern window on eighteenth-century church at Pueblito.

   Querétaro triunfante was not about Colombini's cure. That was left to a footnote, the last of many examples of the Virgin's prowess. Colombini wrote to persuade the literate and the powerful of New Spain that devotion to the Virgin—at Pueblito and elsewhere—was appropriate and essential, even in the age of reason. He offered a prescription for social peace in a world of conflict and polarization. After the title page Colombini began with the 45th Psalm: "Gather, distant peoples, come to see the works of the Lord, and the prodigies he has done for us across the land: He has exiled war to the edges of the world." Amid wars that persisted as the French Revolution gave way to Napoleonic expansion, and while revolution raged in Haiti, the psalm had to read as a utopian dream. War had not been exiled to the edges of the earth in 1801—unless one saw the world from the interior of New Spain. At Querétaro as across the Bajío, peace held and production boomed. Colombini, an enlightened officer who knew the Mediterranean and the Atlantic world in an age of war, found peace at Querétaro. *Querétaro triunfante* aimed to explain that peace and to share it. Colombini began with a disclaimer: "when I speak here of the miracles, marvels, and prodigies of this Sacred Image, I understand them as proven by human faith subject to fallacy; I do not speak for the judgement of the Holy Church." He would report the Virgin's miracles without challenging the Church. He offered a narrative that his readers should engage with "piety and in in the light of nature." His First Song narrated the powers of Our Lady at Pueblito:

> I sing to María, august Mother of
> A great infinite God; our beloved Mother:
> Honor, Glory, and reverence of Pueblito,
> Your special chosen Patroness.
> Happy Querétaro, that in your district
> Come such great and celebrated gains!
> I sing to your beautiful and heavenly Lady,
> To your loving Mother and Protector.

He offered details:

> I sing to María, healing aura
> In times of plagues and ruling ills,
> In times of misfortune, a loving comfort
> For everyone near and far;
> In times of drought come clouds with rain,
> Delivering abundant harvests;
> A sure bright shining star
> On the road of this mortal life.[64]

Our Lady at Pueblito fought plagues and disasters, and brought rains and ample crops. She did good in the world. To men of reason Colombini insisted that her works "exceed the ability of the human mind."[65] To all he insisted that "the power of God, which is infinite, takes to the field in the fields of Pueblito." The martial metaphor emphasized her importance to the people of the countryside. Much of the rest of the First Song recounts her role in bringing Christianity to the Otomí in the seventeenth century, based on Vilaplana's history.[66] But Colombini soon returned to her worldly acts and comforts:

> There the unfortunate and the helpless,
> The sick and the persecuted,
> Find themselves fully relieved
> Of affliction, sadness, and lamentations.[67]

And her powers were not merely local:

> Many distant republicans
> Gain her grace and profit,

Thanks to the resounding fame
Of María's great prodigies.[68]

The result:

The people of Querétaro are so content
All at once are brothers.[69]

Our Lady at Pueblito works in the world to serve the people of Querétaro and beyond; shared devotion unites all in peace and happiness.

Late in the First Song, and through the Second, Colombini adds another dimension to the Virgin's importance. He repeats her acts in the world, her delivery of "health, comfort, peace, grace, and favors."[70] She is even an entrepreneur, noted for "her works, businesses and projects."[71] But he steadily, almost stealthily, links Our Lady at Pueblito to more sacramental, penitential, ultimately salvationist worship.

There the most persistent sinners . . .
Convert suddenly;
Because Mother María full of clemency
Reforms their consciences instantly.[72]

The priests at Atotonilco could not have asked more. From penance came salvation:

To achieve sure eternal life
Under the protection of this pure Virgin.[73]

Was it to persuade men of power and reason of the importance of Our Lady that Colombini linked her cult to the sacramental, penitential, moralizing religion they often preferred?

To end vice, to brake passions;
Virtue and reform are her trophies,
Devotion and faith are her emblems,
Reclaiming many souls captured by sin
Only when they go to Pueblito.[74]

Her power had the effect of "illuminating blind sinners."[75] The result: "She brings lively faith and contrite hearts."[76] Colombini tied propitiatory devotion to penitence.

Near the end of the Second Song he returned to the Virgin's work in the world. She created "Happy Querétaro!" She was "that beautiful favorable cloud, fertilizing your fields."[77] Colombini emphasized devotion by the Sisters of Santa Clara—praying mortgage bankers, heirs to the wealth of don Fernando de Tapia, Querétaro's Otomí founder. The convent most honored by powerful patriarchs, inhabited by their daughters, and devoted to funding their estates, knew the power of Our Lady at Pueblito.[78] Colombini linked propitiatory, penitential, and entrepreneurial Catholicism to Querétaro's chosen Virgin.

The Third Song seems least original, narrating cures reported earlier by Vilalpando. Colombini began with:

> The certain protection of María.[79]

He turned again to penance:

> All have seen infinite people
> Ask pardon with contrite reason.[80]

He then added a link to charitable action, a concern shared by penitential patriarchs and rational reformers:

> She helps unfortunate invalids
> And with liberal kindness
> She shares her treaures with the poor.[81]

Our Lady was sacramental, penitential, and charitable—while she healed the sick, repaired the lame, and brought healthy children in the most difficult deliveries. Among all her cures, all her interventions in epidemics, and all her elicitations of rain, Colombini focused on cures of elite and religious women.[82] The populace would not read the text. His goal was to convince the literate, the rational, and the powerful of the importance of Our Lady. A focus on cures of elite women might help powerful men to see the limit of their powers.

The Third Song ends with a new crisis and a new cure. In 1769 the Franciscan Andrés Picazo, aged, retired, and devoted to the Virgin, was attacked for no known reason by a clockmaker, Manuel Carrera. The assault, narrated in gory detail, was devastating: multiple guns shot bullets into the aging cleric; multiple stab wounds followed. Everyone expected the friar to die. But he called to the Virgin at Pueblito and lived; the constables captured the brutal offender. Our Lady at Pueblito now addressed the great fear of eighteenth-century reformers: urban crime. Even Archbishop Lorenzana in Mexico City, famed as a rational reformer, knew this was a miracle.[83] Colombini offered Our Lady at Pueblito as the solution to the maladies of the times. She would cure all that ailed New Spain.

The Fourth Song brought the power of Our Lady at Pueblito to bear on the challenges of the new nineteenth century:

> Not only in times now past,
> But with abundance in times present
> We see her prodigies and graces

Manifestly multiplied in service
To the afflicted, to unfortunates ill and in pain.[84]

He narrated the epilepsy of a young Querétaro nun and his own debilitating asthma.[85]

Thousands and thousands are the men still alive,
Thousands and thousands the women post-delivery,
Who sing of great and lofty favors.[86]

Then he began what seemed a reiteration—and became another shift of emphasis:

If pains and afflictions assault you,
If plagues and ills devastate you,
If your precious possessions are lost
To ferocious and fatal storms,
She will fill you with a thousand comforts.[87]

Our Lady at Pueblito was famed for powerful interventions: cures, rains, births. But if readers doubted her, they should know that the Virgin also consoled her people in desperate times.

In the worst of bad times,
In moments of total abandon and anxiety,
When the fields are destroyed and without fruits,
Then María sends abundance,
    Protecting her children, who assured,
Cannot doubt her love, her loyalty;
And when hunger attacks and consumes them,
That is when her mercy is most sure.[88]

To leave no doubt,

People must face famines and earthquakes,
Droughts, floods, pestilence,
And other threats, from which MARÍA
Draws vows; then all in Heaven
Come down to console us.[89]

Should her power not allay worldly calamities, Our Lady always consoled the desperate.

Then, as the Fourth Song drew toward a close, Colombini addressed a wider world:

Pure and powerful Mother MARÍA,
Your power is infinite,
Your are not only the beloved Protector

Of Michoacán, Querétaro, and Pueblito,
But of all the world that adores you
With a most contrite and Christian heart;
Your piety leads the whole world
To keep the law of Our Lord, the true God.[90]

Our Lady at Pueblito would lead the world against "malicious impiety."[91]

Cast away, oh beautiful Virgin, the clouds
Of the infernal bloody revolution,
That has ruined so many peoples,
And with its fury aims to subvert
The universe everywhere:
Atrocious fury, driven and promoted by disbelief
Which offends God and his sacred laws,
Bringing down his vassals and his kings.

The problem was revolution—provoked and promoted when "The evil unbelievers of our times" attacked religion.[92] Human pride, misled by reason, warred against God and legitimate sovereigns. Our Lady upheld the faith; she would defeat the unbelievers who brought the plague of revolution. Colombini—raised to honor the Virgin, educated in the light of reason, then drawn back to the Virgin by a disease that only she could cure—saw social destruction in the reason vaunted by the enlightened age:

The refusal to honor God, the true God,
Is the greatest plague on the entire world.[93]

A turn from God brought the plagues of revolution and war to the Atlantic world. Colombini then focused his message on the empire he fought to defend:

To the Royal Monarch of the two Spains,
Who fortunately and justly governs us,
In your works, enterprises, and campaigns
You bring us glory and internal peace,
The fruits of piety and Christian faith,
Emblems of your sovereign house.[94]

Our Lady defended the Monarch of the Spains—Old and New—the core of Spain's vast empire. A just sovereign guided by faith and piety would defend Our Lady:

Because, purest MARÍA
Defends your vast domains.[95]

Colombini insisted that devotion to Our Lady, the sustenance of the Monarchy, began in regional homelands. Querétaro came first:

> Pledge your commitment, Oh Queretanos,
> Begging MARÍA your patroness
> To bring success to our Monarch.[96]

As long as the people of Querétaro honored their Virgin, they would sustain the Empire:

> From Pueblito, beloved mother,
> Carry your holy blessing to the Court.
> Your power, that is infinite,
> Defends Spain, Spain under assault.[97]

To defend the "entire Empire,"[98] the devotion to Mary so strong at Querétaro had to extend across New Spain. Colombini concluded with a tour in praise of other devotions to the Virgin. He honored Guadalupe, whose "miracles and prodigies are so famous," the Virgin of Los Angeles, whose "miraculous image" brings "countless blessings," and Nuestra Señora de los Remedios: "The Mexicanos [people of Mexico City and nearby] devoted to her live free of plagues, hunger, and earthquakes."[99] In provinces beyond the capital, Colombini recognized devotions to the Virgin at Ocotlán near Tlaxcala, and at Xuquila in Oaxaca.[100]

All this, Colombini emphasized, he learned at Pueblito:

> Mother of mine, finally at Pueblito
> You have filled my soul;
> Because here I found an infinte power,
> A fountain of grace and calm.[101]

In a world of war and revolution, Our Lady at Pueblito brought faith and peace to *Querétaro triunfante*. She shared her gift with Colombini; he pledged to share her power. Our Lady offered peace to a world in conflict. The Conde wrote a political and religious tract detailing the essential role of the Virgin among Queretanos, powerful and poor: she mediated deepening polarizations, kept the peace, and sustained the vibrant production that upheld the Spanish empire. All the sovereign's peoples should worship the Virgin; all should enjoy her peace.

Guadalupe's Priest and the Religious Politics of Social Control

Our Lady at Pueblito was not the only virgin honored at Querétaro. Her primacy was unquestioned but not uncontested. In 1803 don José María Zeláa published *Las Glorias de Querétaro*, perhaps in response to Colombini's *Querétaro triunfante*. A priest in Querétaro's Congregation of Guadalupe, Zeláa took the title (and included the text) of don Carlos de Siguenza y Góngora's tribute of 1680, written to dedicate Querétaro's Temple of Guadalupe. The new offering gloried in Guadalupe's cures during the matlazahuatl (typhus) plague of the late 1730s and her subsequent nomination as New Spain's patroness.[102] Yet that was his last reference to Guadalupe's saving interventions in the world. At Querétaro, Guadalupe was a figure of power, promoting penance and providing charity.

Focusing on the centenary of Guadalupe's Querétaro temple in 1780, Zeláa detailed how the city council, the religious communities, and "all the noble citizens of the city" led a procession featuring "many persons of authority."[103] Zeláa honored Guadalupe's recent benefactors: don Manuel de Escandón y Llera, second Conde de la Sierra Gorda, and don José Ygnacio Villaseñor y Cervantes, the landlord and magistrate. Both held valuable entails and, lacking heirs, left rich properties to the congregation; Guadalupe's priests joined the Sisters of Santa Clara as leading mortgage bankers. Zeláa detailed the image of Guadalupe in her temple. Her "main figure" was "entirely of silver, nicely worked," surrounded by a "striking frame, also silver." A new image in a side chapel was kept by a sodality devoted to "Our Lady of Guadalupe of the Poor." Zeláa detailed how "this holy image is surrounded by beautiful rays of gold," gilding that cost 1,700 pesos. Zeláa did not suggest that Querétaro's poor were devoted to such rich images.[104]

A popular image remained in Guadalupe's temple. In another side chapel was "a carved statue, humble and patient, called the Lord of the Little Huerta; its fame comes from its long veneration in a small chapel built on a little huerta and kept by *indios*." In his *Relación peregrina* (1739) the Jesuit Navarrete noted its importance. The image had been moved to Guadalupe's temple "to end the disorders at the old chapel caused by the great numbers that assembled there; the image has long seen much worship and devotion due to the great prodigies experienced by those devoted to it." Popular devotion in Guadalupe's temple focused on a captured image of Christ, taken from Otomí control to limit popular excess.[105]

Querétaro's annual festival of Guadalupe began on 12 December, offering eight days of "magnificent events, with sermons." The goal

Temple of Our
Lady of Guada-
lupe, Querétaro,
seventeenth
to eighteenth
centuries.

was to preach. The temple's estates and loan revenues funded the titu-
lar feast and the second day. Guadalupe's brotherhood of the poor
funded the third, Capitán don Pedro Antonio de Acevedo the fourth,
"some priests of the Congregation" the fifth, "workers at the Royal
Tobacco Factory" the sixth, "leading men of the city" the seventh, and
"the *indios* of city neighborhoods and nearby towns" the eighth and
last.[106] All told the powerful paid for six days of Guadalupe's festival
at Querétaro; tobacco workers and indigenous republics paid for two.

Zeláa exulted in days of festival that were days of preaching. Every
year Guadalupe's priests said 4,000 Masses, 1,500 paid with their own
funds and 2,500 paid by those who had the means. At Querétaro Guadalupe offered sacraments, sermons, and—Zeláa insisted—service: "This
venerable Congregation has always worked and still works in service
of the public, for the good of souls, in assistance to the poor, as is most
evident in the works of virtue and charity it pursues." Guadalupe promoted sacraments, sermons, service, and charity.[107] The nature of the
service reported by Zeláa is revealing. Three of Guadalupe's priests
spent every day in the temple hearing confessions for the "welfare
and consolation of the faithful." The padre Sacristán was ready to give

communion "to all who ask." Guadalupe's priests labored "continually and with great zeal and precision to preach and hear confessions" at her temple, at the convents of Santa Rosa and the Carmelite sisters, "and in the Jail and the obrajes."[108] The goal was to preach and confess, to reform and seek penance—focusing on women in convents and men in confinement. For 125 years, Zeláa reported with pride, Guadalupe's priests said Mass every Sunday and Holy Day at Querétaro's jail, for no pay. Congregation funds fed prisoners every day. On three religious holidays Guadalupe's priests delivered the meals personally.[109] Sermons, penance, and food for the confined characterized the congregation's charitable services.

There was more. On Guadalupe's feast of 12 December the congregation awarded a dowry of three hundred pesos so one orphan girl could join a convent. The priests gave twelve pesos each to twelve "poor women" on the same day. On Holy Thursday another twelve women got such gifts. And on Saint Joseph's day twelve men shared two hundred pesos, just over sixteen pesos each. Linking preaching to charitable distributions, Zeláa noted that every Wednesday small sums were given to "the several beggars" who attended the morning "doctrinal lessons."[110] Zeláa concluded with the congregation's charity to the clergy: "When a poor cleric becomes ill, the Priest-Treasurer provides 4 reales daily for food, physician's care, medicines, and clothing and any other need—even paying for a decent burial in the Church."[111] It might cost two hundred pesos yearly to provide food and care to an aging cleric—far more than the twelve pesos granted to a few penitential poor women, or the sixteen pesos given to fewer poor men.

The contrasts between Our Lady at Pueblito as described by Colombini and Our Lady of Guadalupe at Querétaro as described by Zeláa are clear. The Virgin at Pueblito began as an Otomí devotion; she offered help with the trials of daily life; by the eighteenth century she was as important to Querétaro's powerful as to her poor. Sustained by voluntary alms, she integrated local society. Colombini saw this shared devotion as the base of Querétaro's social harmony—a key to the survival of the kingdom. He argued that the truly enlightened among the devout must join in sustaining that worship, consolidating a religious culture linking the powerful few and the struggling poor.

Devotion to Guadalupe emerged after the conquest among Nahuas near Mexico City. In the 1640s elites and clergy in the viceregal capital claimed her devotion. She journeyed to Querétaro in the 1680s at the behest of provincial Spanish notables. Her congregation lived by investments and commercial estates. Her priests focused on sacraments, penance, preaching, and feeding prisoners. Her charities were small gifts exchanged for attending sermons, along with sustenance for prisoners and aging priests. Zeláa never hints at popular devotion to Guadalupe at Querétaro. Rather, her priests aimed to reform the poor.

The Virgin at Pueblito, Colombini knew, offered aid and comfort to all, rich and poor, Spanish and Otomí. She served and stabilized—to Colombini she pacified—life in a polarizing society. In contrast, Guadalupe as portrayed by Zeláa lived locked in her splendid temple, sustained by the rich, pleading for morality through penance. Our Lady of Pueblito was popular and thus powerful. Guadalupe at Querétaro asserted power; there is no sign that she was popular.

The Corregidor, the Consolidation, and the Threat to Convent Capitalism

Amid economic boom and social polarization, most threats to life and the social order came from disease and drought, as Colombini emphasized. Popular responses focused on the powers of the Virgin at Pueblito. In 1805, however, Querétaro faced a new challenge, a financial threat from the Spanish regime. New Spain had long generated unparalleled revenues for the monarchy. Extractions—taxes, donations, and forced loans—had risen dramatically during the wars that began with the French revolution in the 1790s and continued after 1800 in the Napoleonic era. The Bajío economy paid those exactions without major strain. Mining, textile, and agricultural entrepreneurs still prospered; the majority faced new insecurities and deepening poverty, yet continued to work and survive.

Late in 1804 the regime announced the consolidation of royal bonds. The bonds had been first issued in the 1780s to fund Spain's support for the war for independence in British North America. Long wars through the 1790s and into the 1800s left the monarchy desperate, forced to issue new bonds and unable to pay bondholders. The consolidation ordered church corporations to sell all properties not part of their original foundation and to call in most loans. The proceeds would fill the treasury, which promised 5 percent interest on collected funds. To Madrid it was a solution in desperate times. The treasury would get an infusion of funds; church institutions would survive, dependent on the regime.[112]

The church would now face what the regime earlier had imposed on indigenous community treasuries through the Bank of San Carlos. All knew about the communities' loss of funds, the delayed and missed interest payments. In the summer of 1805 Corregidor Domínguez saw the destruction of the Bajío. He wrote to his superiors arguing the importance of convent capitalism to life at Querétaro. He argued that the first role of the regime was to protect institutions linking the powerful and the poor in the economy that sustained the empire. Soon after Colombini praised mediation by Our Lady at Pueblito, the Corregidor pleaded with the regime to mediate economic life by saving convent capitalism.[113]

Domínguez recognized the "great obligations and clear urgencies" that required "extraordinary actions" to save "the honor of the nation." He did not dispute that the consolidation promised church corporations "sure interest on their capital."[114] But the program was "impracticable in substance." It would bring "the ruin of agriculture, mining, commerce, and industry."[115] The Bajío economy sustained Spain's Atlantic system. Ruining that economy would destroy not only the Bajío but Spanish power.

There was not enough money in circulation to redeem ecclesiastical mortgages. Most loans paid 5 percent interest to convents; most estates produced profits in the same range. If half the value of an estate was mortgaged, it would take ten years to redeem the loan, leaving the operator without income or working capital. Quick redemption was impossible; any attempt would undermine commercial agriculture. If church corporations sold estates at the same time, they would flood the market when few could buy. Prices would plummet, the regime would gain little, and a few among the very rich would buy vast properties cheaply. That, Domínguez noted, was what happened when the regime seized the Jesuit estates in the 1760s. The Conde de Regla got vast holdings at bargain prices; thirty-eight years later many estates remained unsold.[116] The consolidation could not succeed.

It could, however, destroy the Bajío economy. Domínguez instructed his superiors: most estates were mortgaged and most mortages passed on through inheritance, sale, and auction. The capital sustained production; the income supported convents, schools, and hospitals. "The money in pious endowments . . . should be called the common fund, the universal resort, the quick support, and the spirit that moves agriculture, mining, commerce, and industry, . . . It is hard to find a business . . . that is not energized . . . by this permanent flow. To lenders it yields modest interest; among borrowers it stimulates profitable activity—for the state and the public, it yields incalculable benefits."[117] In prose reminiscent of Colombini's song to the Virgin, Domínguez praised convent bankers.

In times of drought, frost, or other crisis, mortgages gave estate operators funds to maintain operations, pay their workers, and plant new crops. In the aftermath mortgages provided capital "to find a new source of water or build a dam to control it, and other works" to ex-

pand and assure production. Such investment served "particular interest and the common good equally."[118] While convent capital funded
mining, trade, and clothmaking, Domínguez focused on commercial
cultivation. In his key metaphor church mortgages were a "full and
flowing river that irrigates and fertilizes an immense land."[119]

In rhetoric reminiscent of legitimations offered by don José Sánchez
Espinosa and other agrarian capitalists, Domínguez saw convent mortgages as works of charity: "In terrible deadly famines and devouring
epidemics, city councils and charitable organizations . . . have . . . no
capital other than the pious funds to fill public granaries, to aid the
indigent, and to provide hospitals to feed and cure the sick." To the
Corregidor convent banks did the service that Colombini attributed to
Our Lady at Pueblito: they sustained the people so that "today there
are many working hands and many taxpayers who animate the kingdom; their efforts and those of their families and businesses increase
the revenues of the king."[120] Church bankers—not penitential or propitiatory devotions—sustained life through the great dearth of 1785 and
1786, a service remembered by all who survived those painful years.[121]

Domínguez knew that the great landed entrepreneurs of the Bajío,
including Sánchez Espinosa, the Conde de Regla, and others, relied
minimally on church mortgages. However powerful, they were not,
the corregidor argued, the real producers at Querétaro and across the
Bajío: "In truth, it is not the great growers, owners of vast estates, who
sustain agriculture and feed the people; it is not the great miners who
extract the greatest part of silver and gold; it is not the powerful merchants who most stimulate commerce, nor view the public with equity,
. . . These are instead men who put obstacles and difficulties in the way
of all kinds of businesses and careers."[122] Domínguez was wrong about
the great miners at Guanajuato; the Rayas and Valenciana mines ruled
production there. In commerce there was a hierarchy of traders, great,
middling, and small, with the powerful often causing the middling
and small to face "obstacles and difficulties." And in agriculture the
pattern is clear. Middling and small growers, owners and tenants, fed
the people when crops were good and prices low. Great growers like
Sánchez Espinosa profited by storing harvests and feeding the hungry
in times of scarcity and peak prices. Arguing against the consolidation,
Domínguez recognized the predatory ways of the most powerful entrepreneurs and defended the many provincial landlords who relied on
convent mortgages.

He added: "It is the middling and poor farmers, miners, and traders
who by their labor, industry, and economy maintain the current course
of these professions, keeping a balance and equilibrium beneficial to
all."[123] Domínguez implied that the church funded the middling and

the poor, sustaining their key role in the economy (against rich and powerful predators). He constructed a partial truth. Convents funded Querétaro's leading estate operators and merchants, middling entrepreneurs only in the context of men like Sánchez Espinosa, Regla, and the Valenciana partners. In Querétaro they were powerful if provincial entrepreneurs. There is no evidence of church mortgages funding the truly poor.

In a rhetorical turn that paralleled Thomas Jefferson's equating of great slave-owning planters with struggling family farmers, unequal men he fused as independent cultivators, Domínguez linked Querétero entrepreneurs, great and small. "If they are deprived of principal, or better said, of the only assistance they have to begin, continue, and prosper . . . inevitably they will come to ruin, at great cost to business, the king, and the public."[124] Amid such calamity, "Many estates will be sold to the rich, who alone can buy them; such an accumulation of properties in few hands contradicts every rule and precept of rational and Christian policy." The result will be "frightening monopolies" and "cruel oppression, . . . miserable slavery." Again Jeffersonian in linking Crown policy to an enslavement of colonial peoples, Domínguez saw only threats to an "unhappy people, who already suffer so much it is hard to explain."[125] He recognized the deepening polarization driven by the continuing dynamism of the Bajío economy. He knew that revenues generated there were essential to Crown coffers. He argued that the consolidation would collect little, yet undermine the economy. It would concentrate capital among the few, undermine the efforts of middling entrepreneurs (including Querétaro elites), and drive the working populace deeper into desperation.

Domínguez sought rational, Christian, and patriarchal policies from the regime. He reminded the monarchy that it prospered by mediating: "The king, by the greatest gift of God, is not only master and mediator of his kingdoms; he is also the father, the loving father, of his subjects, the tutor of his peoples, the guardian of his royal revenues."[126] He attributed to the king what Colombini attributed to Our Lady. Both saw threats to the Bajío economy. Colombini lobbied the literate to reject excessive reason and return to the Virgin, the ultimate recourse of the desperate, the best support of the social order. Domínguez lobbied the regime to end a program that would decapitalize the economy, and to remember its Christian tradition of paternal mediation among subjects powerful and poor.

Across New Spain many joined in protest against the consolidation. Implementation was negotiated and limited. In a famous case the pastor at Dolores, don Miguel Hidalgo y Costilla, saw his one modest estate embargoed. Many have seen that loss at the root of his leadership of the insurgency of 1810. Equally notable, don José Sánchez Espinosa, profiting from valuable estates entailed as an Obra Pía, never mentioned the consolidation in his vast correspondence. To him it was no threat at all. His properties at La Griega east of Querétaro, at Puerto de Nieto on the road to San Miguel, and at Bocas on the vast plateau of San Luis Potosí were all part of the "original foundation" and thus exempt. Others among the powerful negotiated payments stretched over years. When the consolidation ended in 1808 they escaped with limited losses. Many more who held smaller loans—convents, merchants, and estate cultivators alike—faced losses that struck at their limited prosperity.[127]

The consolidation's threat and the fears that it raised among those dependent on convent funds are clear from Domínguez's protest. Its real effects demand careful evaluation. Across New Spain the consolidation took 10,500,000 pesos, two-thirds of collections across the empire. In New Spain 5,000,000 pesos came from the archbishopric of Mexico, including Querétaro, 1,100,000 pesos from the bishopric of Valladolid, including Guanajuato. Such amounts suggest vast extractions of capital and a real assault on religious institutions. The consolidation seems an assault on the commercial economy and a leading cause of discontent leading to the wars for independence that began in 1810.[128]

Over 950,000 pesos were taken from fourteen individual debtors, most based in Mexico City. A few were rich merchants trading with ecclesiastical capital. They paid over 100,000 pesos each with relative ease. A few were entrepreneurial landlords, mixing trade and estate operation, like don Gabriel Yermo, or mining and agricultural operations, like the second Conde de Regla. They too paid sums that seem large, about 86,000 pesos each, but were modest in the context of their vast holdings. The Conde de Regla held entailed commercial properties earlier evaluated at over 2,000,000 pesos. More prejudiced was the Marqués de San Miguel de Aguayo. Holder of vast estates in the far North, he had been burdened with debts by entrepreneurial managers who served themselves more than the Marqués during the eighteenth century. In the early 1800s he remained a rich and powerful man—and lived at the edge of bankruptcy. The 43,200 pesos that he paid the consolidation, negotiated down from a much larger debt, hastened his family's slide to ruin. The consolidation did not cause the longer, larger, and more complex process of that collapse.[129]

Larger sums came from the convents, mostly of nuns, that served as New Spain's investment bankers. They paid nearly 2,000,000 pesos in the viceroyalty, over 1,000,000 in the archbishopric of Mexico. The

Encarnación Convent in Mexico City paid over 250,000 pesos, nearly 175,000 in redeemed loans, over 75,000 as proceeds of an estate sold in 1809. The Santa Clara Convent in the capital paid over 110,000 pesos. The 191,195 pesos paid by Querétaro's Convent of Santa Clara was the second-largest redemption in New Spain.[130] That was a loss to Querétaro's economy. Perhaps Domínguez wrote to defend Santa Clara, heir to the legacy of Querétaro's Otomí founders, the city's leading mortgage bank in the eighteenth century. Other institutions paid far less: at Querétaro other convents and ecclesiastical institutions paid a total of only 84,452 pesos, including 9,775 pesos by the Congregation of Guadalupe and 2,267 by Our Lady at Pueblito. Across the Guanajuato intendancy, convents and other institutions paid 61,176 pesos, including 16,170 pesos from Celaya's Carmelites and only 4,500 pesos in total at San Miguel.[131]

Was the consolidation a mortal blow to the Bajío economy? It weakened Santa Clara, taking important loan capital out of circulation and limiting the nuns' religious activities. The promised interest of 5 percent was soon cut in half; payments ended amid the wars for independence in 1812. Beyond Santa Clara the impact in the Bajío seems limited. Regional commerce peaked between 1801 and 1805 then declined by 7 percent in 1806–9.[132] The fall coincides with the consolidation. But the decline was over 9 percent at Guanajuato, where the consolidation had little impact, and 15 percent at San Miguel, where it was negligible. Perhaps the extractions from Santa Clara help to explain the 8 percent fall at Querétaro. The larger downturn across the Bajío is better explained by escalating costs of mining, as shafts drove deeper while war disrupted Atlantic trade. The consolidation was one part of the exactions in times of war, a part that primarily affected Querétaro in the Bajío.[133]

The consolidation cannot explain the turn toward independence after 1808. In 1810 Querétaro, hardest hit, proved most loyal. San Miguel and Guanajuato, little affected, became insurgent hotbeds. The consolidation challenged commercial capitalism and institutional Catholicism at Querétaro after 1805; it destroyed neither. It did not send the powerful on a rush to independence. It did show that the Spanish regime, facing endless war, could assault key bases of the regional economy that sustained its empire. Neither Our Lady at Pueblito nor Guadalupe in her Querétaro temple could fix that. Surely Domínguez knew Colombini's *Querétaro triunfante* and Zeláa's *Glorias de Querétaro* when he wrote in 1805. He knew that Our Lady at Pueblito could only serve and console and that Guadalupe's priests would only pray, preach, and feed prisoners—if the regime mediated between Spain and New Spain, between convent bankers and Bajío land-lords, between entrepreneurs and families locked in poverty and inse-curity. The consolidation was a threatening lesson.

A Widow's Vision and Legacy:
Sacramental Worship and Social Reform

After 1805 international conflicts persisted, disrupting trade while revenue demands rose. Querétaro and the Bajío faced uncertainties that brought declining commercial activities. Yet production held near historic peaks. The powerful took profits; the majority faced pressures toward poverty worsened by insecurity. The summer of 1808 brought news of Napoleon's capture of the Spanish monarchy, setting off trans-atlantic debates about sovereignty. Claims of popular rights prolifer-ated across the empire, even as assertions of religiously sanctioned monarchy held strong. The years from 1808 to 1810 brought unprece-dented debates about sovereignty and legitimacy, debates that esca-lated from Mexico City to the Bajío while drought and scarcity raised the specter of the catastrophe of 1785 and 1786.[134]

Amid political debates, mounting scarcity, and social uncertainty, the Bajío and New Spain remained at peace and at work into the sum-mer of 1810. As tensions mounted, doña María Josefa Vergara Her-nández wrote a will detailing a vision of social reform. A widow with no children and a rich estate, she allocated her wealth to promote a world commited to sacramental worship, and to charity, education, and social control. Taking a role usually reserved to men, doña María Josefa offers a rich, devout, and enlightened woman's vision of what life and belief should become as the first decade of the nineteenth cen-tury ended.[135]

The origins of her estate are not clear. When she married don José Luis Frías neither brought property to the union. With eighty pesos between them, she insisted that they built their wealth by their own efforts. Still, they were born among the comfortable at Querétaro. One Frías owned the Labor de los Olveras in 1791.[136] Don José Luis had leased an estate before he owned property. Frías and Vergara women joined Querétaro convents, lives that required dowries. Doña María Josefa and don José Luis came from the edge of Querétaro's elite, not poor, not born to landed power. When Frías died in 1798 he left a widow, no children, a fine residence on Querétaro's Calle de Perdón, two adjacent houses, and the valuable hacienda named Nuestra Señora de la Esperanza. The property lay in the Tolimán jurisdiction, east of La Griega.[137] How Frías acquired the estate is unclear. He did not borrow from convent bankers. His only lien was ten thousand pesos owed the Capuchin Mothers of Salvatierra, a bequest he created. Frías may have been a merchant clothier who bought estate property; or he may have found undeveloped land, invested in irrigation, and expanded cultivation during times of high grain prices following the famine of 1785–86. In 1807 Esperanza included the largest population of Otomí in Querétaro's outlying districts, 241 married householders and 57 men yet to marry.[138] Total estate population, including Spaniards, mestizos, and mulattoes, likely approached 1,500—the largest community of producers in the eastern Bajío.

Doña María Josefa began her will at the estate on 8 December 1808; perhaps she was ill. She began with bequests to religious women. The Capuchin Mothers of Salvatierra saw a lien of 10,000 pesos grow to 28,000—a yearly income of 1,400 pesos. Querétaro's Capuchin Mothers got 10,000 pesos to endow two chaplains. Another 1,000 pesos helped a convent of Teresas at Querétaro. Women of prayer and service were the widow's first concern. She gave less to those who served her household: Manuela and her daughter Ignacia, both slaves, got freedom and 200 pesos each; Eusebia and María Josefa, Otomí orphans, got 200 pesos yearly; the orphan doña María Aguilar, of higher status, got 8 pesos weekly, plus 400 pesos a year, for life. Service mattered; status mattered more; kinship mattered most: her husband's three sisters got 1,000 pesos each. Sister María Josefa de San Francisco Frías of the convent of Santa Clara got 6 pesos weekly for religious needs and charitable works. Friar Miguel Frías got 200 pesos yearly. The notary don Juan Fernando Domínguez, who "has served me in so many affairs," got a stipend of 2,000 pesos.

Doña María Josefa then allocated symbols of distinction. She owned four coaches—among the seventy-six that Father Zeláa had counted among Querétaro's glories. One went to the parish of Espíritu Santo to deliver communion to the homebound; the rest would be sold. Apparently none among her beneficiaries deserved to ride Querétaro's streets in style. Household silver and other furnishings went in equal shares to doña María Aguilar (the orphan already given 800 pesos yearly), the "foundling orphan" don José María Frías, don Agustín Piña, and don Ponciano Tinajero. The three men got added bequests, and emphatic directions: Piña got 1,000 pesos for a house, plus 12,000 pesos on condition that he leave Esperanza and "work for himself." Tinajero had to choose between 10,000 pesos cash and service as a lesser manager at the estate. Don José María Frías got a house in Querétaro and 12,000 pesos, without conditions. Perhaps he was a son of her late husband, called an orphan to be polite. All three men had lived in her service; now doña María Josefa provided silver, stipends, and instructions to make their own way. By challenging men to live as independent patriarchs while funding women in convents, the rich widow promoted patriarchy.

Her nephew, don Domíngo Hernández, would serve for life as "general manager" at Esperanza, earning 1,700 pesos yearly plus sustenance from estate produce. He could work the Rancho de Cenizos rent-free. (The manager at La Griega received a 300-peso annual salary, rations, and paid rent for a rancho.) Hernández gained no property but earned a proprietary role in management, an ample salary, and use of valuable land. The executors must keep Esperanza an integrated enterprise. "Never under any pretext" would it be divided. If sale was inevitable all proceeds must go to doña María Josefa's foundations.

She instructed Hernández to build a school for boys and one for girls at Esperanza, and to pay the teachers on estate account. Hernández must also pay three hundred pesos yearly to a priest to say Mass on festival days and twenty-five pesos twice a year to hear residents' confessions. The widow provided for the education and sacramental welfare of estate residents. She also directed three hundred pesos to her landed brother-in-law to buy cloth and other goods to distribute among the workers and families who remained at the Gamboa estate after her late husband ended his lease there. Had her husband provided less than fair remunerations? If so she assuaged her conscience with a small bequest.[139] The first installment of the testament ended there. Doña María Josefa gave bequests to women of prayer and service as she thought their status deserved. She gave funds to men who were her dependents—with instructions to begin to live as men, that is, as independent patriarchs. She gave control at Esperanza to her nephew, instructing him to attend to the education and sacramental lives of workers and their families. She compensated old injustices at Gamboa.

On 22 December, still at Esperanza as Christmas neared, doña María Josefa wrote a second installment.[140] She offered a profession of faith: devotion to God as Trinity, to the sacraments, to her Holy Mother the church, and to her "intermediary and advocate Most Holy María." She asked forgiveness for sins, commended her soul to God, and requested burial in Franciscan habit at the Missionary College of Santa Cruz. She wrote a clear statement of sacramental worship. The Virgin was her advocate; power belonged to God—infinite and distant. She made no mention of Our Lady at Pueblito.[141]

She turned next to charity and education. Her executors would pay two pesos each to the poor who mourned at her funeral. The manager at Esperanza would pay half the tribute owed there, reducing annual burdens on three hundred Otomí men. Produce from Esperanza would feed students at schools run by Teaching Carmelites and the Convent of San José de Gracia in Querétaro. To the primary school at the Franciscan Convent on the plaza, she gave five hundred pesos yearly to raise the pay of two teachers, hire a third, and buy paper for poor students. In addition her estate would found primary schools for girls at Querétaro's four parishes, paying the teachers. The girls enrolled would learn "Christian doctrine, and to read, write, sew, embroider, and other skills appropriate to their sex."[142]

Then doña María Josefa detailed her major bequests. She named the Corregidor don Miguel Domínguez, Alférez Real don Pedro de Septién, and the Querétaro council as executors. She ordered the foundation of a Casa de Hospicio, a poorhouse, following precedents in Madrid, Mexico City, and Guanajuato.[143] She saw an asylum "which would shelter all the poor of both sexes who are truly unable to work for their own upkeep, and thus beg and harass in churches, homes, and streets." Begging would end. "With this foundation aiding the truly disabled, we will also remove every lazy person able to work, but faking needs and taking from the truly poor and disabled what is justly their due." By separating the disabled from the lazy, "people now prejudicial to the republic and the state will become useful and beneficial with working hands."[144] The poorhouse would aid the disabled and take them from sight; the able must labor. With charity came social control.

Doña María Josefa also addressed the problems of women in patriarchal society. The disabled deserving poor, men and women, could live in the poorhouse. Able men must work and fend for themselves. But women needed a place to work (beyond the tobacco factory, which employed thousands, providing day care and mutual aid). She ordered the council to create a Casa de Recogido, where women could live and work in safety.[145] Having attended to the deserving, disabled poor and struggling women, doña María Josefa aimed to do more. Not sure that her wealth could sustain her vision, she ordered several additional foundations, always stating: if funds sufficed. Amid scarcity she would fund a *pósito*, a public granary to limit profiteering from dearth. To fight crime the council should provide urban lighting to ensure "public security," the essence of "good government." Fifteen guards would keep the lights and "contain disorder." Querétaro finally would have lights and a patrol, like Guanajuato.[146]

Doña María Josefa also hoped to help artisans and shopkeepers struggling in time of crisis. She pledged 100,000 pesos to a Monte Pío (modeled on the institution founded in Mexico City by the Conde de Regla, whose wealth originated in Querétaro). For those "who face bankruptcy," or who needed to "cover pending debts . . . to maintain their credit and good reputation," the Monte Pío would take goods on pawn and give short-term loans. To prevent abuse the widow demanded surveillance: the pious lender "will confirm the circumstances and conduct of those who seek credit."[147]

Then doña María Josefa remembered the problem of epidemic disease—when the people of Querétaro, powerful and poor, usually turned to Our Lady of Pueblito. She offered another remedy: "In any year that this city is struck and afflicted by plague, all other works will cease and the profits and produce of the hacienda will go to temporary hospitals for men and women; they will provide everything needed spiritually and materially, with no concern for costs, to cure and assist the unfortunates who suffer."[148] Charity hospitals would care for Queretaranos in time of plague. Plagues left orphans, so doña María Josefa ordered a "nursery for orphan children," raising it to third in her priorities (after the poorhouse and the women's shelter). The orphanage would end placements "in private homes, ending the well known improprieties and other evils this brings to families."[149] The widow knew how weavers and other artisans took in orphans and worked them hard for little more than food and rags, and how others exploited them as servants. Her orphanage aimed to do better.

Her final thought: if the city of Querétaro faced a water shortage, her foundation would fund a remedy.[150] Perhaps doña María Josefa imagined that her bequest, and her instructions to city fathers, would leave her remembered like the Marqués del Villar del Aguíla, honored for the great aqueduct that brought water to the center. Vergara told the council to act wisely by majority vote, and to keep careful account of her wealth and the charities she ordered.[151] The Esperanza estate could not fund all her plans. Before insurgency changed everything in September 1810, the council used her resources to open a poorhouse and feed urban consumers facing worsening scarcity. The immediate crisis postponed her larger goals.

Doña María Josefa returned to Querétaro and lived another seven months, to 22 July 1809. In the interim she made changes.[152] It is possible that Esperanza's profits in times of famine were generating unprecedented earnings. On 29 December doña María Josefa allocated another 72,000 pesos for a convent of Agustinian nuns. She insisted again that Esperanza remain one enterprise—perhaps stopping a council proposal to rent parts of the property. In April she returned to personal issues. The three young men who served her, all orphans, had complained. She answered with sharp reductions: don Agustín Piña would get but 1,000 pesos; don Ponciano Tinajero only 3,000 pesos, and he lost the chance to serve at Esperanza; don José María Frías, still favored, got but 4,000 pesos. All must leave Esperanza and live on their reduced inheritances. Challenging the widow brought costs.[153]

On 20 July doña María Josefa looked again to Esperanza. She ordered: "all who serve in my home and at Esperanza . . . are free of all debts to me at the end of their service; all are pardoned as of today." She relieved workers of obligations created by wage and cloth advances; her charity recognized that workers' debts were rarely collected—she cleared the books of obligations impossible to collect. And charity came with instruction; teachers would distribute printed cards to promote sacramental worship.[154]

Doña María Josefa even instructed Sisters of Santa Clara. They would receive two shipments of devotional tracts, one a life of San Francisco de Sales (patron of the penitential oratorios), the other a meditation on the Santísimo Sacramento. Both would be sold to fund religious activities, perhaps compensating a bit the sisters' losses to the consolidation. Yet the bequest also seems a subtle instruction to the sisters to turn from their famous devotion to Our Lady at Pueblito to more penitential and sacramental worship.

To the end doña María Josefa gave shelter and sustenance to women in distress. The last so favored, the poor María Saturnina Salas, "sheltered in my home," gained two hundred pesos yearly for life.[155] Two days later doña María Josefa Vergara Hernández died. She left a legacy that challenged the Querétaro council to take on new social reforms combining education, charity, and social control. She stressed sacramental and charitable devotion. She focused less on penitence than San Miguel's patriarchs did; she was more committed to charity than Zeláa and his colleagues at Guadalupe's temple. She ignored Our Lady at Pueblito. Sacramental worship, education, hard work for the able, and charity for the disabled were the way to success in a commercial patriarchal society. She instructed Corregidor Domínguez to live up to his commitments to a patriarchal society in which the few would profit, the majority would work with dignity, and the disabled would find Christian charity.

Cultural Polarization and Contending Mediations

While globally linked capitalism accelerated social polarization across the Bajío, a cultural divide deepened after 1770. Many among the powerful and their clerical allies promoted a sacramental religion linked to a new interest in reasoned inquiry; they promoted analysis and action as keys to life in the world. Adherents of sacramental and rational religion saw popular devotions of supplication and service as superstition. Meanwhile proponents of rational worship pressed reform by preaching, promoting education, and promising charities, all to transform or suppress popular worship. Popular communities struggled to keep the independence to control local worship and propitiatory devotions.

A focus on polarizing visions and conflicts over cultural control highlights a widening gap, suggesting a trajectory toward social breakdown. But while polarization deepened after 1770, peace held thanks to patriarchal, judicial, and cultural mediations. Promoters of religious change through preaching and schooling aimed to limit cultural conflict by drawing communities to sacramental worship. Many villages welcomed teachers of Spanish and literacy, then negotiated to control the schools. Reforms that provoked polarization also allowed mediation, tying the powerful and the poor in ongoing negotiations. When advocates of rational religion promised compensation in the world, whether the small charities of Guadalupe's priests or the large commitments of doña María Josefa Vergara, reformers promised to help the people they sought to change. They drew rulers and communities into negotiations that mediated continuing polarization.

At the same time old mediations persisted. The Corregidor Domínguez argued that the regime must continue to negotiate worldly relations among convent bankers, Bajío entrepreneurs, and working families. Colombini pleaded that those who sought peace and prosperity in the Bajío and the Spanish empire must respect and promote mediation by Our Lady at Pueblito. Historically the regime organized power, promoted the commercial economy, took revenues, and offered judicial mediation to those with grievances. Entrepreneurs found favor in the halls of administration; communities sought justice in the courts. Regime mediation was pivotal to all. The church historically symbolized divine truth, promoted sacramental worship, financed commercial production, collected tithes, legitimated power, and allowed subject communities to adapt local Christianities. Regime courts and church-sanctioned popular devotions worked in parallel to negotiate, sustain, and stabilize the polarizations of colonial society. In Spanish Mesoamerica and along the Bajío's Mesoamerican fringe, village clergy and the courts that adjudicated the rights of indigenous republics were essential mediators. Across the Bajío and Spanish North America, where indigenous republics and rural clergy were scarce, managers and devotions to the Virgin were indispensable.

The rational religion offered by Díaz de Gamarra at San Miguel, Querétaro's Congregation of Guadalupe, and the widow Vergara contrasted with the divine interventions promised by Our Lady at Pueblito and honored by the Conde de Colombini. They offered contending ways of mediation. Both promised religious legitimacy and material help in a polarizing world. Our Lady asked devotion and promised cures to the ill, children to families, and rain for abundant crops. Rational reformers demanded sacramental worship and offered material charity. Powerful and educated men and women promoted both visions.

We know most about popular responses to these contending visions in the indigenous republics along the southern and eastern margins of the Bajío. Their pursuit of religious independence and their preference for participatory and propitiatory devotions are clear. We know less about the majority that lived and worked in city neighborhoods and estate communities. We do know that don José Sánchez Espinosa, the powerful priest-patriarch, promoted devotion to Guadalupe at La Griega. We also know that the Otomí majority there looked to a fiscal who oversaw religious life—and threatened to strike at harvest time in 1805 if they were denied permission for a festival. We know that at Esperanza, over the mountains east of La Griega, doña María Josefa Vergara waited to found schools, pay teachers, and promote sacramental devotion until she wrote her will, suggesting that local autonomy prevailed there too. The devotions preferred by families at La Griega and Esperanza remain unknown. Other sources only hint at estate communities' cultural independence: indigenous devotions at San Luis de la Paz reached into the Jofre estate; communities of Hispanized indios and mulattoes from San Miguel to Dolores filed suits seeking status as Repúblicas, demanding land and chapels.

The reforming vision provoked polarization and promised education and charities that could be measured and evaluated. Guadalupe's charities at Querétaro were small. The widow Vergara saw the immensity of the task; her rich estate could not fund her vision. In time of war and demands for revenues that drained church resources, the option of reform sustained by education and charity was limited by the dearth of resources to meet educational and charitable promises. Enlightened reformers demanded change and pressed social controls, making promises they could not keep.

In contrast, regime mediation coupled with the Virgin's assistance and consolations promoted production, power, and social peace around Querétaro. Mediation focused on the Virgin was rooted in the populace and confirmed by Franciscan preachers, the banking nuns of Santa Clara, and the enlightened Conde de Colombini. While rational reformers demanded cultural change and promised services that left the populace dependent, access to the Virgin was direct and independent. In a social environment defined by dependence, deepening poverty, and new insecurities, demands for cultural autonomy remained strong. Propitiatory worship offered independence, assistance, hope, and consolation.

Into the years after 1800 competing visions of mediation, competing projects seeking cultural hegemony and social peace, persisted. They engaged the powerful and the populace in debates about production, social relations, and religious truth. The rational reforms promoted by enlightened elites demanded cultural change and promised worldly gains. Traditional mediations promoted by a few among the powerful, many among the religious, and most of the people promised social peace and stability through regime mediation and the Virgin's care. As long as the worldly promises of rational reformers were slow to materialize, the populace preferred access to the courts and the Virgin. While debates persisted, the regime ruled, and the Virgin reigned at Pueblito, production continued and peace held.

When insurgency exploded from Dolores to San Miguel in September 1810, social negotiations and cultural debates gave way to deadly conflicts. Early in the insurgency Father Hidalgo took a flag of Guadalupe found at Atotonilco as the banner of insurgency.[156] Worship there was not committed to Guadalupe; a ranchero found the flag in the cellar and gave it to Hidalgo. In Spanish North America, Guadalupe was more a Hispanic than an indigenous devotion. Around San Luis Potosí, just north of the insurgent heartland, every rancho reportedly had a shrine to Guadalupe.[157] Guadalupe was probably also honored among rancheros and Hispanized indios around San Miguel and Dolores. She became the sponsor of those who fought for justice and independence after 1810.

The royalist partisans and military forces soon entrenched at Querétaro proclaimed Our Lady of Pueblito their protector. In the face of unimagined popular insurgency, the powerful at Querétaro grasped the essence of Columbini's vision. Widespread rural rebellion endured for a decade around San Miguel, Dolores, and Atotonilco, where priests preached penance and personal responsibility. Most Querétaro communities remained at peace and at work while insurgency raged all around. Did Our Lady at Pueblito's mediation sustain social peace around Querétaro, as the Conde de Colombini insisted? Did Guadalupe promote insurgency around Dolores and San Miguel, as Hidalgo's banner suggested? There was more to the hard, often deadly decision to rebel than Guadalupe's banner, more to remaining at work than Our Lady at Pueblito's mediation. Still, where the Otomí Virgin ruled, social polarization was contained, and insurgency proved limited. Where insurgency was widespread and enduring, Guadalupe reigned. As conflict spread across the Bajío, reformers' promises of education and charity became empty rhetoric. In an unprecedented context of social warfare, dueling Virgins—the insurgent Guadalupe facing the pacifying Lady of Pueblito—legitimated the violence that would remake the Bajío.

Conclusion

The Bajío and North America

in the Atlantic Crucible

BEGINNING IN THE SIXTEENTH CENTURY the peoples of the Bajío built a new society embedded in a new world of global interactions. Strategically located at the intersection of European expansion and Chinese demand for silver, they laid the foundations for a new world. The highland basin watered by a network of rivers offered great agricultural potential, but was little settled around 1500 as Mesoamerican states faced independent Chichimecas across a frontier of conflict and trade. Almost everything began anew after 1520. First came the Otomí escaping Mexica power. Then silver strikes at Zacatecas and Guanajuato brought throngs of Mesoamericans, Europeans, and Africans, and herds of Old World livestock, along with smallpox and other plagues devastating to indigenous Americans. War and epidemic left Chichimecas few in number, and forced to adapt in marginal missions or upland refuges. Meanwhile silver drove profit-seeking commercial development.

Querétaro flourished as a city of huertas, textiles, and trade; early on an Otomí council was the only local government, Spaniards and Otomí shared entrepreneurship, and a labor market shaped by obligation and patriarchy developed around 1600. The seventeenth century brought northward expansion and the consolidation of Spanish North America beyond Querétaro, which finally gained a Spanish council in 1655. Guanajuato was a place of mining, of hope and risk, of ethnic fluidity and social insecurity. Mineworkers mixing Mesoamerican and African ancestry became proud mulattoes. Across rich bottomlands irrigation expanded and communities of cultivators grew. Local elites were Spanish, even as they included people mixing European, Mesoamerican, and African ancestry. Communities working estate lands mixed tenant production and obligated labor, all orchestrated by patriarchy. They too mixed Mesoamericans and Africans, most becoming indios after 1650.

The eighteenth century brought revivals of mining and northward expansion, of textile towns and religious expressions. Guanajuato became a leading silver producer as Chinese demand surged again. San Miguel boomed as an industrial town, making cloth, cutlery, and more. Querétaro's textile industry flourished; its great aqueduct asserted Spanish power; the Otomí council still defended the rights of the majority working valuable huertas. Our Lady of Pueblito, the Otomí Virgin, became a favorite of Querétaro Spaniards. Penitential worship helped the patriarchs of San Miguel know that they did God's work. At Guanajuato, Jesuits and others preached penitence and subordination in a city of disorder and insecurity. Then in the 1760s Atlantic war and its aftermath heightened demands for militias and revenues, provoking resistance at Guanajuato, San Luis Potosí to the north, Pátzcuaro to the south, and outlying towns including San Luis de la Paz. The people of Querétaro and most of the Bajío countryside remained at work, limiting the mid-century insurgent challenge. The risings did remind regime officials and colonial entrepreneurs of their common interests. They inflicted harsh punishments and then drew the majority back into mines and workshops.

Mining drove to new heights from the 1770s and held them past 1800. The economy expanded and stayed strong despite famine in the 1780s and trade disruptions in the 1790s. Great families linking Atlantic trade, mining investment, and landed entrepreneurship ruled from Mexico City. In their shadows provincial elites negotiated power and business in Bajío cities and towns: mining magnates ruled booming Guanajuato; the Canal clan dominated a declining San Miguel; a more integrated elite led trade, textiles, and estate operation at Querétaro. Across the region economic boom came with deepening pressures on the working majority. Mineworkers faced daily danger, sustained global trade, and lost ore shares while wages fell. Textile makers faced the competition of imports promoted by new policies of "free trade" that aimed to draw more silver toward Spain and Europe; obrajes closed while a rising number of household cloth makers worked more to gain less. Estate communities saw rents rise and evictions spread on rich bottomlands; new lands opened only in marginal uplands; obligated labor expanded, yet advances, wages, and rations declined; seasonal wage work allowed boys to help struggling households, but then many had to move on in search of land to clear, only to face declining yields.

Patriarchy shaped social relations everywhere; ethnic complexity made every community, urban and rural, different. Both faced new challenges after 1770. Patriarchy, an ideal promoted by religious leaders and entrepreneurs since the sixteenth century, had long been weak at Guanajuato, where mining labor made working men uniquely prosperous and insecure, caught up in short, dangerous lives that inhibited stable family relations. Patriarchy was long entrenched in agricultural entrepreneurs' organization of estate production, and in merchant financiers' organization of household cloth making. But in the late eighteenth century, while patriarchy remained a dominant ideal (not only among most men but also among powerful women like doña María Josefa Vergara), pressures to maximize profit increasingly led to evictions, declining earnings, and other sources of insecurity that undermined working men's ability to sustain families, threatening their capacity to implement the essential bargain of household patriarchy. It became increasingly difficult to claim household power in exchange for family sustenance as sustenance became scarce and uncertain. Meanwhile the employment of a growing number of women in mining at Guanajuato refineries and Querétaro's tobacco factory served the interests of production, holding earnings low and keeping men constrained. It also challenged the patriarchal hierarchies that for so long had structured and stabilized inequalities in the Bajío.

In the same decades ethnic relations became more complex. Over the centuries ethnic segregation had persisted around Querétaro, its Otomí majority and council facilitating Otomí separation, or at least distinction. Around Guanajuato and San Miguel and across the bottomlands, amalgamations had ruled; but communities there developed different ways of amalgamation and differing ethnic identities. At Guanajuato and San Miguel peoples mixing indigenous and African ancestry were mostly mulatto around 1750; across the bottomlands people of similar origins had often become indios. Enlightened eighteenth-century reformers envisioned new forms of segregation; Gálvez insisted that indios should live like indios and stop mixing with others and claiming new identities. He had little success; many descendants of Guanajuato's mid-century mulattoes were becoming Spaniards by the 1790s, not indios. People of mixed Otomí and African ancestry north of San Miguel, around Dolores, did assert indio status, not to accept subordination but to demand landed republics. The Spaniards, mestizos, mulattoes, and Otomí at Puerto de Nieto, east of San Miguel, kept mixing in patriarchal families and clans.

In the city of Querétaro a growing number of Otomí without huertas dispersed to live and work across an expanding Spanish center, while Hispanic tradesmen and their families built shops among the long Otomí huertas of San Sebastián. A small Hispanic community settled among long-resistant Pames at San Pedro de la Cañada. Yet ethnic distinctions ruled within the burgeoning city, in the canyon, and at La Griega and other estate communities east on the Amascala plain. The Santa Rosa basin was different. There, between segregating Querétaro and amalgamating San Miguel and Guanajuato, the informal town of Santa Rosa saw limited patriarchy and ethnic mixing. But the surrounding estate communities were actively segregating in the 1780s and 1790s. Families moved to create communities of Spaniards and mestizos, others of mulattoes—all with Otomí underclasses of workers and subtenants. The segregation of Hispanics and Otomí within communities was newly complicated by the shift of Spaniards and mestizos to live together in some estate communities, while mulattoes were left separated at others—all among dependent Otomí families. In the Santa Rosa basin enlightened visions did lead to new forms of segregation.

As the eighteenth century drew toward a close, patriarchy remained a dominant ideal and a key to orchestrating structural inequalities. It faced deepening challenges not in ideology but from the social assaults of profit-seeking capitalism. Old patterns of segregation around Querétaro and of amalgamation and negotiated identities elsewhere in the Bajío faced reformers who preferred segregation, while everyday adaptations led to proliferating new complexities. Patriarchal hierarchies aimed to integrate and stabilize deepening exploitations, while working patriarchs faced unprecedented uncertainties that challenged the essence of patriarchal bargains. Newly complex ways of amalgamation and segregation made each community ever more different from its neighbors.

Still, from 1770 to 1810 capitalism flourished across the Bajío. Its silver drove global and Atlantic trade and stimulated European industries. Predatory entrepreneurs ruled mining, commerce, and landed empires from Mexico City. Leading Guanajuato mine owners might escape from, or ally with, financial powers concentrated in the capital. Locally powerful men in Querétaro and San Miguel lived in their shadows. A search for profit drove entrepreneurs, great, provincial, and marginal. Predators abounded, and faced fewer limits after 1770 as the economy soared and population growth made workers more widely available and dependent.

Entrepreneurs and regime officials maintained an alliance for profit and revenues, even as they might dispute some policies. Markets integrated everything. With few indigenous republics, subsistence production was limited in the Bajío, and it shrank as estates replaced tenants with paid hands working commercial fields. Where production for sustenance persisted (and expanded in poor uplands) it was an adjunct of capitalist cropping, sustaining poor families that paid rents, fed themselves, and provided labor for little pay at expanding estate fields.

The Bourbon regime participated throughout, promoting mining, taking increased revenues, and aiming to create new forces of coercion, in the hope of ruling more by assertion and less by conciliation. Mining and revenues soared after 1770, but administration remained limited. To contain the risings of the 1760s the regime depended on colonial militias. When it appointed loyalists from Spain to key posts, they married into the families of leading entrepreneurs in Mexico City and built ties with New Spain's dominant economic interests. When it named intendants to assert power in provincial capitals, at Guanajuato and elsewhere new officials found allies among provincial elites. When new forces of coercion were built in the 1780s and 1790s they were patrols ruled by local councils and militias commanded and funded by entrepreneurial elites. In effort after effort Bourbon reformers promoted administrative powers, and (re)learned the need to negotiate with the entrepreneurs who ruled the silver economy and to conciliate the majority that produced everything.

Thus after 1770, while the Bajío economy flourished, ethnic amalgamations persisted in the face of new segregation, patriarchy still ruled while working patriarchs faced new challenges, and the regime exercised administrative powers while maintaining key ways of negotiation and conciliation. Polarization accelerated, concentrating wealth while forcing insecurity and poverty onto the majority. Yet stability held and capitalism flourished.

Meanwhile new visions and fractures developed in Bajío Catholicism; cultural polarity exacerbated deepening social chasms. Enlightened visionaries saw popular devotion as superstition and argued for change. Many resisted and took worship underground. Yet as divisions deepened in the domains of profit and work, patriarchy, and religion, key mediators understood the need to negotiate: estate managers had to maintain production; priests worked to keep religious peace in diverse communities. An Italian count, Querétaro's corregidor, and the widow Vergara offered differing ways to mediate deepening social and cultural conflicts. In years of concentrating profit and deepening desperation, men powerful and poor still collaborated in negotiating patriarchal inequities. Women resisted sporadically. Everyone debated religious truths and ways to worldly help.

Until 1808 the regime held and the economy flourished. For decades patriarchal power, ethnic fluidity, social fragmentation, and persistent mediations combined to stabilize the polarizing society of the capitalist Bajío. To 1810 it remained an engine of the global economy, the foundation of the continuing expansion of Spanish North America, and the key to the Spanish empire's continuing role in escalating contests over Atlantic power—while much of the rest of Europe and the Americas faced war and revolution. When revolution broke silver production in the Bajío after 1810, European wars moved toward resolution in a British victory that set the stage for British and later Anglo-American eminence in a new world of industrial, imperial capitalism.

Spanish North America after 1770: Consolidation and Expansion

While the Bajío boomed and stabilized deepening polarization after 1770, the northward drive and commercial development of Spanish North America accelerated. The late eighteenth century saw a sustained silver boom at Guanajuato, and new bonanzas at Fresnillo and Sombrerete north of Zacatecas and at Catorce north of San Luis Potosí. Recession at Parral and Chihuahua meant that production receded from the far frontier, but prospecting drove on. The Bajío and regions north remained an integrated North American economy.

From the sixteenth century Zacatecas, San Luis Potosí, Parral, and Chihuahua had focused on mining and grazing while facing independent, often resistant native peoples. The Bajío sent grain and cloth to mining and grazing communities stretching north. When mining boomed anew in the eighteenth century, remaining independent peoples were few and farther north; commercial cultivation developed near Zacatecas at Aguascalientes and east of San Luis Potosí at Río Verde. Outposts once sustained by the Bajío began to mix mining, grazing, and cultivation in integrated commercial societies. The northward shift of livestock raised the costs of wool in the Bajío; growing northern herds and demand for cloth brought obrajes to Durango. The commercial complex begun in the Bajío was replicated ever northward. After 1750 Spanish North America consolidated commercial cropping and grazing from San Antonio to Sonora. It incorporated New Mexico's Spaniards and Pueblos in new commercial ways. And it drove settlement up the coast of California to San Francisco.

By 1800 Spanish North America had developed distinct zones: the Bajío, where it all began, still mixed mining, cloth making, and irrigated cropping, while grazing shifted north; a near North included Zacatecas and San Luis Potosí, where mining boomed, irrigated culti-

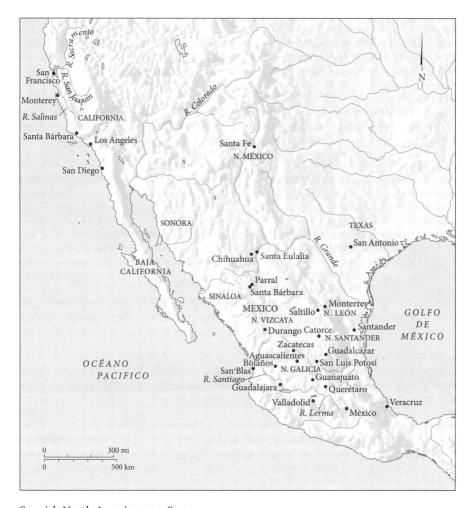

Spanish North America, ca. 1800

vation expanded, and grazing carried on; a far North stretched across
Durango and Chihuahua and reached east to Saltillo and Nuevo León
and west to Sonora, still mixing mining and grazing with limited cultivation; finally, the frontier extended into Texas, New Mexico, and
California. All these zones shared core characteristics: mining focused
commercial ways; mines and towns were sustained by irrigated cultivation where possible, and grazing estates almost everywhere; populations of diverse ancestry, rooted in migration, mixed and forged new
identities; and indigenous republics remained scarce (except in New
Mexico)—missions were transitional communities, drawing natives to
settled subordination and to labor in the money economy while they
faced devastating diseases and eventual marginalization.

Profit drove and commerce integrated everything. Expanding alcabala tax collections document northern expansion. In the Bajío, long-
est settled and holding near peak levels of silver production, taxed
commerce grew 13 percent from 1781 to 1809. Just north, old but still
developing regions showed more growth: 28 percent at Zacatecas and
39 percent at San Luis Potosí. Farther north, expansion was greater.
In Nueva Viscaya, combining Durango and Chihuahua, the increase
was 50 percent despite slow mining. In the northeast, including Coahuila, Nuevo León, and Nuevo Santander, commerce increased by 80
percent. And in northwestern Sinaloa and Sonora, it soared by 360
percent. To a degree increases reflected better collection, notably in
Sonora. Still, only commercial growth could sustain such payments.
By 1800–1809 collection totals in Zacatecas and San Luis Potosí approached those in the Bajío. Far northern revenues rose from 15 percent to nearly 25 percent of the total for Spanish North America.[1] The
northward commercial drive held to 1810.

That thrust consolidated core characteristics of Spanish North
America across vast territories. Mining stimulated everything. We
have seen the historical development of key centers from Guanajuato, Zacatecas, and San Luis Potosí north to Catorce, Sombrerete,
Parral, and Chihuahua. Different mines boom at different times; despite fits and starts, the northward trajectory is clear. Guanajuato's
output peaked as a proportion of all New Spain's silver in the 1740s
and again in the 1770s and 1780s. The colonial peak from 1791 to 1810
saw a slippage of Guanajuato's share (and little production at Real del
Monte and Taxco, the major mines of Spanish Mesoamerica). The late
colonial boom was led by mining north of the Bajío.[2] And mining was
always an economic stimulus and a promise of more. Northward expansion was energized by hopes of what might lie in sierras just beyond.

To sustain mining an archipelago of northern cities and towns recreated much that had begun in Querétaro. From Aguascalientes to Durango and Saltillo, extending to San Antonio, and emerging in Los
Angeles, the towns of Spanish North America were places where district magistrates faced local Spanish councils, traders became landlords (and often sat as councilmen), artisans made craft goods, the
clergy preached, and irrigated huertas made cities into oases of lush
cultivation.[3] Commercial estates shaped the northern countryside.
Entrepreneurs in Mexico City operated the largest properties: don José
Sánchez Espinosa dominated San Luis Potosí around 1800; the Marqués de San Miguel de Aguayo held vast properties around Saltillo.
Provincials based in the Bajío and northern towns created smaller replicas. Where streams allowed irrigation—at Aguascalientes, Río Verde

east of San Luis Potosí, and Saltillo—new crops led to estate communities that mixed tenants and obligated employees. Where the latter ruled cultivation and grazing, men took salaries, rations, and cloth to sustain and rule families. An integrated agro-pastoral sector sold animals, wool, and tallow in northern mines, provincial towns, cities in the Bajío, and Mexico City; Bajío grain fed the arid north and Mexico City when local harvests failed. European, Asian, and Bajío textiles clothed northerners. Merchants in Mexico City, Querétaro, and other towns integrated markets and profited.[4]

As in all of New Spain, the Bourbon regime worked to build administrative power across the North.[5] Yet officials always had to negotiate with local entrepreneurs, especially near frontiers where officials and entrepreneurs together faced independent natives, mission communities, and expanding yet uncertain economic opportunities.[6] Patriarchy orchestrated almost everything in towns like Chihuahua, and in estate communities everywhere.[7] Rural settlement expanded along with cultivation and grazing at estates and in independent ranchero communities; so did reports of Apache incursions as livestock became more valuable to commercial grazers and to independent natives (and diverse others) seeking ways to remain independent. The result was an adamant northern patriarchy that mixed landholding, production, and martial valor.[8]

Meanwhile, across the north as in the Bajío, commercial communities shaped by patriarchy lived ethnic amalgamations and changes. In 1778 mulattoes were 83 percent of residents in the rural Charcas jurisdiction of northern San Luis Potosí. At Durango they were 43 percent in 1770 and 63 percent in 1790, as the number of Spaniards and mestizos fell.[9] At Chihuahua birth registers recorded mostly Spaniards and indios early in the eighteenth century; both groups then diminished, while mestizos peaked at 39 percent in 1775, as did mulattoes at 22 percent in 1780. Then indios and mulattoes all but disappeared as Spaniards rose to 25 percent and mestizos to more than 60 percent.[10]

If commercial dynamism, regime negotiation, patriarchal integration, and ethnic amalgamation and redefinition combined to characterize Spanish North America into the early nineteenth century, so did the dearth of indigenous republics, the demise of missions, and the weak presence of the church outside scattered cities and towns. A few migrant Mesoamerican communities with rights to land and self-governance had settled early to stabilize relations with independent northern natives. Often of Tlaxcalan origins, they saw their rights come under attack in the eighteenth century from commercial accumulators within and land engrossers without. Many of the risings in rural San Luis Potosí in 1767 resulted from such pressures; endemic conflicts at San Miguel Mexquitic revealed that the pressures and conflicts persisted into the nineteenth century.[11]

Missions were planned as transitional institutions. Property, governance, economic rule, and religious oversight belonged to Franciscans, Jesuits, and other clergy. The goal was to teach Christianity, sedentary life, patriarchy, and subordinate production—to help (and induce) independent people to become colonial subordinates. Across the high plateau from the Bajío to Chihuahua, as mining drove estate development from the sixteenth century to the eighteenth, missions began in times of conflict and plague. The missions and their residents often faced short lives. Where mining and commercial development proved slower, as along Pacific foothills from Sinaloa through Sonora, missions and natives lived longer. But there too they eventually faced economic pressures, disease, and collapse; missions rarely became indigenous republics providing land and self-rule to native survivors. Don José de Escandón's eighteenth-century military colonization of the Gulf lowlands used missions and missionaries to back commercial goals; he repeatedly frustrated missionary friars' attempts to cushion adaptations to conquest and disease. Missions were institutions of frontier advance. Their cycle of foundation and demise eased the commercial ways of Spanish North America.[12]

As mission clergy moved northward, the institutional church concentrated in cities and towns. Clergy were scarce in the countryside. But Catholic culture was everywhere, perhaps more contested and diverse because clerical oversight was limited. Zacatecas developed a religious life parallel to the inclusive yet debated culture of the Bajío. The Conde de Santiago de la Laguna, patriarch of a leading mining family, promoted "enlightened" and "rational" Catholicism, believing and asserting that life demanded sacramental morality and rewarded human effort. The majority were devoted to representations of the Virgin, often Our Lady of Sorrows—perhaps an inevitable focus for people living in a place defined by dreams and danger.[13] For the rural north sources for popular religious life remain few, beyond missionaries' constant laments that natives and settlers were uncertain and weak Catholics—a sure sign of underlying religious independence.[14]

Commercial dynamism, patriarchal orchestration, ethnic fluidity, scarce indigenous republics, transitory missions, and contested religious cultures combined to mark Spanish North America as settlement drove north from the Bajío. There were of course endless variations. Local environments, prior indigenous ways, migration patterns, and economic prospects (notably the presence or absence of silver and water) made every community different, as we have seen even in the confines of the eastern Bajío. Two larger patterns of difference deserve note. One differentiated the Bajío from everything to its north; the other shaped differing trajectories of societies marching northward.

The Bajío was unique because of its ample fertile and irrigable lands, sixteenth-century foundations, and proximity to the great markets at Guanajuato, Zacatecas, and Mexico City. A long history of immigration combined with eighteenth-century population growth to end the labor scarcities that had long challenged entrepreneurs and favored the basin's peoples. After 1770 entrepreneurs in mining, textiles, and estate agriculture found new success driving the working majority toward deepening poverty and proliferating insecurities, often threatening the patriarchy that structured social inequality and stabilized regional life. During the late eighteenth century the Bajío became a crucible of economic dynamism and social polarization; entrepreneurs pursuing immediate gain became predators attacking the working families and communities who produced their profits and almost everything else.

Beyond the Bajío migration and population growth still lagged behind labor demands in rapidly expanding commercial regions. In his report on Aguascalientes in 1792, don Félix Calleja emphasized agricultural expansion since the 1780s but lamented that people remained mobile and too independent. In addition to the usual complaint that mineworkers labored only until news of the next bonanza, Calleja added: "Agricultural workers roam no less." The result: "They have formed a character of low liberty, indolence, and self-abandon, which leads to every kind of vice and disorder."[15] Working people remained scarce and mobile from San Luis Potosí northward; social relations there held favorable to workers and producing families. Entrepreneurs still adapted to demands for fair tenancies and salaries with good rations and ample cloth provisions, thus reinforcing patriarchy and bolstering security. Everyday life was contested; frustrated employers might become coercive. Yet the balance of population and production favored workers north of the Bajío. After the regime collapsed in 1808 the Bajío exploded in insurgency in 1810. People to the north rose only sporadically.[16]

Spanish North America expanded in three corridors of northward thrust: the highland plateau between the Sierras, the Pacific hills, and the Gulf lowlands. From the start the highlands led, beginning in the Bajío, gaining dynamism at Zacatecas in the 1550s, and reaching New Mexico by the 1580s, filling the spaces in between during times of expansion and consolidation through the eighteenth century. In contrast, the Gulf lowlands remained marginal until the eighteenth century. There was little silver there, and limited need for coastal pastures before Escandón's military colonization in the 1740s built a ranching culture that soon overwhelmed the missions and drove across the Río Grande.

The Pacific hills from Sinaloa to Sonora had a different history. Mining strikes along the eastern slopes of the Sierras from Zacatecas to Durango sent prospectors across passes toward the coast looking for more silver. They found little in a region of settled cultivators once linked to Mesoamerican states but now independent. Spaniards faced scarce opportunity and much resistance in the Pacific foothills. Jesuits built missions from Sinaloa through Sonora in the seventeenth century, bringing new ways of cultivation (including wheat and livestock) to people facing disease and depopulation. To the mid-eighteenth century missions endured as the social and economic foundation of colonial life along Pacific hills. They sent crops, livestock, and workers to interior mining communities.[17] The highlands remained the dynamic core of Spanish North America. Then after 1770 all three corridors drove north—the Pacific region rapidly commercializing in Sinaloa and Sonora while a new mission frontier thrust north along the coast of California.

After Spain gained Louisiana in 1765, New Spain pulled back in east Texas. A lack of minerals in thick woods inhabited by insistently independent cultivators limited interest among migrants from New Spain. Early missions near Nacodoches, led by Franciscans from Querétaro and Zacatecas, proved costly and frustrating. Retreat consolidated most Spanish settlement near San Antonio, which saw the decline and secularization of its missions and the incorporation of the survivors as workers in a commercial world. People arriving from the south, often mulattoes and mestizos, claimed Spanish status and married Canary Islanders who had settled, built irrigation works, and labored on huertas. Town cultivators were often artisans too. Grazing ranches spread across the countryside. Merchant-ranchers asserted preeminence over missionaries and military officers as all joined the market economy. Cattle drives went south to Saltillo, where Texas livestock traded for cloth from the Bajío, Europe, and Asia. Around 1800 San Antonio was the northeastern outpost of Spanish North America.[18]

The people of San Antonio and outlying ranchos still faced independent peoples. As the livestock economy expanded, Comanches armed by New Mexican Spaniards chased Apaches into Texas, provoking unfathomable conflicts over lands and people, horses and cattle, cloth and firearms. Ranch development, violent conflict, and cultural adaptation were inseparable. Nomads riding horses and hunting cattle ruled the high plains from San Antonio to New Mexico. Independent Tejas and other settled cultivators and traders held the land between San Antonio and Louisiana, trading for arms, ruling local diplomacy, and compelling Europeans to adapt to their power and gender practices, which made warriors of men and diplomats of women.[19]

Between San Antonio and the Gulf new missions engaged the Karankawa. Living scattered along bays from the Nueces River north, they hunted deer and gathered plants inland during spring and summer, then fished and gathered shellfish on the coast in fall and winter. They had long resisted missions. But when livestock invaded their hunting grounds the Karankawa began to hunt cattle, setting off conflicts reminiscent of the Chichimeca wars. After 1780 missions led by Franciscans from Zacatecas approached the Karankawa, whose numbers were falling because of disruption, conflict, and disease. Mounted and armed Apaches, pursued by Comanches, had invaded inland Karankawa hunting grounds. In the face of new threats they proved receptive to Franciscans. They built missions at spring and summer hunting camps. European livestock replaced deer and bison as spring and summer sustenance. Karankawa men learned to cultivate, women to spin and weave. Yet they returned to coastal camps to live on fish and shellfish every fall and winter, frustrating missionaries with their independence. The Karankawa used missions to negotiate adaptations to Spanish North America; they lived for decades in a Franciscan Karankawa world, until depopulation enabled an expansion of ranching—and then opened the way for cotton and slavery in the 1830s.[20]

At the northern limit of the highland plateau, where the Río Grande emerged from the sierras, New Mexico was the northernmost extension of New Spain from the late sixteenth century until the settlement of Monterey and San Francisco in northern California after 1770. In part a replica of Spanish Mesoamerica, where Spaniards ruled Pueblo republics, and in part the northern outpost of Spanish North America, where Spaniards and Pueblos together faced independent peoples in conflict and trade, New Mexico had a long contested history.[21] From the 1580s to the 1680s a small number of Spanish officials, inevitably also warrior-entrepreneurs, joined Franciscan clergy along the Río Grande, where they ruled a native majority composed of cultivating communities with distinct languages and social ways who were facing disease, depopulation, and incursions of European livestock. To Spaniards they were all Pueblos—different from the independent nomadic peoples on the Great Plains stretching east and the high basins reaching north. For a century Spaniards pressed Pueblos to adapt to Christianity; together they joined in conflicts and trade with surrounding peoples who remained adamantly independent while learning the uses of European horses and arms.

In 1680, amid a recession of silver mining that limited Spanish power and frontier trading, that first fragile equilibrium broke. An alliance of

Pueblos and independent peoples rejected Spanish rule in the Pueblo Revolt. Surviving Spaniards fled south. But relations between Pueblos and independent Apaches, Navajos, and others proved uncertain, and all had come to depend on European livestock, tools, and trade. After 1692 Spaniards found allies and began to return. Around 1700, as silver mining boomed anew at Santa Eulalia in Chihuahua, they negotiated new relations with Pueblos, and together they built new ties with their independent neighbors.

The first half of the eighteenth century brought accelerating incorporation into the markets of Spanish North America. Livestock and cloth went south in caravans to supply Chihuahua; Spaniards provided most livestock, Pueblos wove most cloth, and men of both groups traveled together to sell their wares as the Santa Eulalia mines boomed.[22] What returned north was not silver, which still flowed south and then across the oceans toward China, but metal wares, cloth, and ceramics from New Spain (including Querétaro), Europe, and Asia. Spaniards depended on the Pueblos for grain production, and Spaniards and Pueblos again joined in selling livestock and tools to independent peoples. In return they gained hides and human captives, who were often incorporated into families and communities as *genízaros*. This was the era when Navajos settled canyons northwest of the Río Grande to become great grazers of sheep and skilled weavers of wool. It was also a time when most Apaches and Comanche newcomers kept close and peaceful ties with New Mexico, gaining the horses, weapons, and tools of Europe that made them powerful on the plains. For half a century a resurgent silver economy facilitated Spanish rule in New Mexico. Entrepreneurial officials balanced the gains of trade with Chihuahua, dependence on the Pueblos for cloth and grain, and the need for peace and trade with independent peoples—all to sustain an era of commercial growth.

Decades of relative peace and good prosperity collapsed around 1750 into a new era of conflict. As Chinese demand for silver fell mining receded at Santa Eulalia, the first sign of a mid-century recession across New Spain. With the prospects and profits of trade down, independent Apaches and Comanches turned from trading to raiding to gain livestock and weapons. Decades of war kept Spaniards and Pueblos in a continuing alliance, yet the mutual gains of their economic relations waned. Spanish military spending became a prime stimulus to the local economy; officials used the powers of office to press Pueblos to take advances of goods, often cloth, in exchange for grain essential to a growing Hispanic population. Mining recession led to conflicts in the far north a decade before parallel developments contributed to the uprisings in and near the Bajío in the 1760s. The northern outpost of

Spanish North America proved a harbinger of conflicts across the region in the 1680s and again in the 1750s. The profits and power derived from the silver economy were tenuous at the margins.

Peace and economic dynamism returned around 1780. Changing geopolitics and social relations in and around New Mexico shaped a transition, again in the context of the silver economy resurgent across Spanish North America from the 1770s. A campaign in 1779 led by don Juan Bautista de Anza, fresh from California, included 85 regular soldiers stationed at Santa Fe (Bourbon reformers' primary contribution), 205 local Hispanic militiamen, and 259 Pueblo men. They defeated key Comanche forces. In 1780 and 1781 smallpox struck New Mexico, inflicting population losses averaging 25 percent. Afterward a Hispanic population including Spaniards, mestizos, mulattoes, genízaros, and people from the Pueblos who married all of the above recouped its numbers with rapid reproductive growth. Those who remained in the Pueblos did not. As the eighteenth century ended Pueblos became a subordinated minority while Hispanic numbers and commercial activities surged. Pueblos remained important producers of grains and cloth. But the Hispanic majority was ever less dependent on Pueblo production and on Pueblo alliances in wars against their independent neighbors.[23]

Spanish New Mexicans negotiated peace with the Comanches, encouraging them to settle nearby and engage in trade with independent peoples farther out—trade facilitated by Spanish rule at New Orleans and St. Louis after 1765. The peace enabled Comanches to dominate the great plains that stretched east from the Río Grande highlands, and with the tacit acceptance of New Mexico officials, to wage war against ever more isolated Apaches who drove into Texas and raided south toward Chihuahua, even Durango. All that combined to facilitate the commercial dynamism that marked New Mexico from 1780 to 1810, while Pueblos faced new marginalization as subordinated communities.

Thanks to local peace and a resurgent silver economy, in the 1770s New Mexicans sold cloth and livestock in Sonora as it experienced multiple mining strikes, but no sustained bonanza. From the 1780s New Mexican entrepreneurs sent growing herds of sheep south to Chihuahua, along with ever more cloth. Pueblo cloth remained important, as did Navajo weavings. The sheep driven south came from Hispanic and Navajo grazers. But only rich Hispanic New Mexicans organized and profited from the surging trade stimulated by the late colonial boom of Spanish North America.

As the eighteenth century ended, New Mexico joined the economic dynamism, social ways, and cultural conversations of Spanish North

America. It was ruled by entrepreneurs who were also officials and militia commanders—always Spaniards, whatever their ancestry. Commercial ways stimulated by globally linked silver production were sustained locally by irrigated cultivation and extensive grazing. A growing Hispanic society forged a majority mixing Europeans, mestizos, mulattoes, and diverse natives in amalgamations that led to changing identities. Pueblos became a minority facing separation and exploitation (including land losses), yet still able to use republican rights to defend their participation in a complex society that had to mediate inequalities to stabilize commercial dynamism. While commercial ways surged, entrepreneurs funded sodalities that became known as *penitentes*, reflecting a "powerful, self-confident *vecino [citizen]* worldview." People in the Pueblos focused worship on Katchinas expected to bless them with "rain, fertile crops, good hunting, general well being."[24] The penitentes promoted worship reminiscent of devotions funded by San Miguel entrepreneurs at the Oratorio and Atotonilco; Pueblos kept commitments parallel to Otomí worship of Our Lady at Pueblito. As a new century began New Mexico consolidated the commercial ways, social amalgamations, and cultural polarizations of Spanish North America.

The Last Frontier of Spanish North America: Sonora to California

Meanwhile that dynamic colonial society opened a new frontier in California. The Pacific hills and river valleys from Sonora to California lived transforming changes after 1760. In Sonora the mission economy collapsed, accelerating the consolidation of a commercial, patriarchal, culturally fluid society energized by mining and sustained by estate communities. A new mission frontier drove up the California coast from San Diego to San Francisco. The simultaneous collapse of the missions in Sonora and their creation anew across California marked the consolidation of Spanish North America in the former and its beginning in the latter.

The Jesuits built missions from Sinaloa through Sonora during the seventeenth century. Engaging sedentary villagers without states and cultivating fertile river valleys, they began in Sinaloa, reached the Mayos and Yaquis of Sonora by 1620, and extended to include the Pimas and others in the 1690s. The Jesuits imagined that they were forging peasant communities under clerical care. A close look at internal organization and external relations suggests that the Pacific missions were very much in the commercial tradition of Spanish North

America.[25] The Jesuits offered many natives alliance against old enemies, access to new ways of production (tools, livestock, and wheat, which flourished on Pacific floodplains), and new religious resources in times of disruption, disease, and death. Long periods of adaptation to mission life were interrupted by times of resistance—notably in the 1680s and 1690s, at the same time as risings by Pueblos and Tarahumara. During two centuries limited mineral finds contained Hispanic settlement and commercial development in New Spain's Pacific Northwest, while natives faced disease and prolonged decline. In nearby uplands and across northern deserts independent peoples still pressed against sedentary villagers as they negotiated mission life.

For most Pacific cultivators, missions shaped adaptation to the colonial order from the early 1600s to the 1760s. Yet the coastal missions were more like the estates of Spanish North America than the indigenous republics of Mesoamerica. The land was held by the Jesuits in trust for the community; the fathers named local governors and magistrates, intermediaries appointed by priests, not officials with rights to go to court to defend village land and autonomy. Jesuits led religious life, with inevitable negotiations. They ruled production and marketing in ways reminiscent of commercial estates across the North. Mission lands were divided between estate fields and plots allocated to resident families. About half the residents' labor went to family sustenance, men clearing and cultivating crops, women raising children, making meals, and clothing the family. The other half of men's labor went to mission fields, where they raised wheat and maize and cared for livestock that fed the fathers and provided surpluses sold in mining camps and Spanish settlements. The income sustained the mission. For work in estate fields residents gained food rations and cloth allocations. The Jesuits also contracted to send gangs of mission workers to mines and nearby estates. The wages went to the mission, which provided cloth, rations, and sustenance to the workers and their families.

Across Spanish North America estate operators were often clergymen who pursued profit, offered sacraments, and proclaimed charitable intentions. Northern estates mixed market production with family cultivation and crafts; remuneration combined rations and cloth. All this suggests strong parallels between Pacific missions and commercial estates. There were differences, of course: profit served the Jesuits and the missions, not patriarchal families; mission labor brought access to land and sustenance, not salaries calculated in cash. Even so, the mix of family cultivation and labor, the sale of surplus in the commercial economy, and the lack of even limited control by the community over land and production made the coastal missions more like northern estates than Mesoamerican republics.

Through the seventeenth century coastal natives adapted to mission life as they encountered emerging commercial ways and the devastation of smallpox and other diseases. There were negotiations over production, labor, and religious life within the missions; there were conflicts with independent peoples. The risings of independent peoples in the late seventeenth century mostly struck coastal missions as assaults from without that unified communities within. In the eighteenth century the northern economy accelerated and Hispanic settlement spread across Pacific foothills. Pressures for mission produce and labor escalated while mission populations plunged. Widening conflicts began in the 1740s, now mostly within the missions as residents resisted old strictures and new demands. Hispanic settlers and regime officials began to seek an end to the missions (always presumed transitional). The decision to secularize was taken in 1765; the expulsion of the Jesuits in 1767 accelerated the process.[26]

Missions without Jesuits were assigned to Franciscans, many based in Querétaro; other new missionaries, including Junípero Serra, had experience in the Sierra Gorda. In uncertain and disputed processes Franciscans gained religious oversight without control of land and production, except in new missions usually in arid lands. Don José de Gálvez arrived in 1768, fresh from his tour of repression across the Bajío. He aimed to privatize mission lands, advance commercial production, and integrate mission residents as dependent workers in a market economy. He organized a military expedition of over a thousand troops from Spain and New Spain to force independent peoples into submission, with little success.

The first bishop of Sonora, Fray Antonio de los Reyes, a Spaniard trained at Santa Cruz de Querétaro, joined magistrates and commanders in the 1780s to distribute mission lands as private property. Residents got small plots; outsiders got larger mission fields and then bought indigenous plots to create estates. Commercial development came as mining accelerated in fleeting gold placers and limited veins of silver. Settlers poured in: Spaniards, mulattoes, and mestizos sought a chance on a new commercial frontier. Some natives who had lived in missions claimed rights as vecinos, citizens of Hispanic towns, mining camps, and estates. The demise of the missions accelerated commercial ways and ethnic amalgamations. Spanish North America, latent in the mission economy, flourished in Sonora after 1780, as shown in soaring alcabala revenues.

While the mission economy collapsed in Sonora a new mission frontier opened in California. Both developments fit Gálvez's plan: the role of missions as an advance guard of commercial Spanish North America could not be clearer. Gálvez justified funding new missions by the threat of Russian and British incursions on the California coast. The settlers who joined the missionaries had their eyes on the traditional prizes of Spanish North America: mines, landed estates, and subordinate peoples to work them.

Small sea and land expeditions left Baja California in 1769 for San Diego, a bay known to passing Manila galleons since the sixteenth century. The first mission in Alta California began there; in the following year an overland march founded the Presidio at Monterey (also long known to mariners) and the nearby mission of San Carlos Borromeo (now Carmel). Between San Diego and Monterey missions began at San Gabriel, San Luis Obispo, and San Antonio in 1771 and 1772. From a population estimated at 250,000 to 300,000, including coastal fishing peoples and inland hunters and gatherers, the missions attracted perhaps 1,000 neophytes in five years. Thus began the colonial intrusion, cultural interaction, population decline, and ecological transformation that marked the coming of Spanish North America to California.[27]

The challenges and prospects of Spanish California emerge in the diary of Fray Pedro Font. Born in Cataluña in 1738, he studied at Querétaro's Santa Cruz College from 1763 to 1773. (He was thus in the Bajío for the conflicts of 1766 and 1767.) Assigned to the San José de Pimas mission in northern Sonora in 1773, he joined don Juan Bautista de Anza, a Sonora-born Presidio commander, on the second land expedition to California in September 1775. Font kept a revealing record of the soldiers and settlers who joined the trek and their encounters with uncolonized peoples, early missions, and the Monterey Presidio.[28]

The expedition, which left on 29 September, included ten veteran soldiers and twenty new enlistees (with 106 family members) assigned to Monterey, twenty muleteers, and four other families with seventeen members. Font later estimated a total of 240 people and over 1,000 head of livestock. It was a community in transit; there were births and deaths along the way. Our Lady of Guadalupe, "mother and protector of the *indios* of this America," would aid the group on its perilous journey. Heading north by old missions and new ranchos, early on the military escort fended off Apaches. Northern Sonora remained a conflict zone.[29]

In late October the expedition left the last mission and entered "lands of gentiles." Independent Pimas at the Gila River asked the fathers to stay, baptize them, and help fight their enemies; the Pimas cultivated a rich floodplain with irrigation canals, held a festival with the cross a prominent symbol, traded with mission natives (Pimas and others), and fought Apaches. Elsewhere Opatas met the expedition, showing bows and arrows yet ready to share maize and wheat. Cocomaris asked the Spaniards to sanction their leaders. Font met a world of conflict and exchange that linked Spaniards, mission residents, and independent people beyond the frontier.[30]

On 19 November the weary travelers reached the Yumas of the Colorado River basin. They were welcomed by a Captain Palma, who led his people in a dance that Font believed showed their ability to fight and destroy the newcomers—and a preference to negotiate for mutual benefit. The Spaniards answered with gunshots in the air and then offered to judge native disputes, punish transgressors, and facilitate trade, already evident in stacks of cloth from New Spain. The Colorado floodplain was sown in wheat—an adoption of the European staple beyond the frontier. Font offered a mission and Palma "became very pleased." The friar set classic terms: "It was essential that they agreed to learn the doctrine to become Christian; they must also build with brick, work as carpenters, plow the land, and labor, . . that they live together in a town, . . . and that they build a house for the Priest, and a church." Palma answered (according to Font): "with pleasure."[31]

The travelers left a friar among the Yuma, along with gifts and supplies to start a mission. Captain Palma dressed as a Spaniard to see off the caravan. In a long discourse on Yuma ways Font lamented lives "so free"; he was especially bothered by what he saw as a lack of sexual discipline that allowed freedom among youths and polygamy among elders. He abhorred "effeminate men." All would be corrected by the mission. Although they already harvested wheat and wore cotton and woolen cloth, he characterized the Yumas as "very lazy; if they were not they would harvest much more grain. They live content as long as the have enough to eat with abundance." The Colorado floodplain made abundance easy, limiting any dedication to labor that might produce surpluses. That too the mission would fix. Still, Font recognized the Yumas as "most happy, rich, and comfortable; they live on their lands and eat well with little trouble."[32]

In early December the expedition set off west across deserts toward distant peaks. On barren terrain desperate natives were quick to hunt Spanish livestock. To Font they were "thieving *indios*," "the most unfortunate in all the world, . . . so savage, wild, filthy, disheveled, and ugly." Others held back, watching the caravan pass. Font had no thought of a mission here.[33] Just after Christmas the desperate travelers crossed the San Gabriel Mountains. Soldiers scouted for *panino*, soils suggesting silver deposits. Some reported promising finds, and water for mining was everywhere. The dream of Spanish North America was alive as they descended into the San Gabriel (later Los Angeles) basin. Its rich plain seemed a paradise, until they were greeted by a soldier sent from the mission with fresh horses and news that natives had risen and killed a friar at San Diego in November.[34]

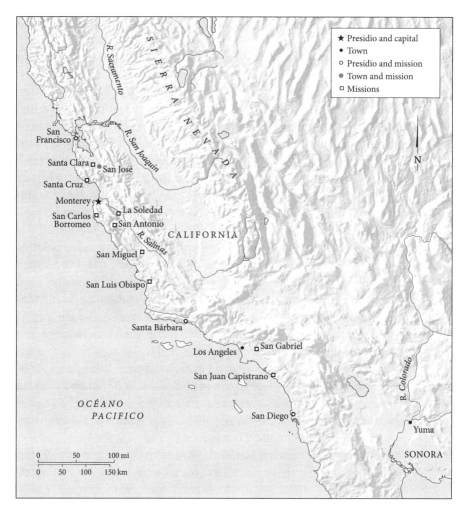

Spanish California, ca. 1800

Font arrived at San Gabriel on 4 January 1776. There were "canals and corn-fields." With irrigation, wheat would soon be planted too. There were cows, sheep, and chickens. Huts housed five hundred adults and children and their clergy, while another served as a church; a *jacalón*, a large hut, stored grain. The granary preceded construction of a mission chapel. To ensure discipline, barracks held eight soldiers. Natives could come and go until they were baptized: then they were not to return to the *rancherías*—free settlements. To enforce Christian monogamy, unmarried adolescent girls, once baptized, lived in a separate shelter.[35] The work of creating a sedentary community of Christian cultivators, organized in patriarchal families and producing a surplus under Franciscan oversight, was under way.

Font detoured south with an expedition sent to finish pacification at San Diego. He saw the problems that led to violence there. The mission had failed to establish cultivation—"it lacks provisions"—and allowed natives to continue to live scattered across the country, hunting, fishing, and bartering fish to support the mission. When a mix of baptized residents and their neighbors found mission demands unacceptable, their independence facilitated resistance and the killing of a friar, a carpenter, and a blacksmith.[36] They targeted men who brought European impositions and innovations without offering secure sustenance.

Late in February the expedition headed north. Crossing the sloping coastal plain of the Santa Bárbara Channel, Font saw a dense population that lived by fishing in large launches. The people were well fed, well armed, and traded with communities as distant as the Yumas of the Colorado floodplain. Earlier Spanish visitors included soldiers led by one Camacho. They had assaulted local women and as a result all soldiers were called "Camachos." Women along the channel hid as the expedition passed. Font noted that the combination of independent sustenance and an aversion to Spanish soldiers would inhibit mission efforts to come.[37] Early in March the travelers reached San Luis Obispo, a mission thriving with fertile lands and well-cultivated fields. A few days later they arrived at San Antonio de Robles, east of the coastal range. There construction had advanced to include adobe buildings, huertas, grain fields, and a corral.[38] Away from the coastal resources that eased native subsistence, early missions flourished by introducing cultivation and Christianity.

On 9 March the caravan found the southern sources of the Monterey (Salinas) River; there Font met "indios who spoke a bit of Spanish." A week later the travelers reached Monterey, where Presidio soldiers greeted them with artillery shot and rifle fire. Armed force, cultivation, European livestock, and Christianity were central to the mission enterprise. The next day Font visited nearby San Carlos Borromeo, the northernmost mission of New Spain, which included four hundred baptized natives who fished, kept huertas, and worked fields of grain. Irrigation works had not begun; Font blamed scarce workers. (Or did neophytes prefer fishing to hard labor digging canals?) Still, rich land and ample rain fed lush fields and a thriving mission. Font noted one problem: "The licentious ways of the soldiers who take up with indias."[39] Ethnic amalgamation began early, and was not always consensual.

On 23 March Anza and Font headed north toward San Francisco. At Cupertino they met armed but peaceful people; at San Mateo residents were so friendly that Font proposed a mission. On reaching the bay on 27 March he reported a vast opening to the sea, a fine anchorage, good land, and clean water—perfect for a fortress.[40] Awed by the vast estuary, the group trekked south around the bay, hiking across mountains on the far shore, only to face a central valley so dense in reed thickets that they could not go on. Around the bay they met villagers who fished from reed launches; many had never before seen a European. East of the bay they saw a canyon recalling "Guanajuato and its mines." The lure of silver was strong. Across the impenetrable central valley Font and Anza saw the Sierra Nevada.[41] Its gold would later complete the development of Spanish North America—under United States rule.

Fray Pedro Font understood the goals and challenges of mission colonization. To turn independent people into sedentary Christian cultivators living in monogamous patriarchal families, missionaries had to assure sustenance. To enforce mission discipline they needed soldiers. But soldiers had to live as Christian patriarchs, or else they alienated the people whom they were urging toward lives of Christian dependence. In California, friars and soldiers had to attempt all that far beyond the northern edge of Spanish North America. All the while, they kept an eye for the gold or silver that might energize the commercial economy they knew was the ultimate goal.

Spanish California developed rapidly after Font visited in 1776. The next year the San Francisco Presidio set a northern anchor for the region; new missions emerged at Santa Clara near San Francisco Bay and at San Juan Capistrano between San Gabriel and San Diego. By 1782 there were four presidios: San Diego, Santa Bárbara, Monterey, and San Francisco; there was a Spanish town at Los Angeles, another at San José near the south end of San Francisco Bay. By 1810 nineteen missions stretched from San Diego to Santa Clara.[42]

Most engaged distinct ethnic peoples, used their labor to build irrigation and plant fields of wheat and maize, introduced them to livestock grazing, and directed them toward sedentary lives of Christianity and patriarchy—men clearing and cultivating; wives making clothing, processing food, and caring for children; unmarried girls isolated to ensure monogamy. While missions defined residents as neophyte indios, most kept native languages and ethnic identities. With men working in estate fields and secondarily in family plots, periodically leaving to hunt and engage kin still in independent villages—and with children often baptized in advance of parents—mission kinship focused on mothers and children; fathers remained dependent insiders or independent outsiders.[43]

The majority of California natives never joined missions. They dealt with soldiers, friars, settlers, livestock, and mission residents in every other way: collaboration and confiscation, assault and adaptation, disease and death. Spanish California's population peaked above 21,000 around 1810, with over 2,500 settlers in presidios and pueblos and about 19,000 mission residents. Far larger, if uncounted, numbers of natives remained independent. Missions were imagined as indigenous communities under clerical care. They operated under Franciscan rule as mission-estates like those developed by the Jesuits in Sinaloa and Sonora. Residents split time between family plots and estate fields; they fed themselves, raised wheat and maize for towns and presidios, and tended growing herds.[44]

That these were estate enterprises was immediately clear to Jean François de la Pérouse, a French mariner who visited Monterey and San Carlos Borromeo in 1786. His first impressions were strong and positive: mission life was "without avarice," California was "inexpressably fertile," the potential for trade with China was "greater . . . than the richest mine of Mexico." The friars were "pious and prudent." Yet when they led him from Monterey to San Carlos, they were greeted "like lords of the manor." A tour of the mission shifted La Pérouse from European manors to colonial plantations. "They brought to our recollection a plantation at Santo Domingo or any other West Indian Island." There was a village of 50 huts for 740 residents, overshadowed by a brick and plaster granary. The common work areas, the numerous livestock, the sight of a few people in irons, the sound of others taking light lashings in the distance—all recalled the plantation experience.[45]

The Franciscans were both spiritual and temporal rulers of a community required to labor seven hours daily, and study and pray for two hours more. Unbaptized natives came and went; once they had been received to Catholicism, departure led to warnings and pursuit by soldiers. What really held people at the mission, however, was warfare with independent neighbors. There was little room for escape, little distance to flee pursuit by loyal residents or soldiers. Indigenous magistrates, elected from lists approved by the friars, were overseers. Men tilled fields and periodically hunted and fished; women ground corn, made cloth and clothing, and tended gardens and children. Mission residents were pressed to dependence, labor, and patriarchy, often the only refuge from conflicts with independent neighbors—"savages" to La Pérouse.[46] Mission-estates like San Carlos thrived into the 1800s. Their populations grew slowly while a larger number of independent people faced livestock invasion and smallpox.

Simultaneously a fully commercial Spanish North America began at presidios and pueblos like Los Angeles, founded in 1782 by migrants from Sinaloa, Sonora, and other regions of Spanish North America. They came in patriarchal households rewarded with house lots and grants of lands that included fields open to irrigation, other lands dependent on rain, and still others to be used for grazing. All was an advance to be repaid with ten years' residence and production; obligated work shaped the foundations of Los Angeles. Of twelve founding households two were headed by Spaniards, one (a bigamist) from Cádiz, the other from Chihuahua; both had married indias. Two founding patriarchs were negros, two mulattoes—all married to mulattas. Four indio patriarchs had wed two indias, a *coyote*, and a mulatta. One chino from Manila had married a girl of twelve—granted no category.[47] The founders of Los Angeles were quintessentially North American: Spaniards of mixed ancestry, mostly mulatto, already amalgamating, and resolutely patriarchal.

On arrival the newcomers stayed a league away from the San Gabriel mission. Several of their children were recovering from smallpox. The attempt to quarantine was surely ineffective; the plague that repeatedly facilitated Spanish colonization and devastated nations had arrived. The group that founded Los Angeles had come overland via Yuma territory and the Colorado crossing. Soon after they passed, a growing number of Hispanic settlers and their livestock invaded the floodplain (likely joined by smallpox); the Yumas rose, expelled their new Spanish neighbors, and closed the land route to California. People who had welcomed Anza and Font in 1775 seeking trade, tools, and alliance against native foes turned to violent resistance when invaded by newcomers who undermined local sustenance. As Fray Simón del Hierro had learned years before and Font well knew, the success of a mission required security of sustenance and alliance against enemies. The Yuma needed no help with sustenance; they already cultivated wheat and traded over long distances. When settlers invaded their economy they rebelled, leaving California a mission society linked by sea to New Spain and Spanish North America.[48]

Los Angeles grew steadily. Soldiers retiring at the Santa Bárbara presidio just north received land grants, settled in Los Angeles, married locally, and developed ranchos across the basin. They reinforced the Hispanic-mulatto community that ruled locally, holding office through early decades. They gained labor by trading with and hiring independent natives from nearby highlands, some baptized and others not (mission discipline had its limits). Sons of the mulatto settlers began to marry local women; their offspring reinforced the mulatto community. In 1790 the town had twenty-four patriarchal households led by twelve labradores (cultivators), five grazers, two shoemakers, a weaver, a blacksmith, a bricklayer, a tailor, and a servant. Spanish North America had arrived—if in small numbers.[49]

The absence of mineral wealth did not deter the development of trade tied to China, as Spanish North America refashioned itself for the last time under Spanish rule. In the 1780s La Pérouse saw promise in trade with China and hoped for a Bourbon alliance for profit. Spanish shipping was limited, mostly tying California to San Blas and South America. British and Russian vessels landed from the 1790s, buying supplies and sea otter skins coveted in Asia. After 1800 ships from Atlantic ports in the young United States, some landing as interlopers, others as neutrals in times of war, linked California to China. Missions and ranchos supplied the trade.[50] Spanish North America again built a commercial society, stimulating trade that reached beyond the empire to Asia.

Every society changes as it engages new environments and different people. Spanish North America began in the Bajío, an exceptionally fertile basin that was a frontier between state-ruled cultivators and nomadic hunters and gatherers. Franciscans accompanied the Otomí who founded Querétaro as a place of irrigation, trade, and textiles. Later, migration and commercial development accelerated as silver production boomed, and Spanish North America drove northward into drier regions. After the Bajío, California was the most fertile, potentially irrigable region incorporated in Spanish North America. Franciscans played a critical role there too. But the native majority in California fragmented into many linguistic groups, never before subject to state rule, unfamiliar with cultivation, and spared the stimulus of precious metals from 1769 to 1849. So California was different.

It began like other regions of Spanish North America where silver was scarce: missions struggled to draw natives to lives of Christian cultivation while stock grazing became the leading commercial activity. In 1810 Old World livestock, mostly cattle and sheep, exceeded 350,000 head in California. They displaced and replaced native people in a deadly transformation accelerated by smallpox and other infections. Simultaneously Hispanic farmers in the Los Angeles basin began to claim lands, build irrigation works, and mix cultivation with grazing—sometimes recruiting mission residents as workers and sometimes contracting with independent people who gained access to cloth, tools, and livestock without the pressures to conversion and cultural conformity that came with mission life. The friars opposed these links, ostensibly because growers dealt with gentiles, and surely also because the ranchos competed with missions in emerging markets. As in regions earlier facing such difficult transformations, long negotiations brought some natives to settled dependence, some to experiment with European ways and beliefs, some to resistance and flight, some to all of these over the years.[51] In 1810 a group of San Gabriel mission residents joined independent Mojaves in a plot against Spanish Los Angeles—until loyal neophytes leaked the plan. Baptized rebels outnumbered gentiles two to one among thirty-three captives; all were sentenced to labor at Presidio Santa Bárbara.[52] Cultural imposition, labor demands, and disease afflicted mission residents while proliferating livestock and disease displaced independent peoples. Imposition provoked resistance; repression aimed to take labor. All the while natives faced an era of death. California in 1810 was well along the trajectory toward mission adaptation, depopulation, livestock invasion, and ethnic amalgamation.

Yet the construction of Spanish North America remained incomplete in California. No rich mines drove the economy; estate-missions ruled near the coast and independent peoples dominated the interior when disputes over sovereignty in the Spanish empire set off the social revolution in the Bajío in 1810. Together they led to Mexican independence in 1821, and stalled the northward drive of the New World's most dynamic economy. Mexican liberals secularized the California missions in the 1830s, distributing their lands to profit-seeking entrepreneurs, freeing native survivors to live as laboring subordinates on commercial ranchos linked to Asian trade. When gold placers in the Sierra hit bonanza in 1849, California took its place at the center of a burgeoning world economy that mixed mining, irrigated agriculture, and commercial grazing, all dependent on native labor, in a society of ethnic complexity. The installation of Spanish North America was completed under United States rule.[53]

The Bajío, Spanish North America, and Spanish Mesoamerica: New Spain after 1780

The Viceroyalty of New Spain, reaching from Mexico City north to California and south into Central America, ruled Spanish North America and Spanish Mesoamerica. Two distinct colonial orders combined in the Americas' richest kingdom; their social and cultural dynamics were fundamentally different. While Spanish North America was thoroughly commercial, socially fluid, deeply patriarchal, and persistently expansive, Spanish Mesoamerica was structured by a Hispanic commercial sector grafted upon enduring indigenous republics. Landed self-governing communities defined Spanish Mesoamerica and included the vast majority of its people. Led by councils of notables who oversaw local justice, worship, and festivals, they regularly went to colonial courts to defend community rights. Regime officials, clergymen, and entrepreneurs dealt with indigenous republics through indigenous intermediaries.

Across New Spain there were reasons to be Spanish; people of mixed ancestry and ample wealth (or just local power) claimed Spanish status. In Spanish Mesoamerica there were enduring reasons to be indio. In native republics indio status brought rights to land, participation in local cultural and political life, and access to channels of judicial mediation that both limited and confirmed subordination. The result was an entrenched bifurcation of Spanish Mesoamerica into Spanish and indigenous sectors.

Spanish North America and Spanish Mesoamerica were different, but not separate. Mexico City, by far the largest city in the Americas in 1800, was the administrative, financial, and commercial capital of all New Spain, home to entrepreneurs who financed mines, ruled trade, and ran vast estates in both domains. The capital concentrated powers integrating North America and Mesoamerica; it showed characteristics of both. A majority of over 100,000 residents were classed as Spaniards, mestizos, and mulattoes in about equal numbers. They shared a commercial society where status depended on wealth and culture as much as on ancestry, reflecting the ways of Spanish North America. Mexico City also included the largest indigenous republics in Spain's Americas: San Juan Tenochtitlan and Santiago Tlatelolco. Indios of diverse ancestry and economic roles—some speaking Nahuatl, many Spanish; some living in barrios rooted in the Mesoamerican past, others fully engaged in the Spanish city—worked as artisans, traders, carriers, and more. Mexico City ruled and linked Spanish North America and Mesoamerica, mixing both in its urban complexity.[54]

Across Spanish Mesoamerica native republics remained the foundation of almost everything. Spanish power and commercial production were grafted onto landed communities, more or less intensely in diverse regions. Spanish commercial ways came first to the Puebla basin, between the Gulf and the capital. Puebla was a new colonial city, a center of trade and production in obrajes and craft shops. In the countryside commercial crops flourished in the seventeenth century. Many indigenous families became estate residents, while most remained villagers, cultivating for sustenance and working seasonally in estate fields. In the eighteenth century Puebla entrepreneurs faced competition from the Bajío; Puebla obrajes closed and its textile sector shrank, sustained as in the Bajío by struggling family producers. Commercial estates stagnated. Indio communities endured, perhaps taking a greater role in the regional economy. In 1810 Puebla led a region marked by enduring indigenous villages and a limited Hispanic overlay that included a growing number of mestizos and mulattoes.[55]

West of Puebla around Mexico City, commercial life concentrated in the city during the first colonial centuries. In the countryside native republics remained strong, supplying maize and pulque to Mexico City into the eighteenth century. Early estates raised European goods: sugar to the south around Cuernavaca, wheat at Chalco, livestock in the dry Mezquital. The commercial overlay in the basins around the capital was limited. Then in the eighteenth century silver soared at Taxco southwest of the capital before 1750, at Real del Monte into the 1760s, and through the century in the Bajío and regions north. Population and commercial life boomed in the capital. Its demand for produce soared while renewed population growth saw villagers consume most of local harvests. After 1750 many began to see land shortages. To meet rising urban demand, estates in the Valleys of Mexico and Toluca expanded maize production. To the northeast, from Otumba to Apan and the Mezquital, grazing estates turned to pulque. The commercial overlay expanded and intensified. But around Mexico City (in contrast to Puebla) estates recruited only small resident populations (often mestizos and mulattoes); they drew most workers seasonally from nearby communities, hiring men and boys to plant and harvest crops. As populations grew, villagers struggling in the face of land shortages remained villagers, cultivating what they could, earning wages as seasonal estate workers. Indigenous notables brokered that key labor relationship.[56]

The late colonial expansion of commercial cultivation near Mexico City depended on landed republics and the mediation of village elites. Spanish Mesoamerica endured, its bifurcation entrenched as commercial life flourished. By the late eighteenth century the valleys around Mexico City were hybrids in which commercial dynamics drove the economy while republics rooted in the Mesoamerican past adapted to sustain everything. Estates profited; republics survived; the economy boomed. Ties between estates and the community became symbiotic exploitations—unequal, exploitative, and stable.

In regions extending south of the central highlands, across Oaxaca, and into Chiapas, Yucatán, and Guatemala, indigenous communities remained the foundation of Spanish Mesoamerica. Commercial activity expanded there too in the eighteenth century, but without the stimulus of silver, market life was less intense. Near cities like Antequera in the Valley of Oaxaca, modest estates tapped community residents to raise crops for urban markets. In the Mixteca uplands of Oaxaca, indigenous communities produced cochineal, a dye valuable to European cloth makers.[57] In Yucatán estates developed among entrenched Maya communities in the late eighteenth century, tapping their workers to raise crops for Mérida and new Cuban sugar and slave plantations.[58] In highland Guatemala communities with staunch native elites upheld the colonial order. They maintained an economy of sustenance and regional markets, supplied the city of Guatemala, and provided workers to indigo estates developing along the coast around San Salvador.[59]

While enclaves of Hispanic society and commercial production expanded across the southern reaches of Spanish Mesoamerica during the late eighteenth century, generating new profits for local elites and new conflicts with indigenous republics, the latter remained the base of colonial life. Spaniards claimed modest profits; indigenous families defended communities, cultivated for sustenance, and sent workers to commercial estates; native notables clung to power and gained small profits as essential brokers; the courts mediated when conflict escaped local brokerage. Stability ruled as the nineteenth century began.[60]

Across Spanish Mesoamerica commercial production remained a graft on native republics. The key axis of power linked a Spanish sector (including minorities of mestizos and mulattoes) and an indigenous domain led by local notables heading communities of diverse Mesoamerican ancestry and language. The district magistrates and provincial clergy, rural traders and estate managers, and especially the indigenous notables who brokered between the sectors were pivotal to orchestrating and stabilizing Spanish Mesoamerica. Ethnic segmentation shaped enduring identities rooted in ancestral and linguistic differences. Religious ways reflected and contested segmented integration. Everyone was Christian, yet Spanish Catholicism tended to be institutional and sacramental while native worship leaned toward propitiatory devotions and festivals of integration. They remained in one church with a common clergy; near the capital they shared Guadalupe. When reformers promoted "rational" beliefs they were engaged and limited by communities led by local notables.[61]

Spanish Mesoamerica was also deeply patriarchal. Yet patriarchy worked differently there. In the Spanish sector it shaped entrepreneurial families and tied them to managers, traders, clerics, and others, replicating the ways of Spanish North America. But personal ties of patriarchy rarely reached from the heights of power to working men in native republics. Community governors and magistrates stood between them; they held lands and offices as community notables, not as awards from landlords, priests, or officials. When outsiders attempted to intervene they set off conflicts as often as they gained power.

Within the republics patriarchal norms ruled: notable men held office, led religious life, and organized work gangs to nearby estates; men worked most lands, and men and boys labored for wages. Women did inherit shares of family lands; they ruled local markets; they often led riots to force judicial mediations. Everyday life saw endless negotiations between men and women over household relations and community affairs. Patriarchy mattered. But in Spanish Mesoamerica the patriarchal order broke at the ethnic divide, reinforcing ethnic segmentation. Was patriarchy more hotly contested in the working families of indigenous republics, or did family conflicts more often get to the courts that mediated to stabilize life there? Brokerage among officials and clergy, estate managers and village notables was pivotal to organizing and stabilizing deepening inequalities in Spanish Mesoamerica.[62]

In Spanish Mesoamerica capitalism shaped Spanish cities and commercial estates, working through diverse brokers to penetrate landed indigenous republics. In the more commercially dynamic regions near the capital, estate managers worked with village labor captains to draw seasonal hands to expanding commercial fields. Across the South district magistrates traded to extract limited produce from villages that still ruled rural production. Tied to the world of silver production and trade by Mexico City financiers, Spanish Mesoamerica remained a bifurcated and brokered society stretching south from Mexico City. Its commercial dynamism was limited by the enduring resilience of the indigenous republics; its social stability was reinforced by the same resilience, backed by the regime's continuing emphasis on judicial mediation and conciliation.

As the nineteenth century began, the kingdom of New Spain combined Spanish North America and Spanish Mesoamerica, each in its way generating great wealth for entrepreneurs and rising revenues for the Spanish Empire. After 1785 commercial growth, rising prices, land shortages, and stagnant or falling earnings forced new pressures on people across the Bajío and in landed republics near the capital. Yet the stabilization of hierarchical patriarchy in the Bajío and the mediations of village notables and colonial courts in the regions around the capital kept both societies at work. The economy grew in both regions.

Soaring silver production still stimulated global trade. Silver taxes, alcabala revenues on commercial sales, and tributes of indios and mulattoes channeled enormous revenues to the regime—funds that sustained its rule across New Spain, Cuba, and the Caribbean (including Louisiana). As Atlantic wars escalated in the 1790s New Spain's revenues funded Madrid, its French allies, and their British foes. The profits and revenues taken from New Spain before 1808 neither undermined the economy, destabilized the polity, nor provoked widespread unrest.[63] The fusion of Spanish North America and Spanish Mesoamerica made New Spain an engine of Atlantic trade to 1810.

The Other North America:
Struggling to Create United States

While New Spain's silver economy integrated Mesoamerica, the Bajío, and North America, and Spanish North America drove north across California after 1770, the rest of the Atlantic world faced unprecedented conflicts and profound uncertainties. The mainland colonies of British North America became the first American nation, only to struggle with deep divisions, enduring difficulties, and uncertain successes. Like New Spain, British North America included diverse societies. In the North most colonists were British (or from other parts of Europe). Most natives were excluded, pushed inland beyond frontiers of conflict and trade, leaving production and labor mostly to colonists. Northerly cities were the domain of traders, officials, clergy, and artisans. The country was home to communities of cultivators who also fished, cut timber, and worked in crafts, producing for sustenance and trade. Cities and villages were integrated by churches, and by a patriarchal order. Like Spanish North America, Northern British America was commercial, patriarchal, and hierarchical. But having excluded natives, and with few African slaves, it lacked the cultural complexity of Spanish North America. And it lacked the engine of silver or any comparable commercial product.[64]

The southern colonies of British North America were mainland variants of the slave societies of the greater Caribbean. Driven by commodity exports, their tobacco, indigo, rice, and wheat were no match for the islands' sugar. These plantation colonies were organized by slave labor and a racial divide. Slavery dominated a bit less in mainland plantation colonies; vast hinterlands allowed room for free farmers and their families. Planters negotiated the difference by creating a sharp racial divide, asserting that whiteness united planters, free farmers, and their families—for none were black or enslaved.[65] Patriarchy was important, but limited as slave men struggled to head families. The southern colonies of mainland British America were bifurcated like Spanish Mesoamerica, but slavery imposed bluntly coercive exploitation, while New Spain's indigenous republics allowed local rights, cultural refuge, and negotiated, often symbiotic exploitation.

British North America, like New Spain, divided between a more socially fluid North organized by patriarchy and a bifurcated South shaped by a sharp cultural divide. The Bajío and Spanish North America, thanks to silver, were far more economically dynamic, profitable to entrepreneurs, and productive of regime revenues than northern British America. Spanish Mesoamerica, with silver and commercial estates around Mexico City and cochineal to the south, was also profitable to entrepreneurs—surely as profitable as the slave colonies of the British American South. And British North America lacked a center like Mexico City, a New World capital that integrated regime rule and financial power, and generated unmatched revenues and trade.

The coastal provinces of British America, poor colonies marginal to the Atlantic economy and costly to the British regime, moved early to independence. In the process they set off persistent conflicts, political, economic, social, and racial, as they struggled to become united states. Resistance to imperial taxes and to limits on westward expansion into independent natives' domains began in the 1760s, escalating into a war for independence in the 1770s. With help from France and Spain (and funds from New Spain), British North America became the United States early in the 1780s. Victory did not bring unity or prosperity, however. Congresses ruling under the Articles of Confederation found consensus rare as war ended. Debates escalated over taxes, tariffs, and economic policies, and over national powers and states rights. Conflicts over slavery and the slave trade allowed northerners to support democratic ideals without fear of economic loss; southern planters saw power, profit, and a way of life threatened.

Removed from empire, the economy struggled. Across the northern interior, farmers who had fought for political independence faced debts; they clashed with urban creditors, who aimed to profit with little concern for producers' autonomy. Conflict peaked during Shays's Rebellion, a rising of Massachusetts farmers who refused to accept that independence meant ceding land to rich financiers. Meanwhile northern farmers joined southern planters and farmers in pursuing settlement beyond the Appalachian ridge. British North Americans sought independence to expand westward; indigenous nations, their independence assaulted, fought back in endless skirmishes and Pontiac's rebellion.[66]

Conflict and uncertainty led to a new constitution in 1787. It strengthened the federal government and limited state autonomy; it protected creditors and slavery, and entrenched the power of slaveholders by denying citizenship (and more) to slaves, even while counting them as two-thirds of a person (giving exceptional representation to their owners). The new constitution, promoted by southern slaveholders and northern merchant-creditors, was controversial and ratified in close, often challenged contests.[67]

Early optimism for the presidency of George Washington gave way to deep division. Alexander Hamilton, secretary of the treasury, led nationalists in promoting banks, commerce, and urban development.

Opposition coalesced around the secretary of state, Thomas Jefferson, author of the Declaration of Independence, wartime governor of Virginia, and ambassador to France at the outbreak of the French Revolution. He assembled a coalition of slaveholding planters and free farmers, defending slavery (which he intellectually rejected) and agrarian independence against a commercializing urban North. Factional conflict heightened in reaction to the French revolution, which Jefferson celebrated as a liberating extension of his Declaration and Hamilton condemned as a threat to order, property, commerce, and profit.[68]

Economic trends in the 1790s sustained both factions: British industrialization stimulated demand for cotton, driving plantations and slavery across the South toward the Mississippi (and escalating conflicts with natives). War between Britain and France left traders and ships from Boston to Baltimore neutrals free to trade (allowing United States merchants to gain silver from the Bajío and sea otter skins from California—both sent to China). A southern society of cotton plantations worked by slaves and sustained by free yeoman farmers expanded. So did a northern world of trade and profit—and few slaves. Both factions strengthened; each presumed a right to displace Native Americans. Some promised missions to incorporate and transform recalcitrant natives; all were quick to crush indigenous resistance.[69]

Factionalism wracked the early republic. Amid wartime prosperity and uncertainty, political divisions deepened. Conflicts over taxes, lands, and western settlement led to insurgency, notably the Whiskey Rebellion of 1793 on the Pennsylvania frontier, a rising crushed by federal armies. Factional strife peaked in the election of 1800. Threats of secession and armed conflict were averted in a compromise that gave Jefferson the presidency, a deal engineered when Gabriel's rebellion at Richmond, Virginia, fueled fears of a Haitian revolution in the Tidewater, reminding the powerful of the need for unity against those they ruled. The Union survived along with political divisions, economic uncertainty, and slavery.[70]

Into the 1800s cotton and slavery spread across the South and into Louisiana territories acquired from Spain (via Napoleon) in 1803. Trade and profit continued to grow in northern ports, provoking conflict with European belligerents who resented Anglo-American profiteering while they fought costly wars. In 1808 embargoes blocked United Sates trade and forced an unwanted shift toward self-reliance and internal development. War with Britain came in 1812.[71] Around 1800 there was no sure sign that the United States would survive as one nation or that it would prosper, even as the slave economy expanded and northern regions responded to embargo with hesitant moves toward industry.

Spanish North America flourished, extending into Texas, consolidating in New Mexico, and building California, while the United States remained a young nation of conflict and uncertain opportunity.

The Bajío and New Spain in the Atlantic Crucible

Conflict escalated across the Atlantic world from the 1770s. While the young United States fought for independence, indigenous uprisings shook the colonial order across the Andean highlands of Spanish South America from Cuzco to Potosí in the early 1780s. They challenged Spanish power and colonial inequities for years, until the powerful reestablished an alliance for repression, allowing the regime to reassert power and reset key institutions. Spanish rule persisted for another four decades, but the silver economy that had been so strong there in the sixteenth and seventeenth centuries never fully revived.[72]

The North American republic had barely written its constitution when elites in Minas Gerais, Brazil's gold region, conspired to plot independence from Portugal. Facing declining mines and Portuguese pressure for revenues, they struggled to imagine how to fight a war for liberation without liberating their slaves. They could not act before they were discovered by authorities in 1789.[73] Later that year France, facing debts left by the costs of supporting the independence of the United States against Britain, collapsed into the revolution that defined all revolutions. Then in the 1790s conflicts in Saint-Domingue over who might claim the rights of Frenchmen led to the Haitian revolution, the end of slavery and plantation production, and the second American nation after 1800.[74] Meanwhile war between England and revolutionary France consumed Europe, facilitated the Haitian revolution, prejudiced the United States, and threatened Spain and its colonies.

From the 1770s to 1810 wars and social conflicts challenged the Atlantic world. The transition from the multi-centered global capitalism—in which the Atlantic empires were key participants—to modern Anglo-centered industrial capitalism—in which Atlantic empires fragmented into nation-states—was under way. Still, the unbroken dynamism of the Bajío and Spanish North America, yielding unprecedented silver flows that sustained Spanish power and global trades, showed that the world of early capitalism carried on. So did the continuing conflicts between Britain, France, and Spain for Atlantic dominance, and enduring Chinese hegemony in Asia. Britain was beginning to pioneer the integration of fossil fuels, machines, and factory labor in ways that would soon define its hegemony and reshape capitalism;

it was already asserting power in India and looking toward China. But until Napoleon invaded Spain in 1808 conflicts escalated—yet the first global commercial order held.

Everything changed between 1808 and 1815: the Spanish empire broke, setting off wars that created new nations with uncertain economies across the Americas. In 1810 the Bajío collapsed into a social revolution that undermined silver production and restructured life in its protean capitalist society. By 1815 Britain was victorious in war and industrialization; its hegemony in Europe and the Atlantic world was set. It recognized United States independence at the end of the War of 1812, enabling its former colonies to consolidate a political stability that allowed cotton and slave plantations to drive across the South, sustaining British industry. Brazil soon proved the one American colony to become a nation without devastating wars and deep economic uncertainties. Its old northern sugar and slave economy and new southern coffee and slave economy flourished in good part thanks to British merchants and markets—again fueling British wealth and power.

In less than a decade the collapse of the Spanish empire, followed by the revolution that brought down silver production in the Bajío and Spanish North America—inseparable conflicts—combined with Britain's victory in Europe, industrial innovation, and new ways to draw resources, wealth, and power from American regions no longer held as colonies—inseparable developments—to set a new course for capitalism. British industry and empire ruled, shaping trade in an Atlantic world redefined by American nations, driving power and trade across South Asia toward China. Meanwhile Mexico struggled to become a nation and forge a new economy. Soon enough the United States would take advantage of Mexico's struggles to claim much of Spanish North America, incorporating its resources and capitalist ways, and accelerating its own rise to global hegemony.[75]

Epilogue

Toward Unimagined Revolution

✦ BEFORE 1808 NO ONE IN THE BAJÍO imagined the breakdown of the Spanish empire, the Hidalgo revolt, or the social revolution that followed. While provincial elites resented escalating demands for revenues, including the recall of ecclesiastical mortgages in the consolidation that began in 1804, they grumbled, negotiated, and paid. Entrepreneurs struggled during uncertain times, especially in textile markets as years of blockade alternated with periods of open trade. Still, most found profits in an economy driven by silver, population growth, and commercial cultivation. Meanwhile working producers, urban and rural, faced deepening poverty, frustrating insecurities, and threats to patriarchy. But while the economy prospered and the regime held on, few challenged prevailing ways. Revenue demands and economic uncertainties frustrated elites, especially those without the resources of a patriarch like don José Sánchez Espinosa. Worsening poverty, insecurity, and threats to patriarchy angered many in working families, creating tensions revealed in local contests at Puerto de Nieto, La Griega, and other communities. Yet frustrations among provincial elites and producing families remained just that—frustrations lived differently in diverse communities, negotiated within patriarchal hierarchies, and debated within evolving religious understandings.

Only after Napoleon invaded Spain, took Madrid in May 1808, and claimed the Crown for his brother, proclaimed José I, did an unforeseen sequence of events set off the conflicts that brought revolution to the Bajío. People in Madrid (memorialized in Goya's famous Third of May paintings) and across the Spanish countryside resisted Napoleonic rule. Legitimate sovereignty broke; resistance fighters—guerrillas—rose across the peninsula. Political actors knew that vacated sovereignty reverted to the pueblos—organized communities. They fought to reconstruct sovereignty, first in local councils called juntas, later by calling a Cortes, the Spanish parliament dormant under Bourbon rule but not forgotten by the political classes. What Napoleon envisioned as a conquest of Spain and a taking of its American revenues set off political and social conflicts that led to peninsular campaigns, the liberal constitution of 1812, wars for independence across Spanish America, and social revolution in the Bajío.[1]

When news of Napoleonic occupation arrived in New Spain in the summer of 1808, the key question was clear to regime officials and colonial elites: how did a colonial kingdom without a legitimate king find, or recreate, sovereignty? The viceroy don José de Iturrigaray and the Mexico city council called for a Mexican junta to join in the reconstitution of sovereignty, and perhaps to rule locally in the interim. The judges of the High Court allied with the merchants of Mexico City's Consulado to reject that call to participation, demanding instead recognition of the political forces moving toward a Cortes in Spain. They deposed Iturrigaray in a coup that blocked the first movement for Mexican sovereignty. Neither the viceroy nor the city council resisted, surely conscious of Haiti, where elites fighting about rights and liberties began conflicts that led to a transforming popular revolution.[2]

From the fall of 1808 officials and entrepreneurs in Mexico City negotiated power in the colonial capital while in Spain diverse groups fought Napoleon and struggled toward a liberal regime. Many provincials, however, rejected the presumption that sovereignty and its reconstruction belonged only to the pueblos of Spain. In Valladollid, capital of the Intendency of Michoacán, seat of the bishopric that included the Bajío, landlords, traders, militia officers, clergy, and indigenous notables met to seek a provincial junta that would allow them a part in remaking sovereignty. When authorities broke their movement another appeared at Querétaro, with extensions into San Miguel and Dolores. Again provincial elites met to discuss sovereignty and debate how to proceed. When officials arrested participants at Querétaro in September 1810, allies at San Miguel (don Ignacio de Allende) and Dolores (the priest don Miguel Hidalgo) provoked an insurgency that soon mobilized thousands of estate residents and mineworkers, who asserted their own visions of popular sovereignty.

Neither the Hidalgo revolt nor the regional revolution that followed came inevitably out of the capitalist trajectory of Bajío development, nor from the polarization that marked the region after 1770. Only after the mounting grievances generated by long developing social pressures and cultural polarization merged with the unprecedented challenge to legitimate sovereignty of 1808, and both mixed with dearth, famine, and profiteering, did the rising that began at Dolores lead to the breakdown of the colonial order and a decade of revolutionary violence. No one envisioned that transforming conflict. Without decades of deepening polarization culminating in challenges to working men's patriarchy, the conflicts that began in 1808 would likely have remained contests among the politically engaged few. Without the Napoleonic intrusion and the political crisis it created, Bajío capitalism and its social and cultural polarities might have carried on indefinitely. Without the desperate scarcities of 1808 to 1810 and the public profiteering by deeply religious entrepreneurs like don José Sánchez Espinosa, would the grievances afflicting so many have come into the sharp relief that led large numbers to take the moral and physical risks of insurgency?

The confluence of all this led to the Hidalgo revolt and its revolutionary aftermath. Those conflicts were never imagined by their leaders or their diverse participants; they were neither planned nor controlled. They did transform the Bajío, North America, and the Atlantic world, and were an important part of the shift of global capitalism from centuries of multi-centered commercial origins to times of Anglo-centered industrial expansion.

The explosion of the Hidalgo revolt in September 1810 is celebrated as Mexico's declaration for independence. After the defeat of that rising in January 1811 José María Morelos and others led a continuing fight for political sovereignty. Its focus shifted south of the Bajío, and by 1813 it was a war for independence. The same year, however, a deadly typhus epidemic struck and inhibited mobilization. The defeat of Napoleon in 1814 brought back the Bourbon monarchy under Fernando VII, who quickly abrogated the much-debated liberal charter proclaimed in his name (and in his absence) at Cádiz in 1812. The drive for political independence was moribund in New Spain after 1815—alive mostly in isolated uplands and coastal lowlands.[3]

The social conflicts that concentrated in the Bajío proved more enduring. During the fall of 1810 Hidalgo and his insurgent populace enabled workers to take over the great mining city of Guanajuato. After the defeat of that first rising, the center of the silver economy was held by loyal forces, yet years of conflict became a decade of siege. Mining carried on, but scarce capital and uncertain supplies from a region held by insurgents kept risks high, yields low, and workers testy. The Bajío countryside seemed in constant turmoil, though years of insurgency alternated with months of peace on the bottomlands and around León. The amalgamating estate communities around Dolores and San

Miguel, including Puerto de Nieto, joined Hidalgo in 1810 and then sustained renewed insurgency from early 1812 into 1820. They took the land, expelled owners and managers, and built ranchos (often run by women while men fought) to support families and insurgent bands. Risings were limited in the ethnically polarized communities of Querétaro. The men of La Griega stayed at work, maintaining estate production, royalist forces, and family patriarchy during years of conflict. Still, insurgency cut mining and assaulted agrarian capitalism across most of the Bajío.[4]

Guanajuato's mines were periodically abandoned and eventually flooded; the great Valenciana drowned for lack of investment in drainage in 1820. Most obrajes collapsed as spinning and weaving dispersed across the countryside. When pacification finally came from 1818 to 1820, insurgents had to recognize estate property. But across a long-contested countryside (including at Puerto de Nieto), families kept the ranchos they had created during the insurgency. They became tenants paying small rents to maintain family production.

When military officers and landed entrepreneurs who had joined forces to end the insurgency in 1820 allied again behind don Agustín Iturbide to break with Spain in 1821, they faced a Bajío transformed by revolution. Large-scale estate cultivation to profit from food scarcity had all but vanished; so had food scarcity. Landlords proclaimed the economy destroyed; new state governments in Guanajuato and Querétaro lamented scarce revenues. Meanwhile families worked the land, paid rents (irregularly), and flooded regional markets with cheap and plentiful food. Women kept roles as heads of tenant households, and apparently found other ways to assert their independence. The first governor of independent Guanajuato complained of insubordinate women. Patriarchy faced challenge as the commercial economy collapsed.

In the wake of wars for independence and a Bajío revolution, efforts to create a Mexican nation brought decades of conflict. Attempts to build a national regime faced the inherent challenge of fusing the differing social and cultural ways of Spanish Mesoamerica and Spanish North America into a homogeneous political system. The sharp decline of silver production inhibited attempts to revive the commercial economy; a decade of revolution in the Bajío, along with less enduring and transforming mobilizations elsewhere, made the reimposition of social subordination after 1820 uncertain and often contested. The post-independence decades of conflict in the new Mexican nation did not result from enduring colonial traditions; they resulted from the attempt to force two societies with radically different pre-Hispanic and colonial histories into one nation—difficulties exacerbated by the revolution that transformed the Bajío, undermining its once dynamic economy, challenging patriarchy, and facilitating assertions of popular autonomy.

The Bajío revolution of 1810 to 1820 turned the most capitalist society in the Americas into a region of family production, entrepreneurial insecurity, and uncertain patriarchy. Popular welfare, the goal of most Bajío insurgents, improved. Predatory profit taking all but collapsed; revenues to sustain state power became scarce; and the provision of silver to the world economy plummeted, marking the end of a long eighteenth century of global expansion. The Spanish North American economy that had integrated regions from Mexico City, through the Bajío, and far to the north broke into fragments. Northward expansion slowed. Frontier zones from Texas to California, long linked to the dynamic Bajío, became isolated. Profit seeking at their core, commercial at their bases—they looked for new links to a changing capitalist world.

The Bajío revolution that inhibited the construction of a Mexican state and slowed northward expansion helped open the way for the westward expansion of a United States finally surmounting post-independence conflicts and uncertainties after 1820. In 1846 the United States—seventy-five years a nation, industrializing in the North, profiting from the expansion of cotton and slavery across the South—provoked a war to claim the northern territories of Mexico— only twenty-five years a nation and facing enduring political conflicts and economic uncertainties (like the United States around 1800). The war allowed the United States to incorporate the commercial ways and vast territories for expansion that shaped Spanish North America.

After 1847 North American power and capitalist dynamism belonged to the United States. As the Haitian revolution freed slaves and ended plantation production in Saint-Domingue, yet opened the way for the expansion of plantations and slavery in Cuba and Brazil, so the Bajío revolution halted mining and turned cultivation and cloth production into family activities, reversing the trajectory of the most capitalist region of the Americas and facilitating the expansion of Anglo-American capitalism. Popular risings claimed essential liberations for the people of Haiti and new control of production for families across the Bajío. The powers of capitalism were deflected locally, only to fill in elsewhere, accelerating where they could.

Bajío revolutionaries, men and women, claimed new autonomy for themselves and many neighbors. Their success slowed the creation of a Mexican nation, a construct imagined mostly by men seeking profit and power. The resulting challenges to national consolidation helped the United States to conquer the northern outposts of Hispanic North

America, accelerating there the capitalist ways that Bajío insurgents fought to constrain. Contradictions rooted in entrepreneurial goals, regime roles, and popular adaptations, and after 1810 in violent confrontations, shaped and reshaped the Bajío, North America, Atlantic power — and capitalism.

Acknowledgments

I NEVER PLANNED TO WRITE THIS BOOK. When I began I thought I had an opportunity to offer a new analysis of popular participation in the decade of insurgency that reshaped life in the Bajío after 1810. Thanks to detailed records of the life and business dealings of don José Sánchez Espinosa from 1780 to 1827, and of production and labor relations at La Griega and Puerto de Nieto between 1811 and 1827, I expected to bring new understanding to the wars that led to Mexican independence and the struggles that shaped the new nation. But as I learned more about the world of entrepreneurship that made Sánchez Espinosa powerful before 1810, and about the lives, work, and cultural conversations of the families living at the two estate communities, I began to see a society more capitalist than I had imagined deep in the interior of New Spain. That conclusion led to this analysis of the Bajío and Spanish North America before 1810. A second volume will focus on the decade of insurrection and its transforming consequences.

As the project became larger and more ambitious my dependence on colleagues and other scholars became greater. My debts are vast.

At the University of Texas, Austin, James Lockhart initiated me into the challenges of research on colonial Latin America and introduced me to many of its sources. He taught me to do social history. We have not always agreed on approaches or conclusions, but I could not have undertaken this project without mobilizing everything he taught me. The late Nettie Lee Benson urged me to appreciate Mexican politics in the independence era; she brought me to nineteenth-century authors and nineteenth-century sources. Scholars of Mexico are returning to questions she raised decades ago. The anthropologist Richard Adams introduced me to social theory and encouraged me to study the big picture over the long term. He insisted that analysis of any community, region, or nation must attend to the hierarchies of power that structure life within—and the external links that aid some and constrain others. My learning with him informs this work in key ways. Richard Graham wrote Brazilian history in Atlantic perspective before it was fashionable; he insisted that there is always another question to ask. Standish Meacham brought me to the debates about Britain, industry, and capitalism that inform the analysis here.

Undergraduate students, first at St. Olaf and Carleton colleges, now at Georgetown, pressed me to do history that takes on questions that matter and to offer my views in accessible ways. I am still trying. Graduate students keep drawing me to new perspectives. At Boston College I was reminded by Erin O'Conner that gender matters and by Jennifer Dorsey that Latin America is part of a larger world, a role she continued at Georgetown. There Theresa Alfaro-Velcamp, Alberto Fierro, Michael Coventry, Gillian McGillivray, Veronica Vallejo, and Larisa Veloz kept politics, gender, and culture together. Theresa and Larisa added migration; Gillian saw working communities as central; Veronica linked gender and religion. Emilio Coral and Luis Fernando Granados insisted that Mexico's cities are as important as rural communities. Rodolfo Fernández joined me in focusing on the North, its differences, and its importance. George Vrtis and Ben Fulwider linked ecological bases, state policies, production, and labor relations. With similar concerns, Linda Ivey brought me to California before I knew that it belonged in this book. Luis Fernando Granados, Elizabeth Chávez, and Fernando Pérez showed new ways to understand indigenous peoples facing state powers. Every student in my colloquium on global power and local culture in Latin America since 1990 helped to advance this project. The real reward of teaching is the chance to learn with students.

Patrick Carroll and Jonathan Brown have been friends and colleagues since graduate school. They read an early version of the full manuscript, providing key suggestions. Brian Owensby, whom I came to know more recently (first as a scholar, then as my daughter María's best teacher), read the full text, reread revisions, and offered encouragement and advice that made this a better book. While the project evolved I was privileged to be part of the international group of scholars brought together by Leticia Reina and Elisa Servín to rethink the long course of Mexican history. We produced two books, leading me to write essays on Mexico in global context. The group shaped perspectives that mark this history.

Opportunities to share sections of the work with others brought challenges and new ideas. Mary Kay Vaughan's seminar at the University of Maryland helped me forward in early going. Colleagues in the annual Washington Area Seminar on the History of Latin America took on my foray into cultural questions; Barbara Weinstein was notably probing and encouraging. Sessions organized by Pat Carroll at Texas A&M, Corpus Christi, and Jon Brown at UT Austin allowed me to offer some of my more far-reaching conclusions—and face the challenges they provoked. Near the end Luis Fernando Granados and Emilio Kourí organized sessions with faculty and students at the University of Chicago, leading me to sharpen the perspectives in the Prologue.

The Georgetown History Department has been pivotal to my ability to write this book. It recruited me nearly two decades ago to join in forging a community of scholars dedicated to seeing history in global perspective. Tom Klubock was at Georgetown when I began this project. He took the time to read drafts of four chapters that later expanded to become this volume. He saw that I was on to something—and that the work needed to improve in many ways. His advice and his perspectives on gender and labor informed the long process that followed. My colleagues then honored and burdened me with the opportunity to chair the department from 2003 to 2009, a role that slowed completion of the book—while the time made it better. Richard Stites, now departed and deeply missed, drew me to become chair, pressed me to finish the book, and in constant banter led me to a title for the book that I could not find without him. John McNeill has been essential, allowing me to survive by serving as director of graduate studies while stimulating me to write a better book. A scholar grounded in the Americas and dedicated to global understanding, he demands that regional histories be understood in global and comparative contexts.

At a pivotal moment John convened a seminar of colleagues to engage the manuscript (a role that he takes regularly). In that gathering, other venues, and continuing conversations, Alison Games pressed me to refine my Atlantic understanding; the late Faruk Tabak insisted that I take the role of silver more seriously; Adam Rothman and Bryan McCann helped me see urban life; Maurice Jackson brought perspective on ethnicity and resistance; Erick Langer challenged me to improve my grasp of rural communities; Meredith McKittrick, Tommaso Astarita, Amy Leonard, and David Collins helped me deal with gender and religion; David Painter and Michael Kazin pressed me to demonstrate, not just assert, that the Bajío and Spanish North America were important to United States history. Chandra Manning, Joe McCartin, and Katie Benton-Cohen have joined me (and Tom Klubock) in placing patriarchy at the center of politically informed, labor-based social histories. Their work convinced me that we are on to something. Early on John McNeill and Adam Rothman made the comparative and conceptual materials in the Introduction clearer. Later John McNeill and Micah Muscolino made the Prologue stronger in its global aspirations.

Jane McAuliffe, now president of Bryn Mawr College, was dean of Georgetown College during most of my time as history chair. She made it possible to continue the work of building a strong department, helping us to recruit and grant tenure to a group of amazing young teaching scholars and enabling us to retain essential senior colleagues. She made being chair worthwhile, and gave me space and encouragement to keep my scholarship alive. She founded the Georgetown Americas Initiative and gave me the opportunity to lead it. Its monthly faculty seminars continue to gather colleagues from many disciplines to share texts that engage problems across the hemisphere. Americas conferences link Georgetown scholars with others in dialogues about challenges facing Americans in global context. Few deans are so effective—and stimulate such creativity.

Financial support for a project that was built on decades of research came from many institutions. Some of the research was done while I was a doctoral student supported by the University of Texas, more while I was a Fulbright-Hays fellow in Mexico in 1973. Most came during the years since. The National Endowment for the Humanities has sustained my work in many ways—most recently with a year of fellowship support in 2002–3. At Georgetown the School of Foreign Service (my other academic home), the Graduate School, and the History Department repeatedly found resources to support this project, sending me to Mexico and to Austin when I needed archives and libraries. I gained essential help from archivists and librarians at the University of Texas (from Nettie Lee Benson to Adán Benavides), Washington State University, the Library of Congress (where Barbara Tenenbaum saved me at a difficult moment), and the Archivo General de la Nación in Mexico City (culminating with its director Aurora Gómez).

Most scholarly acknowledgments would end here. But this work combines my archival research with sources discovered, published, and analyzed by others. I could not have written a history of a complex region covering three centuries without depending on their contributions. Every citation of a scholar's work is an acknowledgment. A few are so important that I must note them here. David Brading's Bajío trilogy inspired my work and made my analysis possible; so did his publication of key sources, his study of Spanish-American intellectual life, his work on Our Lady of Guadalupe. Early on he encouraged me personally. This book builds on everything he has contributed. The same can be said for Felipe Castro Gutiérrez. My portrayal of the conflicts of the 1760s relies on his analysis and his publication of don José de Gálvez's long report. I have gained encouragement, inspiration, and insight from William Taylor throughout my career. Though he studied the Bajío only tangentially, much of my understanding, especially of justice and religion, follows his leads. Brian Owensby's new book on justice solidified everything.

I depend most concretely on Mexican scholars committed to local and regional histories. For Querétaro, I could not have generated my analysis without documents published and analyses offered by José Ignacio Urquiola Permisán and Juan Ricardo Jiménez Gómez. On the Bajío bottomlands I rely on census materials published by Alberto Carrillo Cázares. For Guanajuato, analyses and documents published by Isauro Rionda Arreguín and María Guevara Sangines are essential. María's research and understanding of the African-origin population of Guanajuato turned my hunches into understanding. Her work needs to be engaged by scholars of slavery and African peoples across the Americas.

Many more have contributed essential insights and materials: Steve Stern on patriarchy; Yolanda Lastra on the Otomí; Carlos Sempat Assadurian on early colonization; Susan Deeds and Chantal Cramaussel on seventeenth-century expansion; Patricia Osante on New Santander; Susan Deans-Smith and Carmen Imelda González Gómez on the Querétaro tobacco factory and its women workers; Dorothy Tanck de Estrada and Gerardo Lara Cisneros on eighteenth-century indigenous communities and their religious ways; Juliana Barr on Texas, Ramón Gutiérrez, James Brooks, and Ross Frank on New Mexico; and Marta Soto Ortega and Stephen Hackel on California. All helped me make this work more than a monograph. I have learned from every scholar recognized here, and the many more cited in the notes. I am responsible for my reading of their work—and the history of the Bajío and Spanish North America that I built with their help.

Carlos Preciado de Alba's work on nineteenth-century Guanajuato will inform the sequel to this book. He and Luis Ernesto Camarillo Ramírez took me on a tour of the historic mines of Guanajuato that led to photos and gave me a sense of the unique dimensions of life in the canyon city shaped by the mines (and mineworkers) of its rugged mountain environs.

Valerie Millholland, ably assisted by Miriam Angress, encouraged and facilitated this project in many ways. She was interested before I knew what I was doing; when I thought I saw the dimensions of the work, she offered a contract; she remained patient as I continued to learn about the Bajío, its place in North America, its role in global capitalism. She arranged for readers—anonymous, so I can't thank them personally—who saw importance in the manuscript, pressed me to make it better, and made key suggestions about how to do so. At a pivotal point Valerie gave sage advice: Noting how long I had worked on this project, she told me that it was more important to make it as strong as I could rather than deliver it quickly. I have tried—and I think the gains have been worth the delay.

William Nelson drew the maps with skill and good cheer; Amy Rogers Hays, pursuing her own work in history at Georgetown, made the manuscript ready for press. María Tutino and Israel Gutiérrez joined the excursion to take the photos that illustrate the volume. Fred Kameny, Managing Editor at Duke, took on the challenge of making a long and complex text clearer than I had written it, making suggestions with skill, dealing with my responses with humanity. I expect readers will thank him.

At the end Cherie Westmoreland designed a volume pleasing to read, despite its weight. And Rodolfo Fernández joined me in proofreading when my eye could no longer see.

I dedicate the book to Jane, María, and Gabriela Tutino. We have learned about life together in a journey of challenges, detours, and loving persistence. And yes, I still go to school after all these years.

Appendix A

Employers and Workers at Querétaro, 1588–1609

Thanks to the work of José Ignacio Urquiola Permisán and his associates, a set of nearly three hundred work contracts completed at Querétaro between 1588 and 1609 — most between 1598 and 1609 — allows a revealing exploration of labor relations during formative decades. Urquiola provides an analysis that emphasizes advance payments and judicial findings, creating contractual obligations to labor. He shows that textile workshops, the obrajes, played key roles but were not majority employers. Most workers were indigenous, yet from diverse regions. And while coercion was a tool of employers and the courts, ultimately labor relations were monetized, contested, and repeatedly renegotiated at Querétaro as the seventeenth century began.[1]

Urquiola published the entire set of contracts. They include detailed information on employers, workers, work relations, salaries, ethnic origins, and family relations, the basis of the quantitative analysis offered here and of the social and cultural discussion in chapter 1. Table A.1 summarizes the labor relations revealed in the contracts, distinguishing those employers who appear only as recipients of payment for debts left by unfulfilled work, those only advancing money to gain obligations of work service, and those who did both. Fifty-seven employers, most engaging one or two workers, appeared only as recipients of payment for workers' existing obligations. Most of those previous debts had not been formalized in contracts; previous employers had advanced goods or money valued more than the work performed. When workers sought a new position the new employer paid the old obligation and demanded a contract documenting the amount owed, the salary offered, and the work needed to cover the obligation. The fifty-four employers who only paid advances were usually small employers. The thirty-nine who both received payment for earlier debts and paid advances to acquire new workers were major employers.

Most employers contracted for the work of only one or two workers dur-

TABLE A.1 Employers, Workers, and Financial Transactions, 1588–1609

Workers per Employer	Employer Receives	Employer Advances	Employer Receives and Advances	No Obligation	Total Employers	Total Work Relations
1	45	38	2	6	91	91
2	10	7	10		27	54
3	2	6	4	1	13	39
4		2	5		7	28
5			8		8	40
6			2		2	12
7		1	2		3	21
9			2		2	18
12			1		1	12
20			1		1	20
42			1		1	42
56			1		1	56
TOTAL	57	54	39	7	157	433

Source: Urquiola Permisán, *Trabajadores de campo y ciudad*, 135–396, my calculations.

ing a dozen years of intensive documentation. Only four contracted for more than ten workers: a landed entrepreneur who appeared twelve times, and three textile obraje operators who were the only employers with twenty or more contracts. These three entrepreneurs were leading employers, yet they engaged just over a quarter of the workers in the contracts. In the emerging labor market most employers and workers engaged each other in small numbers. The obrajes were exceptional: large employers in a society ruled by more personal labor relations.

The economic activities of employers are known in 62 of 157 cases, as summarized in table A.2. Larger operators are the best-known; the activities of small employers are less well known.

Entrepreneurs provided most employment. Estates and mines operated outside town and only contracted a portion of their workers in Querétaro. The obrajes were most important in town.

Juan Rodríguez Galán operated a textile obraje that he sold in 1598 for 17,000 pesos to Antón de Arango. Arango complained that he had been cheated but kept the shop for several years before returning it to Rodríguez in 1603.[2] Rodríguez and Arango were leading employers, as was Juan de Chavarría, owner of the other major obraje in Querétaro.

Rodríguez Galán was the obraje operator least involved in work contracts. He never engaged more than four workers in any year.

Antón de Arango proved an energetic contractor once he purchased the obraje in 1598, as seen in table A.4. He raised salaries from a mean of 2.3 pesos monthly in 1598 to 2.7 in 1599 and 2.9 in 1600. As salaries rose, it cost Arango more in advances to claim a steady supply of labor. Arango sharply reduced

TABLE A.2 Employers and Workers by Economic Activity, 1588–1609

Activity	Number of Employers	Total Number of Workers	Mean Number of Workers
ENTREPRENEURS			
Landed	8	43	5.4
Merchant	9	29	3.2
Mining	9	20	2.2
Textile	4	125	31.3
Total entrepreneurs	30	217	7.2
TRANSPORT OPERATORS			
Muleteers	8	21	2.6
Carters	3	4	1.3
Total transport	11	25	2.3
ARTISANS			
Blacksmith	3	4	1.3
Miller	1	4	4
Baker	1	2	2
Butcher	1	3	3
Pastry maker	1	1	1
Shoemaker	2	4	2
Tailor	1	2	2
Hat maker	1	2	2
Master of writing	1	6	6
Surgeon-barber	1	1	1
Total artisans	13	29	2.2
OFFICIALS, ETC.			
District magistrates	2	2	1
Constable	1	2	2
Indigenous officials	2	2	1
Priest	1	1	1
Estate steward	1	1	1
Total officials	8	10	1.3
GRAND TOTAL	62	281	4.5

Source: Urquiola Permisán, *Trabajadores de campo y ciudad*, 135–396, my calculations.

his labor contracting beginning in 1601, a sign of the difficulties that led to the return of the obraje to Rodríguez.

An inspection of Rodríguez's obraje in 1604 showed that workers obligated by contract formed only part of the labor force. Twenty-five workers, 40 percent of the total, worked voluntarily, earning higher salaries and remaining longer than those subject to contract or enclosure. The inspection also reported workers' diverse regional and ethnic origins.

Juan de Chavarría operated his obraje from 1598 to 1609. He contracted fifty-six workers, advanced over 2,200 pesos, and gained 780 months of obli-

TABLE A.3 Employment Relations of Juan Rodríguez Galán, Obrajero, 1589–1609

	Number of Contracts	Total Pesos Advanced	Mean Salary in Pesos	Total Months Owed	Mean Received in Pesos
1589	1	24	2	12	
1598	3	85.5	1.9	46	
1599	1	90	3	30	
1603	2	258	2.5	104	
1605	3	183	2.9	63	
1606	2	101	3	34	
1607	2	82	2.5	33	
1608	4	123	2.3	53	
1609	2	208.5	3.5	60	
TOTAL	20	1,155	2.7	435	58

Source: Urquiola Permisán, *Trabajadores de campo y ciudad*, 135–396, my calculations.

TABLE. A.4 Employment Relations of Antón de Arango, Obrajero, 1598–1607

	Number of Contracts	Total Pesos Advanced	Mean Salary in Pesos	Total Months Owed	Mean Received in Pesos
1598	14	488.5	2.3	210	
1599	11	531	2.7	197	
1600	10	594	2.9	205	
1601	1	120	2.5	48	
1602	1	39	3	13	
1603	3	307	2.9	106	
1605	1			29.5	
1607	1			17	
TOTAL	42	2,079.5	2.6	825.5	49.5

Source: Urquiola Permisán, *Trabajadores de campo y ciudad*, 135–396, my calculations.

gated service—just over five workers yearly. He began paying 2.6 pesos per month in 1598, significantly more than the 2.3 pesos being offered by Arango, then raised salaries to 3 pesos by 1603.

The obrajes were the largest employers in Querétaro. They employed most workers sentenced to fines, and thus to labor, for crimes. The obrajes were also the most important payers of previous debts, moving workers from service based on negotiated advances to labor under contracts. Still, voluntary workers, who gained advances but were not subject to contracts, were a significant minority of obraje employees.

Nearly three hundred salaries recorded in Querétaro work contracts are detailed in table A.7.

TABLE A.5 Workers at Obraje of Juan Rodríguez Galán, 1604

Number of Workers	Voluntary	Contracted	Enclosed	Unknown	Total
Total	25	12	18	6	61
Percent	41	20	30	10	100
Detailed	19		13		32
Percent	59		41		100
Total Owed	59 p		36 p		95 p
Mean Salary	3.1 p		2.8 p		3 p
Months Owed	107		74		181
Mean Months Owed	5.6		5.7		5.7
Mean Years at Obraje	5.8		5.2		5.4
KNOWN ORIGIN					
Querétaro	3		2		5
Otomí	4		2		6
Tarascan	2		1		3
Mexicano	2				2
Guadalajara	2				2
Mulatto	1		1		2
TOTAL	14		6		20

Source: Urquiola Permisán, *Trabajadores de campo y ciudad*, 126–27, my calculations.

TABLE A.6 Employment Relations of Juan de Chavarría, Obrajero, 1598–1609

	Number of Contracts	Total Pesos Advanced	Mean Salary in Pesos	Total Months Owed	Mean Received in Pesos
1598	9	387	2.6	150	
1599	13	446	2.7	163	
1600	2	82.5	2.5	33	
1601	2	104	3.7	28	
1602	4	173	2.8	62	
1603	6	216.5	3.0	72	
1604	1	74.5	3.5	21	
1605	1	81	3.0	27	
1606	6	248.5	3.0	83	
1607	3	84	3.0	28	
1608	7	259.5	2.9	91	
1609	2	66.5	3.0	22	
TOTAL	56	2,223	2.9	780	39.7

Source: Urquiola Permisán, *Trabajadores de campo y ciudad*, 135–396, my calculations.

TABLE A.7 Salaries in Querétaro Work Contracts (in Pesos per Month), 1588–1609

	−2	2+	3+	4+	5+	6+	7+	8+	Total
1588–89		3							3
1596–97		3	3					1	7
1598	4	25	7	3			1	2	42
1599	1	14	16	2			1	2	36
1600	1	9	16	1		1	1	3	32
1601	1	2	4	1	1			2	11
1602		1	9	1		1		1	13
1603		3	12	1		1	1		18
1604–5		2	7	3	1			1	14
1606		3	10	1	1	1		3	19
1607		2	7	3	2		2	4	20
1608	1	2	14	3	4		2	2	28
1609		1	14	5	3	2	1	8	34
TOTAL	8	70	119	24	12	6	9	29	277

Source: Urquiola Permisán, *Trabajadores de campo y ciudad*, 135–396, my calculations.

Salaries held near two pesos monthly through 1598 and then rose to three pesos by 1602; by 1605 many workers earned more, and by 1609 a majority earned at least four pesos.

Table A.8 reports workers' status as categorized by regime officers. The category of indio included and obscured peoples of diverse indigenous ancestry. Mulatto was the category assigned to free people of African origins. Mestizo presumed mixed indigenous and European origins. Chinos were Asians. Vecinos were citizens of European ancestry.

Around 1600 colonial status categories were not ethnic identities. Identity is difficult to document. But work contracts record the place of birth of most who were called indios. They allow tabulation of diverse origins and likely ethnic identities, as detailed in table A.9.

A note on the regional and ethnic identities used here is necessary. Querétaro identifies workers from the city and its immediate neighboring villages, most of whom were of Otomí ethnicity. Chichimeca includes only those explicitly noted as such: their regional origins are uncertain. The category Otomí includes peoples from Otomí regions across the Mezquital and the northern Toluca basin, and around San Juan del Río. Tarascan includes those from towns across Michoacán. Mexica includes workers from the city of Mexico, nearby communities, and the Nahua zones across the core of the old Mexica empire, extending into the Puebla basin. Guadalajara includes those stated as being from there, with no ethnic identity presumed. "Beyond" refers to the few from as far north as Aguascalientes and as far south as Oaxaca.

The work contracts also include the names of indigenous workers and state whether they required an interpreter or rather were ladino, conversant in Spanish. There were three clearly different naming patterns: those retaining

TABLE A.8 Colonial Categories of Querétaro Employees, 1588–1609

	Indios	Mulattoes	Mestizos	Chinos	Vecinos	Total	Percent Non-indigenous
1588–89	3	1				4	25
1596–97	5		1		1	7	29
1598	40	2	1		3	46	13
1599	32	2	3		3	40	20
1600	32	3			1	36	11
1601	8		4			12	33
1602	15					15	0
1603	15	3	2			20	25
1604–5	15					15	0
1606	23	1		1	1	26	12
1607	13	3	3		4	23	43
1608	25		2	1	1	29	14
1609	32	1		1	3	37	14
TOTAL	258	16	16	3	17	310	17

Source: Urquiola Permisán, *Trabajadores de campo y ciudad*, 135–396, my calculations.

TABLE A.9 Regional and Ethnic Origins of Indigenous Workers

	Querétaro	Chichimeca	Otomí	Tarascan	Mexica	Guadalajara	Beyond	Unknown	Total
1588–89	3			1					4
1596–97	1	1	1	1	1				5
1598	18	1	5	8	5	1	1		39
1599	13	1	5	3	7	1		2	32
1600	16	1	4	2	6		1		30
1601	4		1	3					8
1602	5		1	1	7			1	15
1603	8		1		5				14
1604–5	8		2	3	1				14
1606	4		9	1	7			1	22
1607	5		3		2				10
1608	10		1	4	8	1	1		25
1609	9		8		3	1	1		22
TOTAL	104	4	41	27	52	4	4	4	240
Percent of all workers	43	2	17	11	22	2	2	2	100

Source: Urquiola Permisán, *Trabajadores de campo y ciudad*, 135–396, my calculations.

TABLE A.10 Indigenous Workers' Names and Language Use at Querétaro, 1588–1609

	Indigenous Surnames	Hispanic Surnames	Saints' Names	Total
1588–89				
Contracted through interpreter	4			4
Contracted in Spanish				0
1596–97				
Contracted through interpreter	3	2		5
Contracted in Spanish				0
1598				
Contracted through interpreter	18	9	8	35
Contracted in Spanish		1	3	4
1599				
Contracted through interpreter	18	3	7	28
Contracted in Spanish		2	3	5
1600				
Contracted through interpreter	12	7	9	28
Contracted in Spanish	1	1	2	4
1601				
Contracted through interpreter	5	3		8
Contracted in Spanish				0
1602				
Contracted through interpreter	2	4	5	11
Contracted in Spanish		3	1	4
1603				
Contracted through interpreter	3	3	6	12
Contracted in Spanish		2	1	3
1604–5				
Contracted through interpreter	4	6	3	13
Contracted in Spanish		1	1	2
1606				
Contracted through interpreter	1	8	3	12
Contracted in Spanish		7	4	11
1607				
Contracted through interpreter	2		3	5
Contracted in Spanish		3	1	4
1608				
Contracted through interpreter	4	6	8	18
Contracted in Spanish	1	1	4	6
1609				
Contracted through interpreter	6	14	5	25
Contracted in Spanish	1	3	2	6
TOTAL				
Contracted through interpreter	79	66	59	204
Contracted in Spanish	3	24	22	49
GRAND TOTAL	82	90	81	253

Source: Urquiola Permisán, *Trabajadores de campo y ciudad*, 135–396, my calculations.

TABLE A.11 Workers Sentenced for Criminal Offenses, 1596–1609

	Violent Crimes	Property Crimes	Crimes vs. Patriarchy	Unspecified	Criminal Total	Percent of Total Contracts
1596–97	1		1	1	3	60
1598	3		4	5	12	26
1599	2	1	1	1	5	13
1600	3		2	2	7	19
1601		1	1		2	17
1602	1	1		3	5	20
1603	2	1	1	1	5	25
1604–5	1	1	1		3	20
1606	2	2			4	15
1607					0	0
1608			1		1	3
1609		1			1	3
TOTAL	15	8	12	13	48	15

Source: Urquiola Permisán, Trabajadores de campo y ciudad, 135–396, my calculations.

TABLE A.12 Women in Labor Contracts, 1588–1609

	Working Alone	With Husband	Total Working	Percent of Total Workers	Guarantors with Husband	Guarantors Alone	Total Women
1588–89	1		1	25			1
1596–97		1	1	14			1
1598		5	5	11			5
1599	1	6	7	18	2		9
1600	1	4	5	14	1		6
1601		2	2	17			2
1602		3	3	20		1	4
1603	1	1	2	10		1	3
1604–5		1	1	7			1
1606		2	2	8			2
1607		3	3	13	1	1	5
1608		1	1	4	1	1	3
1609	2	4	6	17	1	2	9
TOTAL	6	33	39	13	6	6	51

Source: Urquiola Permisán, Trabajadores de campo y ciudad, 135–396, my calculations.

indigenous surnames; those who had Hispanic surnames; and those who used a combination of two saints' names (or other Christian designators), which was eventually the colonial norm for naming indios. The intersection of naming patterns and language skills is outlined in table A.10.

Sentences to labor for criminal offenses were few in number, totaling forty-six, or about 15 percent of the labor contracts. This was not primarily a system of criminal enforcement to force labor service. Still, the criminal contracts are revealing, as outlined in table A.11.

During the decade from 1596 to 1606 criminal sentences were an important part of generating labor contracts. The nature of the crimes is suggestive. Of the thirty-five detailed cases fifteen involved violence against persons, eight involved property crimes, and twelve offenses to patriarchy.

The link between labor and patriarchy is also evident in contracts that included women, often as wives, sometimes as single workers, and later in the decade as guarantors. It is worth noting that women contracted to work were nearly as numerous as men sentenced to labor for criminal offenses. Adding women who served as guarantors, more women appeared in work contracts than criminals.

Appendix B

Production, Patriarchy, and Ethnicity

in the Bajío Bottomlands, 1670–1685

The analysis of commercial production, patriarchal social relations, and ethnic amalgamation in the Bajío bottomlands that forms the core of chapter 2 depends on two key sources. An inventory of the estate of don Diego de la Cruz Saravia made in 1671 details commercial estate operations and complex social relations of production. That document is published as an appendix in Baroni Boissonas, *La formación de la estructura agraria el el Bajío colonial*, 193–214. Parish censuses for Salamanca, Valle de Santiago, and Salvatierra (and much of León to the northwest) are transcribed and published in Carillo Cázares, *Partidos y padrones del Obispado de Michoacán*. This appendix presents quantitative analyses of the inventory and censuses to support the analysis in chapter 2.

Production and Patriarchy at Valle de Santiago, 1671

The inventory of the estate of don Diego de la Cruz Saravia offers rare detail about land values, estate operations, profitability, and labor relations around Valle de Santiago. The extent and variety of de la Cruz Saravia's properties and activities make the inventory most revealing of the nature of the commercial economy and how patriarchy shaped rural social relations. Table B.1 compiles and organizes all the property included in the document, such as land, livestock, and grains.

The inventory also lists tenants, their rents, and their payment status. The largest group rented small holdings at the Hacienda Grande; most produced just enough for family sustenance and limited marketing. Six tenants owed no

TABLE B.1 Property Values in de la Cruz Saravia Inventory, 1671

Total Estate: 58,427 pesos, 6 reales
    Urban property, Celaya: 6,550 pesos (11%)
        Main home (6,000 pesos)
        Other Celaya lots and houses (550 pesos)
    Slaves (at Celaya home): 10, total 1,800 pesos (3%)
        Lucas, mulatto, 60+ years, 250 pesos
        Pedro de la Cruz, negro, 60, 200 pesos
        Joseph, negro, 40, 300 pesos
        Cristina, 60+ years, 100 pesos
        Ysabel, 60+ years, 100 pesos
        Teresa, 40, ill in bed, 100 pesos
        Ana, mulata, 350 pesos, her sons
            Diego, mulatto, 8, 200 pesos
            Joseph, cuate, 2, 100 pesos
            Francisco, cuate, 2, 100 pesos
    Luxury goods: total 2,950 pesos (5%)
    Subtotal Celaya properties, slaves, luxuries, 11,300 pesos (17.9%)
Rural properties, Valle de Santiago
    Hacienda Grande, 6 caballerías, 6 days water for irrigation, with houses, granaries,
        gardens, 119 oxen, 100 horses: 14,095 pesos
    Hacienda de Santa María, 4 caballerías, 6 days water, hut: 6,000 pesos
    Combined: 20,095 pesos (2,010 pesos per irrigated caballería)
    Hacienda de labor, irrigated, without livestock, etc.: 2,000 pesos
    Tierra de Surumútaro, 2 caballerías plus pasture for oxen: 150 pesos
    3 Criaderos de Tierras, with right to cut (*herido*) for mill: 300 pesos
    2 caballerías, undeveloped, at Valtierra, right to 2 heridos: 450 pesos
Rural properties, Valle de Santa Cruz del Guaje
    Labor de San Juan and San Pablo, 10 caballerías, ranchos, terrazgueros, by river,
        chapel, 2 adobe granaries, house, 59 oxen: 4,404 pesos
    Labor de San Andrés, 20 fanegas de sembradura; 36 oxen; rented to Tomás
        García for 40 pesos: 1,000 pesos
    Labor de San Joseph, 30 fanegas de sembradura (partially cleared),
        45 oxen, with jacales de indios: 1,270 pesos
    Labor de San Joaquín, new, few good lands, 8 oxen, rented to Bartolomé
        Morales for 25 pesos: 248 pesos
    Labor de San Salvador: well and granary, 40 oxen, rented for 250 pesos (100 pesos
        cash; 150 in improvements): 1,742 pesos
    Ranchos in same area: 4,500 pesos
    Sitio del Sauce: 4 ranchos de indios, 500 vacas chichiguas,
        rented to Juan de Bustos: 700 pesos
    Estancia de Mandinga: rented to Juan García de Sotomayor, 30 pesos:
        400 pesos
    Sitio Sotelillos: 7 ranchos de indios arrendatarios, 95 vacas y toros:
        400 pesos
    Estancia Tres Pitayos: oxen, granaries, rented to Tomás Ortega for 25 pesos:
        500 pesos
    Estancia Lagunilla: rented to Nicolás Nieto for 25 pesos: 300 pesos

Estancia El Zapote (disputed with heirs of Francisco de Rayo), rented to
    Juan Ramírez for 25 pesos: 300 pesos.
Estancia de Santiago al Arroyo Grande, rented to Sebastián y Antonio de
    Soto (no rent for land, lease 263 vacas y toros at 6 reales or
    197 pesos): 100 pesos
Total Landed Properties: 38,859 pesos
Additional Livestock
    1,229 vacas y toros at 4 pesos: 4,916 pesos
    18 novillos at 4 pesos: 72 pesos
Total additional livestock: 4,988 pesos
Total productive property: land, livestock, water rights, etc.: 43,847 pesos (75%)
Cereals in Storage
Maize: 200 fanegas at 3 reales (for rations at hacienda Grande): 75 pesos
    1,000 fanegas maíz viejo at Guaje Granaries, at 2 reales: 250 pesos
    2,760 fanegas maíz de un año, at 2 reales: 690 pesos
    400 fanegas maíz, at 2 reales: 100 pesos
Total maize: 4,360 fanegas; 1,115 pesos (2 reales per fanega)
Wheat: 866, cargas not threshed, at 20 reales: 2,165 pesos (962.5 cargas harvested;
    96 to tithe)
Total cereals: 3,280 pesos (6%)

Source: Baroni Boissonas, *La formación de la estructura agraria en el Bajío colonial*,
193–214, my calculations.

TABLE B.2 Rents at Hacienda Grande, 1671

Rents Owed, in Pesos	Number of Tenants	Number of Tenants with Rent Unpaid	Rents Owed, in Pesos	Number of Tenants	Number of Tenants with Rent Unpaid
0	6		31–40	2	1
1–10	1	10	41–50	1	
11–20	25	2	TOTAL TENANTS	45	19
21–30	10	6	TOTAL RENTS	704	70

Source: Baroni Boissonas, *La formación de la estructura agraria en el Bajío colonial*,
193–214, my calculations.

rents as they opened new lands to cultivation. More than half of those who
owed rents had not paid in full.

Eight men leased commercial holdings that generated larger incomes. Their
rents averaged nearly 9 percent of property value (table B.3). Saravia also
leased herds of livestock (table B.4). The estate expected total rents of 1,463
pesos for land and livestock in 1671; it received 1,252 pesos, or 86 percent of
rents due.

TABLE B.3 Property Values and Rents for Commercial Leaseholds

	Property Value	Rent
	1,742	250 pesos (100 cash, 150 improvements)
	1,198	40
	700	[50]
	500	25
	400	30
	300	25
	300	25
	248	25
TOTAL	5,388	470 pesos

Source: Baroni Boissonas, *La formación de la estructura agraria en el Bajío colonial*, 193–214, my calculations.

TABLE B.4 Rents for Livestock

Vacas y Toros: 148 at 6 reales: 111 pesos
    115 at 6 reales: 86 pesos, 2 reales
    68 at 6.5 reales: 55 pesos, 2 reales
TOTAL LIVESTOCK RENTS: 252 pesos, 4 reales

Source: Baroni Boissonas, *La formación de la estructura agraria en el Bajío colonial*, 193–214, my calculations.

The inventory does not offer a full list of workers and wages. Instead it lists those owed income by the estate and those obligated to labor by advances previously received and still outstanding. Those owed for labor performed but not yet compensated were called sirvientes, suggesting Hispanic status. The manager was due a large sum, surely several years' pay. The rest were owed less than a year's earnings, in most cases only a few months' earnings.

A larger group of seventeen workers, called indios, were obligated by debts owed to the estate. The labor captain, charged with organizing work gangs, owed the most. He had received an advance of over a hundred pesos. Presuming salaries of three pesos monthly, several others owed more than a year's service, with the average at around nine months. Advances and obligations remained central to recruiting and retaining indigenous workers in the basin bottomlands around 1670.

Calculating the profitability of de la Cruz Saravia's properties is difficult. The inventory provides the value of his productive holdings, his rental expectations and incomes, and the quantity of grains harvested and in storage, along with their values. It does not provide the costs of labor. I have calculated these costs by assuming the following: the manager earned two hundred pesos yearly (thus he was owed for over three years); the captain earned one hundred pesos annually (thus he had been advanced a full year); and all others earned sal-

TABLE B.5 Sirvientes Owed by the Estate at Hacienda Grande, 1671

624p5r	Cristoval García de León, mayordomo
30p4r	Miguel, hijo de Joseph Ramírez
25p2r	Marcos Macías
14p6r	Esteban Moreno, español
14p2r	Diego de la Cruz
11p1r	Diego Hernández
7p	Sebastián Martín
5p3r	Juan de la Cruz
3p1r	Andres Moreno Tartamudo
2p2r	Joseph Ramírez
TOTAL 738p2r	
TOTAL, MINUS MAYORDOMO: 113p5r (mean: 12p5 per employee)	

Source: Baroni Boissonas, *La formación de la estructura agraria en el Bajío colonial*, 193–214, my calculations.

TABLE B.6 Indios Obligated at Hacienda Grande, 1671

100p1r	Simón, Capitán
63p6r	Miguel, yerno de Juan Ladino
43p3r	Bautista, yerno del Tartamudo
41p	Bartolomé, hijo de Joseph
38p4r	Miguel, Capitán Viejo
36p4r	Baltasar, hijo de Juan Ladino
33p5r	Matheo, yerno de Juan
30p4r	Nicolás Melero
28p7r	Ventura
26p	Sebastián Rodríguez, boyero
25p5r	Pablo Ramírez
16p4	Ignacio
16p2r	Nicolas de Mendoza
14p2r	Juan Vidal
11p2r	Francisco Pedro
3p4r	Agustín Melchor Hernández
1p1r	Miguel, ? de Juan Ramírez
TOTAL 530p6r	
TOTAL DEBTS, MINUS CAPITÁN: 430p5r (mean: 26p7r per worker)	

Source: Baroni Boissonas, *La formación de la estructura agraria en el Bajío colonial*, 193–214, my calculations.

aries of three pesos monthly, thus thirty-six pesos yearly (surely some sirvientes earned more, others among indio youths less), for a total of nine hundred pesos yearly. Manager, captain, and workers earned around twelve hundred pesos yearly. Using those estimates, a calculation of profitability is possible.

The clerical censuses of 1683 for the three basin parishes of Salamanca, Valle de Santiago, and Salvatierra distinguish between Hispanic families,

TABLE B.7 Earnings on Productive Property, Cruz Saravia Estates, 1671

Value, productive rural properties: 43,847 pesos
Rents Received in Cash: 1,152 pesos
Wheat: 2,165 pesos
Maize: 1,115 pesos
Total earnings: 4,432 pesos
Salary costs: 1,200 pesos
Earnings minus salary costs: 3,232 pesos
Profit: 7.4% of value of productive properties

Source: Baroni Boissonas, *La formación de la estructura agraria en el Bajío colonial*, 193–214, my calculations.

TABLE B.8 Hispanic Households in Salamanca: Town Residents, 1683

Size	Male-Headed		Female-Headed		Combined	
	Number	Population	Number	Population	Number	Population
1						
2	1	2	1	2	2	4
3	1	3	2	6	3	9
4	4	16			4	16
5	1	5	1	5	2	10
6	6	36	2	12	8	48
7	2	14			2	14
8	3	24			3	24
9	2	18			2	18
10	1	10			1	10
11	4	44			4	44
12						
13	1	13			1	13
TOTAL	26	185	6	25	32	210

Source: Alberto Carrillo Cázares, *Partidos y padrones del Obispado de Michoacán, 1680–1685*, 416–18, my calculations.

mostly town dwellers plus a few rural cultivators at Salamanca, and a pro-ducing population presumed indigenous and mostly living at estates across the countryside. There were a few small indigenous communities. A very few residents were identified as slaves or mulattoes, thus of African ancestry. Care-ful analysis reveals much about patriarchy and ethnicity as commercial agri-culture consolidated across the Bajío basin in the late seventeenth century. I begin at Salamanca, the oldest of the settlements.

In town, patriarchs headed over 80 percent of Hispanic households at Sala-manca. Patriarchal households averaged over seven residents each, while the few headed by women, mostly widows, included just over four residents each. As a result nearly 90 percent of residents of Hispanic households in urban

TABLE B.9 Hispanic Households at Salamanca: Rural Residents, 1683

Size	Male-Headed		Female-Headed		Combined	
	Number	Population	Number	Population	Number	Population
1						
2	1	2			1	2
3	5	15	1	3	6	18
4	3	12			3	12
5	2	10			2	10
6	6	36	1	6	7	42
7	7	49			7	49
8	4	32			4	32
9	3	27	1	9	4	36
10	3	30			3	30
11	3	33			3	33
12						
13	2	26			2	26
14	3	42			3	42
19			1	19	1	19
27	1	27			1	27
35	1	35			1	35
TOTAL	44	376	4	37	48	413

Source: Alberto Carrillo Cázares, *Partidos y padrones del Obispado de Michoacán, 1680–1685*, 418–21, my calculations.

TABLE B.10 Indigenous Households at Salamanca: Pueblos and Barrios, 1683

	Santa María Nativitas	San Juan de la Presa	San Pedro del Molino	San Nicolás	Total
Patriarchal couples	48	8	9	21	86
Widowers	2	1	2	1	6
Widows	5	3		2	10
Dependents	25	3	2	17	47
Total population	128	23	22	62	235
Mean household	2.6	2.6	2.0	2.8	2.6

Source: Alberto Carrillo Cázares, *Partidos y padrones del Obispado de Michoacán, 1680–1685*, 421–22, my calculations.

Salamanca lived under patriarchal rule. Patriarchy was more dominant among rural Hispanic households around Salamanca.

Across the Salamanca countryside patriarchs headed 92 percent of Hispanic households, accounting for 93 percent of the population. Thanks to a few very large households—probably residential compounds—the household average was larger outside town, at over 8 residents. Combining urban and rural resi-

TABLE B.11 Indigenous Households at Salamanca: Communities and Estates, 1683

	Communities	Estates	Total		Communities	Estates	Total
Patriarchal couples	86	263	349	Dependents	47	130	177
Widowers	6	12	18	Total population	235	679	914
Widows	10	11	21	Mean household	2.6	2.5	2.5

Source: Table B.9 and Alberto Carrillo Cázares, *Partidos y padrones del Obispado de Michoacán, 1680–1685*, 422–27, my calculations.

TABLE B.12 Indigenous Settlements at Salamanca, 1683

Households per Settlement	Number of Settlements	Total Households	Households per Settlement	Number of Settlements	Total Households
1	3	3	11	2	22
2	7	14	12	3	36
3	10	30	16	1	16
4	4	16	Percent, 11–20	11	20
5	6	30	22	1	22
Percent, 1–5	55	25	50	1	50
6	5	30	Percent, 20+	4	20
7	2	14	TOTAL	55	367
8	6	48			
9	4	36			
Percent, 6–10	31	35			

Source: Tables B.10, B.11, my calculations.

dents, Salamanca had 81 Hispanic households with 631 residents, or nearly 8 each. Women headed only 10 households with 62 residents. Patriarchy ruled in nearly 90 percent of Hispanic households in the Salamanca parish, and patriarchs ruled over 90 percent of the population in Hispanic households there.

The Salamanca census reported four indigenous settlements. The largest, Santa María Nativitas, was founded in the 1650s on lands abandoned by Hispanic residents who moved to more productive fields at nearby Valle de Santiago. The census reports these communities in less detail, listing married couples, widowers, widows, and diverse dependents separately. Still, it documents the patriarchal organization of indigenous life.

The calculations in this and subsequent tables on communities presume that married men and widowers headed households and that widows did not. It is likely that some widows did head households—perhaps half—and that some widowers did not. That leaves the overall calculation of household size less certain, but it errs in the direction of a high estimate (in a population of small households). If half of widows led households, they led about 5 percent

TABLE B.13 Hispanic Households at Valle de Santiago, 1683

	Male-Headed		Female-Headed		Combined	
Size	Number	Population	Number	Population	Number	Population
1						
2	33	66	6	12	39	78
3	17	51	7	21	24	72
4	11	44	2	8	13	52
5	12	60	2	10	14	70
6	8	48	3	18	11	66
7	4	28	2	14	6	42
8	1	8			1	8
13	1	13			1	13
16	1	16			1	16
17	1	17			1	17
TOTAL	89	351	22	83	111	434

Source: Alberto Carrillo Cázares, *Partidos y padrones del Obispado de Michoacán, 1680–1685*, 418–21, my calculations.

of households in Salamanca's indigenous communities. What emerges clearly is the predominance of patriarchs who were married and headed very small households—averaging a husband, a wife, and less than one dependent each. The contrast with Hispanic households that were equally patriarchal, but far larger, is striking. The inclusion of children under the age of confession would increase the size of both Hispanic and indigenous households, but the contrast would remain.

The Salamanca census also reports on indigenous families living at fifty-one rural ranchos, grazing properties, and cereal farms, most operated by Hispanic proprietors. Patriarchal family relations remained strong, parallel to those at the indigenous communities.

The indigenous population at Salamanca in 1683 lived in small patriarchal households in small settlements—the great majority on private properties operated by Hispanic residents. These residents lived in much larger patriarchal households, in town and especially across the countryside.

Valle de Santiago was a new town and parish, south of Salamanca near fields long developed by residents of the older town. Valle de Santiago in 1683 was a younger society in rapid development. Hispanic households there were smaller and less patriarchal.

At Valle de Santiago 80 percent of households were patriarchal and 20 percent were headed by women. All were small, averaging under four residents each—with women heading households only slightly smaller. Patriarchy ruled less fully at the new town. All indigenous households at Valle de Santiago lived at private properties, most called labores, or irrigated grain farms. They maintained small and thoroughly patriarchal households similar to those at Salamanca.

TABLE B.14 Indigenous Households at Valle de Santiago, 1683

Patriarchal couples	277	Dependents	121
Widowers	9	Total population	704
Widows	20	Mean household	2.5

Source: Alberto Carrillo Cázares, *Partidos y padrones del Obispado de Michoacán, 1680–1685*, 430–34, my calculations.

TABLE B.15 Indigenous Settlements at Valle de Santiago, 1683

Households per Settlement	Number of Settlements	Total Households	Households per Settlement	Number of Settlements	Total Households
2	2	4	11	1	11
3	2	6	12	1	12
4	1	4	13	2	26
5	2	10	16	1	16
Percent, 1–5	24	8	17	2	34
6	2	12	Percent, 11–20	24	35
7	4	28	28	1	28
8	3	24	33	1	33
9	2	18	Percent, 20+	7	21
10	2	20	TOTAL	29	286
Percent, 6–10	45	36			

Source: Table B.14, my calculations.

At the new estates of Valle de Santiago most indigenous residents lived at larger estate communities with eleven or more households.

Salvatierra was founded in the 1640s south of Salamanca and Valle de Santiago, on the banks of the River Santiago that irrigated the Bajío bottomlands. Also a zone of recent settlement, it included two indigenous communities already present near the northern edge of Mesoamerica. Salvatierra's Hispanic households in 1683 were smaller than those at the older town of Salamanca, larger than those at recently founded Valle de Santiago, and notably less patriarchal.

Patriarchy shaped most Hispanic households at Salvatierra, but the proportion was only 68 percent, notably less than the 80 percent at Valle de Santiago and the 92 percent at Salamanca. Hispanic household size held under five at Salvatierra, smaller than at older Salamanca, larger than at Valle de Santiago. Patriarchal households were generally larger or smaller than the mean; women headed households concentrated at the mean.

A majority of residents at Salvatierra were indigenous, divided between two older communities and thirty-two newer private properties. Again, small patriarchal households ruled.

The predominance of patriarchal households persisted at the new labores, with very small households indeed: the vast majority included an indigenous

TABLE B.16 Hispanic Households at Salvatierra, 1683

	Male-Headed		Female-Headed		Combined	
Size	Number	Population	Number	Population	Number	Population
2	18	36	4	8	22	44
3	18	54	7	21	25	75
4	10	40	11	44	21	84
5	11	55	7	35	18	90
6	19	114	10	60	29	174
7	8	56	2	14	10	70
8	5	40	2	16	7	56
9	4	36	2	18	6	54
10	2	20			2	20
11			1	11	1	11
14	1	14			1	14
TOTAL	96	465	46	227	142	692

Source: Alberto Carrillo Cázares, *Partidos y padrones del Obispado de Michoacán, 1680–1685*, 404–8, my calculations.

TABLE B.17 Indigenous Households at Salvatierra, Pueblos, 1683

	San Miguel de Menguaro	Nuestra Señora de la Asunción de Urineo	Total
Patriarchal couples	70	40	110
Widowers	1	5	6
Widows	7	5	12
Dependents	26	27	53
Total population	174	117	291
Mean household	2.4	2.6	2.5

Source: Alberto Carrillo Cázares, *Partidos y padrones del Obispado de Michoacán, 1680–1685*, 408–10, my calculations.

patriarch, his wife, and no dependents other than infants and children not yet admitted to confession. The labores at Salvatierra appear to have been very new, and very patriarchal, settlements. They were not small, confirming the trend toward larger estate communities revealed at Valle de Santiago.

At Salvatierra the majority of indigenous settlements at labores remained small; nearly 80 percent included ten or fewer households. But the majority of indigenous residents, over 60 percent, lived at seven large properties; nearly half lived at the three largest. Estate dependence, small and young patriarchal families, and a concentration at larger estates defined rural life for the indigenous majority at Salvatierra in 1683.

TABLE B.18 Indigenous Households at Salvatierra:
Communities and Labores, 1683

	Communities (2)	Labores (32)	Total
Patriarchal couples	110	353	463
Widowers	6	8	14
Widows	12	12	24
Dependents	53	50	103
Total population	291	776	1,067
Mean household	2.5	2.1	2.1

Source: Table B. 16 and Alberto Carrillo Cázares, *Partidos y padrones del Obispado de Michoacán, 1680–1685*, 410–13, my calculations.

TABLE B.19 Indigenous Settlements at Salvatierra: Labores, 1683

Households per Settlement	Number of Settlements	Number of Households	Households per Settlement	Number of Settlements	Number of Households
1	1	1	11	1	11
2	2	4	13	1	13
3	3	9	16	2	32
4	4	16	Percent 11–20	13	16
5	2	10	29	1	29
Percent, 1–5	38	11	48	1	48
6	3	18	81	1	81
7	4	28	Percent 20+	9	45
8	2	16	TOTAL	32	353
9	3	27			
10	1	10			
Percent, 6–10	41	28			

Source: Table B.18, my calculations.

Slaves and People of African Ancestry in the Bottomlands, 1683

Slavery brought people of African origins into the Bajío in large but uncertain numbers. In the census lists from the basin parishes only forty-four people are noted explicitly as slaves, black, or mulatto, indicating African ancestry. The sample is small, yet there are hints of a larger presence. Of the forty-four people twenty-six were town dwellers and eighteen rural—nearly all at private properties. Notably, women were twenty-two of the twenty-six town dwellers, half noted as enslaved, the other half probably free. Seven of the free women and two slaves were mulattas; two slaves and one free mother with three children were called negras; three women were only called esclavas. Of the four men in towns two were slaves (one a mulatto, the other just an esclavo); one

TABLE B.20 The de la Cruz in Hispanic Households, 1683

| | Household Heads | | Dependents | | | | Percent of |
	Male	Female	Male	Female	Total	Population	Population
Salamanca Town	1		7	15	23	210	11
Salamanca Rural	1		15	18	34	412	8
Salamanca TOTAL	2		22	33	57	622	9
Valle de Santiago			2	15	17	434	4
Salvatierra	1	3	8	58	70	692	10
TOTAL	3	3	32	106	144	1,748	8

Source: Alberto Carrillo Cázares, *Partidos y padrones del Obispado de Michoacán, 1680–1685*, 404–13, 416–34, my calculations.

mulatto and one negro were listed without status as slave or free. The census taker had two interests: slave status and African ancestry. Other distinctions were irregularly noted. Of the eighteen people of African ancestry at rural properties, fourteen were men, four women. Eight men and one woman were slaves; six men and three women were free. Ten men (four slaves and six free men) and three women (all free) were mulattoes. In sum, rural people of African ancestry were mostly male and mulatto, divided evenly between the enslaved and the free.

There was a reflection of the patriarchy prevailing across the larger society: men of African ancestry, slaves and free, were mostly rural producers. Women of African ancestry (twenty-two of twenty-six) served in urban households. That separation of residence and roles ensured that women of African origin had regular contacts with Hispanic patriarchs and their families, and that men of African origin lived among the indigenous majority. Such residence patterns facilitated cultural and biological interaction.

One last characteristic of the few identified as having African roots raises a revealing suggestion. Among the forty-four, eleven (25 percent) had a saint's name followed by de la Cruz (of the Cross). Seven were slaves: six women and one man. Five were negros, five mulattoes, and one noted only as a slave. A quarter of the population identified as having African origins shared a surname that is not a traditional patronym, yet refers to Christ's sacrifice and perhaps calls for his protection. An analysis of the roles of all people named de la Cruz is suggestive.

Two points are notable: 80 percent of those with the name de la Cruz in urban households are dependent women, parallel to the roles of the few explicitly noted as having African ancestry. In rural Salamanca, the one zone of

TABLE B.21 The de la Cruz in Indigenous Communities, 1683

	Salamanca	Salvatierra	Total
Patriarchs	9	7	16
Wives	11	12	23
Widowers	1		1
Widows	1	1	2
Dependent males	2	7	9
Dependent females	3	3	6
TOTAL	27	30	57
Total population	235	291	526
Percent of population	11	10	11

Source: Table B.19, my calculations.

TABLE B.22 The de la Cruz in Rural Communities:
Ranchos and Labores, 1783

	Salamanca	Valle de Santiago	Salvatierra	Total
Patriarchs	19	18	34	71
Wives	30	28	30	88
Widowers			1	1
Widows		7		7
Dependent males	10	1	4	15
Dependent females	14	10	5	29
TOTAL	73	64	74	211
Total population	914	704	1,042	2,660
Percent of population	8	9	7	8

Source: Table B.20, my calculations.

rural Hispanic households, the number of de la Cruz men nearly equaled the number of women. Like the smaller numbers explicitly listed as being of African origin, in Hispanic households most de la Cruz women were urban dependents and most de la Cruz men rural producers. Life was different for the de la Cruz in indigenous settlements.

De la Cruz men led 11 percent of indigenous community households; de la Cruz women were 11 percent of indigenous patriarchs' wives. Yet there were very few de la Cruz children. It appears that men and women of African ancestry were merging into indigenous communities, marrying indigenous mates, and not naming their children de la Cruz—perhaps to assert indigenous status. Ethnic status was fluid and negotiated in basin communities.

A majority of the de la Cruz lived at rural estates, though they formed a smaller part of the population there than in the indigenous communities. At estates and communities de la Cruz patriarchs were outnumbered by de la

TABLE B.23 Indigenous Communities at San Francisco del Rincón, 1683

	San Francisco del Rincón	Nuestra Señora de la Limpia Concepción	Total
Patriarchal couples	211	136	347
Widowers	12	2	14
Widows	37	15	52
Dependents	142	168	310
Total population	613	457	1,070
Mean household	2.7	3.3	3.0

Source: Alberto Carrillo Cázares, *Partidos y padrones del Obispado de Michoacán, 1680–1685*, 457–62, my calculations.

TABLE B.24 Population and Patriarchy at Rincón Haciendas, 1683

	Santiago, Sauz de Armento	Cañada de los Negros	Pedregal	San Nicolás Buenaventura	Total
Patriarchal couples	30	20	4	10	64
Widowers	4				4
Widows	1		3	1	5
Dependents	16	8	15	12	51
Total population	81	48	26	33	188
Mean household	2.4	2.4	6.5	3.3	2.8

Source: Alberto Carrillo Cázares, *Partidos y padrones del Obispado de Michoacán, 1680–1685*, 454–55, my calculations.

Cruz wives in patriarchal families. Across the rural settlements of the bottomlands the de la Cruz were bringing African ancestry and culture into a population amalgamating as indio.

Patriarchy at León Communities, 1683–1685

West and northwest of the bottomlands lay the district of León. Limited irrigation watered lands along the Turbio river that ran through the jurisdiction; León thus developed more as a zone mixing cultivation and grazing. The censuses from León in 1683 report only the populations of San Francisco del Rincón and its neighbors: two indigenous communities, five haciendas, and fourteen ranchos. Only the ranchos included numerous Hispanic families, most classed as mestizos. Still patriarchy ruled, with revealing variations.

In the two León communities families were patriarchal and small, yet

TABLE B.25 Population and Patriarchy at Rincón, Haciendas, and Ranchos, 1683

	Communities (2)	Haciendas (5)	Ranchos (14)	Rincón (Total)
Patriarchal couples	347	64	80	491
Widowers	14	4	5	23
Widows	52	5	4	61
Dependents	310	51	191	552
Total population	1,070	188	360	1,618
Mean household	3.0	2.8	4.2	3.2

Source: Tables B.19 and B.20, and Alberto Carrillo Cázares, *Partidos y padrones del Obispado de Michoacán, 1680–1685*, 455–56, my calculations.

TABLE B.26 Households per Settlement: Rincón Haciendas and Ranchos, 1683

Households per Settlement	Number of Settlements	Total Households	Households per Settlement	Number of Settlements	Total Households
1			11	1	11
2	3	6	14	1	14
3	2	6	Percent, 11–15	10	16
4	3	12	22	1	22
5	2	10	25	1	25
Percent, 1–5	50	22	Percent, 16+	10	30
6	1	6	TOTAL	20	154
7	2	14			
8					
9	2	18			
10	1	10			
Percent, 6–10	30	31			

Source: Tables B.20, B.21, my calculations.

larger than at the bottomlands. The greater presence of households headed by widows at Rincón perhaps reflected greater access to community lands there.

The Rincón census also lists families at five haciendas, two populated mostly by indios (Santiago and Sauz de Armento); one settled by indios and mestizos (Cañada de los Negros, despite the name owned or managed by a Spaniard with a Spanish wife); one populated by mestizos (Pedregal, owned or managed by an indio married to an india); and one mixing a majority of indios with a significant number of mulattoes (San Nicolás de Buenavista, owned or managed by a mestizo married to an india).

Among hacienda residents, where indios predominated patriarchal households remained small; among mestizos and mulattoes they were larger. At the fourteen ranchos near Rincón, mestizos, mulattoes, and Spaniards lived in larger patriarchal households.

TABLE B.27 Indigenous Households at León Pueblos, 1685

Size	Male-Headed		Female-Headed		Combined	
	Number	Population	Number	Population	Number	Population
1	4	4	3	3	7	7
2	24	48			24	48
3	32	96	6	18	38	114
4	48	192	3	12	51	204
5	36	180	2	10	38	190
Total 1–5	144	520	14	43	158	563
Percent	44	24	61	31	45	24
6	39	234	2	12	41	246
7	33	231	1	7	34	238
8	32	256	1	8	33	264
9	20	180			20	180
10	12	120	2	20	14	140
Total 6–10	136	1,021	6	47	142	1,068
Percent	42	47	26	34	41	45
11	14	154			14	154
12	9	108	1	12	10	120
13	4	52	1	13	5	65
14	8	112			8	112
15	4	60			4	60
Total 11–15	39	486	2	25	41	511
Percent	12	22	9	18	12	22
16	2	32			2	32
17	1	17			1	17
18	1	18			1	18
Total 16–20	4	67			4	67
Percent	1	3			1	3
21	1	21			1	21
23	1	23	1	23	2	46
25	2	50			2	50
Total 21–25	4	94	1	23	5	117
Percent	1	4	4	17	1	5
TOTAL	327	2,188	23	138	350	2,326
Mean household		6.7		6		6.6
Dependent patriarchs		113		18		131
Mean per patriarch		5		3.4		4.8

Source: Alberto Carrillo Cázares, *Partidos y padrones del Obispado de Michoacán, 1680–1685*, 439–50, my calculations.

TABLE B.28 Indios Laboríos, Mulattoes, and Mestizos at León, 1685

	Indios laboríos	Mulattoes, Blacks	Mestizos
Patriarchal couples	637	169	96
Widowers	48	18	13
Dependents	1,095	368	272
Total population	2,417	724	477
Mean household	3.5	3.9	4.4

Source: Alberto Carrillo Cázares, *Partidos y padrones del Obispado de Michoacán, 1680–1685*, 457, my tabulations.

TABLE B.29 Household and Patriarchy at León, 1685

	Indios Laboríos	Indios de Pueblo	Free Mulattoes and Negroes	Mestizos	Total
Total population	2,417	2,326	724	277	5,744
Percent of population	42	40	13	5	100
Mean per household	3.5	6.6	3.9	4.4	4.3
Mean per patriarch	3.5	4.8	3.9	4.4	3.9

Source: Tables B.27, B.28, my calculations.

At Rincón estates small, diverse settlements prevailed.

A different census completed at León in 1685 included more communities and estates but still excluded the Hispanic town of León. It reported entire populations, including children below the age of confession.

Patriarchy again ruled: women headed only 7 percent of households, accounting for only 6 percent of the population. Yet the census of 1685 reported households far larger than those reported in 1683. The inclusion of children under the age of seven in 1685 might account for an increase in the size of the average indigenous household from 2.5 to 4, but not to the 6.6 reported. The larger households of 1685 resulted from multigenerational patriarchal families. Young patriarchs, married and often with children, lived with their fathers and less often with their widowed mothers. The population per patriarch was 5.0 in households headed by men, 3.4 in those headed by women, and 4.8 overall. Patriarchal indigenous families at León were similar in size to those across the bottomlands (allowing for the inclusion at León of the youngest children). What differed in the count at León in 1685 was the reporting of extended family households.

That census provided summary reports on indigenous peoples at private properties, on persons of African ancestry, and on mestizos. They confirm that at León too, indigenous estate dependents outnumbered pueblo residents. Mulattoes and mestizos formed significant minorities.

A summary table suggests the relative size and household dimensions of the complex population of León (excluding Spaniards).

Over 80 percent of the population at León remained classed as indio, but only 40 percent lived in pueblos with rights to land and local rule. Thus 60 percent of the total population lived at commercial estates: where two-thirds were categorized as indigenous, a fifth were of African ancestry, and fewer than a tenth were mestizo. Household size was 4.4 among mestizos, 3.9 among those of African origin, and 3.5 among the indigenous majority at León estates. Was this also the rank order of prosperity in León rural communities — apparently not amalgamating as rapidly as those on the bottomlands?

Appendix C

Bajío Population, 1600–1800

The Bajío was a region of diverse communities, cities, towns, villages, and estates, settled in the aftermath of the Spanish conquest. Population figures are essential to understanding its historical development. They are also scarce and often uncertain, are open to various interpretations, and require manipulation before they can become the basis for comparisons across zones within the region and for measuring change over the centuries. This appendix examines the available figures, discusses their uncertainties and implications, and presents tables to support the analysis presented in the text.

I begin with Querétaro and its district. Under Spanish rule that jurisdiction was smaller than the state that emerged after independence in 1821. It included the City of Querétaro and its surrounding basins, San Juan del Río to the southeast and its countryside, and San Pedro Tolimán in the drier and hillier country to the northeast. The colonial jurisdiction of Querétaro thus included the key southeastern extension of the Bajío, and little of the rugged uplands that became part of the state in the nineteenth century.

There are no known censuses for Querétaro and its district before the middle of the eighteenth century. John Super estimates a population of one thousand for the late sixteenth century and an increase to five thousand by the middle of the seventeenth. Those figures are accurate for the town and perhaps its immediate vicinity, but do not represent the larger jurisdiction, including San Juan del Río and its outlying pueblos. I propose a district population of three thousand for the late sixteenth century, based on the more than three hundred adult workers in the labor contracts detailed in appendix A, and the knowledge that such workers were but part of a community primarily cultivating huertas. I use a population figure of eighteen thousand for 1630, presuming that Querétaro's population was over half that reported for Celaya in the census of 1631, a jurisdiction just west that included outlying towns.

The first good report of Querétaro's population came in 1743 from the Corregidor, don José Gómez de Acosta. He reported the number of families or households, and suggested that each included an average of eight residents. Diverse sources, including other regional censuses from the eighteenth century, suggest that five was a more appropriate average household size. Thus I have multiplied Gómez's figures by five to produce the following population figures:

TABLE C.1 Querétaro District Population, 1743

Jurisdiction	Spaniards	Mestizos, Mulattoes	Indios	Total
Querétaro	5,745	9,475	14,025	29,245
San Juan del Río	1,515	1,865	13,310	16,690
San Pedro Tolimán	450	560	3,160	4,170
DISTRICT TOTAL	7,710	11,900	30,495	50,105

Source: Gómez de Acosta, *Querétaro en 1743: Informe presentado al rey por el Corregidor*, 126–27, 176.

A far more detailed census is available for Querétaro and its jurisdiction for 1778. It reports the populations of the city, rural villages, and estates, separating Spaniards, mestizos, mulattoes, and indios. It documents the substantial population growth of the middle decades of the eighteenth century.

Subsequent population figures are less detailed and sometimes uncertain, but still suggestive. In his mid-nineteenth-century report on Querétaro, José del Raso offered regional totals for 1790. They suggest some decline since 1778, a possibility given the great famine years of 1785 and 1786.

If Raso's figures for 1790 seem low, those offered by Carlos de Urrutía in 1794 appear high. Without additional breakdown he reports a population of 46,388 for Querétaro and its district, and another 42,393 for San Juan del Río and San Pedro Tolimán and their district, bringing the jurisdiction total to 88,781. Urrutía's report seems more credible when we note that his report for Querétaro and its district closely parallels Raso's from 1790. What is different is Urrutía's far higher population for the outlying districts. It seems reasonable, then, to use a mean of Raso's and Urrutía's totals—80,246—as a population estimate for the early 1790s. Raso added that the population of the city and its district alone rose to 58,000 by 1810, suggesting a population for the entire jurisdiction of about 93,000 that year.

The result of this combination of estimates, censuses, and calculations is an outline of the population history of the Querétaro jurisdiction from 1590 to 1810:

1590	3,000
1630	18,000
1743	50,000
1778	76,000
1792	80,000
1810	93,000

TABLE C.2 Querétaro District Population, 1778

	Spaniards	Mestizos	Mulattoes	Indios	Total
Querétaro	6,735	4,521	3,009	5,874	20,139
San Sebastián	345	708	549	5,596	7,198
CITY TOTAL	7,080	5,229	3,558	11,470	27,337
La Cañada	134	100	52	2,909	3,195
San Francisco	42	33		2,571	2,646
Huimilpan	8			1,091	1,099
PUEBLOS TOTAL	184	133	52	6,571	6,940
Haciendas	1,954	2,359	820	7,195	12,328
QRO. JURIS. TOTAL	9,218	7,721	4,430	25,236	46,605
San Juan del Río	1,328	532	520	2,346	4,726
Tequisquiapan	134	150	244	1,978	2,506
Pueblos (4)	67	8		1,242	1,317
Haciendas	1,573	1,639	1,213	6,849	11,274
SAN JUAN JURIS. TOTAL	3,102	2,329	1,977	12,415	19,823
San Pedro Tolimán	273			1,375	1,648
Tolimanejo	350	46	78	1,165	1,639
Pueblos (3)				3,924	3,924
Haciendas	994	163	378	610	2,145
TOLIMÁN JURISDICTION TOTAL	1,617	209	456	7,074	9,356
QUERÉTARO DISTRICT TOTAL	13,937	10,259	6,863	44,725	75,784

Source: Urquiola Permisán, "La región centro-sur de Querétaro," table at p. 158, my calculations.

TABLE C.3 Querétaro District Population, 1790

	Urban	Rural	Total
Querétaro	29,702	15,657	45,359
San Juan del Río	7,476	10,359	17,835
San Pedro Tolimán	2,641	5,876	8,517
TOTAL	39,819	31,892	71,711

Source: Raso, *Notas estadísticas del departamento de Querétaro, año de 1845*, 97.

If these figures are accurate the population of Querétaro and its jurisdiction continued to expand until the year that insurgency began.

The population history of the regions of the central and western Bajío that in 1786 became the Intendancy of Guanajuato and later the state of the same name can be traced over a longer time, but without the detail provided by the census of Querétaro of 1778. An ecclesiastical survey by the bishop of Michoacán in 1631 offers reports of numbers of families and households. I have used the multiplier of five to calculate population estimates. The *Theatro americano* of don José Antonio Villaseñor y Sánchez offers reports for 1742 requiring the same multiplier. A round of ecclesiastical visits produced detailed counts for the 1750s and 1760s, sometimes offering total populations, sometimes communicants (those over the age of seven). These counts convert to populations by adding 25 percent. Finally, Carlos de Urrutía provides population totals for the early 1790s.

The District of Celaya, just west of Querétaro, was the first settled, most diverse, and most populous region of Guanajuato. In addition to the district capital at Celaya there were important nearby towns at Apaseo and Chamacuero, along with the outlying centers of Acámbaro to the south, Yuriria to the southwest, and Salamanca and Salvatierra in the basin to the west. Four subdistricts had different population histories.

The subdistrict of Celaya in 1631 remained mostly indigenous, primarily Otomí:

TABLE C.4 Celaya Subdistrict Population, 1631

	Spaniards	Indians	Total
Celaya	1,000	12,500	13,500
Apaseo	0	2,000	2,000
Chamacuero	50	3,000	3,050
TOTAL	1,050	17,500	18,550

Source: López Lara, ed., *El Obispado de Michoacán en el siglo XVII*, 156–65, my calculations.

When Villaseñor y Sánchez surveyed the zone over a century later, the population had grown and become more complex. The report recognized two groups: *gente de razón*, including Spaniards, mestizos, and mulattoes; and indios.

TABLE C.5 Celaya Subdistrict Population, 1743

	Gente de Razón	Indios	Total
Celaya	10,100	14,575	24,675
Apaseo	1,000	6,625	7,625
Chamacuero	150	3,450	3,600
TOTAL	11,250	24,650	35,900

Source: Villaseñor y Sánchez, *Theatro americano*, vol. 2, 30–33.

TABLE C.6 Celaya Subdistrict, 1755

	Gente de Razón	Indios	Total
Celaya town	4,925	4,710	9,635
Celaya country	735	7,520	8,255
Celaya total	5,660	12,230	17,890
PUEBLOS DE CELAYA			
Rincón village		840	840
Rincón country	395	980	1,375
Rincón total	395	1,820	2,215
Otopam village	145	1,195	1,340
Otopam country	240	765	1,005
Otopam total	385	1,960	2,345
Santa Cruz village	10	2,285	2,295
Santa Cruz country	785	2,980	3,765
Santa Cruz total	795	5,265	6,060
Neutla village	45	750	795
Neutla country	105	2,000	2,105
Neutla total	150	2,750	2,900
Amoles village		1,500	1,500
Amoles country	625	7,860	8,485
Amoles total	625	9,360	9,985
San Juan Vega village	245	915	1,160
San Juan Vega country	80	1,500	1,580
San Juan Vega total	325	2,415	2,740
Pueblos (6) villages total	445	7,485	7,930
Pueblos (6) country total	2,230	16,085	18,315
Pueblos (6) total	2,675	23,570	26,245
Apaseo village	705	1,590	2,295
Apaseo country	270	3,250	3,520
Apaseo total	975	4,840	5,815
Chamacuero village	615	2,090	2,705
Chamacuero country	270	8,010	8,280
Chamacuero total	885	10,100	10,985
Celaya urban	6,690	15,875	22,565
Celaya country	3,505	34,865	38,370
Celaya subdistrict total	10,195	50,740	60,935

Source: González Sánchez, *El Obispado de Michoacán en 1765*, 307–8, my calculations.

The ecclesiastical census of 1755 provides exceptional detail for the Celaya subdistrict. It separates town and village centers from outlying estate populations. For urban and outlying Celaya it reports only gente de razón and indios. For surrounding communities it separates Spaniards, mestizos, and mulattoes, and reveals that most of the population classed as de razón in the countryside around Celaya identified as mulatto. Still, outside the city center the overwhelming preponderance was of indios. I have thus listed only figures for the

TABLE C.7 Acámbaro Subdistrict Population, 1631

	Spaniards	Indios	Total
Acámbaro	20	10,500	10,520

Source: López Lara, ed., *El Obispado de Michoacán en el siglo XVII*, 168–72.

population that was de razón—including Spaniards, mestizos, and mulattoes—and indios.

Finally, Urrutía reports a total of 67,867 people for the subdistrict of Celaya around 1790. That leads to the following long-term estimates for that zone:

1630	18,550
1740	35,900
1755	60,900
1790	68,000

Given the detail of the ecclesiastical census of 1755, it seems accurate and indicates that the estimates from 1742 are an undercount. It appears that most population growth in the Celaya subdistrict occurred before 1755, and that there was slowing after that date.

Acámbaro, including the nearby town of Jerécuaro, lay at the southern margin of the Celaya District—and the Bajío. Available population figures are limited and often uncertain.

The figures reported for 1743 by Villaseñor seem partial and very low:

TABLE C.8 Acámbaro Subdistrict, 1743

	Gente de Razón	Indios	Total
Acámbaro	400	2,450	2,850
Jerécuaro	100	250	350
ACÁMBARO TOTAL	500	2,700	3,200

Source: Villaseñor y Sánchez, *Theatro americano*, vol. 2, 32–33.

They suggest a jurisdiction still overwhelmingly indigenous—and one that had lost population while all surrounding zones had grown.

The ecclesiatical census report of 1754 may solve the problem. It explicitly states that it includes Acámbaro, Jerécuaro, six other villages, and several estates. It offers only the following totals:

TABLE C.9 Acámbaro Subdistrict Population, 1754

	Gente de Razón	Indios	Total
Acámbaro	6,875	16,250	23,125

Source: González Sánchez, El Obispado de Michoacán en 1765, 306.

These figures suggest that Villaseñor had estimates only for the two main towns. The report, adding both outlying villages and estates, reveals that Acámbaro had experienced developments parallel to those at Celaya and Querétaro: population growth, an expanded presence of Spaniards, mestizos, and mulattoes, and a shift of the rural majority to estates.

Urrutía's report for the 1790s offers a population of only 10,074—either a serious undercount or the result of a shift of rural areas to reporting in other zones (a real possibility, as we shall see). For now the long-term estimates for Acámbaro are as follows:

1630   10,520
1743   3,200
1754   23,125
1790   10,074

The Tarascan zones around Yuriria are equally problematic in the sources, though at least one census report, from 1766, is exceptionally revealing of local demographic structures. Again, the bishop's census of 1631 is limited but straightforward:

TABLE C.10 Yuririapúndaro Subdistrict Population, 1631

	Gente de Razón	Indios	Total
San Nicolás		2,225	2,225
Yuririapúndaro		555	555
TOTAL		2,780	2,780

Source: López Lara, ed., El Obispado de Michoacán en el siglo XVII, 201–3.

The figures offered for 1743 by Villaseñor suggest that the zone remained deeply indigenous and experienced little growth during the century after 1630—or excluded the many residents of the San Nicolás estate:

TABLE C.11 Yuririapúndaro Subdistrict Population, 1743

Jurisdiction	Gente de Razón	Indios	Total
Yuririapúndaro		2,425	2,425
S. Mig. Emenguaro		475	475
Urireo		485	485
TOTAL		3,385	3,385

Source: Villaseñor y Sánchez, Theatro americano, vol. 2, 32.

TABLE C.12 San Nicolás Subdistrict Population, 1754

	Spaniards	Mestizos, Mulattoes	Indios	Total
San Nicolás	250	443	3,038	3,731
Emenguaro		21	443	464
Urireo	5	50	564	619
Pejo			99	99
Haciendas y Ranchos			1,795	1,795
TOTAL	255	514	5,939	6,708

Source: González Sánchez, El Obispado de Michoacán en 1765, 299.

The ecclesiastical report for the parish of San Nicolás in 1754 reveals for the first time the presence of Spaniards, mestizos, and mulattoes in the zone, still in small numbers. It indicates steady mid-century growth, especially on estates. The report specifies that most of the three thousand people at San Nicolás lived on estates, and like the eighteen hundred indigenous residents of outlying settlements were divided among families headed by men serving for salaries, tenants paying rents, and arrimados—squatters neither regularly employed nor leasing lands.

A church census from 1766 gives more detail. It ignores ethnic status but includes families and total populations, and distinguishes villages, estates, and informal settlements called *puestos*. It reveals either that there was a rapid surge of growth—or that earlier counts missed many outside of communities. It shows five as the mean household size for the rural population, with smaller families in villages and larger ones at estates and puestos.

Urrutía provides a total for the early 1790s of 11,814, suggesting only modest late-century growth. The estimates of long-term population for Yuriria are as follows:

1630	555
1743	3,385
1766	10,113
1790	11,814

TABLE C.13 Yuririapúndaro Subdistrict Population, 1766

	Families	Population	Mean Family Size
PUEBLOS			
Yuririapúndaro	492	2,234	4.5
Maravatío	46	187	4.1
Magdalena	125	440	3.5
Ozumbilla	22	102	4.6
Piníquaro	76	304	4.0
San Lucas	10	40	4.0
Curambatío	37	171	4.6
Uriangato	168	807	4.8
Emenguaro	40	195	4.9
Buena Vista	6	25	4.2
Parangarico	40	156	3.9
Pueblos total	1,062	4,661	4.4
Pueblos mean	97	424	4.4
ESTATES			
Pastores	60	300	5.0
Joya Grande	12	60	5.0
Zempoala	9	50	5.6
San Joseph	8	40	5.0
La Virgen	15	87	5.8
Santa Mónica	34	178	5.2
Quanamuco	55	322	5.9
Estates total	193	1,037	5.4
Estates mean	28	148	5.3
PUESTOS			
60 total	833	4,415	5.3
60 mean	14	73	5.2
SUBDISTRICT			
TOTAL	2,088	10,113	4.8

Source: González Sánchez, El Obispado de Michoacán en 1765, 166–69, my calculations.

Yuriria, like the Celaya zone settled by indigenous peoples soon after the conquest, showed most growth early, then limited expansion during the late eighteenth century.

The adjacent zone of San Nicolás had the following trajectory:

1630	2,225
1754	6,708

For 1790 Urrutía included San Nicolás in his report for Salamanca. Late-century growth thus cannot be gauged locally, but the shift should not affect our understanding of the trajectory of the larger Celaya District.

TABLE C.14 Salamanca Subdistrict Population, 1631

	Spaniards	Mestizos, Mulattoes	Indios	Total
Salamanca	130	35	250	415

Source: López Lara, ed., *El Obispado de Michoacán en el siglo XVII*, 77–81.

TABLE C.15 Communicant Population, Salamanca-Salvatierra Subdistrict, 1683

Jurisdiction	Hispanic Households	Indio Households	Total Communicants	Total Estimated Population
Salamanca	622	1,139	1,761	2,201
Valle de Santiago	434	704	1,138	1,423
Salvatierra	692	1,333	2,025	2,531
TOTAL	1,748	3,176	4,924	6,155

Source: Tables B.8–B.19.

TABLE C.16 Salvatierra Subdistrict Population 1743

	Gente de Razón	Indios	Total
Salvatierra	1,500	4,525	6,025

Source: Villaseñor y Sánchez, *Theatro americano*, vol. 2, 34.

The last subdistrict included the rich basin lands around Salamanca and Salvatierra. Again the reports are limited, but the long-term trajectory seems clear. For 1631 the bishop reported figures only for Salamanca; Salvatierra and Valle de Santiago had not yet been founded.

The basins lands were less settled early in the seventeenth century, with less indigenous populations. They were a region of growth and settlement from the 1640s, documented by unique and revealing parish censuses in 1683 (analyzed in appendix B). They report only communicants, above the age of seven. I report the census totals, then my estimates of total population in table C.28 (increased by 25 percent).

For 1743, once again Villaseñor appears to offer only a partial report, limited to Salvatierra—whether the figures include Salamanca and Valle de Santiago is unclear.

He does note that the population of Spaniards, mestizos, and mulattoes had grown, divided between the city and outlying estates. He added that the indigenous majority was of Otomí origin, and that most were fluent in Spanish.

TABLE C.17 Salvatierra Population, 1754

	Gente de Razón	Indios	Total
Ciudad	2,386	180	2,566
Estates (45)	3,008		3,008
TOTAL	5,394	180	5,574

Source: González Sánchez, El Obispado de Michoacán en 1765, 298–99.

Again the ecclesiastical censuses of the 1750s and 1760s provide the clearest picture of the Salvatierra population as the late eighteenth century began.

The same survey offered the following for Salamanca:

TABLE C.18 Salamanca Population, 1754

	Gente de Razón	Indios	Total
Villa	1,408		1,408
Pueblos (4)		1,221	1,221
Estates (55)	3,209	4,414	7,623
TOTAL	4,617	5,635	10,252

Source: González Sánchez, El Obispado de Michoacán en 1765, 302–5.

Around the middle of the eighteenth century Salvatierra was more Hispanic, with the report adding that about two-thirds of the estate population was "de color quebrado"—mostly mulatto. Salamanca retained an indigenous majority. In both places the majority lived as estate dependents. Another report from 1766 added that the population of Valle de Santiago, the more recent settlement outside Salamanca, was then 8,000—in town and at surrounding estates. I use that estimate to bring the total for 1755 to 23,826 (González Sánchez, El Obispado de Michoacán en 1765, 175–76).

In 1794 Urrutía reported the population of Salvatierra at 25,021, and that of Salamanca, including Valle de Santiago, at 27,234. The Salvatierra report includes San Nicolás, limiting the apparent late-century population advance. The resulting estimates of the Salamanca-Salvatierra population history are as follows:

1630	415
1683	6,155
1743	6,025
1755	23,826
1790	52,255

Even if we presume that 12,000 of the additional inhabitants reported for 1790 reflect the inclusion of San Nicolás and its surrounding countryside, the increase after 1755 is substantial—the greatest in the Celaya District in the late eighteenth century.

Finally, it is possible to offer general estimates of the population history of the Celaya District in the seventeenth and eighteenth centuries:

TABLE C.19 Celaya District Population, 1600–1800

	Celaya	Acámbaro	Yuriria/ San Nicolás	Salamanca/ Salvatierra	Total
1630	18,600	10,500	2,800	400	32,300
1740	35,900	3,200	3,400	6,000	48,500
1755	60,900	23,100	16,800	23,800	124,600
1790	68,000	10,100	11,800	52,300	142,200

Source: Tables C.4–C.18, my calculations.

This summary confirms again that the population figures provided by Villaseñor y Sánchez for the Celaya district for 1743 are an extreme undercount. Using the more accurate reports from 1630, 1683 for the bottomlands, 1755, and 1790 clarifies several trends. Early-seventeenth-century population concentrated around Celaya and Acámbaro. Over the next century and a half populations grew across the district—more slowly around Celaya and Acámbaro, rapidly in the basin lands around Salamanca and Salvatierra.

The San Miguel District lay north of Celaya. The first region settled in the northern Bajío, the district included San Miguel, and San Felipe to the northwest. Dolores was founded after 1700. The bishop's report of 1631 shows limited settlement:

TABLE C.20 San Miguel District Population, 1631

	Spaniards	Indios	Total
San Miguel	350	250	600
San Felipe	200	120	320
TOTAL	550	370	920

Source: López Lara, ed., *El Obispado de Michoacán en el siglo XVII*, 48–52, 172–74.

The District had a Spanish majority; the report mentions but does not count mulattoes.

Villaseñor's report of 1743 included Spaniards, mestizos, and mulattoes—gente de razón. He mentioned indios, with no count. The ecclesiastical census of San Miguel from 1754 shows indigenous people as a third of the population.

The population in San Miguel and its countryside had grown enormously in the previous century, that of the regions to the north around Dolores and San Felipe much less.

The ecclesiastical census of 1754 reported only the San Miguel subdistrict.

TABLE C.21 San Miguel District Population, 1743

	Gente de Razón	Indios (estimated)	Total
San Miguel	15,000	7,500	22,500
Dolores	1,000	500	1,500
San Felipe	200	120	320
TOTAL	16,200	8,120	24,320

Source: Villaseñor y Sánchez, Theatro americano, vol. 2, 35–37.

TABLE C.22 San Miguel Subdistrict Population, 1754

	Gente de Razón	Indios	Total
San Miguel	16,812	8,406	25,218

Source: González Sánchez, El Obispado de Michoacán en 1765, 297–98.

The detail is revealing, and confirms the value of Villaseñor's reports from 1743 for this area.

The increase suggested from 1743 to 1754 seems reasonable. The Hispanic predominance and the strong indigenous minority are clear.

In 1794 Urrutía reported the population of San Miguel at 22,583, of Dolores at 15,661, and of San Felipe at 17,721, for a district total of 55,965. The increase slowed at San Miguel after mid-century, while the district grew by rapid settlement to the north at Dolores and San Felipe. The estimated historical trajectory of the San Miguel District is as follows:

1630	920
1743	24,320
1755	35,000
1790	55,965

Guanajuato held the center of the intendancy—and the regional economy. Its district included outlying refining zones at Marfil and agricultural areas at Silao and Irapuato. Again the bishop's report provides a baseline for 1631:

TABLE C.23 Guanajuato District Population, 1631

	Spaniards	Indios	Total
Guanajuato			1,067
Marfil	10	40	50
Silao			120
Irapuato	60	60	120
TOTAL	70	100	1,357

Source: López Lara, ed., El Obispado de Michoacán en el siglo XVII, 70–72, 74–77.

The figures seem low for an important, if secondary, mining center. But they confirm the late and limited settlement of the northern and western zones of the Bajío.

Villaseñor's report for 1743 reveals ample growth in the intervening century, driven by the surge of mining after 1700:

TABLE C.24 Guanajuato District Population, 1743

	Gente de Razón	Indios	Total
Guanajuato	25,000		25,000
Marfil	5,000		5,000
Silao	7,500		7,500
Irapuato	1,110	5,000	6,110
TOTAL	38,610	5,000	43,610

Source: Villaseñor y Sánchez, Theatro americano, vol. 2, 41.

TABLE C.25 Guanajuato District Population, 1755

	Spaniards	Mestizos, Mulattoes	Indios	Total
Guanajuato	6,313	23,303	2,957	32,573
Marfil	480	2,160	4,351	6,991
Silao	500	1,000	11,250	12,750
Irapuato (1743)	100	122	5,000	5,222
TOTAL	7,393	26,585	23,558	57,536

Source: González Sánchez, El Obispado de Michoacán en 1765, 296–97, 309.

TABLE C.26 Guanajuato District Population, 1792

	Spaniards	Mestizos, Mulattoes	Indios	Total
Guanajuato	18,068	9,645	4,385	32,098
Rest of District	6,092	9,393	7,429	22,914
TOTAL	24,160	19,038	11,814	55,012

Source: Brading, Miners and Merchants in Bourbon Mexico, 249.

The ecclesiastical censuses of 1755 provided greater detail, but exclude Irapuato—which can be added (and not overestimated) using the report for 1743. Villaseñor missed, as he did at San Miguel, important indigenous minorities. The censuses of 1755 confirm the mulatto majority at the mining center, with large minorities nearby.

Urrutía reports a population of 32,998 in 1794, clearly including only the city. David Brading offers the results of the census of 1792, in two versions: from the manuscript and from the summaries. He prefers the manuscript totals, which indicate a decline in population for the city to 21,766 and for the district to 51,510, unlikely during the late-century mining boom. The summaries are more persuasive yet still suggest little growth after mid-century.

These figures seem low. Even with more use of blasting powder and other innovations to save labor, it is improbable that Guanajuato's mines doubled silver production while the population remained unchanged. The explanation is clear. The census of 1792 was a militia count. The people of Guanajuato were known for deep opposition to militia service. Many surely found ways not to register, easier in the raucous mining center than in settled towns and estate communities. The result was an undercount. How large an undercount is unknown. I estimate a city population of 36,000 and a district population of 65,000.

One key change does emerge in the census of 1792 for Guanajuato. The mulatto majority of 1755 had become a Spanish majority. The census also reported that among adult men, 78 percent of Spaniards, 79 percent of mulattoes, and 86 percent of mestizos were born in the city. Many offspring of the mining city's mulatto majority of 1755 had claimed Spanish status by 1792.

The historical trajectory of the Guanajuato district population is estimated as follows:

1630	1,357
1743	43,610
1755	57,563
1792	65,000

The district of León lay west and southwest of Guanajuato, the mining center's immediate hinterland. Like other northern Bajío zones León settled late and grew rapidly in the eighteenth century. We begin again with the bishop's report of 1631:

TABLE C.27 León District Population, 1631

	Spaniards	Mestizos, Mulattoes	Indios	Total
León	375	60	110	545
Rincón			750	750
Pénjamo				270
TOTAL	375	60	860	1,565

Source: López Lara, ed., *El Obispado de Michoacán en el siglo XVII*, 69, 143–44, 175–78.

Rapid growth in the middle of the seventeenth century is shown in the Rincón parish of 1683, reporting only those above the age of communion. I estimate a total.

TABLE C.28 Communicant Population, Rincón Parish, 1683

Pueblos (2)	Haciendas and Ranchos	Total Communicants	Estimated Population
1,070	1,617	2,687	3,359

Source: Appendix B, tables B.23–B.25.

TABLE C.29 León District Non-Spanish Population, 1685

Indios de Pueblo	Indios Laboríos	Mulattoes	Mestizos	Total
2,326	2,417	724	277	5,744

Source: Appendix B, tables B.27–B.29.

As in 1631, the residents of Rincón remain indigenous. By 1683 their numbers increased four times over, with the majority at outlying estates.

A more complete census reports the León district in 1685, including young children but excluding Spaniards concentrated in León's town center.

An estimate that those claiming Spanish status made up 20 percent of the population would bring the total for 1685 to 6,900. The next report comes from Villaseñor for 1743:

TABLE C.30 León District Population, 1743

	Spaniards	Mestizos, Mulattoes	Indios	Total
León	2,605 de razón		750	3,355
Rincón, Purísima Concepión	45	430	2,715	3,190
Pénjamo			270	270
Piedragorda	2,070	635		2,705
TOTAL	5,785 de razón		3,735	9,520

Source: Villaseñor y Sánchez, Theatro americano, vol. 2, 42–45.

Again, Villaseñor seems to undercount. The ecclesiastical censuses of the 1750s and 1760s, incomplete for the León District, suggest rapid growth and dispersal onto estates.

These are obviously estimates. Hispanic peoples, mostly mestizo and mulatto, predominate in 1755.

More revealing is a report for Rincón and its parish from 1765.

This count shows residents of the two indigenous villages and the small mining camp at Comanjo as a small part of the parish. Nearly 80 percent lived on estates. In the village, status as Hispanic or indigenous still mattered. The

TABLE C.31 León Parish Population, 1755

Spaniards	Mestizos, Mulattoes	Indios	Total
3,000	8,000	4,000	15,000

Source: González Sánchez, *El Obispado de Michoacán en 1765*, 311.

TABLE C.32 Rincón Parish Population, 1765

	Gente de Razón	Indios	Total
Rincón village	58	550	608
Rincón country			2,118
Purísima village		400	400
Purísima country			1,523
Real de Comanja			600
TOTAL	58	950	5,249

Source: González Sánchez, *El Obispado de Michoacán en 1765*, 179–80.

TABLE C.33 León Parish Population, 1781

	Spaniards	Mestizos, Mulattoes	Indios	Total
León	1,585	3,544	378	5,507
San Miguel			1,386	1,386
Coecillo			2,472	2,472
Haciendas y Ranchos	1,619	5,482	2,109	9,210
TOTAL	3,204	9,026	6,345	18,575

Source: Brading, *Haciendas and Ranchos in the Mexican Bajío*, 41.

clergyman who reported the figures saw the rural majority as people—most Hispanic in culture and of unknown formal status.

Brading reports another census of the Léon parish from 1781.

There had been modest growth since 1755, confirming the general reliability of both León parish reports. Hispanic predominance in the town of León and across the countryside is clear. The indigenous minority concentrated in villages at San Miguel and Coecillo.

Urrutía offers populations for the entire district in 1794: León, 23,736; Pénjamo, 20,952; Piedragorda, 10,289; thus a León District total of 54,977. The report for the León subdistrict includes three pueblos, San Miguel, Coecillo, and Rincón. There was little growth since the reports of 1755–65, because of the great famine of 1785–86. Expansion at Pénjamo and Piedragorda drove population growth in the western Bajío in the late eighteenth century.

TABLE C.34 San Luis de la Paz District Population, 1743

	Spaniards	Mestizos, Mulattoes	Indios	Total
San Luis de la Paz	210	40	3,070	3,320
Pozos, Palmar	75	180	10	265
Xichú	200	505	910	1,615
Real de Targea	275	375		650
Tierra Blanca		2,965		2,965
TOTAL	760	4,065	3,990	8,815

Source: Villaseñor y Sánchez, *Theatro americano*, vol. 2, 45–47.

TABLE C.35 San Luis de la Paz Parish Populations, 1755

	Spaniards	Mestizos, Mulattoes	Indios	Total
San Luis de la Paz	1,023	1,369	6,063	8,455
Pozos, Palmar	183	741	829	1,753
TOTAL	1,206	2,110	6,892	10,208

Source: González Sánchez, *El Obispado de Michoacán en 1765*, 312.

The overall population estimates for the León District are as follows:

1,565	6,900
1740	9,520
1755	35,000
1790	55,000

Finally we turn to the District of San Luis de la Paz—east of San Miguel, north of Querétaro, where the Bajío met the Sierra Gorda. At the time of the bishop's survey of 1631, San Luis de la Paz was a settlement of recently pacified Chichimecas, estimated at 400 people. The small mining camps at Los Pozos and El Palmar were said to include 150 Hispanic settlers, plus an uncounted number of indigenous newcomers. Xichú, within the archbishopric of Mexico City, was not reported. I estimate the total population within the Hispanic sector at 900—excluding the unknown number of unincorporated indigenous peoples in the rugged Sierra Gorda uplands just east. (López Lara, *El obispado de Michoacán en el siglo XVII*, 53–53, 67–68.)

Villaseñor's report for 1743 came just before the second pacification of the Sierra Gorda, allowing the beginning of a rapid settlement in the San Luis de la Paz District.

The district remained at the margin of the Bajío, with a vast indigenous majority and an emerging Hispanic minority. The ecclesiastical censuses of 1755, again excluding Xichú, show the continuation of both trends.

TABLE C.36 Guanajuato Intendancy Population, 1600–1800

	Celaya	San Miguel	Guana-juato	León	San Luis de la Paz	Total
1630	32,300	900	1,400	1,600	900	37,100
1740	48,500	24,300	43,600	9,500	8,800	134,700
1755	123,600	35,000	57,600	35,000	12,200	263,400
1790	142,200	56,000	65,000	56,000	30,800	350,000

TABLE C.37 Bajío Population History, 1600–1800

	Querét.	Celaya	San Miguel	Guana-juato	León	San Luis de la Paz	Total
1630	18,000	32,300	900	1,400	1,600	900	55,100
Percent	33	59	2	3	3	2	100
1740	50,000	48,500	24,300	43,600	9,500	8,800	184,700
Percent	27	26	13	24	5	5	100
1755	60,000	123,600	35,000	57,600	35,000	12,200	323,400
Percent	19	38	11	18	11	4	100
1790	80,000	142,200	56,000	65,000	56,000	30,800	430,000
Percent	19	33	13	15	13	7	100

Estimating a population of 2,000 for Xichú suggests a district population of 12,200 in 1755.

Urrutía reports a district population of 30,759 in 1794, consonant with the known surge of settlement and development in San Luis de la Paz and the adjacent sierras in the late eighteenth century. The resulting long-term estimates are as follows:

1630	900
1740	8,815
1754	12,200
1790	30,755

We can now compile general population estimates for the region that became the Intendancy of Guanajuato (table C.36).

It is also possible to include the Querétaro District, creating an estimate for 1755 by calculating a mean of the censuses of 1743 and 1778 (63,000), then reducing it to 60,000. See table C.37.

Several trends are clear. After the first century of settlement and development, the Bajío population still concentrated in southeastern zones around Querétaro and Celaya in 1630. The bottomlands and the northern areas around San Miguel and León developed steadily during the following century. Growth in the peripheries—San Luis de la Paz and the Sierra Gorda to the northeast,

Dolores and San Felipe to the north, and Pénjamo and Piedragorda to the west—accelerated after 1750. Given the indigenous, mostly Otomí, majorities around Querétaro and Celaya, into the seventeenth century the Bajío remained an extension and adaptation of Mesoamerica into Chichimeca territories under Spanish sovereignty. The rapid development of the central, northern, and western Bajío after 1650, zones of Hispanic, indio, and mulatto peoples, brought about the demographic dominance of Hispanic North America in the eighteenth century.

Appendix D

Eighteenth-Century Economic Indicators:

Mining and Taxed Commerce

Silver Production: Guanajuato and New Spain, 1691–1810

Mining drove the economies of the Bajío, New Spain, the Atlantic, and the world during the eighteenth century. Mining output, overwhelmingly of silver and secondarily of gold, is the best-documented economic activity of eighteenth-century New Spain, thanks to the regime's interest in promoting and taxing its primary source of revenue. Figures for all of New Spain are available for 1691 to 1810. Figures for Guanajuato exist for 1716 to 1800—plus a few reports for the first decade of the nineteenth century. To follow long-term trends I calculate five-year means for both sets of indicators to trace the growth of mining across New Spain after 1690 and the role of Guanajuato in that growth after 1715.

Most notable is long-term growth across New Spain and at Guanajuato. Guanajuato's expansion began slowly, hovering around 15 percent of New Spain's production to 1725. It accelerated to between 25 and 30 percent through the 1740s. Then Guanajuato faced a decline that held for two decades, contributing to a plateau in production across New Spain. From the 1770s both experienced boom; Guanajuato's share approached 25 percent of historically high levels—until the crisis and insurgency of 1810.

There is no sign of an industry on the verge of collapse before 1810. Brading's analysis of Valenciana reveals rising costs, mostly labor for ever deeper excavations and drainage, pressing against thinning profits in the early 1800s. Such pressures were, however, a standard part of the mining cycle: early excavations with few profits; if fortunate, a time of boom production and great

TABLE D.1 Silver Production, New Spain and Guanajuato, 1691–1810
(Five-Year Means, in Pesos)

	New Spain	Guanajuato	Guanajuato as Percentage of Total
1691–95	4,482,128		
1696–1700	3,570,848		
1701–5	5,138,460		
1706–10	5,913,881		
1711–15	6,281,424		
1716–20	7,117,022	1,173,572	16
1721–25	8,326,930	1,228,561	15
1726–30	8,877,724	1,852,570	21
1731–35	8,922,145	1,964,248	22
1736–40	9,845,385	2,161,670	22
1741–45	9,925,010	2,835,410	29
1746–50	12,459,617	3,215,834	26
1751–55	12,777,106	2,422,930	19
1756–60	12,814,206	2,248,779	18
1761–65	11,713,842	2,361,837	20
1766–70	12,626,630	2,658,575	21
1771–75	16,235,937	3,356,735	21
1776–80	19,303,964	4,946,962	26
1781–85	20,249,114	4,374,763	22
1786–90	18,541,481	4,505,469	24
1791–95	23,246,840	5,231,388	23
1796–1800	23,093,612	5,042,503	22
1801–5	22,559,968		
1806–10	22,771,278		
1801–3	19,519,315	4,662,037	24
1809	26,172,982	5,220,000	20

Source: For New Spain, Lerdo de Tejada, *Comercio exterior de México desde la conquista hasta hoy*, table 54; for Guanajuato, Morín, *Michoacán en la Nueva España del siglo XVIII*, 94; my calculations of means and percentages.

profits; then an era of lesser ores, deeper shafts, rising costs, and falling profits. After 1800 Valenciana was approaching the end of such a cycle. Whether its difficulties portended industry collapse or just another bonanza going bust is ultimately unknowable. What is clear is that mining at Guanajuato and across New Spain collapsed after 1810 because of the combination of regime crisis, civil war, and popular insurgencies. What might have happened without those conflicts can only be imagined

Taxed Commerce in the Bajío, 1781–1811

Calculating activity in the commercial economy during the eighteenth century is uncertain. Thanks to regionally specific collection reports for the alcabala, a tax on commercial sales, it is possible to estimate the direction, if not the size, of commercial production in the Bajío and its subregions during the decades before 1810. Before 1776 alcabalas were farmed to independent collectors. Regime receipts reflected the value of farm contracts; relationships with real economic activity remain difficult to discern. After that date, as part of reforms aimed to tighten state power and increase revenue, collectors were regime agents. From 1778 to 1780 the alcabala was calculated as 6 percent of the value of sales. From 1781 to 1790 the rate was 8 percent—in an attempt to raise revenues. The attempt failed, primarily because of the famine of 1785 and 1786, leading to a reduction to 6 percent in 1791, a rate that held to 1811. The levels of taxed commerce reported in the tables take reported receipts and calculate production based on the prevailing rate. (I do not use the figures for 1778 to 1780. They report years of experiment and uncertainty. The figures for subsequent years follow patterns that suggest a set system of collection.)

It is important to know what the alcabala did and did not tax. It did not tax silver production—which paid its own tax, the quinto (about 13 percent), thus enabling separate analysis of the silver sector. Production by people classified as indio and sales in village markets were exempt, as were sales by indigenous growers in city markets. Thus alcabala reports are good economic indicators for Spanish North America, very partial indicators for Mesoamerica. Part of the Bourbon reform effort applied the alcabala to maize harvested by commercial growers for sale in town markets. In general alcabalas taxed commercial sales of food, cloth, and artisan wares.

To compensate for annual fluctuations I calculate five-year averages. I separate 1810, when insurgency began in September, and 1811, the first year of widespread year-long disruptions. My analysis of pre-insurgency trends reflects the figures through 1809. The figures for 1810 and 1811 are useful to gauge the early location and impact of insurgent disruptions. To facilitate comparisons with population figures I have combined the collection figures for Celaya, Acámbaro, and Salamanca into Celaya district figures. The collection district of San Miguel included San Luis de la Paz, just east.

Querétaro and Guanajuato ruled commercial life in the late-eighteenth-century Bajío. Together they accounted for 60 percent of collections. Commercial production dropped across the region during and after the famine of 1785 and 1786. The early 1790s brought sharp recovery, then a decline after 1795, mostly because of low collections at Guanajuato. The region sustained high levels of commercial activity from 1801 to 1809.

To gauge long-term trends across diverse zones I use the five-year mean for 1781–85 and the nine-year mean for 1801–9, when the regional economy had recovered from the great famine and adapted to the Atlantic warfare that had begun in the 1790s.

As a region the Bajío experienced commercial expansion of about 13 percent

TABLE D.2 Taxed Commerce in the Bajío, 1781–1811 (in 1,000 Pesos)

	Querétaro	Celaya	San Miguel	Guanajuato	León	Total
1781–85	1,232	1,167	560	1,771	347	5,077
Percent	24	23	11	35	7	100
1786–90	884	865	344	1,472	271	3,836
Percent	23	23	9	38	7	100
1791–95	1,192	1,114	520	2,176	373	5,375
Percent	22	21	10	40	7	100
1796–1800	1,291	1,084	571	1,609	462	5,017
Percent	26	22	11	32	9	100
1801–5	1,678	1,282	553	1,856	540	5,909
Percent	28	22	9	31	9	100
1806–9	1,544	1,234	470	1,699	573	5,520
Percent	28	22	9	31	10	100
1810	1,310	659	577	1,131	362	4,039
Percent	32	16	14	28	9	100
1811	1,610	250	0	841	453	3,154
Percent	51	8	0	27	14	100

Source: Garavaglia and Grosso, Las alcabalas novohispanas, 229–36, my calculations.

TABLE D.3 Commercial Expansion in the Bajío, 1781–1809 (in 1,000 Pesos)

	Querétaro	Celaya	San Miguel	Guanajuato	León	Total
1781–86	1,232	1,167	560	1,771	347	5,077
1801–9	1,611	1,259	524	1,778	557	5,729
Percent change	+31	+8	−6	0	+61	+13

Source: Table D.2, my calculations of percentages.

from the early 1780s to the decade after 1800—probably in line with population expansion (which experienced a sharp fall in the late 1780s, then grew from the 1790s). More notable are the exceptional expansions at Querétaro and especially León, the decline at San Miguel, and the lack of commercial growth at Guanajuato during decades when silver production reached and held a peak. There is every reason to assume that the trends for Querétaro, León, and San Miguel reflected real tendencies. The trajectory for Guanajuato is puzzling. Did the regime relax collections—unofficially—to promote mining? Did efforts to drive down workers' remuneration succeed, limiting sales of basic goods such as food and cloth even as silver production held near peak levels? Did lower remuneration and relaxed collections combine to favor production and facilitate pay reductions?

It is revealing to compare subregional relations between population and

TABLE D.4 Subregional Variations in Commercial Activity in the Bajío, 1781–1785

	Querétaro	Celaya	San Miguel	Guanajuato	León	Total
Population	80,000	142,200	86,800	65,000	56,000	430,000
Taxed commerce (in thousand pesos)	1,232	1,167	560	1,771	347	5,077
Per capita commerce	15.4 p	8.2 p	6.5 p	27.2 p	6.2 p	11.8 p

Source: Tables C.37, D.2, my calculations.

commercial activity. That can be done most accurately for 1781 to 1785. We have figures for mean taxed commerce then. And the population estimates for 1790 should apply to that period as well, as is confirmed by the similarity of the Querétaro censuses of 1778 and 1790.

The mean per capita commerce of about twelve pesos for the entire Bajío suggests that a family of five would need fifty to sixty pesos to live if they bought everything in the market. As we shall see, that is remarkably close to prevailing salaries across the countryside before the late-century decline. More revealing is the concentration of commercial activity in Querétaro and Guanajuato. That was expected for the mining center: wages were high and nearly everyone lived in the market. But the high figure for Querétaro, a jurisdiction including the great commercial and textile city and a larger rural countryside, indicates especially intense commercial economy there. In contrast, the low level of commercial activity per capita in Celaya, San Miguel (including San Luis de la Paz), and León suggests larger subsistence sectors, with only a part of economic activity—perhaps half—focused on the market. That likely reflects the still large number of landed growers. Around Celaya many landed villages remained; there and around San Miguel and León many rural tenants raised goods first for sustenance, then to market. In contrast, in and around Querétaro commercial farming ruled on the many huertas. As a result, even Otomí family agriculture was deeply commercial.

It is possible, with less accuracy, to estimate parallel figures for 1801 to 1809, using the mean taxed commerce for those years, and increasing population figures to reflect a general growth rate of 13 percent, as is suggested by the general increase in alcabala revenues. (Population reports for Querétaro, noted in appendix B, suggest growth there of 16 percent, not far from my estimate. Variation of this magnitude should not invalidate subregional comparisons.)

These calculations must be interpreted carefully. It seems likely that population growth was greater at León than across the Bajío, thus reducing the apparent increase of per capita commercial activity there. Still, the increases at Querétaro and León, and declines at San Miguel and Guanajuato, likely reflected real developments—though not precisely at the levels indicated. As discussed in chapter 6, Querétaro and León probably saw commercial expansion, for quite different reasons. Guanajuato's decline remains difficult to explain, unless workers' earnings were driven down while mining peaked. The decline at

TABLE D.5 Subregional Commercial Activity in the Bajío, 1801–9

	Queré-taro	Celaya	San Miguel	Guana-juato	León	Total
Population	90,400	160,700	98,100	73,500	63,300	486,000
Taxed commerce (in 1,000 pesos)	1,611	1,259	524	1,778	557	5,729
Per capita commerce	17.8 p	7.8 p	5.3 p	24.2 p	8.8 p	11.8 p
Percent change since 1785	+16	−5	−18	−11	+42	0

Source: Tables C.37, D.2, my calculations.

TABLE D.6 Mining and Commerce in the Bajío and Guanajuato, 1781–1809 (in 1,000 Pesos)

	Silver Production		Taxed Commerce	
	New Spain	Guanajuato	Bajío	Guanajuato
1781–85	20,219	4,375	5,077	1,771
1786–90	18,541	4,505	3,830	1,472
1791–95	23,207	5,231	5,375	2,176
1796–1800	23,094	5,042	5,017	1,609
1801–5	19,519*	4,662*	5,909	1,856
1806–9	26,173**	5,220**	5,520	1,699

* Figures are for 1801–3.
** Figures are for 1809.

Source: Tables D.1, D.2.

San Miguel reflected weak textile production there, while rural development in its district was oriented to settling tenants who were struggling to generate subsistence. There is no simple link between per capita commercial activity and insurgency. Yet the growth of commercial activity at Querétaro and León, where insurgency was limited and late, and the commercial declines at San Miguel and Guanajuato, where insurgency was early and massive in 1810, suggest important correlations and questions to explore.

Mining and Commerce at Guanajuato, 1780–1810

It is possible to gauge the link between mining and commerce at Guanajuato and across the Bajío. When we compare the growth of mining across New Spain and locally with the expansion of commercial activity across the Bajío and in Guanajuato, it is clear that silver stimulated commercial life across the region more than in the city that produced it.

The deadly famine of 1785 and 1786 struck commercial life far harder than

TABLE D.7 Source of Taxed Goods at Guanajuato (in 1,000 Pesos), 1779–1804

	Total Taxed Commerce, Guanajuato	Intendancy of Guanajuato	New Spain	Europe	China
1779–81	2,093	792 (38%)	239 (11%)	431 (21%)	58 (3%)
1785–86	1,099	365 (33%)	189 (17%)	274 (25%)	12 (1%)
1791–92	2,587				
1797–98	1,485	424 (29%)	349 (24%)	126 (8%)	54 (4%)
1800–1808	1,487	324 (22%)	300 (20%)	191 (13%)	58 (4%)
1804–5	1,983				

Source: Alvarado Gómez, *Comercio interior de la Nueva España*, cuadro 1, 146; cuadro 5, 150.

TABLE D.8 Sources of Taxed Goods at San Miguel, 1798 (in 1,000 Pesos)

San Miguel	New Spain	Europe	China	Total
15 (10%)	66 (44%)	27 (18%)	42 (28%)	150 (100%)

Source: Alvarado Gómez, *Comercio interior de Nueva España*, cuadro 9, 157–58.

mining. Then regional commerce rebounded to match or exceed the value of mining at Guanajuato until 1810; commerce at Guanajuato peaked in the early 1790s, then fell and fluctuated at lower levels to 1810. Pressure on mineworkers' earnings appears to have limited the local economy; regionally, mining and commerce held high together until the insurgency.

The sources of commercial goods taxed at Guanajuato also reveal key trends. The available information begins with years of boom, followed mostly by times of difficulty. I report total commerce for selected years of prosperity in table D.7, for context.

Goods from the four sources are 65 to 75 percent of the total; the remainder is accounted for by taxed goods made in the city. The share drawn from the intendancy was declining; the share from across New Spain grew, suggesting a widening integration stimulated by Guanajuato silver. Goods from Europe declined in total yet grew as a percentage in the crisis years of 1785 and 1786; during the trade blockages after 1793, goods from Europe dropped precipitously. Imports from China held steady at a low level, but plummeted in the crisis of the 1780s. The huge Chinese imports lamented by Monségur in 1706 are not in evidence. Had he exaggerated? Or had the Bourbons redirected most silver and trade to Europe?

Parallel information for San Miguel in 1798, a year of blockage due to war, suggests different consumption patterns in a town of rich aristocrats (table D.8).

In the smaller town local production provided less—and China much more.

TABLE D.9 Taxed Commerce in the North, 1781–1809 (Five-Year Means, in 1,000 Pesos)

	San Luis Potosí	Zacatecas	Nueva Vizcaya	Northeast	Northwest	Total
1781–85	1,398	2,233	888	417	200	5,136
1786–90	1,301	1,640	912	370	276	4,499
Percent change	−7	−27	+3	−11	+38	−12
1791–95	1,776	2,706	1,417	465	716	7,080
Percent change	+37	+65	+55	+26	+160	+57
1796–1800	1,886	2,806	1,555	531	764	7,542
Percent change	+6	+4	+10	+14	+7	+7
1801–5	2,012	2,828	1,456	659	881	7,836
Percent change	+7	+1	−6	+24	+15	+4
1806–9	1,881	2,872	1,211	838	958	7,760
Percent change	−7	+2	−17	+27	+9	−1
Percent change, 1781–85 to 1801–9	+39	+28	+50	+80	+360	+51

Note: San Luis Potosí also includes Guadalcázar, Charcas, and Valles. Zacatecas includes Fresnillo, Aguascalientes, Sombrerete, Bolaños, Mazapil, Sierra de Pinos, and Xerez. Nueva Vizcaya consists of Durango and Chihuahua. Northeast consists of Saltillo, Coahuila, Monterrey, and Santander. Northwest consists of Alamos, Rosario, Arispe, San Antonio Huerta, Sinaloa, Culiacán, Cosalá, Horcasitas, and Cieneguilla.

Source: Garavaglia and Grosso, *Las alcabalas novohispanas*, 229–36, my calculations.

Either the Canals and their kin who concentrated so much wealth focused consumption on Chinese luxuries, or Asian imports remained larger than records at Guanajuato suggested, in a year when European trade was limited.

Taxed Commerce: The Bajío and Spanish North America, 1781–1809

Alcabala collections also recorded the growth of commercial activity in the rapidly developing regions that stretched north of the Bajío. The farther north, the more accelerated the increase in taxed commerce.

From 1781 to 1809 commercial activity increased modestly in the Bajío, substantially in the regions just north, and enormously in the far reaches of Spanish North America. The increase in the Bajío kept pace with population growth, while holding at historically high levels. Whether commercial expansion in the near and far North exceeded population growth is not known. What the figures for taxed commerce demonstrate is the northward expansion of commercial society. Population and commercial production drove northward as the eighteenth century ended and the nineteenth began.

The relative economic weight of the three zones of Spanish North America was changing. In the early 1780s half of all commercial activity was in the

TABLE D.10 Commerce in the Bajío and the North, 1781–1809
(Five-Year Means, in 1,000 Pesos)

	Bajío	Near North	Far North	Total
1781–85	5,077	3,632	1,504	10,213
Percent	50	36	15	100
1786–90	3,856	2,941	1,558	8,355
Percent	46	35	19	100
1791–95	5,375	4,481	2,598	12,454
Percent	43	36	21	100
1796–1800	5,017	4,692	2,850	12,559
Percent	40	37	23	100
1801–5	5,909	4,840	2,996	13,745
Percent	43	35	22	100
1806–9	5,520	4,753	3,007	13,280
Percent	42	36	23	100
Percent change, 1781–85 to 1800–1809	+13	+32	+100	+32

Source: Bajío figures from table D.2; Near North combines San Luis Potosí and Zacatecas; Far North combines Nueva Vizcaya, the Northeast, and Northwest, all from table D.9.

Bajío, with 35 percent in the near North and only 15 percent in the zones beyond. While market activity increased in all three zones, the accelerated expansion in the far North meant that around 1800 commercial activity in the Bajío fell to around 40 percent, that of San Luis Potosí and Zacatecas held around 35 percent, and in the far North—the Northeast, Nueva Vizcaya, and the Northwest—commerce doubled to become a quarter of the activity of Spanish North America. Into the 1800s commercial life remained strong in the Bajío, vibrant in the near North, and expansively dynamic in the most northerly zones of Spanish America.

Appendix E

The Sierra Gorda and New Santander, 1740–1760

The years from 1740 to 1760 saw an energetic thrust northward from Querétaro through the Sierra Gorda and along the Gulf lowlands to the Río Grande Valley. The lands from the Río Pánuco to the Nueces were constituted as a new Colony of New Santander. The entire enterprise was led by don José de Escandón, a Spanish immigrant who had made a fortune in trade and textile production and claimed military command at Querétaro. Regions that had remained enclaves of indigenous independence after the Chichimeca wars of the sixteenth century now were settled in a rapid thrust that combined military rule, a mission presence, and commercial goals in new ways intended to promote the silver economy and accelerate Atlantic capitalism.

Two surveys provide revealing portraits of the process. In 1743 Escandón reported on the state of missions, military forces, and indigenous peoples in the Sierra Gorda, just after an expedition in which he had bolstered the military presence and just before he engineered the replacement of many established missionaries with newcomers more subject to his military rule and commercial interests. Then don Agustín López de la Cámara Alta, a lieutenant colonel and engineer in the Spanish military sent to survey the state of settlement and development in New Santander, wrote a detailed account of his visit in 1757, less than a decade into the development of the new colony. This appendix offers tabular summaries of key aspects of their reports, to sustain the analysis in the last section of chapter 3.

In his survey Escandón focused on military forces, the affiliations of missionary clergy, and the population of indigenous nations. It is clear that military forces far exceeded the missionary presence, and that native peoples fragmented into many small groups.

Escandón's thrust into the Sierra Gorda militarized settlements and missions long in place and long contested. His later drive into the Gulf lowlands

TABLE E.1 The Sierra Gorda in 1743

Pueblo/Mission	Military			Religious		Peoples	
	Officers	Soldiers	Number	Base		Nación	Number
Jurisdicción Querétaro							
Pueblo San Pedro Tolimán	2	62					
Misión Santo Domingo Soriano			unknown	Santo Domingo, México		De razón	22
						Otomí	100
						Jonaces	171
Cadereita, Villa de Cadereita	4	200					
Pueblo de Vizarrón	1	7					
Misión de Vizarrón			3	San Fernando, México		Jonaces	121
Misión Guadalupe Aguacatlán			1	Santo Domingo,		De razón	36
						Pames	183
Misión Santiago Xalpan	2	20	unknown	San Agustín, México		Spaniards, mestizos, mulattoes	408
						Mexicanos	122
						Pames, Pisquintla	159
						Tancama	652
						Tongo, Landa	562
						Soyapilca	386
						Tancoyol	255
						Mallila	599
						Amatlan	260

Hacienda San Nicolás Concá	1	42			Razón, Esclavos	215
					Indios	234
Misión San Juan Bautista Pacula	2	40			Spaniards, mestizos, mulattoes	477
					Pames	1,234
Jurisdicción San Luis de la Paz						
Pueblo San Luis de la Paz			unknown	S.J.	Jonaces	245
Misión San Miguel de la Cruz Milagrosa	1		1	Santo Domingo, México	Jonaces	234
Pueblo San Juan Bautista Xichú		10	1	San Francisco, Michoacán	Jonaces	249
Real San Francisco Xichú				Chichimecas	Chichimecas	30
South-East Margins Real de Zimapán	1					
Misión de Tolimán		46	3	San Francisco, Pachuca	Chichimecas	67
Jurisdicción de Meztitlán						
Pueblo Jacala-Otupilla	90 Españoles voluntarios					
M. Chapulhuacan				unknown	unknown	
Villa de Valles						
M. Xilitla, Tilaco, Labor						

Source: AGN, Historia, vol. 522, f. 133–36; Mendoza Muñoz, *El Conde de Sierra Gorda, don José de Escandón y Helguera*, 104–9.

TABLE E.2 Spanish New Santander in 1757 (with Dates of Founding)

	Population		Calidades			Economy				
	Families	Total	Sp.	Mest.	Mul.	Ag.	Irr.	Salt	Silver	Livestock
SIERRA GORDA										
Santa Bárbara	85	424	x		x	x			x	3,083
Palmilla (1755)	25	67				x				3,667
Jaumave (1743)	88	428				x	x		x	7,799
R. Infantes (1749)	32	234				x	x		x	4,709
S. Gorda Total	230	1,154	1		1	4	2		3	19,445
SW TRANSITION										
Altamira (1749)	81	361	x		x			x		4,363
Horcasitas	73	367	x		x	x			x	1,790
Escandón (1751)	65	264				x	x	x	x	1,432
Llera (1742)	82	296	x	x	x	x	x		x	1,749
Aguayo (1750)	178	989	x		x	x	x		x	6,919
Guemes	79	373	x		x	x	x		x	11,647
SW Tran. Total	558	2,650	5	1	5	5	4	2	5	27,900
CENTRAL CORREDOR										
Soto la Marina (1750)	66	340	x	x	x	x		x		27,681
Santillana	17	71	x		x	x	x	x		5,963
Santander (1749)	126	496	x	x	x	x	x			3,221
Padilla	67	370	x		x	x				12,356
Real de Borbón	107	455				x			x	3,397
Hoyos	69	444				x	x			34,396
Cent Cor. Total	452	2,176	4	2	4	5	4	2	1	87,396
RÍO CONCHOS										
San Fernando (1749)	69	365	x		x	x		x		18,420
Burgos (1749)	52	214				x	x			10,155
Río Conchos Total	121	579	1		1	2	1	1		28,575
RÍO GRANDE										
Reynosa (1749)	57	310				x		x		17,970
Camargo (1749)	95	679	x		x	x		x		82,252
Mier (1757)	39	258				x	x	x		40,740
Revilla (1750)	61	400	x	x	x	x	x	x		50,523
Rancho Dolores (1750)	30	123								9,050
Laredo (1755)	12	84								10,201
Río Grande Total	294	1,854	2	1	2	4	2	4		210,716
N. Santander Total	1,655	8,413	13	4	13	20	13	9	9	326,305

Sp. = Spaniards; Mest. = Mestizos; Mul. = Mulattoes; Ag. = cultivation under way; Irr. = irrigation used..

"x" denotes activity present; blank denotes no activity.

Source: López de la Cámara Alta, Descripción general de la Colonia de Nuevo Santander, my calculations.

began the enduring settlement and commercial development of coastal regions long left to independent native peoples. López de Cámara Alta's report aimed to capture a complex, fluid, often conflictive situation.

The thrust along the Gulf lowlands to settle New Santander was a military enterprise with religious accompaniment and commercial goals. Salaried officers and soldiers far outnumbered religious personnel (including those assigned to missions). Officers were always estate builders; soldiers expected to become landed settlers. Their salaries compensated for the risks of facing native warriors defending independence and home communities; the same funds facilitated commercial development, large and small. Most notably, soldiers, missionary clergy, and natives were far outnumbered by European livestock, the primary "settlers" of New Santander, especially in the north along the Río Grande and beyond. Table E.3 details the military presence, the salaries of officers and soldiers, and the presence of clergy in Spanish settlements.

The project to settle New Santander did include missions, aiming to fulfill their usual role of bringing once independent peoples to lives of settled, cultivating, laboring Christianity. The missions increased the presence and role of clergy, but they remained far less a presence than the military. By 1757 missionaries engaged few of the independent peoples of the Gulf lowlands, and fewer had been baptized. Table E.4 summarizes the state of missions that year.

Many more indigenous nations and people remained independent. Some fought the thrust of colonization, some tried to ignore it, others engaged it on their own terms.

All the effort and expense of settling soldiers and building missions was aimed at accelerating a commercial economy. While most indigenous peoples remained independent and many resisted, less than a decade after Escandón's drive began, a complex commercial economy mixed cultivation, stock grazing, the extraction of salt, and a search for silver.

TABLE E.3 Officers, Soldiers, and Clergy in Spanish New Santander, 1757

	Captains		Lieutenants		Sergeants		Soldiers		Clergy		
	No.	Salaried	No.	Salaried	No.	Salaried	No.	Salaried	No.	Stipend	Base
SIERRA GORDA											
Santa Bárbara	1	800	1	no	1	no	settlers	no	1		
Palmillas											
Jaumave			1	no	1	no	settlers	no			
Real Infantes	1	no			1	no					
SOUTHWEST TRANSITION											
Altamira	1	500			1	250	8	225			
Horcasitas	1	500			1	250	9	225	1		Zacatecas
Escandón	1	500			1	250	6	225			
Llera											
Aguayo	1	500	1	no	1	no	settlers	no			
Guemes	1	500			1	no	2	225	1		Zacatecas
CENTRAL CORRIDOR											
Soto la Marina	1	500			1	250	9	225			
Santillana											
Santander	1	500	2	250	15	225					

	Captains		Lieutenants		Sergeants		Soldiers		Clergy		
	No.	Salaried	No.	Salaried	No.	Salaried	No.	Salaried	No.	Stipend	Base
CENTRAL CORRIDOR											
Padilla	1	500	1	400	2	250	18	225			
Real de Borbón											
Hoyos	1	no	1	no	1	no	settlers	no			
RÍO CONCHOS											
San Fernando	1	500			1	250	8	225			
Burgos	1	500			1	250	10	225	1	350	Zacatecas
RÍO GRANDE											
Reynosa	1	500			1	250	9	225	1	350	Zacatecas
Camargo	1	500			1	250	11	225	1		
Mier	1	no									
Revilla	1	no									
Rancho											
Dolores											
Laredo											

Source: López de la Cámara Alta, *Descripción general de la Colonia de Nuevo Santander*, my calculations.

TABLE E.4 New Santander Missions, 1757

			Population			Clergy		
Mission		Indigenous Nations	Families	Total	Baptized	No.	Stipend	Base
SIERRA GORDA								
Santa Bárbara	yes	Janambres Pames						
Palmillas	Nuestro Señora de Nieves	Pisones	25		all	1		Michoacán
Jaumave	San Juan Bautista	Pisones	15	67	all	1	no	
Real Infantes	yes	Pisones	7		45	1	yes	
					25			
SOUTHWEST TRANSITION								
Altamira	yes	Anacaná	38		34	1		
Horcasitas	San Francisco Xavier	Palagueques	37	95	12	1		Zacatecas
Escandón	yes	Pames		166		1	350	Zacatecas
Llera	Divina Pastora	Pisones		150	all	1	350	
Aguayo	unknown	Pisones	50		53			
Guemes								

			Population			Clergy		
	Mission	Indigenous Nations	Families	Total	Baptized	No.	Stipend	Base
CENTRAL CORRIDOR								
Soto la Marina	Purísima Concepción			210	all			
SANTILLANA								
Santander Padilla	Helguera	Bocas Prietas		300	none	unknown		
R. Borbón								
Hoyos	San Pedro Alcántara		100	400	none	1	no	Zacatecas
Río Conchos								
San Fernando	yes	Pintos		173	12			
Burgos	no							
Río Grande								
Reynosa	San Joaquín Monte	Nazos, Narices, Comecrudos, Texanos		188	20	1		
Camargo								
Mier								
Revilla	no							
Rancho Dolores								
Laredo								

Source: López de la Cámara Alta, *Descripción General de la Colonia de Nuevo Santander*, my calculations.

TABLE E.5 Independent Natives, New Santander, 1757

		Population				
	Nations	Families	Total	Bowmen	Economy	War or Peace
Sierra Gorda						
Santa Bárbara						
Palmillas	Pisones			100		unknown
Jaumave	Pisones					mix
R. Infantes	Pisones					peace
Southwest Transition						
Altamira	Mapalcaná, Cataicaná, Anacaná, Caramiguay, Panguay, Zapoteros					
Horcasitas	Olives	21	71			war, Spanish alli
	Huastecas	30	107			peace
	Mariguanes					war and peace
	Martínez		3,000			peace
	Caramariguanes					peace
	Positos, Oretines					war
	Panguanes					war
	Zapateros					war
Escandón	Pames					
Llera	Pisones					war and peace
	Janambres	60	250			war
	Neolinas					war
	Mariguanes					war
Aguayo	Janambres					war and peace
	Pisones					war and peace
Guemes	no hay Cong.				hunt	
Central Corridor						
Soto la Marina	Mariguanes				cultivate	peace
	Positos				cultivate	peace
	Caribay,				coast gather	war
	Comecamotes,				coast gather	war
	Anacariguayes,				coast gather	war
	Tagualiles,				coast gather	war
	Positos				coast gather	war
Santillana	Tumapacanas			350	Gentiles, serve Spaniards	peace
	Positos					
Santander	Mariguanes		10,000 in highlands, 3,000 along coast		cultivate	war and peace
	Martínez					

	Nations	Population			Economy	War or Peace
		Families	Total	Bowmen		
lla	Gentiles de Tamaulipas,				do not serve	
	Mezquitas, Serrones				Spaniards	war
de Borbón	Indios de Sierra Madre					
	Tamaulipas					war
os	Gentiles y apostates					war
Conchos						
Fernando	Comecrudos			160	at Lagunas	war and peace
	Tedejeños		73		at coast	war and peace
os	Apóstatas de N. León:				all in Sierra	war
	Guajalotes,					war
	Códimas,					war
	Canaynenas,					war
	Borrodos					war
Grande						
osa	Pintos				nearby	peace
	Tanaquiapenes		1,700		downriver	peace
	Soulapaguemes				downriver	peace
	Juayapemes,				downriver	peace
	Jaupaguanes,				downriver	peace
	Huscapemes,				downriver	peace
	Comesecapemes,				downriver	peace
	Catoromepaques				downriver	peace
	Negros con Indios				island at mouth	war
argo	Carrizos				all in rancherías;	peace
	Catamanos				visit town	peace
	Cocolares					peace
	Garzas,					
	Malaguecos	60	220		work for Spaniards	
						peace
lla	Carrizos, Catamanos,					unknown
	Cacalotes,					
res	no Indios					
do	no fear of Indios					peace

ce: López de la Cámara Alta, *Descripción General de la Colonia de Nuevo Santander,* my calculations.

TABLE E.6 The Economy of Spanish New Santander, 1757

Place	Maize			Other	Agriculture			Livestock		Mineral	
	Irrigation	Planted	Yield (in fanegas)	Frijol	Chile	Caña	Frutas	Total	Primary	Salt	Silver
SIERRA GORDA											
Santa Bárbara		80f	150	x				3,083			
Palmillas		45f	150	x		x		3,667			
Jaumave	x	50f	180	x	x			7,799	5,406 sheep		x
Real de Infantex		50f	200	x	x			4,709	3,799 sheep		x
SOUTHWEST TRANSITION											
Altamira (trade prime)								4,363		x	
Horcasitas		6f		x				1,790			x
Escandón	x							1,422		x	x
Llera	x	40f	100	x	x		x	1,749			x
Aguayo	x	70f	100			x	x	6,919			x
Guemes	x	40f	180	x				11,647	7,235 sheep		x
CENTRAL CORRIDOR											
Soto la Marina		2f	70					27,681	20,900 sheep	x	
Santillana	x	7f	200					5,963	4,240 sheep		
Santander	x	30f	200				x	3,221	1,160 sheep	x	

Place									
Padilla					x		12,356	10,808 sheep	x
Real de Borbón	x	x	2f				3,397		x
Hoyos	x	x	75f	150	x	x	34,396	27,024 sheep	x
RÍO CONCHOS San Fernando	x		5f		x		18,420	11,600 sheep	x
Burgos	x						10,155	6,960 sheep	
RÍO GRANDE Reynosa							17,976	13,890 sheep	x
Camargo			40f	100	x	x	82,252	71,770 sheep	x
Mier	x		3f	180			40,720	38,659 sheep	
Revilla	x		2f		x		50,523	43,770 sheep	x
Dolores							9,050	3,000 steers, 3,000 mares	
Laredo							10,201		

"x" denotes activity present; blank denotes no activity.

Source: López de la Cámara Alta, *Descripción General de la Colonia de Nuevo Santander*, my calculations.

Appendix F

Population, Ethnicity, Family, and Work

in Rural Communities, 1791–1792

The analysis of rural communities in chapter 4 focuses on La Griega and Puerto de Nieto, Bajío estates within the Obra Pía properties controlled by don José Sánchez Espinosa from the 1780s to the 1820s. The two communities are open to analysis thanks to a unique confluence of sources: census manuscripts from 1791–92, managers' letters from 1780 to 1826, and operating accounts covering production, prices, sales, work, wages, and rents from 1811 to 1826 for La Griega and from 1820 to 1826 for Puerto de Nieto.

But could the two communities represent the region, the eastern Bajío? Chapter 7 shows that La Griega and Puerto de Nieto participated in the same regional economy and shared general economic operations. Yet the two estate communities differed sharply in social composition: La Griega was divided between a large Spanish minority and an indigenous majority, while Puerto de Nieto integrated Spaniards, mestizos, mulattoes, and indios. To place the two communities in context this appendix offers quantitative portraits of ten estates (and two towns) from La Griega, east of Querétaro, northwest to Puerto de Nieto, at the eastern edge of the jurisdiction of San Miguel, based on the militia census of 1791–92.

The census reports are exceptionally detailed, yet limited. Militia service excluded indio men. The census thus reports only households headed by men classed as Spaniards, mestizos, and mulattoes. It reports name, age, ethnic status, place of birth, and economic role, wives' names and ethnic categories, plus the ages and economic roles of adult male children. It also reports the number of adult dependent women and minor children, male and female. Because indigenous men and the households they headed are excluded, we can only estimate the indigenous presence in estate communities. But because the census does include indigenous women married to men of other categories, it allows calculations of intermarriage among ethnic groups, including indigenous peoples. For the estates in the Querétaro jurisdiction (all but Puerto de Nieto) the tribute census of 1807 allows an approximation of the size of the indigenous population. See appendix G, especially table G.16.

Close analysis of the census manuscripts reveals that different enumerators at different communities paid more or less attention to different questions. Some carefully noted places of birth; others reported nearly everyone the same way. Some precisely detailed economic roles; others left ambiguities. As a result, this appendix explores each community separately, highlighting local variations. I have not combined the results from different communities into a general analysis. Doing so would offer a vision of life that no community experienced. Within broad regional parameters, local variation defined life across the eastern Bajío as the eighteenth century ended—a key conclusion.

The República of La Cañada and Amascala Basin Estates

Between Querétaro and the Amascala basin to the east lay the canyon town of San Pedro de la Cañada. Originally a Pame settlement, it was the first site of Querétaro, before the Otomí moved to the bottomlands just west. In the 1750s the corregidor described La Cañada's lush huertas and luxurious baths, and complained that the community blocked Spanish settlement. The canyon that concentrated the waters sustaining Querétaro remained an indigenous enclave into the eighteenth century. The census totals for 1778 (appendix C, table C.2) showed 134 Spaniards, 100 mestizos, and 52 mulattoes, totaling 286 non-indigenous peoples—9 percent of a community of nearly 3,200. A small Hispanic population gained a place at La Cañada after 1750.

The militia census of 1791 reported only 36 non-indigenous households with 136 residents. (In 1778 only totals had been reported, not household listings; the census likely included outlying ranchos with Hispanic residents.) As the eighteenth century ended, the non-indigenous population at La Cañada remained small and lived in small households, averaging only 3.5 members. There were no households of one, and very few of five or more. Most Hispanic residents at La Cañada were young newcomers, still forming families in a community with an indigenous majority.

In that emerging minority community marriage patterns are also revealing. Most heads of non-indigenous households at La Cañada were classed as Spaniards. Two-thirds married women of the same category, a third married mestizas, and one married an india.

While nearly half the non-indigenous men at La Cañada cultivated the land, having gained access to huertas by purchase or marriage (perhaps explaining ties to mestizas), the rest pursued a variety of occupations typical of a rural town: there were priests, a schoolteacher, small traders, managers and specialists at a mill powered by the waters rushing down the canyon, and a variety of craftsmen. None engaged in textile production. Perhaps cloth making had

TABLE F.1 Non-indigenous Population and Family Size at La Cañada, 1791

Family Size	Number of Families	Total Population	Percentage	Family Size	Number of Families	Total Population	Percentage
1				6	2	12	9
2	10	20	16	7	1	7	6
3	11	33	26	8	1	8	6
4	8	32	25	TOTAL	36	127	100
5	3	15	12				

Source: AGN, Padrones, vol. 39, ff. 207v–209; vol. 40, 69, my calculations.

TABLE F.2 Marriage in Non-indigenous Households at La Cañada, 1791

Male Head	Spouse					Total
	Spaniard	Mestiza	Mulata	Cacica	India	
Spaniard	18	8			1	27
Mestizo	1	1				2
Mulatto					1	1
Cacique	1					1
TOTAL	20	9			2	31

Source: AGN, Padrones, vol. 39, ff. 207v–209; vol. 40, 69, my calculations.

TABLE F.3 Economic Roles of Non-indigenous Men at La Cañada, 1791

Priest	2	Shoe maker	1
School master	1	Tailor	1
Storekeeper	1	Mill administrator	1
Tobacco agent	1	Mill steward	1
Peddler	1	Miller	1
Candle maker	3	Granary keeper	1
Hat maker	3	Laborer	1
Blacksmith	2	Labrador	18
Sculptor	1	TOTAL	40

Source: AGN, Padrones, vol. 39, ff. 207v–209; vol. 40, 69, my calculations.

been monopolized by native households combining weaving and spinning with huerta cultivation. Surely there were also indigenous traders and craftsmen. Still, the emerging Hispanic minority at La Cañada focused on professional, commercial, and craft roles.

The listings for La Cañada clearly differentiate places of birth for male heads of household. Twenty were born in La Cañada, eight in Querétaro, and five elsewhere.

TABLE F.4 Non-indigenous Heads of Household Born at La Cañada, 1791

Age	Craftsmen	Labradores	Total	Age	Craftsmen	Labradores	Total
≤20				51–60	2	3	5
21–30	1	4	5	61+		2	2
31–40	2	4	6	TOTAL	6	14	20
41–50	1	1	2				

Source: AGN, Padrones, vol. 39, ff. 207v–209; vol. 40, 69, my calculations.

TABLE F.5 Extended Non-indigenous Families at La Cañada, 1791

Families in Clan	Number of Clans	Total Families	Total Population	Population per Clan
1	19	19	80	4
2	2	4	12	6
3	3	9	22	7
4	1	4	13	13
TOTAL	25	36	127	5

Source: AGN, Padrones, vol. 39, ff. 207v–209; vol. 40, 69, my calculations.

The presence of men born in La Cañada more than fifty years before 1791 suggests that the corregidor exaggerated the exclusion of Spaniards in the 1750s. The majority of Hispanic craftsmen and cultivators had been born in La Cañada, suggesting that local roots were key to gaining customers and huertas. Professionals and managers came from outside. The six migrants from nearby Querétaro were young, between twenty-one and thirty-four, and included the priests, the schoolmaster, and all three traders, but only two cultivators. Among craftsmen only the tailor, born at Irapuato, came from outside. The mill also engaged outsiders: the administrator, only thirty-one, came from Castile; the steward, fifty-two, came from Jilotepec to the south; the miller, forty, was a cacique from San Miguel el Grande; and the forty-four-year-old granary keeper came from the Ajuchitlán estate to the southeast. The mill, between Querétaro and La Cañada, was operated by outsiders rooted in neither community.

Patriarchal extended family clans often organized life in rural communities in the eastern Bajío. At La Cañada, however, they were rare among nonindigenous residents. A young Hispanic minority lived mostly in single-family households.

La Griega lay eight miles (thirteen kilometers) east of La Cañada, twelve miles (nineteen kilometers) east of Querétaro. Operated in 1791 by don José Sánchez Espinosa, it was a large, estate-based community in the center of the Amascala basin. It had a larger non-indigenous population, with larger households and larger extended family clans than La Cañada.

Among non-indigenous families at La Griega the mean household size was

TABLE: F.6 Non-indigenous Population and Family Size at La Griega, 1791

Family Size	Number of Families	Total Population	Percent of Population	Family Size	Number of Families	Total Population	Percent of Population
1	4	4	1	7			
2	12	24	7	8	2	16	5
3	10	30	9	9	3	27	8
4	15	60	19	10	1	10	3
5	9	45	14	11	2	22	7
6	14	84	26	TOTAL	72	322	100

Source: AGN, Padrones, vol. 39, 202v–206; vol. 40, 68–69.

TABLE F.7 Ethnic Category and Intermarriage at La Griega, 1791

Male Head	Spouse				Total
	Spanish	Mestiza	Mulata	India	
Spanish	51	3			54
Mestizo	2	3			5
Mulatto			1	2	3
TOTAL	53	6	1	2	62

Source: AGN, Padrones, vol. 39, 202v–206; vol. 40, 68–69.

4.5, clearly larger than at La Cañada. More than half the population lived in households of five or more. The Hispanic families at La Griega were large and well established.

Men classed as Spaniards, including three immigrants from Spain, headed fifty-four of the sixty-two non-indigenous households there. Those Spaniards were exceptionally endogamous, all but three marrying women also classed as Spaniards. Whatever the attraction of mestizo wives at La Cañada (probably access to land), it did not operate at La Griega.

Both the census totals from 1778 and labor accounts from 1811 indicate that indigenous people formed a 60 percent majority at La Griega (appendix C, table C.2; AGN, Bienes Nacionales, v. 558, La Griega Accounts, 1811–12). The tribute count of 1807 (table G.16) indicates an even larger Otomí presence. In that context the 94 percent endogamy rate of Spanish men indicates a sharp ethnic divide.

The enumerator at La Griega was not careful with economic roles. He reported fifteen households at the estate center, then added fifty-seven tenants. Among the latter every man is a labrador—a cultivator. It is not clear that all were tenants. Administrative letters note cultivation on estate account and separate tenants from sirvientes—employed cultivators. Most Hispanic men at La Griega were cultivators: some tenants, others employees; we cannot know

TABLE F.8 Economic Roles of Non-indigenous Men at La Griega, 1791

	Number	Percent
ADMINISTRATIVE		
Mayordomo	3	4
Ayudante	1	1
CRAFTSMEN		
Blacksmith	1	1
Ventero	1	1
STOCKHERDERS		
Caporal	1	1
Vaquero	5	6
Guardamonte	1	1
CULTIVATORS		
Labrador	67	84
TOTAL	80	100

Source: AGN, Padrones, vol. 39, 202v–206; vol. 40, 68–69.

TABLE F.9 Age of Non-indigenous Labradores at La Griega, 1791

	Number	Percent		Number	Percent
≤20	7	10	51–60	11	16
21–30	21	31	61+	7	10
31–40	8	12	TOTAL	67	100
41–50	13	19			

Source: AGN, Padrones, vol. 39, 202v–206; vol. 40, 68–69.

exact numbers. The few who were not cultivators were craftsmen or herders working on estate account. There were no traders.

The enumerator at La Griega listed nearly every male head of household as having been born in Querétaro—not in the city, but in the jurisdiction, which included Querétaro, La Cañada, La Griega, and nearby estates. The only exceptions were the three men born in Spain and the two from San Juan del Río, just south. An indication of the longevity of the Hispanic community at La Griega is the ages of the men listed as labradores—working the land as tenants or employees, household heads and dependent youths.

Over 45 percent of cultivators were over forty; another 41 percent were thirty or younger. The La Griega community was established and expanding, with several large clans.

A large and long-established Hispanic population at La Griega had created extended families. Only 36 percent lived in households without male kin heading other households; 41 percent were part of small clans of two or three households; and 28 percent lived in the four clans of four to six households.

TABLE F.10 Non-indigenous Extended Family Clans at La Griega, 1791

Families in Clan	Number of Clans	Number of Families	Total Population	Percentage of Population	Population per Clan
1	28	28	116	36	4.1
2	3	6	25	8	8.3
3	6	18	92	29	15.3
4	1	4	13	4	13.0
5	2	10	51	16	25.5
6	1	6	25	8	25.0
TOTAL	41	72	322	100	7.9

Source: AGN, Padrones, vol. 39, 202v–206; vol. 40, 68–69.

TABLE F.11 Population and Family Size at Chichimequillas, 1791

Household Size	Number of Families	Total Population	Percentage of Population	Household Size	Number of Families	Total Population	Percentage of Population
1	5	5	1	8	5	40	10
2	11	22	6	9	7	63	17
3	9	27	7	10	1	10	3
4	11	44	12	11			
5	7	35	9	12	1	12	3
6	10	60	16	TOTAL	76	381	100
7	9	63	17				

Source: AGN Padrones, vol. 39, ff. 194–98; vol. 40, pp. 63–64;, my calculations.

Kinship ties were surely more extensive. The largest clan, the six Franco households (headed by the resident manager), was linked by marriage to the Guerrero family of five households, the Mendoza clan of four households, and the Burgos and Sandi of three households each, creating a complex managerial clan of at least twenty-one households and ninety-six people, accounting for 30 percent of the estate's Hispanic population. The only large clan not related to the Francos was the Rangels, a group of five families recently displaced from management.

The Chichimequillas estate lay north of La Griega, at the limits of the Amascala basin, eighteen miles (twenty-nine kilometers) northeast of Querétaro. The estate was owned by Querétaro's Carmelite convent, and its Hispanic community included a few more family households and many more people than La Griega. Large households ruled at Chichimequillas. Not only was the mean household size five, but two-thirds of the non-indigenous population lived in families of six or more.

Spaniards headed most non-indigenous households at Chichimequillas, as at La Cañada and La Griega. But by making up only 57 percent of the popula-

TABLE F.12 Ethnic Categories and Marriage at Chichimequillas, 1791

	Spouse					
Male Head	Spaniard	Mestiza	Mulatta	Cacica	India	Total
Spaniard	30	7		2		39
Mestizo	2	13		2		17
Mulatto	5	2	2		1	10
Cacique		1		1		2
TOTAL	37	23	2	5	1	68

Source: AGN Padrones, vol. 39, ff. 194–98; vol. 40, pp. 63–64; my calculations.

tion, Spaniards dominated far less than at La Griega. Similarly, Spaniards at Chichimequillas were generally endogamous (77 percent), yet less so than at La Griega (94 percent).

The Hispanic population at Chichimequillas included significantly more mestizos and mulattoes than at La Griega. Spaniards and mestizos shared endogamy rates of 76 to 77 percent—if mestizos marrying mestizas was endogamy. The small mulatto population was notably exogamous: five of the ten men married Spaniards and only two married mulattas. The one characteristic shared with La Griega was the near-absence of marriage between Hispanic and indigenous people, with most exceptions involving caciques. While at La Griega a sharp ethnic line separated Spaniards from an indigenous majority, at Chichimequillas the hard line divided a more diverse Hispanic community from indigenous residents who cannot be counted for 1971, but totaled at least 167 households in 1807 (table G.16).

The enumerator at Chichimequillas paid close attention to men's economic roles, carefully delineating tenants (listed as arrendatarios) from employed cultivators (listed as labradores). In addition, the number and diversity of craftsmen at Chichimequillas and the differing roles of men of different ethnic categories reveal a complex estate community:

TABLE F.13 Non-indigenous Economic Roles at Chichimequillas, 1791

	Spaniard	Mestizo	Mulatto	Cacique	Total	Percentage
ADMINISTRATIVE						
Mayordomo	3				3	
Ayudante			1		1	
Servant	1				1	
TOTAL	4		1		5	5
CRAFTSMEN						
Herrero	1	2			3	
Panadero	1				1	
Sastre	1				1	
Hat maker	3				3	
TOTAL	6	2			8	9

	Spaniard	Mestizo	Mulatto	Cacique	Total	Percentage
TEXTILES						
Tejedor	8		2		10	
Cardador	3	1			4	
Hilador	2	3			5	
Dorador	1				1	
TOTAL	14	4	2		20	22
LIVESTOCK						
Arriero			1		1	
Caporal		2	1		3	
Vaquero		1	4		5	
Pastor	1				1	
Guardamonte	1				1	
TOTAL	2	3	6		11	12
AGRICULTURE						
Arrendatario	11	9			20	
Labrador	11	14	2	2	29	
TOTAL	22	23	2	2	49	53
GRAND TOTAL	48	32	11	2	93	100

Source: AGN Padrones, vol. 39, ff. 194–98; vol. 40, pp. 63–64; my calculations.

The managers, blacksmiths, muleteer, stock herders, and cultivators held roles common at estates, including La Griega. But the textile makers and men devoted to tailoring, hat making, and baking were different. Some appear to have provided goods and services to the estate community. Others, notably the cloth makers, sustained household manufacturing that supplied local needs and outside markets. Chichimequillas was becoming a diverse economic community—while still an estate enterprise.

The economic roles of men of differing ethnic categories are revealing. Spaniards dominated management and craftwork, rarely participated in stock grazing, and joined with mestizos in cultivation, equally divided between tenants and employees. Mestizos appeared among the small number of craftsmen and livestock workers and mostly worked in agriculture (twenty-three of thirty-two). Among mestizo cultivators nine were tenants and fourteen served as employees. Mulattoes concentrated in livestock activities; only two were employed as cultivators. The two caciques were agricultural employees. Ethnic status mattered in work and production.

The enumerator at Chichimequillas also noted that all had been born in Querétaro. The age distribution of tenants and employees reveals much about community development.

Among the tenants, 75 percent were over forty. Nearly 50 percent of employees were under thirty.

TABLE F.14 Age Distribution of Non-indigenous Cultivators at Chichimequillas, 1791

Age	Arrendatarios	Labradores	Total	Age	Arrendatarios	Labradores	Total
≤20	1	4	5	51–60	5	4	9
21–30	1	10	11	61+	1	3	4
31–40	3	2	5	TOTAL	20	29	49
41–50	9	6	15				

Source: AGN Padrones, vol. 39, ff. 194–98; vol. 40, pp. 63–64; my calculations.

TABLE F.15 Non-indigenous Extended Family Clans at Chichimequillas, 1791

Families in Clan	Number of Clans	Total Families	Total Population	Percentage of Population
1	25	25	132	35
2	11	22	98	26
3	5	15	85	22
4				
5	1	5	22	6
6				
7				
8				
9	1	9	44	12
TOTAL	43	76	381	100

Source: AGN Padrones, vol. 39, ff. 194–98; vol. 40, pp. 63–64; my calculations.

Chichimequillas had not developed large clans, perhaps because of dispersed settlement.

Chichimequillas, like La Griega, had a large managerial clan. The Lozada clan included nine households: three mayordomos, three hat makers, a baker, two carders, and two weavers. Lozadas had married with the Ruiz, a clan of five households, twenty-two people, including a weaver; the Pereas and the Campos, each with three households and together totaling thirty-six people, including a weaver and a spinner; and the Ximénez, a clan of two families, ten people, and a weaver. In total the Lozadas and their kin included 24 households and 128 people—34 percent of the estate's Hispanic population. The clan ruled management and textile production. The managerial Lozadas used their role to build a family-based cloth industry at Chichimequillas.

The Santa Rosa Basin: Segregating Estates and a Free Community

Extending from Querétaro along the road to San Luis Potosí, a series of basins gained altitude as they reached northward. Small streams coming down from

TABLE F.16 Non-indigenous Population and Family Size at Juriquilla, 1791

Family Size	Number of Families	Total Population	Percentage of Population	Family Size	Number of Families	Total Population	Percentage of Population
1	1	1	1	6	6	36	25
2	3	6	4	7	2	14	10
3	8	24	17	8	1	8	6
4	7	28	20	TOTAL	33	142	100
5	5	25	18				

Source: AGN, Padrones, vol. 39, ff. 238–39; vol. 40, pp. 63–64; my calculations.

TABLE F.17 Ethnic Category and Marriage at Juriquilla, 1791

Male Head	Spouse				Total
	Spaniard	Mestiza	Mulatta	India	
Spaniard	8				8
Mestizo	1	3			4
Mulatto			16	3	19
TOTAL	9	3	16	3	31

Source: AGN, Padrones, vol. 39, ff. 238–39; vol. 40, pp. 63–64; my calculations.

surrounding uplands allowed irrigation. The basins were ruled by two sets of estates: don Pedro de Septién's Juriquilla, Solana, and San Isidro, in the southern basin and nearby uplands; and don Francisco de Velasco's Santa Catarina, Monte del Negro, and Buenavista to the north. Amid those estates the town of Santa Rosa (now de Jáuregui) was developing. These estates were smaller yet more socially diverse than La Griega and Chichimequillas. At the northern limit of the zone lay Jofre, the largest, most diverse of the Querétaro communities analyzed here.

Juriquilla sat nine miles (fifteen kilometers) northwest of Querétaro, the first of three Septién properties that a northward traveler encountered. La Solana and San Isidro extended his holdings toward hills northeast and northwest. Juriquilla's non-indigenous community included 33 families and 142 people, or 4.3 per household. Nearly 60 percent lived in households of five people or more.

Compared to La Griega and Chichimequillas, Juriquilla was a diverse community that included Spaniards, mestizos, and many mulattoes. Still, endogamy ruled.

Spaniards were almost fully endogamous. Spaniards and mestizos were fully endogamous among themselves. Mulatto men were 84 percent endogamous—the three exceptions had married indias. The community divided between a few Spaniards and mestizos and a larger group of mulattoes, who formed links

TABLE F.18 Economic Roles of Non-indigenous Men at Juriquilla, 1791

	Spaniards	Mestizos	Mulattoes	Total
ADMINISTRATION				
Administrator	1			1
Mayordomo	1			1
Ayudante	1			1
Servant	1			1
SPECIALISTS				
Herrero	1			1
Perchero	1			1
Arriero		1	3	4
Vaquero			1	1
AGRICULTURE				
Labrador	5	1	5	11
Arrendatario		1	13	14
Arrendatario Cantero		1		1
TOTAL	11	4	22	37

Source: AGN, Padrones, vol. 39, ff. 238–39; vol. 40, pp. 63–64; my calculations.

TABLE F.19 Age and Ethnic Category of Non-indigenous Men Born at Juriquilla, 1791

	Spaniards	Mestizos	Mulattoes	Total
≤20				
21–30	1		6	7
31–40			5	5
41–50	1	1	1	3
51–60			4	4
61+				
TOTAL	2	1	16	19

Source: AGN, Padrones, vol. 39, ff. 238–39; vol. 40, pp. 63–64; my calculations.

to uncounted indigenous families. The latter included at least sixty-six house-holds in 1807 (table G.16).

There were also economic separations. Spaniards ruled administration; a minority were employed cultivators, favored with security through salaries and food rations. Most mulattoes were tenants. Was Juriquilla opening new uplands, offering mulattoes limited independence along with inevitable inse-curity?

The enumerator at Juriquilla paid close attention to the place of birth. Nearly all the mulattoes had been born at the estate. Most Spaniards and mes-tizos were newcomers.

The number and age distribution of mulattoes confirm that they were a group established at the estate. The adminstrator and two kinsmen came from Apaseo, three Spaniards and two mestizos from Querétaro, a mestizo and a mulatto from Santa Rosa, and a Spaniard and a mulatto from Jurica, an estate just south. Juriquilla had a core of mulatto tenants, long at the estate, perhaps descended from an earlier slave population. Spaniards managed—probably overseeing uncounted indigenous workers on estate fields.

As a community of mulattoes (some perhaps newly freed) and recent arrivals, Juriquilla lacked large clans:

TABLE F.20 Non-indigenous Extended Family Clans at Juriquilla, 1791

Number of Households	Number of Clans	Total Familes	Total Population	Population per Clan
1	24	24	107	4.5
2	3	6	22	7.3
3	1	3	8	8.0
TOTAL	28	33	137	4.9

Source: AGN, Padrones, vol. 39, ff. 238–39; vol. 40, pp. 63–64; my calculations.

TABLE F.21 Non-indigenous Population and Family Size at La Solana, 1791

Family Size	Spaniards		Mestizos		Total	
	Number	Population	Number	Population	Number	Population
1	1	1			1	1
2	1	2	2	4	3	6
3	1	3			1	3
4	4	16	3	12	7	28
5	2	10	1	5	3	15
6	2	12	2	12	4	24
7	1	7	1	7	2	14
8						
9			1	9	1	9
11			1	11	1	11
TOTAL	12	51	11	60	23	111

Source: AGN, Padrones, vol. 39, ff. 243–45, my calculations.

The few clans of two or three households were mostly mulattoes. In contrast to La Griega and Chichimequillas where managers dominated through large clans, at Juriquilla the steward was an outsider tied by marriage to one household and two migrants from his hometown of Apaseo. Ruling mulatto tenants was different.

Six miles (ten kilometers) northeast of Juriquilla lay La Solana, also owned by don Pedro Septién. It was a small community of 23 families and 111 residents, divided between Spaniards and mestizos—and no mulattoes. There were sixty-eight Otomí households there in 1807, and many youths seeking work too (table G.16). Ethnic segregation among Hispanic residents marked Septién's estates—which all included an indigenous underclass.

Households headed by Spaniards were a majority. But they were smaller, leaving families led by mestizos a majority of the population.

Ethnic endogamy ruled at La Solana:

TABLE F.22 Ethnic Category and Marriage at La Solana, 1791

Male Head	Spouse					Total
	Spaniard	Mestiza	Mulata	Cacica	India	
Spaniard	11					11
Mestizo	1	6		1		8
Mulato						
Cacique						
Indio		1				1
TOTAL	12	7		1		20

Source: AGN, Padrones, vol. 39, ff. 243–45, my calculations.

TABLE F.23 Non-indigenous Economic Roles at La Solana, 1791

	Spaniards		Mestizos		Total		Total
	Arren-datario	Labrador	Arren-datario	Labrador	Arren-datario	Labrador	
≤20	1	3	1	6	2	9	11
21–30	4	3	3		7	3	10
31–40		1		1		2	2
41–50	5	1	3		8	1	9
51–60	1		1		2		2
61+			1		1		1
TOTAL	11	8	9	7	20	15	35

Source: AGN, Padrones, vol. 39, ff. 243–45, my calculations.

Juriquilla and Solana were ethnically segregated: mulattoes concentrated at Juriquilla, Spaniards and mestizos at Solana. Yet both were settlements of tenant families.

While Spaniards and mestizos held similar economic roles, the community faced a generational divide. Most men over forty were tenants, working lands on their own account. A larger group of men thirty and younger included a few tenants, while most lived as household dependents. Would young cultivators soon gain lands? Or did a new generation face life as employed cultivators?

Places of birth are reported in detail at Solana and show an immigrant community. Only five heads of household in 1791 were born at the estate. The great majority, eighteen of twenty-three, were from elsewhere: six Spaniards

TABLE F.24 Place of Birth of Non-indigenous Heads of Household
at La Solana, 1791

	La Solana		Juriquilla		Other	
	Spaniard	Mestizo	Spaniard	Mestizo	Spaniard	Mestizo
≤20					1	1
21–30			2	1	2	2
31–40	1		1			
41–50	1	2	3	1	2	
51–60		1			1	
61+				1		
TOTAL	2	3	6	3	6	3

Source: AGN, Padrones, vol. 39, ff. 243–45, my calculations.

and three mestizos from Septién's Juriquilla; three Spaniards from Querétaro, two from Puerto de Nieto, and one from Chamacuero; and two mestizos from Jurica and one from La Rochera. The migrants from Juriquilla came first; the others followed. Segregation had not happened; it was created by migration.

Clan formation at La Solana clarifies much:

TABLE F.25 Non-indigenous Extended Family Clans at La Solana, 1791

Families in Clan	Number of Clans	Total Families	Total Population	Population per Clan
1	8	8	32	4.0
2	4	8	39	9.8
7	1	7	40	40.0
TOTAL	13	23	111	8.5

Source: AGN, Padrones, vol. 39, ff. 243–45, my calculations.

Like most small new communities La Solana included mostly single families and small clans. Like established communities it had one large clan—the Aguilars, with seven households and forty members, over a third of the entire population—led by the estate manager. The manager and four other Aguilar patriarchs came from Juriquilla; two others, including the only mestizo, were among the minority born at La Solana. The Aguilars had led a migration from Juriquilla to Solana. That Antonio Aguilar was a steward in 1791 suggests that Septién had organized and sanctioned the migration. The Aguilar clan's departure left Juriquilla a mulatto community. It made La Solana an estate of Spanish and mestizo tenants, soon joined by Spaniards and mestizos from Querétaro and nearby communities. Segregation was a process created by managerial sanction.

A pattern of estate society in rural Querétaro emerges: Spaniards, mestizos, and mulattoes often engaged in parallel economic activities, though Spaniards

TABLE F.26 Non-indigenous Population and Family Size at
Santa Catarina, 1791

Family Size	Spaniards	Mestizos	Mulattoes	Total	Total Population	Percentage of Population
1						
2	2			2	4	7
3	1		2	3	9	16
4		1	1	2	8	15
5			3	3	15	27
6		1	1	2	12	22
7			1	1	7	13
TOTAL	3	2	8	13	55	100

Source: AGN, Padrones, vol. 39, ff. 240v–241; vol. 40, pp. 93–94; my calculations.

dominated management. Endogamy simultaneously maintained social separation, with exceptions linking Spaniards and mestizos. In larger communities, especially where Spaniards and mestizos dominated, managers led large clans that were key to their power and the integration of estate communities. Where mulattoes were a majority, as at Juriquilla, the Spanish manager remained an outsider, overseeing production without the links created by a large managerial clan.

Don Pedro Septién's third property, San Isidro, was six miles (ten kilometers) northwest of Juriquilla. It included only four non-indigenous households with sixteen people. The manager was a Spaniard from San Geronimo Aculco to the south. The two Uribes, father and son, were mestizo labradores, born in Querétaro. Pascual Alvarez was a mulatto labrador born at La Solana, perhaps forced to move so that La Solana could be segregated as a Spanish-mestizo community. Four families, all outsiders, did not make a community—and surely could not make San Isidro a productive estate. We must assume that the Spanish manager and the three mestizo-mulatto labradores oversaw production by indigenous workers, excluded from the militia census of 1791 but totaling forty-five households in 1907 (table G.16). In that case don Pedro Septién had forged three ethnically distinct estate communities in the basin northwest of Querétaro: Juriquilla, where Spaniards ruled a few mestizos and many mulatto tenants; La Solana, a community of Spanish and mestizo tenants, living but not marrying together; and San Isidro, where a Spanish manager and mestizo-mulatto assistants ruled indigenous workers. Segregation was an active process at the Septién estates.

The three estates of don Francisco Velasco, just north of Septién's properties, show similar segregation. Santa Catarina lay in the center of the basin, closest to Querétaro, fifteen miles (twenty-four kilometers) south. Like Juriquilla, Santa Catarina had a small non-indigenous community: only 13 households and 55 people, or 4.2 per household. Like Juriquilla too, Santa Catarina

TABLE F.27 Ethnic Category and Marriage at Santa Catarina, 1791

Male Head	Spouse				
	Spaniard	Mestiza	Mulata	India	Total
Spaniard	2				2
Mestizo	1	1			2
Mulatto			6	2	8
TOTAL	3	1	6	2	12

Source: AGN, Padrones, vol. 39, ff. 240v–241; vol. 40, pp. 93–94; my calculations.

TABLE F.28 Non-indigenous Economic roles at Santa Catarina, 1791

	Spaniards	Mestizos	Mulattoes	Total
ADMINISTRATION				
Administrator	1			1
Mayordomo	1			1
Ayudante	1		1	2
LIVESTOCK				
Vaquero		2	2	4
Boeyero			1	1
AGRICULTURE				
Labrador	1	1	7	9
TOTAL	4	3	11	18

Source: AGN, Padrones, vol. 39, ff. 240v–241; vol. 40, pp. 93–94; my calculations.

included a few Spaniards and mestizos, and a mulatto majority among Hispanic residents.

Again endogamy ruled: Spanish men married Spanish women; mestizos married Spaniards and mestizas. Most mulattoes married mulattas; a few married indias.

Also as at Juriquilla, Spaniards managed Santa Catarina while mulattoes cultivated, though whether as tenants or employees is not clear. The nearly sixty Otomí households there in 1807 divided evenly between employees and tenants (table G.16).

Managers at Santa Catarina also came from outside; workers divided between those born at the estate and migrants from nearby.

TABLE F.29 Birthplace of Non-indigenous Male Household Heads at Santa Catarina, 1791

	La Solana			Other		
	Spaniards	Mestizos	Mulattoes	Spaniards	Mestizos	Mulattoes
≤20			1			
21–30			2		1	1
31–40				1		2
41–50		1	1	1		1
51–60						
61+				1		
TOTAL	0	1	4	3	1	4

Source: AGN, Padrones, vol. 39, ff. 240v–241; vol. 40, pp. 93–94; my calculations.

Half the mulattoes were born at Santa Catarina, likely descendants of former slaves there. One mulatto came from the same owner's Buenavista estate, just north, reinforcing ethnic segregation. All four managers, including the mulatto ayudante, were outsiders.

Extended families were limited at this small and mostly immigrant community:

TABLE F.30 Non-indigenous Extended Family Clans at Santa Catarina, 1791

Families in Clan	Number of Clans	Total Families	Total Population	Population per Clan
1	7	7	32	4.6
3	2	6	23	11.5
TOTAL	9	13	55	6.1

Source: AGN, Padrones, vol. 39, ff. 240v–241; vol. 40, pp. 93–94; my calculations.

Where mulattoes accounted for the majority of Hispanic working families, managers came from outside, and extended families were limited. Of two clans of three households each, one was headed by the Spanish mayordomo, Manuel Núñez, sixty-five years old; he was a widower from Querétaro with two mulatto sons working under his supervision. He had broken the norm of endogamy to create a small interethnic variant of the managerial clans that dominated in Spanish-mestizo estate communities. The other was the Guzmán clan of a father and two sons: all mulattoes, all labradores.

Velasco's Monte del Negro estate, east of Santa Catarina, seems an extension of that estate. There was no resident manager, and most non-indigenous residents were mulattoes. In 1807 there were fifty indigenous households, mostly employees (table G.16).

The small population was perfectly endogamous. There were two herdsmen and nine labradores (not distinguishing tenants or employed cultivators). Most

TABLE F.31 Non-indigenous Population and Family Size at Monte del Negro, 1791

Family Size	Spaniards	Mestizos	Mulattoes	Total Families	Total Population
1			1	1	1
2			2	2	4
3	1			1	3
4			1	1	4
5					
6		1		1	6
7			1	1	7
8					
9		1		1	9
TOTAL	1	2	5	8	34

Source: AGN, Padrones, vol. 39, f. 245; vol. 40, p. 95; my calculations.

TABLE F.32 Ethnic Category and Marriage at Monte del Negro, 1791

| Male Head | Spouse | | | Total |
	Spaniard	Mestiza	Mulata	
Spaniard	1			1
Mestizo		2		2
Mulatto			3	3
TOTAL	1	2	3	6

Source: AGN, Padrones, vol. 39, f. 245; vol. 40, p. 95; my calculations.

were recent migrants: a Spaniard, nineteen, from Querétaro; a mestizo from Jofre to the north, and another from Santa Rosa; one mulatto from Velasco's Buenavista (again, consolidating segregation) and four from the Jalpa estate, south of Puerto de Nieto (west of the mountains in the San Miguel district—Monte del Negro seems to have been a place of refuge for mulattoes and others).

Typically for small, mostly mulatto communities, extended families were limited:

TABLE F.33 Non-indigenous Extended Family Clans at Monte del Negro, 1791

Families in Clan	Number of Clans	Total Families	Total Population	Population per Clan
1	5	5	24	4.8
3	1	3	10	10.0
TOTAL	6	8	34	5.7

Source: AGN, Padrones, vol. 39, f. 245; vol. 40, p. 95; my calculations.

TABLE F.34 Non-indigenous Population and Family Size at Buenavista, 1791

Family Size	Spanish	Mestizo	Mulatto	Indio	Total Familes	Total Population
1	2				2	2
2	2	1			3	6
3	3			1	4	12
4	5	4	1	1	11	44
5		3			3	15
6	3	1			4	24
7	1	2			3	21
8		1			1	8
9			1		1	9
11		1			1	11
TOTAL	16	13	2	2	33	152

Source: AGN, Padrones, vol. 39, ff. 241–43; vol. 40, pp. 94–95; my calculations.

TABLE F.35 Ethnic Category and Marriage at Buenavista, 1791

Male Head	Spouse					
	Spaniard	Mestiza	Mulatta	Cacica	India	Total
Spaniard	10	2			2	14
Mestizo	1	9		1	1	12
Mulatto			2			2
Indio		2				2
TOTAL	11	13	2	1	3	30

Source: AGN, Padrones, vol. 39, ff. 241–43; vol. 40, pp. 94–95; my calculations.

TABLE F.36 Age of Non-Indigenous Cultivators at Buenavista, 1791

Age	Tenants	Dependents	Total	Age	Tenants	Dependents	Total
≤20	3	10	13	51–60	4		4
21–30	9	1	10	61+	1		1
31–40	4	2	6	TOTAL	23	14	37
41–50	2	1	3				

Source: AGN, Padrones, vol. 39, ff. 241–43; vol. 40, pp. 94–95; my calculations.

The three Nuñez households were the core of the group of migrant mulattoes from Jalpa.

Buenavista was the most northerly of Velasco's estates, near the pass to Puerto de Nieto just west. Velasco's most populous estate, Buenavista, was a Spanish-mestizo community overseeing an emerging Otomí majority that approached one hundred households, mostly tenants, in 1807 (table G.16). As at La Solana, Spaniards headed the largest group of households, while households led by mestizos were larger, making the mestizos a majority. As was typical of Querétaro communities, endogamy ruled. Yet at Buenavista a few Spaniards married mestizos, even indios. As at Monte del Negro there was no resident manager, suggesting that tenants paid rents at Santa Catarina. There was a schoolmaster: Spaniards and mestizos aimed to educate their children.

Most tenants were young: 70 percent forty or younger, 52 percent thirty or younger. Most dependent cultivators were twenty or younger. Everything suggests a community of recent settlement.

The distribution of tenants and dependents by ethnic category is also revealing:

TABLE F.37 Ethnic Status of Non-Indigenous Cultivators at Buenavista, 1791

	Spaniards	Mestizos	Mulattoes	Total
Tenants	13	8	2	23
Dependents	4	6	4	14
TOTAL	17	14	6	37

Source: AGN, Padrones, vol. 39, ff. 241–43; vol. 40, pp. 94–95; my calculations.

TABLE F.38 Place of Birth of Non-indigenous Heads of Household at Buenavista, 1791

	Buenavista			Santa Catarina		Querétaro		Other	
	Spaniards	Mestizos	Mulattoes	Spaniards	Mestizos	Spaniards	Mestizos	Spaniards	Mestizos
≤20	1	1			1				
21–30	4				3	1	1		2
31–40	2	2				1		2	
41–50		1	1			1			1
51–60			1	1			2		
61+						1			
TOTAL	7	4	2	1	4	4	3	2	3

Source: AGN, Padrones, vol. 39, ff. 241–43; vol. 40, pp. 94–95; my calculations.

Spaniards had preferred access to tenancies at Buenavista; few were dependent cultivators. Fewer mestizos were tenants, leaving a nearly equal number of dependent cultivators in their households. Only two mulattoes had tenancies (others had moved to Velasco's segregated mulatto estates), leaving four sons to work as dependents.

The place of birth of male heads of household reveals that Buenavista mixed established residents and immigrants to create a segregated Spanish-mestizo community.

The men born at Buenavista, thirteen heads of household, appear to have been a cross-section of rural society north of Querétaro: seven Spaniards, four mestizos, and two mulattoes. The mulattoes were elders who remained while others left (willingly?) for segregated communities at Santa Catarina and

Monte del Negro. The Spaniards and mestizos born at Buenavista were young: new heads of household in a population that stayed. Five migrant tenants from Velasco's Santa Catarina were also young and mostly mestizos, reinforcing Buenavista as a Spanish-mestizo community. The seven migrants from Querétaro, in contrast, were mostly Spaniards and older. They had moved to claim tenancies. Because we only know their place of birth, not the date of migration, we cannot know if they were early migrants or new arrivals. The five migrants from other places (two from Maravatío to the south, one from Chamacuero, one from Jalpa, and one from Juriquilla), were Spaniards and mestizos, neither young nor old. With twenty of thirty heads of tenant households forty or younger, Buenavista was a young community, settled mostly during the 1780s. Amid the regional collapse of slavery and the famine of 1785–86, Spaniards and mestizos moved to tenant ranchos in a segregated community.

In a new and young estate community, extended family clans were limited:

TABLE F.39 Non-indigenous Extended Family Clans at Buenavista, 1791

Families in Clan	Number of Clans	Number of Families	Total Population	Population per Clan
1	17	17	73	4.3
2	2	4	22	11
3				
4	3	12	57	19
TOTAL	22	33	152	6.9

Source: AGN, Padrones, vol. 39, ff. 241–43; vol. 40, pp. 94–95; my calculations.

Most residents at Buenavista lived in single-family households; the two clans of two included a patriarchal household and one headed by a widow. The three clans of four households are revealing. With no manager resident at Buenavista, there was no managerial clan. (The schoolmaster was a single young man from Querétaro.) The Solís clan included four men aged twenty to thirty, all Spaniards, all tenants, all born at Buenavista. Their elders had either moved or died; the four brothers (or cousins) were the beginning of a potentially powerful extended family rooted in the estate community. The Yáñez, in contrast, had migrated from Querétaro. They headed four tenant households and included a fifty-three-year-old patriarch, sons aged thirty-two and thirty, and a mestizo, thirty-five, born at Buenavista, who may have been a cousin who drew Spanish kin to the estate, or a son of the patriarch by an indigenous or mestizo woman.

The Sánchez clan is most interesting. The patriarch, Pedro Donoso Sánchez, was a Spaniard, sixty, born at Santa Catarina and married to a mestiza. His eldest son, Ermenegildo, thirty, mestizo, was born in Querétaro. Two younger sons, twenty and sixteen, were also mestizos, the elder born at Santa Catarina and the younger at Buenavista. The births trace the migrations of a patriarch and the clan that he fathered: Pedro Donoso was born at Santa Catarina

TABLE F.40 Non-indigenous Population and Family Size at Santa Rosa, 1791

Family Size	Number of Households	Total Population	Percentage of Population	Family Size	Number of Households	Total Population	Percentage of Population
1	2	2	3	6	1	6	8
2	4	8	11	7	2	14	19
3	4	12	17	8	1	8	11
4	3	12	17	TOTAL	19	72	100
5	2	10	14				

Source: AGN, Padrones, vol. 39, ff. 239v–240v; vol. 40, pp. 92–93; my calculations.

around 1731; his first son was born in Querétaro in 1761, the second during a stay back at Santa Catarina around 1771, and the last around 1775 at Buenavista, where all lived and worked as tenant cultivators in 1791. The Sánchez clan settled at Buenavista between 1771 and 1775. Early migration consolidated their role in the estate community. Those who followed during the difficult years of the 1780s had little opportunity to create clans before 1791.

The six estate communities of Santa Rosa basin northwest of Querétaro, three to the south owned by don Pedro Septién, three to the north owned by don Francisco Velasco, reveal key trends. Population and production were expanding, combining commercial harvesting on irrigated bottomlands with tenancies on uplands. Spaniards, mestizos, and mulattoes all participated in tenant cultivation. Migrations expanded tenant production and created newly segregated communities: Spaniards and mestizos living and working—but rarely marrying—together at La Solana and Buenavista; mulattoes working (beside or among indigenous majorities?) under Spanish managers at Juriquilla, Santa Catarina, and Monte del Negro; Spaniards and mestizos overseeing indigenous workers at San Isidro. Managerial power organized segregation. Spaniards, mestizos, and mulattoes seeking land joined the process, suggesting a complex (and unknowable) intersection of cultural prejudice and managerial interest.

Amid those six segregating estates, near Santa Catarina, the informal community of Santa Rosa (now Santa Rosa de Jáuregui) was developing. The census lists Santa Rosa as an *auxiliar de* San Sebastián, the indigenous parish that included the huertas on the north side of Querétaro. The priest at Santa Rosa was an assistant to the pastor at San Sebastián. With nineteen non-indigenous households including seventy-two residents, most people at Santa Rosa were likely indigenous. Perhaps many had come out from the densely settled huertas of the city. Santa Rosa had no community lands. Many residents engaged in agriculture, renting lands and laboring for wages at nearby estates. The presence of Santa Rosa helps to explain the small populations at Juriquilla and Santa Catarina.

Diversity ruled the small non-indigenous community at Santa Rosa. The average family size was four, but that masked a far greater variety. Most households had three members or fewer; most residents lived in households of five or more.

Ethnic diversity also ruled, and intermarriage was more common than at nearby estates:

TABLE F.41 Ethnic Category and Marriage at Santa Rosa, 1791

Male Head	Spouse					
	Spaniard	Mestiza	Mulatta	Cacica	India	Total
Spaniard	4	2				6
Mestizo	1					1
Mulatto			1		1	2
Cacique	1	1				2
TOTAL	6	3	1		1	11

Source: AGN, Padrones, vol. 39, ff. 239v–240v; vol. 40, pp. 92–93; my calculations.

TABLE F.42 Age of Non-indigenous Labradores at Santa Rosa, 1791

Age	Number	Percentage	Age	Number	Percentage
≤20	7	39	51–60	1	6
21–30	4	22	61+	1	6
31–40	2	11	TOTAL	18	100
41–50	3	17			

Source: AGN, Padrones, vol. 39, ff. 239v–240v; vol. 40, pp. 92–93; my calculations.

Spaniards still tended toward endogamy; others married with little regard for ethnic status.

Many heads of household were not married, limiting the role of traditional patriarchal families. The widowed cacique, the single cacique, and a single mulatto perhaps reflected a new and still informal community. The four women among nineteen heads of household (over 20 percent) included a Spaniard, two mestizas, and a cacica.

The occupations of men suggest an agricultural settlement. The priest, a shoemaker, and a shepherd joined eighteen labradores. The census makes no distinction between tenants and employed cultivators. Most labradores at Santa Rosa were young. Some perhaps rented nearby lands, many surely labored as employees or day workers. Workers perhaps gained independence by not living at estates; they likely also lost security.

Among male heads of household only five had been born at Santa Rosa and ten had migrated from elsewhere. The Spanish priest, a Spanish labrador married to a mestiza, and a cacique labrador widower came from Querétaro. Two Galváns, father and son, labradores, were from San Luis Potosí to the north (the only case of southward migration in any community). A single cacique, a sixty-year-old labrador, came all the way from Mexico City. A mulatto shoe-maker had been born at Puerto de Nieto. Three other labradores—a Spaniard from Celaya, a mestizo from Apaseo, and a cacique from San Diego—had settled at Santa Rosa.

We can only wonder about the origins and economic roles of the four women heads of household. One, the widow Guzmán, was a mestiza linked to a mulatto of the same name born at Santa Rosa. The other three widows had no apparent kin in the community. The census never noted women's economic activities. Living near Querétaro left spinning for merchant clothiers a possibility, but no textile activities are reported for Hispanic men at Santa Rosa. Did the women run inns or taverns for travelers on the road to San Luis Potosí?

Santa Rosa shared with neighboring estate communities the limited development of extended family clans:

TABLE F.43 Non-indigenous Extended Family Clans at Santa Rosa, 1791

Number of Households	Number of Clans	Number of Familes	Total Population	Population per Clan
1	11	11	37	3.4
2	4	8	35	8.8
TOTAL	15	19	72	4.8

Source: AGN, Padrones, vol. 39, ff. 239v–240v; vol. 40, pp. 92–93; my calculations.

Still, nearly half the small community lived in pairs of households; such links eased life in the emerging informal settlement, and pointed to future clan development.

TABLE F.44 Non-indigenous Population and Families at Jofre, 1791

Family Size	Spaniards	Mestizos	Mulattoes	Caciques	Total Familes	Total Population
1	5	1	1		7	7
2	17	5	7		29	58
3	11	19	2		32	96
4	16	11	5		32	128
5	16	11	2		29	145
6	12	10	3	2	27	162
7	8	4	1		13	91
8	8	3	1		12	96
9		1			1	9
10	1	2			3	30
13		1			1	13
TOTAL	94	68	22	2	186	835

Source: AGN, Padrones, vol. 39, ff. 245v–257; vol. 40, pp. 95–99; my calculations.

Santa Rosa, neither a formal republic nor a commercial property, was less endogamous, more heavily immigrant, more diverse, and more female than communities on estate lands. The greater diversity and independence of life at Santa Rosa suggests that the norms of organized estate communities were not just cultural tendencies; they were standards linked to managerial power. People not subject to estate power found other ways to live.

North of Santa Rosa and the Velasco estates, at the edge of Querétaro's district, lay don Francisco Aldama's Jofre—eighteen miles (twenty-nine kilometers) from the city, not far west of Chichimequillas and the northern end of the Amascala basin, separated by a range of hills.

Jofre included the largest Hispanic community in the Querétaro countryside, with over 180 households in 1791. Half were headed by Spaniards, 38 percent by mestizos (including the two caciques), and 12 percent by mulattoes. Spanish households averaged 4.4 members, mestizos (plus caciques) 4.8 members, and mulattoes only 3.8 members, accentuating the Spanish-mestizo character of the community and confirming the mulattoes' minority status.

Marriage patterns at Jofre are endogamous, with revealing exceptions:

TABLE F.45 Ethnic Category and Marriage at Jofre, 1791

Male Head	Spouse					
	Spaniard	Mestiza	Mulatta	Cacica	India	Total
Spaniard	69	10			1	80
Mestizo	7	46			1	54
Mulatto			16			16
Cacique		1		1		2
TOTAL	76	57	16	1	2	152

Source: AGN, Padrones, vol. 39, ff. 245v–257; vol. 40, pp. 95–99; my calculations.

The rate of endogamy was 85 percent for Spaniards and mestizos. As at Querétaro estates, most exceptions saw Spaniards marrying mestizos. Mulattoes were fully endogamous, socially excluded despite their numerical presence. The unions linking a Spaniard and a mestizo with indias indicate sharp segregation—as a growing indigenous population included more than 130 households by 1807 (table G.16).

Jofre was a community of cultivators. There were two mayordomos, one Spanish and one mestizo, plus an assistant (Spanish) to collect rents. Two mulatto vaqueros and a Spanish mulero cared for livestock. All other men were tenants or cultivators. Their distribution by age and ethnicity is revealing. Young men labored as dependent cultivators, awaiting the chance to become tenants and heads of households. Among Spaniards and mestizos 65 percent were tenants. Among mulattoes only half were tenants. Spanish and mestizo tenants were young; mulatto tenants were aging—most mulattoes under forty remained dependents. Mulattoes remained at Jofre, but they faced discrimi-

TABLE F.46 Age and Ethnic Category of Non-Hispanic Cultivators at Jofre, 1791

	Spaniards		Mestizos		Mulattoes		Total	
	Arren-datario	Labrador	Arren-datario	Labrador	Arren-datario	Labrador	Arren-datario	Labrador
≤20	6	38	3	23	2	11	11	72
21–30	27	10	22	5	3	2	52	17
31–40	27	4	12	4	3	2	42	10
41–50	13	1	13		3		29	1
51–60	9		8		5	1	22	1
61+	9		4		1		14	
TOTAL	91	53	62	32	17	16	170	101

Source: AGN, Padrones, vol. 39, ff. 245v–257; vol. 40, pp. 95–99; my calculations.

TABLE F.47 Place of Birth of Non-indigenous Heads of Household at Jofre, 1791

	Jofre				Querétaro			Other		
	Spaniard	Mestizo	Mulatto	Total	Spaniard	Mestizo	Total	Spaniard	Mestizo	Total
≤20	2		2	4						
21–30	23	15	2	40	2	4	6	1		1
31–40	24	13	4	41	3	1	4	4		4
41–50	19	11	4	34		2	2	1	1	2
51–60	8	6	5	19	1	1	2			
61+	7	3	1	11	1	2	3	1		1
TOTAL	83	48	18	149	7	10	17	7	1	8

Source: AGN, Padrones, vol. 39, ff. 245v–257; vol. 40, pp. 95–99; my calculations.

nation in access to land, and perhaps residential segregation within estate boundaries.

Places of birth confirm the trend toward discrimination against mulattoes. Over 85 percent of men heading households were born at Jofre. Two-thirds of the immigrant minority came from Querétaro, mostly mestizos. The rest, nearly all Spaniards, came from diverse places: one each from Castile, Celaya, Comanja (near León), and Chichimequillas just east. Two managers were born at a place named Coyote, probably a rancho. No mulattoes had migrated to Jofre. A minority might remain at the estate to face limited opportunities, but no newcomers were welcomed. Jofre too was moving toward segregation in 1791.

As a large and long-established estate, Jofre had important extended family clans. At the same time, the large minority of immigrants added families without kin at the estate community. As a result, 27 percent of families and 29 percent of the population lived in single-family groups; 32 percent of families and

TABLE F.48 Non-indigenous Extended Family Clans at Jofre, 1791

Families in Clan	Number of Clans	Total Families	Total Population	Population per Clan
1	51	51	242	4.7
2	11	22	94	8.5
3	11	33	154	14.0
4	1	4	16	16.0
5	3	15	64	21.3
6	2	12	45	22.5
7	1	7	41	41.0
8	1	8	35	35.0
9	1	9	32	32.0
12	1	12	58	58.0
13	1	13	57	57.0
TOTAL	84	186	838	10.0

Source: AGN, Padrones, vol. 39, ff. 245v–257; vol. 40, pp. 95–99; my calculations.

of the population were in small clans of two to four households; 41 percent of families and 40 percent of the population were in large clans of five to thirteen households.

Jofre lacked a dominant managerial clan. The two mayordomos, the Spaniard Hernández and the mestizo Martínez, headed clans of three households and fourteen people each. Hernández was born at Jofre; Martínez came from Coyote, bringing a young cousin, a Spaniard, to assist. Did the Spanish steward collect rents from Spaniards, the mestizo from mestizos? If so segregation was a key to management. For the Spanish steward Hernández the lack of a large clan was compensated for when a young kinsman married into the Vargas clan of twelve mostly Spanish households. The mestizo steward Martínez made a similar link to the Campos clan of seven households, including five Spaniards and eight mestizos.

Jofre was unique among Querétaro estate communities for the number of women heads of households: 15 of 186, or 8 percent—a notable number, but a smaller percentage than at Santa Rosa. Eleven of the fifteen women headed households within large, male-dominated clans. Four lived without a patriarch nearby: three heading isolated households and one widow heading a clan of five families. Patriarchy ruled at Jofre.

The full report of the militia census for the Querétaro district places the diverse rural communities in context. It separates the city center, including indigenous San Sebastián, and four rural sectors: (1) La Cañada and the Amascala basin estates; (2) Huimilpan to the south; (3) El Pueblito and estates to the west; and (4) the Santa Rosa basin.

Several conclusions emerge. Most of the non-indigenous population concentrated in and near the city. The tendency for mestizo families to be large, mulatto families to be small, and Spanish families to hold near the mean characterized the entire region, urban and rural.

TABLE F.49 Non-indigenous Population of the Querétaro Jurisdiction, 1791

	Families	Men	Women	Boys	Girls	Total	Mean Family Population
CITY							
Spaniards	2,254	2,317	3,657	1,095	877	7,946	3.5
Mestizos	1,370	2,244	2,214	825	684	5,967	4.4
Mulattoes	607	572	801	235	147	1,755	2.9
TOTAL	4,231	5,133	6,672	2,155	1,708	15,668	3.7
LA CAÑADA							
Spaniards	211	244	235	171	153	803	3.8
Mestizos	112	142	132	120	111	505	4.5
Mulattoes	71	83	63	83	56	285	4.0
TOTAL	394	469	430	374	320	1,593	4.0
HUIMILPAN							
Spaniards	139	179	170	133	124	606	4.4
Mestizos	54	83	96	89	69	337	6.2
Mulattoes	56	73	52	30	40	195	3.5
TOTAL	249	335	318	252	233	1,138	4.6
PUEBLITO							
Spaniards	32	35	41	23	16	115	3.6
Mestizos	25	38	46	24	27	135	5.4
Mulattoes	6	7	7	4	5	23	3.8
TOTAL	63	80	94	51	48	273	4.3
SANTA ROSA							
Spaniards	185	273	220	147	114	754	4.1
Mestizos	137	188	179	165	126	658	4.8
Mulattoes	85	117	90	68	49	324	3.8
TOTAL	407	578	489	380	289	1,736	4.3
COMBINED							
Spaniards	2,821	3,048	4,323	1,569	1,284	10,224	3.6
Mestizos	1,698	2,695	2,667	1,223	1,017	7,602	4.5
Mulattoes	825	852	1,013	420	297	2,582	3.1
TOTAL	5,344	6,595	8,003	3,212	2,598	20,408	3.8

Source: AGN, Padrones, vol. 39, f. 358; vol. 40, pp. 62, 74, 83, 85, 99; my calculations.

Rural society around Querétaro fell into distinct zones. The areas to the south and west, around Huimilpan and Pueblito, had few non-indigenous residents. Estates there rarely became communities. Instead they had small resident populations and recruited seasonal workers from indigenous communities, including Querétaro's barrios. The southern zones of Querétaro's hinterland thus remained like Spanish Mesoamerica.

TABLE F.50 Spanish and Mestizo Households at Puerto de Nieto, 1792

Family Size	Number of Families	Total Population	Percentage of Population	Family Size	Number of Families	Total Population	Percentage of Population
1	6	6	1	7	9	63	10
2	34	68	11	8	9	72	12
3	28	84	14	9	1	9	1
4	28	112	18	12	1	12	2
5	13	65	11	TOTAL	150	617	100
6	21	126	20				

Source: AGN, Padrones, vol. 36, 137–58.

To the east, north, and northwest, Hispanic populations were larger. To the east they formed large minorities at estates like La Griega and Chichimequillas in the Amascala basin. To the north and northwest they probably formed small majorities. In addition, the census totals demonstrate that the communities analyzed in detail above—La Cañada, La Griega, and Chichimequillas in the first sector; the Septién and Velasco properties, plus Jofre, around Santa Rosa in the fourth sector—included the majority of the non-indigenous people in their zones. The complexities of the communities studied here were the complexities that defined and differentiated rural society in the Amascala and Santa Rosa basins.

Puerto de Nieto and Rural San Miguel

Puerto de Nieto lay just west over the pass from Buenavista, twenty miles (thirty-two kilometers) northwest of Querétaro and the same distance east of San Miguel (it was the easternmost estate in San Miguel's jurisdiction). Like La Griega east of Querétaro, Puerto de Nieto belonged to the Obra Pía estates assembled by don Juan Caballero y Ocío and operated in 1792 by the priest-patriarch don José Sánchez Espinosa. The militia census of Spanish and mestizo households conducted in 1792 survives. The companion listing of mulattoes does not, if it was even taken. Quantitative comparisons with estates in the Querétaro jurisdiction are not possible. Still, the Puerto de Nieto census is revealing.

With 150 families and a population of 617, Puerto de Nieto was the second-largest community analyzed and would probably have been the largest had mulattoes and indios been fully counted.

The mean family size (just over four) hides a huge range of difference. Numerous households of two kept the mean low. Nearly 75 percent of residents lived in families of four to twelve.

Marriage patterns demonstrate the uniqueness of Puerto de Nieto relative to Querétaro estate communities. Endogamy was much less prevalent at Puerto de Nieto, and intermarriage reached beyond Spaniards and mestizos to include a small yet significant number of mulatto and indigenous spouses.

TABLE F.51 Ethnic Category and Marriage at Puerto de Nieto, 1792

Male Head	Spouse				
	Spaniard	Mestiza	Mulatta	India	Total
Spaniard	44	17		4	65
Mestizo	15	26	4	4	49
Mulatto	9	7			16
TOTAL	68	50	4	8	130

Source: AGN, Padrones, vol. 36, 137–58.

Overall endogamy was only 54 percent, Spanish endogamy only 68 percent, mestizo endogamy merely 53 percent. The only exclusion was that Spanish men did not marry mulattas. But nine mulatto men married Spanish women, and another seven married mestizas.

The sixteen mulatto men appeared in the census only because they had married Spaniards and mestizas. If we assume that overall mulatto endogamy held around 60 percent, the total number of mulatto-headed households at Puerto de Nieto approached forty. The eight indias only appear because they had married Spanish and mestizo men. Assuming 75 percent indigenous endogamy, there were perhaps a similar number of families headed by indigenous men at Puerto de Nieto. The eighty additional households, at four members each, would add over three hundred members to the counted community, bringing the population to over nine hundred.

Puerto de Nieto remained an agrarian community: 137 of 165 men were listed as cultivators. There were the usual managers—two mayordomos and two assistants—and thirteen vaqueros and other herdsmen. Still, a group of eleven craftsmen lived at Puerto de Nieto, mostly trapicheros engaged in textile production, along with a hat maker and a *gamusero*. The census does not distinguish tenants and employed cultivators (the managers' letters show both present). It does differentiate between household heads and dependent youths:

TABLE F.52 Spanish and Mestizo Labradores at Puerto de Nieto, 1792

	Spaniards		Mestizos		Total	
	Heads	Dependents	Heads	Dependents	Dependents	Heads
≤20	3	15		12	3	27
21–30	14	3	12	5	26	8
31–40	17	1	18	1	35	2
41–50	10		8		18	
51–60	2		4		6	
61+	9		3		12	
TOTAL	55	19	45	18	100	37

Source: AGN, Padrones, vol. 36, 137–58.

TABLE F.53 Place of Birth of Spaniards and Mestizos at
Puerto de Nieto, 1792

	Puerto de Nieto		Other	
	Spaniards	Mestizos	Spaniards	Mestizos
≤20	2		1	1
21–30	12	8	5	4
31–40	18	16	4	2
41–50	15	11	2	2
51–60	4	2		1
60+	10	4	2	
TOTAL	61	41	14	10

Source: AGN, Padrones, vol. 36, 137–58.

Among cultivators, Spaniards and mestizos held parallel economic roles, though Spaniards gained independence at a younger age and were slightly favored as heads of cultivating households.

The great majority of cultivators at Puerto de Nieto, 102 of 126, or 80 percent, were born at the estate. It was a far more settled, less heavily migrant community than those across the mountains in the Santa Rosa basin of Querétaro.

Migrants reinforced an existing community. Newcomers were younger, divided among Spaniards and mestizos in almost perfect proportion to the groups' presence in the established community. In addition, while a few managers came from San Miguel, nearly all the newcomers came from nearby ranchos; most shared kinship ties with clans already at Puerto de Nieto. No migrants came from Querétaro or estates in the Santa Rosa basin just east. People there faced sharp segregation and the near-exclusion of mulattoes. Were they reluctant to migrate to a community so open to ethnic intermarriage? For whatever reason, migration at Puerto de Nieto was limited and primarily reflected movements by kin between the hacienda and nearby ranchos. It demonstrates the integration of the estate and nearby settlements. (We have seen a few migrants from Puerto de Nieto to estates in the Santa Rosa basin just east. Most were mulattoes joining segregating communities. Surely life was not ideal for mulattoes at Puerto de Nieto, despite greater integration there.)

As Puerto de Nieto was a large and long-settled estate community, extended family clans were well developed:

Spanish and Mestizo Extended Family Clans at
Puerto de Nieto, 1792

Families in Clan	Number of Clans	Total Families	Total Population	Population per Clan
1	30	30	134	4.5
2	11	22	88	8.0
3	3	9	34	11.3
4	4	16	63	15.8
5	3	15	48	16.0
6	1	6	32	32.0
7	4	28	122	30.5
8	1	8	48	48.0
TOTAL	57	134	569	10.0

Source: AGN, Padrones, vol. 36, 137–58.

This is a partial tabulation; the census does not give the names of mulatto men married to Spanish and mestizo women: only their wives' kinship ties can be traced. Among the sixteen mulatto-headed households, ten wives linked mulatto husbands to Spanish (nine) and mestizo (seven) clans: two clans of four, two of five, one of seven, and one of eight households. The last was the clan of the managerial Ricos, whose clan consisted mostly of Spaniards yet also included mestizos and mulattoes. The Puerto de Nieto census documents an estate community engaged in amalgamation, in contrast to the segregation across rural Querétaro.

A close examination of key clans demonstrates their importance at Puerto de Nieto. The manager in 1792 was don Manuel Puente, born in San Miguel and head of a small clan of two households. His only son and a daughter had married into the Licea clan of seven households, creating a larger managerial clan of nine households and forty-four members—all Spaniards. The steward at the Labor was don José Toribio Rico, a member of the largest clan at Puerto de Nieto. The eight Rico households had forty-eight members, and Ricos had married with several other clans to create direct links with a kinship community of nineteen households and ninety-three people, accounting for 15 percent of the population counted by the census. Members of the Rico clan married mestizos and mulattoes. The majority of adults remained Spaniards, but the Ricos and their kin joined in the intermarriages that made Puerto de Nieto an integrated community. That large and complex clan helped don José Toribio Rico rise to rule estate management from the 1790s to 1810.

Both managerial clans (which together linked over 20 percent of the community) engaged in management, cultivation, and livestock care—all estate-dependent activities. Managerial clans facilitated management through kinship and favored managerial kin in estate production. In contrast to Chichimequillas, where managerial kin monopolized textiles, at Puerto de Nieto men belonging to clans separated from management made cloth. The linked Alamilla, Arias, López, Monzón, Rodríguez, and Ceballos clans, together includ-

TABLE F.55 Spanish and Mestizo Population
of San Miguel el Grande, 1792

	Families	Population
City	866	3,043
RURAL SECTORS		
First	46	183
Second	199	814
Third	88	349
Fourth	67	237
RURAL TOTAL	400	1,583
TOTAL	1,266	4,626

Source: AGN, Padrones, vol. 36, 264.

ing 23 households and 105 members, mixed cultivation with textile production. There were twenty-one cultivators, ten cloth makers, and two shepherds in families that mixed twenty-five Spaniards, fifteen mestizos, two indios, and a mulatto among their adults—and two Monzón women, one Spanish and the other mestiza, had married mulatto men. While the Puentes worked to manage through a clan fully Spanish and dependent on estate production, and the Ricos remained dependent on estate production while engaging in amalgamation, the clans that were engaged in textile production sought economic activities less dependent on estate management and resources—while also joining in ethnic amalgamation. Managers' clans aimed to implement estate power. Among dependent families, parallel clans emerged to negotiate life in the estate community.

Puerto de Nieto differed from Querétaro estate communities. Was it typical of communities west and north around San Miguel? With no formal repúblicas de indios, all San Miguel rural communities lived on estate lands. Still, Puerto de Nieto was different. The census of 1792 showed that it alone had a large population of Spaniards and mestizos.

With 150 households and 617 members, Puerto de Nieto included 75 percent of the Spanish and mestizo population of the second sector, extending east from San Miguel. And that single estate included nearly 40 percent of the Spaniards and mestizos reported across the entire San Miguel countryside.

This uniqueness must be considered from several perspectives. First, the Spanish-mestizo population of San Miguel—4,626—was only 20 percent of the total population of the jurisdiction, reported at 22,583 in 1794 (appendix C). Thus 80 percent of residents there were mulattoes or indios, in numbers and proportions that we cannot know. With 40 percent of the rural Spanish and mestizo population concentrated at Puerto de Nieto, and with no indigenous communities outside urban San Miguel, the inevitable conclusion is that at the rest of San Miguel's twenty-nine estate communities, most residents were mulattoes and indios.

We must therefore conclude that Puerto de Nieto's mix of Spanish, mestizo, mulatto, and indigenous families was unique—transitional between Querétaro communities just east, where Hispanic residents were also numerous and segregation prevailed, and rural San Miguel, where Spaniards and mestizos were rare, mulatto and indigenous families dominated, and mulatto-indio mixing was common.

The conclusion of this quantitative analysis is this: there was no "typical" estate community in this limited zone of the eastern Bajío. There were discernible social processes: separation within divided communities in the Amascala basin; segregation between communities around Santa Rosa; and amalgamation at Puerto de Nieto. Patriarchy ruled everywhere at estates—yet was weak at the "free" community of Santa Rosa. Patriarchal clans developed most among Spanish and mestizo residents; they were often used by managers to assert power, yet also forged by dependents to negotiate that power. Ultimately patriarchy engaged complex differences of ethnic separation and integration to orchestrate production, power, and social relations in communities from La Griega to Puerto de Nieto. In an integrated regional economy orchestrated by patriarchy, diverse ethnic relations made every community different.

Appendix G

Tributes and Tributaries in the Querétaro District, 1807

Even as tributes became a head tax that funded local schools and otherwise sent funds to the general treasury, and as levies on full tributaries (married male heads of household) and half-tributaries (unmarried men and widowers) were equalized at 1.5 reales each, the tributary list (*matrícula*) completed for the Querétaro district in 1807 distinguished full payers from halves. It also listed tributaries by residence and employment, distinguishing residents of pueblos and barrios from those working in large obrajes and tanneries, those employed in small shops, and those at estates (and sometimes separating employed residents from tenants and informal residents). The resulting count allows analysis of men classified as indios by residence and employment, distinguishing the roles of married and single men—the latter mostly youths yet to establish households. That the count came in 1807, the last year before the combination of political crisis and drought that led to the insurgency of 1810, makes the results all the more informative.

The count covers the full tribute district of Querétaro: the city and its environs as well as regions south around San Juan de Río and east toward Tolimán and the edges of the Sierra Gorda. It does not include the Cadereyta district, more fully of the Sierra. I present the results in tables that distinguish the city of Querétaro, its near countryside, the San Juan region, and the Tolimán area. Within each I separate town, village, and barrio residents from those linked to workshops and estates. The results are revealing: urban workshops, large and small, had become places of unmarried youths; rural estates were worked by married men and a few youths; only towns and villages mixed both in balance.

Among indios in the Spanish city the concentration of youths in workshops emerges clearly. In the city's Espíritu Santo parish youths were a majority of indio workers in three large obrajes.

TABLE G.1 Tributaries in the Parish of Santiago de Querétaro, 1807

Place of Work or Residence	Full Tributaries	Half Tributaries	Total Tributaries	Percentage of Halves
City and Barrios (3)	295	84	379	22
Obrajes (6)	184	125	309	40
Trapiches (4)	28	22	50	44
Hacienda and Tenería de Carretas	80	20	100	20
PARISH TOTAL	587	251	838	30

Source: Jiménez Gómez, ed., *La República de Indios de Querétaro*, no. 121, 711–34, my calculations.

TABLE G.2 Tributaries in the Parish of Santa Ana, 1807

Place of Work or Residence	Full Tributaries	Half Tributaries	Total Tributaries	Percentage of Halves
City and Barrio (2)	168	85	253	34
Obrajes (6) and Tenerías (1)	127	91	218	42
PARISH TOTAL	295	176	471	37

Source: Jiménez Gómez, ed., *La República de Indios de Querétaro*, no. 121, 711–34, my calculations.

TABLE G.3 Tributaries in the Parish of Espíritu Santo, 1807

Place of Work or Residence	Full Tributaries	Half Tributaries	Total Tributaries	Percentage of Halves
City and Barrio (2)	104	29	133	22
Obrajes (3)	63	98	161	61
PARISH TOTAL	167	127	294	43

Source: Jiménez Gómez, ed., *La República de Indios de Querétaro*, no. 121, 711–34, my calculations.

TABLE G.4 Tributaries in the Parish of Divina Pastora, 1807

Place of Work or Residence	Full Tributaries	Half Tributaries	Total Tributaries	Percentage of Halves
City (1)	175	64	239	27
Obraje (1)	25	10	35	29
Trapiches (29)	77	68	145	47
PARISH TOTAL	277	142	419	34

Source: Jiménez Gómez, ed., *La República de Indios de Querétaro*, no. 121, 711–34, my calculations.

TABLE G.5 Tributaries in the Four Parishes of Spanish Querétaro, 1807

Place of Work or Residence	Full Tributaries	Half Tributaries	Total Tributaries	Percentage of Halves
City and Barrios (8)	742	262	1,004	26
Obrajes (16) and Tenerías (2)	479	344	823	42
Trapiches (31)	105	90	195	46
CITY TOTAL	1,326	696	2,022	34

Source: Tables G.1–G.4, my calculations.

TABLE G.6 Tributaries in the Pueblo de San Sebastián, 1807

Place of Work or Residence	Full Tributaries	Half Tributaries	Total Tributaries	Percentage of Halves
San Sebastián and Barrios (7)	742	170	912	19

Source: Jiménez Gómez, ed., *La República de Indios de Querétaro*, no. 121, 711–34, my calculations.

TABLE G.7 Tributaries at Pueblo de San Pablo and Nearby Estates, 1807

Place of Work or Residence	Full Tributaries	Half Tributaries	Total Tributaries	Percentage of Halves
Pueblos (2)	296	93	389	24
Tenerías (4)	26	29	55	53
Haciendas (22)	937	304	1,241	24
TOTAL	1,259	426	1,685	25

Source: Jiménez Gómez, ed., *La República de Indios de Querétaro*, no. 121, 711–34, my calculations.

In the city parish with the greatest concentration of small workshops, Divina Pastora, the employment of youths was again clearly concentrated. A table combining the tributaries for the four city parishes is most revealing.

Among over two thousand indio tributaries in the Spanish city, the concentration of unmarried youths in the obrajes and smaller workshops is notable. Urban labor was becoming work for men without families to sustain.

The parish of San Sebastián, the indigenous community set in the huertas on the north back of the river, was different. There youths were becoming scarce in 1807, suggesting that many had crossed the river to work in city workshops, large and small.

Linked by the matrícula to the Pueblo de San Pablo was the series of basins around Santa Rosa that rose northwest of Querétaro. It was a much more rural

TABLE G.8 Tributaries at Pueblito, Huimilpan, and Nearby Estates. 1807

Place of Work or Residence	Full Tributaries	Half Tributaries	Total Tributaries	Percentage of Halves
Pueblito (San Francisco Galileo)	420	78	498	16
Pueblo de San Miguel Huimilpan	146	40	186	22
Obraje de Batán	49	8	57	14
Operarios	25	8	33	24
Haciendas (18)	746	143	889	16
TOTAL	1,386	277	1,663	17

Source: Jiménez Gómez, ed., *La República de Indios de Querétaro*, no. 121, 711–34, my calculations.

TABLE G.9 Tributaries in the Amealco region, 1807

Place of Work or Residence	Full Tributaries	Half Tributaries	Total Tributaries	Percentage of Halves
Pueblos (4)	410	93	503	18
Haciendas (3)	36	12	48	25
TOTAL	446	105	551	19

Source: Jiménez Gómez, ed., *La República de Indios de Querétaro*, no. 121, 711–34, my calculations.

district in 1807. Married men and unmarried youths balanced in pueblos and at estates; youths went to tanneries.

In areas west and southwest of Querétaro, generally dry and tending toward uplands, a scarcity of unmarried tributaries is clear—especially at Pueblito and nearby haciendas. The trend was also notable in the pueblos around Amealco, at the southern limits of Querétaro's district.

East of Querétaro, administratively linked to the canyon town of San Pedro de la Cañada, lay the Amascala basin, the district's best agricultural lands, long subject to estate development.

Thanks to the retention of huertas, San Pedro and its barrios had a balance of married men and unmarried youths. Meanwhile few estates on the Amascala plain offered opportunity to youths. La Griega, with 214 tributaries, included only 23 youths beside 191 married tributaries (11 percent); Chichimequillas approached the norm with 17 percent youths among 190 tributaries; and Atongo proved the exception, with 84 youths in a total of 280 tributaries (30 percent).

The plains that begin east of Querétaro around Amascala extend southeast to reach San Juan del Río, the second-largest town in the district. Estates ruled the country in between, with those nearest San Juan having favored access to

TABLE G.10 Tributaries at San Pedro de la Cañada and Amascala Basin Estates, 1807

Place of Work or Residence	Full Tributaries	Half Tributaries	Total Tributaries	Percentage of Halves
Pueblo de la Cañada and Barrios (8)	498	143	641	22
Haciendas (17)	417	80	497	16
TOTAL	915	223	1,138	20

Source: Jiménez Gómez, ed., *La República de Indios de Querétaro*, no. 121, 711–34, my calculations.

TABLE G.11 Tributaries at San Juan del Río and Estates on its Plain, 1807

Place of Work or Residence	Full Tributaries	Half Tributaries	Total Tributaries	Percentage of Halves
San Juan del Río, Pueblos and Barrios (12)	773	334	1,107	30
Haciendas and Ranchos (33)	417	101	518	19
TOTAL	1,190	435	1,625	27

Source: Jiménez Gómez, ed., *La República de Indios de Querétaro*, no. 121, 711–34, my calculations.

TABLE G.12 Tributaries at Tequisquiapan and Nearby Estates, 1807

Place of Work or Residence	Full Tributaries	Half Tributaries	Total Tributaries	Percentage of Halves
Pueblo Santa María Tequisquiapan	520	140	660	21
Haciendas (6)	544	136	680	20
TOTAL	1,064	276	1,340	21

Source: Jiménez Gómez, ed., *La República de Indios de Querétaro*, no. 121, 711–34, my calculations.

TABLE G.13 Tributaries at Soriano, Tolimanejo, and Nearby Estates, 1807

Place of Work or Residence	Full Tributaries	Half Tributaries	Total Tributaries	Percentage of Halves
Pueblos (2)	738	251	989	25
Haciendas (3)	430	129	559	23
TOTAL	1,168	380	1,548	25

Source: Jiménez Gómez, ed., *La República de Indios de Querétaro*, no. 121, 711–34, my calculations.

TABLE G.14 Tributaries in Sierra Pueblos and Haciendas, 1807

Place of Work or Residence	Full Tributaries	Half Tributaries	Total Tributaries	Percentage of Halves
Pueblos (4)	1,322	481	1,803	27
Haciendas (2)	44	21	65	32
TOTAL	1,366	502	1,868	27

Source: Jiménez Gómez, ed., *La República de Indios de Querétaro*, no. 121, 711–34, my calculations.

TABLE G.15 Tributaries in the Querétaro District, 1807

Place of Work or Residence	Full Tributaries	Half Tributaries	Total Tributaries	Percentage of Halves
Pueblos and Barrios (50)	6,607	1,992	8,599	23
Workshops (58)	684	479	1,163	41
Haciendas and Ranchos (104)	3,571	926	4,497	21
TOTAL	10,862	3,397	14,259	24

Source: Jiménez Gómez, ed., *La República de Indios de Querétaro*, no. 121, 711–34, my calculations.

the Mexico City market. Again it is clear that estates were short on opportunity for young men.

North and northeast of San Juan del Río were Tequisquiapan, San Francisco Tolimanejo, and Santo Domingo Soriano. Estate development was long established near Tequisquiapan and was accelerating rapidly as new lands opened and settlers arrived farther north and east. Youths found limited opportunity at these newly developed properties.

Farther north and east, on a frontier of eighteenth-century estate development, youths found opportunity at least in balance with their general portion in the population.

Here opportunities for youths were better, though they were concentrated at the Juchitlán el Grande estate, where youths accounted for 54 of 166 tributaries (33 percent). At the large Esperanza hacienda, the base of doña María Josefa de Vergara's endowment discussed in chapter 8, youths were only 57 among 298 tributaries (19 percent), suggesting a closing of opportunities there.

In the Sierra Gorda regions around San Pedro Tolimán, most tributaries lived in pueblos. In zones newly opened to development, youths did find opportunities.

Finally I combine the figures for pueblos, workshops, and estates across the district.

The combined totals suggest that unmarried youths formed just under a quarter of the indigenous tributary population of the Querétaro district in

TABLE G.16 Tributaries at Haciendas in Amascala and Santa Rosa Basins, 1807

Place of Work or Residence	Full Tributaries	Half Tributaries	Total Tributaries	Percentage of Halves
Amascala				
La Griega				
Hacienda	37	1	38	3
Arrimados	6	6	0	
Labores (2)	58	5	63	8
Arrimados	11	2	13	13
Ranchos (7)	79	15	94	16
TOTAL	191	23	214	11
Chichimequillas				
Hacienda	67	11	78	14
Labores (2)	46	2	48	4
Tenants and Arrimados	54	20	74	27
TOTAL	167	33	200	17
Santa Rosa				
Septién Estates				
Juriquilla	66	24	90	27
San Isidro	43	2	45	4
La Solana	68	33	101	33
TOTAL	177	59	236	25
Velasco Estates				
Santa Catarina	28	19	47	40
Tenants and Arrimados	30	13	43	30
Monte del Negro	38	10	48	20
Tenants and Arrimados	10	5	15	33
Buenavista	33	14	47	29
Tenants and Arrimados	64	19	83	23
TOTAL	203	80	283	28
Jofre: Hacienda	43	27	70	39
Tenants and Arrimados	89	39	128	30
TOTAL	132	66	198	33

Source: Jiménez Gómez, ed., *La República de Indios de Querétaro*, no. 121, 715–17, my calculations.

1807, and that the population of the city, towns, and their barrios approximated that proportion. At rural estates there was an emerging dearth of opportunity for tributary youths—a deepening difficulty in older estate communities, less of a problem in regions of newer development. Meanwhile in the city large obrajes and smaller workshops offered work to young men in search of employment, leaving married men a shrinking portion of the manufacturing work force. The conclusion: married men in the city and unmarried younger men at rural estates faced declining prospects as the first decade of the nineteenth century ended.

Notes

Abbreviations

AGN   Archivo General de la Nación, Mexico City
BN   Ramo de Bienes Nacionales, Archivo General de la Nación, Mexico City
CPP   Conde de Peñasco Papers, Benson Latin American Collection, University of Texas, Austin
FEN   Don Francisco de Espinosa y Navarijo Papers, Benson Latin American Collection, University of Texas, Austin (formerly a separate collection; now filed by date among CPP)
GM   *Gaceta de México*
JSE   Don José Sánchez Espinosa Papers, Benson Latin American Collection, University of Texas, Austin (formerly a separate collection; now filed by date among CPP)
PCR   Papeles de los Condes de Regla, Washington State University, Pullman

Prologue: Making Global History in the Spanish Empire

1. This is the essence of the argument made by Dennis Flynn and Arturo Giráldez in "Born with a 'Silver Spoon.'"

2. See Wallerstein, *The Modern World-System*; Wolf, *Europe and the People without History*; and Braudel, *Civilization and Capitalism*.

3. Flynn and Giráldez, "Born with a 'Silver Spoon'" and "Cycles of Silver"; Frank, *ReOrient*; and Pomeranz, *The Great Divergence*.

4. Pomeranz, *The Great Divergence*, engages those debates effectively.

5. See Bakewell, *Miners of the Red Mountain*; Cole, *The Potosí Mita*; Spalding, *Huarochirí*; and Mangan, *Trading Roles*.

6. Notably Bakewell, *Silver Mining and Society in Colonial Mexico*, and Salvucci, *Textiles and Capitalism in Mexico*.

7. Such visions mark David Brading's otherwise essential *Miners and Merchants in Bourbon Mexico* and J. H. Elliott's magisterial synthesis, *Empires of the Atlantic World*.

8. Much of this claims roots in Max Weber's *The Protestant Ethic and the Spirit of Capitalism*.

9. Flynn and Giráldez, "Born with a 'Silver Spoon'" and "Cycles of Silver," make this case powerfully; William Schell opens an essential rethinking of Mexican history in "Silver Symbiosis."

10. Read Kamen, *Empire*, in the context of Flynn and Giráldez, "Cycles of Silver."

11. Read Bakewell, *A History of Latin America*, in the context of Braudel, *The Mediterranean*, and Tabak, *The Waning of the Mediterranean*.

12. Read Stein and Stein, *Silver, War, and Trade*, in the context of Braudel, *Civilization and Capitalism* (and Crosby, *The Columbian Exchange*).

13. This era of conflictive transformation opens C. H. Bayly's magisterial *The Birth of the Modern World*. Like so many global analysts, Bayly sees Europe and Asia better than the Americas. To complement his analysis see Tutino, "The Revolution in Mexican Independence"; Dubois, *Avengers of the New World*; and Adelman, *Sovereignty and Revolution in the Iberian Atlantic*.

14. Wallerstein, *The Modern World-System*, vol. 1.

15. Wolf, *Europe and the People without History*. Wolf early wrote a seminal essay famous among scholars of Mexico, "The Mexican Bajío in the Eighteenth Century," showing the region as a center of capitalism.

16. North, *Institutions, Institutional Change, and Economic Performance*, maintained that Anglo-Protestant political and religious ways were pivotal to capitalism; Grafe and Irigoin, "The Spanish Empire and Its Legacy," offers a strong critique.

17. Braudel, *The Wheels of Commerce*, 229–30.

18. I make the point in a very different context in Tutino, "The Revolutionary Capacity of Rural Communities."

19. Such emphases mark Pomeranz, *The Great Divergence*, and the debates that he engages so effectively.

20. The larger challenges of contemporary capitalism are discussed in a balanced way in my colleague John McNeill's magisterial *Something New under the Sun*.

21. In a vast literature note Gibson, *The Aztecs under Spanish Rule*; Lockhart, *The Nahuas after the Conquest*; and Spalding, *Huarochirí*.

22. See Williams, *Capitalism and Slavery*, and Blackburn, *The Making of New World Slavery*.

23. Kamen, *Empire*.

24. In *Empires of the Atlantic World* J. H. Elliot offers a sophisticated rendition of this vision. Such views face challenge in Pomeranz, *The Great Divergence*, which focuses on resources, production, social relations, and state powers, and shows that imperial interventions (so often blamed for Spain's demise) were pivotal to Britain's rise.

25. Irigoin and Grafe, "Bargaining for Absolutism" and "A Stakeholder Empire." Their view seems compatible with Pomeranz's emphasis on imperial facilitation of Britain's nineteenth-century rise. Mutually beneficial ties between an empire and its commercial stakeholders, broadly defined, operated there too. On the limits (or absence) of absolutism in its supposed home see my colleague James Collins's *The State in Early Modern France*.

26. The inclusion of proprietary officeholders as stakeholders is based on the chapters that follow.

27. The limits of military power are blatant in Archer, *The Army in Bourbon Mexico*, and in the history of the Bajío.

28. Pomeranz, *The Great Divergence*, moves us toward comparisons that engage global processes and interactions.

29. Braudel, *The Perspective of the World*, 352–85.

30. Bayly, *The Birth of the Modern World*.

31. Dubois, *Avengers of the New World*.

32. Tutino, "The Revolution in Mexican Independence."

33. Dubois, *Avengers of the New World*.

34. Ávila, *En nombre de la nación*; Tone, *The Fatal Knot*; Tutino, "Soberanía quebrada, insurgencias populares y la independencia de México."

35. Braudel, *The Perspective of the World*, 77–79.

36. See Tutino, "The Revolution in Mexican Independence," and Schell, "Silver Symbiosis."

37. Work summarized in North, *Institutions, Institutional Change, and Economic Performance*.

38. A point I learned from Richard Adams years ago; see his *Energy and Structure*.

39. North, Wallis, and Wiengast, *Violence and Social Orders*.

40. Clifford Geertz, in the first chapter of *The Interpretation of Cultures*, argues for the importance of thick descriptions. In *The Last Colonial Massacre* Greg Grandin offers a model analysis linking thick descriptions and interpretive syntheses.

Introduction: A New World

1. Eric Wolf recognized the importance of the Bajío in his seminal essay "The Mexican Bajío in the Eighteenth Century." David Brading's Bajío trilogy revealed the complexity of the region's eighteenth-century history; see *Miners and Merchants in Bourbon Mexico*, *Haciendas and Ranchos in the Mexican Bajío*, and *Church and State in Bourbon Mexico*. Recently Felipe Castro Gutiérrez has refocused understanding of New Spain's eighteenth century on the Bajío and nearby zones in *Nueva ley y nuevo rey*. Their essential contributions made this history possible.

2. The figures are from materials in appendices C and D.

3. The role of New Spain's silver in the age of Atlantic war and revolution is detailed in Marichal, *La bancarrota del virreinato*.

4. I offered a preliminary analysis of the Bajío revolution in "The Revolution in Mexican Independence."

5. My colleague John McNeill, responding to a draft of this introduction, pointed out that Mesoamerica was as much an old world as Europe in the sixteenth century—leading me to this vision of old and new worlds.

6. The key distinction between Mesoamerica and the arid zones to the north in pre-contact times is emphasized in Alfredo López Austin and Leopoldo López Luján. To sample the fine historical work on Spanish Mesoamerica see Gibson, *The Aztecs under Spanish Rule*; Farriss, *Maya Society under Colonial Rule*; Carmagnani, *El regreso de los dioses*; Lockhart, *The Nahuas after the Conquest*; Taylor, *Magistrates of the Sacred*; Dorothy Tanck de Estrada, *Pueblos de indios y educación en el México colonial*; Pastor, *Cuerpos sociales, cuerpos sacrificiales*; and Castro Gutiérrez, *Los tarascos bayo el imperio español*.

7. This interpretation previews the analysis to come; for an introduction to the early Bajío and the foundation of Spanish North America see Powell, *Soldiers, Indians, and Silver*, and Bakewell, *Silver Mining and Society in Colonial Mexico*.

8. On early sugar colonies see Charles Verlinden's classic *The Origins of Modern Colonization* and the recent collection edited by Stuart Schwartz, *Tropical Babylons*.

9. This is clear in the opening of Edmund Morgan's classic *American Slavery, American Freedom*.

10. On the spread of slave colonies in the British Atlantic see Richard Dunn's also classic *Sugar and Slaves*; on diversity in the early British colonies see Games, *Migration and the Origins of the English Atlantic World*.

11. See White, *The Middle Ground*; Brooks, *Captives and Cousins*; Gallay, *The Indian Slave Trade*; Ethridge, *Creek Country*; Weber, *Bárbaros*; and Barr, *Peace Came in the Form of a Woman*.

12. Flynn and Giráldez, "Born with a 'Silver Spoon.' "

13. See Wallerstein, *The Modern World-System*, and Wolf, *Europe and the People without History*.

14. See Kamen, *Empire*; Israel, *Dutch Primacy in World Trade*; Stein and Stein, *Silver, War, and Trade*; and Stein and Stein, *Apogee of Empire*.

15. Flynn and Giráldez, "Cycles of Silver," and Stein and Stein, *Apogee of Empire*.

16. See McNally, *Political Economy and the Rise of Capitalism*; Wallerstein, *The Modern World-System*; and Wolf, *Europe and the People without History*.

17. Verlinden, *The Origins of Modern Colonization*.

18. On the persistence of community rights and challenges to seigneurial powers see Blum, *The End of the Old Order in Europe*. On the reconstitution and survival of community rights in the Andes see Stern, *Peru's Indian Peoples and the Challenge of Spanish Conquest*, and Spalding, *Huarochirí*. On Mesoamerica see note 5, above.

19. Kamen, *Empire*.

20. Stein and Stein, *Silver, War, and Trade* and *Apogee of Empire*.

21. This vision marks Wallerstein, *The Modern World-System*. The empha-

sis on the view that Iberian America was defined by enduring coercive labor regimes persists in Romano, *Mecanismo y elementos del sistema económica colonial americano.*

22. On the transatlantic dynamics of British industrialization such classics as Deane, *The First Industrial Revolution,* and Perkin, *The Origins of Modern English Society,* must link to studies of cotton and slavery ranging from Genovese's *The Political Economy of Slavery* to Rothman's *Slave Country,* which in turn must link to studies of still independent indigenous peoples such as Usner, *Indians, Settlers, and Slaves in a Frontier Exchange Economy,* and Ethridge, *Creek Country.* On the role of slavery in the origins of capitalism see Williams, *Capitalism and Slavery,* and Blackburn, *The Making of New World Slavery.*

23. See for example Schwartz, *Sugar Plantations in the Formation of Brazilian Society,* and Childs, *The 1812 Aponte Rebellion in Cuba and the Struggle against Atlantic Slavery.*

24. My search for ways to integrate material and cultural approaches to history began in graduate seminars led by Richard Adams in the early 1970s at the University of Texas, Austin. He brought his students into the process that led to *Energy and Structure,* a work that placed energy and ecology at the base of power relations and cultural constructions, an analysis that was ahead of its time—but that was too often set aside as anthropology and history took sharp cultural turns.

25. Steward, *Theory of Culture Change,* 57.

26. Geertz, *The Interpretation of Cultures,* 30, 44.

27. Weber, *The Theory of Social and Economic Organization,* 156.

28. North, Wallis, and Weingast, *Violence and Social Orders.*

29. These limits are clear in Kamen's *Empire* and brilliantly detailed in Owensby, *Empire of Law and Indian Justice in Colonial Mexico.*

30. Owensby, *Empire of Law,* 130–32.

31. This reflects Barrington Moore Jr.'s two classic works. In *Social Origins of Dictatorship and Democracy* he focused on political economy, the historic interactions of powers of life and death, to explain the roots of modern regimes. In *Injustice* he offered the notion of "moral outrage" to explain power breaks and turns to revolt. The linkage of material powers and cultural legitimacy could not be clearer.

32. The role of culture as both organizing and legitimating is exemplified in Pastor, *Cuerpos sociales, cuerpos sacrificiales.*

33. Geertz, *The Interpretation of Cultures,* 15, 93, 126.

34. For a reinforcing vision see Rosaldo, *Culture and Truth.*

35. Scott, *Domination and the Arts of Resistance.*

36. Morgan, *Inventing the People.*

37. Taylor, *Drinking, Homicide, and Rebellion in Colonial Mexican Villages*; Borah, *Justice by Insurance*; and now Owensby, *Empire of Law and Indian Justice in Colonial Mexico.*

38. Stern, *The Secret History of Gender.*

39. Christian, *Local Religion in Sixteenth-Century Spain.*

40. Debatable reciprocities also are evident in slavery, as analyzed by Geno-

vese in *Roll, Jordan, Roll* and in the negotiation of brokered power in Andean societies as revealed in Spalding, *Huarochirí*; Thomson, *We Alone Will Rule*; and Serulnikov, *Subverting Colonial Authority*.

41. See Stern, *Peru's Indian Peoples and the Challenge of Spanish Conquest* for a clear case anslysis.

42. For the Andes see Spalding, *Huarochirí*; for Mesoamerica see Tutino, "Urban Power and Agrarian Society" and "Haciendas y comunidades en el valle de México."

43. This is the key emphasis of Farriss, *Maya Society under Colonial Rule*.

44. For the Andes see Bowser, *The African Slave in Colonial Peru*; for the Bajío, Guevara Sanginés, *Guanajuato diverso*.

45. This is evident in every analysis from Ricard, *The Spiritual Conquest of Mexico*, to Spalding, *Huarochirí*; Farriss, *Maya Society under Colonial Rule*; Lockhart, *The Nahuas after the Conquest*; and Taylor, *Magistrates of the Sacred*.

46. Such views shape North's work in *Institutions* and *Violence and Social Orders*.

47. Wallerstein, *The Modern World-System*.

48. I discovered these key emphases in Adams's seminars; they are presented in *Energy and Structure*.

49. This is evident in any good history of the rise of Spain, from Elliott, *Imperial Spain*, to Kamen, *Empire*.

50. See Grafe and Irigoin, "The Spanish Empire and Its Legacy."

51. See Wallerstein, *The Modern World-System*, and Stein and Stein, *Silver, War, and Trade*.

52. This is my reading of Stein and Stein, *Apogee of Empire*.

53. Tutino, *From Insurrection to Revolution in Mexico*.

54. This is clear in Lockhart, *Spanish Peru*, and for the Bajío in Super, *La vida en Querétaro durante la colonia*.

55. See Owensby, *Empire of Law and Indian Justice in Colonial Mexico*, especially chapter 8, "Rebellious Subjects," and Vinson, *Bearing Arms for His Majesty*.

56. Adelman, *Sovereignty and Revolution in the Iberian Atlantic*, emphasizes negotiations among entrepreneurs and officials; Owensby, *Empire of Law and Indian Justice in Colonial Mexico*, details mediations between the powerful and the populace. A comprehensive understanding of the Spanish American regime must merge both perspectives.

57. This understanding is illustrated throughout the analysis that follows. The judicial focus of colonial government is evident in Borah, *Justice by Insurance*, in Taylor, *Drinking, Homicide, and Rebellion in Colonial Mexican Villages*, and now most persuasively in Owensby, *Empire of Law and Indian Justice in Colonial Mexico*. Relations between entrepreneurs and officials in the formative seventeenth century are seen in Hoberman, *Mexico's Merchant Elite*, and Cramaussel, *Poblar la frontera*. On the eighteenth-century attempt to create military forces see Archer, *The Army in Bourbon Mexico*; on the resistance the key work is Castro Gutiérrez, *Nueva ley y nuevo rey*.

58. The importance and complexity of ethnic and racial ranks and cate-

gories have been widely studied across the Americas; see the sources on Meso-america, the slave colonies, and the Andes in notes 6, 8–11, and 41, above. Patrick Carroll, author of *Blacks in Colonial Veracruz*, is completing a study that will shed new light on ethnic stratifications in coastal and Mesoameri-can regions of New Spain. Conversations with him have helped refine my understanding of the different ways of the Bajío and Spanish North America. Owensby, *Empire of Law and Indian Justice in Colonial Mexico*, details how Mesoamericans engaged regime courts to make *indio* a category of limited rights and benefits—how some northerners grasped for those rights.

59. In many Amerindian societies patriarchy ruled warfare and the hunt, while matrilineal relations organized families and communities, creating more complex and less patriarchal relationships. Europeans pressed Amer-indian peoples toward their visions of patriarchy whenever possible. See Eth-ridge, *Creek Country*, and Barr, *Peace Came in the Form of a Woman*—the latter illustrating Spaniards' limited success in early Texas.

60. This understanding of patriarchy is rooted in Stern, *The Secret History of Gender*.

61. The importance of patron-client relationships to organizing social in-equality in Latin America is long recognized. The links between patronage and household patriarchy are less noted, removing the gendered essence of hier-archical rule. Perhaps the best analysis, and a strong influence on my under-standing, is Graham, *Patronage and Politics in Nineteenth-Century Brazil*.

62. This is my synthesis of the detailed analysis in Silva Prada, *La política de una rebellion*.

63. An understanding that the only effective class was the ruling class shaped Marc Bloch's classic *Feudal Society*. Writing in an era of powerful, al-most presumptive Marxism, Bloch expected that popular class consciousness came with capitalism. This analysis suggests that polarized two-class societies were a Marxian dream, an ideological and political utopia. Elite unity and popular fragmentations integrated by axes of hierarchal power seem a more common outcome in capitalist societies.

64. Notably in *Domination and the Arts of Resistance*.

65. My colleague Adam Rothman challenged me to clarify my notion of mediators. It derives from the research for this work, viewed in the context of historical studies of Spanish Mesoamerica that focus on key mediators: Farriss, *Maya Society under Colonial Rule*, Lockhart, *The Nahuas after the Conquest*, and Taylor, *Magistrates of the Sacred*, emphasize colonial developments; Mallon, *Peasant and Nation*, and Guardino, *Peasants and the Formation of Mexican Na-tional Politics*, bring analyses focused on mediators into the national era; and Grandin, *Blood of Guatemala*, analyzes indigenous notables from the colonial era to the late twentieth century.

Chapter 1. Founding the Bajío

1. The challenges and conflicts inherent in constructing regime power in sixteenth-century New Spain are explored in fine detail in Martínez Baracs's *Convivencia y utopia*, which details the long and uncertain process by which regime officers and church prelates contested each other and diverse indigenous factions to establish a colonial order in Michoacán, just south of the Bajío. For the Bajío see Wright Carr, *La conquista del Bajío y los orígenes de San Miguel de Allende*, and Cruz Rangel, *Chichimecas, misioneros, soldados y terratenientes*, 73–142.

2. This geographic sketch reflects Wright Carr, *La conquista del Bajío y los orígenes de San Miguel de Allende*, 7; Murphy, *Irrigation in the Bajío Region of Colonial Mexico*, 3–5; Tovar Rangel, *Geografía de Guanajuato*; and my travels.

3. Carrasco, *Estructura político-territorial del imperio tenochca*, makes plain the ideological shaping of the indigenous chronicles produced before and after the conquest. He also shows how a critical reading can elicit a vision of power and production, conflict and instability—and an appreciation of contested legitimations. On the Bajío as a frontier of both interaction and conflict see Cruz Rangel, *Chichimecas, misioneros, soldados y terratenientes*.

4. This outline of pre-Hispanic history in the Bajío reflects López Austin and López Luján, *El pasado indígena*, and relies heavily on the new vision in Wright Carr, *La conquista del Bajío y los orígenes de San Miguel de Allende*, 11–20.

5. My knowledge of Plazuelas, recently excavated, comes from a day there in November 2008, arranged and accompanied by the historians of the University of Guanajuato.

6. Soustelle, *La familia otomí-pame del México central*, 13–39, 445–507; Lastra, *Los Otomíes*, 72–106.

7. Carrasco, *Estructura político-territorial del imperio tenochca*.

8. This outline of the Bajío on the eve of conquest is based on Wright Carr, *La conquista del Bajío y los orígenes de San Miguel de Allende*, 20–35, and Ruíz Guadalajara, *Dolores antes de la independencia*, vol. 1, 77–87.

9. The classic study of smallpox and the conquest of Mesoamerica remains Crosby, *The Columbian Exchange*.

10. García Castro, *Indios, territorio y poder en la provincial matlatzinca*. For Spanish struggles to rule the former Tarascan polity see Martínez Baracs, *Convivencia y utopia*.

11. The narrative that follows is my synthesis of the essential research of Somohano Martínez, *La versión histórica de la conquista y la organización política del pueblo de Querétaro*; Wright Carr, *La conquista del Bajío y los orígenes de San Miguel de Allende*; and Lastra, *Los Otomíes*, all in the context of García Castro, *Indios, territorio y poder en la provincial matlatzinca*, and Martínez Baracs, *Convivencia y utopia*.

12. Guzmán and his violent ways are detailed in Sempat Assadourian, *Zacatecas*, 27–34.

13. Cruz Rangel, *Chichimecas, misioneros, soldados y terratenientes*, 73–111.

14. Sempat Assadourian, *Zacatecas*, 34–47; Becerra Jiménez, *Gobierno, justicia y instituciones en la Nueva Galicia*, 39–67.

15. Lastra, *Los Otomíes*, 134; Ayala Calderón, *Yuriria*, 50–78.

16. Urquiola Permisán, "Estructura urbana y agua."

17. Jiménez Gómez, ed., *La República de Indios de Querétaro*, no. 22, 30 April 1550, 420–21; no. 123, 26 August 1550, 737.

18. Ibid., no. 65, 22 August 1550, 563; no. 66, 27 August 1550, 563–64; no. 83, 26 August 1550, 610; no. 67, 9 October 1551, 564.

19. Ibid., no. 124, 4 October 1550, 737–38; no. 125, 4 April 1551, 738–39.

20. Ibid., no. 126, 3 July 1551, 739–40; no. 23, 10 November 1551, 421–22; no. 127, 8 April 1552, 740–41.

21. Cruz Rangel, *Chichimecas, misioneros, soldados y terratenientes*, 76–106.

22. Jiménez Gómez, ed., *La República de Indios de Querétaro*, no. 24, 20 December 1555, 422–23.

23. Ibid., no. 25, 23 June 1558, 423–26.

24. Ibid., no. 26, 25 June 1564, 426.

25. Cruz Rangel, *Chichimecas, misioneros, soldados y terratenientes*, 85.

26. Flynn and Giráldez, "Born with a 'Silver Spoon.'"

27. Bakewell, *Silver Mining and Society in Colonial Mexico*; Powell, *La guerra chichimeca*.

28. Castro Rivas, Rangel López, and Tovar Rangel, *Desarrollo socio-demográfico de la ciudad de Guanajuato durante el siglo XVII*, 21.

29. *Registro de la primeras minas de Guanajuato*, 30–31.

30. Ibid.

31. On the complexities of refining that shaped Guanajuato's colonial history see Torres, *El beneficio de la plata en Guanajuato*, and Lara Meza, *Haciendas de beneficio en Guanajuato*.

32. *Registro de la primeras minas de Guanajuato*, 37, 85.

33. Rionda Arreguín, "Los hospitales en el Real de Minas de Guanajuato."

34. Guevara Sanginés, *Guanajuato diverso*, 97, 202–3.

35. Ibid., 202–3, provides the longer original text.

36. Ibid., 144–45.

37. Castro Gutiérrez, "La resistencia indígena."

38. This reads Powell, *La guerra chichimeca*, in the context of analyses of Spanish relations with North American indigenous peoples in Ricklis, *The Karankawa of Texas*, and Brooks, *Captives and Cousins*.

39. Sempat Assadourian, *Zacatecas*, 56–68.

40. Cruz Rangel, *Chichimecas, misioneros, soldados y terratenientes*, 203.

41. Wright Carr, *La conquista del Bajío y los orígenes de San Miguel de Allende*, 54–55; Rubio Mañé, "Títulos de las villas."

42. Sempat Assadourian, *Zacatecas*, 79–84.

43. This is a key point made by Sempat Assadourian in ibid., 70–71.

44. Ibid., 336–47, quotes at 341 (from Archivo General de Indias, Seville, Patronato, 182, ramo 5).

45. Ibid., 86–103.

46. Murphy, *Irrigation in the Bajío Region of Colonial Mexico*, 41–42; Ayala Calderón, *Yuriria*; Baroni Boissonas, *La formación de la estructura agraria en el Bajío colonial, siglos XVI y XVII*, 10–37, 41–47.

47. Wright Carr, *La conquista del Bajío y los orígenes de San Miguel de Allende*, 59–60; Murphy, *Irrigation in the Bajío Region of Colonial Mexico*, 47–50.

48. This is evident throughout Baroni Boissonas, *La formación de la estructura agraria en el Bajío colonial, siglos XVI y XVII*, and Guevara Sanginés, *Guanajuato diverso*.

49. Sempat Assadourian, *Zacatecas*, 414–24 (Carta del Arzobispo, Archivo General de Indias, Seville, 336A), quotes at 415, 420, 421.

50. Ibid., 104–7, quotes at 105–6.

51. Ibid., 131–37.

52. This view of pacification reflects Powell, *Capitán mestizo*, also read against Ricklis, *The Karankawa of Texas*, and Brooks, *Captives and Cousins*.

53. Becerra Jiménez, *Gobierno, justicia y instituciones en la Nueva Galicia*, 103–13, emphasized the importance of the diseases that devastated settled natives and resistant Chichimecas on the frontier.

54. Sego, *Aliados y adversos*.

55. "Relación de Juan Antonio Velázquez," Archivo General de Indias, Seville, 110; reprinted in Sempat Assadourian, *Zacatecas*, 449–88.

56. Ibid., 482.

57. Ibid., 449–50.

58. Ibid., 451.

59. Ibid., 455–56.

60. Ibid., 456–57.

61. Ibid., 455.

62. Ibid., 455, 457.

63. Ibid., 458.

64. Ibid., 462.

65. Ibid., 467–70.

66. Ibid., 471–73.

67. Ibid., 473–81.

68. Ibid., 486.

69. Ibid.

70. "Relación Geográfica de Querétaro." The materials on authorship are at 120 and 154.

71. Ibid., 121–22, 138–40, 145–46, 152, quote at 140.

72. Ibid., 122–26.

73. Ibid., quotes at 129, 130, 131.

74. Ibid., 130.

75. Ibid., 130–33.

76. Ibid., 133.

77. Ibid.

78. Ibid., 132.

79. Ibid., 133–34.

80. Ibid., 134.

81. Ibid., 135.

82. Ibid., 140.

83. Ibid., 140–41.

84. Ibid., 141.

85. Ibid., 141–42.

86. Ibid., 144.

87. Ibid., 142.

88. Ibid., 143.

89. Ibid., 135.

90. Ibid., 146.

91. Ibid., 149, 152.

92. Ibid., 145, 151.

93. Ibid., 149.

94. Ibid., 148, 150.

95. Ibid., 148–49.

96. Bakewell, *Silver Mining and Society in Colonial Mexico*, table 5 (p. 246).

97. Ibid., table 1 (p. 237).

98. Guevara Sanginés, *Guanajuato diverso*, 147–48.

99. On Mexico City merchants financing mining see Hoberman, *Mexico's Merchant Elite*.

100. Cruz Rangel, *Chichimecas, misioneros, soldados y terratenientes*, 263.

101. Rionda Arreguín, *La Compañía de Jesús en la provincia guanajuatense*, 19–23, quote at 23.

102. Ibid., 25–34.

103. Ibid., 28–39.

104. Ibid., 34.

105. I synthesize ibid., 37–55, Solís de la Torre, *Bárbaros y ermitanos*, Mendoza Muñoz, *Historia eclesiástica de Cadereyta*, and Cruz Rangel, *Chichimecas, misioneros, soldados y terratenientes*.

106. Rangel Silva, *Capitanes a guerra, linajes de frontera*, 14–15, 18.

107. Carbajal López, *La minería en Bolaños*, 40–43.

108. My view of Querétaro reflects Super, *La vida en Querétaro durante la colonia*, and Jiménez Gómez, "Instituciones sociales, mentalidades y vida cotidiana en Querétaro."

109. Jiménez Gómez, *La República de Indios de Querétaro*, no. 16, 29 May 1590, 412.

110. Ibid., 27, 15 January 1591, 426–27.

111. Urquiola Permisán, *Trabajadores de campo y ciudad*, 138–39, 182–83, 223–24, 251–52, 257–58, 286, 321–22, 332, 387–88.

112. Jiménez Gómez, *La República de Indios de Querétaro*, no. 68, 10 April 1576, 565–66; no. 69, 30 April 1591, 566.

113. Super, *La vida en Querétaro durante la colonia*.

114. Jiménez Gómez, *La República de Indios de Querétaro*, no. 85, 3 March 1591 to 31 August 1596, 611–13.

115. Ibid., no. 86, 22 June 1595 to 8 August 1595, 613–19.

116. Ibid., no. 87, 14–22 February 1598, 620–21; no. 88, 12 March 1598, 622.

117. Ibid., no. 89, 30 June 1598, 622–23.

118. Ibid., no. 90, 26 July 1598, 623–28.

119. Ibid., no. 7, 5 December 1605, 346–57; no. 8, 7 October 1608, 358–59.

120. Ibid., no. 91, 27 October 1598, 628–29.

121. Ibid., no. 92, 22 January 1599, 629–31.

122. Super, *La vida en Querétaro durante la colonia*, 41, 45, 68, 111.

123. Ibid., 66–68.

124. Ibid, 59.

125. Rangel Silva, *Capitanes a guerra, linajes de frontera*, 86–88.

126. Super, *La vida en Querétaro durante la colonia*, 62–64.

127. Ibid., 80–84.

128. This is a key conclusion of Bakewell, *Silver Mining and Society in Colonial Mexico*.

129. Super, *La vida en Querétaro durante la colonia*, 275.

130. The outline above and the discussion that follows build upon documents published by Urquiola Permisán, *Trabajadores de campo y ciudad*, analyzed and presented in tables in Appendix A.

131. Here I differ with Ruggiero Romano, who in *Mecanismo y elementos del sistema económica colonial americano* sees coercion at the heart of nearly all Iberian colonial labor relations. For the role of incentives in slavery see Schwartz, *Sugar Plantations in the Formation of Brazilian Society*.

132. See Appendix A, table A.1.

133. See the seminal analysis of Viquiera Palerm and Urquiola Permisán, *Los obrajes de la Nueva España*.

134. Pérez-Mallaína, *Spain's Men of the Sea*.

135. Urquiola Permisán, *Trabajadores de campo y ciudad*, 299–399.

136. Ibid., 369.

137. For employers see Appendix A, table A.2.

138. Urquiola Permisán, *Trabajadores de campo y ciudad*, 139–40, 178–79, 180, 222, 258, 291–92, 355.

139. Ibid., 242.

140. Ibid., 327–28.

141. Ibid., 252–53, 286, 278–79, 388.

142. Ibid., 282–83.

143. Ibid., 312–13.

144. Ibid., 311–12.

145. Ibid., 376–77, 386–87.

146. See Appendix A, table A.1.

147. On obraje labor see Appendix A, tables A.3–A.6.

148. Appendix A, table A.5.

149. Appendix A, table A.7.

150. Appendix A, table A.8.

151. On indigenous peoples' regional and ethnic origins see Appendix A, table A.9.

152. Appendix A, table A.10.

153. Urquiola Permisán, *Trabajadores de campo y ciudad*, 276.

154. Ibid., 301–2.

155. Appendix A, table A.11.

156. Urquiola Permisán, *Trabajadores de campo y ciudad*, 279–80.

157. Appendix A, table A.12.

158. Urquiola Permisán, *Trabajadores de campo y ciudad*, 196–97.

159. Ibid., 359.

160. Super, *La vida en Querétaro durante la colonia*, 212–23; Guevara Sanginés, *Guanajuato diverso*.

161. Jiménez Gómez, "Instituciones sociales, mentalidades y vida cotidiana en Querétaro," 100; Lavrin, "El convento de Santa Clara de Querétaro."

162. Jiménez Gómez, *La República de Indios de Querétaro*, no. 128, 13 June 1618, 741–47.

163. In 1626 and 1627 a deal with tribute maize linked the republic to two local entrepreneurs; Jiménez Gómez, *La República de Indios de Querétaro*, no. 129, 29 August 1627, 747–48.

164. Ibid., no. 94, 3 January 1622, 635; no. 95, 5 January 1622, 635–36.

165. Ibid., no. 96, 14 June 1624 to 16 July 1628, 636–46.

166. Ibid., no. 97, 12 June-10 July 1629, 646–54.

167. Super, *La vida en Querétaro durante la colonia*, 70–71.

168. Jiménez Gómez, "Instituciones sociales, mentalidades y vida cotidiana en Querétaro"; and López Lara, ed., *El obispado de Michoacán en el siglo XVII*.

169. This builds on Pastor, *Crisis y recomposición social* and *Cuerpos sociales, cuerpos sacrificiales*. My view of monogamous patriarchy relies on Bennett, *Africans in Colonial Mexico*, and Stern, *The Secret History of Gender*.

170. Gálvez Jiménez, *Celaya*; Alberro, *Inquisición y sociedad en México*, 283–334.

171. Zeláa y Hidalgo, *Glorias de Querétaro*, 167.

172. Taylor, "The Virgin of Guadalupe," 9–33; Poole, *Our Lady of Guadalupe*.

173. Vilaplana, *Histórico, y sagrado novenario de la milagrosa imagen de Nuestra Señora del Pueblito*, 14–15.

174. Ibid., 17.

175. Ibid., 20.

176. Ibid.; Acosta and Munguía, *La milagrosa imagen de Ntra. señora del pueblito*.

177. Jiménez Gómez, *La República de Indios de Querétaro*, no. 14, 1 September 1621, 410.

178. Ibid., no. 15, 6 March 1631, 410–11.

179. Ibid., no. 138, 27 March 1640, 748–49.

180. Murphy, *Irrigation in the Bajío Region of Colonial Mexico*, 92–99; Jiménez Gómez, *La República de Indios de Querétaro*, no. 99, 25 February 1654, 657–59.

181. The foundation of Querétaro's Spanish Council is detailed in Ferrusca Beltrán, *Querétaro*.

Chapter 2. Forging Spanish North America

1. Hoberman, *Mexico's Merchant Elite*, details key developments in trade and government.

2. Stein and Stein, *Silver, War, and Trade*, 3–105.

3. Owensby, *Empire of Law and Indian Justice in Colonial Mexico*, provides a detailed and persuasive new understanding of this process.

4. Bakewell, *Silver Mining and Society in Colonial Mexico*, remains the essential study of Zacatecas.

5. Ibid., 9–12, 38–39.

6. Ibid., 27.

7. Ibid., 46, 68, 74, 95, 114–15; on Mateos, the Rincón Gallardo, and Ciénega de Mata see Alcaide Aguilar, *La hacienda "Ciénega de Mata" de los Rincón Gallardo*, 31–44, 268–87, 426–30.

8. Bakewell, *Silver Mining and Society in Colonial Mexico*, 122–23, 137.

9. Ibid., 55, 125–26, 201, 211.

10. Flynn and Giráldez, "Cycles of Silver"; Bakewell, *Silver Mining and Society in Colonial Mexico*, 58, 60, 75, 90–95, 179, 213.

11. The literature on New Mexico is vast. Three complementary studies provide innovative perspectives and access to scholarly debates: Gutiérrez, *When Jesus Came the Corn Mothers Went Away*; Brooks, *Captives and Cousins*; and Frank, *From Settler to Citizen*.

12. Three key works guide this analysis of northward expansion: Robert West's classic *The Mining Community in Northern New Spain*; Susan Deeds's recent and innovative *Defiance and Deference in Mexico's Colonial North*; and Chantal Cramaussel's massive and deeply researched *Poblar la frontera*.

13. Cramaussel, *Poblar la frontera*, 30–78, details all this; for Santa Bárbara see 38.

14. Deeds, *Defiance and Deference in Mexico's Colonial North*, 11–26; Vargas-Lobsinger, *Formación y decadencia de una fortuna*, 11–28.

15. Cramaussel, *Poblar la frontera*, 207–9.

16. Deeds, *Defiance and Deference in Mexico's Colonial North*, 30–36.

17. Bakewell, *Silver Mining and Society in Colonial Mexico*, 79.

18. This sketch builds on the detailed reseach of Cramaussel, *Poblar la frontera*.

19. Owensby, *Empire of Law and Indian Justice in Colonial Mexico*, 130–33, 164–65, details Concho collaborations, an attempt to gain redress in Mexico City's General Indian Court as coercions mounted in 1541, then the turn to resistance.

20. West, *The Mining Community in Northern New Spain*; Deeds, *Defiance and Deference in Mexico's Colonial North*, 72–84.

21. Deeds, *Defiance and Deference in Mexico's Colonial North*, 77.

22. Ibid., 86–101.

23. This vision of Santa Bárbara around 1700 relies on Cramaussel, *Poblar la frontera*. Parallel developments ruled in eastern San Luis Potosí; see Rangel Silva, *Capitanes a guerra, linajes de frontera*, 102.

24. Rionda Arreguín, *La Compañía de Jesús en la provincia guanajuatense*, 245.

25. Ibid., 246–49.

26. Torres, *El beneficio de la plata en Guanajuato*, 22–24, 33–34.

27. Brading, *Haciendas and Ranchos in the Mexican Bajío*, 29–30; Israel, *Race, Class, and Politics in Colonial Mexico*, 33, 157–58, 177; López Lara, ed., *El obispado de Michoacán en el siglo XVII*, 76–77 and passim.

28. López Lara, *El obispado de Michoacán en el siglo XVII*, ed., 76–77.

29. Castro Rivas, Rangel López, and Tovar Rangel, *Desarrollo socio-demográfico de la ciudad de Guanajuato durante el siglo XVII*, 27–28; my calculations.

30. Ibid., 29–30.

31. Ibid., 62–63.

32. Ibid.

33. Brading, *Haciendas and Ranchos in the Mexican Bajío*, 29–30; López Lara, ed., *El obispado de Michoacán en el siglo XVII*, 49–51, 71, 76, 178; Ladd, *The Mexican Nobility at Independence*, 193–95.

34. López Lara, ed., *El obispado de Michoacán en el siglo XVII*, 76–78; Castro Rivas, Rangel López, and Tovar Rangel, *Desarrollo socio-demográfico de la ciudad de Guanajuato durante el siglo XVII*, 39–45, 46–49.

35. Castro Rivas, Rangel López, and Tovar Rangel, *Desarrollo socio-demográfico de la ciudad de Guanajuato durante el siglo XVII*, 62–63.

36. Ibid., 64.

37. Ibid., 33; my calculations.

38. Rionda Arreguín, *La Compañía de Jesús en la provincia guanajuatense*, 250–56.

39. Ibid., 46–48; my calculations.

40. Ruíz Guadalajara, *Dolores antes de la independencia*, vol. 1, 67–160, details this process with exceptional clarity.

41. López Lara, ed., *El obispado de Michoacán en el siglo XVII*, 48–52; Wright Carr, *La conquista del Bajío y los orígenes de San Miguel de Allende*, 63–65, 106–7; Ruíz Guadalajara, *Dolores antes de la independencia*, vol. 1, 185.

42. This portrait of the uplands and La Erre synthesizes Ruíz Guadalajara, *Dolores antes de la independencia*, vol. 1, 161–237; the suit for rights is on 200–201; the analysis of the parish registers is on 228–29. On Ciénega de Mata see Alcaide Aguilar, *La hacienda "Ciénega de Mata" de los Rincón Gallardo*; on San Nicolás de Tierranueva see Rivera Villanueva, *Los otomíes de San Nicolás de Tierranueva*.

43. Murphy, *Irrigation in the Bajío Region of Colonial Mexico*, 9–27.

44. Ibid., 41–87.

45. Bakewell, *Silver Mining and Society in Colonial Mexico*, 63, 209, 250.

46. López Lara, ed., *El obispado de Michoacán en el siglo XVII*, 77–80.

47. The inventory is in Baroni Boissonas, *La formación de la estructura agraria en el Bajío colonial, siglos XVI y XVII*, 193–214; I analyze the quantitative materials in appendix B.

48. Appendix B, table B.1.

49. Baroni Boissonas, *La formación de la estructura agraria en el Bajío colonial, siglos XVI y XVII*, 194–98.

50. Appendix B, table B.1.

51. Appendix B, table B.7.

52. Appendix B, tables B.5, B.6.

53. Baroni Boissonas, *La formación de la estructura agraria en el Bajío colonial, siglos XVI y XVII*, 203–4.

54. Appendix B. table B.2.

55. Appendix B, tables B.1, B.3.

56. The censuses are in Carrillo Cázares, *Partidos y padrones del obispado de Michoacán*, 403–34; my quantitative analyses are in appendix B.

57. Baroni Boissonas, *La formación de la estructura agraria en el Bajío colonial, siglos XVI y XVII*, 65.

58. Appendix B, tables B.8, B.9, B.13.

59. Appendix B, table B.10.

60. Appendix B, tables B.11, B.12, B.14, B.15.

61. Carrillo Cázares, *Partidos y padrones del obispado de Michoacán*, 431–32.

62. Ibid., 416, 426.

63. Ibid., 427, 430; Baroni Boissonas, *La formación de la estructura agraria en el Bajío colonial, siglos XVI y XVII*, 199.

64. Carrillo Cázares, *Partidos y padrones del obispado de Michoacán*, 416–18.

65. Ibid., 418–19, 425.

66. Ibid., 428, 429, 432.

67. Torre Villar, ed., *Instrucciones y memorias de los virreyes novohispanos*, vol. 1, 524.

68. Appendix B, table B.16.

69. Carrillo Cázares, *Partidos y padrones del obispado de Michoacán*, 404–7, 411–13.

70. Ibid., 404, 407, 411, 412.

71. Ibid., 404.

72. Ibid., 404–8, 411.

73. Ibid., 406.

74. Baroni Boissonas, *La formación de la estructura agraria en el Bajío colonial, siglos XVI y XVII*, 66.

75. Appendix B, tables B.23, B. 24, B.25, B.26.

76. Appendix B, table B.27.

77. Brading, *Haciendas and Ranchos in the Mexican Bajío*, 19.

78. López Lara, ed., *El obispado de Michoacán en el siglo XVII*, 69.

79. Ibid., 48–52, 76–77, 172–174.

80. Ruíz Guadalajara, *Dolores antes de la independencia*, vol. 1, 228.

81. Appendix B, tables B.27–B.29.

82. Baroni Boissonas, *La formación de la estructura agraria en el Bajío colonial, siglos XVI y XVII*, 82–86.

83. Appendix B.22–B.23.

84. Carrillo Cázares, *Partidos y padrones del obispado de Michoacán*, 417, 432.

85. Ibid., 417, 423.

86. Support for de la Cruz as an indicator of African ancestry came from two sources. I asked Patrick Carroll, who arguably has read more sources on people of African origins in New Spain than any other scholar, if any surnames

stood out. He immediately offered de la Cruz. Recently the recurrence of de la Cruz in Velázquez Gutiérrez, *Mujeres de origen africano en la capital novohispana*, confirms the usefulness of the indicator.

87. Carrillo Cázares, *Partidos y padrones del obispado de Michoacán*, 420.

88. Ibid., 433.

89. Ibid., 405–8.

90. Appendix B, table B.20.

91. Appendix B, table B.22.

92. Appendix B, table B.21.

93. Carrillo Cázares, *Partidos y padrones del obispado de Michoacán*, 422.

94. Ibid., 430.

95. Ibid., 404, 405, 407, 408.

96. Bakewell, *Silver Mining and Society in Colonial Mexico*, 225–36, and Stein and Stein, *Silver, War, and Trade*, 19–23, preceded me in emphasizing the capitalist dynamics of New Spain's North as the seventeenth century ended.

97. This is detailed in Stein and Stein, *Silver, War, and Trade*, 3–103. Native resistance reached eastern San Luis Potosí and the Gulf lowlands; see Rangel Silva, *Capitanes a guerra, linajes de frontera*, 98.

98. The assault is noted in Gunnarsdóttir, *Mexican Karismata*, 80–81; the news traveled quickly with a group of friars who landed just after the event and then moved inland.

99. The riots are detailed in Silva Prado, *La política de una rebelion*.

100. Jaffary, *False Mystics*, 4.

101. These are noted in Gunnarsdóttir, *Mexican Karismata*, 45–48, and treated here in chapter 3.

102. Again, Stein and Stein, *Silver, War, and Trade*, 19–23, 92–93, emphasized the link between dynamic New World silver societies and the rising capitalism of northwestern Europe, mediated by the economic and political decline of Spain.

Chapter 3. New World Revivals

1. Escamilla González, "La nueva alianza," 45–46.

2. Ibid., 47.

3. Ibid., 49–56.

4. Stein and Stein, *Silver, War, and Trade*, 3–144, offers a detailed examination.

5. Berthe, ed., *Las nuevas momorias del Capitán Jean de Monségur*, 31.

6. Ibid., 44.

7. Ibid., 60–76.

8. Ibid., 133.

9. Ibid., 143–99.

10. Ibid., 200.

11. Ibid., 200–201.

12. Ibid., 204.

13. Flynn and Giráldez, "Cycles of Silver."

14. See appendix D, table D.1.

15. Ibid.

16. López Lara, ed., *El obispado de Michoacán en el siglo XVII*, 51.

17. On Caballero y Medina see Ferrusca Beltrán, *Querétaro*, 159; the will is in Rincón Frías, "Testamento de don Juan Caballero y Ocío," 5–11.

18. Rincón Frías, "Testamento de don Juan Caballero y Ocío," 11.

19. Ibid., 10.

20. Ibid.

21. See chapter 7.

22. José Fernando Alcaide Aguilar found the records that document the Rincón Gallardo's suits and inventories in archives in Seville and Mexico; he published the details and his interpretations in *La hacienda "Ciénega de Mata" de los Rincón Gallardo*. I recalculated his numbers and offer my own interpretations in the following paragraphs.

23. Alcaide Aguilar, *La hacienda "Ciénega de Mata" de los Rincón Gallardo*, 424–25.

24. Ibid., 425; he does not provide numbers for those no longer working.

25. The inventories of workers and their debts are in Alcaide Aguilar, *La hacienda "Ciénega de Mata" de los Rincón Gallardo*, 411–17.

26. Brading, *Haciendas and Ranchos in the Mexican Bajío*, 73–82; 119–48; Rionda Arreguín, *La Compañía de Jesús en la provincia guanajuatense*, 260–61, 280.

27. Brading, *Haciendas and Ranchos in the Mexican Bajío*, 70–88.

28. See appendix C, tables C.17, C.18.

29. These developments are documented in Brading, *Haciendas and Ranchos in the Mexican Bajío*; Morín, *Michoacán en la Nueva España del siglo XVIII*; and Rodríguez Gómez, *Jalpa y San Juan de los Otates*. On the proliferation of estate communities see Gómez de Acosta, *Querétaro en 1743*, 170–74; and González Sánchez, *El Obispado de Michoacán en 1765*, 166–69, 175–76, 298–99, 302–8.

30. Ruíz Guadalajara, *Dolores antes de la independencia*, I, 237–62.

31. Ibid., I, 279–301, 347–48.

32. Brading, *Haciendas and Ranchos in the Mexican Bajío*, 34–38, 183; Espinosa Morales, "Análisis de los precios de los productos diezmados," 122–72.

33. Appendix D, table D.1.

34. This discussion is based upon Rionda Arreguín, *La mina de san Juan de Rayas*; the quote is from 16–17.

35. Brading, *Miners and Merchants in Bourbon Mexico*, 263; Jáuregui, *Los Marqueses de Rayas*, 21–24; Rodríguez Gómez, *Jalpa y San Juan de los Otates*, 79–83.

36. Brading, *Miners and Merchants in Bourbon Mexico*, 264–65; Jáuregui de Cervantes, *Los Marqueses de Rayas*, 24–33, 59–84.

37. This description of Guanajuato builds on Torres, *El beneficio de la plata en Guanajuato*; numbers are on 62 and in anexo 5, 174–76.

38. Again, this synthesizes Torres, *El beneficio de la plata en Guanajuato*.

39. This selling of *cuadrilla* compounds is documented in Lara Meza, *Haciendas de beneficio en Guanajuato*.

40. Morín, *Michoacán en la Nueva España del siglo XVIII*, 94; Rionda Arreguín, *La Compañía de Jesús en la provincia guanajuatense*, 276; Villaseñor y Sánchez, *Theatro americano*, vol. 2, 39–41; Jáuregui de Cervantes, *Los Marqueses de Rayas*, 32, 36; Brading, *Miners and Merchants in Bourbon Mexico*, 276.

41. Brading, *Miners and Merchants in Bourbon Mexico*, 277.

42. Appendix C, table C.25, on Guanajuato.

43. Guevara Sanginés, *Guanajuato diverso*, 104–5, 150–53.

44. Rionda Arreguín, *La Compañía de Jesús en la provincia guanajuatense*, 272.

45. This is a key conclusion of Vinson, *Bearing Arms for His Majesty*, 223, 227.

46. Guevara Sanginés, *Guanajuato diverso*, 128–29.

47. Ibid., 129–32.

48. Ibid., 210.

49. The will is reproduced in ibid., 233–40.

50. Nicolasa's will is in ibid., 241–49.

51. The case is brilliantly analyzed by Guevara Sanginés in *Guanajuato diverso*, 175–85; she reproduces the correspondence on 223–32.

52. Cervantes Aguilar, *Fray Simón del Hierro*, offers the narrative of one missionary friar, including a stop in Guanajuato in 1745.

53. Rionda Arreguín, *La Compañía de Jesús en la provincia guanajuatense*, 260.

54. Ibid., 260–68.

55. Rodríguez Frausto, "La Universidad de Guanajuato en su origen," 71–98, quote at 72.

56. Ibid., 78.

57. Ibid., 78–80.

58. Ibid., 80–81.

59. Ibid., 82–83.

60. Ibid., 83–84.

61. Rionda Arreguín, *La Compañía de Jesús en la provincia guanajuatense*, 264; Rodríguez Frausto, "La Universidad de Guanajuato en su origen," 75.

62. Rionda Arreguín, *La Compañía de Jesús en la provincia guanajuatense*, 280, 290–91.

63. Ibid., 312.

64. Ibid., 322–24.

65. Ibid., 340, 347–48.

66. Ibid., 340–41.

67. Ibid., 341–44.

68. Quoted in Rodríguez Frausto, "La Universidad de Guanajuato en su origin," 95.

69. Ajofrín, *Diario del viaje . . . a la América septentrional*, vol. 1, 277.

70. Ibid., vol. 1, 265, 267.

71. Ibid., vol. 1, 267; for the mining recession see appendix D, table D.1.

72. Ajofrín, *Diario del viaje . . . a la América septentrional*, vol. 1, 267.

73. Ibid., 272.

74. Huerta, "Comercio en tierra adentro," 34–35.

75. Salvucci, "Aspectos de un conflicto empresarial," 410–21.

76. Villaseñor y Sánchez, *Theatro americano*, vol. 2, 37.

77. Appendix C, tables C.20–C.21; Salvucci, "Aspectos de un conflicto empresarial," 408–9.

78. Hernández, *La soledad del silencio*, 23–132; the inscriptions are reproduced in photos on 78, 87.

79. Zárate Toscano, *Los nobles ante la muerte en México*, 147.

80. Chowning, *Rebellious Nuns*, 22–59.

81. Correa, "La Cofradía de Indios de la Limpia Concepción en la Villa de San Miguel el Grande en el siglo XVIII."

82. Brading, *Una iglesia asediada*, 178; Veronica Vallejo's Georgetown dissertation probes curing at San Miguel.

83. This pivotal conflict is detailed in Salvucci, "Aspectos de un conflicto empresarial."

84. Chowning, *Rebellious Nuns*, 62–145.

85. Ajofrín, *Diario del viaje . . . a la América septentrional*, vol. 1, 291.

86. Ibid., 293.

87. Lavrin, "El convento de Santa Clara de Querétaro," 76–119.

88. The foundation is famously celebrated in Siguenza y Góngora, *Glorias de Querétaro*.

89. Vilaplana, *Historico, y sagrado novenario de la milagrosa imagen de Nuestra Señora del Pueblito*, 26–30.

90. On the foundation see McCloskey, *The Formative Years of the Missionary College of Santa Cruz de Querétaro*, 15–33; for Ocío's will see Rincón Frías, "Testamento de don Juan Caballero y Ocío," 5–11.

91. McCloskey, *The Formative Years of the Missionary College of Santa Cruz de Querétaro*, 54–56.

92. This analysis builds on Alberro, *Inquisición y sociedad en México*, 508–25, and Buelna Serrano, "Las endemoniadas."

93. Alberro, *Inquisición y sociedad en México*, 512–18.

94. Ibid., 519–21.

95. Ibid., 521–24.

96. I am guided by Norton, *In the Devil's Snare*, and Lewis, *Hall of Mirrors*. Both detail how accusations and assumptions of witchcraft permeated and negotiated power in ethnically complex societies.

97. Gunnarsdóttir, *Mexican Karismata*, 17–138.

98. Super, *La vida en Querétaro durante la colonia*, 242; Gómez de Acosta, *Querétaro en 1743*, 165. On the persistence of slavery in the obrajes see Armas Briz and Solís Hernández, *Esclavos negros y mulatos en Querétaro, siglo XVIII*, 11–22, 23–92.

99. The details of sixty-one slave sales are reported in Mendoza Muñoz, *El Conde de Sierra Gorda, don José de Escandón y Helguera*, 83–84, 228–47; the calculations and interpretations are mine.

100. Ibid., 33–34, reports the case; the speculations are mine.

101. Jiménez Gómez, ed., *La República de Indios de Querétaro*, docs. 100–103, 659–68.

102. Ibid., doc. 71, 568–69.

103. Gunnarsdóttir, "The Convent of Santa Clara, the Elite, and Social Change in Eighteenth-Century Querétaro," 261–74.

104. Mendoza Muñoz, *El Conde de Sierra Gorda, don José de Escandón y Helguera*, 11–82, 163, 179–82, details Escandón's life and business.

105. See Couturier, *The Silver King*, 24–73.

106. Gómez, *Querétaro en 1743*, 126–27.

107. Navarrete, *Relación peregrina de la agua corriente . . .*, 41.

108. Gómez de Acosta, *Querétaro en 1743*, 119–20.

109. Ibid., 169–70.

110. Navarrete, *Relación peregrina de la agua corriente . . .*, 42; Gómez de Acosta, *Querétaro en 1743*, 121–22.

111. Navarrete, *Relación peregrina de la agua corriente . . .*, 28.

112. Gómez de Acosta, *Querétaro en 1743*, 165.

113. Navarrete, *Relación peregrina de la agua corriente . . .*, 42.

114. Gómez de Acosta, *Querétaro en 1743*, 169.

115. Ibid., 168–69.

116. Navarrete, *Relación peregrina de la agua corriente . . .*, 58–61.

117. Ibid., 69–70.

118. Ibid., 78–86.

119. Ibid., 86–90.

120. Gómez de Acosta, *Querétaro en 1743*, 128–31.

121. Ibid., 150–52.

122. Ibid., 154–58.

123. Ibid., 140–42; Nuestra Señora del Pueblito is also the first devotion addressed in the Corregidor's will, 183.

124. Navarrete, *Relación peregrina de la agua corriente . . .*, 43–47.

125. Ibid., 47–50.

126. Ibid., 50.

127. Reproduced in Medina Medina, "Noticias de Querétaro en las *Gacetas de México*, 61–69; quotes at 64.

128. Ibid., 66.

129. Vilaplana, *Historico, y sagrado novenario de la milagrosa imagen de Nuestra Señora del Pueblito*, 83–85.

130. Ibid., 69.

131. Ibid., 96.

132. Ibid., 27–32.

133. Ibid., 48, 54, 77.

134. Ibid., 48–96.

135. On the great epidemic see Molina del Villar, *La Nueva España y el matlazahuatl*.

136. Ajofrín, *Diario del viaje . . . a la América septentrional*, vol. 1, 185.

137. Ibid., vol. 1, 187–88.

138. Ibid., vol. 1, 189–93, 199–201.

139. Hadley, *Minería y sociedad*; Swann, *Tierra Adentro*; Martin, *Governance and Society in Colonial Mexico*.

140. Frank, *From Settler to Citizen*, 7–22; Ortelli, *Trama de una guerra conveniente*.

141. Wade, *The Native Americans of the Texas Edwards Plateau*, 1–133, details engagements along the Río Grande after 1650; Cruz Rangel, *Chichimecas, misioneros, soldados y terratenientes*, shows a century of stalemate in the Sierra Gorda.

142. Chipman, *Spanish Texas*, 70–85.

143. Ibid., 86–104; Barr, *Peace Came in the Form of a Woman*.

144. Río, *El régimen jesuítico de la Antigua California*, 158–60, 170–71, 190.

145. McCloskey, *The Formative Years of the Missionary College of Santa Cruz de Querétaro*, 98–99; Cervantes Aguilar, *Fray Simón del Hierro*, 15.

146. Chipman, *Spanish Texas*, 104–12.

147. Barr, *Peace Came in the Form of a Woman*.

148. Chipman, *Spanish Texas*, 104–26; Teja, *San Antonio de Béjar*.

149. Carbajal López, *La minería en Bolaños*, 45–49, quote at 49.

150. On the "conquest" of Nayarit see Meyer, *El gran Nayar*. Jesuits dealing with frustrations and constructing texts of success are analyzed brilliantly by Irene del Valle in *Escribiendo desde los márgenes*.

151. Osante, *Orígenes del Nuevo Santander*, treats the full process; also McCloskey, *The Formative Years of the Missionary College of Santa Cruz de Querétaro*, 108–13.

152. Mendoza Muñoz, *El Conde de Sierra Gorda, don José de Escandón y Helguera*, 95–98, 103; early-eighteenth-century incursions and conflicts are detailed in Cruz Rangel, *Chichimecas, misioneros, soldados y terratenientes*.

153. Rangel Silva, *Capitanes a guerra, linajes de frontera*.

154. Osante, *Orígenes del Nuevo Santander*, 102–5; Domínguez Paulín, *Querétaro en la conquista de las Californias*, 97–122.

155. Mendoza Muñoz, *El Conde de Sierra Gorda, don José de Escandón y Helguera*, 85, 99–100.

156. Ibid., 104.

157. That report is synthesized in appendix E, table E.1; it is summarized here.

158. Mendoza Muñoz, *El Conde de Sierra Gorda, don José de Escandón y Helguera*, 109–12.

159. Ibid., 98–99.

160. Gómez de Acosta, *Querétaro en 1743*, 166–67; Osante, *Orígenes del Nuevo Santander*, 102–5; Domínguez Paulín, *Querétaro en la conquista de las Californias*, 125–54.

161. Mendoza Muñoz, *El Conde de Sierra Gorda, don José de Escandón y Helguera*, 115–19; see also Osante, *Orígenes del Nuevo Santander*.

162. AGN, Bandos, vol. 4, exp. 3, reproduced in Mendoza Muñoz, *El Conde de Sierra Gorda, don José de Escandón y Helguera*, 117–19.

163. Osante, *Orígenes del Nuevo Santander*, 93–268.

164. López de la Cámara Alta, *Descripción general de la Colonia de Nuevo Santander*. In appendix E, tables E.2–E.6 offer summaries of his report.

165. Ibid., 126–27. A late-eighteenth-century chronicle reported that the Olives had come in the 1540s from Florida. The dates of their arrival might be uncertain; their adaptation to Spanish ways and alliance with Escandón

were not. See Cruz Rangel, *Chichimecas, misioneros, soldados y terratenientes*, 34–35.

166. López de la Cámara Alta, *Descripción general de la Colonia de Nuevo Santander*, 146.

167. Ibid., 111.

168. Ibid., 64, 79–80.

169. Note the constant references in ibid., introduction, 52–62; the verb repeats throughout his report.

170. Ibid., 57, 58–59.

171. Ibid., 123, 127–28.

172. Ibid., 142–58.

173. Sánchez García, *Crónica del Nuevo Santander*.

174. Ibid., 63.

175. Ibid., 64–65.

176. Ibid., 67–69, 77–78, 80–81, 94–96, quote on 84.

177. Ibid., 90.

178. Ibid., 128.

179. Osante, *Orígenes del Nuevo Santander*, 198–206.

180. Teja, *San Antonio de Bejár*; Chipman, *Spanish Texas*, 126–70; Couturier, *The Silver King*.

181. Cervantes Aguilar, *Fray Simón del Hierro*, 15–49.

182. Ibid., 124–25, 139–95.

183. Ibid., 234.

184. Ibid., 237–38.

Chapter 4. Reforms, Riots, and Repressions

1. Flynn and Giráldez date the end of the Chinese premium and what they call the Mexican cycle about 1750; see "Cycles of Silver."

2. Appendix D, table D.1.

3. This chapter builds upon the work of Felipe Castro Gutiérrez in *Movimientos populares en Nueva España* and *Nueva ley y nuevo rey*, plus his publication of key documents in Gálvez, *Informe sobre las rebeliones populares de 1767*. I also depend upon materials in Rionda Arreguín, *La Compañía de Jesús en la provincia guanajuatense*, and the analysis of Doris Ladd in *The Making of a Strike*. My interpretations build on theirs—in the context of my analysis of the Bajío and Spanish North America.

4. Liss, *Atlantic Empires*.

5. For an overview of the conflicts that led to United States independence see Countryman, The *American Revolution*.

6. Stein and Stein, *Silver, War, and Trade*.

7. Mazín, *Entre dos magistades*; Castro Gutiérrez, *Nueva ley y nuevo rey*.

8. My understanding of politics and policy in Spain reflects the essential work of Stanley Stein and Barbara Stein in *Apogee of Empire*, 3–80.

9. Ibid., 81–115.

10. Mazín, *Entre dos magistades*, and Castro Gutiérrez, *Movimientos populares en Nueva España*, 53–76.

11. Velázquez, *El estado de guerra en Nueva España*.

12. Ibid., 215–17; on deadly coasts, see McNeill, *Mosquito Empires*.

13. Ibid.; Castro Gutiérrez, *Nueva ley y nuevo rey*.

14. Mazín, *Entre dos magistades*; Castro Gutiérrez, *Nueva ley y nuevo rey*.

15. Castro Gutiérrez, *Nueva ley y nuevo rey*.

16. Jáuregui de Cervantes, *Los Marqueses de Rayas*, 51.

17. The early colonial history of the region is detailed in Melville, *A Plague of Sheep*.

18. Ladd, *The Making of a Strike*.

19. Ibid.

20. Vinson, *Bearing Arms for His Majesty*, 63, 114–15.

21. Castro Gutiérrez, *Movimientos populares en Nueva España*, 94–111; Vinson, *Bearing Arms for His Majesty*, 91–92.

22. William Taylor, *Drinking, Homicide, and Rebellion in Colonial Mexican Villages*, revealed that judicial mediation formed the core of rule in Spanish Mesoamerica. Castro Gutiérrez in *Nueva ley y nuevo rey* showed that the same approach shaped Spanish North America—and argued that a turn against mediation lay at the heart of the conflicts of the 1760s.

23. Castro Gutiérrez, *Movimientos populares en Nueva España*, 111–25.

24. Ibid., 156.

25. Ibid., 148–52.

26. Ibid., 120–37.

27. The documents are reprinted by Castro in Gálvez, *Informe sobre las rebeliones populares de 1767*, 95–98.

28. There is an overview in Castro Gutiérrez, *Nueva ley y nuevo rey*, 141–45; quotes are from the report reprinted by Castro in Gálvez, *Informe sobre las rebeliones populares de 1767*, 99–102.

29. Castro Gutiérrez, *Nueva ley y nuevo rey*, 146–52.

30. Lara Cisneros, *El cristianismo en el espejo indígena*; population figures are on 113.

31. Rionda Arreguín, *La Compañía de Jesús en la provincia guanajuatense*, 461–63, narrates the events at San Luis de la Paz.

32. Quotes are from Cleere's report, reprinted by Castro in Gálvez, *Informe sobre las rebeliones populares de 1767*, 87–90.

33. Barreda's report is reprinted by Castro in Gálvez, *Informe sobre las rebeliones populares de 1767*, 91–92.

34. The July events at Guanajuato are narrated in fine detail in Rionda Arreguín, *La Compañía de Jesús en la provincia guanajuatense*, 463–73.

35. Torijo's letter is published by Castro in Gálvez, *Informe sobre las rebeliones populares de 1767*, 103–6.

36. Torijo, in Gálvez, *Informe sobre las rebeliones populares de 1767*, 104.

37. Rionda Arreguín, *La Compañía de Jesús en la provincia guanajuatense*, 463–69.

38. Ibid., 469–73.

39. Castro, *Los tarascos bajo el imperio español, 1600–1740*, 305–44, offers a brilliant delineation of the process of breakdown of community solidarity in the Tarascan highlands, providing the first persuasive explanation of the precocious resistance there in the 1760s—while most Mesoamerican communities held back.

40. Gálvez, *Informe sobre las rebeliones populares de 1767*, 22.

41. Ibid., 25.

42. This is a key emphasis of Castro Gutiérrez in *Nueva ley y nuevo rey*.

43. Gálvez, *Informe sobre las rebeliones populares de 1767*, 29–30; Rionda Arreguín, *La Compañía de Jesús en la provincia guanajuatense*, 476–83.

44. Castro Gutiérrez, *Nueva ley y nuevo rey*, 188.

45. Gálvez, *Informe sobre las rebeliones populares de 1767*, 46–47.

46. Rionda Arreguín, *La Compañía de Jesús en la provincia guanajuatense*, 488–90.

47. Cited in Castro Gutiérrez, *Nueva ley y nuevo rey*, 189.

48. Gálvez, *Informe sobre las rebeliones populares de 1767*, 42.

49. Ibid., 43–46; Castro Gutiérrez, *Nueva ley y nuevo rey*, 190–91.

50. Gálvez, *Informe sobre las rebeliones populares de 1767*, 51–52.

51. Ibid., 58–60.

52. Castro Gutiérrez, *Nueva ley y nuevo rey*, 183–201.

53. Gálvez, *Informe sobre las rebeliones populares de 1767*, 61.

54. Gálvez, cited in Rionda Arreguín, *La Compañía de Jesús en la provincia guanajuatense*, 496.

55. Rionda Arreguín, *La Compañía de Jesús en la provincia guanajuatense*, 496–500.

56. Gálvez, *Informe sobre las rebeliones populares de 1767*, 62.

57. Ibid., 63–64.

58. Rionda Arreguín, *La Compañía de Jesús en la provincia guanajuatense*, 508–10.

59. Gálvez, cited in ibid., 502.

60. Gálvez, cited in ibid., 502–3.

61. Ibid., 503.

62. Ibid., 504.

63. Ibid., 505–6.

64. Gálvez, cited in ibid., 510–11.

65. Gálvez, cited in Castro Gutiérrez, *Movimientos populares en Nueva España*, 135.

66. Ibid., 135–36.

67. Ibid., 137–38.

68. The literature on United States independence is vast. In addition to Countryman, *The American Revolution*, my views have been shaped by Morgan and Morgan, *The Stamp Act Crisis*; Morgan, *Inventing the People*; Wood, *The Creation of the American Republic*; Egnal, *A Mighty Empire*; and Nash, *The Unknown American Revolution*. Among many studies of popular assertions in regional context see Holton, *Forced Founders*; Kors, *Breaking Loose Together*; and Szatmary, *Shays' Rebellion*.

69. Greene, *Pursuits of Happiness*; McCusker and Menard, *The Economy of British America.*

70. The sources in note 68, above, and many more are the basis of this vision.

71. Morgan, *Inventing the People.*

72. Guarisco, *Los indios del valle de México y la construcción de una nueva sociabilidad Política,* and Owensby, *Empire of Law and Indian Justice in Colonial Mexico,* make this unmistakably clear.

Chapter 5. Capitalist, Priest, and Patriarch

1. Brading, *Miners and Merchants in Bourbon Mexico,* made this case most persuasively, a position confirmed by Kicza in *Colonial Entrepreneurs* and by Pérez Rosales in *Familia, poder, riqueza y subversión.*

2. Brading, in *Miners and Merchants in Bourbon Mexico,* is the leading proponent of this view—one of the few points in his monumental contributions that I find unsustainable.

3. Granados, "Cosmopolitan Indians and Mesoamerican Barrios in Bourbon Mexico City," provides a new view of life in city neighborhoods.

4. Cruz Rangel, *Chichimecas, misioneros, soldados y terratenientes,* 305.

5. Brading, *Miners and Merchants in Bourbon Mexico*; Ladd, *The Mexican Nobility at Independence*; Kicza, *Colonial Entrepreneurs*; Zárate Toscano, *Los nobles ante la muerte en México.*

6. The correspondence of don Francisco de Espinosa y Navarijo (FEN), don José Sánchez Espinosa (JSE), and don Mariano Sánchez y Mora, third Conde de Peñasco (CPP) was kept in separate collections at the Benson Latin American Library of the University of Texas, Austin, when I read it. Recently the items have been refiled together by date. I cite them by collection (usually indicating the recipient of the letter), then date.

7. JSE, 24 August 1774.

8. JSE, 5 August 1778, 15 August 1778.

9. JSE, 1 March 1779, 2 May 1779, 1 November 1779.

10. JSE, 24 February 1781.

11. JSE, 23 January 1783.

12. AGN, BN, vol. 164, 1782.

13. JSE, 12 October 1783.

14. AGN, BN, vol. 164, 1782.

15. JSE, vol. 215, no. 458, n.d. (where letters had no date, I cite the original volume and document number); Fernández de Recas, *Aspirantes Americanos a cargos de Santo Oficio,* 65.

16. JSE, 27 May 1808.

17. FEN, 7 October 1753.

18. FEN, 16 September 1759, 2 December 1763; JSE, 9 October 1768, 29 June 1792.

19. On trade: JSE, 26 November 1773; FEN, 18 March 1779; JSE, 7 May 1783.

On the store: FEN, 26 March 1773; JSE, 5 November 1784. On loans: AGN, BN, vol. 164, 1782. On Rivascacho: JSE, 24 August 1774.

20. JSE, 9 October 1768, 24 August 1774; FEN, 29 August 1777; JSE, 5 August 1778, 24 August 1778.

21. JSE, vol. 213, no. 384, n.d.

22. JSE, 24 August 1774, 5 August 1778; FEN, 29 August 1777.

23. The first son was born at Peñasco, San Luis Potosí, in January 1777. Zárate Toscano, *Los nobles ante la muerte en México*, 419.

24. JSE, 30 January 1789; CPP, 18 May 1825; Castro Gutiérrez, *Nueva ley y nuevo rey*; Rangel Silva, *Capitanes a guerra, linajes de frontera*, 132–36.

25. JSE, 13 December 1778.

26. JSE, 22 August 1787, 18 March 1789.

27. JSE, 1 March 1779, 2 May 1779, 27 October 1784, 18 March 1789; GM, 18 June 1783; AGN, BN, vol. 549, 1794.

28. JSE, 25 November 1781; AGN, BN, vol. 164, 1782.

29. JSE, 27 May 1808.

30. JSE, 15 February 1782, 15 July 1782, 9 October 1782, 31 October 1782, December 1782.

31. JSE, 14 March 1781, 24 February 1781, 30 October 1782, 19 March 1783.

32. JSE, 23 January 1782, 2 September 1783, 12 October 1783, 15 October 1783.

33. JSE, 21 May 1783, 10 September 1783, 15 October 1783, 4 January 1784.

34. JSE, 16 November 1784.

35. On Borda: Pérez Rosales, *Minería y sociedad en Taxco durante el siglo XVIII*, 75–84; Langue, *Los señores de Zacatecas*, 145–50. On Jala: Tutino, "Creole Mexico," 75. Zárate Toscano, *Los nobles ante la muerte en México*, 187, reports that only 7 percent of noble families included an ordained priest.

36. JSE, 19 January 1785.

37. JSE, 27 August 1786, 30 August 1786, 27 September 1786, 3 October 1787, 10 December 1787.

38. JSE, 19 January 1785, 22 August 1787, 25 February 1789.

39. AGN, BN, vol. 164, 1782.

40. JSE, 5 April 1786, 19 April 1786, 26 April 1786, 10 May 1786, 25 October 1786.

41. JSE, 20 June 1804, 15 September 1804.

42. Zárate Toscano, *Los nobles ante la muerte en México*, 60.

43. JSE, 22 August 1787, 7 April 1789.

44. JSE, 9 June 1794.

45. JSE, 9 August 1799.

46. JSE, 18 January 1806.

47. JSE, 23 January 1782; vol. 213, no. 385, n.d.

48. JSE, 21 November 1805.

49. JSE, 16 May 1786, 16 July 1786, 13 September 1786, 20 September 1786, 16 November 1786, 3 June 1789, 19 August 1789, 16 October 1804, 15 June 1806, 4 May 1807.

50. JSE, 29 July 1799.

51. Báez Macías, ed., "Planos y censos de la Ciudad de México," 632.

52. JSE, October 1789, 10 March 1795, 2 September 1814.

53. JSE, 22 July 1789, October 1789, 10 March 1793, 13 December 1804, 20 May 1805, 26 September 1805, 13 September 1807, 22 December 1807, 6 April 1810, 16 February 1812.

54. The other great entrepreneurial priest of the age, the mining magnate don José de la Borda, left two sons whom he legitimated in 1785 by petition and payment to the regime. See Twinam, *Public Lives, Private Secrets*, 280–81. I found no hint that Sánchez Espinosa produced children after ordination.

55. JSE, 23 July 1784, 27 October 1787, 19 February 1788, 1 November 1800.

56. JSE, 4 April 1787, 15 August 1787, 22 August 1787.

57. JSE, 5 September 1787.

58. JSE, 30 January 1789, 11 September 1789.

59. JSE, 12 October 1790, 18 November 1792.

60. Archer, The *Army in Bourbon Mexico*, 212.

61. JSE, 11 December 1795, 4 March 1796; *GM*, 10 June 1797.

62. Tutino, "Life and Labor on North Mexican Haciendas."

63. JSE, 6 April 1798.

64. JSE, 21 February 1800.

65. JSE, 21 November 1799.

66. JSE, 18 January 1800.

67. JSE, 28 March 1800, 20 April 1800, 15 July 1800, 24 March 1802.

68. JSE, 22 July 1805.

69. JSE, 24 September 1805.

70. AGN, Vínculos, vol. 54, n. 1, f. 203, 13 November 1805.

71. CPP, 3 October 1805; JSE, 21 October 1805, 16 December 1805, 18 December 1805.

72. JSE, 23 December 1805.

73. JSE, 27 December 1805.

74. JSE, 13 January 1806, 21 January 1806, 7 April 1806, 14 April 1806, 10 May 1806.

75. JSE, 13 February 1806.

76. JSE, 4 April 1806.

77. JSE, 17 October 1807.

78. CPP, 25 May 1800, 16 August 1800; JSE, 11 April 1801, 29 April 1803; CPP, 4 April 1808; JSE, 4 April 1808.

79. CPP, 29 September 1808, 21 November 1808, 9 January 1809.

80. JSE, 11 October 1809.

81. On trade and revenues see Marichal, *La bancarrota del virreinato*; on trade and mining, Brading, *Miners and Merchants in Bourbon Mexico*, and Pérez Rosales, *Familia, poder, riqueza y subversion*; on mining, Pérez Rosales, *Minería y sociedad en Taxco durante el siglo XVIII*; Langue, *Los señores de Zacatecas*; and Carbajal López, *La minería en Bolaños*; on Veracruz, Souto Mantecón, *Mar abierto*.

82. Appendix D, table D.1; Marichal, *La bancarrota del virreinato*.

83. Brading, *Miners and Merchants in Bourbon Mexico*; Vargas-Lobsinger, *Formación y decadencia de una fortuna*.

84. Brading, *Miners and Merchants in Bourbon Mexico*; Marichal, *La bancarrota del virreinato*.

85. Hoberman, *Mexico's Merchant Elite*; Brading, *Miners and Merchants in Bourbon Mexico*.

86. Brading, whose *Miners and Merchants in Bourbon Mexico* has done so much to reveal the complexities of mining and merchant financing, and who documents the repeated turn to the land, offers such a perspective—one that he modifies by noting the risks of mining and the security of landed investment. Zárate Toscano, *Los nobles ante la muerte en México*, 99–100, offers the broadest analysis of New Spain's eighteenth-century elite and concludes that titled members, old and new, were entrepreneurs committed to honor, status, and legitimacy.

87. Ladd, *The Mexican Nobility at Independence*, 29–30; on the Condes de Santiago in the seventeenth century see Israel, *Race, Class, and Politics in Colonial Mexico*.

88. PCR, vol. 54, 19 December 1736.

89. PCR, vol. 71, 29 December 1773; vol. 105, 6 September 1785; vol. 121, f. 126, October 1800.

90. PCR, vol. 101, 1784; vol. 103, 6 September 1785; vol. 115, 20 March 1795; vol. 121, f. 121, 1 October 1800; vol. 124, f. 12, 17 February 1805. On doña María Josefa's years of power see Tutino, "Power, Class, and Family."

91. García Collection, Benson Latin American Collection, University of Texas, Austin, v. 257, "Instancia de d. Ygnacio Leonel Gómez de Cervantes," 1995. PCR, vol. 118, f. 46, 1799; f. 93, 8 October 1799; vol. 124, f. 16–17, 10–13 March 1802; f. 29, 5 May 1802; vol. 129, f. 8, 7 August 1805; vol. 132, f. 10, 9 June 1806; vol. 138, 4 February 1809. PCR, uncatalogued, folder dated 1810, "Autos seguidos por el Señor Marqués de Salvatierra."

92. PCR, vol. 118, f. 81, 4 September 1799; vol. 123, f. 57, 22 July 1801; vol. 124, f. 54, 3 July 1802; f. 64, 24 July 1802; f. 65, 25 July 1802; f. 73, 18 August 1802; vol. 125, f. 17, 18 July 1803.

93. Brading, *Miners and Merchants in Bourbon Mexico*, 183–85. Couturier, *The Silver King*, offers a family history.

94. PCR, uncatalogued materials, "Ynventario de . . . la Casa del Señor Conde de Santa María de Regla"; PCR, "Testamento del Señor Conde de Regla, Cuenta de División . . ."; *Testimonios relativos . . . de D. Pedro Romero de Terreros* (Mexico City, 1803).

95. Riley, "Santa Lucía," 272; Couturier, "Hacienda de Hueyapan," 78–80.

96. PCR, "Testamento, Cuenta"; the inheritance is detailed in Tutino, "Creole Mexico," table 2.5, 78–79.

97. Fernández de San Salvador, *Defensa jurídica de la Señora Doña María Micaela Romero de Terreros*; Romero de Terreros, "Los hijos de los primeros Condes de Regla"; Couturier, "Hacienda de Hueyapan," 97–98; PCR, vol. 120, 11 October 1788; *GM*, 19 December 1801.

98. Romero de Terreros, "Los hijos de los primeros Condes de Regla," 197–200; Zárate Toscano, *Los nobles ante la muerte en México*, 121; Humboldt, *Ensayo político sobre el Reino de la Nueva España*, 83.

99. *Testimonios relativos . . . de D. Pedro Romero de Terreros* (Mexico City, 1803), 43.

100. PCR, "Testimonio, Cuenta."

101. Romero de Terreros, "La Condesa escribe," 456; on the Jala family see Tutino, "Creole Mexico," 62–75.

102. Brading, *Miners and Merchants in Bourbon Mexico*, 207. The Fagoagas, leaders in silver banking, landed operations, and the politics of independence, finally have a family biography in Pérez Rosales, *Familia, poder, riqueza y subversion*.

103. PCR, vol. 118, f. 52, 26 June 1799; vol. 123, f. 58, 27 June 1801.

104. Lafuente Ferrari, *El Virrey Iturrigaray y los orígenes de la independencia en México*, 144–52; Romero de Terreros, "La Condesa escribe," 458–67.

105. PCR, "Condado de Jala . . . 1836," f. 92; vol. 118, f. 85, 4 September 1799; "Ymposición."

106. PCR, vol. 121, f. 76, July 1800; vol. 124, f. 41, 28 May 1802; vol. 127, f. 9, 13 June 1803; PCR, uncatalogued, folder dated 1770; PCR, "Testimonio, Cuenta"; Brading, *Miners and Merchants in Bourbon Mexico*, 69–70, 162.

107. Brading, *Miners and Merchants in Bourbon Mexico*, 43, 46–47; García Collection, Benson Latin American Collection, University of Texas, Austin, vol. 257, "Instancia de don Ygnacio Leonel Gómez de Cervantes . . . 1793."

108. PCR, vol. 109, 1 March 1788; vol. 115, 20 March 1795; vol. 123, f. 46, 9 June 1801; vol. 124, f. 58, 13 July 1802; vol. 125, f. 3, January 1803; vol. 129, f. 4, 8 May 1805; GM, 4 June 1805.

109. PCR, "El Condado de Jala . . . 1836," fol. 36–37, 105–6, 108–10; PCR, vol. 82, 1777; AGN, BN, vol. 1844, exp. 2, 1778; AGN, Intendentes, vol. 65, exp. 411, f. 343, 1778.

110. Romero de Terreros, "Los hijos," 193.

111. Brading, *Miners and Merchants in Bourbon Mexico*, 39–48.

112. PCR, vol. 46, 9 September 1775; vol. 52, 18 May 1775; PCR, "Testamento, cuenta"; Fernández de Recas, *Mayorazgos de la Nueva España*, 215.

113. Brading, *Miners and Merchants in Bourbon Mexico*, 64–66.

114. The compilation is detailed in Tutino, "Creole Mexico," table 1.3, 30, and table 1.8, 41.

115. Zárate Toscano in *Los nobles ante la muerte en México* identifies about forty titled families based in Mexico City (counting is imprecise as families intermarried and moved). Her work suggests that I have counted the properties of at least half the great landed families (some with titles were lesser landholders), a fair "sample" to characterize the elite.

116. Pérez Rosales, *Familia, poder, riqueza y subversion*, 127.

117. Barrett, *The Sugar Hacienda of the Marqueses del Valle*.

118. Tutino, "Creole Mexico," table 2.1, 56, table 2.2, 59.

119. Konrad, *A Jesuit Hacienda in Colonial Mexico*, 203–8.

120. Tutino, "Creole Mexico," table 2.4, 67, table. 2.5, 78–79.

121. Vargas-Lobsinger, *Formación y decadencia de una fortuna*.

122. This view is shared by Zárate Toscano, *Los nobles ante la muerte en México*, 15–16.

123. On council roles see Tutino, "Creole Mexico," 26–28; on professionals as provincial elites, table 4.1, 195.

124. For a discussion of Mexico City's provincial elites see Tutino, "Creole Mexico," 193–231.

125. Barrett, "Morelos and Its Sugar Industry in the Late Eighteenth Century"; Martin, *Rural Society in Colonial Morelos*; Scharrer Tamm, *Azúcar y trabajo*.

126. The classis study of maize marketing is Florescano, *Precios del maíz y crisis agrícolas en México*. On great families see Tutino, "Creole Mexico," 128–32; on Sánchez Espinosa and La Teja, JSE, 23 September 1807.

127. Tutino, "Creole Mexico," 134–41; Tutino, "Buscando independencias populares."

128. On the abasto and the supply of meat to Mexico City, including its importance to the population from elites to the working poor, see Quiroz, *Entre el lujo y la subsistencia*.

129. Tutino, "Creole Mexico," 148–49.

130. JSE, 15 August 1787, 22 July 1800, 5 August 1800, 18 August 1801, 25 April 1805, 27 July 1807, 24 May 1808, 27 May 1808.

131. JSE, 18 January 1800, 9 September 1800.

132. Condes de Santiago Calimaya Papers, Biblioteca Nacional, Mexico City, "Libro de Caja de don Martín Angel Michaus, 1777–1797."

133. Tutino, "Creole Mexico," 156.

134. Ibid., 152–54.

135. JSE, 12 April 1780, 16 November 1795, 11 April 1801, 20 June 1804.

136. Marketing at La Griega, Puerto de Nieto, and across the Bajío is detailed in chapters 3 and 4 of Tutino, "Creole Mexico."

137. Accounts in PCR, "Testamento, Cuenta," detailed in Tutino, "Creole Mexico," table 3.10, 169.

138. AGN, Vínculos, vol. 213, no. 4; detailed in Tutino, "Creole Mexico," table 3.11, 171, table 3.12, 173.

139. AGN, Vínculos, vol. 55, no. 18; detailed in Tutino, "Creole Mexico," table 3.13, 176.

140. JSE, 27 May 1808.

141. Humboldt, *Ensayo político sobre el Reino de la Nueva España*, 68–69.

142. Zárate Toscano's *Los nobles ante la muerte en México* documents that religious commitments were most evident in public ceremonies and funeral practices, less in financial allocations and lives lived under religious vows.

143. JSE, 27 May 1808.

144. Zárate Toscano, *Los nobles ante la muerte en México*, 170–91, documents that these were regular but not pervasive practices, each present in fewer than 20 percent of nobles' wills.

145. AGN, Intendentes, vol. 73, exp. 8, f. 506, November 1809.

146. PCR, vol. 121, f. 149, 7 December 1800.

147. JSE, 12 September 1797; PCR, vol. 18, f. 7, 23 January 1793; vol. 121, f. 49, 9 April 1800; f. 78, 9 Jul, 1800; vol. 132, f. 17, 10 December 1806.

148. Florescano, *Precios del maíz y crisis agrícolas en México*.

149. PCR, vol. 118, f. 18, 9 March 1799.

150. JSE, 29 April 1801; also PCR, vol. 127, f. 8, 6 June 1804.

151. PCR, vol. 118, f. 18, 6 March 1799; f. 74, 14 August 1799; f. 90, 2 October 1799; f. 94, 16 October 1799.

152. JSE, 23 September 1807.

153. PCR, vol. 118, f. 16, 27 February 1799; f. 24, 13 April 1799; f. 27, 23 April 1799; f. 34, 25 May 1799; f. 49, 22 June 1799; f. 69, 7 August 1799; vol. 121, f. 19, 8 February 1800; f. 81, 19 July 1800; f. 96, 20 August 1800.

154. PCR, vol. 121, f. 102, 30 August 1800; f. 114, 17 September 1800.

155. This too is confirmed by Zárate Toscano's broad study *Los nobles ante la muerte en México*, 125, 128.

Chapter 6. Production, Patriarchy, and Polarization

1. Flynn and Giráldez, "Cycles of Silver."

2. Stern, *The Secret History of Gender*, defined the debates of household patriarchy and explored its internal conflicts in eighteenth-century New Spain.

3. See appendix D, table D.1.

4. Mining entrepreneurship at Guanajuato is detailed in Brading, *Miners and Merchants in Bourbon Mexico*.

5. Ibid., 141.

6. Ibid., 235; Castro Rivas and Rangel López, *Relación histórica de la intendencia de Guanajuato*, 29–30.

7. Brading, *Miners and Merchants in Bourbon Mexico*, 274–78.

8. Domínguez de la Fuente, *Leal informe político-legal*, 82–89, 190–95.

9. Ibid., 190–95.

10. Ibid., 222–24.

11. Brading, *Miners and Merchants in Bourbon Mexico*, 278–98; Zárate Toscano, *Los nobles ante la muerte en México*, 178.

12. This is the portrait that emerges from Ada Marina Lara Meza in *Haciendas de beneficio en Guanajuato*.

13. Castro Rivas and Rangel López, *Relación histórica de la intendencia de Guanajuato*, 31, 36–37.

14. Revillagigedo, "Carta al excelentísimo señor don Antonio Valdés, 1789," *El ocaso novohispano*, ed. Brading, 273–75.

15. Brading, ed., *El ocaso novohispano*, 19–22.

16. Mourelle, "Viaje a las minas de Guanajuato, noviembre de 1790," *El ocaso novohispano*, ed. Brading, 23–76, quote at 33–34.

17. Ibid., 36.

18. Ibid., 37–38.

19. Ibid., 41–43.

20. Ibid., 44, 46.

21. Ibid., 47.

22. Ibid., 64.

23. Ibid., 39–40.

24. Ibid., 64.

25. Ibid., 66.

26. Ibid., 65.

27. Brading. *Miners and Merchants in Bourbon Mexico*, appendix C, table C.

28. Castro Rivas and Rangel López, *Relación histórica de la intendencia de Guanajuato*, 48.

29. Ibid., 57.

30. Brading, *Miners and Merchants in Bourbon Mexico*, 243–44; Castro Rivas and Rangel López, *Relación histórica de la intendencia de Guanajuato*, 48, 51, 57–60, 126–27.

31. Mourelle, "Viaje a las minas de Guanajuato, noviembre de 1790," *El ocaso novohispano*, ed. Brading, 52.

32. Brading, *Miners and Merchants in Bourbon Mexico*, 285–90.

33. Castro Rivas and Rangel López, *Relación histórica de la intendencia de Guanajuato*, 124, anexo II, 189–90.

34. Humboldt, *Ensayo político sobre el Reino de la Nueva España*, 49.

35. Brading, *Miners and Merchants in Bourbon Mexico*, 290.

36. Castro Rivas and Rangel López, *Relación histórica de la intendencia de Guanajuato*, 93.

37. Appendix D, table D.1.

38. Appendix D, table D.6.

39. Tutino, "Guerra, comercio colonial y textiles mexicanos," 39.

40. On the development of commercio libre the essential work is Stein and Stein, *Apogee of Empire*. On the rise of the Catalan textile industry and its search for colonial markets see Martínez Shaw, "Los orígenes de la industria algodonera catalana y del comercio colonial"; García-Barquero, "Comercio colonial y producción industrial en Cataluña a fines del siglo XVIII"; and Izard, "Comercio libre, guerras coloniales y mercado americano."

41. Tutino, "Guerra, comercio colonial y textiles mexicanos," table 3, 40, table 5, 43.

42. Ibid., table 4, 41.

43. Nor did all slave workers. A census in 1791 listed fifty-three still working in ten obrajes, mostly in small numbers. Only one workshop with nine and another with twelve still relied on significant numbers of slaves. Wu, "The Population of the City of Querétaro in 1791," 296–97.

44. Tutino, "Guerra, comercio colonial y textiles mexicanos."

45. Ibid., cuadro 1, 37, and Miño Grijalva, *Obrajes y tejedores de Nueva España*.

46. Tutino, "Guerra, comercio colonial y textiles mexicanos," table 4, 41.

47. Domínguez, "Descripción de la industrial textile en Querétaro," 197–99, *El ocaso novohispano*, ed. Brading; Zeláa y Hidalgo, *Glorias de Querétaro*, 167.

48. Brading, *Haciendas and Ranchos in the Mexican Bajío*.

49. See Brading, *Miners and Merchants in Bourbon Mexico* and *Haciendas and Ranchos in the Mexican Bajío*.

50. Agustín Morfi, quoted in Sánchez de Tagle, *Por un regimento, el regimen*, 68–69.

51. Maza, *San Miguel de Allende*, 20–21.

52. AGN, Padrones, vol. 24, f. 3, 1792; vol. 36, 204, 1792. Tierras, vol. 1370, exp. 1, f. 27, 1804.

53. AGN, Padrones, vol. 24, f. 3, 1792; vol. 36, 104, 1792. Tierras, vol. 1370, exp. 1, f. 27, 1804.

54. Sánchez de Tagle, *Por un regimento, el regimen*, 45.

55. Ibid., 83.

56. Ibid., 85; Maza, *San Miguel de Allende*, 187–88.

57. This is my reading of Chowning, *Rebellious Nuns*, 151–218.

58. JSE, 5 March 1759, 19 February 1788; CPP, 7 June 1808.

59. JSE, 29 May 1786, 1 April 1793, 29 May 1798.

60. JSE, 17 March 1784, 9 December 1784; CPP, 20 December 1784; JSE, 27 December 1784, 12 November 1799.

61. JSE, 7 August 1790, 15 February 1793, 28 February 1788, 10 November 1803, 10 February 1804.

62. JSE, 25 May 1804, 4 June 1804, 14 November 1804; CPP, 9 September 1808, 17 October 1809.

63. JSE, 9 July 1802, 9 August 1802, 8 October 1802.

64. Mourelle, "Viaje a las minas de Guanajuato, noviembre de 1790," 28–29.

65. Urrutía, "Noticia geográfica del Reino de la Nueva España," 103.

66. Wu, "The Population of the City of Querétaro in 1791," 281–86.

67. AGN, Padrones, vol. 39, f. 1–2, 1791, lists Querétaro proprietors; AGN, Padrones, vol. 35, 1–8, 1791, does the same for San Juan del Río.

68. Ladd, *The Mexican Nobility at Independence*, 60, 82, 227; AGN, Padrones, vol. 39, 1, 1791; AGN, Alcabalas, vol. 37, 26 March 1793, f. 2–3; GM, 8 November 1785, 429–30, 6 December 1785, 431–32; JSE, 13 April 1797.

69. Brading, *Miners and Merchants in Bourbon Mexico*, 312–16; AGN, Padrones, vol. 39, f. 1–2, 1791; GM, 17 February 1789, 3 January 1808. AGN, Tierras, vol. 764, exp. 3, f. 4, 1751; vol. 939, exp. 4, f. 11, 3 November 1793; vol. 1373, exp. 4, f. 11, 1806.

70. PCR, uncatalogued materials, "Méritos de don Pedro Romero de Terreros"; AGN, Padrones, vol. 35, f. 1, 1791; AGN, Alcabalas, vol. 37, 13 April 1793; GM, 16 May 1793; AGN, Tierras, vol. 1351, exp. 9, f. 1, 3 October 1801.

71. GM, 5 January 1787, 18 August 1798, 24 February 1801; PCR, 121-11, 31 January 1801; Romero de Terreros, *Antiguas haciendas de México*, 171.

72. AGN, Padrones, vol. 39, f. 2, 1791; GM, 17 February 1789; AGN, Tierras, vol. 1341, exp. 3, f. 22, 1803.

73. AGN, Padrones, vol. 39, f. 2, 1791; GM, 8 November 1785.

74. AGN, Padrones, vol. 39, f. 1–2, 1791; AGN, Alcabalas, vol. 37, 13 April 1793; GM, 8 November 1785, 11 January 1799, 7 January 1804.

75. AGN, Padrones, vol. 39, f. 1, 1791; AGN, Alcabalas, vol. 37, 13 April 1793; GM, 11 January 1799, 19 September 1804.

76. AGN, Padrones, vol. 39, f. 1–2, 1791; GM, 8 November 1785.

77. Gunnarsdóttir, "The Convent of Santa Clara, the Elite, and Social Change in Eighteenth-Century Querétaro," 273, 279–89.

78. Suárez Muñoz and Jiménez Gómez, eds., *Del Reino a la República*, vol. 1, no. 86, 692–95; vol. 2, no. 91, 34–36.

79. JSE, 25 October 1808, 29 October 1808, 15 November 1808.

80. JSE, 10 February 1804; CPP, 7 June 1808, 29 October 1808; JSE, 28 July 1810.

81. FEN, 16 September 1778, 28 January 1779, 7 May 1779, 13 May 1779, 24 May 1779, 22 November 1779; JSE, 2 July 1784, 29 July 1784, 9 December 1784, 27 December 1784, 15 August 1785; *GM*, 8 November 1785.

82. Library of Museo Nacional de Antropología, Mexico City, microfilm collection, San Luis Potosí, roll 6.

83. AGN, Alcabalas, vol. 37, 12 April 1793; JSE, 9 July 1792, 11 December 1795, 4 March 1796, 1 April 1796, 21 February 1800, 22 July 1802.

84. *GM*, 21 January 1807; JSE, 8 March 1808, 28 March 1808, 27 May 1808, 12 November 1808, 3 December 1808, 22 April 1809.

85. Super, "Querétaro Obrajes."

86. Zeláa y Hidalgo, *Glorias de Querétaro*, 8–9.

87. Urquiola Permisán, "Querétaro," 57–77.

88. Zeláa y Hidalgo, *Glorias de Querétaro*, 10.

89. Suárez Muñoz and Jiménez Gómez, eds., *Del Reino a la República*, vol. 1, no. 75, 570–71.

90. Ibid., vol. 1, no. 73, 570–83.

91. Suárez Muñoz and Jiménez Gómez, eds., *Del Reino a la República*, vol. 1, no. 1, 284–90; no. 33, 447–49; no. 36, 455–60.

92. Jiménez Gómez, *La República de Indios de Querétaro*, no. 13, 398–409; no. 106, 669–71.

93. Ibid., no. 107, 672–73; nos. 109–11, 677–88.

94. Ibid., nos. 113–15, 698–702.

95. Ibid., no. 117, 704.

96. Ibid., no. 119, 707–10.

97. Suárez Muñoz and Jiménez Gómez, eds., *Del Reino a la República*, vol. 1, no. 21, 288–96.

98. Ibid., vol. 2, no. 143, 626–30.

99. Jiménez Gómez, *La República de Indios de Querétaro*, no. 118, 705–6; no. 120, 710–11.

100. Suárez Muñoz and Jiménez Gómez, eds., *Del Reino a la República*, no. 1, 80–96.

101. Appendix G, tables G.1–G.5.

102. For obrajes and slave labor in the eighteenth century see Super, *La vida en Querétaro durante la colonia*, 88, 96; Salvucci, *Textiles and Capitalism in Mexico*, 87–88, 90–91, 101, 140; Miño Grijalva, *Obrajes y tejedores de Nueva España*, 33, 68–73; and Armas Briz and Solís Hernández, *Esclavos negros y mulatos en Querétaro, siglo XVIII*, 11–22, 23–92 (the documents on the Durango transactions are at 103–14).

103. Somohano Martínez, *Sistemas de aprendizaje gremial en obrajes y talleres artesanos en Querétaro*; Armas Briz and Solís Hernández, *Esclavos negros y mulatos en Querétaro, siglo XVIII*, 115–16.

104. Suárez Muñoz and Jiménez Gómez, eds., *Del Reino a la República*, vol. 3, nos. 156–60, 52–76.

105. Wu, "The Population of the City of Querétaro in 1791," 294–97, tables 8, 9.

106. AGN, Alcabalas, vol. 37, 13 April 1793; on merchants and cotton see Hernández Jaimes, "El comercio de algodón en las cordilleras y costas de la mar del sur de Nueva España en el siglo XVIII," 238, 243–44.

107. Suárez Muñoz and Jiménez Gómez, eds., *Del Reino a la República*, vol. 3, nos. 161–63, 78–88.

108. Somohano Martínez, *Sistemas de aprendizaje gremial en obrajes y talleres artesanos en Querétaro*.

109. Urquiola Permisán, "Querétaro," 82.

110. Zeláa y Hidalgo, *Glorias de Querétaro*, 9.

111. Domínguez, "Descripción," *El ocaso novohispano*, ed. Brading, 197.

112. Ibid.

113. Somohano Martínez, *Sistemas de aprendizaje gremial en obrajes y talleres artesanos en Querétaro*.

114. Deans-Smith, *Bureaucrats, Planters, and Workers*, 54.

115. González Gómez, *El tabaco virreinal*, 118.

116. Deans-Smith, *Bureaucrats, Planters, and Workers*, 219–26; González Gómez, *El tabaco virreinal*, 80–83.

117. Deans-Smith, *Bureaucrats, Planters, and Workers*, 153.

118. Deans-Smith, *Bureaucrats, Planters, and Workers*, table 20, 176; González Gómez, *El tabaco virreinal*, cuadro II.3, 109–10.

119. The text is reproduced in González Gómez, *El tabaco virreinal*, anexo VII, 218–19.

120. Humboldt, *Ensayo político sobre el Reino de la Nueva España*, 453; González Gómez, *El tabaco virreinal*, cuadro II.3, 109–10.

121. Wu, "The Population of the City of Querétaro in 1791," 277–307; Somohano Martínez, *Sistemas de aprendizaje gremial en obrajes y talleres artesanos en Querétaro*.

122. Taylor, *Drinking, Homicide, and Rebellion in Colonial Mexican Villages*.

123. Zeláa y Hidalgo, *Glorias de Querétaro*, 10–11. On judicial districts see Serrano Contreras, "La ciudad de Santiago de Querétaro a fines del siglo XVIII," 529.

124. Miguel Domínguez, "Memorial sobre los obrajes en Querétaro," *El ocaso novohispano*, ed. Brading, 215.

125. Ibid., 202.

126. Ibid., 204–5.

127. Ibid., 205–6.

128. Ibid., 206.

129. Ibid., 207.

130. Ibid., 214.

131. Ibid., 208–10.

132. Ibid., 210.

133. Ibid.

134. Ibid., 209, 211.

135. Ibid., 210.

136. Ibid., 212.

137. Ibid., 212–13.

138. Ibid., 213.

139. Ibid., 216.

140. Ibid., 215.

141. Ibid., 216–17.

142. Ibid., 217.

143. Ibid., 218.

144. Ibid., 215.

145. Super, *La vida en Querétaro durante la colonia*, 243.

146. Tutino, "Guerra, comercio colonial y textiles mexicanos," cuadros 5 and 6, 43.

147. Ibid.

148. See appendix G.

149. Suárez Muñoz and Jiménez Gómez, eds., *Del Reino a la República*, no. 77, 632–38.

150. AGN, Tierras, vol. 764, exp. 3, f. 1–14, 1751–58; vol. 1296, exp. 3, f. 1–6, 1798. Wu, "The Population of the City of Querétaro in 1791," 301.

151. Zeláa y Hidalgo, *Glorias de Querétaro*, 57.

Chapter 7. The Challenge of Capitalism

1. This section integrates Brading, "La estructura de la producción agraria en el Bajío de 1750–1850"; Brading, *Haciendas and Ranchos in the Mexican Bajío*; Super, *La vida en Querétaro durante la colonia*; Morín, *Michoacán en la Nueva España del siglo XVIII*; and Murphy, *Irrigation in the Bajío Region of Colonial Mexico*. All but Murphy are synthesized in Tutino, *From Insurrection to Revolution in Mexico*.

2. JSE, 9 December 1784.

3. FEN, 9 January 1779.

4. JSE, 1 May 1782, 28 August 1782.

5. JSE, 28 September 1782.

6. JSE, 4 November 1782.

7. *GM*, 1785–88.

8. JSE, 26 March 1783.

9. The census reports, my calculations, and analyses are in appendix F.

10. Appendix F, tables F.50, F.51.

11. Appendix F, tables F.34, F.35.

12. Jiménez Gómez, *La República de Indios de Querétaro*, no. 121, 711–34.

13. Appendix F, tables F.44, F.45; Appendix G, table G.16.

14. Jimémez Gómez, *La República de Indios de Querétaro*, no. 75, 584–90.

15. Appendix C, table C.2.

16. Appendix C, table C.2; Appendix F, table F.1.

17. Appendix F, tables F.1–F.5.

18. Appendix F, tables F.6, F.7; Appendix G, table G.16.

19. Appendix C, table C.2; AGN, BN, vol. 558, La Griega accounts, 1811–12.

20. Appendix F, tables F.11, F.12; Appendix G, table G. 16.

21. Appendix F, tables F.16–F.25; Appendix G, table G. 16.

22. Appendix F, tables F.26–F.30; Appendix G, table G. 16.

23. Appendix F, tables F. 45–F.48; Appendix G, table G. 16.

24. Appendix F, tables F.40–F.43.

25. Appendix F, tables F.50, F. 55.

26. Ruíz Guadalajara, *Dolores antes de la independencia*, vol. 2, 282; I explore the suits later in this chapter.

27. Appendix F, tables F.50, F.51.

28. Velázquez Gutiérrez, *Mujeres de origen africano en la capital novohispana*, 300–307.

29. Appendix F, tables F.10, F.15, F.25, F.54.

30. Appendix F, table F.15.

31. Appendix F, tables F.20, F.30, F.33.

32. Appendix F, table F.54.

33. FEN, 29 April 1773, 22 November 1779; JSE, 13 December 1778, 16 May 1783, 27 September 1786, 2 November 1786, 1 December 1786, 31 August 1787.

34. JSE, 29 February 1788.

35. JSE, 16 January 1792, 25 November 1793, 13 April 1797, 13 November 1799, 24 November 1801, 15 March 1802, 15 April 1805, 27 May 1808.

36. JSE, 17 March 1801.

37. AGN, BN, Vol. 558, La Griega accounts, 1811–12.

38. JSE, 11 July 1801.

39. JSE, 30 June 1804.

40. JSE, 16 May 1793, 3 May 1787, 31 August 1787, 15 January 1792.

41. Tutino, *From Insurrection to Revolution in Mexico*, 74–80.

42. JSE, 15 January 1792, 1 March 1792, 10 March 1792, 23 December 1792.

43. JSE, 15 January 1792.

44. JSE, 28 May 1792. On Oyarzábal see *GM*, 8 November 1785; AGN, Padrones, vol. 39, f. 1, 1791.

45. JSE, 8 January 1792.

46. JSE, 16 March 1792.

47. JSE, 24 June 1792.

48. JSE, 11 July 1801.

49. JSE, 14 March 1802.

50. JSE, 20 September 1802.

51. JSE, 15 July 1805.

52. JSE, 21 March 1806.

53. AGN, BN, vol. 558, La Griega accounts, 1811–12: my calculations.

54. The tribute counts from La Griega are in Jiménez Gómez, *La República de Indios de Querétaro*, no. 121, 711–34; they are analyzed for the entire district in appendix G.

55. FEN, 12 October 1754; JSE 24 August 1792, 6 April 1802, 19 May 1805, 15 July 1805; CPP, 18 October 1808.

56. AGN, Padrones, vol. 39, f. 1. 1791.

57. Jiménez Gómez, *La República de Indios de Querétaro*, no. 121, 711–34.

58. AGN, Tierras, vol. 1351, exp. 9, f. 7, 1801.

59. Ibid., f. 9.

60. Ibid., f. 10.

61. Ibid., f. 14.

62. Ibid., f. 24.

63. Ibid., f. 1.

64. Ibid., f. 1–2.

65. Ibid., f. 3.

66. Ibid., f. 4.

67. Ibid., f. 4.

68. Ibid., f. 5.

69. Ibid., f. 5.

70. Ibid., f. 5.

71. Ibid., f. 6.

72. JSE, December 1805.

73. Ibid.

74. Spanish and native views of alcohol and religion are probed in Taylor, *Drinking, Homicide, and Rebellion in Colonial Mexican Villages*.

75. FEN, 11 December 1778; JSE, 30 July 1779, 30 August 1781, 3 December 1781, 4 February 1782, 15 July 1782, 16 July 1783, 22 January 1784.

76. JSE, 1 May 1782.

77. JSE, 17 March 1784.

78. JSE, 9 December 1784.

79. JSE, 27 September 1789.

80. JSE, 8 February 1787.

81. AGN, Padrones, vol. 36, 156, 1792.

82. JSE, 29 November 1786, 23 January 1787.

83. JSE, 2 June 1781, 13 June 1781, 23 June 1783, 21 March 1787, 21 January 1799, 28 May 1799, 12 November 1799, 24 November 1801.

84. JSE, 1 August 1790, 22 March 1793, 10 March 1794, 24 November 1801, 5 March 1802, 17 December 1802.

85. Appendix F, tables F.53–F.54.

86. Ibid.

87. JSE, 2 November 1786, 13 December 1786, 24 November 1801, 8 December 1809.

88. Appendix F, tables F.53–F.54.

89. JSE, 20 May 1799, 29 July 1799.

90. JSE, 4 November 1799.

91. JSE, 9 July 1802, 17 December 1802.

92. JSE, 13 May 1798, 24 March 1802, 9 August 1792, 22 October 1802.

93. JSE, 24 March 1802.

94. JSE, 20 June 1803.

95. CPP, 20 April 1799.

96. JSE, 10 February 1804, 13 March 1804.

97. JSE, 2 August 1804.

98. JSE, 15 October 1804.

99. JSE, 12 April 1805.

100. CPP, 1 April 1808, 4 April 1808.

101. Appendix F, table F.55.

102. For Charco de Araujo accounts see Tutino, *From Insurrection to Revolution in Mexico*, 82–90 and appendix B, 383–89.

103. This synthesizes the important work of Ruíz Guadalajara, *Dolores antes de la independencia*, vol. 2.

104. AGN, Padrones, vol. 24, f. 3, 1792.

105. The suit is documented in AGN, Tierras, vol. 1332, exp. 3, 1801–7.

106. AGN, Padrones, vol. 24, f. 2, 1792.

107. The suit is in AGN, Tierras, vol. 1370, exp. 1, 1804–7.

108. Ibid., f. 1, 22 September 1804.

109. Ibid., f. 12.

110. Ibid., f. 13.

111. Ibid., f. 59.

112. Ibid., f. 41.

113. Ibid., f. 23.

114. Ibid., f. 73–74.

115. CPP, 3 May 1808.

116. JSE, 1 April 1808.

117. JSE, 1 April 1808; CPP, 3 May 1808.

118. CPP, 9 September 1808, 20 September 1808.

119. CPP, 17 October 1808.

120. CPP, 18 October 1808; JSE, 25 October 1808; CPP, 1 November 1808.

121. CPP, 31 March 1809, 1 April 1809; JSE, 4 November 1809.

122. JSE, 24 November 1809, 3 January 1810, 25 January 1810.

123. JSE, 14 July 1810.

124. This reflects Tutino, *From Insurrection to Revolution in Mexico*, 99–137, and "The Revolution in Mexican Independence."

125. This is detailed in Ruíz Guadalajara, *Dolores antes de la independencia*, vol. 2, 542–44, 574–83.

126. Appendix G documents a shortage of Otomí youths at Amascala estates (table G.10), while they increased in city workshops (table G.5) and held strong at outlying estates (tables G.9, G.13, G.14).

127. Ruíz Guadalajara, *Dolores antes de la independencia*, vol. 2, 583–85, make a strong case for that among Hidalgo's Dolores parishioners.

Chapter 8. Enlightened Reformers and Popular Religion

1. This is a key conclusion of Voekel, *Alone before God*, and Herrejón Peredo, *Del sermon al discurso cívico*. Covarrubías, *En busca del hombre útil*, details how enlightened thinkers in New Spain pursued utilitarian visions grounded in religious understandings—in concert with contemporaries across Europe, yet without the intense debates common among Old World philosophers.

2. This section synthesizes Taylor, *Magistrates of the Sacred*, and Tanck de Estrada, *Pueblos de indios y educación en el México colonial*.

3. Taylor, *Magistrates of the Sacred*, 6, 18–19, 50.

4. Tanck de Estrada, *Pueblos de indios y educación en el México colonial*, 18–24.

5. Taylor, *Magistrates of the Sacred*, 275, 279.

6. Ibid., 292, 297.

7. Tanck de Estrada, *Pueblos de indios y educación en el México colonial*, 32.

8. Ibid., 107, 247–48.

9. Ibid., 436.

10. Taylor, *Magistrates of the Sacred*, 81.

11. Tanck de Estrada, *Pueblos de indios y educación en el México colonial*, 51, 68, 79, 248, 250, 486.

12. Ibid., 250, 384, 525.

13. Ibid., 403.

14. Ibid., 405.

15. Ibid., 36, 83, 121, 199.

16. Ibid., 96–97, 218–20, 226, 287, 298.

17. Ibid., 387.

18. Ibid., 398.

19. Ibid., 322–24.

20. Ibid., 446.

21. Taylor, *Magistrates of the Sacred*, 43.

22. Ibid., 184.

23. Tanck de Estrada, *Pueblos de indios y educación en el México colonial*, 526.

24. Suárez Muñoz and Jiménez Gómez, eds., *Del Reino a la República*, vol. 1, no. 1, 80–96.

25. Appendix G, tables G.1–G.6.

26. Suárez Muñoz and Jiménez Gómez, eds., *Del Reino a la República*, vol. 1, no. 21, 288–96.

27. Taylor, *Magistrates of the Sacred*, 324–28, 332–33.

28. Ibid., 233.

29. Lara Cisneros, *El cristianismo en el espejo indígena*, 27–125.

30. Ibid., 113–14.

31. Ibid., 75–76.

32. Ibid., 129–31; Taylor, *Magistrates of the Sacred*, 86.

33. Lara Cisneros, *El cristianismo en el espejo indígena*, 132–36.

34. Ibid., 136.

35. Ibid., 135.

36. Ibid., 138–39.

37. Taylor, *Magistrates of the Sacred*, 91–96.

38. Lara Cisneros, *El cristianismo en el espejo indígena*, 140, 142–44; Tanck de Estrada, *Pueblos de indios y educación en el México colonial*, 515; Taylor, *Magistrates of the Sacred*, 183.

39. Lara Cisneros, *El cristianismo en el espejo indígena*, 149.

40. Ibid., 149.

41. Ibid.

42. Ibid., 150.

43. Ibid., 151–52.

44. Ibid., 152.

45. Ibid., 154.

46. Ibid., 159.

47. Ibid., 154, 156–57, 161.

48. Ibid., 161–62.

49. Ibid., 162.

50. This synthesizes Brading, *Una iglesia asediada*, 59–76; Herrejón Peredo, *Del sermón al discurso cívico*, 109–16; and Covarrubías, *En busca del hombre útil*, 384–401.

51. Covarrubías, *En busca del hombre útil*, 384–401, links Díaz's philosophical visions to the worldly science of don José Antonio Alzate.

52. Brading, *Una iglesia asediada*, 60.

53. Herrejón Peredo, *Del sermón al discurso cívico*, 114.

54. See Behar, "Sex and Sin, Witchcraft and the Devil in Late Colonial Mexico"; Behar, "Sexual Witchcraft, Colonialism, and Women's Power"; Ramírez Leyva, "El decir que condena"; and Pappe, "Pretender la verdad? Imponer el orden!" See also Taylor, *Magistrates of the Sacred*, 18–19.

55. Serrano Contreras, "La ciudad de Santiago de Querétaro a fines del siglo XVIII," 545–50.

56. The statistics are in Castro Rivas and Rangel López, *Relación histórica de la intendencia de Guanajuato*, 106–8.

57. Zeláa y Hidalgo, *Glorias de Querétaro*.

58. Ibid., 67–69.

59. Ibid., 69–70.

60. Ibid., 72.

61. Suárez Muñoz and Jiménez Gómez, eds., *Del Reino a la República*, vol. 1, no. 21, 288–96.

62. Colombini y Camayori, *Querétaro triunfante en los caminos del Pueblito*.

63. Ibid., 89–90.

64. Ibid., 1–2.

65. Ibid., 3.

66. Ibid., 10–14; Vilaplana, *Histórico, y sagrado novenario de la milagrosa imagen de Nuestra Señora del Pueblito*.

67. Colombini y Camayori, *Querétaro triunfante en los caminos del Pueblito*, 19.

68. Ibid.

69. Ibid., 21.

70. Ibid., 29.

71. Ibid., 37.

72. Ibid., 19.

73. Ibid., 22.

74. Ibid., 38.

75. Ibid., 42.

76. Ibid., 44.

77. Ibid., 45.

78. Ibid., 45–50.

79. Ibid., 51.

80. Ibid., 52.

81. Ibid., 53.

82. Ibid., 58–70.

83. Ibid., 71–77.

84. Ibid., 81.

85. Ibid., 81–91.

86. Ibid., 92.

87. Ibid., 93.

88. Ibid.

89. Ibid., 94.

90. Ibid., 94–95.

91. Ibid., 95.

92. Ibid., 95–96.

93. Ibid., 97.

94. Ibid., 100.

95. Ibid.

96. Ibid., 101.

97. Ibid., 102.

98. Ibid.

99. Ibid., 102–3.

100. Ibid., 104–5.

101. Ibid., 107.

102. Zeláa y Hidalgo, *Glorias de Querétaro*, 158.

103. Ibid., 161.

104. Ibid., 163–66.

105. Ibid., 167; Navarrete, *Relación peregrina de la agua corriente . . .* , 47.

106. Zeláa y Hidalgo, *Glorias de Querétaro*, 170.

107. Ibid.

108. Ibid., 170–71.

109. Ibid., 171.

110. Ibid., 171–72.

111. Ibid., 172.

112. On the Consolidation in general see Wobeser, *Dominación colonial*.

113. Domínguez, "La representación contra la consolidación, 1805," 229–51.

114. Ibid., 229.

115. Ibid., 230.

116. Ibid., 231–35.

117. Ibid., 237.

118. Ibid., 238.

119. Ibid., 239.

120. Ibid., 240.

121. Ibid., 241.

122. Ibid., 245.

123. Ibid., 243.

124. Ibid., 243–44.

125. Ibid., 245.

126. Ibid., 249.

127. Wobeser, *Dominación colonial.*

128. Ibid., cuadro 4, 48, cuadro 49, 195.

129. Ibid., cuadro 43, 183; Vargas-Lobsinger, *Formación y decadencia de una fortuna.*

130. Calculations based on Wobeser, *Dominación colonial,* cuadro 19, 132–33, and appendice 2, 286–313.

131. Calculations from Wobeser, *Dominación colonial,* appendice 2, 286–313; appendice 5, 330–39.

132. Appendix D, table D.2.

133. See Marichal, *La bancarrota del virreinato,* 168–72.

134. The prevailing view of sovereignty is linked to the origins of insurgency in 1810 in the introductory essay by Herrejón Peredo in *Hidalgo,* and to the politics of independence broadly in Ávila, *En nombre de la nación.*

135. Vergara Hernández, *Testamento.*

136. AGN, Padrones, vol. 39, f. 1, 1791.

137. Vergara Hernández, *Testamento,* 14.

138. Jiménez Gómez, *La República de Indios de Querétaro,* no. 121, 711–34.

139. Vergara Hernández, *Testamento,* 24–29.

140. Ibid., 13–22.

141. Ibid., 13–14.

142. Ibid., 17.

143. Arrom, *Containing the Poor.*

144. Vergara Hernández, *Testamento,* 16–17.

145. Ibid., 17.

146. Ibid., 18.

147. Ibid.

148. Ibid., 19.

149. Ibid.

150. Ibid., 22.

151. Ibid., 19–21.

152. Ibid., 22–23.

153. Ibid., 29–33.

154. Ibid., 35–36.

155. Ibid.

156. Hernández, *La soledad del silencio,* 106–7.

157. Taylor, *Magistrates of the Sacred,* 287.

Conclusion: The Bajío and North America

1. Appendix D, tables D.6, D.7.

2. Appendix D, table D.1.

3. On northern towns see Calleja, "Descripción de la Subdelegación de Aguascalientes," 200–203; Olmedo, *Dinero para el rey*; Swann, *Tierra Adentro*; Offutt, *Saltillo*; Teja, *San Antonio de Béjar*; Ríos-Bustamante, *Los Angeles*.

4. In addition to the sources in note 3, above, see chapter 5; Tutino, "Life and Labor on North Mexican Haciendas"; Harriss, *A Mexican Family Empire*; Vargas-Lobsinger, *Formación y decadencia de una fortuna*; and Rangel Silva, *Capitanes a guerra, linajes de frontera*.

5. This is the focus of Weber, *The Spanish Frontier in North America*.

6. This is clear in Weber's important *Bárbaros* and now in Ortelli, *Trama de una guerra conveniente*.

7. This is best evidenced and analyzed in Martin, *Governance and Society in Colonial Mexico*.

8. See Alonso, *Thread of Blood*, on rural patriarchy in the face of the Apache threat. Ortelli, *Trama de una guerra conveniente*, argues that the "Apache" threat was inflamed to keep state revenues flowing northward while commercial grazing stimulated cattle rustling among diverse peoples often denigrated as "Apaches."

9. Tutino, "Life and Labor on North Mexican Haciendas," 347; Cook and Borah, *Essays in Population History*, vol. 2, 220, 243–44.

10. Martin, *Governance and Society*, table 5, 208–9, my calculations.

11. See chapter 4 and David Frye, *Indians into Mexicans*, 42–110.

12. In addition to the discussions of northward expansion in chapters 2 and 3, on Sonora and Sinaloa see the essays in Ortega Noriega and del Río, eds., *Tres siglos de historia sonorense*.

13. García González, *Familia y sociedad en Zacatecas*, 66–81.

14. See Valle, *Escribiendo desde los márgenes*, for a penetrating analysis of such laments.

15. Calleja, "Descripción de la Subdelegación de Aguascalientes," 202.

16. The differing social relations in estate communities are detailed in Tutino, "Life and Labor on North Mexican Haciendas." The benefits gained by scarce workers farther north are clear in Offutt, *Saltillo*, 114–16. I began to explore differing participations in insurgency in Tutino, *From Insurrection to Revolution in Mexico*, 99–182.

17. See the essays in Ortega Noriega and del Río, eds., *Tres siglos de historia sonorense*.

18. Teja, *San Antonio de Béjar*, and Chipman, *Spanish Texas*.

19. This is brilliantly developed in Barr, *Peace Came in the Form of a Woman*.

20. Ricklis, *The Karankawa of Texas*, quote at 158.

21. My understanding of the long history of New Mexico is shaped by Gutié-rrez, *When Jesus Came the Corn Mothers Went Away*, and Brooks, *Captives and Cousins*. The synthesis of eighteenth-century economic, social, and cultural change that follows builds on the innovative analysis in Frank, *From Settler to Citizen*.

22. On Santa Eulalia see Hadley, *Minería y sociedad.*

23. This key conjuncture is detailed in Frank, *From Settler to Citizen*, 55–62, 72–75. See Fenn, *Pox Americana*, for the continental importance of this epidemic.

24. The first quote is from Frank, *From Settler to Citizen*, 188, the second at 6.

25. The following discussion of the coastal missions builds on Ortega Noriega, "El sistema de misiones jesuíticas" and "Crecimiento y crisis del sistema misional"; Atondo Rodríguez and Ortega Soto, "Entrada de colonos españoles en Sonora durante el Siglo XVII"; Ortega Soto, "La colonización española en la primera mitad del siglo XVIII"; and Radding, *Wandering Peoples*, 2–88.

26. The analysis of Sonora after 1767 builds on Río, "El noroeste novohispano y la nueva política imperial española"; López Mañon and del Río, "La reforma institucional borbónica"; Escandón, "La nueva administración misional y los pueblos de indios" and "Economía y sociedad en Sonora"; and Radding, *Wandering Peoples.*

27. The first trek is detailed in Sweet, *Beasts of the Field*, 3–20; he goes on to explore mission life in California, focusing on the transformation of independent natives into workers. My understanding depends on Hackel's exceptional analysis of the complexities of mission life in *Children of Coyote, Missionaries of Saint Francis* in the context of Ortega Soto's detailed overview of economic and social developments in *Alta California.*

28. Font, *Diario íntimo.*

29. Ibid., 45–65, quote at 47.

30. Ibid., 65–90, quote at 65.

31. Ibid., 97.

32. Ibid., 118–21.

33. Ibid., 128–45.

34. Ibid., 152–58.

35. Ibid., 163–67, 205.

36. Ibid., 175–86.

37. Ibid., 210–16. Chávez-García in *Negotiating Conquest*, 3–24, emphasizes Spanish soldiers' assaults on native women and the later pressure to form patriarchal families in mission projects.

38. Ibid., 229–32.

39. Ibid., 236–52, quote at 252.

40. Ibid., 263–74.

41. Ibid., 282–316.

42. See the details in Ortega Soto, *Alta California*, 23–239, and Hackel, *Children of Coyote, Missionaries of Saint Francis*, 15–366.

43. Hackel, *Children of Coyote*; Ríos-Bustamente, *Los Angeles*, 27–83; Haas, *Conquests and Historical Identities in California*, 13–32, on San Juan Capistrano.

44. Ortega Soto, *Alta California*; Haas, *Conquests and Historical Identities in California*; and Hackel, *Children of Coyote, Missionaries of Saint Francis*, all make this clear.

45. La Pérouse, *Life in a California Mission*, quotes at 63, 67, 70, 77.

46. Ibid., 81–93, quote at 93.

47. Ríos-Bustamente, *Los Angeles*, 87–92.

48. Ibid., 98–101.

49. Ibid., 108–30.

50. Ortega Soto, *Alta California*, 174–85, 216–42.

51. Such diverse adaptations are detailed in Sweet, *Beasts of the Field*.

52. Ibid., 213, on livestock; Ríos-Bustamente, *Los Angeles*, 146; Hackel, *Children of Coyote, Missionaries of Saint Francis*, 258–67, on the uprising.

53. Anyone steeped in the history of Spanish North America can only read Sweet's narrative of the impact of mining in California with a powerful sense of déjà vu. Compare *Beasts of the Field*, 21–134, with Cramaussel, *Poblar la frontera*, on seventeenth-century Nueva Vizcaya. Sweet, grounded in United States labor history, sees a new capitalism emerging in California, rather than the extension and adaptation in the United States of a capitalism long developing in Spanish North America. Johnson, *Roaring Camp*, and Isenberg, *Mining California*, also show how gold rush California emerged from Spanish North America.

54. The role of Mexico City as the entrepreneurial and administrative capital of Spanish North America is clear in chapter 5; on life in the city see Gibson, *The Aztecs under Spanish Rule*, and Lira, *Comunidades indígenas frente a la ciudad de México*. My interpretation is shaped by Granados, "Cosmopolitan Indians and Mesoamerican Barrios in Bourbon Mexico City."

55. On the Puebla basin see Thomson, *Puebla de los Ángeles*; Grosso and Garavaglio, *La región de Puebla en la economía Novohispana*; and Castillo Palma, *Cholula*.

56. See Tutino, "Urban Power and Agrarian Society" and "Haciendas y comunidades en el valle de México."

57. Taylor, *Landlord and Peasant in Colonial Oaxaca*, and Pastor, *Campesinos y reformas*.

58. Farriss, *Maya Society under Colonial Rule*; Patch, *Maya and Spaniard in Yucatán*.

59. McCreery, *Rural Guatemala*; Grandin, *Blood of Guatemala*.

60. Taylor, *Drinking, Homicide, and Rebellion in Colonial Mexican Villages*; Grandin, *Blood of Guatemala*.

61. Taylor, *Magistrates of the Sacred*; Tanck de Estrada, *Pueblos de indios y educación en el México colonial*.

62. I build upon Stern, *The Secret History of Gender*; Tutino, "Creole Mexico" and "Haciendas y comunidades en el valle de México"; Guarisco, *Los indios del valle de México y la construcción de una nueva sociabilidad Política*; and Kanter, *Hijos del Pueblo*.

63. Garner, *Economic Growth and Change in Bourbon Mexico*, offers similar visions of growth, social pressure, and state exaction. Marichal, *La bancarrota del virreinato*, details the extraction of revenues during the decades of war after 1790.

64. The scholarship on colonial- and independence-era British North America is immense and strong. Key works that guide me include Taylor,

American Colonies; Greene, *Pursuits of Happiness*; McCusker and Menard, *The Economy of British America*.

65. The classic work is Morgan, *American Slavery, American Freedom*.

66. Again, to cite a small part of vast scholarship, see Countryman, *The American Revolution*; Nash, *The Unknown American Revolution*; and Richards, *Shays' Rebellion*.

67. Morgan, *Inventing the People*.

68. See McDonald, *Alexander Hamilton*; and McCoy, *The Elusive Republic*.

69. For example see Wallace, *Jefferson and the Indians*; and Rothman, *Slave Country*.

70. Newman, *Fries's Rebellion*; Egerton, *Gabriel's Rebellion*; and Horn, Lewis, and Onuf, eds., *The Revolution of 1800*.

71. See Brown, *The Republic in Peril*; and Rothman, *Slave Country*.

72. Walker, *Smoldering Ashes*; Thomson, *We Alone Will Rule*; and Serulnikov, *Subverting Colonial Authority*.

73. Maxwell, *Conflicts and Conspiracies*.

74. Dubois, *Avengers of the New World*.

75. Marichal, *La bancarrota del virreinato*, details how Spain, France, and Britain all extracted bullion, showing how New Spain sustained all the belligerents in Europe's wars from 1790 to 1808. On the rest of Spain's empire see Adelman, *Sovereignty and Revolution in the Iberian Atlantic*; on the larger global vision Hobsbawm, *Industry and Empire*, Pomeranz, *The Great Divergence*, and Bayly, *The Birth of the Modern World*.

Epilogue: Toward Unimagined Revolution

1. On the independence era in Spain and New Spain see Guerra, *Modernidades y independencias*.

2. Analysis of politics in New Spain during the conflicts that led to independence must start with Ávila, *En nombre de la nación*.

3. This interpretation summarizes Tutino, "Soberanía quebrada."

4. The analysis of the Bajío Revolution and its consequences, to be developed in *Remaking the New World*, is previewed in Tutino, "The Revolution in Mexican Independence." On challenges to the silver economy, see Romero Sotelo, *Minería y guerra*.

Appendix A: Employers and Workers at Querétaro

1. Urquiola Permisán, *Trabajadores de campo y ciudad*, 15–131.

2. Super, *La vida en Querétaro durante la colonia*, 91.

Bibliography

Acosta, Vicente, and Cesárea Munguía. *La milagrosa imagen de Ntra. señora del pueblito*. Mexico City: Jus, 1962.

Adams, Richard N. *Energy and Structure: A Theory of Social Power*. Austin: University of Texas Press, 1975.

Adelman, Jeremy. *Sovereignty and Revolution in the Iberian Atlantic*. Princeton: Princeton University Press, 2006.

Ajofrín, Francisco de. *Diario del viaje . . . a la América septentrional*. Madrid: Real Academia de la Historia, 1958.

Alberro, Solange. *Inquisición y sociedad en México, 1571–1700*. Mexico City: Fondo de Cultura Económica, 1988.

Alcaide Aguilar, José Fernando. *La hacienda "Ciénega de Mata" de los Rincón Gallardo*. Guadalajara: Universidad de Guadalajara, 2004.

Alonso, Ana. *Thread of Blood: Colonialism, Revolution, and Gender on Mexico's Northern Frontier*. Tucson: University of Arizona Press, 1995.

Alvarado Gómez, Armando. *Comercio interior en la Nueva España: El abasto en la ciudad de Guanajuato, 1773–1816*. Mexico City: Instituto Nacional de Antropología e Historia, 1995.

Archer, Christon. *The Army in Bourbon Mexico, 1760–1810*. Albuquerque: University of New Mexico Press, 1977.

Armas Briz, Luz Amelia, and Olivia Solís Hernández. *Esclavos negros y mulatos en Querétaro, siglo XVIII: Antología documental*. Querétaro: Archivo Histórico de Querétaro, 2001.

Arrom, Sylvia. *Containing the Poor: The Mexico City Poor House, 1774–1871*. Durham: Duke University Press, 2000.

Atondo Rodríguez, Ana María, and Martha Ortega Soto. "Entrada de colonos españoles en Sonora durante el siglo XVII." *Tres siglos de historia sonorense, 1530–1830*, ed. Sergio Ortega Noriega and Ignacio del Río, 95–136. Mexico City: Universidad Nacional Autónoma de México, 1993.

Ávila, Alfredo. *En nombre de la nación*. Mexico City: Taurus, 2002.

Ayala Calderón, Javier. *Yuriria, 1522–1580: Organización del espacio y acultura-ción en un pueblo de indios*. Guanajuato: La Rana, 2005.

Báez Macías, Eduardo, ed. "Planos y censos de la Ciudad de México, 1753." *Boletín del Archivo General de la Nación* 8, nos. 3–4 (1967).

Bakewell, P. J. *A History of Latin America*. Oxford: Blackwell, 2003.

———. *Miners of the Red Mountain: Indian Labor in Potosí*. Albuquerque: University of New Mexico Press, 1984.

———. *Silver Mining and Society in Colonial Mexico: Zacatecas, 1546–1700*. Cambridge: Cambridge University Press, 1971.

Baroni Boissonas, Ariana. *La formación de la estructura agraria en el Bajío colonial, siglos XVI y XVII*. Mexico City: La Casa Chata, 1990.

Barr, Juliana. *Peace Came in the Form of a Woman: Indians and Spaniards in the Texas Borderlands*. Chapel Hill: University of North Carolina Press, 2007.

Barrett, Ward. "Morelos and Its Sugar Industry in the Late Eighteenth Century." *Provinces of Early Mexico*, ed. Ida Altman and James Lockhart, 155–75. Los Angeles: UCLA Latin American Center, 1976.

———. *The Sugar Hacienda of the Marqueses del Valle*. Minneapolis: University of Minnesota Press, 1970.

Bayly, C. A. *The Birth of the Modern World, 1780–1914*. Oxford: Blackwell, 2004.

Becerra Jiménez, Celina. *Gobierno, justicia y instituciones en la Nueva Galicia: La alcaldía mayor de Santa María de los Lagos, 1563–1750*. Guadalajara: Universidad de Guadalajara, 2008.

Behar, Ruth. "Sex and Sin, Witchcraft and the Devil in Late Colonial Mexico." *American Ethnologist* 14, no. 1 (1987), 34–54.

———. "Sexual Witchcraft, Colonialism, and Women's Power: Views from the Mexican Inquisition." *Sexuality and Marriage in Colonial Latin America*, ed. Asunción Lavrin. Lincoln: University of Nebraska Press, 1989.

Bennett, Herman. *Africans in Colonial Mexico: Absolutism, Christianity, and Afro-Creole Consciousness, 1570–1640*. Bloomington: Indiana University Press, 2003.

Berthe, Jean-Pierre, ed. *Las nuevas momorias del Capitán Jean de Monségur*, trans. Florence Oliver, Blanca Pulido, and Isabelle Vérical. Mexico City: Universidad Nacional Autónoma de México, 1994.

Blackburn, Robin. *The Making of New World Slavery*. London: Verso, 1997.

Bloch, Marc. *Feudal Society*, trans. L. A. Manyon. Chicago: University of Chicago Press, 1966.

Blum, Jerome. *The End of the Old Order in Europe*. Princeton: Princeton University Press, 1978.

Borah, Woodrow. *Justice by Insurance*. Berkeley: University of California Press, 1982.

Bowser, Frederick. *The African Slave in Colonial Peru, 1524–1650*. Stanford: Stanford University Press, 1974.

Brading, D. A. *Church and State in Bourbon Mexico: The Diocese of Michoacán, 1749–1810*. Cambridge: Cambridge University Press, 1994.

———. "La estructura de la producción agraria en el Bajío de 1750–1850." *Historia mexicana* 22, no. 3 (1973), 197–237.

————. *Haciendas and Ranchos in the Mexican Bajío: León, 1680–1860*. Cambridge: Cambridge University Press, 1978.

————. *Una iglesia asediada: El obispado de Michoacán, 1749–1810*. Mexico City: Fondo de Cultura Económica, 1994.

————. *Miners and Merchants in Bourbon Mexico, 1763–1810*. Cambridge: Cambridge University Press, 1971.

————, ed. *El ocaso novohispano: Testimonios documentales*. Mexico City: Instituto Nacional de Antropología e Historia, 1996.

Braudel, Fernand. *Civilization and Capitalism, 15th–18th Century*, trans. Siân Reynolds.

Vol. 1, *The Structure of Everyday Life*. New York: Harper and Row, 1982.

Vol. 2, *The Wheels of Commerce*. New York: Harper and Row, 1982.

Vol. 3, *The Perspective of the World*. New York: Harper and Row, 1984.

————. *The Mediterranean and the Mediterranean World in the Age of Phillip II*. 2 vols., trans. Sian Reynolds. Berkeley: University of California Press, 1996.

Brooks, James. *Captives and Cousins: Slavery, Kinship, and Community in the Southwest Borderlands*. Chapel Hill: University of North Carolina Press, 2002.

Brown, Roger. *The Republic in Peril, 1912*. New York: W. W. Norton, 1971.

Buelna Serrano, María Elvira. "Las endemoniadas de Querétaro." *Heterodoxia y inquisición en Querétaro*, ed. Buelna Serrano. Querétaro: Universidad Autonoma de Querétaro, 1997.

Calleja, Félix. "Descripción de la Subdelegación de Aguascalientes." *Relaciones geográficas de 1792*, ed. Lourdes Romero Nararrete and Felipe Echenique Marsh, 200–203. Mexico City: Instituto Nacional de Antropología e Historia, 1994.

Cañizares-Esguerra, Jorge. *Puritan Conquistadores: Iberianizing the Atlantic, 1550–1700*. Stanford: Stanford University Press, 2006.

Carbajal López, David. *La minería en Bolaños, 1748–1810*. Zamora: Colegio de Michoacán, 2002.

Carmagnani, Marcelo. *El regreso de los dioses*. Mexico City: Fondo de Cultura Económica, 1988.

Carrasco, Pedro. *Estructura político-territorial del imperio tenochca*. Mexico City: Fondo de Cultura Económica, 1996.

Carrillo Cázares, Alberto. *Partidos y padrones del obispado de Michoacán, 1680–1685*. Zamora: Colegio De Michoacán, 1996.

Carroll, Patrick. *Blacks in Colonial Veracruz: Race, Ethnicity, and Regional Development*. Austin: University of Texas Press, 1991.

Castillo Palma, Norma. *Cholula: Sociedad mestiza en la ciudad india*. Mexico City: Universidad Autónoma Metropolitana, Ixtapalapa, 2001.

Castro Gutiérrez, Felipe. *Movimientos populares en Nueva España: Michoacán, 1766–1767*. Mexico City: Universidad Nacional Autónoma de México, 1990.

————. *Nueva ley y nuevo rey: Reformas borbónicas y rebellion popular en Nueva España*. Zamora: Colegio de Michoacán, 1996.

————. "La resistencia indígena al repartimiento minero de Guanajuato y la introducción de la mita en Nueva España." *Colonial Latin American Historical Review* 11, no. 3 (2002), 229–58.

———. *Los tarascos bajo el imperio español, 1600–1740*. Mexico City: Universidad Nacional Autónoma de México, 2004.

Castro Rivas, Jorge Arturo, and Matilde Rangel López. *Relación histórica de la intendencia de Guanajuato, 1787–1809*. Guanajuato: Universidad de Guanajuato, 1998.

Castro Rivas, Jorge, Matilde Rangel López, and Rafael Tovar Rangel. *Desarrollo socio-demográfico de la ciudad de Guanajuato durante el siglo XVII*. Guanajuato: Universidad de Guanajuato, 1999.

Cervantes Aguilar, Rafael. *Fray Simón del Hierro*. Mexico City, UNAM, 1986.

Chávez-García, Miroslava. *Negotiating Conquest: Gender and Power in California, 1770s to 1880s*. Tucson: University of Arizona Press, 2004.

Childs, Matt. *The 1812 Aponte Rebellion in Cuba and the Struggle against Atlantic Slavery*. Chapel Hill: University of North Carolina Press, 2006.

Chipman, Donald. *Spanish Texas, 1519–1821*. Austin: University of Texas Press, 1992.

Chowning, Margaret. *Rebellious Nuns: The Troubled History of a Mexican Convent, 1752–1863*. New York: Oxford University Press, 2006.

Christian, William. *Local Religion in Sixteenth-Century Spain*. Princeton: Princeton University Press, 1981.

Cole, Jeffrey. *The Potosí Mita, 1573–1700: Compulsory Indian Labor in the Andes*. Stanford: Stanford University Press, 1985.

Collins, James. *The State in Early Modern France*. 2nd edn. Cambridge: Cambridge University Press, 2009.

Colombini y Camayori, Francisco María. *Querétaro triunfante en los caminos del Pueblito: Poema histórico-sagrado en quatro cantos, de la milagrosa imagen de Nuestra Señora del Pueblito*. Mexico City: Zúñiga y Ontiveros, 1801.

Cook, Sherburne, and Woodrow Borah. *Essays in Population History*, vol. 2. Berkeley: University of California Press, 1974.

Correa, Phyllis. "La Cofradía de Indios de la Limpia Concepción en la Villa de San Miguel el Grande en el siglo XVIII." Paper presented to XI Colloquium on Otopame Peoples, University of South Florida, St. Petersburg, September 2009.

Countryman, Edward. *The American Revolution*. New York: Hill and Wang, 2003.

Couturier, Edith. "Hacienda de Hueyapan: The History of a Mexican Social and Economic Institution." Ph.D. diss., Columbia University, 1965.

———. *The Silver King: The Remarkable Life of the Count of Regla in Colonial Mexico*. Albuquerque: University of New Mexico Press, 2003.

Covarrubías, José Enrique. *En busca del hombre útil: Un estudio comparativo del utilitarismo neomercantilista en México y Europa, 1748–1833*. Mexico City: Universidad Nacional Autónoma de México, 2005.

Cramaussel, Chantal. *Poblar la frontera: La provincia de Santa Bárbara en Nueva Vizcaya durante los siglos XVI y XVII*. Zamora: Colegio de Michoacán, 2006.

Crosby, Alfred. *The Columbian Exchange: Biological and Cultural Consequences of 1492*. Westport, Conn.: Greenwood, 1972.

Cruz Rangel, José Antonio. *Chichimecas, misioneros, soldados y terratenientes: Estrategías de colonización, control y poder en Querétaro y la Sierra Gorda, siglos XVI–XVIII*. Mexico City: Archivo General de la Nación, 2003.

Deane, Phyllis. *The First Industrial Revolution*. Cambridge: Cambridge University Press, 1965.

Deans-Smith, Susan. *Bureaucrats, Planters, and Workers: The Making of the Tobacco Monopoly in Bourbon Mexico*. Austin: University of Texas Press, 1992.

Deeds, Susan. *Defiance and Deference in Mexico's Colonial North: Indians under Spanish Rule in Nueva Vizcaya*. Austin: University of Texas Press, 2003.

Domínguez, Miguel. "La representación contra la consolidación, 1805." *El ocaso novohispano: Testimonios documentales*, ed. D. A. Brading, 229–51. Mexico City: Instituto Nacional de Antropología e Historia, 1996.

Domínguez de la Fuente, Manuel José. *Leal informe político-legal, 1774*. Guanajuato: La Rana, 1999.

Domínguez Paulín, Arturo. *Querétaro en la conquista de las Californias*. Mexico City: Sociedad Mexicana de Geografía y Estadística, 1966.

Dubois, Laurent. *Avengers of the New World: The Story of the Haitian Revolution*. Cambridge: Harvard University Press, 2005.

Dunn, Richard. *Sugar and Slaves: The Rise of the Planter Class in the English West Indies, 1624–1713*. Chapel Hill: University of North Carolina Press, 1972.

Egerton, Douglas. *Gabriel's Rebellion: The Virginia Slave Conspiracies of 1800 and 1802*. Chapel Hill: University of North Carolina Press, 1993.

Egnal, Marc. *A Mighty Empire: The Origins of the American Revolution*. Ithaca: Cornell University Press, 1988.

Elliott, J. H. *Empires of the Atlantic World: Britain and Spain in the Americas, 1492–1830*. New Haven: Yale University Press, 2006.

———. *Imperial Spain, 1469–1716*. Harmondsworth: Penguin, 1970.

Escamilla González, Iván. "La nueva alianza: El Consulado de México y la monarquía borbónica durante la guerra de sucesión." *Mercaderes, comercio y consulados de Nueva España en el siglo XVIII*, ed. Guillermina del Valle Pavón. Mexico City: Instituto Mora, 2003.

Escandón, Patricia. "Economía y sociedad en Sonora, 1767–1821." *Tres siglos de historia sonorense, 1530–1830*, ed. Sergio Ortega Noriega and Ignacio del Río, 367–403. Mexico City: Universidad Nacional Autónoma de México, 1993.

———. "La nueva administración misional y los pueblos de indios." *Tres siglos de historia sonorense, 1530–1830*, ed. Sergio Ortega Noriega and Ignacio del Río, 327–65. Mexico City: Universidad Nacional Autónoma de México, 1993.

Espinosa Morales, Lydia. "Análisis de los precios de los productos diezmados: El Bajío oriental, 1665–1786." *Los precios de alimentos y manufacturas novohispanos*, ed. Virginia García Acosta. Mexico City: CIESAS, 1995.

Ethridge, Robbie. *Creek Country: The Creek Indians and Their World*. Chapel Hill: University of North Carolina Press, 2003.

Farriss, Nancy. *Maya Society under Colonial Rule*. Princeton: Princeton University Press, 1984.

Fenn, Elizabeth. *Pox Americana: The Great Smallpox Epidemic of 1775–1782*. New York: Hill and Wang, 2002.

Fernández de Recas, Guillermo. *Aspirantes americanos a cargos de Santo Oficio.* Mexico City: Porrúa, 1956.

———. *Mayorazgos de la Nueva España.* Mexico City: Instituto Bibliográfico Mexicano, 1965.

Fernández de San Salvador, Fernando. *Defensa jurídica de la Señora Doña María Micaela Romero de Terreros.* Mexico City, 1796.

Ferrusca Beltrán, Rita. *Querétaro: De pueblo a ciudad, 1655–1733.* Querétaro: Archivo Histórico de Querétaro, 2004.

Florescano, Enrique. *Etnia, estado y nación: Esayos sobre las identidades colectivas en México.* Mexico City: Aguilar, 1997.

———. *Precios del maíz y crisis agrícolas en México, 1708–1816.* Mexico City: Colegio de México, 1969.

Flynn, Dennis, and Arturo Giráldez. "Born with a 'Silver Spoon': The Origins of World Trade in 1571." *Journal of World History* 6, no. 2 (1995), 201–21.

———. "Cycles of Silver: Global Unity through the Mid-Eighteenth Century." *Journal of World History* 13, no. 2 (2002), 391–427.

Font, Fray Pedro. *Diario íntimo,* ed. Julio César Montañé. Mexico City: Plaza y Valdéz, 2000.

Frank, Andre Gunder. *ReOrient: Global Economy in the Asian Age.* Berkeley: University of California Press, 1998.

Frank, Ross. *From Settler to Citizen: New Mexican Economic Development and the Creation of Vecino Society, 1750–1820.* Berkeley: University of California Press, 2000.

Frye, David. *Indians into Mexicans: History and Identity in a Mexican Town.* Austin: University of Texas Press, 1996.

Gallay, Alan. *The Indian Slave Trade: The Rise of the English Empire in the American South, 1670–1713.* New Haven: Yale University Press, 2002.

Gálvez, José de. *Informe sobre las rebeliones populares de 1767,* ed. Felipe Castro Gutiérrez. Mexico City: Universidad Nacional Autonóma de México, 1990.

Gálvez Jiménez, Mónica Leticia. *Celaya: Sus raíces africanas.* Guanajuato: La Rana, 1995.

Games, Alison. *Migration and the Origins of the English Atlantic World.* Cambridge: Harvard University Press, 1999.

Garavaglia, Juan Carlos, and Juan Carlos Grosso. *Las alcabalas novohispanas, 1776–1821.* Mexico City: Archivo General de la Nación, 1987.

García-Barquero, Antonio. "Comercio colonial y producción industrial en Cataluña a fines del siglo XVIII." *Agricultura, comercio colonial y crecimiento económico en la España contemporánea,* ed. Jordi Nadal and Gabriel Tortella, 268–94. Barcelona: Ariel, 1974.

García Castro, René. *Indios, territorio y poder en la provincial matlatzinca: La negociación del espacio politico en los pueblos otomianos, siglos XV–XVII.* Zinacatepec: Colegio Mexiquense, 1999.

García González, Francisco. *Familia y sociedad en Zacatecas: La vida en un microcosmos minero novohispano, 1750–1830.* Mexico City: Colegio de México, 2000.

Garner, Richard, with Spiro Stefanou. *Economic Growth and Change in Bourbon Mexico.* Gainesville: University of Florida Press, 1993.

Geertz, Clifford. *The Interpretation of Cultures*. New York: Basic Books, 1973.

Genovese, Eugene. *The Political Economy of Slavery*. New York: Pantheon, 1965.

———. *Roll, Jordan, Roll: The World the Slaves Made*. New York: Pantheon, 1974.

Gibson, Charles. *The Aztecs under Spanish Rule*. Stanford: Stanford University Press, 1964.

Gómez de Acosta, Estéban. *Querétaro en 1743: Informe presentado al rey por el corregidor*, ed. Mina Ramírez Montes. Querétaro: Archivo Histórico de Querétaro, 1997.

González Gómez, Carmen Imelda. *El tabaco virreinal: monopolio de una costumbre*. Querétaro: Universidad Autónoma de Querétaro, 2002.

González Sánchez, Isabel. *El Obispado de Michoacán en 1765*. Morelia: Gobierno de Michoacán, 1985.

Grafe, Regina, and Alejandra Irigoin. "The Spanish Empire and Its Legacy: Fiscal Redistribution and Political Conflict in Colonial and Post-Colonial Spanish America." *Journal of Global History* 1 (2006), 241–67.

Graham, Richard. *Patronage and Politics in Nineteenth-Century Brazil*. Stanford: Stanford University Press, 1990.

Granados, Luis Fernando. "Cosmopolitan Indians and Mesoamerican Barrios in Bourbon Mexico City." Ph.D. diss., Georgetown University, 2008.

Grandin, Greg. *Blood of Guatemala: A History of Race and Nation*. Durham: Duke University Press, 2000.

———. *The Last Colonial Massacre: Latin America in the Cold War*. Chicago: University of Chicago Press, 2005.

Greene, Jack. *Pursuits of Happiness: The Social Development of the Early British Colonies and the Formation of American Culture*. Chapel Hill: University of North Carolina Press, 1988.

Grosso, Juan Carlos, and Juan Carlos Garavaglia. *La región de Puebla en la economía novohispana*. Mexico City: Instituto Mora, 1996.

Guardino, Peter. *Peasants and the Formation of Mexican National Politics: Guerrero, 1800–1857*. Stanford: Stanford University Press, 1997.

Guarisco, Claudia. *Los indios del valle de México y la construcción de una nueva sociabilidad Política, 1770–1835*. Zinacatepec: Colegio Mexiquense, 2003.

Guerra, Francois-Xavier. *Modernidades y independencias*. Mexico City: Fondo de Cultura Económica, 1993.

Guevara Sanginés, María. *Guanajuato diverso: Sabores y sinsabores de su ser mestizo*. Guanajuato: La Rana, 2001.

Gunnarsdóttir, Ellen. "The Convent of Santa Clara, the Elite, and Social Change in Eighteenth-Century Querétaro." *Journal of Latin American Studies* 33, no. 2 (2001), 257–90.

———. *Mexican Karismata: The Baroque Vocation of Francisca de los Angeles, 1664–1744*. Lincoln: University of Nebraska Press, 2004.

Gutiérrez, Ramón. *When Jesus Came the Corn Mothers Went Away: Marriage, Sexuality, and Power in New Mexico, 1500–1846*. Stanford: Stanford University Press, 1991.

Haas, Lisbeth. *Conquests and Historical Identities in California, 1769–1936*. Berkeley: University of California Press, 1995.

Hackel, Steven. *Children of Coyote, Missionaries of Saint Francis: Indian-Spanish Relations in Colonial California, 1769–1850*. Chapel Hill: University of North Carolina Press, 2005.

Hadley, Philip. *Minería y sociedad en el centro minero de Santa Eulalia, Chihuahua, 1709–1750*. Mexico City: Fondo de Cultura Económica, 1979.

Harriss, Charles. *A Mexican Family Empire: The Latifundio of the Sánchez Navarro Family, 1765–1867*. Austin: University of Texas Press, 1975.

Hernández, Jorge. *La soledad del silencio: Microhistoria del santuario de Atotonilco*. Mexico City: Fondo de Cultura Económica, 1991.

Hernández Jaimes, Jesús. "El comercio de algodón en las cordilleras y costas de la mar del sur de Nueva España en el siglo XVIII." *Mercaderes, comercio y consulados de Nueva España en el siglo XVIII*, ed. Guillermina del Valle Pavón. Mexico City: Instituto Mora, 2003.

Herrejón Peredo, Carlos. *Del sermon al discurso cívico: México, 1760–1834*. Zamora: Colegio de Michoacán, 2003.

——, ed. *Hidalgo*. Mexico City: Secretaría de Educación Pública, 1986.

Hoberman, Louisa. *Mexico's Merchant Elite, 1590–1660: Silver, State, and Society*. Durham: Duke University Press, 1991.

Hobsbawm, Eric. *Industry and Empire: The Birth of the Industrial Revolution*, rev. edn. New York: New Press, 1999.

Holton, Woody. *Forced Founders: Indians, Debtors, and Slaves in the Making of the American Revolution*. Chapel Hill: University of North Carolina Press, 1999.

Horn, James, Jan Ellen Lewis, and Peter Onuf, eds. *The Revolution of 1800*. Charlottesville: University of Virginia Press, 2002.

Huerta, María Teresa. "Comercio en tierra adentro." *Mercaderes, comercio y consulados de Nueva España en el siglo XVIII*, ed. Guillermina del Valle Pavón. Mexico City: Instituto Mora, 2003.

Humboldt, Alejandro de. *Ensayo político sobre el Reino de la Nueva España*. Paris: Rosa, 1822; repr. Mexico City: Porrúa, 1966.

Irigoin, Alejandra, and Regina Grafe. "Bargaining for Absolutism: A Spanish Path to Nation-State and Empire Building." *Hispanic American Historical Review* 88, no. 2 (2008), 173–209.

——. "A Stakeholder Empire: The Political Economy of Spanish Imperial Rule in America." Working paper presented to Washington Area Seminar on the History of Latin America, University of Maryland, March 2009.

Isenberg, Andrew. *Mining California: An Ecological History*. New York: Hill and Wang, 2006.

Israel, Jonathan. *Dutch Primacy in World Trade, 1585–1748*. Oxford: Oxford University Press, 1989.

——. *Race, Class, and Politics in Colonial Mexico, 1610–1670*. Oxford: Oxford University Press, 1975.

Izard, Miguel. "Comercio libre, guerras coloniales y mercado americano." *Agricultura, comercio colonial y crecimiento económico en la España contemporánea*, ed. Jordi Nadal and Gabriel Tortella, 295–321. Barcelona: Ariel, 1974.

Jaffary, Nora. *False Mystics: Deviant Orthodoxy in Colonial Mexico*. Lincoln: University of Nebraska Press, 2008.

Jáuregui de Cervantes, Aurora. *Los Marqueses de Rayas*. Guanajuato: La Rana, 1987.

Jiménez Gómez, Juan Ricardo. "Instituciones sociales, mentalidades y vida cotidiana en Querétaro, 1575–1625." *Indios y Franciscanos en la construcción de Santiago de Querétaro, siglos XVI–XVII*, ed. José Antonio Cruz Rangel et al. Querétaro: Archivo Historíco de Querétaro, 1997.

————, ed. *La República de Indios de Querétaro, 1550–1820*. Querétaro: Instituto de Estudios Constitucionales, 2006.

Johnson, Susan. *Roaring Camp: The Social World of the California Gold Rush*. New York: W. W. Norton, 2001.

Kamen, Henry. *Empire: How Spain Became a World Power, 1492–1763*. New York: Harper Collins, 2003.

Kanter, Deborah. *Hijos del Pueblo: Gender, Family, and Community in Rural Mexico, 1730–1850*. Austin: University of Texas Press, 2009.

Kicza, John. *Colonial Entrepreneurs: Family and Business in Bourbon Mexico City*. Albuquerque: University of New Mexico Press, 1983.

Konrad, Herman. *A Jesuit Hacienda in Colonial Mexico: Santa Lucía, 1576–1767*. Stanford: Stanford University Press, 1980.

Kors, Marjoleine. *Breaking Loose Together: The Regulator Rebellion in Pre-revolutionary North Carolina*. Chapel Hill: University of North Carolina Press, 2002.

Ladd, Doris. *The Making of a Strike: Mexican Silver Workers' Struggles in Real del Monte, 1766–1775*. Lincoln: University of Nebraska Press, 1988.

————. *The Mexican Nobility at Independence, 1780–1826*. Austin: University of Texas Press, 1976.

Lafuente Ferrari, Enrique. *El Virrey Iturrigaray y las orígenes de la independencia en México*. Madrid: Consejo Superior de Investigación Científica, 1941.

Langue, Frederique. *Los señores de Zacatecas: Una aristocracía minera del siglo XVIII novohispano*. Mexico City: Fondo de Cultura Económica, 1999.

La Pérouse, Jean-François de Galaup, comte de. *Life in a California Mission: Monterey in 1786: The Journals of Jean-François de La Pérouse*, ed. Malcolm Margolin. Berkeley: Heyday, 1989.

Lara Cisneros, Gerardo. *El cristianismo en el espejo indígena: Religiosidad en el occidente de Sierra Gorda, siglo XVIII*. Mexico City: Archivo General de la Nación, 2002.

Lara Meza, Ada Marina. *Haciendas de beneficio en Guanajuato: Tecnología y usos del suelo, 1770–1780*. Guanajuato: Presidencia Municipal, 2001.

Lastra, Yolanda. *Los Otomíes: Su lengua y su historia*. Mexico City: Universidad Nacional Autonóma de México, 2006.

Lavrin, Asunción. "El convento de Santa Clara de Querétaro: La administración de sus propiedades en el siglo XVII." *Historia mexicana* 25, no. 1 (1975), 76–117.

Lerdo de Tejada, Miguel. *El comercio exterior de México desde la conquista hasta hoy*. 1853; reprint, Mexico City: Banco Nacional de Comercio Exterior, 1967.

Lewis, Laura. *Hall of Mirrors: Power, Witchcraft, and Caste in Colonial Mexico.* Durham: Duke University Press, 2003.

Lira, Andrés. *Comunidades indígenas frente a la ciudad de México.* Zamora: Colegio de Michoacán, 1983.

Liss, Peggy. *Atlantic Empires: The Networks of Trade and Revolution, 1713–1826.* Baltimore: Johns Hopkins University Press, 1982.

Lockhart, James. *The Nahuas after the Conquest.* Stanford: Stanford University Press, 1992.

———. *Spanish Peru, 1532–1562.* Madison: University of Wisconsin Press, 1968.

López Austin, Alfredo, and Leonardo López Luján. *El pasado indígena.* 2nd edn. Mexico City: Fondo de Cultura Económica, 2001.

López de la Cámara Alta, Agustín. *Descripción general de la Colonia de Nuevo Santander*, ed. Patricia Osante. Mexico City: Universidad Nacional Autónoma de México, 2006.

López Lara, Ramón, ed. *El obispado de Michoacán en el siglo XVII.* Morelia: Fimax Publicistas, 1973.

López Mañón, Edgardo, and Ignacio del Río. "La reforma institucional borbónica." *Tres siglos de historia sonorense, 1530–1830*, ed. Sergio Ortega Noriega and Ignacio del Río, 287–325. Mexico City: Universidad Nacional Autónoma de México, 1993.

Mallon, Florencia. *Peasant and Nation: The Making of Post-colonial Mexico and Peru.* Berkeley: University of California Press, 1992.

Mangan, Jane. *Trading Roles: Gender, Ethnicity, and the Urban Economy in Colonial Potosí.* Durham: Duke University Press, 2005.

Marichal, Carlos. *La bancarrota del virreinato: Nueva España y las finanzas del Imperio español, 1780–1810.* Mexico City: Fondo de Cultura Económica, 1999.

Martin, Cheryl. *Governance and Society in Colonial Mexico: Chihuahua in the Eighteenth Century.* Stanford: Stanford University Press, 1996.

———. *Rural Society in Colonial Morelos.* Albuquerque: University of New Mexico Press, 1985.

Martínez Baracs, Rodrigo. *Convivencia y utopia: El gobierno indio y español de la "ciudad de Mechuacan," 1521–1580.* Mexico City: Fondo de Cultura Económica, 2005.

Martínez Shaw, Carlos. "Los orígenes de la industrial algodonera catalana y del comercio colonial." *Agricultura, comercio colonial y crecimiento económico en la España contemporánea*, ed. Jordi Nadal and Gabriel Tortella, 243–67. Barcelona: Ariel, 1974.

Maxwell, Kenneth. *Conflicts and Conspiracies: Brazil and Portugal, 1750–1808.* Cambridge: Cambridge University Press, 1973.

Maza, Francisco de la. *San Miguel de Allende, su historia, sus monumentos.* 2nd edn. Mexico City: Frente de Afirmación Hispanista, 1972.

Mazín, Oscar. *Entre dos magistades: El obispo y la iglesia del Gran Michoacán ante las reformas borbónicas, 1758–1772.* Zamora: Colegio de Michoacán, 1986.

McCloskey, Michael. *The Formative Years of the Missionary College of Santa*

Cruz de Querétaro, 1683–1733. Washington: American Academy of Franciscan History, 1955.

McCoy, Drew. *The Elusive Republic: Political Economy in Jeffersonian America*. New York: W. W. Norton, 1980.

McCreery, David. *Rural Guatemala, 1750–1940*. Stanford: Stanford University Press, 1994.

McCusker, John, and Russell Menard. *The Economy of British America, 1607– 1789*. Chapel Hill: University of North Carolina Press, 1991.

McDonald, Forrest. *Alexander Hamilton: A Biography*. New York: W. W. Norton, 1982.

McNally, David. *Political Economy and the Rise of Capitalism: A Reinterpretation*. Berkeley: University of California Press, 1988.

McNeill, J.R. *Mosquito Empires: Ecology and War in the Greater Caribbean, 1620–1914*. Cambridge: Cambridge University Press, 2010.

———. *Something New under the Sun: An Environmental History of the Twentieth-Century World*. New York: W. W. Norton, 2001.

Medina Medina, Alejandra. "Noticias de Querétaro en las *Gacetas de México*, 1722–1742." *Investigación*, 61–69. Querétaro: Universidad Autónoma de Querétaro, 1985.

Melville, Elinor. *A Plague of Sheep: Environmental Consequences of the Conquest of Mexico*. Cambridge: Cambridge University Press, 1994.

Mendoza Muñoz, Jesús. *El Conde de Sierra Gorda, don José de Escandón y Helguera: Militar, noble y caballero*. Cadereyta: Fomento de Historia y Cultura de Cadereyta, 2005.

———. *Historia eclesiástica de Cadereyta*. Querétaro: Gobierno del Estado, 2002.

Meyer, Jean. *El gran Nayar*. Mexico City: Centro de Estudios Mexicanos y Centroamericanos, 1989.

Miño Grijalva, Manuel. *El mundo novohispano: Población, ciudades y economía, siglos XVII y XVIII*. Mexico City: Fondo de Cultura Económica, 2001.

———. *Obrajes y tejedores de Nueva España: La industria urbana y rural de una economía colonial*. Mexico City: Colegio de México, 1998.

Molina del Villar, América. *La Nueva España y el matlazahuatl*. Zamora: Colegio de Michoacán, 2001.

Moore, Barrington, Jr. *Injustice: The Social Bases of Obedience and Revolt*. White Plains, N.Y.: M. E. Sharpe, 1978.

———. *Social Origins of Dictatorship and Democracy: Lord and Peasant in the Making of the Modern World*. Boston: Beacon, 1966.

Morgan, Edmund. *American Slavery, American Freedom: The Ordeal of Colonial Virginia*. New York: W. W. Norton, 1975.

———. *Inventing the People*. New York: W. W. Norton, 1989.

Morgan, Edmund, and Helen Morgan. *The Stamp Act Crisis: Prologue to Revolution*. Chapel Hill: University of North Carolina Press, 1953; repr. 1995.

Morín, Claude. *Michoacán en la Nueva España del siglo XVIII: Crecimiento y desigualdad en una economía colonial*. Mexico City: Fondo de Cultura Económica, 1979.

Murphy, Michael. *Irrigation in the Bajío Region of Colonial Mexico*. Boulder: Westview, 1986.

Nadal, Jordi, and Gabriel Tortella, eds. *Agricultura, comercio colonial y crecimiento económico en la España contemporánea*. Barcelona: Ariel, 1974.

Nash, Gary. *The Unknown American Revolution: The Unruly Birth of Democracy and the Struggle to Create America*. New York: Viking, 2005.

Navarrete, Francisco Antonio. *Relación peregrina de la agua corriente que para beber y vivir goza la muy noble, leal y florida ciudad de Santiago de Querétaro*. Mexico City: José Bernardo de Hogal, 1739; repr. Querétaro: Gobierno del Estado, 1987.

Newman, Paul Douglas. *Fries's Rebellion: The Enduring Struggle for the American Revolution*. Philadelphia: University of Pennsylvania Press, 2004.

North, Douglass. *Institutions, Institutional Change, and Economic Performance*. Cambridge: Cambridge University Press, 1990.

North, Douglass, John Joseph Wallis, and Barry Weingast. *Violence and Social Orders: A Conceptual Framework for Interpreting Recorded Human History*. Cambridge: Cambridge University Press, 2009.

Norton, Mary Beth. *In the Devil's Snare: The Salem Witchcraft Crisis of 1692*. New York: Alfred A. Knopf, 2002.

Offutt, Leslie. *Saltillo, 1770–1810: Town and Region in the Mexican North*. Albuquerque: University of New Mexico Press, 1995.

Olmedo, José. *Dinero para el rey: El padrón de 1781 y los artesanos de Zacatecas*. Mexico City: Instituto Nacional de Antropología e Historia, 2009.

Ortega Noriega, Sergio. "Crecimiento y crisis del sistema misional, 1591–1699." *Tres siglos de historia sonorense, 1530–1830*, ed. Sergio Ortega Noriega and Ignacio del Río, 137–85. Mexico City: Universidad Nacional Autónoma de México, 1993.

———. "El sistema de misiones jesuíticas, 1591–1699." *Tres siglos de historia sonorense, 1530–1830*, ed. Sergio Ortega Noriega and Ignacio del Río, 41–94. Mexico City: Universidad Nacional Autónoma de México, 1993.

Ortega Noriega, Sergio, and Ignacio del Río, eds. *Tres siglos de historia sonorense, 1530–1830*. Mexico City: Universidad Nacional Autónoma de México, 1993.

Ortega Soto, Martha. *Alta California: Una frontera olvidada del noroeste de México, 1769–1846*. Mexico City: Universidad Autónoma Metropolitana, Ixtapalapa, 2001.

———. "La colonización española en la primera mitad del siglo XVIII." *Tres siglos de historia sonorense, 1530–1830*, ed. Sergio Ortega Noriega and Ignacio del Río, 187–245. Mexico City: Universidad Nacional Autónoma de México, 1993.

Ortelli, Sara. *Trama de una guerra conveniente: Nueva Vizcaya y la sombra de los Apaches, 1748–1790*. Mexico City: Colegio de México, 2007.

Ortíz Escamilla, Juan. *El teatro de la guerra: Veracruz, 1750–1825*. Castelló de la Plana, Valencia: Universitat Jaume-1, 2008.

Osante, Patricia. *Orígenes del Nuevo Santander*. Mexico City: Universidad Nacional Autónoma de México, 1997.

Owensby, Brian. *Empire of Law and Indian Justice in Colonial Mexico*. Stanford: Stanford University Press, 2008.

Pappe, Sylvia. "Pretender la verdad? Imponer el orden!" *Heterodoxia y Inquisición en Querétaro*, 195–219. Querétaro: Universidad Autónoma de Querétaro, 1997.

Pastor, María Alba. *Crisis y recomposición social: Nueva España en el trásito del siglo XVI al XVII*. Mexico City: Fondo de Cultura Económica, 1999.

———. *Cuerpos sociales, cuerpos sacrificiales*. Mexico City: Fondo de Cultura Económica, 2004.

Pastor, Rodolfo. *Campesinos y reformas: La mixteca, 1700–1856*. Mexico City: Colegio de México, 1987.

Patch, Robert. *Maya and Spaniard in Yucatán, 1648–1812*. Stanford: Stanford University Press, 1993.

Pérez-Mallaína, Pablo. *Spain's Men of the Sea: Daily Life on the Indies Fleet in the Sixteenth Century*, trans. Carla Rahn Phillips. Baltimore: Johns Hopkins University Press, 1998.

Pérez Rosales, Laura. *Familia, poder, riqueza y subversion: Los Fagoagas novohispanos, 1730–1830*. Mexico City: Universidad Iberoamericana, 2003.

———. *Minería y sociedad en Taxco durante el siglo XVIII*. Mexico City: Universidad Iberoamericana, 1996.

Perkin, Harold. *The Origins of Modern English Society, 1780–1880*. London: Routledge, 1969.

Pomeranz, Kenneth. *The Great Divergence: China, Europe, and the Making of the Modern World Economy*. Princeton: Princeton University Press, 2000.

Poole, Stafford. *Our Lady of Guadalupe: The Origins and Sources of a Mexican National Symbol*. Tucson: University of Arizona Press, 1995.

Powell, Philip Wayne. *Capitán mestizo: Miguel Caldera y la frontera norteña: La pacificación de las chichimecas*, trans. Juan José Utrillo. Mexico City: Fondo de Cultura Económica, 1977.

———. *La guerra chichimeca, 1550–1600*, trans. Juan José Utrillo. Mexico City: Fondo de Cultura Económica, 1977.

———. *Soldiers, Indians, and Silver: The Northward Advance of New Spain, 1550–1600*. Berkeley: University of California Press, 1969.

Quiroz, Enriqueta. *Entre el lujo y la subsistencia: Mercado, abastecimiento y precios de la carne en la ciudad de México, 1750–1812*. Mexico City: Colegio de México, 2005.

Radding, Cynthia. *Wandering Peoples: Colonialism, Ethnic Spaces, and Ecological Frontiers in Northwestern Mexico, 1700–1850*. Durham: Duke University Press, 1977.

Ramírez Leyva, Edelmira. "El decir que condena." *Heterodoxia y Inquisición en Querétaro*, 1–47. Querétaro: Universidad Autónoma de Querétaro, 1997.

Rangel Silva, José Alfredo. *Capitanes a guerra, linajes de frontera: Asenso y consolidación de los elites en el oriente de San Luís Potosí, 1617–1823*. Mexico City: Colegio de México, 2008.

Raso, José Antonio del. *Notas estadísticas del departamento de Querétaro, año de 1845*. Mexico City: Imprenta de José Mariano Lara, 1848.

Registro de la primeras minas de Guanajuato, 1556–1557. Guanajuato: Archivo General de Estado, 1992.

"Relación Geográfica de Querétaro." *Querétaro en el siglo XVI: Fuentes documentales primarias*, ed. David Wright, 95–219. Querétaro: Gobierno del Estado, 1989.

Ricard, Robert. *The Spiritual Conquest of Mexico*. Berkeley: University of California Press, 1982.

Richards, Leonard. *Shays' Rebellion: The American Revolution's Final Battle*. Philadelphia: University of Pennsylvania Press, 2002.

Ricklis, Robert. *The Karankawa of Texas: An Ecological Study of Cultural Tradition and Change*. Austin: University of Texas Press, 1996.

Riley, James. "Santa Lucía: Desarrollo y administración de una hacienda jesuíta en el siglo XVIII." *Historia mexicana* 23, no. 2 (1973).

Rincón Frías, Gabriel. "Testamento de don Juan Caballero y Ocío." *Investigación*, 5–1. Querétaro: Universidad Autónoma de Querétaro, 1985.

Ringrose, David. *Spain, Europe, and the "Spanish Miracle," 1700–1900*. Cambridge: Cambridge University Press, 1996.

Río, Ignacio del. "El noroeste novohispano y la nueva política imperial española." *Tres siglos de historia sonorense, 1530–1830*, ed. Sergio Ortega Noriega and Ignacio del Río, 247–86. Mexico City: Universidad Nacional Autónoma de México, 1993.

———. *El régimen jesuítico de la Antigua California*. Mexico City: Universidad Nacional Autónoma de México, 2003.

Rionda Arreguín, Isauro. *La Compañía de Jesús en la provincia guanajuatense, 1590–1767*. Guanajuato: Universidad de Guanajuato, 1996.

———. "Los hospitales en el Real de Minas de Guanajuato." *Guanajuato: La cultura en el tiempo*, ed. Mariano González Leal, 15–44. León: Colegio del Bajío, 1988.

———. *La mina de San Juan de Rayas, 1676–1727*. Guanajuato: Universidad de Guanajuato, 1982.

Ríos-Bustamente, Antonio. *Los Angeles: Pueblo y región, 1781–1850*. Mexico City: Instituto Nacional de Antropología y Historia, 1991.

Rivera Villanueva, José Antonio. *Los otomíes de San Nicolás de Tierranueva: Río de Jofre, 1680–1794*. San Luis Potosí: Colegio de San Luis, 2007.

Rodríguez Frausto, Jesús. "La Universidad de Guanajuato en su origin." *Guanajuato: La cultura en el tiempo*, ed. Mariano González Leal, 71–98. León: Colegio del Bajío, 1988.

Rodríguez Gómez, María Guadalupe. *Jalpa y San Juan de los Otates: Dos haciendas en el Bajío colonial*. León: Colegio del Bajío, 1984.

Romano, Ruggiero. *Mecanismo y elementos del sistema económica colonial americano: Siglos XVI–XVIII*. Mexico City: Fondo de Cultura Económica, 2004.

Romero de Terreros, Manuel. *Antiguas haciendas de México*. Mexico City: Patria, 1956.

———. "La Condesa escribe." *Historia mexicana* 1, no. 3 (1951).

———. "Los hijos de los primeros Condes de Regla." *Memorias de la Academia Mexicana de Historia* 3, no. 2 (1944).

Romero Sotelo, María Eugenia. *Minería y guerra: La economía de Nueva España, 1810–1821*. Mexico City: El Colegio de México, 1997.

Rosaldo, Renato. *Culture and Truth: The Remaking of Social Analysis*. Boston: Beacon, 1993.

Rothman, Adam. *Slave Country: American Expansion and the Origins of the Deep South*. Cambridge: Harvard University Press, 2005.

Rubio Mañé, J. Ignacio. "Títulos de las villas de San Miguel (1559) y de San Felipe (1562)," *Boletín del Archivo General de la Nación* 2, no. 3 (1961), 233–54.

Ruíz Guadalajara, Juan Carlos. *Dolores antes de la independencia*. Zamora: Colegio de Michoacán, 2004.

Salvucci, Richard. "Aspectos de un conflicto empresarial: El obraje de Baltásar de Sauto y la historia social de San Miguel el Grande." *Asuario de Estudios Americanos* 36 (1979), 405–43.

———. *Textiles and Capitalism in Mexico: An Economic History of the Obrajes, 1539–1810*. Princeton: Princeton University Press, 1987.

Sánchez de Tagle, Estéban. *Por un regimento, el regimen: Política y sociedad, la formación del Regimento de la Reina en San Miguel el Grande*. Mexico City: Instituto Nacional de Antropología e Historia, 1982.

Sánchez García, José Hermenegildo. *Crónica del Nuevo Santander*. Mexico City: Conacyt, 1990.

Scharrer Tamm, Beatríz. *Azúcar y trabajo: Tecnología de los siglos XVII y XVIII en el actual Estado de Morelos*. Mexico City: Porrúa, 1997.

Schell, William. "Silver Symbiosis: ReOrienting Mexican Economic History." *Hispanic American Historical Review* 81, no.1 (2001), 90–133.

Schwartz, Stuart. *Sugar Plantations in the Formation of Brazilian Society: Bahia, 1550–1835*. Cambridge: Cambridge University Press, 1985.

———, ed. *Tropical Babylons: Sugar in the Making of the Atlantic World*. Chapel Hill: University of North Carolina Press, 2004.

Scott, James. *Domination and the Arts of Resistance*. New Haven: Yale University Press, 1990.

Sego, Eugene. *Aliados y adversarios: Los colonos tlaxcaltecos en la frontera septentrional de Nueva España*. San Luís Potosí: Colegio de San Luis, 1998.

Sempat Assadourian, Carlos. *Zacatecas: Conquista y transformación de la frontera en el siglo XVI: Minas de plata, guerra, y evangelización*. Mexico City: Colegio de Mexico, 2008.

Serrano Contreras, Ramón María. "La ciudad de Santiago de Querétaro a fines del siglo XVIII." *Anuario de Estudios Americanos* 30 (1973), 489–555.

Serulnikov, Sergio. *Subverting Colonial Authority: Challenges to Spanish Rule in the Eighteenth-Century Southern Andes*. Durham: Duke University Press, 2003.

Siguenza y Góngora, Carlos. *Glorias de Querétaro*. Mexico City, 1680.

Silva Prada, Natalia. *La política de una rebellion: Las indígenas frente al tumulto de 1692 en la Ciudad de México*. Mexico City: Colegio de México, 2007.

Solís de la Torre, Jesús. *Bárbaros y ermitanos: Chichimecas y Agustinos en la Sierra Gorda, siglos XVI–XVIII*. Querétaro: Gobierno del Estado, 2004.

Somohano Martínez, Lourdes. *Sistemas de aprendizaje gremial en obrajes y talleres artesanos en Querétaro, 1780–1815*. Querétaro: Archivo Histórica de Querétaro, 2001.

———. *La versión histórica de la conquista y la organización política del pueblo de Querétaro*. Querétaro: Instituto Tecnológico de Estudios Superiores de Monterrey, Querétaro, 2003.

Soustelle, Jacques. *La familia otomí-pame del México central*. Mexico City: Fondo de Cultura Económica, 1993.

Souto Mantecón, Matilde. *Mar abierto: la política y el comercio del consulado de Veracruz en el ocaso del sistema imperial*. Mexico City: El Colegio de México, 2001.

Spalding, Karen. *Huarochirí: An Andean Society under Inca and Spanish Rule*. Stanford: Stanford University Press, 1983.

Stein, Stanley, and Barbara Stein. *Apogee of Empire: Spain and New Spain in the Age of Charles III, 1759–1789*. Baltimore: Johns Hopkins University Press, 2003.

———. *Silver, War, and Trade: Spain and America in the Making of Early Modern Europe*. Baltimore: Johns Hopkins University Press, 2000.

Stern, Steve. *Peru's Indian Peoples and the Challenge of Spanish Conquest*. Madison: University of Wisconsin Press, 1982.

———. *The Secret History of Gender: Men, Women, and Power in Late Colonial Mexico*. Chapel Hill: University of North Carolina Press, 1995.

Steward, Julian. *Theory of Culture Change*. Urbana: University of Illinois Press, 1953.

Suárez Muñoz, Manuel, and Juan Ricardo Jiménez Gómez, eds. *Del Reino a la República*. Querétaro: Instituto de Estudios Constitucionales, 2001.

Super, John. "Querétaro Obrajes: Industry and Society in Provincial Mexico, 1600–1800," *Hispanic American Historical Review* 56, no. 2 (1976), 197–216.

———. *La vida en Querétaro durante la colonia, 1521–1810*. Mexico City: Fondo de Cultura Económica, 1983.

Swann, Michael. *Tierra Adentro: Settlement and Society in Colonial Durango*. Boulder: Westview, 1982.

Sweet, Richard Steven. *Beasts of the Field: A Narrative History of California Farmworkers, 1769–1913*. Stanford: Stanford University Press, 2004.

Szatmary, David. *Shays' Rebellion: The Making of an Agrarian Insurgency*. Amherst: University of Massachusetts Press, 1980.

Tabak, Faruk. *The Waning of the Mediterranean, 1550–1870: A Geohistorical Approach*. Baltimore: Johns Hopkins University Press, 2008.

Tanck de Estrada, Dorothy. *Pueblos de indios y educación en el México colonial*. Mexico City: Colegio de México, 1999.

Taylor, Alan. *American Colonies: The Settling of North America*. New York: Penguin, 2001.

Taylor, William. *Drinking, Homicide, and Rebellion in Colonial Mexican Villages*. Stanford: Stanford University Press, 1979.

———. *Landlord and Peasant in Colonial Oaxaca*. Stanford: Stanford University Press, 1972.

———. *Magistrates of the Sacred: Priests and Parishioners in Eighteenth-Century Mexico*. Stanford: Stanford University Press, 1996.

———. "The Virgin of Guadalupe: An Inquiry into the Social History of Marian Devotion." *American Ethnologist* 14, no. 1 (1987), 9–33.

Teja, Jesús Frank de la. *San Antonio de Béjar: A Community on New Spain's Northern Frontier*. Albuquerque: University of New Mexico Press, 1995.

Thomson, Guy. *Puebla de los Ángeles: Industria y sociedad en una ciudad mexicana, 1700–1850*. Puebla: Universidad Autónoma de Puebla, 2002.

Thomson, Sinclair. *We Alone Will Rule: Native Andean Politics in the Age of Insurgency*. Madison: University of Wisconsin Press, 2003.

Tone, John. *The Fatal Knot: The Guerrilla War in Navarre and the Defeat of Napoleon in Spain*. Chapel Hill: University of North Carolina Press, 2005.

Torres, Eugenio Martín. *El beneficio de la plata en Guanajuato, 1686–1740*. Guanajuato: Presidencia Municipal, 2001.

Torre Villar, Ernesto de la, ed. *Instrucciones y memorias de los virreyes novohispanos*. Mexico City: Porrúa, 1991.

Tovar Rangel, Rafael. *Geografía de Guanajuato: Escenario de su Historia*. Guanajuato: Universidad de Guanajuato, 2003.

Tutino, John. "Buscando independencias populares: Conflicto agrario y insurgencia indígena en el Mezquital mexicano, 1800–1815." *Las Guerras de independencia en la América Española*, ed. Marta Terán and José Antonio Serrano, 295–321. Zamora: Colegio de Michoacán, 2002.

———. "Creole Mexico: Spanish Elites, Haciendas, and Indian Towns, 1750–1810." Ph.D. diss., University of Texas, 1976.

———. *From Insurrection to Revolution in Mexico: Social Bases of Agrarian Violence, 1750–1940*. Princeton: Princeton University Press, 1986.

———. "Guerra, comercio colonial y textiles mexicanos: El Bajío, 1785–1810." *Historias* 11 (1985).

———. "Haciendas y comunidades en el valle de México: El crecimiento commercial y la persistencia de los pueblos a la sombra del capital colonial, 1600–1800." *Historia General del Estado de México*, ed. Maria Theresa Jarquin Ortega and Manuel Miño Grijalva. Zinacatepec: Colegio Mexiquense, 2011.

———. "Life and Labor on North Mexican Haciendas: The Querétaro-San Luis Potosí Region, 1775–1810." *El trabajo y los trabajadores en la historia de México*, ed. Elsa Cecilio Frost et al., 339–78. Mexico City: Colegio de México, 1979.

———. "Power, Class, and Family: Women and Men in the Mexico City Elite, 1750–1810." *Americas* 39, no. 3 (1983), 359–81.

———. "The Revolutionary Capacity of Rural Communities: Ecological Autonomy and Its Demise." *Cycles of Conflict, Centuries of Change: Crisis, Reform, and Revolution in Mexico*, ed. Elisa Servín, Leticia Reina, and John Tutino, 211–68. Durham: Duke University Press, 2007.

———. "The Revolution in Mexican Independence: Insurgency and the Renegotiation of Property, Production, and Patriarchy in the Bajío, 1800–1855." *Hispanic American Historical Review* 78, no. 3 (1998), 367–418.

———. "Soberanía quebrada, insurgencies populares y la independencia de México: La guerra de Independencias, 1808–1821." *Historia mexicana* 59, no. 1 (2009), 11–75.

———. "Urban Power and Agrarian Society: Mexico City and Its Hinterland in the Colonial Era." *La ciudad y el campo en la historia de México*, vol. 2, 507–22. Mexico City: Universidad Nacional Autonóma de México, 1992.

Twinam, Ann. *Public Lives, Private Secrets: Honor, Sexuality, and Illegitimacy in Colonial Spanish America*. Stanford: Stanford University Press, 1999.

Urquiola Permisán, José Ignacio. "Estructura urbana y agua: La fase inicial del asentamiento de Querétaro: El núcleo, huertas, labores y conducción de agua." *Las ciudades y sus estructuras: Población, espacio y cultura en México, siglos XVIII y XIX*, ed. Sonia Pérez Toldeo and Luis Pérez Cruz, 63–91. Mexico City: Universidad Autónoma Metropolitana, Ixtapalapa, 1999.

———. "La región centro-sur de Querétaro: colonización y desarrollo ganadero y agrícola durante la época colonial." *Historia de la cuestión agraria mexicana: Estado de Querétaro*, vol. 1, ed. José Ignacio Permisán, 27–197. Mexico City: Juan Pablos, 1989.

———. "Querétaro: Aspectos agrarios en los últimos años de la colonia." *Historia de la cuestión agrarian mexicana: Estado de Querétaro*, vol. 2, ed. José Ignacio Urquiola Permisán. Mexico City: Juan Pablos, 1989.

———. *Trabajadores de campo y ciudad: Las cartas de servicio como forma de contratación en Querétaro, 1588–1609*. Querétaro: Gobierno del Estado, 2001.

Urrutía, Carlos de. "Noticia geográfica del Reino de la Nueva España." *Descripciones económicas generales de Nueva España*, ed. Enrique Florescano and Isabel Gil. Mexico City: Instituto Nacional de Antropología y Historia, 1973.

Usner, Daniel. *Indian, Settlers, and Slaves in a Frontier Exchange Economy: The Lower Mississippi Valley before 1783*. Chapel Hill: University of North Carolina Press, 1992.

Valle, Irene del. *Escribiendo desde los márgenes: Colonialismo y jesuitas en el siglo XVIII*. Mexico City: Siglo XXI, 2009.

Vargas-Lobsinger, María. *Formación y decadencia de una fortuna: Los mayorazgos de San Miguel de Aguayo y de San Pedro de Álamo, 1583–1823*. Mexico City: Universidad Nacional Autónoma de México, 1992.

Velázquez, María del Carmen. *El estado de guerra en Nueva España, 1760–1808*. Mexico City: Colegio de México, 1950; repr. 1997.

Velázquez Gutiérrez, María Elisa. *Mujeres de origen africano en la capital novohispana, siglos XVII y XVIII*. Mexico City: Universidad Nacional Autónoma de México, 2006.

Vergara Hernández, María Josefa. *Testamento*. Querétaro: Gobierno del Estado, 1987.

Verlinden, Charles. *The Origins of Modern Colonization*, trans. Yvonne Freccero. Ithaca: Cornell University Press, 1970.

Vilaplana, Hermenegildo de. *Histórico, y sagrado novenario de la milagrosa imagen de Nuestra Señora del Pueblito, de la santa provincia de Religiosos Observantes de San Pedro, y San Pablo de Michoacán*. Mexico City, 1765; repr. Mexico City: Luis Abadiano y Valdés, 1840.

Villaseñor y Sánchez, José Antonio. *Theatro americano*, 1748; reprint, Guanajuato: Gobierno del Estado, 1989.

Vinson, Ben. *Bearing Arms for His Majesty: The Free-Colored Militia in Colonial Mexico*. Stanford: Stanford University Press, 2001.

Viquiera Palerm, Carmen, and José Ignacio Urquiola Permisán. *Los obrajes de la Nueva España, 1539–1630*. Mexico City: Conaculta, 1990.

Voekel, Pamela. *Alone before God: The Religious Origins of Modernity in Mexico*. Durham: Duke University Press, 2002.

Wade, María. *The Native Americans of the Texas Edwards Plateau, 1582–1799*. Austin: University of Texas Press, 2003.

Walker, Charles. *Smoldering Ashes: Cuzco and the Creation of Republican Peru, 1780–1840*. Durham: Duke University Press, 1999.

Wallace, Anthony. *Jefferson and the Indians: The Tragic Fate of the First Americans*. Cambridge: Harvard University Press, 1999.

Wallerstein, Immanuel. *The Modern World-System*, vol. 1. New York: Academic, 1974.

Weber, David. *Bárbaros: Spaniards and Their Savages in the Age of Enlightenment*. New Haven: Yale University Press, 2005.

———. *The Spanish Frontier in North America*. New Haven: Yale University Press, 1992.

Weber, Max. *The Protestant Ethic and the Spirit of Capitalism*, ed. and trans. Stephen Kolberg. Oxford: Blackwell, 2002 [orig. pubd. 1905].

———. *The Theory of Social and Economic Organization*, ed. Talcott Parsons, trans. A. M. Henderson and Talcott Parsons. New York: Free Press, 1964.

West, Robert. *The Mining Community in Northern New Spain: The Parral Mining District*. Berkeley: University of California Press, 1949.

White, Richard. *The Middle Ground: Indians, Empires, and Republic in the Great Lakes Region, 1650–1815*. Cambridge: Cambridge University Press, 1991.

Williams, Eric. *Capitalism and Slavery*. Chapel Hill: University of North Carolina Press, 1944.

Wobeser, Gisela von. *Dominación colonial: La consolidación de vales reales, 1804–1812*. Mexico City: Universidad Nacional Autónoma de México, 2003.

Wolf, Eric. *Europe and the People without History*. Berkeley: University of California Press, 1982.

———. "The Mexican Bajío in the Eighteenth Century." *Synoptic Studies of Mexican Culture*, 178–99. New Orleans: Tulane University, Middle American Research Institute, 1957.

Wood, Gordon. *The Creation of the American Republic, 1776–1789*. Chapel Hill: University of North Carolina Press, 1969.

Wright Carr, David Charles. *La conquista del Bajío y los orígenes de San Miguel de Allende*. Mexico City: Fondo de Cultura Económica, 1998.

Wu, Celia. "The Population of the City of Querétaro in 1791." *Journal of Latin American Studies* 16, no. 2 (1984), 277–307.

Zárate Toscano, Verónica. *Los nobles ante la muerte en México: Actitudes, ceremonias y memoria, 1750–1850*. Mexico City: Colegio de México, 2000.

Zeláa y Hidalgo, José María. *Glorias de Querétaro*. Mexico City: Mariano Joseph de Zúñiga y Ontiveros, 1803; repr. Querétaro: Calle del Hospital, 1860.

Index

350–51; commercial vs. industrial, 485–86

Capitalist societies, 43–44

Catalan textiles, 317

Cárdenas, Gonzalo de, 102

Carlos I, king of Castille (Carlos V, Holy Roman Emperor), 80–81

Carlos III, king of Spain, 230–32

Carrillo Altamirano, don Hernán, 133–34

Carvallo, Pedro, 101–2

Casas, Bartolomé de las, 81

Casas estate, 376–80

Castillo, don Pedro Lorenzo de, 134

Castillo y Llata, don Juan Antonio, 328–30

Castro Gutiérrez, Felipe, 16

Caxcanes, 74, 82

Celaya: founding of, 83, 140; popular religion in, 116; tributary population in, 149; commercial economy of, 319–20; religious reform and schools in, 408–9; population in, 532–34, 540

Chapingo estate, 294

Charco de Araujo estate, 390–91

Chavarría, Juan de, 106, 501–3

Chichimecas, 32, 68–71; Mexica definition of, 67; resistance by, 78–80; ecological transformation and, 86; history, society, and culture of, 87–88; war and, 88–89, 91; pacification of, 89–90; postwar life of, 95

Chichimequillas estate: ethnic segregation at, 363; managerial patriarchy at, 366–67; population and economic activities at, 579–82; tributaries and labor at, 612

Chihuahua: silver boom in, 210–11; New Mexico trade with, 464

China: New World silver economies and, 1–2, 8–10, 36, 77–78, 160–62, 228; as potential source of mercury, 311; California trade with, 475–76

Chupícuaro culture, 67

Ciénega de Mata estates, 124–25, 139, 166–68

Ciprián, Juan, 244, 253–54

Class relations, 59–60

Cleere, don Felipe, 242–43

Coercion, 20–21

Colombini, Conde de (don Francisco María Colombini y Camayori), 6, 25, 448; on Our Lady of Pueblito, 424–32

Comanches, 211, 213, 462–66

Comercio libre (free trade), 316–22

Commerce, 458, 551–57

Concha, don Vicente de la, 330–31; as tenant at La Griega, 372

Conchos, 127–29

Connín (don Fernando de Tapia), 3–4, 52; founding of Querétaro led by, 72–74; challenges to, 75–77; Chichimecas fought by, 83, 91

Conquest, Spanish, 71–72

Consolidation of royal bonds, 436–42

Convent capitalism: Querétaro origins of, 115–16; consolidation of royal bonds and, 437–42

Cortés, don Fernando, 71

Coruña, Conde de, viceroy, 85

Crisis of 1680s, 157

Crisis of 1760s, 228–31; in British North America, 256–59

Croix, Marqués de, viceroy, 238

Cruillas, Marqués de, viceroy, 233

Cuadrillas, 78

Cumano, doña Juana María, 272

Cumano, don Domingo, 272

Degollado, don Juan José, 384

De la Cruz, Diego, 141, 145

De la Cruz name, 152–54, 176, 531–23

De la Cruz Saravia, don Diego, 4–5, 52, estate operations of, 141–45, 509–13; African ancestry of, 153–54

Geertz, Clifford, 45, 47–48, 419
Giráldez, Arturo, 2, 14
Gómez de Acosta, corregidor, 199–203
González, Felipe, 412–13
González Carvajal, don Ciriaco, 283
Grafe, Regina, 15, 18
Great familias, 285–88
Griega, La, estate, 5, 165; Toltec settlement and, 67; production at, 292–93, 298, 369–72, 380; ethnic segregation at, 362–63; managerial patriarchy at, 366–67; religious life at, 369; workers, tenants, and evictions at, 370–72; labor and patriarchy at, 373–75; Otomí community at, 374–76; labor and religious disputes at, 380–82; Bajío revolution and, 490; population and economic roles at, 576–79; tributaries and labor at, 612
Guachichiles, 70
Guadalcázar: popular resistance in, 240–41; repression in, 250
Guadalupe, congregation of, 205; as mortgage banker, 332; consolidation of royal bonds and, 441
Guadalupe, Our Lady of, 117, 192–93; 433–36; insurgency and, 450
Guadalupe Mission College, Zacatecas, 213, 223
Guamaraes, 70
Guanajuato, 23–24; settlement of, 78–79, 94–95, 131–38; labor in, 134, 252–53, 313; ethnic relations in, 135–37, 175–76, 253, 312; Spanish council and, 135, 175; silver production in, 163, 302, 549–50; commercial life in, 175, 319; population in, 175, 312, 541–43, mission preaching in, 223; popular risings in, 235, 238; repression in, 251–52; reforms in, 252–54; urban patrols in, 303, 313; forest depletion in, 311, 314; guilds abolished in, 313;

smallpox and inoculation in, 421; mining and commerce in, 555
Guanajuato, Our Lady of, 79, 137
Guatemala, 479–80
Guatemala, Ana María, 242, 249
Guinea family, 155
Gutiérrez, Altamirano y Velasco, don Juan Lorenzo, Conde de Santiago, 280–81, 284
Gutiérrez, don Bernadino, 393–94
Gutiérrez, don José, 391–93
Guzmán, Nuño de, 71–74

Haitian revolution, 9–10, 18, 485
Hamilton, Alexander, 483–84
Hedionda, La, 241
Hegemony, 49
Hernández, don Domingo, 414
Hernández, Francisco, 100–101
Herrera, don Vicente, 282, 284
Hidalgo y Costilla, don Miguel, 18; indios of Tequisquiapan supported by, 395; sovereignty crisis and, 400; consolidation of royal bonds and, 439–40; Guadalupe and, 450; revolt and, 488–90
Hierro, Fray Simón del, 223–24
Hiervas, don Juan de: Jesuits at Guanajuato funded by, 181; Canal family and, 184
Huertas, 4, 94, 99, 119
Huertecilla, El Señor de la: founding of, 117; at Temple of Guadalupe, 205, 433
Hueyapan estate, 268
Huimilpan, San Miguel, 76, 201–2
Humboldt, Alexander von: on inequality, 296; on Guanajuato labor, 314; on Querétaro tobacco factory, 341

Ibarra, don Diego de, 76, 124
Ibarra, don Francisco de, 81
Ibarra family, 127
Indios: as colonial category, 27–28; emerging identity of, 108–10, 150–53

Mariscales de Castilla estates, 139, 323; elite rivalry and, 392–93

Martín, don Baltázar, 114–15

Martín, Francisco, 138

Martín family: Querétaro Otomí led by, 98–99; as employers, 105; demise of, 112; religious endowments and, 115

Martínez, Andres, 413–16

Martínez, Gregorio, 413–16

Martínez de Lejarza, don Juan José, 274; wool deals and, 292, 330–31

Martínez Moreno, don José: land and power at Querétaro of, 328, 376; suit by workers at Casas against, 377

Marx, Karl, 2, 10, 38, 42

Mediators, 56–67, 61

Medrano family, 147–48

Mejía Altamirano, don Rodrigo, 134

Mendoza, don Antonio, viceroy, 74, 75

Merino Pablo, don Tomás, 292, 338

Merino y Arellano, don Joseph, 145–46

Mesoamerica, 67–71

Mestizo, as colonial category, 28

Mexica: power and expansion of, 69–71; at early Guanajuato, 79; as workers at Querétaro, 108–9

Mexicano identity, 28

Mexico City, 27–28; riots in, 58; merchants and Bourbon succession in, 161; in silver economy, 161–62; government and finance in, 263–64, 277; abasto (mutton supply) in, 291; Spanish Mesoamerica and North America linked by, 478

Michaus, don Martin Ángel, 292

Mier y Trespalacios, don Cosme de, 284–86

Militia, mulatto, 176, 233–35

Missions: founding at San Luis de la Paz of, 95–97; at Santa Bárbara, 129–31; as bases of success and failure, 224–25; on north-

west coast, 467–68; in California, 473–74

Molino de Flores estate, 280

Monségur, Jean de, 161–62

Monte del Negro estate: ethnic segregation at, 364; population and economic activities at, 590–92

Monterey, California, presidio, 472

Mora, doña Mariana de la, 266–69

Mora, don Francisco de, Conde de Peñasco: resistance in San Luis Potosí fought by, 239–40; repression engaged in by, 249–51; don José Sánchez Espinosa and, 268, 273, 279

Morality, 46–48

Morgan, Edmund, 48

Morelos, José María, 489

Mourelle, don Francisco Antonio: on Guanajuato mines, 308–12; on Querétaro, 326

Moya y Contreras, don Pedro de, archbishop, 83–86

Mulatto, as colonial category, 28

Mulattoes: as Querétaro employers, 106; as Guanajuato workers, 175–79; women at Guanajuato, 177–79; militias and, 235; in conflicts at Valladolid and Pátzcuaro, 236

Nacodoches missions, 213

Naming, and indigenous identity, 108–9, 504–8

Napoleon I, emperor of the French, 9–10, 276, 487–88

Navajos, 127, 211, 464

Navarrete, don Fancisco Antonio, 199–207

Nayarit, Sierra de, 97, 211, 213

New Mexico, 126–27, 211, 463–66

New Orleans, 212

New Santander: missions in, 216; apostate natives in, 218; economy of, 219; ethnic groups in, 219; native resistance and collaboration in, 220–22; settlement, economy, and population in, 561–71

New Spain: dual social organization in, 257–58; republican rights in, 259–60; expansion and stabilization in, 481; silver production in, 549–50

Noriega, don Melchor, 422

North, Douglass, 12, 20–21, 46

Oaxaca, 479

Obrajes: defined, 99; employment in, 107; labor and conflict at San Miguel and, 189–90; expansion, slave labor, and, 196; decline of, 317–18; end of slavery and, 336–37; life and labor in, 343–47

Obra Pía estates, 265–66; profits of, 294–95; charitable distributions by, 296

Obregón, don Antonio, 305

Obregón family, 279, 321

Ocío y Ocampo, don Álvaro, 169–70

Ocío y Ocampo, don Antonio, 197–98

Ojo de Agua estate, 294

Olid, don Cristóbal de, 124

Olives (Florida natives in New Santander), 218

Oñate family: at Zacatecas, 124; in New Mexico, 126

Oratorio de San Felipe Neri, San Miguel, 186

Otero, don Pedro Luciano de, 305

Otomí: founding of Querétaro and, 3–4, 23, 32–33, 65–67; ethnic identity of, 57; pre-conquest life of, 68–69; at early Guanajuato, 79; Chichimeca war and, 81; rule and economy at Querétaro and, 91–94; religion of, 92–93; labor at Querétaro by, 108–9; at La Griega, 165; at Dolores, 170; at Guanajuato, 176; protest at La Griega by, 381–82; religious reform and, 410

Otomí republic: founding of, 74–76; challenges and resistance to, 113–15, 332–35; jurisdiction retained by, 120; aqueduct built by, 203–5;

huertas and, 324; revenues, religion, and schools of, 399–411

Oviedo, don Juan Nepomuceno de, 274–75

Owensby, Brian, 16

Oyarzábal, don José Antonio, 328, 370

Palau, Fray Francisco, 215

Pames, 70; at San Pedro de la Cañada, 73–74, 201, 362

Parral, 123, 128–31

Patriarchy: defined, 54, 58; Chichimeca wars and, 85; labor at Querétaro and, 109–11; labor at Valle de Santiago and, 143–44; penitential worship and, 183, 189; social hierarchy and, 227–28, 301–2, 329; challenges to, 301–2; rural communities and, 353; end of slavery and, 358–59; estate management and, 366–67, 384; obligated labor and, 379–80; Otomí subordination and, 382; insurrection and, 401; in Vergara testament, 443–44; in Spanish Mesoamerica, 480–81

Pátzcuaro: conflict of 1760s in, 236–38; repression in, 254–55; reforms in, 255

Penitential worship, 185–89

Peñasco, Conde de, second, 273–74; bankruptcy of, 330–31

Peñasco, Condesa de, 275

Peñasco estate, 268, 291

Pérez de Espinosa, don Juan Antonio, 185–86

Pérez de Hoyos family, 146

Pérez Gálvez, Conde de, 272–73

Pérouse, Jean François de la, 474–76

Pimas, 469–70

Pious Fund for the Californias, 218

Plaza, don José Antonio, 358; firing of, 383–84

Plazuelas, 67

Political relations, 53, 55–57

402; consolidation of royal bonds and, 440

Sánchez García, José Hermenegildo, 220–22

Sánchez y Mora, don Joaquín, 271, 276

Sánchez y Mora, don Mariano, third Conde de Peñasco, 271, 274–77

San Diego, California, 470–72

Sandi family, 147–48

San Felipe: in Chichimeca wars, 81; resistance in, 238; repression in, 250

San Fernando Mission College, Mexico City, 214

San Francisco Bay, 472–73

San Gabriel, California, 470–71; mission and Mojave rebellion in, 476–77

San Isidro estate: ethnic segregation at, 264, population and economic activities at, 588

San Juan del Río, 612–13

San Luis de la Paz: founding of, 95–97; popular resistance in, 241–43; defense of Jesuits in, 246–47; repression in, 249; religious conflict in, 411–16; population in, 546–47

San Luis Potosí: founding and settlement of, 94–95, 214; resistance in, 238–41; repression in, 249–51

San Mateo Valparaiso, Conde de, 291

San Miguel, el Grande (de Allende), 23–24; founding of, 73, 81; in Chichimeca wars, 86–89; early development of, 138–39; industry in, 184–85; ethnic relations in, 185, 191, 365; popular devotion in, 189; industrial conflict in, 189–90; reforms in, 254; economic decline in, 318–21; municipal policies in, 321; militia in, 322–23; religion and enlightenment in, 416–17; population in, 540–41; taxed commerce in, 555; population and ethnic relations in, 606–7

San Miguel de Aguayo, Marqués de: Texas and, 213; New Santander and, 215; don José Sánchez Espinosa and, 271; landed power of, 287; Bassoco's dealings with, 291; consolidation of royal bonds and, 440

San Pedro de la Cañada: early Otomí settlement and, 73–74; Pame independence and, 201, 208–9; ethnic relations in, 362; religious resistance in, 411; population and economic activities in, 574–76; tributaries and labor in, 612–12

San Pedro estate, 268

San Pedro mines, San Luis Potosí, 239, 250–51

San Sebastián, 611. *See also* Otomí Republic; Querétaro

Santa Ana, don Juan Antonio, 305

Santa Bárbara, 127–30

Santa Bárbara, California, 472

Santa Bárbara estate, 391–93

Santa Catarina estate: ethnic segregation at, 364; population and economic activities at, 588–90

Santa Clara de Jesús (convent), 4; founding of, 112–13; water rights dispute and, 119; estates, banking, and, 192; as bank, 198, 205–6, Our Lady of Puedblito and, 208, 428–29; consolidation of royal bonds and, 441; Vergara legacy and, 447

Santa Cruz mission college: founding of, 193, 211–12; mission college of Guadalupe and, 212; Apaches and, 223

Santa Lucía estate, 281

Santa Rosa basin: ethnic relations in, 363–65; segregating estates in, 595; tributaries and labor in, 611

Santa Rosa town: ethnic relations in, 364–65; population and economic activities in, 595–98

JOHN TUTINO TEACHES THE HISTORY
OF MEXICO AND THE AMERICAS IN THE
HISTORY DEPARTMENT AND SCHOOL OF
FOREIGN SERVICE AT GEORGETOWN
UNIVERSITY.

Library of Congress Cataloging-in-Publication Data
Tutino, John, 1947–
Making a new world : founding capitalism in the Bajío and
Spanish North America / John Tutino.
p. cm.
Includes bibliographical references and index.
ISBN 978-0-8223-4974-7 (cloth : alk. paper)
ISBN 978-0-8223-4989-1 (pbk. : alk. paper)
1. Bajío Region (Mexico)—History. 2. Bajío Region
(Mexico)—Economic conditions. 3. New Spain—History.
4. New Spain—Economic conditions. 5. Capitalism—Mexico—
Bajío Region—History. 6. Capitalism—New Spain—History.
I. Title.
F1246.6.T88 2011
972'.41—dc22 2010054509